Angular for Enterprise-Ready Web Applications

Second Edition

Build and deliver production-grade and cloud-scale evergreen web apps with Angular 9 and beyond

Doguhan Uluca

BIRMINGHAM - MUMBAI

Angular for Enterprise-Ready Web Applications
Second Edition

Copyright © 2020 Packt Publishing

All rights reserved. No part of this book may be reproduced, stored in a retrieval system, or transmitted in any form or by any means, without the prior written permission of the publisher, except in the case of brief quotations embedded in critical articles or reviews.

Every effort has been made in the preparation of this book to ensure the accuracy of the information presented. However, the information contained in this book is sold without warranty, either express or implied. Neither the author, nor Packt Publishing or its dealers and distributors, will be held liable for any damages caused or alleged to have been caused directly or indirectly by this book.

Packt Publishing has endeavored to provide trademark information about all of the companies and products mentioned in this book by the appropriate use of capitals. However, Packt Publishing cannot guarantee the accuracy of this information.

Producer: Jonathan Malysiak
Acquisition Editor – Peer Reviews: Suresh Jain
Content Development Editor: Alex Patterson
Technical Editor: Aniket Shetty
Project Editor: Carol Lewis
Copy Editor: Safis Editing
Proofreader: Safis Editing
Indexer: Pratik Shirodkar
Presentation Designer: Pranit Padwal

First published: May 2018
Second edition: May 2020

Production reference: 1280520

Published by Packt Publishing Ltd.
Livery Place
35 Livery Street
Birmingham B3 2PB, UK.

ISBN 978-1-83864-880-0

www.packt.com

packt.com

Subscribe to our online digital library for full access to over 7,000 books and videos, as well as industry leading tools to help you plan your personal development and advance your career. For more information, please visit our website.

Why subscribe?

- Spend less time learning and more time coding with practical eBooks and Videos from over 4,000 industry professionals
- Learn better with Skill Plans built especially for you
- Get a free eBook or video every month
- Fully searchable for easy access to vital information
- Copy and paste, print, and bookmark content

Did you know that Packt offers eBook versions of every book published, with PDF and ePub files available? You can upgrade to the eBook version at www.Packt.com and as a print book customer, you are entitled to a discount on the eBook copy. Get in touch with us at customercare@packtpub.com for more details.

At www.Packt.com, you can also read a collection of free technical articles, sign up for a range of free newsletters, and receive exclusive discounts and offers on Packt books and eBooks.

Contributors

About the author

Doguhan Uluca is a technical fellow for Excella in Washington, DC, and a Google Developers Expert in Angular and web technologies. He is a software development, agile, and cloud engineering expert. Doguhan is passionate about teaching technology and open source software. He is a speaker, an author whose work includes the best-selling *Angular 6 for Enterprise-Ready Web Applications*, and an active contributor in the OSS community. Doguhan enjoys recording music, playing Go, building Lego, and mixology. Find him on Twitter as `@duluca`.

> Dear Chanda and Ada, thank you for your great sacrifice and amazing support in making this second edition happen. Mr. Caulkins, "What doesn't kill you makes you stronger," so now we're stronger. Also, thanks to Kenton Bocock, Brendan Sawyer, Andrej Rasevic, Alex Hoffman, Jan-Niklas Wortmann, Gleb Bahmutov, Mamadou Toure, and my mentor Fadi Stephan for all the ideas, OSS contributions, and collaboration.

About the reviewers

Brendon Caulkins is a full-stack developer based in the Washington DC area. He has over a decade of product testing experience evaluating hardware and software systems, including writing custom test applications. He is focused on delivering high-quality and well-tested line-of-business applications that leverage JavaScript, Java, Ruby, and Docker. He enjoys mentoring and developing innovative and efficient solutions as a Technical Lead on internal, commercial, and federal projects. He speaks at local conferences and meetups about agile software processes, Angular, and automated testing best practices. Brendon enjoys hiking, science fiction, board games, video games, and still plays with LEGO and toy soldiers. He can be found on the interwebs via Twitter, as `@BrendonCaulkins`.

Aayush Arora is a Google Developer Expert and the founder of FilterPixel, an AI-based photography start-up. An innovation strategist and Massachusetts Institute of Technology Bootcamp graduate, he brings more than 5 years of experience in web development and accessibility with his expertise in Angular framework.

He has made open source contributions in repositories including NASA, CloudCV, and FOSSASIA, and has been continuously contributing to the growth of these communities.

Table of Contents

Preface	**xv**
Chapter 1: Introduction to Angular and Its Concepts	**1**
A brief history of web frameworks	**4**
Introduction to Angular	**10**
Angular's philosophy	13
Angular Evergreen	14
TypeScript	16
Basic Angular architecture	17
The reactive development paradigm	**19**
RxJS	21
Reactive data streams	21
Advanced Angular architecture	**23**
The Angular Router	24
Lazy loading	25
State management	26
The Flux pattern	27
NgRx	27
React.js architecture	29
Notable Angular features	**30**
Angular 6	30
Angular 8	32
Angular 9	32
Summary	**34**
Further reading	**35**
Questions	**35**

Table of Contents

Chapter 2: Setting Up Your Development Environment — 37
CLI package managers — 38
- Installing Chocolatey for Windows — 39
- Installing Homebrew for macOS — 40

Installing development tools — 41
- Git and GitHub Desktop — 41
  - Why use GitHub? — 42
  - Why use GitHub Desktop? — 42
  - Installing Git and GitHub Desktop — 43
  - Using your GitHub credentials in Git — 44
- Node.js — 45
- Existing Node.js installation — 46
- Installing Node.js — 46
  - Global npm packages — 47
- Visual Studio Code — 48
  - Installing Visual Studio Code — 48
- Docker — 49
  - Installing Docker — 49
- Cloud services — 50
  - Vercel Now — 50
  - Google Firebase — 50
  - Google Cloud — 51
  - Amazon Web Services — 51

Setup automation for Windows and macOS — 52
- PowerShell script — 52
- Bash script — 54

The Angular CLI — 57
- Setting up your development directory — 57
- Generating your Angular application — 58
  - Installing the Angular CLI — 58
  - Initializing your Angular app — 59
  - Publishing a Git repository using GitHub Desktop — 61
  - Inspecting and updating package.json — 62
  - Committing code using VS Code — 67
- Running your Angular app — 68
- Verifying your code — 70

Optimizing VS Code for Angular — 70
- Configuring your project automatically — 71
  - VS Code auto save — 72
  - IDE settings — 72
  - IDE extensions — 74
- Scripting code styling and linting — 75
  - Configuring tooling — 76
  - Implementing a style checker and fixer — 78

Implementing a lint checker and fixer	79
Configuring Angular CLI autocomplete	80
VS Code Auto Fixer	81
Summary	**81**
Further reading	**82**
Questions	**82**

Chapter 3: Creating a Basic Angular App — 83

Planning using Kanban and GitHub projects	**85**
Setting up a GitHub project	86
Configuring a Kanban board	87
Creating a backlog for the Local Weather app	88
Wireframe design	90
High-level architecture	91
Crafting UI elements using components and interfaces	**93**
Adding an Angular component	94
Demystifying Angular components	99
Defining your model using interfaces	100
Using Angular Services and HttpClient to retrieve data	**105**
Creating a new Angular service	106
Injecting dependencies	107
Discovering OpenWeatherMap APIs	108
Storing environment variables	111
Implementing an HTTP GET operation	112
Retrieving service data from a component	114
Transforming data using RxJS	**117**
Implementing Reactive transformations	117
Null guarding in Angular	**121**
Property initialization	122
The safe navigation operator	123
Null guarding with *ngIf	124
Summary	**125**
Further reading	**126**
Questions	**126**

Chapter 4: Automated Testing, CI, and Release to Production — 127

Unit testing	**129**
Angular unit tests	**132**
Jasmine	133
Fixtures	133
Matchers	134
Anatomy of auto-generated unit tests	135

Unit test execution	**136**
Compilation errors	137
Test results	138
Configuring TestBed	**139**
Declarations	139
Providers	141
Imports	142
Test doubles	**143**
Fakes	144
Mocks, stubs, and spies	146
Angular e2e tests	**152**
e2e test execution	154
The e2e page object and spec	154
Production readiness	**156**
Building for production	156
Setting environment variables	157
Continuous Integration	**157**
CircleCI	158
GitHub flow	161
Deploying to the Cloud	**166**
Vercel Now	166
Deploying static files	166
Summary	**169**
Further reading	**170**
Questions	**170**
Chapter 5: Delivering High-Quality UX with Material	**171**
Angular Material	**173**
Angular Material setup and performance	**176**
Installing Angular Material	178
Automatically	178
Manually	181
Understanding Material's components	181
Manually configuring Angular Material	182
Importing modules	182
Importing themes	184
Adding the Material Icon font	185
Angular Flex Layout	**185**
Responsive layouts	187
Installing Angular Flex Layout	189
Layout basics	189
Flex Layout APIs for DOM containers	190
Flex Layout APIs for DOM elements	191
Flex Layout APIs for any element	191

Using Material components — **192**
  Angular Material schematics — 192
  Modifying the landing page with Material Toolbar — 193
  Material cards — 195
    Card header and content — 198
  Material typography — 199
    Applying typography — 200
  Flex Layout Align — 201
  Flex Layout — 202
    Implementing layout scaffolding — 203
  Aligning elements with CSS — 205
    Individually styling elements — 206
    Fine-tuning styles — 207
    Tweaking to match design — 209
  Custom themes — 212
  Unit testing with Material — 217
Accessibility — **219**
  Configuring automated pa11y testing — 220
Building an interactive prototype — **223**
  MockFlow WireframePro — 223
  Building a mock-up — 223
    Home screen — 225
    Search results — 225
    Settings pane — 226
  Adding interactivity — 227
    Exporting the functional prototype — 228
Summary — **230**
Further reading — **231**
Exercises — **231**
Questions — **231**

Chapter 6: Forms, Observables, and Subjects — 233

Reactive forms versus template-driven forms — **236**
  Adding Angular reactive forms — 237
  Adding and verifying components — 238
  Adding a search option to the weather service — 241
  Implementing a search — 243
  Limiting user inputs with throttle/debounce — 245
  Input validation and error messages — 246
    Template-driven forms with two-way binding — 247
Component interaction with BehaviorSubject — **249**
  Global events — 249
  Child-parent relationships with event emitters — 250

Parent-child relationships with input binding	252
Sibling interactions with subjects	253
Managing subscriptions	**258**
Exposé of a memory leak	258
Unsubscribing from a subscription	259
Unsubscribing using SubSink	260
Implementing the reactive style	**261**
Binding to an observable with an async pipe	261
Tapping into an observable stream	263
Multiple API calls	**264**
Implementing a postal code service	265
Chaining API calls	267
Summary	**269**
Exercises	**270**
Questions	**270**
Chapter 7: Creating a Router-First Line-of-Business App	**271**
The 80-20 solution	**274**
Understanding Line-of-Business apps	275
Disciplined and balanced approach	277
Router-first architecture	**279**
Feature modules	280
Developing a roadmap and scope	282
Designing with lazy loading in mind	282
Implementing a walking-skeleton	283
Achieve a stateless, data-driven design	283
Enforce a decoupled component architecture	284
Differentiate between user controls and components	285
Maximize code reuse with TypeScript and ES	285
Creating LemonMart	**287**
Creating a router-first app	288
Configuring Angular and VS Code	290
Configuring Material and Styles	291
Designing LemonMart	292
Identifying user roles	293
Identifying high-level modules with a site map	293
Generating router-enabled modules	**295**
Designing the home route	298
Setting up default routes	300
RouterLink	301
Router outlet	301

Branding, customization, and Material icons	**302**
Branding	302
Color palette	302
Implementing browser manifest and icons	303
Custom themes	305
Custom icons	306
Material icons	307
Feature modules with lazy loading	**309**
Configuring feature modules with components and routes	312
Eager loading	314
Lazy loading	317
Completing the walking skeleton	**320**
The manager module	320
User module	324
POS and inventory modules	326
POS module	327
Inventory module	328
Inspect the router tree	329
Common testing module	**331**
Designing around major data entities	**334**
Defining entities	334
High-level UX design	**335**
Creating an artifacts Wiki	335
Leveraging mock-ups in your app	338
Summary	**339**
Further reading	**340**
Questions	**340**

Chapter 8: Designing Authentication and Authorization — 341

Designing an auth workflow	**343**
JWT life cycle	344
TypeScript operators for safe data handling	**347**
Null and undefined checking	348
The conditional or ternary operator	349
The null coalescing operator	350
The nullish coalescing operator	350
Optional chaining	351
Reusable services leveraging OOP concepts	**352**
JavaScript classes	353
Abstraction and inheritance	358
Create the auth service	360

Implement an abstract auth service	361
Abstract functions	364
Abstract caching service using localStorage	368
Caching the JWT	371
Implement an in-memory auth service	373
Simple login	376
Logout	379
Resuming a JWT session	380
HTTP interceptor	383
Dynamic UI components and navigation	**385**
Implementing the login component	386
Conditional navigation	391
Common validations for forms	394
UI service	395
Side navigation	400
Role-based routing using guards	**407**
Router guards	408
Auth guards	409
Auth service fake and common testing providers	413
Firebase authentication recipe	**414**
Add an application	416
Configure authentication	418
Implement Firebase authentication	419
Providing a service using a factory	**424**
Summary	**425**
Further reading	**426**
Questions	**427**
Chapter 9: DevOps Using Docker	**429**
DevOps	**432**
Containerizing web apps using Docker	**434**
Anatomy of a Dockerfile	434
Installing Docker	439
Setting up npm scripts for Docker	439
Build and publish an image to Docker Hub	440
NPM scripts in VS Code	447
Docker extensions in VS Code	448
Deploying a Dockerfile to the cloud	**449**
Google Cloud Run	449
Configuring Docker with Cloud Run	453
Troubleshooting Cloud Run	454

Continuous deployment	**455**
Deploying to Vercel Now using CircleCI	456
Deploying to GCloud using orbs	459
Gated CI workflows	464
Advanced continuous integration	**465**
Containerizing build environments	466
Multi-stage Dockerfiles	466
Builder	467
Tester	469
Web server	472
CircleCI container-in-container	473
Code coverage reports	**476**
Code coverage in CI	478
Summary	**481**
Exercise	**481**
Further reading	**482**
Questions	**482**
Chapter 10: RESTful APIs and Full-Stack Implementation	**483**
Full-stack architecture	**487**
Minimal MEAN	488
Angular	489
Express	489
Node	490
Mongo	490
Tooling	490
Configuring a monorepo	491
Monorepo structure	492
Git submodules	492
Configuring a Node project with TypeScript	494
CircleCI config	498
Docker Compose	500
Using Nginx as the web server	501
Containerizing the server	502
Configuring environment variables with DotEnv	503
Define Docker-Compose YAML	505
Orchestrating the Compose launch	507
Compose on CircleCI	508
RESTful APIs	**510**
API design with Swagger	511
Defining a Swagger YAML file	512
Preview Swagger file	516
Implementing APIs with Express.js	517
Bootstrapping the server	520
Routes and versioning	521

[ix]

Services	523
Configuring Swagger with Express	524
MongoDB ODM with DocumentTS	**527**
About DocumentTS	528
Connecting to the database	529
Models with IDocument	531
Implementing JWT auth	**536**
Login API	537
Authenticating middleware	539
Custom server auth provider	543
GET User by ID	546
Generating users with Postman	**547**
Configuring Postman for authenticated calls	548
Postman automation	550
Put User	555
Pagination and filtering with DocumentTS	556
Summary	**559**
Exercise	**559**
Further reading	**560**
Questions	**560**
Chapter 11: Recipes – Reusability, Routing, and Caching	**561**
Implementing a user service with GET	**563**
Implementing PUT with caching	565
Multi-step responsive forms	**566**
Form controls and form groups	569
Stepper and responsive layout	571
Reusing repeating template behavior with directives	576
Attribute directives	576
Field error attribute directive	576
Calculated properties and DatePicker	584
Typeahead support	586
Dynamic form arrays	587
Creating shared components	590
Reviewing and saving form data	592
Scaling architecture with reusable form parts	**595**
Base form component as an abstract class	597
Implementing a reusable form part	599
Input masking	**604**
Custom controls with ControlValueAccessor	**606**
Implementing a custom rating control	606
Using custom controls in forms	611

Layouts using grid list	612
Restoring cached data	615
Exercise	618
Summary	619
Further reading	619
Questions	620
Chapter 12: Recipes – Master/Detail, Data Tables, and NgRx	**621**
Editing existing users	624
Loading data with resolve guard	624
Reusing components with binding and route data	627
Master/detail view auxiliary routes	629
Data table with pagination	632
Updating unit tests	641
NgRx Store and Effects	643
Implementing NgRx for LocalCast Weather	644
Comparing BehaviorSubject and NgRx	646
Setting up NgRx	648
Defining NgRx actions	648
Implementing NgRx Effects	650
Implementing reducers	652
Registering with Store using selector	653
Dispatching store actions	654
Unit testing reducers and selectors	655
Unit testing components with MockStore	656
NgRx Data	658
Implementing NgRx/Data in LemonMart	658
Configuring proxy in Angular CLI	660
Using Entity Service	661
Customizing Entity Service	663
Summary	665
Further reading	666
Questions	666
Chapter 13: Highly Available Cloud Infrastructure on AWS	**667**
Creating a secure AWS account	670
Securing secrets	672
Right-sizing infrastructure	672
Optimizing instances	674
Simple load testing	674
Deploying to AWS ECS Fargate	675
Configuring ECS Fargate	676

Table of Contents

    Creating a Fargate cluster   676
    Creating a container repository   678
    Creating a task definition   680
    Creating an elastic load balancer   682
    Creating a cluster service   686
    Configuring the DNS   689
Adding npm scripts for AWS   691
Publish   695
Deploying to AWS using CircleCI   699

AWS billing   **702**
Summary   **703**
Exercise   **704**
Further reading   **704**
Questions   **704**

Chapter 14: Google Analytics and Advanced Cloud Ops   705

Collecting analytics   **707**
Adding Google Tag Manager to your Angular app   710
    Setting up Google Tag Manager   710
    Setting up Google Analytics   713

Budgeting and scaling   **717**
Calculating the per-user cost   717

Advanced load testing   **719**
Reliable cloud scaling   **723**
Cost per user in a scalable environment   724
    Calculating target server utilization   725
    Revising estimates with metrics   728

Measuring actual use   **728**
Creating a custom event   729
Adding custom events in Angular   734
Advanced analytics events   738

Summary   **740**
Further reading   **741**
Questions   **741**

Appendix A : Debugging Angular   743

The most useful shortcut   **744**
Troubleshooting errors in the browser   **744**
Leveraging Browser DevTools   745
Optimizing dev tools   747
Troubleshooting network issues   748
Investigating console errors   750

Karma, Jasmine, and unit testing errors	**751**
NetworkError	751
Generic ErrorEvents	751
Debugging with Dev Tools	**752**
Debugging with Visual Studio Code	**754**
Debugging with Angular Augury	**757**
Component Tree	758
Router Tree	760
NgModules	760
Debugging with Redux DevTools	**763**
Implement NgRx Console Logger	763
Configuring NgRx Store DevTools	764
Debugging RxJS	**766**
Tapping an RxJS Event Stream	766
Breakpoint debugging an RxJS Event Stream	769
Further advice	**770**
Appendix B : Angular Cheat Sheet	**771**
Built-in directives	**772**
Common pipes	**772**
Starter commands, major components, and CLI scaffolds	**773**
Starter commands	773
Major component scaffolds	773
TypeScript scaffolds	775
Common RxJS functions/operators	**775**
Functions	775
Operators	776
Further Reading	**777**
Another Book You May Enjoy	**779**
Index	**781**

Preface

Welcome to the wonderful world of web development! This book has been designed to teach you the fundamentals of the Angular platform and equip you with useful recipes and practical code examples, so you can create rich and scalable line-of-business applications. The book emphasizes a minimalist approach, by maximizing the use of built-in libraries and avoiding the introduction of additional third-party dependencies to achieve the desired outcome. As a result of this approach, your code will be easier to maintain and upgrade, as new versions of Angular are released frequently. You may continue using this book as a learning resource, as the fundamental concepts, technologies, and samples included in the book will remain relevant for some time to come, albeit with slight modifications. The tools and services recommended in the book have been updated to their latest versions, circa 2020, however, tools and services continually evolve, change, and sometimes outright disappear. If and when this happens, feel free to reach out to me for alternatives.

This book will also aim to instill an Agile and DevOps mindset in you so that you confidently create reliable and flexible solutions. Whether you consider yourself a freelancer developing software for small businesses, a full-stack developer, an enterprise developer, or a web developer, what you need to know to design, architect, develop, maintain, deliver, and deploy a web application, and the best practices and patterns you need to apply to achieve those things, don't vary all that much. If you are delivering an application to an audience of users, in a sense, you are a full-stack developer, since you must be aware of a lot of server technologies. In fact, if you master how to deliver Angular applications using TypeScript, it won't be difficult for you to write your own RESTful APIs using Node.js, Express.js, and TypeScript, which is demonstrated through a concrete implementation later in the book.

Preface

By some definitions, a full-stack developer needs to know everything from catering to international copyright law to successfully create and operate an application on today's web. If you're an entrepreneur, in a sense, this is true. However, in this book, your culinary skills and law degrees need not apply. This book assumes that you already know how to work with web development basics and have familiarity working with RESTful APIs with the tech stack of your choice, and if not, fear not, just follow the hands-on step-by-step instructions and you will be able to create your first API-enabled Angular app in no time.

Who this book is for

This book is for beginners and experienced developers alike who are looking to learn Angular or web development in general. If you are an Angular developer, you will be exposed to the entire gamut of designing and deploying an Angular application to production. You will learn about Angular patterns that are easy to understand and teach others. If you are a freelancer, you will pick up effective tools and technologies to deliver your Angular app in a secure, confident, and reliable way. If you're an enterprise developer, you will learn patterns and practices to write Angular applications with a scalable architecture.

What this book covers

Chapter 1, Introduction to Angular and Its Concepts, introduces the reader to the world of Angular and web development.

Chapter 2, Setting Up Your Development Environment, goes over a scriptable way to set up your environment.

Chapter 3, Creating a Basic Angular App, introduces the Kanban method of software development with easy-to-use design tools used to communicate ideas, going over Angular fundamentals, and leveraging CLI tools to maximize your impact.

Chapter 4, Automated Testing, CI, and Release to Production, covers unit testing, continuous integration, and rapid cloud deployments.

Chapter 5, Delivering High-Quality UX with Material, introduces you to Angular Material and explains how to use it to build great-looking apps.

Chapter 6, Forms, Observables, and Subjects, teaches you to become comfortable using Angular forms and reactive programming with RxJS.

Chapter 7, Creating a Router-First Line-of-Business App, focuses on the Router-first architecture, a seven-step approach to the design and development of mid-to-large line-of-business applications.

Chapter 8, Designing Authentication and Authorization, dives into authentication and authorization related patterns in Angular and RESTful applications.

Chapter 9, DevOps Using Docker, dives deep into containerization with Docker to enable repeatable development and operational workflows across diverse ecosystems.

Chapter 10, RESTful APIs and Full-Stack Implementation, walks you through the implementation of a real-world MEAN stack application to support line-of-business applications.

Chapter 11, Recipes – Reusability, Routing, and Caching, contains recipes around capturing and manipulating user data commonly needed for line-of-business applications.

Chapter 12, Recipes – Master/Detail, Data Tables, and NgRx, contains recipes around presenting user data commonly needed for line-of-business applications and an introduction to implementing the Flux pattern in Angular using NgRx.

Chapter 13, Highly Available Cloud Infrastructure on AWS, moves beyond application features to go over provisioning a highly-available cloud infrastructure on AWS.

Chapter 14, Google Analytics and Advanced Cloud Ops, goes over the nuances of owning, operating, and optimizing your cloud infrastructure, and using Google Analytics to capture user behavior.

Appendix A, Debugging Angular, covers how to deal with common Angular errors and breakpoint debugging using Chrome DevTools.

Appendix B, Angular Cheat Sheet, is a quick reference for Angular CLI commands, major Angular components, and common RxJS operators.

Appendix C, Keeping Angular and Tools Evergreen, includes detailed information about how to keep your development environment, Angular, and its dependencies up to date. You can read this appendix at `https://static.packt-cdn.com/downloads/9781838648800_Appendix_C_Keeping_Angular_and_Tools_Evergreen.pdf`. You can alternatively read this appendix at `https://expertlysimple.io/stay-evergreen`.

Appendix D, Self-Assessment Answers, has the answers to the test questions at the end of each chapter. You can read this appendix at `https://static.packt-cdn.com/downloads/9781838648800_Appendix_D_Self-Assessment_Answers.pdf`. You can alternatively read this appendix at `https://expertlysimple.io/angular-self-assessment/`.

To get the most out of this book

- Follow the instructions at the beginning of each chapter and section.
- Check the latest code examples on GitHub.
- It helps to be familiar with full-stack web development, but it is not a pre-requisite.
- If you are a beginner, follow the book in the published order, coding your solution alongside the content in each chapter.
- You can begin going through any chapter, so long as you clone the prior chapter's implementation from GitHub and understand the assumptions covered in *Chapter 2, Setting Up Your Development Environment*.

Download the example code files

You can get the latest version of the example code files for this book on GitHub. There are four projects that directly supports the content in this book:

1. Web development environment setup scripts at `https://github.com/duluca/web-dev-environment-setup`
2. Local Weather App at `https://github.com/duluca/local-weather-app`
3. LemonMart at `https://github.com/duluca/lemon-mart`
4. LemonMart Server at `https://github.com/duluca/lemon-mart-server`

In each chapter you can find specific instructions to access chapter specific versions of code examples. When demonstrating continuous integration and continuous deployment configuration, Git branches and GitHub pull requests are utilized to demonstrate specific configuration elements.

You can download a snapshot of example code files for this book at the time of publishing from your account at `http://www.packtpub.com`. If you purchased this book elsewhere, you can visit `http://www.packtpub.com/support` and register to have the files emailed directly to you.

You can download the code files by following these steps:

1. Log in or register at `http://www.packtpub.com`.
2. Select the **SUPPORT** tab.
3. Click on **Code Downloads & Errata**.
4. Enter the name of the book in the **Search** box and follow the on-screen instructions.

Once the file is downloaded, please make sure that you unzip or extract the folder using the latest version of:

- WinRAR / 7-Zip for Windows
- Zipeg / iZip / UnRarX for Mac
- 7-Zip / PeaZip for Linux

The code bundle for the book is also hosted on GitHub at `https://github.com/PacktPublishing/Angular-for-Enterprise-Ready-Web-Applications-Second-Edition`. We also have other code bundles from our rich catalog of books and videos available at `https://github.com/PacktPublishing/`. Check them out!

Download the color images

We also provide a PDF file that has color images of the screenshots/diagrams used in this book. You can download it here: `http://www.packtpub.com/sites/default/files/downloads/9781838648800_ColorImages.pdf`.

Conventions used

There are a number of text conventions used throughout this book.

`CodeInText`: Indicates code words in text, database table names, folder names, filenames, file extensions, pathnames, dummy URLs, user input, and Twitter handles. For example; "Mount the downloaded `WebStorm-10*.dmg` disk image file as another disk in your system."

A block of code is set as follows:

```
{
  "name": "local-weather-app",
  "version": "0.0.0",
  "license": "MIT",
  ...
}
```

When we wish to draw your attention to a particular part of a code block, the relevant lines or items are set in bold:

```
"scripts": {
  "ng": "ng",
  "start": "ng serve",
  "build": "ng build",
  "test": "ng test",
  "lint": "ng lint",
  "e2e": "ng e2e"
},
```

Any cross-platform or macOS specific command-line input or output is written as follows:

```
$ brew tap caskroom/cask
```

Windows specific command-line input or output is written as follows:

```
PS> Set-ExecutionPolicy AllSigned; iex ((New-Object System.Net.WebClient).DownloadString('https://chocolatey.org/install.ps1'))
```

Bold: Indicates a new term, an important word, or words that you see on the screen, for example, in menus or dialog boxes, also appear in the text like this. For example: "Browser vendors are supposed to implement these technologies as defined by the **World Wide Web Consortium (W3C)**."

Warnings or important notes appear like this.

Tips and tricks appear like this.

Get in touch

Feedback from our readers is always welcome.

General feedback: Email `feedback@packtpub.com`, and mention the book's title in the subject of your message. If you have questions about any aspect of this book, please email us at `questions@packtpub.com`.

Errata: Although we have taken every care to ensure the accuracy of our content, mistakes do happen. If you have found a mistake in this book we would be grateful if you would report this to us. Please visit, http://www.packtpub.com/submit-errata, selecting your book, clicking on the Errata Submission Form link, and entering the details.

Piracy: If you come across any illegal copies of our works in any form on the Internet, we would be grateful if you would provide us with the location address or website name. Please contact us at copyright@packtpub.com with a link to the material.

If you are interested in becoming an author: If there is a topic that you have expertise in and you are interested in either writing or contributing to a book, please visit http://authors.packtpub.com.

Reviews

Please leave a review. Once you have read and used this book, why not leave a review on the site that you purchased it from? Potential readers can then see and use your unbiased opinion to make purchase decisions, we at Packt can understand what you think about our products, and our authors can see your feedback on their book. Thank you!

For more information about Packt, please visit packtpub.com.

1
Introduction to Angular and Its Concepts

At first, there was HTML, then DHTML. Technologists invented new technologies like Java, JavaScript, PHP, and many others to deliver interactive experiences over the browser. The holy grail of programming was writing a program once and running it everywhere. In a flash, the era of **Single-Page Applications (SPAs)** was born. SPAs tricked the browser into thinking that a single `index.html` could house entire applications containing many pages. Backbone.js, Knockout.js, and Angular.js all came and went. Everyone reeling from unmanaged complexity and JavaScript-framework-of-the-week syndrome looked for a savior. Then came React, Angular, and Vue. They promised to fix all problems, bring about universally reusable web components, and make it easier to learn, develop, and scale web applications. And, so they did! Some better than others. The adolescent history of the web has taught us a couple of essential lessons. First, change is inevitable, and second, the developer's happiness is a precious commodity that can make or break entire companies.

This chapter covers:

- The history of web frameworks
- Angular and the philosophy behind it
- The reactive development paradigm
- Advanced Angular features, including state management
- Major Angular releases and features

Introduction to Angular and Its Concepts

This first chapter is meant to give you a theoretical and historical background for the rest of the book. Feel free to use it as a reference as you go through the rest of the book. *Chapter 2, Setting Up Your Development Environment,* covers how you can configure your development environment for a great development experience. With *Chapter 3, Creating a Basic Angular App,* you begin implementing your first Angular application. If you're already experienced with Angular, you may start with *Chapter 7, Creating a Router-First Line-of-Business App,* to dive into creating scalable applications ready for the enterprise.

Each chapter in the book introduces you to new concepts and reinforces best practices while covering optimal ways of working with widely used and open source tools. Along the way, tips and information boxes cover the bases to close any knowledge gaps you may have about web and modern JavaScript development basics. As you go through the content, pay attention to numbered steps or bullet points as they describe actions you need to take. If you skip a section or a chapter, you may miss subtle changes in configuration or techniques that may confuse you later on.

> The code samples provided in this book have been developed using Angular 9, which is planned to be in **Long-Term Support** (**LTS**) until August 2021. The chances are that you are reading this book after new versions have superseded Angular 9. However, worry not. This book adopts the Angular evergreen motto of always keeping the version of Angular up to date with the latest release. Keeping up to date is made possible by sticking to platform fundamentals and avoiding unnecessary third-party libraries. The example projects for the book were initially written for Angular 5 and updated over time without major rewrites by following a proactive and incremental Angular upgrade schedule. I anticipate these projects to survive with minor modifications for years to come. This reliability is a testament to the excellent compatibility work done by the Angular team.

The world of JavaScript, TypeScript, and Angular is constantly changing. It is normal for there to be some differences between code samples in the book and the code that is generated for you by the tools you use. For this reason, most of the best practices and configuration items recommended by this book are applied using tools that I created, so they can be updated. Below is a high-level overview of the collection of libraries, extensions, and open source projects that support the content of the book:

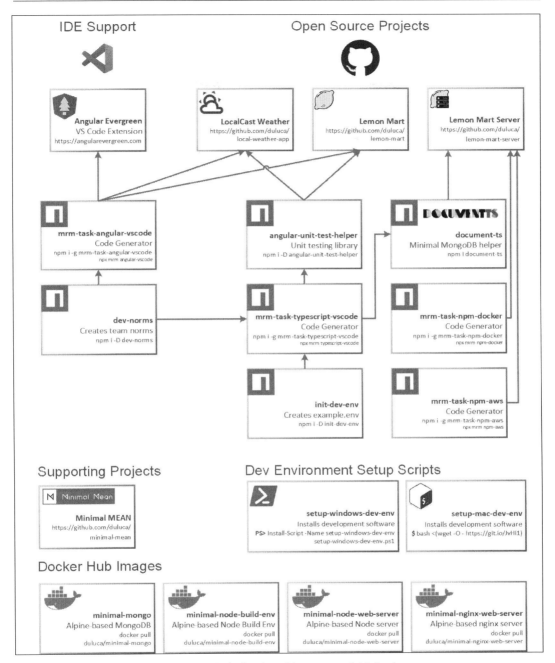

Figure 1.1: Code developed in support of this book

The preceding diagram is to give you a quick glance at some of the moving parts. Each component is detailed in the coming chapters. The most up-to-date versions of the sample code for the book are on GitHub, at the repositories linked below. These repositories contain the final and completed state of the code. To make it easier to verify your progress at the end of a chapter, the `projects` folder in each repository contains chapter-by-chapter snapshots reflecting the current state of the code:

- For *Chapters 2* to *6*, and *12*, LocalCast Weather: https://github.com/duluca/local-weather-app
- For *Chapters 7* to *14*, Lemon Mart: https://github.com/duluca/lemon-mart
- For *Chapter 10*, Lemon Mart Server: https://github.com/duluca/lemon-mart-server

You may read more about updating Angular in *Appendix C, Keeping Angular and Tools Evergreen*. You can find this appendix online from https://static.packt-cdn.com/downloads/9781838648800_Appendix_C_Keeping_Angular_and_Tools_Evergreen.pdf or at https://expertlysimple.io/stay-evergreen.

Let's take a look at the last 20 or so years of web development history, so you can contextualize how Angular came to be and evolved.

A brief history of web frameworks

It is essential to consider why we use frameworks such as Angular, React, or Vue in the first place. Web frameworks came to rise as JavaScript became more popular and capable in the browser. In 2004, the **Asynchronous JavaScript and XML (AJAX)** technique became very popular in creating websites that did not have to rely on full-page refreshes to create dynamic experiences utilizing standardized web technologies like HTML, JavaScript/ECMAScript, and CSS. Browser vendors are supposed to implement these technologies as defined by the **World Wide Web Consortium (W3C)**.

Internet Explorer (IE) was the browser that the vast majority of internet users relied on at the time. Microsoft used its market dominance to push proprietary technologies and APIs to secure IE's edge as the go-to browser. Things started to get interesting when Mozilla's Firefox challenged IE's dominance, followed by Google's Chrome browser. As both browsers successfully gained significant market share, the web development landscape became a mess. New browser versions appeared at breakneck speed. Competing corporate and technical interests led to the diverging implementation of web standards.

This fracturing created an unsustainable environment for developers to deliver consistent experiences on the web. Differing qualities, versions, and names of implementations of various standards created an enormous challenge, which was successfully writing code that could manipulate the **Document Object Model (DOM)** of a browser consistently. Even the slightest difference in the APIs and capabilities of a browser would be enough to break a website.

In 2006, jQuery was developed to smooth out the differences between APIs and capabilities for browsers. So instead of repeatedly writing code to check browser versions, you could use jQuery, and you were good to go. It hid away all the complexities of vendor-specific implementations and gracefully filled the gaps when there were missing features. For a good 5 to 6 years, jQuery became the web development framework. It was unimaginable to write an interactive website without using jQuery.

To create vibrant user experiences, however, jQuery alone was not enough. Native web applications ran all their code in the browser, which required fast computers to run the dynamically interpreted JavaScript and render web pages using the complicated object graphs. Back in the 2000s, many users ran outdated browsers on relatively slow computers, so the user experience wasn't great.

Traditionally, software architecture is described in three primary layers, as shown in the diagram that follows:

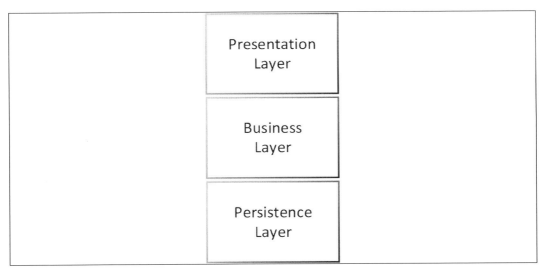

Figure 1.2: Three-tiered software architecture

The presentation layer contains **user interface (UI)** related code, the business layer contains business logic, and the persistence layer contains code related to data storage. It is an overall design goal to aim for low coupling and high cohesion between the components of our architecture. Low coupling means that pieces of code across these layers shouldn't depend on each other and should be independently replaceable. High cohesion means that pieces of code that are related to each other, like code regarding a particular domain of business logic, should remain together. For example, when building an app to manage a restaurant, the code for the reservation system should be together and not spread across other systems like inventory tracking or user management. Modern web development has more moving parts than a basic three-tiered application. The diagram that follows shows additional layers that fit around the presentation, business, and persistence layers:

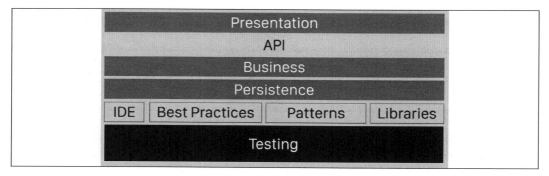

Figure 1.3: Modern web architecture

In the preceding diagram, you can see an expanded architecture diagram that includes essential components of modern web development, which include an API layer that usually transforms data between the presentation and business layers, a tools and best practices layer that defines various methodologies used to develop the software, and an automated testing layer that is crucial in today's iterative and fast-moving development cycles.

In the 2000s, many internet companies relied on server-side rendered web pages. The server dynamically created all the HTML, CSS, and data needed to render a page. The browser acted as a glorified viewer that would display the result. The following is a diagram that shows a sample architectural overview of a server-side rendered web application in the ASP.NET MVC stack:

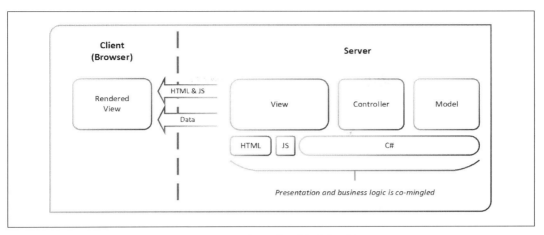

Figure 1.4: Server-side rendered MVC architecture

Model-View-Controller (MVC) is a typical pattern of code that has data manipulation logic in models, business logic in controllers, and presentation logic in views. In the case of ASP.NET MVC, the controller and model are coded using C#, and views are created using a templated version of HTML, JavaScript, and C#. The result is that the browser receives HTML, JavaScript, and data that is needed, and through jQuery and AJAX magic, web pages look to be interactive. Server-side rendering and MVC patterns are still popular and in use today. There are justified niche uses, such as Facebook.com. Facebook serves billions of devices that range from the very slow to the very fast. Without server-side rendering, it would be impossible for Facebook to guarantee a consistent **user experience (UX)** across its userbase. I find the combination of server-side rendering and MVC to be an intricate pattern to execute. To ensure the low coupling of components, every member of the engineering team must be very experienced. Teams with a high concentration of senior developers are hard to come by, and that would be an understatement.

Further complicating matters is that C# (or any other server-side language) cannot run natively in the browser. So, developers who work on server-side rendered applications must be equally skilled at using frontend and backend technologies. It is easy for inexperienced developers to co-mingle presentation and business logic in such implementations unintentionally. When this happens, the inevitable UI modernization of an otherwise well-functioning system becomes impossible. Put in other terms, to replace the sink in your kitchen with a new one, you must renovate your entire kitchen. Due to insufficient architecture, organizations routinely spend millions of dollars every 10 years writing and rewriting the same applications.

Introduction to Angular and Its Concepts

During the 2000s, it was possible to build rich web applications that were decoupled from their server APIs using Java Applets, Flash, or Silverlight. However, these technologies relied on browser plugins that needed a separate installation. Most often, these plugins were out of date, created critical security vulnerabilities, and consumed too much power on mobile computers. Following the iPhone revolution in 2008, it was clear such plugins wouldn't run on mobile phones, despite best attempts by the Android OS. Besides, Apple CEO Steve Jobs' disdain for such inelegant solutions marked the beginning of the end for the support of such technologies in the browser.

In the early 2010s, frameworks like Backbone and AngularJS started showing up, demonstrating how to build rich web applications with a native feel and speed to them and do so in a seemingly cost-effective way. The diagram that follows shows a **Model-View-ViewModel (MVVM)** client with a **Representational State Transfer (REST)** API. When we decouple the client from the server via an API, then we can architecturally enforce the implementation of presentation and business logic separately. In theory, this RESTful web services pattern should allow us to replace the kitchen sink as often as we want to without having to remodel the entire kitchen.

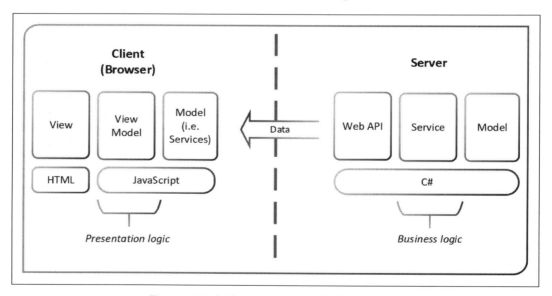

Figure 1.5: Rich-client decoupled MVVM architecture

Observe the near doubling of boxes in the preceding diagram. Just because we separate the client from the server, we don't end up simplifying the architecture. If anything, the architecture surrounding the presentation logic becomes a lot more complicated. Both the client and server must implement their presentation/API, business, and persistence layers.

Unfortunately, many early development efforts leveraging frameworks like Backbone and AngularJS collapsed under their own weight because they failed to implement the client-side architecture properly.

These early development efforts also suffered from ill-designed RESTful Web APIs. Most APIs didn't version their URIs, making it very difficult to introduce new functionality while supporting existing clients. Further, APIs often returned complicated data models exposing their internal relational data models to web apps. This design flaw creates a tight coupling between seemingly unrelated components/views written in HTML and models created in SQL. If you don't implement additional layers of code to translate or map the structure of data, then you create an unintentional and uncontrolled coupling between layers. Over time, dealing with such coupling becomes very expensive very quickly, in most cases necessitating significant rewrites.

Today, we use the API layer to flatten the data model before sending it down to the client to avoid such problems. Newer technologies like GraphQL go a step further by exposing a well-defined data model and letting the consumer query for the exact data it needs. Using GraphQL, the number of HTTP requests and the amount of data transferred over-the-wire is optimal without the developers having to create many specialized APIs.

Backbone and AngularJS proved that it was viable to create web applications that run natively in the browser. All SPA frameworks at the time relied on jQuery for DOM manipulation. Meanwhile, web standards continued to evolve, and evergreen browsers that support new standards started to become commonplace. However, change is constant, and the evolution of web technologies made it unsustainable to evolve this first generation of SPA frameworks gracefully.

The next generation of web frameworks needed to solve many problems; they needed to enforce good architecture; be designed to evolve with web standards; and be stable and scalable to enterprise needs without collapsing. Also, these new frameworks needed to gain acceptance from developers, who were burned out with too many rapid changes in the ecosystem. Remember, unhappy developers do not create successful businesses. Achieving these goals required a clean break from the past, so Angular and React emerged as platforms to address the problems of the past in different ways.

Introduction to Angular

Angular is an open source project maintained by Google and a community of developers. The new Angular platform is vastly different from the legacy framework you may have used in the past. In collaboration with Microsoft, Google made TypeScript the default language for Angular. TypeScript is a superset of JavaScript that enables developers to target legacy browsers such as Internet Explorer 11, while allowing them to write modern JavaScript code that works in evergreen browsers such as Chrome, Firefox, and Edge. The legacy versions of Angular, versions in the 1.x.x range, are referred to as AngularJS. Version 2.0.0 and higher versions are called Angular. Where AngularJS is a monolithic JavaScript SPA framework, Angular is a platform that is capable of targeting browsers, hybrid-mobile frameworks, desktop applications, and server-side rendered views.

Upgrading to the new AngularJS was risky and costly because even minor updates introduced new coding patterns and experimental features. Each update introduced deprecations or the refactoring of old features, which required rewriting large portions of code. Also, updates were delivered in uncertain intervals, making it impossible for a team to plan resources to upgrade to a new version. The release methodology eventually led to an unpredictable, ever-evolving framework with seemingly no guiding hand to carry code bases forward. If you used AngularJS, you likely were stuck on a particular version, because the specific architecture of your code base made it very difficult to move to a new version. In 2018, the Angular team released the last major update to AngularJS with version 1.7. This release marked the beginning of the end for the legacy framework, with planned end-of-life in July 2021.

Angular improves upon AngularJS in every way imaginable. The platform follows semver, as defined at `https://semver.org/`, where minor version increments denote new feature additions and potential deprecation notices for the second next major version, but no breaking changes. Furthermore, the Angular team at Google has committed to a deterministic release schedule with major versions released every 6 months. After this 6-month development window, starting with Angular 4, all major releases receive LTS with bug fixes and security patches for an additional 12 months. From release to end-of-life, each major version receives updates for 18 months. Refer to the following chart for the tentative release and support schedule for AngularJS and Angular:

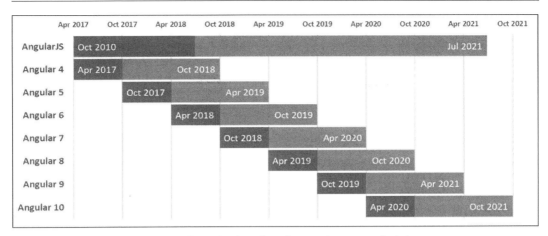

Figure 1.6: Tentative Angular release and support schedule

So, what does this mean for you? You can be confident that your Angular code is supported and backward compatible for an approximate time frame of 24 months, even if you make no changes to it. So, if you wrote an Angular app in version 9 in February 2020, your code is runtime compatible with Angular 10 and will be supported until October 2021. To upgrade your Angular 9 code to Angular 11, you need to ensure that you're not using any of the deprecated APIs that receive a deprecation notice in Angular 10.

In practice, most deprecations are minor and are straightforward to refactor. Unless you are working with low-level APIs for highly specialized user experiences, the time and effort it takes to update your code base should be minimal. However, this is a promise made by Google and not a contract. The Angular team has a significant incentive to ensure backward compatibility because Google runs around 1,000+ Angular apps with a single version of Angular active at any one time throughout the organization. So, by the time you read this, all of Google's 1,000+ apps will be running on the latest version of Angular.

You may think Google has infinite resources to update thousands of app regularly. Like any organization, Google too has limited resources, and not every app is actively maintained by a dedicated team. So, the Angular team must ensure compatibility through automated tests and make it as painless as possible to move through major releases going forward. In Angular 6, the update process was made much simpler with the introduction of `ng update`.

The Angular team continually improves its release process with automated CLI tools to make upgrades of deprecated functionality a mostly automated, reasonable endeavor. The benefits of this strategy were demonstrated by Air France and KLM being able to reduce their upgrade times from 30 days in Angular 2 to 1 day in Angular 7.

A predictable and well-supported upgrade process is excellent news for developers and organizations alike. Instead of being perpetually stuck on a legacy version of Angular, you can plan and allocate the necessary resources to keep moving your application to the future without costly rewrites. As I wrote in a 2017 blog post, *The Best New Feature of Angular 4*, at bit.ly/NgBestFeature, the message is clear:

> **For Developers and Managers**: *Angular is here to stay, so you should be investing your time, attention, and money in learning it – even if you're currently in love with some other framework.*
>
> **For Decision Makers (CIOs, CTOs, and so on)**: *Plan to begin your transition to Angular in the next 6 months. It'll be an investment you'll be able to explain to business-minded people, and your investment will pay dividends for many years to come, long after the initial LTS window expires, with graceful upgrade paths to Angular vNext and beyond.*

So, why do Google (Angular) and Microsoft (TypeScript and Visual Studio Code) give away such technologies for free? There are multiple reasons:

- A sophisticated framework that makes it easy to develop web apps is a demonstration of technical prowess, which retains and attracts developer talent
- An open source framework enables the proving and debugging of new ideas and tools with millions of developers at scale
- Allowing developers to create great web experiences more quickly, ultimately drives more business for Google and Microsoft

I don't see any nefarious intent here and welcome open, mature, and high-quality tools that, if necessary, I can tinker with and bend to my own will. Not having to pay for a support contract for a proprietary piece of tech is a welcome bonus.

Beware, looking for Angular help on the web may be tricky. You'll note that sometimes Angular is referred to as Angular 2 or Angular 4. At times, both Angular and AngularJS are referred to as AngularJS. This is incorrect. The documentation for Angular is at angular.io. If you land on angularjs.org, you'll be reading about the legacy AngularJS framework.

> For the latest updates on the upcoming Angular releases, view the official release schedule at `https://angular.io/guide/releases`.

Angular's philosophy

Your time is valuable, and your happiness is paramount, so you must be careful in choosing the technologies to invest your time in. With this in mind, we need to answer the question of why learn Angular, but not React, Vue, or some other framework? Angular is a great framework to start learning. The framework and the tooling help you get off the ground quickly and continue being successful with a vibrant community and high-quality UI libraries you can use to deliver exceptional web applications. React and Vue are great frameworks, with their strengths and weaknesses. Every tool has its place and purpose.

In some cases, React is the right choice for a project, and in other cases, Vue is the right one. Regardless, becoming somewhat proficient in other web frameworks can only help further your understanding of Angular and make you a better developer overall. SPAs such as Backbone and AngularJS grabbed my full attention in 2012 when I realized the importance of decoupling frontend and backend concerns. Server-side rendered templates are nearly impossible to maintain and are the root cause of many expensive rewrites of software systems. If you care about creating maintainable software, then you must abide by the prime directive; keep business logic implemented behind the API decoupled from presentation logic implemented in the UI.

Angular neatly fits the Pareto principle or the 80-20 rule. It has become a mature and evolving platform, allowing you to achieve 80% of tasks with 20% of the effort. As mentioned in the previous section, every major release is supported for 18 months, creating a continuum of learning, staying up to date, and the deprecation of old features. From the perspective of a full-stack developer, this continuum is invaluable, since your skills and training will remain relevant and fresh for many years to come.

The philosophy behind Angular is to err on the side of configuration over convention. Convention-based frameworks, although they may seem elegant from the outside, make it difficult for newcomers to pick up the framework. Configuration-based frameworks, however, aim to expose their inner workings through explicit configuration and hooks, where you can attach your custom behavior to the framework. In essence, where AngularJS had tons of magic, which can be confusing, unpredictable, and challenging to debug, Angular tries to be non-magical.

Configuration over convention results in verbose coding. Verbosity is a good thing. Terse code is the enemy of maintainability, only benefiting the original author. As Andy Hunt and David Thomas put it in *The Pragmatic Programmer*:

> *Remember that you (and others after you) will be reading the code many hundreds of times, but only writing it a few times.*

Further, Andy Hunt's *Law of Design* dictates:

> *If you can't rip every piece out easily, then the design sucks.*

Verbose, decoupled, cohesive, and encapsulated code is the key to future-proofing your code. Angular, through its various mechanisms, enables the proper execution of these concepts. It gets rid of many custom conventions invented in AngularJS, such as `ng-click`, and introduces a more natural language that builds on the existing HTML elements and properties. As a result, `ng-click` becomes `(click)`, extending HTML rather than replacing it.

Next, we'll go over Angular's evergreen mindset and the reactive programming paradigm, which are the latest extensions of Angular's initial philosophy.

Angular Evergreen

When you're learning Angular, you're not learning one specific version of Angular, but a platform that is continually evolving. Since the first drafts, I designed this book with the idea of deemphasizing the specific version of Angular you're using. The Angular team champions this idea. Over the years, I have had many conversations with the Angular team and thought leaders within the community and listened to many presentations. As a result, I can affirm that you can depend on Angular as a mature web development platform. Angular frequently receives updates with great attention to backward compatibility. Furthermore, any code that is made incompatible by a new version is brought forward with help from automated tools or explicit guidance on how to update your code via `update.angular.io`, so you're never left guessing or scouring the internet for answers. The Angular team is committed to ensuring you – the developer – have the best web development experience possible.

To bring this idea front and center with developers, several colleagues and I have developed and published a Visual Studio Code extension called Angular Evergreen.

Figure 1.7: Angular Evergreen VS Code extension

This extension detects your current version of Angular and compares it to the latest and next releases of Angular. Releases that are labeled next are meant for early adopters and for testing the compatibility of your code with an upcoming version of Angular. Do not use next-labeled releases for production deployments.

 Find more information, feature requests, and bug reports on the Angular Evergreen extension at https://AngularEvergreen.com.

One of the critical components of Angular that allows the platform to remain evergreen is TypeScript. TypeScript allows new features to be implemented efficiently while providing support for older browsers, so your code can reach the widest audience possible.

TypeScript

Angular is coded using TypeScript. TypeScript was created by Anders Hejlsberg of Microsoft to address several major issues with applying JavaScript at the enterprise-scale.

Anders Hejlsberg is the creator of Turbo Pascal and C#, and is the chief architect of Delphi. Anders designed C# to be a developer-friendly language built upon the familiar syntax of C and C++. As a result, C# became the language behind Microsoft's popular .NET Framework. TypeScript shares a similar pedigree with Turbo Pascal and C# and their ideals, which made them a great success.

JavaScript is a dynamically interpreted language, where the code you write is parsed and understood by the browser at runtime. Statically typed languages like Java or C# have an additional compilation step, where the compiler can catch programming and logic errors during compile time. It is much cheaper to detect and fix bugs at compile time versus runtime. TypeScript brings the benefits of statically typed languages to JavaScript by introducing types and generics to the language. However, TypeScript does not include a compilation step, but instead a transpilation step. A compiler builds code into machine language with C/C++ or **intermediary language** (IL) with Java or C#. A transpiler, however, merely translates code from one dialect to another. So, when TypeScript code is built, compiled, or transpiled, the result is pure JavaScript.

JavaScript's official name is ECMAScript. The feature set and the syntax of the language is maintained by the ECMA Technical Committee 39 or TC39 for short.

Transpilation has another significant benefit. The same tooling that converts TypeScript to JavaScript can be used to rewrite JavaScript with a new syntax to an older version that older browsers can parse and execute. Between 1999 and 2009, the JavaScript language didn't see any new features. ECMAScript abandoned version 4 due to various technical and political reasons. Starting with the introduction of ES5 and then ES2015 (also known as ES6), browser vendors have struggled to implement new JavaScript features within their browsers. As a result, user adoption of these new features has remained low. However, these new features meant developers could write code more productively. This created a gap known as the JavaScript Feature Gap, as demonstrated by the graphic that follows:

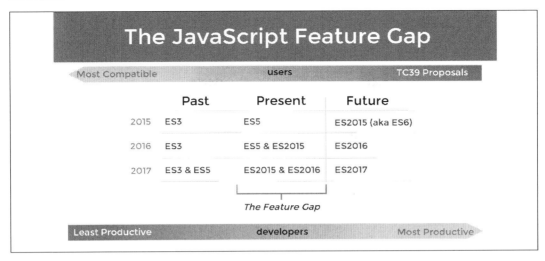

Figure 1.8: The JavaScript Feature Gap

The JavaScript Feature Gap is a sliding one, as TC39 has committed to updating JavaScript every year going forward. As a result, TypeScript represents the past, present, and future of JavaScript. You can use future features of JavaScript today and still be able to target browsers of the past to maximize the audience you can reach.

Now, let's go over Angular's underlying architecture.

Basic Angular architecture

Angular follows the MV* pattern, which is a hybrid of the MVC and MVVM patterns. Previously, we went over the MVC pattern. At a high-level, the architecture of both patterns is relatively similar, as shown in the diagram that follows:

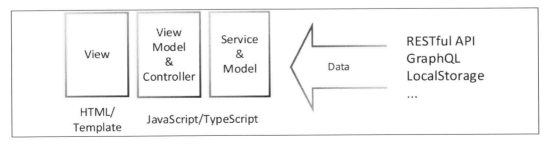

Figure 1.9: MV* architecture

The new concept here is the ViewModel, which represents the glue code that connects your view to your model or service. In Angular, this glue is known as binding. Whereas MVC frameworks like Backbone or React have to call a `render` method to process their HTML templates, in Angular, this process is seamless and transparent for the developer. Binding is what differentiates an MVC application from an MVVM one.

The most basic unit of an Angular app is a component. A component is the combination of a JavaScript class written in TypeScript and an Angular template written in HTML, CSS, and TypeScript. The class and the template fit together like a jigsaw puzzle through bindings, so that they can communicate with each other, as shown in the diagram that follows:

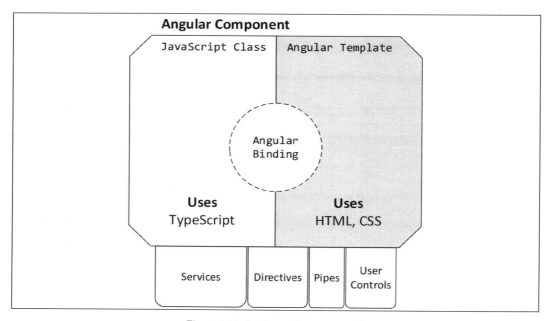

Figure 1.10: Anatomy of a component

Classes are an **Object-Oriented Programming (OOP)** construct. If you invest the time to dig deeper into the OOP paradigm, you are going to improve your understanding of how Angular works vastly. The OOP paradigm allows for the **dependency injection (DI)** of dependent services in your components, so you can make HTTP calls or trigger a toast message to be displayed to the user without pulling that logic into your component or duplicating your code. DI makes it very easy for developers to use many interdependent services without having to worry about the order of instantiation, initialization, or destruction of such objects from memory.

Angular templates also allow similar reuse of code via directives, pipes, user controls, and other components. These are pieces of code that encapsulate highly interactive end user code. This kind of interactivity code is often complicated and convoluted and must be kept isolated from business logic or presentation logic to keep your code maintainable.

All Angular components, services, directives, pipes, and user controls are organized under modules. Each Angular app is bootstrapped by a root module that renders your first component and injects any services and prepares dependencies it may require. You may introduce children modules to enable capabilities like lazy loading so that you don't have to deliver all components of your web application to the browser all at once. For instance, there is no use sending code for the admin dashboard to a user without admin privileges.

Angular makes heavy use of the RxJS library, which introduces reactive development patterns to Angular, as opposed to more traditional imperative development patterns.

The reactive development paradigm

Angular supports multiple styles of programming. The plurality of coding styles is one of the great reasons why it is approachable to programmers with varying backgrounds. Whether you come from an object-oriented programming background or you're a staunch believer of functional programming, you can build viable apps using Angular. In *Chapter 3, Creating a Basic Angular App*, you'll begin leveraging reactive programming concepts in building the LocalCast Weather app.

As a programmer, you are most likely used to imperative programming. Imperative programming is when you, as the programmer, write sequential code describing everything that must be done in the order that you've defined them and the state of your application depending on just the right variables to be set to function correctly. You write loops, conditionals, and call functions; you fire off events and expect them to be handled. Imperative and sequential logic is how you're used to coding.

Reactive programming is a subset of functional programming. In functional programming, you can't rely on variables you've set previously. Every function you write must stand on its own, receive its own set of inputs and return a result without being influenced by the state of an outer function or class. Functional programming supports **Test Driven Development** (**TDD**) very well because every function is a unit that can be tested in isolation. As such, every function you write becomes composable. So, you can mix, match, and combine any function you write with any other and construct a series of calls that yield the result you expect.

Reactive programming adds a twist to functional programming. You no longer deal with pure logic, but an asynchronous data stream that you transform and mold into any shape you need with a composable set of functions. So, when you subscribe to an event in a reactive stream, then you're shifting your coding paradigm from reactive programming to imperative programming.

Later in the book, when implementing the LocalCast Weather app, you'll leverage `subscribe` in action in two places, in the `CurrentWeather` and `CitySearch` components.

Consider the following example, aptly put by Mike Pearson in his presentation *Thinking Reactively: Most Difficult*, of providing instructions to get hot water from the faucet to help understand the differences between imperative and reactive programming:

Instructions to get hot water from the faucet		
	Imperative	**Reactive**
0	Initial state: Water is off	Initial state: Water is off
1	Grab a hose	Turn on the faucet for hot water
2	Spray water into the heater	
3	Turn on the faucet for hot water	
4	Send a text to the utility company to get gas	
5	Wait for hot water	
6	Undo your steps to restore the initial state	Undo your steps to restore the initial state

As you can see, with imperative programming, you must define every step of the code execution. Every step depends on the previous step, which means you must consider the state of the environment to ensure a successful operation. In such an environment, it is easy to forget a step and very difficult to test the correctness of every individual step. In functional reactive programming, you work with asynchronous data streams resulting in a stateless workflow that is easy to compose with other actions.

RxJS is the library that makes it possible to implement your code in the reactive paradigm.

RxJS

RxJS stands for Reactive Extensions, which is a modular library that enables reactive programming, which itself is an asynchronous programming paradigm and allows the manipulation of data streams through transformation, filtering, and control functions. You can think of reactive programming as an evolution of event-based programming.

Reactive data streams

In event-driven programming, you would define an event handler and attach it to an event source. In more concrete terms, if you had a **Save** button, which exposes an onClick event, you would implement a confirmSave function which, when triggered, would show a popup to ask the user **Are you sure?**. Look at the following diagram for a visualization of this process.

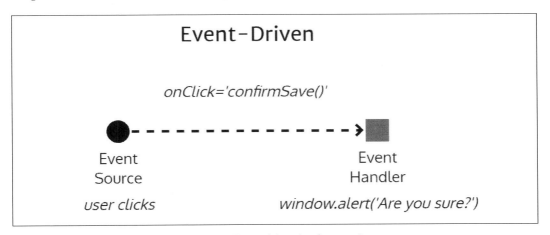

Figure 1.11: Event-driven implementation

In short, you would have an event firing once per user action. If the user clicks on the **Save** button many times, this pattern will gladly render as many popups as there are clicks, which doesn't make much sense.

The publish-subscribe (pub/sub) pattern is a different type of event-driven programming. In this case, we can write multiple handlers to all act on the result of a given event simultaneously. Let's say that your app just received some updated data. The publisher goes through its list of subscribers and passes on the updated data to each of them.

Refer to the following diagram on how the updated data event triggers multiple functions:

- An `updateCache` function updates your local cache with new data
- A `fetchDetails` function retrieves further details about the data from the server
- A `showToastMessage` function informs the user that the app just received new data

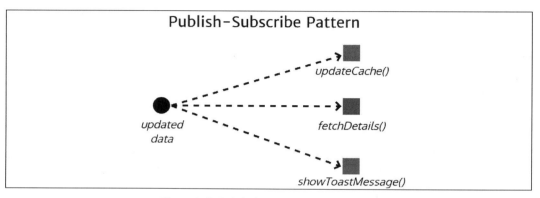

Figure 1.12: Pub/sub pattern implementation

All these events can happen asynchronously; however, the `fetchDetails` and `showToastMessage` functions will be receiving more data than they need, and it can get convoluted to try to compose these events in different ways to modify application behavior.

In reactive programming, everything is treated as a stream. A stream will contain events that happen over time and these events can contain some data or no data. The following diagram visualizes a scenario where your app is listening for mouse clicks from the user. Uncontrolled streams of user clicks are meaningless. You exert some control over this stream by applying the `throttle` function to it, so you only get updates every 250 **milliseconds (ms)**. If you subscribe to this new event, every 250 ms, you will receive a list of click events. You may try to extract some data from each click event, but in this case, you're only interested in the number of click events that happened. We can shape the raw event data into a number of clicks using the `map` function.

Further down the stream, we may only be interested in listening for events with two or more clicks in it, so we can use the `filter` function to only act on what is essentially a double-click event. Every time our filter event fires, it means that the user intended to double-click, and you can act on that information by popping up an alert.

The true power of streams comes from the fact that you can choose to act on the event at any time as it passes through various control, transformation, and filter functions. You can choose to display click data on an HTML list using *ngFor and Angular's async pipe, so the user can monitor the types of click data being captured every 250 ms.

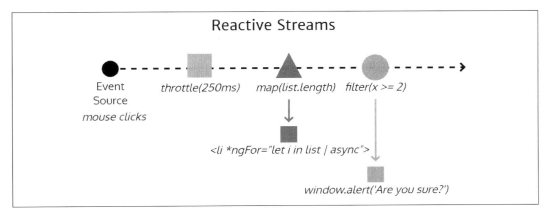

Figure 1.13: A reactive data stream implementation

Now let's consider some more advanced Angular architectural patterns.

Advanced Angular architecture

As mentioned earlier, in the *Basic Angular architecture* section, Angular components, services, and dependencies are organized into modules. Angular apps are bootstrapped via their root module, as shown in the diagram that follows:

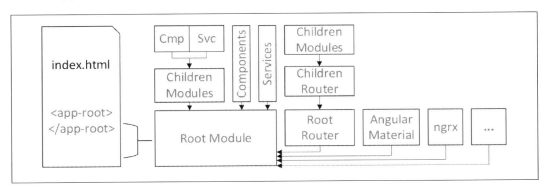

Figure 1.14: Angular Bootstrap process showing major architectural elements

The root module can import other modules and also declare components and provide services. As your application grows, you need to create sub-modules that contain their components and services. Organizing your application in this manner allows you to implement lazy loading, allowing you to control which parts of your application get delivered to the browser and when. As you add more features to your application, you import modules from other libraries, like Angular Material or NgRx. You implement the router to enable rich navigational experiences between your components, allowing your routing configuration to orchestrate the creation of components.

Chapter 7, Creating a Router-First Line-of-Business App, introduces router-first architecture, where I encourage you to start the development of your application by creating all your routes ahead of time.

In Angular, services are provided as singletons to a module by default. You'll quickly get used to this behavior. However, you must keep in mind that if you provide the same service across multiple modules, then each module has its own instance of the provided service. In the case of an authentication service, where we wish to have only one instance across our entire application, you must be careful to only provide that instance of the authentication service at the root module level. Any service, component, or module provided at the root level of your application becomes available in the feature module.

Beyond modules, the router is the next most powerful technology you must master in Angular.

The Angular Router

The Angular Router, shipped in the `@angular/router` package, is a central and critical part of building **single-page applications** (**SPAs**) that act and behave like regular websites that are easy to navigate using browser controls or the zoom or micro zoom controls.

The Angular Router has advanced features such as lazy loading, router outlets, auxiliary routes, smart active link tracking, and the ability to be expressed as an `href`, which enables a highly flexible Router-first app architecture leveraging stateless data-driven components using RxJS `BehaviorSubject`.

Large teams can work against a single code base, with each team responsible for a module's development, without stepping on each other's toes, while enabling easy continuous integration. Google, with its billions of lines of code, works against a single code base for a very good reason: integration after the fact is very expensive.

Small teams can remix their UI layouts on the fly to quickly respond to changes without having to rearchitect their code. It is easy to underestimate the amount of time wasted due to late game changes in layout or navigation. Such changes are easier to absorb by larger teams but a costly endeavor for small teams.

Consider the diagram that follows, where app.ts contains the module. It has a rootRouter; components a, master, detail, and c; services; pipes; and directives provided and declared for it. All of these components will be parsed and eagerly loaded by the browser when a user first navigates to your application.

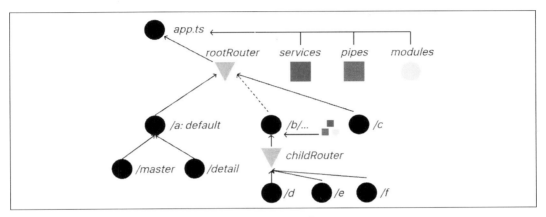

Figure 1.15: Angular architecture

If you were to implement a lazily loaded route /b, you would need to create a feature module named b, which would have its own childRouter; components d, e, and f; services; pipes; and directives provided and declared for it. During transpile-time, Angular will package these components into a separate file or bundle and this bundle will only be downloaded, parsed, and loaded if the user ever navigates to a path under /b.

Let's look into lazy loading in more detail.

Lazy loading

The dashed line connecting /b/... to rootRouter demonstrates how lazy loading works. Lazy loading allows developers to achieve a sub-second first meaningful paint quickly. By deferring the loading of additional modules, we can keep the bundle size delivered to the browser to a minimum. The size of a module impacts download and loading speeds, because the more a browser has to do, the longer it takes for a user to see the first screen of the app. By defining lazily loaded modules, each module is packaged as separate files, which can be downloaded and loaded individually and on demand.

The Angular Router provides smart active link tracking, which results in a superior developer and user experience, making it very easy to implement highlighting features to indicate to the user the current tab or portion of the app that is currently active. Auxiliary routes maximize the reuse of components and help pull off complicated state transitions with ease. With auxiliary routes, you can render multiple master and detail views using only a single outer template. You can also control how the route is displayed to the user in the browser's URL bar and compose routes using `routerLink`, in templates, and `Router.navigate`, in code, driving complicated scenarios.

In *Chapter 7, Creating a Router-First Line-of-Business App*, I cover implementing router basics, and advanced recipes are covered in *Chapter 11, Recipes – Reusability, Routing, and Caching*.

Beyond routing, state management is another crucial concept to master if you would like to build sophisticated Angular applications.

State management

A class backs every component and service in Angular. When instantiated, a class becomes an object in memory. As you work with an object, if you store values in object properties, then you're introducing state to your Angular application. If unmanaged, the state becomes a significant liability to the success and maintainability of your application.

I'm a fan of stateless design both in the backend and frontend. From my perspective, state is evil, and you should pay careful attention not to introduce state into your code. Earlier, we discussed how services in Angular are singletons by default. This is a terrible opportunity to introduce state into your application. You must avoid storing information in your services. In *Chapter 7, Creating a Router-First Line-of-Business App*, I introduce you to BehaviorSubjects, which act as data-anchors for your application. In this case, we store these anchors in services, so they can be shared across components to synchronize data.

In Angular components, the class is a ViewModel acting as the glue code between your code and the template. Compared to services, components are relatively short-lived, and it is okay to use object properties in this context.

However, beyond design, there are specific use cases for introducing robust mechanisms to maintain complicated data models in the state of your application. Progressive web applications and mobile applications are one use case where connectivity is not guaranteed. In these cases, being able to save and resume the entire state of your application is a must to provide a great **user experience (UX)** for your end user.

The NgRx library for Angular leverages the Flux pattern to enable sophisticated state management for your applications. In *Chapter 6*, *Forms, Observables, and Subjects* and *Chapter 12*, *Recipes – Master/Detail, Data Tables, and NgRx*, I provide alternative implementations for various features using NgRx to demonstrate the differences in implementation between more lightweight methods.

The Flux pattern

Flux is the application architecture that was created by Facebook to assist in building client-side web applications. The Flux pattern defines a series of components that manage a store that stores the state of your application via dispatchers that trigger/handle actions and view functions that read values from the store. Using the Flux pattern, you keep the state of your application in a store where access to the store is only possible through well-defined and decoupled functions, resulting in architecture that scales well because, in isolation, decoupled functions are easy to reason with and write automated unit tests for.

Consider the diagram that follows to understand the flow of information between these components:

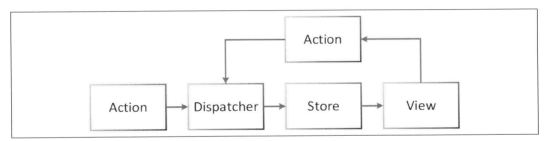

Figure 1.16: NgRx data flow

NgRx implements the Flux pattern in Angular using RxJS.

NgRx

The NgRx library brings Redux-like (a popular React.js library) reactive state management to Angular based on RxJS. State management with NgRx allows developers to write atomic, self-contained, and composable pieces of code creating actions, reducers, and selectors. This kind of reactive programming allows side-effects in state changes to be isolated and feels right at home with the general coding patterns of React.js. NgRx ends up creating an abstraction layer over already complex and sophisticated tooling like RxJS.

There are excellent reasons to use NgRx, like if you deal with 3+ input streams into your application. In such a scenario, the overhead of dealing with so many events makes it worthwhile to introduce a new coding paradigm to your project. However, most applications only have two input streams: REST APIs and user input. To a lesser extent, NgRx may make sense if you are writing offline-first **Progressive Web Apps (PWAs)**, where you may have to persist complicated state information, or architecting a niche enterprise app with similar needs.

Here's an architectural overview of NgRx:

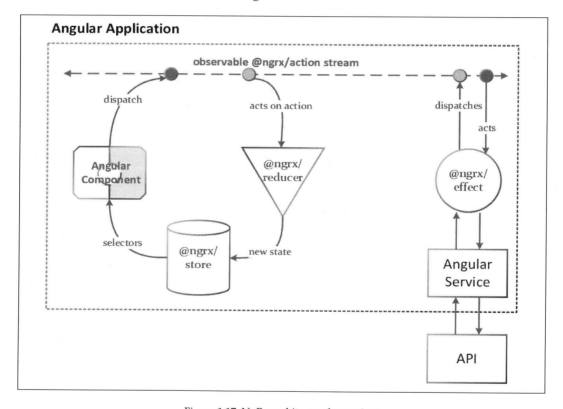

Figure 1.17: NgRx architectural overview

Consider the very top of the diagram as an observable action stream, where actions can be dispatched and acted upon as denoted by the circles. Effects and components can dispatch an action. Reducers and effects can act upon these actions to either store values in the store or trigger an interaction with the server. Selectors are leveraged by components to read values from the store.

Given my positive attitude toward minimal tooling and a lack of definite necessity for NgRx beyond the niche audiences previously mentioned, I do not recommend NgRx as a default choice. RxJS/BehaviorSubjects are powerful and capable enough to unlock sophisticated and scalable patterns to help you build great Angular applications, as is demonstrated in the chapters that lead up to *Chapter 12, Recipes – Master/Detail, Data Tables, and NgRx*.

You can read more about NgRx at `https://ngrx.io`.

React.js architecture

In contrast to Angular, React.js, as a whole, implements the Flux pattern. Following is a router-centric view of a React application, where components/containers and providers are represented in a strict tree-like manner.

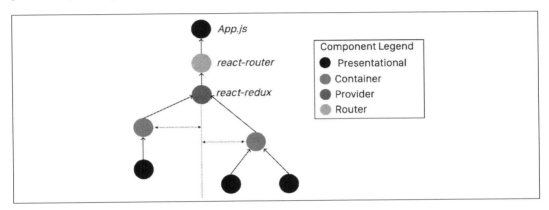

Figure 1.18: React.js architectural overview

In the initial releases of React, one had to laboriously pass values up/down the inheritance tree of every component for even the most basic functionality to work. Later on, react-redux was introduced, so each component can read/write values directly to the store without having to traverse the tree.

This basic overview should give you a sense of the significant architectural differences between Angular and React. However, keep in mind that just like Angular, React, its community, patterns, and practices are continually evolving and getting better over time.

You can learn more about React at `https://reactjs.org`.

Notable Angular features

Specific Angular versions introduce noteworthy changes to advance the philosophy of the platform and make it more seamless and comprehensive. I recommend checking out the unique changes that these seminal releases have introduced.

Angular 6

Most, if not all, of the content, patterns, and practices in this book are compatible with Angular 4 and up. However, Angular 6 was a seminal release of Angular, which brought a lot of under-the-covers improvements to the platform and the overall stability and cohesion across the ecosystem. The development experience is vastly improved with additional CLI tools that make it easier to update versions of packages and faster build times to improve your code-build-view feedback cycle. With Angular 6, all platform tools are version synced to 6.0, making it easier to reason about the ecosystem. In the following table, you can see how this makes it easier to communicate tooling compatibility:

	Previously	With v6
CLI	1.7	6.0
Angular	5.2.10	6.0
Material	5.2.4	6.0

Angular CLI 6.0 comes with major new capabilities, such as `ng update` and `ng add` commands; `ng update` makes it much easier to update your version of Angular, npm dependencies, RxJS, and Angular Material, including some deterministic code rewriting capabilities to apply name changes to APIs or functions. The topic of updating your version of Angular is covered in depth in *Appendix C, Keeping Angular and Tools Evergreen*. You can find this appendix online from https://static.packt-cdn.com/downloads/9781838648800_Appendix_C_Keeping_Angular_and_Tools_Evergreen.pdf or at https://expertlysimple.io/stay-evergreen. `ng add` brings schematics support to the Angular CLI. With schematics, you can write custom code to add new capabilities to an Angular app, adding any dependencies, boilerplate configuration code, or scaffolding. A great example is to be able to add Angular Material to your project by executing `ng add @angular/material`. The topic of adding Angular Material to your project is covered in depth in *Chapter 5, Delivering High-Quality UX with Material*. A standalone Material Update tool aims to make Angular Material updates less painful, found at `Github.com/angular/material-update-tool`, but expect this functionality to be merged into `ng update`. Further schematics can bring their own `generate` commands to CLI, making your life easier and your code base more consistent over time. In addition, version 4 of webpack is configured to build your Angular application into smaller modules with scope hosting, shortening the first-paint time of your app.

The major theme of Angular 6 is under-the-hood performance improvements and Custom Elements support. Version 6 improves upon v5 in terms of the base bundle size by 12% at 65 KB, which improves load times by a whopping 21-40% from fast 3G to fiber connections. As your applications grow, Angular takes advantage of a better tree-shaking technique to further prune unused code out of your final deliverable. Speed is a UX feature in Angular 6. This is accomplished with better support for the Angular **Component Development Kit (CDK)**, Angular Material, Animations, and i18n. Angular Universal allows for server-side assisted fast startup times, and Angular PWA support takes advantage of native platform features such as caching and offline storage, so in subsequent visits, your app remains fast. RxJS 6 support allows the tree-shakeable pipe command, reducing bundle sizes more often, and fixes the behavior of `throttle` as I caution you in *Chapter 6, Forms, Observables, and Subjects*, among numerous bug fixes and performance improvements. TypeScript 2.7 brings in better support for importing different types of JavaScript packages and more advanced features to catch coding errors during build time.

Angular Material 6 added new user controls such as tree and badge while making the library a lot more stable with a slew of bug fixes, completeness of functionality, and theming in existing components. Angular Flex Layout 6 brought in polyfills, enabling Internet Explorer 11 to support CSS Flexbox. This makes Angular apps using Material and Flex Layout fully compatible with the last major legacy browser technology that still persists in enterprises and governments despite leaving mainstream support in January 2018 alongside Windows 8.1 and being superseded 18 times by Microsoft Edge. Angular 6 itself can be configured to be compatible down to IE9 using polyfills. This is great for developers who must support such legacy browsers and still be able to use modern technologies to build their solutions.

Some exciting, new ancillary tooling was also released to enable high-frequency, high-performance, or large enterprise use cases. The Angular ecosystem welcomed the NgRx library, bringing Redux-like reactive state management to Angular based on RxJS. The Nx CLI tool, built by former Angular team members, brings an opinionated development environment setup to Angular, suitable for consultants and large organizations that must ensure a consistent environment. This book follows a similar pattern and aims to educate you in establishing a consistent architecture and design pattern to apply across your applications. Google's Bazel build tool enables incremental builds, so portions of your application that haven't changed don't need to be rebuilt, vastly improving build times for large projects and allowing the packaging of libraries to be shared between Angular applications.

Angular 8

As mentioned in the *Preface* of this book, this book has been designed to be effective with any new version of Angular. This is an idea that is championed by the Angular team, who wishes to deemphasize the specific version of Angular you're currently using, instead of focusing and investing in continually staying up to date with every minor and major release of Angular. The Angular team is spending considerable energy and effort to ensure that as much of the code you have written remains compatible, as the performance and feature set of Angular improve over time. Any breaking change is either supported by automated tools, helping you rewrite portions of your code, or planned deprecations, giving you ample time to phase out unsupported code.

Angular 7 brought performance, accessibility, and dependency updates for TypeScript, RxJS, and Node, along with a significant update and the expansion of Angular Material controls; Angular 8 continuous these trends. Angular 8 introduces differential loading and support for minimal polyfills for evergreen browsers, saving somewhere between 7-20% of the payload delivered to the client.

Angular 9

Angular 9 and its subsequent 9.1 update brings some of the most significant updates to the framework to date by delivering the Ivy rendering engine and TypeScript 3.8 support. This update tackles a lot of tech debt removal, brings 100 bug fixes and features, and greatly expands automated test coverage of the framework. The Ivy rendering engine results in smaller package sizes and faster load times for your apps. In addition, Angular 9.1 brings 40% faster build times, 40-50% improved unit test run-times, and better debugging capabilities with simpler stack traces and template binding. TypeScript 3.8 brings in new syntactical benefits like optional chaining and the nullish operator to make it dramatically easier to deal with null or undefined values in Angular's strict mode.

The full benefits of the Ivy rendering engine will be felt with future updates. Ivy will allow the creation of tiny and lean Angular applications. Prior to Ivy, the metadata needed to describe an Angular component was stored within a module. With Ivy, components implement the locality principle, so they can be self-describing. This allows Ivy to lazily load individual components and creation of standalone components. Imagine an Angular library that can render components with a single function call and only be a few kilobytes in size. This miniaturization makes it feasible to implement Angular Elements using the Custom Elements, part of the Web Components spec.

Angular Elements, introduced in version 6, allows you to code an Angular component and reuse that component in any other web application using any web technology, in essence declaring your very own custom HTML element. These Custom Elements are cross-compatible with any HTML-based tool-chain, including other web application libraries or frameworks. To make this work, the entire Angular framework needs to be packaged alongside your new custom element. This was not feasible in Angular 6, because that meant tacking on at least 65 KB each time you created a new user control.

In early 2020, Chrome, Edge, and Firefox support Custom Elements natively, a significant change from the status quo in early 2018. Angular 9 enables the Ivy rendering engine by default, and future updates to Angular should drive base bundle sizes to be as small as 2.7 KB, so wide-spread use of Angular-based Custom Elements could soon become reality. In 2020, all major browsers natively support Custom Elements, leaving Safari the last browser implement the standard.

Always check `https://caniuse.com` before getting too excited about a new web technology to ensure that you are indeed able to use that feature in browsers that you must support.

`Angular.io` leverages Custom Elements to demonstrate the feasibility of the technology. The documentation site attracts 1 million+ unique visitors per month, so it should help work out some of the kinks as it matures. Custom Elements are great for hosting interactive code samples alongside static content. For example, in early 2018, `Angular.io` started using `StackBlitz.io` for interactive code samples.

`StackBlitz.io` is an amazing tool, a rich IDE right in the browser, so you can experiment with different ideas or run GitHub repositories without needing to pull or execute any code locally.

Other significant updates include the differential loading of JavaScript bundles to improve loading times and **time-to-interactive** (**TTI**) for modern browsers. Angular Router adds backward compatibility to make it feasible to perform piecemeal upgrades of legacy AngularJS projects.

Google mandates that the 2000+ Angular projects they have must all be on the same version of Angular. This means that every new update to Angular is well tested and there are no backward compatibility surprises.

With all the groundwork laid in version 9, we can expect a more agile and capable framework with Angular 10. I hope you are as excited as I am about Angular and the future possibilities it unlocks. Buckle up your seatbelt Dorothy, 'cause Kansas is going bye-bye.

Summary

In summary, web technologies have evolved to a point where it is possible to create rich, fast, and native web applications that can run well on the vast majority of desktop and mobile browsers that are deployed today. Angular has evolved to become a mature and stable platform, applying lessons learned from the past. It enables sophisticated development methodologies that enable developers to create maintainable, interactive, and fast applications. Technologies like TypeScript, RxJS, and NgRx enabled patterns from object-oriented programming, reactive programming, and the Flux pattern.

Angular is engineered to be reactive through and through and, therefore, you must adjust your programming style to fit this pattern. In addition, Angular is meant to be consumed in an evergreen manner, so it is a great idea always to keep your Angular up to date.

Leveraging promises in an Angular app, instead of observables and the async pipe, is equivalent to disregarding all the advice and documentation that the Angular team and thought leaders in the community have communicated. It is easy to fall into bad practices and habits following shallow or wildly out-of-context advice you may glean from self-help sites or blog posts written with an experimental mindset. The official documentation should be your bible, found at `https://angular.io/docs`.

In the next chapter, you will be configuring your development environment to optimize it for a great and consistent Angular development experience across macOS and Windows operating systems. In the following chapters, you will learn how to create a basic Angular app, deploy it on the internet, then learn about advanced architectural patterns to create scalable applications, learn how to create a full-stack TypeScript application using Minimal MEAN, and leverage advanced DevOps and Continuous Integration techniques. The book wraps up by introducing you to Amazon Web Services and Google Analytics.

Further reading

- *Design Patterns: Elements of Reusable Object-Oriented Software*, Erich Gamma, Richard Helm, Ralph Johnson, John Vlissides, 1994, Addison Wesley, ISBN 0-201-63361-2.
- Human JavaScript, Henrik Joreteg, 2013, http://read.humanjavascript.com.
- What's new in TypeScript x MS Build 2017, Anders Hejlsberg, 2017, https://www.youtube.com/watch?v=0sMZJ02rs2c.
- *The Pragmatic Programmer, 20th Anniversary Edition*, David Thomas and Andrew Hunt, 2019, Addison Wesley, ISBN 978-0135957059.
- *Thinking Reactively: Most Difficult*, Mike Pearson, 2019, https://www.youtube.com/watch?v=-4cwkHNguXE.
- *Data Composition with RxJS, Deborah Kurata*, 2019, https://www.youtube.com/watch?v=Z76QlSpYcck.
- Flux Pattern In-Depth Overview, Facebook, 2019, https://facebook.github.io/flux/docs/in-depth-overview.

Questions

Answer the following questions as best as you can to ensure that you've understood the key concepts from this chapter without Googling. Do you need help answering the questions? See *Appendix D, Self-Assessment Answers* online at https://static.packt-cdn.com/downloads/9781838648800_Appendix_D_Self-Assessment_Answers.pdf or visit https://expertlysimple.io/angular-self-assessment.

1. What is the concept behind Angular Evergreen?
2. Using the double-click example for reactive streams, implement the following steps using RxJS: Listen to click events from an HTML target with the `fromEvent` function. Determine if the mouse was double-clicked within a 250ms timeframe using `throttleTime`, `asyncScheduler`, `buffer`, and `filter` operators. If a double-click is detected, display an alert in the browser. Hint: Use https://stackblitz.com or implement your code and use https://rxjs.dev/ for help.
3. What is NgRx, and what role does it play in an Angular application?
4. What is the difference between a module, a component, and a service in Angular?

2
Setting Up Your Development Environment

This chapter demonstrates how you and your team members can create a consistent development environment so that your entire team has the same great web development experience – the importance of which is highlighted in the preface of the book. It can be tough for beginners to create the right development environment, which is essential for a frustration-free development experience. For seasoned developers and teams, achieving a consistent and minimal development environment remains a challenge. Once achieved, such a development environment helps avoid many IT-related issues, including ongoing maintenance, licensing, and upgrade costs.

Instructions on installing GitHub Desktop, Node.js, the Angular CLI, and Docker are a useful reference for those from absolute beginners to seasoned teams, along with strategies for how to automate and ensure the correct and consistent configuration of your development environment.

Feel free to skip this chapter if you already have a robust development environment set up; however, beware that some of the environmental assumptions declared in this chapter may result in some instructions not working for you in later chapters. Come back to this chapter as a reference if you run into issues or need to help a colleague, pupil, or friend to set up their development environment. Automated installation scripts to set up your development environment can be found at https://github.com/duluca/web-dev-environment-setup.

Setting Up Your Development Environment

To make the most of this book, you should be familiar with JavaScript ES2015+, frontend development basics, and RESTful APIs.

The recommended operating systems are Windows 10 Pro v1903+ with PowerShell v7+, or macOS Sierra v10.15+ with Terminal (Bash or Oh My Zsh). Most of the suggested software in this book also works on Linux systems, but your experience may vary depending on your particular setup.

It is standard practice for developers to use Google Chrome 80+ when developing web applications. However, you may also use the Chromium-based Microsoft Edge browser 80+. You should definitely install the cross-platform PowerShell on Windows from `https://github.com/PowerShell/PowerShell/releases`, which gives you access to chain operators `&&` and `||`. Additionally, get the new Windows Terminal from the Microsoft Store for a superior command-line experience on Windows.

In this chapter, you are going to learn how to do the following:

- Work with the CLI package managers Chocolatey and Homebrew to install and update software
- Use those package managers to install GitHub, Node.js, and other essential programs
- Use scripting to automate installation using PowerShell or Bash
- Generate an Angular application using the Angular CLI
- Achieve a consistent and cross-platform development environment using automated tools

Let's start by learning about CLI-based package managers that you can use to install your development tools. In the next section, you'll see that using CLI tools is a superior method compared to dealing with individual installers. It is much easier to automate CLI tools, which makes setup and maintenance tasks repeatable and fast.

CLI package managers

Installing software through a **Graphical User Interface** (**GUI**) is slow and challenging to automate. As a full-stack developer, whether you're a Windows or a Mac user, you must rely on **Command-Line Interface** (**CLI**) package managers to efficiently install and configure the software you depend on.

> Remember, anything that can be expressed as a CLI command can also be automated.

Installing Chocolatey for Windows

Chocolatey is a CLI-based package manager for Windows that can be used for automated software installation. To install Chocolatey on Windows, you need to run an elevated command shell:

1. Launch the **Start** menu
2. Start typing in `PowerShell`
3. You should see **Windows PowerShell Desktop App** as a search result
4. Right-click on **Windows PowerShell** and select **Run as Administrator**
5. This triggers a **User Account Control (UAC)** warning; select **Yes** to continue
6. Execute the install command found at `https://chocolatey.org/install` in **PowerShell** to install the Chocolatey package manager:

   ```
   PS> Set-ExecutionPolicy Bypass -Scope Process -Force; [System.Net.
   ServicePointManager]::SecurityProtocol = [System.Net.ServicePointM
   anager]::SecurityProtocol -bor 3072; iex ((New-Object System.Net.
   WebClient).DownloadString('https://chocolatey.org/install.ps1'))
   ```

7. Verify your Chocolatey installation by executing `choco`
8. You should see a similar output to the one shown in the following screenshot:

Figure 2.1: Successful installation of Chocolatey

> All subsequent Chocolatey commands must also be executed from an elevated command shell. Alternatively, it is possible to install Chocolatey in a non-administrator setting that doesn't require an elevated command shell. However, this results in a non-standard and less secure development environment, and certain applications installed through the tool may still require elevation.

> Scoop is an alternative to Chocolatey that provides a more Unix-like experience. If you prefer Unix-style tools and commands, you can install Scoop at `https://scoop.sh/` or by executing:
>
> ```
> $ iwr -useb get.scoop.sh | iex
> ```

For more information on Chocolatey, refer to `https://chocolatey.org/install`.

Installing Homebrew for macOS

Homebrew is a CLI-based package manager for macOS that can be used for automated software installation. To install Homebrew on macOS, you need to run a command shell:

1. Launch Spotlight Search with ⌘ + *Space*
2. Type in `terminal`
3. Execute the following command in Terminal to install the Homebrew package manager:

   ```
   $ /usr/bin/ruby -e "$(curl -fsSL https://raw.githubusercontent.com/Homebrew/install/master/install)"
   ```

4. Verify your Homebrew installation by executing `brew`
5. You should see a similar output to the following:

```
[du@dougi-mbp13 ~> brew
Example usage:
  brew search [TEXT|/REGEX/]
  brew (info|home|options) [FORMULA...]
  brew install FORMULA...
  brew update
  brew upgrade [FORMULA...]
  brew uninstall FORMULA...
  brew list [FORMULA...]
```

Figure 2.2: Successful installation of Homebrew

6. To enable access to additional software, execute the following command:

   ```
   $ brew tap caskroom/cask
   ```

On macOS, if you run into permissions issues while installing brew packages, related to chown'ing `/usr/local`, you need to execute the `sudo chown -R $(whoami) $(brew --prefix)/*` command. This command reinstates user-level ownership to brew packages, which is more secure than broad superuser/`su`-level access.

For more information, check out `https://brew.sh/`.

Installing development tools

In this section, you'll install all the development tools you need to start developing a web application. Git and GitHub Desktop establish a source code repository on your machine and allow you to sync your code with a remote repository. Node.js is a JavaScript runtime for your PC and it ships with the **Node Package Manager** or **npm**. Npm manages third-party source code including Angular. Visual Studio Code is an **Integrated Development Environment** or **IDE**.

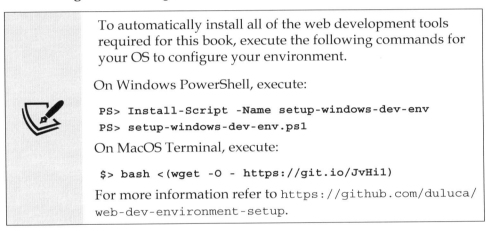

To automatically install all of the web development tools required for this book, execute the following commands for your OS to configure your environment.

On Windows PowerShell, execute:

`PS> Install-Script -Name setup-windows-dev-env`
`PS> setup-windows-dev-env.ps1`

On MacOS Terminal, execute:

`$> bash <(wget -O - https://git.io/JvHi1)`

For more information refer to `https://github.com/duluca/web-dev-environment-setup`.

Once you install your IDE, you're ready to start development. This section also contains instructions to install Docker, a lightweight containerization platform, and configure various cloud services. These tools will become relevant in later chapters. If you want a quicker start to your Angular adventure, you can skip them for now.

Git and GitHub Desktop

This section aims to establish a best practice Git configuration that's suitable for the broadest audience possible. To make the best use of this section and subsequent chapters of this book, I presume you have the following prerequisites fulfilled:

- An understanding of what source code management and Git actually are
- A free account created on `GitHub.com`

Why use GitHub?

If you are a Git user, the chances are that you also use an online repository, such as GitHub, Bitbucket, or GitLab. Each repository has a free tier for open source projects, coupled with robust websites with different feature sets, including on-premise Enterprise options that you can pay for. GitHub, with 38+ million repositories hosted in 2016, is by far the most popular online repository. It is widely considered a baseline utility that never goes offline by the community.

Over time, GitHub has added many rich features that have transformed it from a mere repository to an online platform. Throughout this book, I'll be referencing GitHub features and functionalities so you can leverage its capabilities to transform the way you develop, maintain, and release software.

Why use GitHub Desktop?

The Git CLI tool is indeed powerful, and you will be just fine if you stick to it. However, we full-stack developers are worried about a variety of concerns. In a rush to complete the task at hand, you can easily ruin your, and sometimes your team's, day by following incorrect or incomplete advice.

See the following screenshot for an example of such advice from Stack Overflow (http://stackoverflow.com/questions/1125968/force-git-to-overwrite-local-files-on-pull):

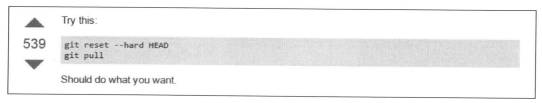

Figure 2.3: An example of a command not to run blindly

If you execute the preceding command, be prepared to lose uncommitted local changes. Unfortunately, novice users tend to follow the most straightforward and most direct instructions, potentially leading to lost work. If you think your past commits are safe, think twice! When it comes to Git, if you can imagine it, it can be done through the CLI.

Thankfully, with GitHub, you can protect branches and implement the GitHub workflow, which entails branching, committing, merging, updating, and submitting pull requests. The protections and the workflow help prevent harmful Git commands from making irreversible changes and enable a level of quality control so that your team remains productive. Performing all of these actions through the CLI, especially when there are merge conflicts, can get complicated and tedious.

>  Note that Git ships with a CLI tool named Git Bash, which is a Unix-based shell that you can use to execute `git` and other commands. Bash is readily available on Linux and macOS computers. Windows 10 is rapidly improving its terminal support with **Windows Subsystem for Linux (WSL)** and alias to Unix commands in PowerShell, so the need to use Git Bash on Windows is rapidly disappearing. If you would like to learn more about Git Bash see the tutorial at Atlassian's website at https://www.atlassian.com/git/tutorials/git-bash.

For a more in-depth understanding of the benefits and pitfalls of Git and GitHub, you can read my 2016 article on the topic at `Bit.ly/InDepthGitHub`.

Installing Git and GitHub Desktop

GitHub Desktop provides an easy-to-use GUI to execute the GitHub workflow in a manner that is consistent across Windows and macOS. Consistency is highly valuable when onboarding new or junior team members, or if you're not a frequent contributor to the code base. We recommend you install GitHub Desktop 2.2+.

1. Execute the installation command:

   For Windows:
   ```
   PS> choco install git github-desktop -y
   ```

   For macOS:
   ```
   $ brew install git && brew cask install github
   ```

2. Verify your Git installation by executing `git --version` and observe the version number returned

   > You need to restart your Terminal after the installation of a new CLI tool. However, you can avoid relaunching your Terminal and save some time by refreshing or sourcing your environment variables. On Windows, execute `refreshenv`; on macOS, execute `source ~/.bashrc` or `source ~/.zshrc`.

3. Verify your GitHub Desktop installation by launching the application
4. Sign in to `https://github.com/` on GitHub Desktop
5. Once you have created a repository, you can launch the application from your Terminal by executing this:
   ```
   $ github path/to/repo
   ```

Setting Up Your Development Environment

6. If you are already in the correct folder, you can type in the following command instead:

   `$ github .`

   > For Windows, on GitHub Desktop launch, if you get stuck on the sign in screen, close the application, relaunch it as an administrator, complete the setup, and then you may use it normally, without having to launch it as an administrator again. For more information, refer to `https://desktop.github.com/`.

Next, we'll go over several strategies for having a smoother experience with Git by properly registering your GitHub credentials.

Using your GitHub credentials in Git

When you interact with your repository on GitHub, the `git` command is leveraged by the tools you're using, like your IDE, to push or pull content. To have a smooth experience with Git, it is a good idea to register your GitHub credentials with Git properly.

There are three major strategies to accomplish this:

1. **Configure SSH** – which is the best and most secure way to interact with any remote computer system, because no passwords are exchanged. You can follow the latest guide from GitHub to configure SSH at `https://help.github.com/articles/connecting-to-github-with-ssh`.

2. **Cache your GitHub password in Git** – sometimes SSH won't be supported by the tool you use, so you may need to cache your password. You can do so by executing the following command:

   For Windows:

   `PS> git config --global credential.helper wincred`

   For macOS:

   `$ git credential-osxkeychain`
   `$ git config --global credential.helper osxkeychain`

   For further guidance, refer to the GitHub guide at `https://help.github.com/articles/caching-your-github-password-in-git`.

3. **Create a personal access token** – this is a strategy that falls in between SSH and password usage from a security perspective because SSH keys and tokens can be revoked at any time from GitHub, but once your password is leaked or compromised, you may lose control of everything.

If you're using two-factor authentication, which you absolutely should, then instead of caching your password, you need to create a personal access token at `https://github.com/settings/tokens` and use the token instead of your password. In *Chapter 3, Creating a Basic Angular App,* we cover how you can set up a token to work with Visual Studio Code, the preferred IDE for this book.

> Check out TJ Holowaychuk's git-extras tool, which can provide repo summary, changelog population, author commit percentage, and more useful information about your repos at `https://github.com/tj/git-extras`.

Node.js

This section aims to establish a best practice JavaScript development environment. I presume that you have an awareness of the modern JavaScript ecosystem and tools. At a minimum, make sure to familiarize yourself with the following resources:

- Node.js's website: `https://nodejs.org`
- Npm's website: `https://www.npmjs.com`
- Angular's website: `https://angular.io`
- The legacy AngularJS website: `https://angularjs.org/`
- Yarn's website: `https://yarnpkg.com`
- React's website: `https://facebook.github.io/react`

Node.js is JavaScript that runs anywhere. It's an open source project that aims to run JavaScript on the server, built on Google Chrome's V8 JavaScript engine. In late 2015, Node.js stabilized and announced enterprise-friendly 18-month LTS cycles that brought predictability and stability to the platform, paired with a more frequently updated, but more experimental, latest branch.

Node also ships bundled with npm, the Node Package Manager, and as of 2018, npm is the largest repository of JavaScript packages in the world.

For a more detailed look into Node's history, read my two-part article on Node at `Bit.ly/NodeJSHistory`.

> You may have heard of Yarn and how it's faster or better than npm. As of npm 5, which ships bundled with Node 8, npm is more feature-rich, easier to use, and on par with Yarn in terms of performance. Yarn is published by Facebook, which also created React. It must be noted that Yarn relies on the npm repository, so whichever tool you use, you get access to the same library of packages.

Existing Node.js installation

If you have installed Node.js before, when installing a new version of Node using choco or brew, ensure that you read the command outputs carefully. Your package manager may return caveats or additional instructions to follow so you can successfully complete the installation.

It is also highly likely that your system or folder permissions have been edited manually in the past, which may interfere with the frustration-free operation of Node. If the following commands do not resolve your issues, use the GUI installer from Node's website as a last resort.

To see a list of your global install packages, execute `npm list -g --depth=0`. To uninstall a global package, execute `npm uninstall -g package-name`. I would recommend that you uninstall all globally installed packages and restart from scratch with the suggestions provided in the next section.

Regardless, you must take care to uninstall all global tools that were installed using `npm -g` previously. With every major Node version, there's a chance that native bindings between your tool and Node have been invalidated. Further, global tools rapidly fall out of date and project-specific tools quickly go out of sync. As a result, installing tools globally is now an anti-pattern that has been replaced with better techniques, which are covered in the next section and in the Angular CLI section in *Chapter 3, Creating a Basic Angular App*.

Installing Node.js

This book presumes that you're using Node 12.13 or a later version. Odd-numbered versions of Node are not meant to be long-lived. 8.x.x, 10.x.x, 12.x.x, and so on are okay, but avoid 9.x.x, 11.x.x, and so on, at all costs, as they are meant to be experimental.

1. Execute the installation command:

    For Windows:
    ```
    PS> choco install nodejs-lts -y
    ```
    For macOS:
    ```
    $ brew install node@10
    ```
2. Verify the installation of Node by executing `node -v`
3. Verify npm by executing `npm -v`

> Note that on Windows, you should never upgrade your npm version using npm install -g npm, as highlighted in *Appendix C, Keeping Angular and Tools Evergreen*. You can find this appendix online from https://static.packt-cdn.com/downloads/9781838648800_Appendix_C_Keeping_Angular_and_Tools_Evergreen.pdf or at https://expertlysimple.io/stay-evergreen. It is highly recommended that you use the npm-windows-upgrade npm package.

For this book, make sure that you've got npm v.6.12+. Now, let's go over some handy npm packages you may want to install globally.

Global npm packages

The npm repository contains numerous useful and mature CLI commands that are often cross-platform. Listed here are the ones I rely on frequently and choose to install globally for performance reasons:

- npx: Executes CLI tools by downloading the latest version on-demand or the project-specific local node_modules folder. Npx ships with npm 5+ and allows you to run code generators that frequently update without a global install.
- rimraf: The Unix command rm -rf works on Windows as well. It's very useful for deleting the node_modules folder, especially when Windows is unable to do so due to the nested folder structure.
- npm-check-updates: Analyzes your project folder and reports on which package has newer versions or not, with the option to be able to update all of them if you so wish. ncu for short.
- n: A dead easy to tool to switch between versions of Node quickly, without having to remember the specific version number, which works on macOS/Linux. For Windows, you can use the choco package, nvs; both n and nvs are covered in the *Appendix C, Keeping Angular and Tools Evergreen*.
- http-server: A simple, zero-configuration command-line HTTP server, which is a great way to locally test static HTML/CSS pages or even the dist folder of your Angular or React project.
- npm-windows-upgrade: Necessary to upgrade npm on Windows.
- npkill: Easily find and remove old and heavy node_modules folders and reclaim gigabytes of disk space.

> You can use npm-check-updates to keep all of your global packages up to date by executing ncu -g.

If you run into EACCES permissions errors while installing global packages on macOS, refer to the guide from npm at `https://docs.npmjs.com/getting-started/fixing-npm-permissions`.

Visual Studio Code

Visual Studio Code (VS Code) is one of the best code editors/IDEs out there, built and maintained by Microsoft. It's free and cross-platform. The remarkable thing is that VS Code has the lightning-fast performance of a code editor – think NotePad++ or Sublime Text – but the feature set and convenience of costly IDEs – think Visual Studio or WebStorm. For JavaScript development, this speed is essential and is a tremendous quality-of-life improvement for a developer who frequently switches back and forth between different projects. VS Code brings together an integrated terminal, easy-to-use extension system, transparent settings, excellent search and replace functionalities, and, in my opinion, the best Node.js debugger that exists.

> This book does not require you to use VS Code. If you wish to use another IDE like WebStorm you may do so. WebStorm is a paid product and delivers a great development experience out of the box, whereas VS Code requires a lot of customization. This book offers automated scripts to configure VS Code for an optimal Angular development experience.
>
> You can find more about WebStorm at https://www.jetbrains.com/webstorm.

Installing Visual Studio Code

For Angular development, this book leverages VS Code v1.42+. I highly recommend that you also use the latest version of VS Code.

1. Execute the installation command:

    For Windows:

    ```
    PS> choco install VisualStudioCode -y
    ```

    For macOS:

    ```
    $ brew cask install visual-studio-code
    ```

    > One of the best features of VS Code is that you can also launch it from the CLI. If you're in a folder that you'd like to be editing, simply execute `code .` or a particular file by executing `code ~/.bashrc` or `code readme.md`.

2. Verify the installation by launching VS Code
3. Navigate to a folder and execute `code`
4. This opens up a new VS Code window with the **Explorer** displaying the contents of the current folder

For more information, refer to `https://code.visualstudio.com`.

With VS Code installed, you're ready to start development. If you want a quicker start to your Angular adventure, skip ahead to the Angular CLI section and refer back to this section when you need Docker and the tools for various cloud services.

Docker

Docker is a *lightweight* container virtualization platform with workflows and tooling that help manage and deploy applications.

Installing Docker

To be able to build and run containers, you must first install the Docker execution environment on your computer.

Windows support for Docker can be challenging. You must have a PC with a CPU that supports virtualization extensions, which is not a guarantee on laptops. You must also have a Pro version of Windows with Hyper-V enabled. On the flip side, Windows Server has native support for Docker, which is an unprecedented amount of support shown by Microsoft toward the industry initiative to adopt Docker and containerization.

1. Install Docker by executing the following command:

   For Windows:
   ```
   PS> choco install docker docker-for-windows -y
   ```
   For macOS:
   ```
   $ brew install docker
   ```
2. Execute `docker -v` to verify the installation

Cloud services

Throughout the book, we'll use various cloud providers to perform deployments of the apps that you are going to build. Each service ships with a CLI tool that facilities the deployment of your app from your Terminal or a **continuous integration** (**CI**) environment in the cloud.

Vercel Now

Vercel Now is a cloud platform for static sites and serverless functions. With a simple CLI command, you host websites and deploy web services instantly. This book leverages a free-tier Vercel Now account.

1. Create a Vercel Now account at `https://vercel.com`.
2. Install the CLI tool by executing:

    ```
    $ npm i -g now
    ```

3. Verify the installation by executing:

    ```
    $ now login
    ```

4. Follow the instructions to complete the login process. You should see a message similar to the one that follows:

    ```
    > We sent an email to xxxxx@gmail.com. Please follow the steps
    provided inside it and make sure the security code matches
    Classical Slow Worm
    √ Email confirmed
    > Congratulations! You are now logged in. In order to deploy
    something, run `now`
    ```

For more information, refer to `https://vercel.com`.

Google Firebase

Firebase is Google's cloud platform tailored for hosting mobile and web apps with authentication, push notifications, cloud functions, databases, machine learning, and analytics support. This book leverages a free-tier Firebase account.

1. Create a Firebase account at `https://firebase.google.com/`.
2. Install the CLI tool by executing:

    ```
    $ npm i -g firebase-tools
    ```

3. Verify the installation by executing:

    ```
    $ firebase login
    ```

4. Follow the instructions to complete the login process. You should see a message similar to the one that follows:

   ```
   Waiting for authentication...

   + Success! Logged in as xxxxxx@gmail.com
   ```

For more information, refer to `https://firebase.google.com/`.

Google Cloud

Google Cloud is Google's world-class cloud infrastructure for enterprises. This book leverages Google Cloud Run for managed container deployments to the cloud. When you first sign up, you may receive free credits to use Google Cloud. However, this is an optional exercise, as you may incur charges while using this service if you forget to tear down your deployment.

1. Create a Google Cloud account at `https://cloud.google.com/`
2. Execute the installation command:

   For Windows:

   ```
   PS> choco install gcloudsdk -y
   ```

   > If you have trouble installing `gcloudsdk` from `choco`, then try `scoop`, as mentioned earlier in the chapter. Execute the commands that follow:
   >
   > ```
   > $ scoop bucket add extras
   > $ scoop install gcloud
   > ```

   For macOS:

   ```
   $ brew install google-cloud-sdk
   ```

3. Verify the installation by executing `gcloud --version`
4. Execute `gcloud init` to finish the setup

For more information, refer to `https://cloud.google.com/run/`.

Amazon Web Services

Amazon Web Services (AWS) is a globally deployed cloud infrastructure provided by Amazon. AWS is a widely popular tool with businesses and governments, making it a lucrative service for IT professionals. *Chapter 13, Highly Available Cloud Infrastructure on AWS*, goes in-depth on how to work with AWS and perform a scalable container-based deployment.

1. Execute the installation command:

   For Windows:

   ```
   PS> choco upgrade awscli -y
   ```

   For macOS:

   ```
   $ brew install awscli
   $ brew upgrade awscli
   ```

   > Note that running the upgrade command on choco and brew ensures that you have the latest version of any given tool if they were previously installed on your environment.

2. Verify the installation by executing `aws --version`

For more information, refer to https://aws.amazon.com/.

Setup automation for Windows and macOS

At the beginning of the chapter, I proclaimed *anything that can be expressed as a CLI command can also be automated*. Throughout the setup process, we have ensured that every tool being used was set up and its functionality was verifiable through a CLI command. This means we can easily create a PowerShell or bash script to string these commands together and ease the task of setting up and verifying new environments.

Let's implement rudimentary but effective scripts to help set up your development environment.

PowerShell script

For Windows-based development environments, you need to create a PowerShell script.

1. Create a file named `setup-windows-dev-env.ps1`
2. Insert the following text, also available at https://github.com/duluca/web-dev-environment-setup, in the file:

   setup-windows-dev-env.ps1

   ```
   # This script is intentionally kept simple to demonstrate basic
   ```

automation techniques.

Write-Output "You must run this script in an elevated command shell, using 'Run as Administrator'"

$title = "Setup Web Development Environment"
$message = "Select the appropriate option to continue (Absolutely NO WARRANTIES or GUARANTEES are provided):"

$yes = New-Object System.Management.Automation.Host.ChoiceDescription "&Install Software using Chocolatey", `
"Setup development environment."

$no = New-Object System.Management.Automation.Host.ChoiceDescription "&Exit", `
"Do not execute script."

$options = [System.Management.Automation.Host.ChoiceDescription[]]($yes, $no)

$result = $host.ui.PromptForChoice($title, $message, $options, 1)

switch ($result) {
  0 {
    Write-Output "Installing chocolatey"
    Set-ExecutionPolicy Bypass -Scope Process -Force; Invoke-Expression ((New-Object System.Net.WebClient).DownloadString('https://chocolatey.org/install.ps1'))
    Write-Output "Refreshing environment variables. If rest of the script fails, restart elevated shell and rerun script."
    $env:Path = [System.Environment]::GetEnvironmentVariable("Path", "Machine") + ";" + [System.Environment]::GetEnvironmentVariable("Path", "User")

    Write-Output "Assuming chocolatey is already installed"
    Write-Output "Installing Git & GitHub Desktop"
    choco.exe upgrade git github-desktop -y

    Write-Output "Installing NodeJS and NVS"
    choco.exe upgrade nodejs-lts nvs -y

    Write-Output "Installing Docker"
    choco.exe upgrade docker docker-for-windows -y

    Write-Output "Installing AWS"
    choco.exe upgrade awscli -y
```
```

```
        Write-Output "Installing VS Code"
        choco.exe upgrade VisualStudioCode -y

        RefreshEnv.cmd
        Write-Output "Results:"
        Write-Output "Verify installation of AWS, Docker, GitHub
    Desktop and VS Code manually."
        $gitVersion = git.exe --version
        Write-Output "git: $gitVersion"
        $nodeVersion = node.exe -v
        Write-Output "Node: $nodeVersion"
        $npmVersion = npm.cmd -v
        Write-Output "npm: $npmVersion"
    }
    1 { "Aborted." }
}
```

3. To execute the script, run:

   `PS> Set-ExecutionPolicy Unrestricted; .\setup-windows-dev-env.ps1`

Alternatively, you can install and execute the script directly from the PowerShell Gallery, located at https://www.powershellgallery.com, by executing the following command:

`PS> Install-Script -Name setup-windows-dev-env`

`PS> setup-windows-dev-env.ps1`

By executing this script, you have successfully set up your development environment on Windows.

If you're interested in publishing your own scripts to the PowerShell Gallery or generally interested in advancing your PowerShell skills, I suggest you install PowerShell Core, a multi-platform version of PowerShell. from https://github.com/PowerShell/PowerShell.

Now, let's look into how you can achieve a similar setup on Mac.

Bash script

For Mac-based development environments, you need to create a bash script.

1. Create a file named `setup-mac-dev-env.sh`

2. Run `chmod a+x setup-mac-dev-env.sh` to make the file executable
3. Insert the following text, also available at https://github.com/duluca/web-dev-environment-setup, in the file:

setup-mac-dev-env.sh

```bash
#!/bin/bash

echo "Execute Installation Script"
read -r -p "Absolutely NO WARRANTIES or GUARANTEES are provided. Are you sure you want to continue? [y/N] " response
if [[ "$response" =~ ^([yY][eE][sS]|[yY])+$ ]]
then
    echo "Installing brew"

    /usr/bin/ruby -e "$(curl -fsSL https://raw.githubusercontent.com/Homebrew/install/master/install)"

    echo "Installing git"
    brew install git
    brew upgrade git

    echo "Installing GitHub Desktop"
    brew cask install github
    brew cask upgrade github

    echo "Installing NodeJS"
    brew install node@12
    brew upgrade node@12

    echo "Installing Docker"
    brew cask install docker
    brew cask upgrade docker

    echo "Installing AWS"
    brew install awscli
    brew upgrade awscli

    echo "Installing VS Code"
    brew cask install visual-studio-code
    brew cask upgrade visual-studio-code

    echo "Results:"
    echo "Verify installation of AWS, Docker, GitHub Desktop and VS Code manually."
```

```
            gitVersion=$(git --version)
            echo "git: $gitVersion"
            nodeVersion=$(node -v)
            echo "Node: $nodeVersion"
            npmVersion=$(npm -v)
            echo "npm: $npmVersion"
    else
            echo "Aborted."
    fi
```

4. To execute the script, run:

    ```
    $ ./setup-mac-dev-env.sh
    ```

By executing this script, you have successfully set up your development environment on Mac. Here is an example of a more sophisticated install and verify routine, where you can check to see if a particular program, like brew or node, is already installed, before attempting to install them:

```
echo "Checking if brew is installed"
which -s brew
if [[ $? != 0 ]] ; then
    echo "Installing brew"
    /usr/bin/ruby -e "$(curl -fsSL https://raw.githubusercontent.com/Homebrew/install/master/install)" < /dev/null
else
    echo "Found brew"
fi

echo "Checking for Node version ${NODE_VERSION}"
node -v | grep ${NODE_VERSION}
if [[ $? != 0 ]] ; then
    echo "Installing Node version ${NODE_VERSION}"
    brew install nodejs
else
    echo "Found Node version ${NODE_VERSION}"
fi
```

Now, you have a pretty good idea of what it looks like to automate the execution of your scripts. The harsh reality is that these scripts do not represent a very capable or resilient solution. Scripts can't be executed or managed remotely, and they can't quickly recover from errors or survive machine boot cycles. Besides, your IT requirements may be above and beyond what is covered here.

If you deal with large teams and have a frequent turnover of staff, an automation tool pays dividends handsomely, whereas if you're on your own or part of a smaller, stable team, it is overkill. I encourage you to explore tools such as Puppet, Chef, Ansible, and Vagrant to help you decide which one best fits your needs or whether a simple script is just good enough.

The Angular CLI

The Angular CLI tool, ng, is an official Angular project to ensure that newly created Angular applications have a uniform architecture, following the best practices perfected by the community over time. This means that any Angular application you encounter going forward should have the same general shape.

Setting up your development directory

Setting up a dedicated `dev` directory is a lifesaver. Since all the data under this directory is backed up using GitHub, you can safely configure your antivirus, cloud sync, or backup software to ignore it. This helps significantly reduce CPU, disk, and network utilization. As a full-stack developer, you're likely to be multitasking a lot, so avoiding unnecessary activity has a net positive impact on performance, power, and data consumption daily, especially if your development environment is a laptop that is resource-starved or you wish to squeeze as much battery life as possible when you're on the move.

> Creating a `dev` folder directly in the `c:\` drive is very important on Windows. Earlier versions of Windows, or rather NTFS, can't handle file paths longer than 260 characters. This may seem adequate at first, but when you install npm packages in a folder structure that is already deep in the hierarchy, the `node_modules` folder structure can get deep enough to hit this limit very easily. With npm 3+, a new, flatter package installation strategy was introduced, which helps with npm-related issues, but being as close to the root folder as possible helps tremendously with any tool.

Create your `dev` folder using the following commands:

For Windows:

```
PS> mkdir c:\dev
PS> cd c:\dev
```

For macOS:

```
$ mkdir ~/dev
$ cd ~/dev
```

> In Unix-based operating systems, ~ (pronounced tilde) is a shortcut to the current user's home directory, which resides under `/Users/your-user-name`.

Now that your development directory is ready, let's start with generating your Angular application.

Generating your Angular application

The Angular CLI is an official Angular project to ensure that newly created Angular applications have a uniform architecture, following the best practices perfected by the community over time. This means that any Angular application you encounter going forward should have the same general shape. The Angular CLI goes beyond initial code generation; you'll use it frequently to create new components, directives, pipes, services, modules, and more. The Angular CLI also helps during development, with live-reloading features so that you can quickly see the results of your changes. The Angular CLI can also test, lint, and build optimized versions of your code for a production release. Furthermore, as new Angular versions are released, the Angular CLI helps you upgrade your code by automatically rewriting portions of it so that it remains compatible with potential breaking changes.

Installing the Angular CLI

The documentation at `https://angular.io/guide/quickstart` guides you on how to install `@angular/cli` as a global npm package. Do not do this. Over time, as the Angular CLI is upgraded, it is a constant irritant to have to keep the global and the in-project version in sync. If you don't, the tool complains endlessly. Additionally, if you are working on multiple projects, you end up with varying versions of the Angular CLI over time. As a result, your commands may not return the results you expect or the results your team members get.

The strategy detailed in the next section makes the initial configuration of your Angular project a bit more complicated than it needs to be; however, you'll more than make up for this pain if you have to return to a project a few months or a year later. In that case, you could use the version of the tool that you last used on the project, instead of some future version that may require upgrades that you're not willing to perform. In the next section, you'll use this best practice to initialize your Angular app.

Initializing your Angular app

The main way to initialize your app is by using the Angular CLI. Let's initialize the application for development using `npx`, which is already installed on your system from when you installed the latest version of Node LTS, from PowerShell/Terminal:

1. Under your `dev` folder, execute `npx @angular/cli new local-weather-app`
2. Select **No**, when asked **Would you like to add Angular routing?**
3. Select **CSS**, when asked **Which stylesheet format would you like to use?**
4. On your terminal, you should see a success message similar to this:

   ```
   $ npx @angular/cli new local-weather-app
   ...
   CREATE local-weather-app/src/environments/environment.ts (662 bytes)
   CREATE local-weather-app/src/app/app-routing.module.ts (245 bytes)
   CREATE local-weather-app/src/app/app.module.ts (393 bytes)
   CREATE local-weather-app/src/app/app.component.html (1152 bytes)
   CREATE local-weather-app/src/app/app.component.spec.ts (1086 bytes) CREATE local-weather-app/src/app/app.component.ts (207 bytes) CREATE local-weather-app/src/app/app.component.css (0 bytes)
   CREATE local-weather-app/e2e/protractor.conf.js (752 bytes) CREATE local-weather-app/e2e/tsconfig.e2e.json (213 bytes) CREATE local-weather-app/e2e/src/app.e2e-spec.ts (632 bytes) CREATE local-weather-app/e2e/src/app.po.ts (251 bytes)
   added 1076 packages from 1026 contributors and audited 42608 packages in 62.832s
   found 0 vulnerabilities Successfully initialized git.
   Project 'local-weather-app' successfully created.
   ```

Your project folder—`local-weather-app`—has been initialized as a Git repository and scaffolded with the initial file and folder structure, which should look like this:

```
local-weather-app
├── .editorconfig
├── .git
├── .gitignore
├── angular.json
├── e2e
│   ├── protractor.conf.js
```

```
|   ├── src
|   |   ├── app.e2e-spec.ts
|   |   └── app.po.ts
|   └── tsconfig.e2e.json
├── package.json
├── README.md
├── src
|   ├── app
|   |   ├── app-routing.module.ts
|   |   ├── app.component.css
|   |   ├── app.component.html
|   |   ├── app.component.spec.ts
|   |   ├── app.component.ts
|   |   └── app.module.ts
|   ├── assets
|   |   └── .gitkeep
|   ├── browserslist
|   ├── environments
|   |   ├── environment.prod.ts
|   |   └── environment.ts
|   ├── favicon.ico
|   ├── index.html
|   ├── karma.conf.js
|   ├── main.ts
|   ├── polyfills.ts
|   ├── styles.css
|   ├── test.ts
|   ├── tsconfig.app.json
|   ├── tsconfig.spec.json
|   └── tslint.json
├── tsconfig.json
└── tslint.json
```

The alias for @angular/cli is ng. If you were to install the Angular CLI globally, you would execute ng new local-weather-app, but we didn't do this. So, it is essential to remember that, going forward, you execute the ng command, but this time under the local-weather-app directory. The latest version of the Angular CLI has been installed under the node_modules/.bin directory so that you can run ng commands such as npx ng generate component my-new-component and continue working efficiently.

> If you are on macOS, you can further improve your development experience by implementing shell auto-fallback, which removes the necessity of having to use the npx command. If an unknown command is found, npx takes over the request. If the package already locally exists under node_modules/.bin, npx passes along your request to the correct binary. So, you can run commands like ng g c my-new-component as if they're globally installed. Refer to npx's readme on how to set this up, at npmjs.com/package/npx#shell-auto-fallback.

Publishing a Git repository using GitHub Desktop

GitHub Desktop allows you to create a new repository directly within the application:

1. Open GitHub for Desktop
2. **File | Add local repository...**
3. Locate the local-weather-app folder by clicking on **Choose...**
4. Click on **Add repository**
5. Note that the Angular CLI already created the first commit for you in the **History** tab

Setting Up Your Development Environment

6. Finally, click on **Publish repository**, marked in the following screenshot as **6**:

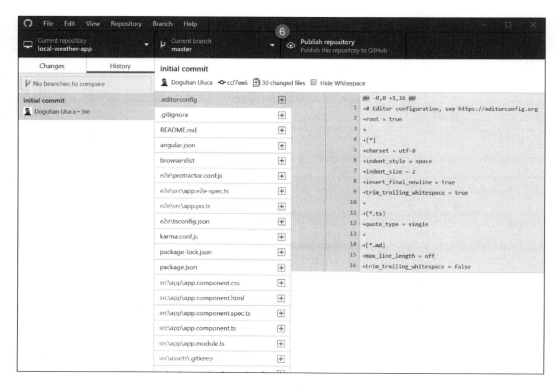

Figure 2.4: GitHub Desktop

Inspecting and updating package.json

Package.json is the single most important configuration file that you should be keenly aware of at all times. Your project's scripts, runtime, and development dependencies are stored in this file.

1. Open package.json and locate the name and version properties:

    package.json
    ```
    {
      "name": "local-weather-app",
      "version": "0.0.0",
      "license": "MIT",
    ...
    ```

2. Rename your app to whatever you wish; I used `localcast-weather`
3. Set your version number to `1.0.0`

> npm uses semantic versioning (semver), where version number digits represent Major.Minor.Patch increments. Semver starts version numbers at `1.0.0` for any published API, though it doesn't prevent `0.x.x` versioning. As the author of a web application, the versioning of your app has no real impact on you, outside of internal tooling, team, or company communication purposes. However, the versioning of your dependencies is critical to the reliability of your application. In summary, patch versions should just be bug fixes. Minor versions add functionality without breaking the existing features, and major version increments are free to make incompatible API changes. However, any update is risky to the tested behavior of your application. Therefore, the `package-lock.json` file stores the entire dependency tree of your application, so the exact state of your application can be replicated by other developers or CI servers. For more information, visit: https://semver.org/.

In the following code block, observe that the `scripts` property contains a collection of helpful starter scripts that you can expand on. The `start` and `test` commands are npm defaults, so they can just be executed by `npm start` or `npm test`. However, the other commands are custom commands that must be prepended with the `run` keyword. For example, in order to build your application, you must use `npm run build`:

package.json

```
...
"scripts": {
  "ng": "ng",
  "start": "ng serve",
  "build": "ng build",
  "test": "ng test",
  "lint": "ng lint",
  "e2e": "ng e2e"
},
...
```

Setting Up Your Development Environment

 Before the introduction of npx, if you wanted to use the Angular CLI without a global install, you would have to run it with `npm run ng -- g c my-new-component`. The double-dashes are needed to let npm know where the command-line tool name ends and the options begin. For example, in order to start your Angular application on a port other than the default 4200, you need to run `npm start -- --port 5000`.

4. Update your `package.json` file to run your development version of the app from a little-used port like 5000 as the new default behavior:

package.json
```
...
  "start": "ng serve --port 5000",
...
```

Under the dependencies property, you can observe your runtime dependencies. These are libraries that get packaged up alongside your code and shipped to the client browser. It's essential to keep this list to a minimum:

package.json
```
...
  "dependencies": {
    "@angular/animations": "~9.0.0",
    "@angular/common": "~9.0.0",
    "@angular/compiler": "~9.0.0",
    "@angular/core": "~9.0.0",
    "@angular/forms": "~9.0.0",
    "@angular/platform-browser": "~9.0.0",
    "@angular/platform-browser-dynamic": "~9.0.0",
    "@angular/router": "~9.0.0",
    "rxjs": "~6.5.3",
    "tslib": "^1.10.0",
    "zone.js": "~0.10.2"
  },
...
```

> In the preceding example, all Angular components are on the same version. As you install additional Angular components or upgrade individual ones, it is advisable to keep all Angular packages on the same version. This is especially easy to do since npm doesn't require the `--save` option anymore to permanently update the package version. For example, just executing `npm install @angular/router` is sufficient to update the version in `package.json`. This is a positive change overall, since what you see in `package.json` matches what is actually installed. However, you must be careful, because npm also automatically updates `package-lock.json`, which propagates your, potentially unintended, changes to your team members.

Your development dependencies are stored under the `devDependencies` property. When installing new tools for your project, you must take care to append the command with `--save-dev` so that your dependency is correctly categorized. Dev dependencies are only used during development and not shipped to the client browser. You should familiarize yourself with every single one of these packages and their specific purpose. If you are unfamiliar with a package shown as we move on, your best resource to learn more about them is https://www.npmjs.com/:

package.json

```
...
  "devDependencies": {
    "@angular-devkit/build-angular": "~0.900.0",
    "@angular/cli": "~9.0.0",
    "@angular/compiler-cli": "~9.0.0",
    "@angular/language-service": "~9.0.0",
    "@types/node": "^12.11.1",
    "@types/jasmine": "~3.4.0",
    "@types/jasminewd2": "~2.0.3",
    "codelyzer": "^5.1.2",
    "jasmine-core": "~3.5.0",
    "jasmine-spec-reporter": "~4.2.1",
    "karma": "~4.3.0",
    "karma-chrome-launcher": "~3.1.0",
    "karma-coverage-istanbul-reporter": "~2.1.0",
    "karma-jasmine": "~2.0.1",
    "karma-jasmine-html-reporter": "^1.4.2",
    "protractor": "~5.4.2",
    "ts-node": "~8.3.0",
```

```
    "tslint": "~5.18.0",
    "typescript": "~3.6.4"
}
...
```

The characters in front of the version numbers have specific meanings in semver:

- The tilde, ~, enables tilde ranges when all three digits of the version number are defined, allowing patch version upgrades to be automatically applied
- The up-caret character, ^, enables caret ranges, allowing minor version upgrades to be automatically applied
- A lack of any character signals npm to install that exact version of the library on your machine

You may notice that major version upgrades aren't allowed to happen automatically. In general, updating packages can be risky. In order to ensure no package is updating without your explicit knowledge, you may install exact version packages by using npm's `--save-exact` option. Let's experiment with this behavior by installing an npm package that I published called `dev-norms`, a CLI tool that generates a markdown file with sensible default norms for your team to have a conversation about, as shown here:

1. Under the `local-weather-app` directory, execute `npm install dev-norms --save-dev --save-exact`. Note that `"dev-norms": "1.7.0"` or similar has been added to `package.json` with `package-lock.json` automatically updated to reflect the changes accordingly.
2. After the tool is installed, execute `npx dev-norms create`. A file named `dev-norms.md` has been created containing the developer norms mentioned previously.
3. Save your changes to `package.json`.

Working with stale packages comes with its risks. With npm 6, the `npm audit` command has been introduced to make you aware of any vulnerabilities discovered in packages you're using. During `npm install`, if you receive any vulnerability notices, you may execute `npm audit` to find out details about any potential risk.

In the next section, you'll commit the changes you have made to Git.

Committing code using VS Code

To commit your changes to Git and then synchronize your commits to GitHub, you can use VS Code:

1. Switch over to the **Source Control** pane, marked as **1** here:

Figure 2.5: Visual Studio Code Source Control pane

2. Enter a commit message in the box marked as **2**
3. Click on the check-mark icon, marked as **3**, to commit your changes
4. Finally, synchronize your changes with your GitHub repository by clicking on the refresh icon, marked as **4**

Setting Up Your Development Environment

If you have two-factor authentication enabled, as you should, GitHub may ask for your credentials. In this case, you need to create a personal access token. Follow the instructions below to get this done:

1. Go to the page `https://github.com/settings/tokens`
2. Generate a new token and copy it
3. Attempt to re-sync your change within VS Code
4. Ignore the GitHub authentication window, which presents you with VS Code's credential input bar
5. Enter your GitHub username, not your email
6. Paste in the token as your password
7. The sync should succeed, and subsequent syncs shouldn't prompt for a password

See the Git and Github Desktop section earlier in this chapter for a wider discussion of the various methods you can use to connect your Git client to GitHub.

Going forward, you can do most Git operations from within VS Code.

Running your Angular app

Run your Angular app to check whether it works. During development, you can execute `npm start` through the `ng serve` command; this action transpiles, packages, and serves the code on localhost with live-reloading enabled:

1. Execute `npm start`
2. Navigate to `http://localhost:5000`
3. You should see a rendered page similar to this:

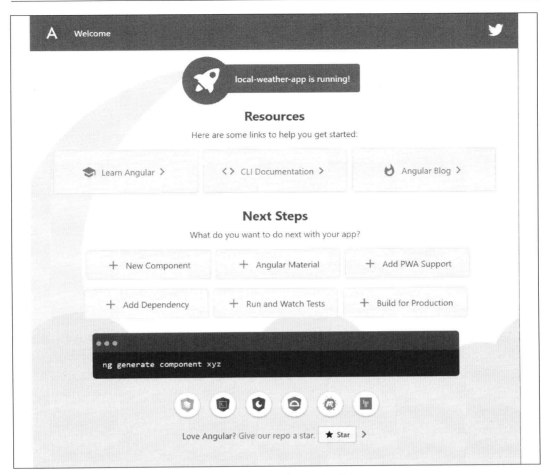

Figure 2.6: Default Angular CLI landing page

4. Stop your application by pressing *Ctrl + C* in the integrated terminal

Congrats! You're ready to start developing your web application. If you ran into any trouble during your setup, see the next section on how you can verify your code against the sample project on GitHub.

Verifying your code

The most up-to-date versions of the sample code for the book are on GitHub at the repository linked following. The repository contains the final and completed state of the code. You can verify your progress at the end of a chapter by looking for the end-of-chapter snapshot of code under the `projects` folder.

For *Chapter 2*:

1. Clone the repo https://github.com/duluca/local-weather-app
2. Execute `npm install` on the root folder to install dependencies
3. The code sample for this chapter is under the sub-folder:
   `projects/ch2`
4. To run the Angular app for this chapter, execute:
   `npx ng serve ch2`
5. To run Angular Unit Tests for this chapter, execute:
   `npx ng test ch2 --watch=false`

> Beware that the source code in the book or on GitHub may not always match the code generated by Angular CLI. There may also be slight differences in implementation between the code in the book and what's on GitHub because the ecosystem is ever evolving. It is natural for the sample code to change over time. Also on GitHub, expect to find corrections, fixes to support newer versions of libraries, or side-by-side implementations of multiple techniques for the reader to observe. The reader is only expected to implement the ideal solution recommended in the book. If you find errors or have questions, please create an issue or submit a pull request on GitHub for the benefit of all readers.

In the next section, I'll cover how you can optimize VS Code for Angular for the best possible development experience.

Optimizing VS Code for Angular

It is essential to optimize your IDE to have a great development experience. If you leverage the automated tools that I present in this section, you can quickly configure your IDE and your Angular project with dozens of settings that work well together.

Configuring your project automatically

To quickly apply configuration steps covered in the upcoming chapters, run the commands that follow:

1. Install the Angular VS Code task:

   `npm i -g mrm-task-angular-vscode`

2. Apply the Angular VS Code configuration:

   `npx mrm angular-vscode`

3. Install the npm Scripts for the Docker task:

   `npm i -g mrm-task-npm-docker`

4. Apply the npm Scripts for Docker configuration:

   `npx mrm npm-docker`

> These settings are continually tweaked to adapt to the ever-evolving landscape of extensions, plugins, Angular, and VS Code. Always make sure to install a fresh version of the task by rerunning the install command to get the latest version.

5. Execute `npm run style:fix`
6. Execute `npm run lint:fix`

For more information on the mrm tasks, refer to:

- `https://github.com/expertly-simple/mrm-task-angular-vscode`
- `https://github.com/expertly-simple/mrm-task-npm-docker`
- `https://github.com/expertly-simple/mrm-task-npm-aws`

> Note that `mrm-task-npm-aws` sets up npm scripts for AWS ECS, which is used in *Chapter 13, Highly Available Cloud Infrastructure on AWS*.

> You may verify your configuration against the sample projects on GitHub. However, note that the configuration pieces will be applied at the root of the repository and not under the `projects` folder.

VS Code auto save

Saving files all the time can get tedious. You can enable automatic saving by doing the following:

1. Open VS Code
2. Toggle the setting under **File | Auto Save**

You can further customize many aspects of VS Code's behavior by launching **Preferences**. The keyboard shortcut to launch **Preferences** is [*Ctrl* + ,] on Windows and [⌘ + ,] on macOS.

IDE settings

You can share such settings with your coworkers by creating a `.vscode` folder in the root of your project directory and placing a `settings.json` file in it. If you commit this file to the repository, everyone will share the same IDE experience. Unfortunately, individuals aren't able to override these settings with their local preferences, so ensure that shared settings are minimal and are agreed upon as a team norm.

Here are the customizations that I use for an optimal, battery-life-conscious Angular development experience:

```
.vscode/settings.json
{
  "debug.openExplorerOnEnd": true,

  "editor.tabSize": 2,
  "editor.rulers": [90],
  "editor.autoIndent": "full",
  "editor.cursorBlinking": "solid",

  "editor.formatOnType": false,         // Adjust the intensity of
  "editor.formatOnPaste": false,           auto-formatting to taste
  "editor.formatOnSave": true,

  "editor.minimap.enabled": false,
  "editor.codeActionsOnSave": {
    "source.organizeImports": false,
    "source.fixAll.tslint": true,
  },
```

```
  "explorer.openEditors.visible": 0,

  "files.trimTrailingWhitespace": true,
  "files.autoSave": "onFocusChange",

  "git.confirmSync": false,
  "git.enableSmartCommit": true,

  "npm.enableScriptExplorer": true,

  "typescript.tsdk": "node_modules/typescript/lib",
  "workbench.iconTheme": "material-icon-theme",     // Requires
                                                       Material Icon
                                                       Theme Extension
  "auto-close-tag.SublimeText3Mode": true,          // Requires Auto
                                                       Close Tag Extension
  "html.autoClosingTags": false,

  "peacock.affectActivityBar": true,                // Requires Peacock
  "peacock.affectStatusBar": true,                     Extension
  "peacock.affectTitleBar": false,
  "workbench.colorCustomizations": {
    "activityBar.background": "#d04649",
    "activityBar.activeBorder": "#37cb34",
    "activityBar.foreground": "#e7e7e7",
    "activityBar.inactiveForeground": "#e7e7e799",
    "activityBarBadge.background": "#37cb34",
    "activityBarBadge.foreground": "#15202b",
    "statusBar.background": "#b52e31",
    "statusBarItem.hoverBackground": "#d04649",
    "statusBar.foreground": "#e7e7e7"
  },

  "peacock.color": "#b52e31",
  "gitlens.menus": {                                // Requires GitLens
    "editorGroup": false                               Extension
  },

  "ng-evergreen.upgradeChannel": "Latest"           // Requires Angular
                                                       Evergreen Extension
}
```

In later sections, as we add tools that enforce our coding style, be careful not to introduce new settings that overlap or contradict each other.

IDE extensions

For a magical development experience with VS Code and Angular, you should install the Angular Essentials extension pack created and curated by John Papa. John Papa is one of the leading champions and thought leaders in the Angular community. He continuously and relentlessly seeks the best possible development experience you can attain so that you are more productive and happier as a developer. To learn more about Angular Essentials, see this blog post at `https://johnpapa.net/rec-ng-extensions` and the GitHub repo at `https://github.com/johnpapa/vscode-angular-essentials`.

I highly recommend you follow John Papa on Twitter at @john_papa.

Similar to settings, you can also share recommended extensions via a JSON file. These are the extensions that I use for Angular development:

`.vscode/extensions.json`
```
{
  "recommendations": [
    "johnpapa.angular-essentials",
    "PKief.material-icon-theme",
    "formulahendry.auto-close-tag",
    "ms-azuretools.vscode-docker",
    "eamodio.gitlens",
    "WallabyJs.quokka-vscode",
    "amatiasq.sort-imports",
    "DSKWRK.vscode-generate-getter-setter",
    "esbenp.prettier-vscode",
    "HookyQR.beautify",
    "expertly-simple.ng-evergreen",
    "msjsdiag.debugger-for-edge"
  ]
}
```

VS Code also recommends some extensions for you to install. I would caution against installing too many extensions, as these noticeably start slowing down the launch performance and optimal operation of VS Code.

The VS Code ecosystem is an ever-evolving, dynamic, and rich ecosystem. As such, certain extensions or settings may disappear, stop working, or have bugs in them. If you run into any trouble or are simply curious, you can find the latest versions of my preferred VS Code configuration files on GitHub at `http://bit.ly/ngCodeSettings`.

Scripting code styling and linting

You can customize the code styling enforcement and code generation behavior in VS Code and the Angular CLI. The most crucial goal of automating the enforcement of code styling and linting rules is to set common ground between developers. If the team can't agree on what styling to follow, a coin toss is better than no agreement. Development teams should be focused on code quality and let automated tools worry about the indentation of their code, location of brackets, and spaces between parentheses. In large teams, any deviation in styling can cause significant headaches with merge conflicts. It is highly recommended that you implement mechanisms to enforce standards.

I prefer StandardJS settings for JavaScript, which codify a minimal approach to writing code while maintaining high readability. This means two spaces for tabs and no semicolons. In addition to the reduced keystrokes, StandardJS also takes less horizontal space, which is especially valuable when your IDE can only utilize half of the screen, with the other half taken up by the browser. You can read more about StandardJS at: `https://standardjs.com/`.

With the default settings, your code looks like:

```
import { AppComponent } from "./app.component";
```

With StandardJS settings, your code looks like:

```
import { AppComponent } from './app.component'
```

If you don't like this style, it is okay. While I'll be sharing my preferred settings following, feel free to tweak them to your liking. The mechanism we implement to enforce the rules remains the same regardless.

To apply and enforce code styling rules, we use some tools that provide both a CLI tool and a VS Code extension:

- Prettier – used to format `.ts` files
- ImportSort/SortImports – used to organize TypeScript import statements

- Beautify – used to format `.html` files,
- TSLint – used as a static code analysis tool to check code readability, maintainability, and functionality errors

Our goal is to end up with four scripts:

1. `style` – to check if our code adheres to styling rules
2. `style:fix` – to automatically format code files as per styling rules
3. `lint` – to check if our code has any linting errors
4. `lint:fix` – to automatically fix auto-fixable linting errors

The style and lint commands would be utilized by our CI server to ensure that every team member is adhering to the same coding standards. The `style:fix` and `lint:fix` commands would help developers adhere to coding standards with as little effort as possible.

These tools are constantly updated. The behavior of these tools may shift over time, so keep an eye out and don't hesitate to experiment with adding/removing tools to this mixture to achieve the configuration that works for you.

Before we set up our dependencies and configuration files, ensure that all the extensions recommended in the IDE extensions section are installed.

Configuring tooling

You can start making the configuration changes by following these steps:

1. Make sure the **Prettier – Code formatter**, **TSLint**, **sort-imports**, and **Beautify** extensions are installed (already included in `extensions.json` from the previous section)
2. Install the CLI tools by executing the following command:

```
npm i -D prettier tslint-config-prettier tslint-plugin-prettier
npm i -D js-beautify
npm i -D import-sort import-sort-cli import-sort-parser-typescript import-sort-style-module
npm i -D tslint tslint-etc
```

With npm, you can use i as an alias for install and -D instead of the more verbose --save-dev option. However, if you mistype -D as -d, you end up saving the package as a production dependency.

3. Edit package.json by appending an importSort attribute at the end of the file:

   package.json
   ```
   ...
     "importSort": {
       ".ts, .tsx": {
         "parser": "typescript",
         "style": "module",
         "options": {}
       }
     }
   ...
   ```

4. Update the tslint.json rules for integration with Prettier and tslint-etc:

   tslint.json
   ```
   {
     "extends": [
       "tslint:recommended",
       "tslint-config-prettier",
       "tslint-plugin-prettier",
       "tslint-etc"
     ],
     "rules": {
       "prettier": true,
       "no-unused-declaration": true,
   ...
   "quotemark": [true, "single", "avoid-escape"],
   ...
   "semicolon": [ true, "never"],
   ...
   "max-line-length": [ true, 90],
   ...
   }
   ```

5. Add a new file to the root of your project, named `.jsbeautifyrc`:

   .jsbeautifyrc
   ```
   {
     "indent_size": 2,
     "wrap_line_length": 90,
     "language": {
       "html": [
         "html"
       ]
     }
   }
   ```

6. Add a new file to the root of your project, named `.prettierrc`:

   .prettierrc
   ```
   {
     "tabWidth": 2,
     "useTabs": false,
     "printWidth": 90,
     "semi": false,
     "singleQuote": true,
     "trailingComma": "es5",
     "jsxBracketSameLine": true
   }
   ```

7. Add a new file to the root of your project, named `.prettierignore`. Note that this file doesn't have curly brackets:

   .prettierignore
   ```
   **/*.html
   ```

Now we are done configuring all the tooling necessary to implement our style and lint scripts.

Implementing a style checker and fixer

Let's implement npm scripts for style and `style:fix` commands. Npm scripts are a great way to document CLI scripts that your team needs to execute across different platforms and even on a CI server.

Now, let's add our first script:

1. Edit the `package.json` scripts attribute to add `style` and `style:fix` commands:

   package.json
   ```
   ...
     "scripts": {
   ```

```
    "style:fix": "import-sort --write \"**/{src,tests,e2e}/*.
ts\" && prettier --write \"**/{src,tests,e2e}/*.{*css,ts}\" && js-
beautify \"src/**/*.html\"",
    "style": "import-sort -l \"**/{src,tests,e2e}/*.ts\" &&
prettier --check \"**/{src,tests,e2e}/*.{*css,ts}\"",  ...
  }
...
```

2. Execute `npm run style` to see the files that do not adhere to styling rules
3. Execute `npm run style:fix` to update all your files to the new style
4. Observe all the file changes in GitHub Desktop
5. Commit your changes

> When you utilize inline templates in Angular, the inlined portion of HTML is formatted by Prettier instead of Beautify. In most of these cases, your code will look good, but if your HTML elements have too many attributes, your code will be formatted in a very verbose manner. In order to prevent this from happening, you may select the relevant HTML code and run the **Beautify selection** command within VS Code. If you add `// prettier-ignore` above the template property, Prettier will stop messing up your beautified HTML.

Now, let's configure our linting scripts.

Implementing a lint checker and fixer

A `lint` command already exists in `package.json`. We overwrite the existing `lint` command with our own and implement an additional `lint:fix` command.

Add the new scripts:

1. Edit the `package.json` scripts attribute to replace `lint` and add `lint:fix` commands:

    package.json
    ```
    ...
      "scripts": {
        ...
        "lint": "tslint --config tslint.json --project . -e \"**/
    {test,polyfills}.ts\"",
        "lint:fix": "tslint --config tslint.json --fix --project . -e
    \"**/{test,polyfills}.ts\"",  ...
      }
    ...
    ```

Setting Up Your Development Environment

Note that unlike the style scripts, we're excluding `test.ts` and `polyfills.ts` from being linted. These files ship with linting errors; they are unlikely to be edited frequently and since they have no bearing on the quality of our code, we can safely ignore them.

2. Execute `npm run lint` to see the files that have linting errors
3. Execute `npm run lint:fix` to fix any auto-fixable errors
4. If there are further errors, then *Ctrl/cmd + click* on the files and manually fix the errors
5. Observe all the file changes in GitHub Desktop
6. Commit your changes
7. Don't forget to push your changes to your repository!

Sometimes, as you type in new code or generate new components using the Angular CLI, you may encounter double-quotes or semicolons being underlined with a red squiggly line to indicate an issue. We have configured VS Code to automatically format files on saving, which happens automatically when the window loses focus. When auto-formatting is triggered, the file updates and formatting related errors disappear.

When we cover CI in *Chapter 4, Automated Testing, CI, and Release to Production*, we are going to run our style and lint checker as part of our pipeline.

Next, configure the ng tool to get the autocomplete functionality in the terminal.

Configuring Angular CLI autocomplete

You can get an autocomplete experience in your terminal when using the Angular CLI. Execute the appropriate command for your `*nix` environment:

- For the bash shell:
    ```
    $ ng completion --bash >> ~/.bashrc
    $ source ~/.bashrc
    ```

- For the zsh shell:
    ```
    $ ng completion --zsh >> ~/.zshrc
    $ source ~/.zshrc
    ```

- For Windows users using the Git bash shell:

    ```
    $ ng completion --bash >> ~/.bash_profile
    $ source ~/.bash_profile
    ```

Next, let's learn about the VS Code Auto Fixer.

VS Code Auto Fixer

Sometimes, a yellow bulb icon appears next to a line of code. This might happen because you have typed some code that violates a rule defined in `tslint.json`. If you click on the bulb, you will see an action labeled as a **Fix**. You can take advantage of these auto-fixers to allow VS Code to fix your code automatically. The screenshot that follows shows an example of an **Unnecessary semicolon** issue:

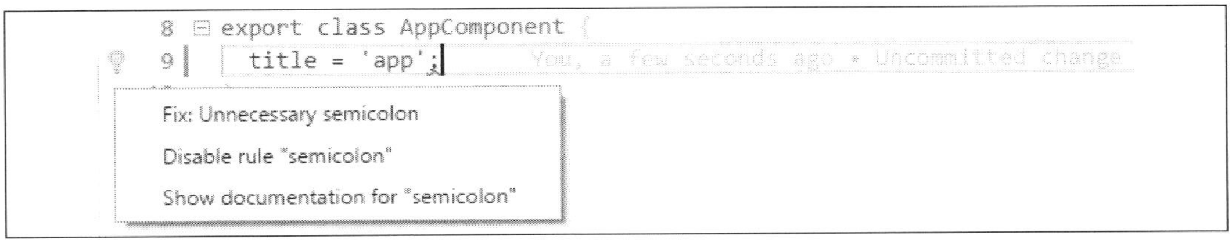

Figure 2.7: VS Code Auto Fixer

Congratulations – you're done setting up your development environment!

Summary

In this chapter, you mastered the use of CLI-based package managers for both Windows and macOS to speed up and automate the setup of development environments for you and your colleagues. You also created your first Angular project and optimized its configuration for development using Visual Studio Code. You then implemented automated style checkers and fixers to enforce coding standards and styling across your team. The lint checker and fixer you implemented will automatically catch potential coding errors and maintainability issues.

The automated scripts you have created codify your team norms and document them for new and existing members alike. By reducing variance from one developer's environment to the next, your team can overcome any individual configuration issue more efficiently and remain focused on the execution of the task at hand. With a collective understanding of a common environment, no single individual on the team carries the burden of having to help troubleshoot everyone else's issues. The same idea applies to the shape and style of your code files.

When a team member looks at another team member's code, it looks stylistically identical, which makes it easier to troubleshoot and debug an issue. As a result, your team is more productive. By leveraging more sophisticated and resilient tools, mid-to-large sized organizations can achieve considerable savings in their IT budgets.

In the next chapter, you're going to learn more about the Angular platform, leverage Kanban using GitHub projects and GitHub issues, learn Angular fundamentals to build a simple web app with a full-stack architecture in mind, and get introduced to reactive programming with RxJS.

Further reading

The article on Automating the Setup of the Local Developer Machine by Vishwas Parameshwarappa is a great place to start for using Vagrant, found at `https://www.vagrantup.com`. You can find the article at `https://Red-gate.com/simple-talk/sysadmin/general/automating-setup-local-developer-machine`.

Other tools include Chef, found at `https://www.chef.io/`, and Puppet, found at `https://puppet.com`. Some developers prefer to work within Docker containers during coding, found at `https://www.docker.com`. This is done to isolate different versions of SDKs from each other. Specific development tools cannot be scoped to a given folder and must be installed globally or OS-wide, making it very difficult to work on multiple projects at the same time. I recommend staying away from this type of setup if you can avoid it. In the future, I expect such chores are going to be automated by IDEs, as CPU core counts increase, and virtualization tech has better hardware acceleration.

We'll leverage Docker a little later in this book, but we'll use it to isolate our production software dependencies from their surrounding elements, like our local development environment or a server in the cloud.

Questions

Answer the following questions as best as you can to ensure that you've understood the key concepts from this chapter without Googling. Do you need help answering the questions? See *Appendix D, Self-Assessment Answers* online at `https://static.packt-cdn.com/downloads/9781838648800_Appendix_D_Self-Assessment_Answers.pdf` or visit `https://expertlysimple.io/angular-self-assessment`.

1. What are the motivations for using a CLI tool as opposed to a GUI?
2. For your specific operating system, what is the suggested package manager to use?
3. What are some of the benefits of using a package manager?
4. What are the benefits of keeping the development environments of the members of your development team as similar to one another as possible?

3
Creating a Basic Angular App

In this chapter, we'll design and build a simple Local Weather app using Angular and a third-party web API with an iterative development methodology. We'll focus on delivering value first while learning about the nuances and optimal ways of using Angular, TypeScript, Visual Studio (VS) Code, Reactive Programming, and RxJS. Before we dive into coding, we need to build a roadmap of features, create a mock-up of the application we intend to build, and diagram the high-level architecture of our app.

You'll be introduced to Angular fundamentals to build a simple web app and become familiar with the new Angular platform and full-stack architecture.

In this chapter, you are going to learn the following:

- Planning out your roadmap using GitHub projects
- Using a Kanban board to enable collaboration and effortless information radiation
- Crafting a new UI element to display current weather information using Angular components and TypeScript interfaces
- Using Angular services and `HttpClient` to retrieve data from `OpenWeatherMap` APIs
- Leveraging observable streams to transform data using RxJS
- Null guarding in Angular

Creating a Basic Angular App

The most up-to-date versions of the sample code for the book are on GitHub at the repository linked below. The repository contains the final and completed state of the code. You can verify your progress at the end of this chapter by looking for the end-of-chapter snapshot of code under the `projects` folder.

For *Chapter 3*:

1. Clone the repository `https://github.com/duluca/local-weather-app`.
2. Execute `npm install` on the root folder to install dependencies.
3. The code sample for this chapter is under the sub-folder:
   `projects/ch3`
4. To run the Angular app for this chapter, execute:
   `npx ng serve ch3`

Beware that the source code in the book or on GitHub may not always match the code generated by Angular CLI. There may also be slight differences in implementation between the code in the book and what's on GitHub because the ecosystem is ever-evolving. It is natural for the sample code to change over time. Also, on GitHub, expect to find corrections, fixes to support newer versions of libraries, or side-by-side implementations of multiple techniques for the reader to observe. The reader is only expected to implement the ideal solution recommended in the book. If you find errors or have questions, please create an issue or submit a pull request on GitHub for the benefit of all readers.

You can read more about updating Angular in *Appendix C, Keeping Angular and Tools Evergreen*. You can find this appendix online from `https://static.packt-cdn.com/downloads/9781838648800_Appendix_C_Keeping_Angular_and_Tools_Evergreen.pdf` or at `https://expertlysimple.io/stay-evergreen`.

Let's start by creating a high-level plan to understand what to implement before you start coding.

Planning using Kanban and GitHub projects

Having a roadmap before getting on the road is critical in ensuring that you reach your destination. Similarly, building a rough plan of action before you start coding is very important in ensuring project success. Building a plan early on enables your colleagues or clients to be aware of what you're planning to accomplish. However, any initial plan is guaranteed to change over time.

Agile software development aims to account for the change of priorities and features over time. Kanban and Scrum are the two most popular methodologies that you can use to manage your project. Each methodology has a concept of a backlog and lists that capture planned, in progress, and completed work. A backlog, which contains a prioritized list of tasks, establishes a shared understanding of what needs to be worked on next. Lists that capture the status of each task act as information radiators, where stakeholders can get updates without interrupting your workflow. Whether you're building an app for yourself or someone else, keeping a live backlog and tracking the progress of tasks pays dividends and keeps the focus on the goal you're trying to achieve.

In implementing the Local Weather app, we are going to leverage a GitHub project to act as a Kanban board. In an enterprise, you can use ticketing systems or tools that can keep a backlog, implement the Scrum methodology, and display Kanban boards. In GitHub, issues represent your backlog. You can leverage the built-in **Projects** tab to define a scope of work that represents a release or a sprint to establish a Kanban board. A GitHub project directly integrates with your GitHub repository's issues and keeps track of the status of issues via labels. This way, you can keep using the tool of your choice to interact with your repository and still, effortlessly, radiate information. In the next section, you are going to set up a project to achieve this goal.

Setting up a GitHub project

Let's set up a GitHub project:

1. Navigate to your GitHub repository in your browser.
2. Switch over to the **Projects** tab.
3. Click on **Create a new project**, as shown in the screenshot that follows:

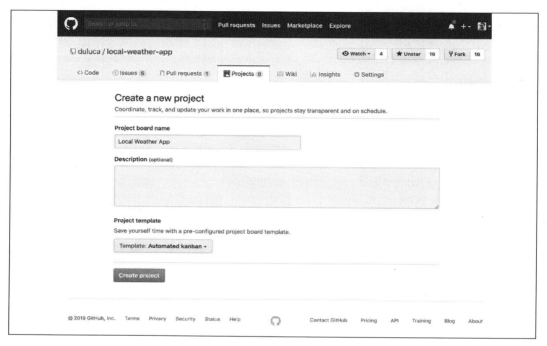

Figure 3.1: Creating a new project in GitHub

4. Provide a name in the **Project board name** box.
5. Select a **Project template**, such as **Automated Kanban**.
6. Later in the book, we'll enable GitHub flow for your GitHub projects. With GitHub flow, changes to your repository are processed through **Pull Requests (PR)**. In the future, you may want to select the **Automated Kanban with reviews** template, which automatically keeps track of the status of a PR, radiating more detailed information about the inner workings of the software development process.
7. Click on **Create project**.

Observe your Kanban board, which should appear as follows:

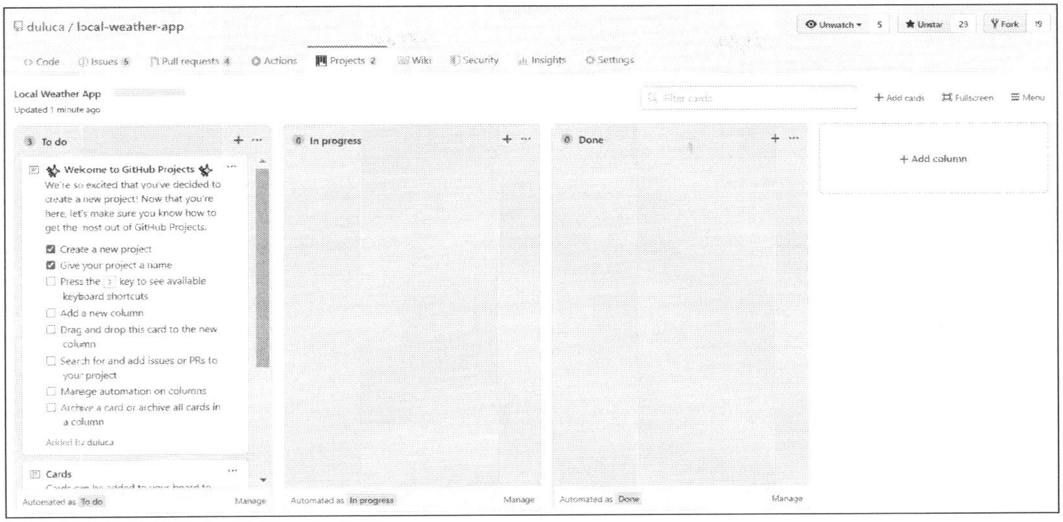

Figure 3.2: The Kanban board for your project

If you have existing issues on your repository, you may be prompted to add cards to your board. You can safely ignore this for now and return to it with the **+ Add cards** button. You are also presented with several **To do** cards. Feel free to review and dismiss these cards to clear out your board.

If you would like to keep track of every release or sprint, you can create a new project for each one. Creating new projects helps keep track of percentage completion for a given release or sprint, at the cost of introducing additional management overhead.

Next, we are going to configure the project as a Kanban board instead of a GitHub Project, which is a lightweight methodology to organize your work you might choose over other methodologies like Scrum.

Configuring a Kanban board

Kanban does not define formal iterations or releases of your work. If you would like to have a low-overhead process, where you only work with a single project, you can do this by introducing a Backlog column to your project.

Creating a Basic Angular App

Now let's add a Backlog column:

1. Click on **+ Add column**.
2. For **Column name** enter `Backlog`.
3. For **Preset** select **To do**.
4. Under **Move issues here when...**, select **Newly added**, as shown here:

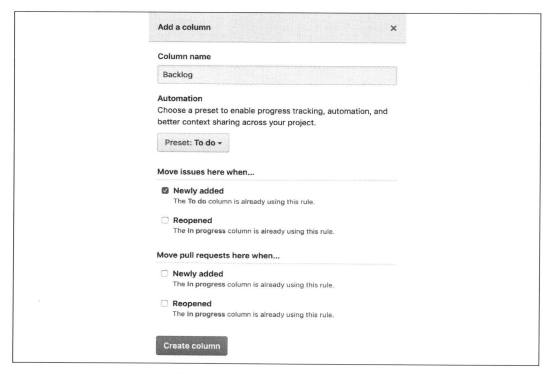

Figure 3.3: Where to select "Newly added"

5. Click on **Create column**.
6. Drag the column to become the leftmost column.

With this setup, new issues are added to the **Backlog**, allowing you to manually maintain the items you intend to work on in the **To do** column.

Creating a backlog for the Local Weather app

Let's create a backlog of issues to keep track of your progress as you implement the design of your application. When creating issues, you should focus on delivering functional iterations that bring some value to the user.

The technical hurdles you must clear to achieve those results are of no interest to your users or clients.

Here are the features we plan to build in our first release:

- Display current location weather information for the current day
- Display forecast information for the current location
- Add city search capability so that users can see weather information for other cities
- Add a preferences pane to store the default city for the user
- Improve the UX of the app with Angular Material

Let's also add some features that we won't implement in this book as a way to demonstrate how a backlog can capture your ideas:

- Add authentication so that users can retrieve data from any browser
- Add HTML5 Geolocation support
- Use `localStorage` to cache user preferences

Feel free to add other features you can think of to your backlog.

Begin by creating the preceding features as issues on GitHub. Make sure to assign each new issue to the project you created earlier in the chapter. Once created, move the preceding defined features to the **To do** column. When you begin working on a task, move the card into the **In progress** column and when it's completed, move it to the **Don**e column. The following is what the board looks like as we plan to begin working on the first feature – *Display Current Location weather information for the current day*:

Figure 3.4: A snapshot of the initial state of the board on GitHub

Creating a Basic Angular App

Note that I also added an issue to **Create a mock-up for the app** and moved it to **Done**, which is something I'll cover in the next section. Also, GitHub might automatically move a card from one state to another as you open and close them.

Ultimately, GitHub projects provide an easy-to-use GUI so that non-technical people can easily interact with GitHub issues. By allowing non-technical people to participate in the development process on GitHub, you unlock the benefits of GitHub becoming the single source of information for your entire project. Questions, answers, and discussions about features and issues are all tracked as part of GitHub issues, instead of being lost in emails. You can also store wiki-type documentation on GitHub. So, by centralizing all project-related information, data, conversations, and artifacts on GitHub, you are greatly simplifying the potentially complicated interaction of multiple systems that require continued maintenance at a high cost. For private repositories and on-premise enterprise installations, GitHub has a very reasonable cost. If you're sticking with open source, as we are in this chapter, all these tools are free.

As a bonus, I created a rudimentary wiki page on my repository at https://github.com/duluca/local-weather-app/wiki. Note that you can't upload images to README.md or wiki pages. To get around this limitation, you can create a new issue, upload an image in a comment, and copy and paste the URL for it to embed images to README.md or wiki pages. In the sample wiki, I followed this technique to embed the wireframe design into the page.

With a roadmap in place, you're now ready to create a mock-up of your application.

Wireframe design

There are some great tools out there to do rough-looking mock-ups to demonstrate your idea with surprising amounts of rich functionality. If you have a dedicated UX designer, such tools are great for creating quasi prototypes. However, as a full-stack developer, I find the best tool out there to be pen and paper. This way, you don't have to learn **yet another tool** (**YAT**), and it is a far better alternative to having no design at all. Putting things on paper saves you from costly coding detours down the line and if you can validate your wireframe design with users ahead of time, even better. My app is called LocalCast Weather, but get creative and pick your own name. Behold, the wireframe design for your weather app:

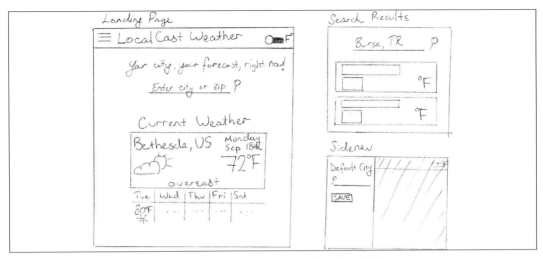

Figure 3.5: Hand-drawn wireframe for LocalCast. (Tip: I did use a ruler!)

The wireframe shouldn't be anything fancy. I recommend starting with a hand-drawn design, which is very quick to do and carries over the rough outlines effectively.

There are great wireframing tools out there. I suggest and use a couple of them throughout this book, however, in the first days of your project, every hour matters.

Granted, this kind of rough design may never leave the boundaries of your team, but please know that nothing beats getting that instantaneous feedback and collaboration by putting your ideas down on paper or a whiteboard.

High-level architecture

No matter how small or large your project is, it is critical to start with a sound architecture that can scale if duty calls. Most of the time, you can't accurately predict the size of your project ahead of time. Sticking to the architectural fundamentals discussed in *Chapter 1, Introduction to Angular and Its Concepts*, results in an architecture that is not overly burdensome, so you can quickly execute a simple app idea. The key is to ensure proper decoupling from the get-go.

In my view, there are two types of decoupling. One is soft-decoupling, where a "Gentlemen's Agreement" is made not to mix concerns and you try and not mess up the code base. This can apply to the code you write, all the way to infrastructure-level interactions. If you maintain your frontend code under the same code structure as your backend code, and if you let your REST server serve up your frontend application, then you are only practicing soft-decoupling.

You should instead practice hard-decoupling, which means frontend code lives in a separate repository, never calls the database directly, and is hosted on its web server altogether. This way, you can be sure that, at all times, your REST APIs or your frontend code is entirely replaceable and independent of other code. Practicing hard-decoupling has monetary and security benefits as well. The serving and scaling needs of your frontend application are guaranteed to be different from your backend, so you can optimize your host environment appropriately and save money. If you whitelist access to your REST APIs to only the calls originating from your frontend servers, you will vastly improve your security. Consider the following high-level architecture diagram for our LocalCast Weather app:

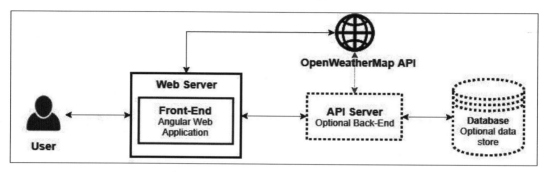

Figure 3.6: LocalCast high-level architecture

The high-level architecture shows that our Angular web application is completely decoupled from any backend. It is hosted on its web server, can communicate with a web API such as **OpenWeatherMap**, or optionally be paired with a backend infrastructure to unlock rich and customized features that a web API alone can't provide, such as storing per-user preferences or complementing the OpenWeatherMap API's dataset with our own.

Regardless of your backend technology, I recommend that your frontend always resides in its repository, and is served using its web server that does not depend on your API server.

 In *Chapter 10, RESTful APIs and Full-Stack Implementation*, you'll deep-dive into learning how a MEAN stack application, using MongoDB, Express, Angular, and Node, comes together in practice.

Now that we have our features, wireframe designs, and high-level architecture in place, we can start implementing our app.

Crafting UI elements using components and interfaces

In *Chapter 2, Setting Up Your Development Environment*, you should have created an Angular application. We'll use that as our starting point. If you haven't done so, please go back to *Chapter 2, Setting Up Your Development Environment*, and create your project.

In this section, you'll leverage Angular components, interfaces, and services to build the current weather feature in a decoupled, cohesive, and encapsulated manner.

The landing page of an Angular app, by default, resides in `app.component.html`. So, start by editing the template of `AppComponent` with basic HTML, laying out the initial landing experience for the application.

We are now beginning the development of Feature 1: **Display Current Location weather information for the current day** so you can move the card in the Github project to the **In progress** column.

1. Delete any existing code in the template file `app.component.html`
2. Add a header as an `h1` tag, followed by the tagline of our app as a `div`, and placeholders for where we may want to display the current weather, demonstrated as shown in the following code block:

   src/app/app.component.html
   ```
   <div style="text-align:center">
     <h1>
       LocalCast Weather
     </h1>
     <div>Your city, your forecast, right now!</div>
     <h2>Current Weather</h2>
     <div>current weather</div>
   </div>
   ```

3. Remove the unused `title` property from the `component` class, so it's empty

   src/app/app.component.ts
   ```
   import { Component } from '@angular/core'

   @Component({
     selector: 'app-root',
     templateUrl: './app.component.html',
     styleUrls: ['./app.component.css'],
   })
   export class AppComponent {}
   ```

4. In the terminal, execute `npm start`
5. Navigate to `http://localhost:5000` on your browser

You should now be able to observe the changes you're making in real time in the browser.

> Note that you should use the integrated terminal within VS Code to run commands, so you don't have to jump around different windows. Use [*CTRL+`*] on Windows or [*^+`*] on Mac to bring the terminal up. In case you're not familiar, ` is a backtick and is usually on the same key as ~ (tilde).

Adding an Angular component

We need to display the current weather information, where `<div>current weather</div>` is located. To achieve this, we need to build a component that is responsible for displaying the weather data.

The reason behind creating a separate component is an architectural best practice that is codified in the **Model-View-ViewModel (MVVM)** design pattern. You may have heard of the **Model-View-Controller (MVC)** pattern before. The vast majority of web-based code written circa 2005-2015 was written following the MVC pattern. MVVM differs from the MVC pattern in meaningful ways, as I explained in my 2013 article on DevPro:

> *An effective implementation of MVVM inherently enforces proper separation of concerns. Business logic is clearly separated from presentation logic. So, when a View is developed, it stays developed, because fixing a bug in one View's functionality doesn't impact other views. On the flip side, if [you use] visual inheritance effectively and [create] reusable user controls, fixing a bug in one place can fix issues throughout the application.*

Angular provides a practical implementation of MVVM:

> *ViewModels neatly encapsulate any presentation logic and allow for simpler View code by acting as a specialized version of the model. The relationship between a View and ViewModel is straightforward, allowing more natural ways to wrap UI behavior in reusable user controls.*

Chapter 3

You can read more about the architectural nuance, with illustrations, at http://bit.ly/MVVMvsMVC.

Next, you create your very first Angular component, which includes the View and the ViewModel, using the Angular CLI's ng generate command:

1. In the terminal, execute npx ng generate component current-weather

 Ensure that you are executing ng commands under the local-weather-app folder, and not under the parent folder where you initialized the project. Also, note that npx ng generate component current-weather can be rewritten as ng g c current-weather. This book utilizes the shorthand format going forward and expects you to prepend npx, if necessary.

2. Observe the new files created in your app folder:

   ```
   src/app
   ├── app.component.css
   ├── app.component.html
   ├── app.component.spec.ts
   ├── app.component.ts
   ├── app.module.ts
   ├── current-weather
   │   ├── current-weather.component.css
   │   ├── current-weather.component.html
   │   ├── current-weather.component.spec.ts
   │   └── current-weather.component.ts
   ```

   A generated component has four parts:
   - current-weather.component.css contains any CSS that is specific to the component and is an optional file.
   - current-weather.component.html contains the HTML template that defines the look of the component and rendering of the bindings and can be considered the View, in combination with any CSS styles used.
   - current-weather.component.spec.ts contains Jasmine-based unit tests that you can extend to test your component functionality.

Creating a Basic Angular App

- `current-weather.component.ts` contains the `@Component` decorator above the class definition and is the glue that ties together the CSS, HTML, and JavaScript code. The class itself can be considered the ViewModel, pulling data from services and performing any necessary transformations to expose sensible bindings for the View, shown as follows:

src/app/current-weather/current-weather.component.ts
```
import { Component, OnInit } from '@angular/core'

@Component({
  selector: 'app-current-weather',
  templateUrl: './current-weather.component.html',
  styleUrls: ['./current-weather.component.css'],
})
export class CurrentWeatherComponent implements OnInit {

  constructor() {}

  ngOnInit() {}
}
```

If the component you're planning to write is a simple one, you can write it using inline styles and an inline template to simplify the structure of your code. If we were to rewrite the component above using inline templates and styles, it would look like the following example:

example
```
import { Component, OnInit } from '@angular/core'

@Component({
  selector: 'app-current-weather',
  template: `
  <p>
    current-weather works!
  </p>
  `,
  styles: []
})
export class CurrentWeatherComponent implements OnInit {
  constructor() {}

  ngOnInit() {}
}
```

However, we won't be inlining this template. So, keep your generated code as-is.

Note that the template is surrounded by the backtick character, `, instead of a single-quote character. The backtick character defines a template literal, which allows newlines to be defined without having to concatenate strings with a plus operator. You can read more about template literals at https://developer.mozilla.org/en-US/docs/Web/JavaScript/Reference/Template_literals.

When you executed the `generate` command, in addition to creating the component, the command also added the new component you created in the app's root module, `app.module.ts`, avoiding the otherwise tedious task of wiring up components together:

src/app/app.module.ts

```
...
import {
  CurrentWeatherComponent
} from './current-weather/ current-weather.component'
...
@NgModule({
declarations: [
    AppComponent,
    CurrentWeatherComponent
  ],
...
```

The bootstrap process of Angular is, admittedly, a bit convoluted. This is the chief reason the Angular CLI exists. `index.html` contains an element named `<app-root>`. When Angular begins execution, it first loads `main.ts`, which configures the framework for browser use and loads the app module. The app module then loads all its dependencies and renders within the aforementioned `<app-root>` element. In *Chapter 7, Creating a Router-First Line-of-Business App*, when we build a line-of-business app, we create feature modules to take advantage of the scalability features of Angular.

Now, we need to display our new component on the initial `AppComponent` template, so it is visible to the end user.

3. Add the `CurrentWeatherComponent` to `AppComponent` by replacing `<div>current weather</div>` with `<app-current-weather></app-current-weather>`:

src/app/app.component.html
```html
<div style="text-align:center">
  <h1>
    LocalCast Weather
  </h1>
  <div>Your city, your forecast, right now!</div>
  <h2>Current Weather</h2>
  <app-current-weather></app-current-weather>
</div>
```

4. If everything worked correctly, you should see this:

Figure 3.7: Initial render of your Local Weather app

Note the icon and name in the tab of the browser window. As a web development norm, in the `index.html` file, update the `<title>` tag and the `favicon.ico` file with the name and icon of your application to customize the browser tab information. If your favicon doesn't update, append the `href` attribute with a unique version number, such as `href="favicon.ico?v=2"`. As a result, your app will start to look like a real web app, instead of a CLI-generated starter project.

Now that you have seen an Angular component in action, let's cover some basics of what is going on under the covers.

Demystifying Angular components

As discussed in *Chapter 1, Introduction to Angular and Its Concepts*, an Angular component is implemented as an ES2015 class, which allows us to leverage OOP concepts. Classes are traditionally present in strongly-typed languages, so it is excellent that JavaScript implements classes as a dynamically typed language. Classes allow us to group (encapsulate) functionality and behavior in self-contained units (objects). We can define the behavior in very generalized and abstract ways and implement an inheritance hierarchy to share and morph behavior into differing implementations.

Considering the `CurrentWeatherComponent` class that follows, I can highlight some benefits of classes:

```
@Component(...)
export class CurrentWeatherComponent implements OnInit {
  constructor() {}

  ngOnInit() {}
}
```

Unlike a function, you can't directly use code within a class. It must be instantiated as an object with the new keyword. This means that we can have multiple instances of any given class and each object can maintain its internal state. In this case, Angular instantiates a component for us behind the scenes. A `constructor` of a class is executed at the time of its instantiation. You can put any code that initializes other classes or variables inside a constructor. However, you shouldn't make an HTTP call or attempt to access DOM elements from a constructor. This is where the `OnInit` life cycle hook comes into play.

As Angular is initializing `CurrentWeatherComponent` as an object, it is also going through the entire graph of modules, components, services, and other dependencies to ensure all interdependent code is loaded into memory. During this time, Angular can't yet guarantee the availability of HTTP or DOM access. After all classes are instantiated, Angular goes through the classes that are decorated with `@Component`, implements the `OnInit` interface, and calls the `ngOnInit` function within our class. This is why we need to put any code that needs HTTP or DOM access during the first load of our component into `ngOnInit`.

Classes can have properties, variables, and functions. From an Angular template, you can access any property, variable, or function inside of an expression. The syntax of an expression looks like `{{ expression }}`, `[target]="expression"`, `(event)="expression"` or `*ngIf="expression"`.

Now you have a good understanding of how the code, or the ViewModel, behind the template, the View, is instantiated and how you can access that code from the template. In the next section, we'll build an interface, which is a contract that defines the shape of an object.

Defining your model using interfaces

Now that your View and ViewModel are in place, you need to define your model. If you look back on the design, you'll see that the component needs to display:

- City and country
- Current date
- Current image
- Current temperature
- Current weather description

You first need to create an interface that represents this data structure. We are creating an interface instead of a class because an interface is an abstraction that does not contain any implementation. When creating touchpoints or passing data between various components, we can ensure a decoupled design if we rely on an abstract definition over an object that may implement unpredictable custom behavior, leading to bugs.

Start by creating the interface:

1. In the terminal, execute `npx ng generate interface ICurrentWeather`
2. Observe a newly generated file named `icurrent-weather.ts` with an empty interface definition that looks like this:

   src/app/icurrent-weather.ts
   ```
   export interface ICurrentWeather {
   }
   ```

   This is not an ideal setup, since we may add numerous interfaces to our app, and it can get tedious tracking down various interfaces. Over time, as you add concrete implementations of these interfaces as classes, it makes sense to put classes and their interfaces in their files.

Why not just call the interface `CurrentWeather`? This is because, later on, we may create a class to implement some interesting behavior for `CurrentWeather`. Interfaces establish a contract, establishing the list of available properties on any class or interface that implements or extends the interface. It is always important to be aware of when you're using a class versus an interface. If you follow the best practice of always starting your interface names with a capital I, you will always be conscious of what type of object you are passing around. Hence, the interface is named `ICurrentWeather`.

3. Rename `icurrent-weather.ts` to `interfaces.ts`
4. Also, implement the interface as follows:

   src/app/interfaces.ts
   ```
   export interface ICurrentWeather {
     city: string
     country: string
     date: Date
     image: string
     temperature: number
     description: string
   }
   ```

   This interface and its eventual concrete representation as a class is the Model in MVVM. So far, I have highlighted how various parts of Angular fit the MVVM pattern; going forward, I'll refer to these parts by their actual names.

   Now, we can import the interface into the component and start wiring up the bindings in the template of `CurrentWeatherComponent`.

5. Import `ICurrentWeather`
6. Switch back to `templateUrl` and `styleUrls`
7. Define a local variable called `current` with type `ICurrentWeather`:

   src/app/current-weather/current-weather.component.ts
   ```
   import { Component, OnInit } from '@angular/core'
   import { ICurrentWeather } from '../interfaces'

   @Component({
     selector: 'app-current-weather',
     templateUrl: './current-weather.component.html',
     styleUrls: ['./current-weather.component.css'],
   })
   ```

Creating a Basic Angular App

```
export class CurrentWeatherComponent implements OnInit {
  current: ICurrentWeather

  constructor() {}
  ngOnInit() {}
}
```

If you just type `current:ICurrentWeather`, you can use the Auto Fixer in VS Code to automatically insert the `import` statement.

In the constructor, you need to temporarily populate the `current` property with dummy data to test your bindings.

8. Implement dummy data as a JSON object and declare its adherence to `ICurrentWeather` using the `as` operator:

   `src/app/current-weather/current-weather.component.ts`

```
...
constructor() {
  this.current = {

    city: 'Bethesda',
    country: 'US',
    date: new Date(),

    image: 'assets/img/sunny.svg',
    temperature: 72,

    description: 'sunny',
  } as ICurrentWeather
}
...
```

In the `src/assets` folder, create a subfolder named `img` and place an image of your choice to reference in your dummy data.

You may forget the exact properties in the interface you created. You can get a quick peek at them by holding *Ctrl* + hovering over the interface name with your mouse, as shown:

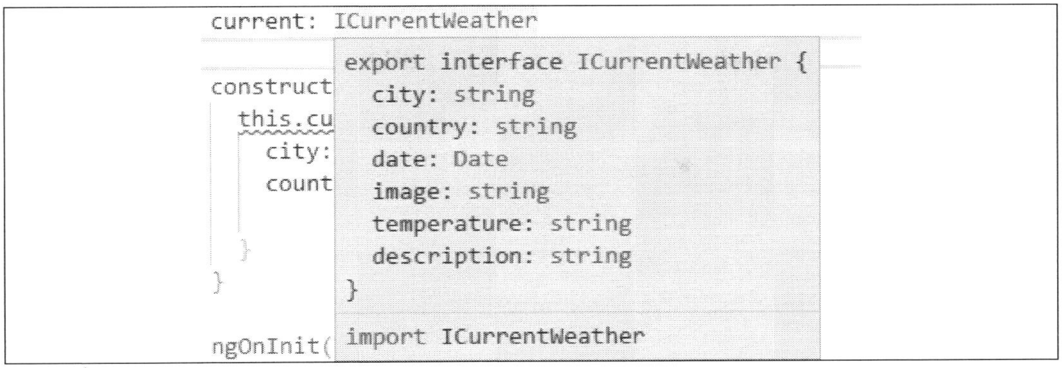

```
current: ICurrentWeather

construct   export interface ICurrentWeather {
  this.cu     city: string
     city:    country: string
     count    date: Date
                image: string
                temperature: string
                description: string
              }
            }
ngOnInit(   import ICurrentWeather
```

Figure 3.8: *Ctrl* + hover over the interface

Now, update the template to wire up your bindings with a basic HTML-based layout.

9. Begin implementing the template:

   `src/app/current-weather/current-weather.component.html`

   ```
   <div>
     ...
   </div>
   ```

10. Within the parent `div`, define another `div` to display the city and country information using binding:

    ```
    <div>
      <span>{{current.city}}, {{current.country}}</span>
      ...
    </div>
    ```

    Note that within the `span`, you can use static text to position the two properties. In this case, the `city` and `country` are separated by a comma, followed by a space.

11. Below `city` and `country`, display the `date` using binding and a `DatePipe` to define a display format for the property:

    ```
    <span>{{current.date | date:'fullDate'}}</span>
    ```

    To change the display formatting of `current.date`, we used the `DatePipe` above, passing in `'fullDate'` as the format option. In Angular, various out-of-the-box and custom pipe | operators can be used to change the appearance of data without actually changing the underlying data. This is a very powerful, convenient, and flexible system to share such user interface logic without writing repetitive boilerplate code.

Creating a Basic Angular App

In the preceding example, we could pass in `'shortDate'` if we wanted to represent the current date in a more compact form. For more information on various `DatePipe` options, refer to the documentation at https://angular.io/api/common/DatePipe.

12. Define another `div` to display the temperature information, formatting the value using `DecimalPipe` and bind an image of the current weather to an `img` tag:

    ```
    <div>
      <img [src]='current.image'>
      <span>{{current.temperature | number:'1.0-0'}}°F</span>
    </div>
    ```

    We bind the image property to the `img` tag's `src` attribute using the square bracket syntax. Next, we format `current.temperature` so that no fractional values are shown, using `DecimalPipe`. The documentation is at https://angular.io/api/common/DecimalPipe.

    > Note that you can render °C and °F using their respective HTML codes: `&#8451;` for °C and `&#8457;` for °F.

13. Create a final `div` to display the description property:

    ```
    <div>
      {{current.description}}
    </div>
    ```

14. Your final template should look as follows:

    `src/app/current-weather/current-weather.component.html`
    ```
    <div>
      <div>
        <span>{{current.city}}, {{current.country}}</span>
        <span>{{current.date | date:'fullDate'}}</span>
      </div>
      <div>
        <img [src]='current.image'>
        <span>{{current.temperature | number:'1.0-0'}}°F</span>
      </div>
      <div>
        {{current.description}}
      </div>
    </div>
    ```

15. If everything worked correctly, your app should be looking similar to this screenshot:

Figure 3.9: App after wiring up bindings with dummy data

Congratulations – you have successfully wired up your first component!

Now let's update the app so that we can pull live weather data from a Web API.

Using Angular Services and HttpClient to retrieve data

Now you need to connect your `CurrentWeather` component to the `OpenWeatherMap` APIs to pull live weather data. However, we don't want to insert this code directly into our component. If we did this, we would have to update the component if the API changed. Now imagine an app with dozens or hundreds of views and imagine how this would create a significant maintainability challenge.

Instead, we'll leverage an Angular service, a singleton class, which can provide the current weather information to our component and abstract away the source of the data. The abstraction decouples the UI from the Web API. Leveraging this separation of concerns, in the future, we could enhance our service to pull from multiple APIs or a local cache to load weather information without having to change the UI code.

In the upcoming sections, we'll go over the following steps to accomplish this goal:

1. Creating a new Angular service
2. Importing `HttpClientModule` and injecting it into the service
3. Discovering the `OpenWeatherMap` API
4. Creating a new interface that conforms to the shape of the API
5. Writing a `get` request
6. Injecting the new service into the `CurrentWeather` component
7. Calling the service from the `ngOnInit` function of the `CurrentWeather` component
8. Finally, mapping the API data to the local `ICurrentWeather` type using RxJS functions so that your component can consume it

Creating a new Angular service

Any code that goes outside of the boundaries of a component should exist in a service; this includes inter-component communication (unless there's a parent-child relationship), API calls of any kind, and any code that caches or retrieves data from a cookie or the browser's `localStorage`. This is a critical architectural pattern that keeps your application maintainable in the long term. I expand upon this idea in my DevPro MVVM article at link `https://www.itprotoday.com/microsoft-visualstudio/mvvm-and-net-great-combo-web-application-development`.

To create an Angular service, use the Angular CLI:

1. In the terminal, execute `npx ng g s weather --flat false`
2. Observe the new `weather` folder that's created:

   ```
   src/app
   ...
   └── weather
       ├── weather.service.spec.ts
       └── weather.service.ts
   ```

A CLI-generated service has two parts:

- `weather.service.spec.ts` contains Jasmine-based unit tests that you can extend to test your service's functionality.

- `weather.service.ts` contains the `@Injectable` decorator above the class definition, which makes it possible to inject this service into other components, leveraging Angular's provider system. This ensures that our service is a singleton, meaning it is instantiated once, no matter how many times it is injected elsewhere.

The service is generated as shown here:

src/app/weather/weather.service.ts

```
import { Injectable } from '@angular/core'

@Injectable({
  providedIn: 'root',
})
export class WeatherService {
  constructor() {}
}
```

Note that the `providedIn` property ensures that the root module provides the weather service in `app.module.ts`.

Next, let's see the dependency injection mechanism in Angular, which allows services and modules to be used by other services, components, or modules without the developer having to manage the instantiation of the shared objects.

Injecting dependencies

To make API calls, you need to leverage the `HttpClient` module in Angular. The official documentation (https://angular.io/guide/http) explains the benefits of this module succinctly:

> "With HttpClient, @angular/common/http provides a simplified API for HTTP functionality for use with Angular applications, building on top of the XMLHttpRequest interface exposed by browsers. Additional benefits of HttpClient include testability support, strong typing of request and response objects, request and response interceptor support, and better error handling via APIs based on Observables."

Let's start by importing the `HttpClientModule` into our app so we can inject the `HttpClient` provided by the module into the `WeatherService`:

1. Add `HttpClientModule` to `app.module.ts`, as follows:

    src/app/app.module.ts
    ```
    ...
    import { HttpClientModule } from '@angular/common/http'
    ...
    @NgModule({
      ...
      imports: [..., HttpClientModule]
      ...
    })
    ```

2. Inject `HttpClient`, provided by the `HttpClientModule` in the `WeatherService`, as follows:

    src/app/weather/weather.service.ts
    ```
    import { HttpClient } from '@angular/common/http'
    import { Injectable } from '@angular/core'

    @Injectable()
    export class WeatherService {
      constructor(private httpClient: HttpClient) {}
    }
    ```

Now, `httpClient` is ready for use in your service.

Discovering OpenWeatherMap APIs

Since `httpClient` is strongly typed, we need to create a new interface that conforms to the shape of the API we'll call. To be able to do this, you need to familiarize yourself with the Current Weather Data API:

1. Read the documentation by navigating to `http://openweathermap.org/current`:

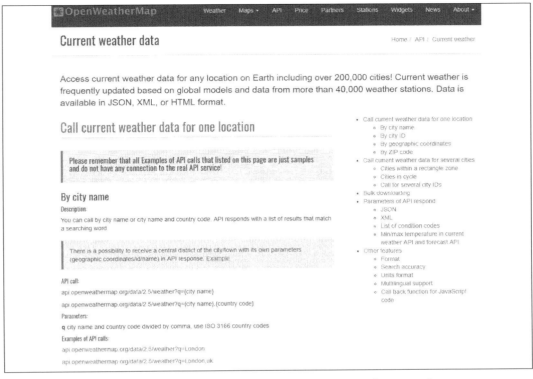

Figure 3.10: OpenWeatherMap Current Weather Data API documentation

You need to use the API named **By city name**, which allows you to get current weather data by providing the city name as a parameter so that our web request looks as follows:

```
api.openweathermap.org/data/2.5/weather?q={city name},{country code}
```

2. On the documentation page, click on the link under **Example of API calls**, and you will see a sample response like the following:

```
http://samples.openweathermap.org/data/2.5/weather?q=London,uk&app
id=b1b15e88fa797225412429c1c50c122a1
```

```
{
  "coord": {
    "lon": -0.13,
    "lat": 51.51
  },
  "weather": [
    {
      "id": 300,
```

```
      "main": "Drizzle",
      "description": "light intensity drizzle",
      "icon": "09d"
    }
  ],
  "base": "stations",
  "main": {
    "temp": 280.32,
    "pressure": 1012,
    "humidity": 81,
    "temp_min": 279.15,
    "temp_max": 281.15
  },
  "visibility": 10000,
  "wind": {
    "speed": 4.1,
    "deg": 80
  },
  "clouds": {
  "all": 90
  },
  "dt": 1485789600,
  "sys": {
    "type": 1,
    "id": 5091,
    "message": 0.0103,
    "country": "GB",
    "sunrise": 1485762037,
    "sunset": 1485794875
  },
  "id": 2643743,
  "name": "London",
  "cod": 200
}
```

Given the existing `ICurrentWeather` interface that you have already created, this response contains more information than you need. You need to write a new interface that conforms to the shape of this response, but only specify the pieces of data you intend to use. This interface only exists in the `WeatherService` and we won't export it since the other parts of the application don't need to know about this type.

3. Create a new interface named `ICurrentWeatherData` in `weather.service.ts` between the `import` and `@Injectable` statements
4. The new interface should like this:

src/app/weather/weather.service.ts
```
interface ICurrentWeatherData {
  weather: [{
    description: string,
    icon: string
  }],
  main: {
    temp: number
  },
  sys: {
    country: string
  },
  dt: number,
  name: string
}
```

> With the `ICurrentWeatherData` interface, we are defining new anonymous types by adding children objects to the interface with varying structures. Each of these objects can be individually extracted out and defined as their own named interface. Especially note that `weather` is an array of the anonymous type that has the `description` and `icon` properties.

Next, let's learn how you can introduce environment variables into your Angular application, so the test and production versions of your app can rely on different values.

Storing environment variables

It's easy to miss, but the sample URL in the previous sections—http://samples.openweathermap.org/data/2.5/weather?q=London,uk&appid=b1b15e88fa797225412429c1c50c122a1—contains a required `appid` parameter. You must store this key in your Angular app. You can store it in the weather service, but in reality, applications need to be able to target different sets of resources as they move from development to testing, staging, and production environments. Out of the box, Angular provides two environments: one `prod` and the other one as the default.

Before you can continue, you need to sign up for a free `OpenWeatherMap` account and retrieve your `appid`. You can read the documentation for `appid` at http://openweathermap.org/appid for more detailed information.

1. Copy your `appid`, which is a long string of characters and numbers
2. Store your `appid` in `environment.ts`
3. Configure `baseUrl` for later use:

    src/environments/environment.ts
    ```
    export const environment = {
      production: false,
      appId: 'xxxxxxxxxxxxxxxxxxxxxxxxxxxxxxxx',
      baseUrl: 'http://',
    }
    ```

> In code, we use a camel-case `appId` to keep our coding style consistent.
>
> Since URL parameters are case-insensitive, `appId` works as well as `appid`.

Next, let's implement an HTTP GET to get the current weather data.

Implementing an HTTP GET operation

Now, we can implement the GET call in the `WeatherService` class:

1. Add a new function to the `WeatherService` class named `getCurrentWeather`
2. Import the `environment` object
3. Implement the `httpClient.get` function
4. Return the results of the HTTP call:

    src/app/weather/weather.service.ts
    ```
    import { HttpClient } from '@angular/common/http'
    import { environment } from '../../environments/environment'
    ...

    export class WeatherService {
      constructor(
        private httpClient: HttpClient
      ) { }
    ```

Chapter 3

```
getCurrentWeather(city: string, country: string) {
  return this.httpClient
    .get<ICurrentWeatherData>(
    `${environment.baseUrl}api.openweathermap.org/data/2.5/weather?` +
        `q=${city},${country}&appid=${environment.appId}`
    )
  }
}
```

Note the use of ES2015's String Interpolation feature. Instead of building your string by appending variables to one another like `environment.baseUrl + 'api.openweathermap.org/data/2.5/weather?q=' + city + ',' + country + '&appid=' + environment.appId`, you can use the backtick syntax to wrap `your string`. Inside the backticks, you can have newlines and directly embed variables in the flow of your string by wrapping them with the `${dollarbracket}` syntax. However, when you introduce a newline in your code, it is interpreted as a literal newline \n. To break up the string in your code, you can add a backslash \, but then the next line of your code can have no indentation. It is easier to just concatenate multiple templates, as shown in the preceding code sample.

Using a long and complicated string is an error-prone process. Instead, we can use the `HttpParams` object to build the URL programmatically.

5. Leverage `HttpParams` to simplify the URL:

src/app/weather/weather.service.ts
```
import { HttpClient, HttpParams } from '@angular/common/http'
import { environment } from '../../environments/environment'
...

export class WeatherService {
  constructor(private httpClient: HttpClient) { }

  getCurrentWeather(city: string, country: string) {
    const uriParams = new HttpParams()
      .set('q', `${city},${country}`)
      .set('appid', environment.appId)

    return this.httpClient
      .get<ICurrentWeatherData>(
```

[113]

Creating a Basic Angular App

```
      `${environment.baseUrl}api.openweathermap.org/data/2.5/weather`,
        { params: uriParams }
      )
  }
}
```

Now let's connect the dots so that we can get the current weather data from the CurrentWeather component leveraging the Weather service.

Retrieving service data from a component

To be able to use the `getCurrentWeather` function in the `CurrentWeather` component, you need to inject the service into the component:

1. Inject the `WeatherService` into the constructor of the `CurrentWeatherComponent` class

2. Remove the existing code that created the dummy data in the constructor:

   src/app/current-weather/current-weather.component.ts
   ```
   constructor(private weatherService: WeatherService) { }
   ```

    Note the use of TypeScript generics with the `get` function using the caret syntax, like `<TypeName>`. Using generics is a development-time quality-of-life feature. By providing the type information to the function, input and/or return variable types of that function display as you write your code and are validated during development and also at compile time.

3. Call the `getCurrentWeather` function inside the `ngOnInit` function:

   src/app/current-weather/current-weather.component.ts
   ```
   ngOnInit() {
     this.weatherService.getCurrentWeather('Bethesda', 'US')
       .subscribe((data) => this.current = data)
   }
   ```

Fair warning: do not expect this code to be working just yet, because `data` is of type `ICurrentWeatherData` and `current` is of type `ICurrentWeather`. You can observe the error, which should say "`error TS2322: Type 'Observable<ICurrentWeatherData>' is not assignable to type 'Observable<ICurrentWeather>'.`" Let's look at what's goes in the next segment.

> Angular components have a rich collection of life cycle hooks that allow you to inject your custom behavior when a component is being rendered, refreshed, or destroyed. `ngOnInit()` is the most common life cycle hook you're going to use. It is only called once, when a component is first instantiated or visited. This is where you want to perform your service calls. For a deeper understanding of component life cycle hooks, check out the documentation at https://angular.io/guide/lifecycle-hooks.

> Note that the anonymous function you have passed to subscribe is an ES2015 arrow function. If you're not familiar with arrow functions, it may be confusing at first. Arrow functions are quite elegant and simple. Consider the following arrow function:
>
> ```
> (data) => { this.current = data }
> ```
>
> You can rewrite it simply as:
>
> ```
> function(data) { this.current = data }
> ```
>
> There's a special condition—when you write an arrow function that transforms a piece of data, such as:
>
> ```
> (data) => { data.main.temp }
> ```
>
> This function effectively takes `ICurrentWeatherData` as an input and returns the `temp` property. The return statement is implicit. If you rewrite it as a regular function, it looks as follows:
>
> ```
> function(data) { return data.main.temp }
> ```

When the `CurrentWeather` component loads, `ngOnInit` fires once, which calls the `getCurrentWeather` function, which returns an object with the type `Observable<ICurrentWeatherData>`.

An Observable *is the most basic building block of RxJS* and represents an event emitter, which emits any data received over time with the type of `ICurrentWeatherData` as described in the official documentation.

The Observable object by itself is benign and won't send a request over the network unless it is being listened to. You can read more about Observables at https://reactivex.io/rxjs/class/es6/Observable.js~Observable.html.

Creating a Basic Angular App

By calling `.subscribe` on the Observable, you're essentially attaching a listener to the emitter. You've implemented an anonymous function within the `subscribe` method, which gets executed whenever a new piece of data is received and an event is emitted. The anonymous function takes a data object as a parameter, and the specific implementation, in this case, assigns the piece of data to the local variable named `current`. Whenever `current` is updated, the template bindings you implemented earlier pull in the new data and render it on the View. Even though `ngOnInit` executes only once, the subscription to the Observable persists. So, whenever there's new data, the current variable updates and the View rerenders to display the latest data.

The root cause of the error at hand is that the data that is being emitted is of type `ICurrentWeatherData`; however, our component only understands data that is shaped as described by the `ICurrentWeather` interface. In the next section, you'll need to dig deeper into RxJS to understand how best to accomplish that task.

Beware, VS Code and the CLI sometimes stop working. As previously noted, as you code, the `npm start` command is running in the integrated terminal of VS Code. The Angular CLI, in combination with the Angular Language Service plugin, continuously watches for code changes and transpiles your TypeScript code to JavaScript so that you can observe your changes with live-reloading in the browser. The great thing is that when you make coding errors, in addition to the red underlining in VS Code, you also see some red text in the terminal, or even the browser, because the transpilation has failed. In most cases, when correcting the error, the red underlining goes away and the Angular CLI automatically re-transpiles your code and everything works. However, in specific scenarios, note that VS Code fails to pick typing changes in the IDE so that you won't get autocompletion help, or the CLI tool may get stuck with a message saying **webpack: Failed to compile**.

You have two main strategies to recover from such conditions:

- Click on the terminal and hit *Ctrl* + *C* to stop running the CLI task and restart by executing `npm start`.
- If that doesn't work, quit VS Code with *Alt* + *F4* for Windows or ⌘ + *Q* for macOS and restart it. Given Angular and VS Code's monthly release cycles, I'm confident that in time the tooling will only improve.

Let's resolve the type mismatch issue by transforming the shape of the data.

Transforming data using RxJS

We are going to use an RxJS reactive pipe (or data stream) to reshape the structure of data coming from the external API to fit the shape of the data we expect within our Angular app. If we don't do this, then our code will fail due to a type mismatch error.

Refer to *Chapter 1, Introduction to Angular and Its Concepts*, to get a deeper understanding of RxJS and reactive programming.

Implementing Reactive transformations

To avoid future mistakes such as returning an unintended type of data from your service, you need to update the `getCurrentWeather` function to define the return type as `Observable<ICurrentWeather>` and import the `Observable` type, as shown:

```
src/app/weather/weather.service.ts
import { Observable } from 'rxjs'
import { ICurrentWeather } from '../interfaces'
...

export class WeatherService {
  ...
  getCurrentWeather(city: string, country: string):
    Observable<ICurrentWeather> {
  }
  ...
}
```

Now, VS Code lets you know that the type `Observable<ICurrentWeatherData>` is not assignable to the type `Observable<ICurrentWeather>`:

1. Write a transformation function named `transformToICurrentWeather` that can convert `ICurrentWeatherData` to `ICurrentWeather`

2. Also, write a helper function named `convertKelvinToFahrenheit` that converts the API-provided Kelvin temperature to Fahrenheit:

    ```
    src/app/weather/weather.service.ts
    export class WeatherService {
    ...
      private transformToICurrentWeather(data: ICurrentWeatherData):
    ICurrentWeather {
        return {
          city: data.name,
          country: data.sys.country,
    ```

```
      date: data.dt * 1000,
      image:
`http://openweathermap.org/img/w/${data.weather[0].icon}.png`,
      temperature: this.convertKelvinToFahrenheit(data.main.temp),
      description: data.weather[0].description,
    }
  }

  private convertKelvinToFahrenheit(kelvin: number): number
  {
    return kelvin * 9 / 5 - 459.67
  }
}
```

Note that you need to be converting the icon property to an image URL at this stage. Doing this in the service helps preserve encapsulation; binding the icon value to the URL in the View template breaks the **Separation of Concerns (SoC)** principle. If you wish to create truly modular, reusable, and maintainable components, you must remain vigilant and strict in terms of enforcing SoC. The documentation for Weather Icons and details of how the URL should be formed, including all the available icons, can be found at http://openweathermap.org/weather-conditions.

On a separate note, the argument could be made that Kelvin to Fahrenheit conversion is a View concern, but we have implemented it in the service. This argument holds water, especially considering that we have a planned feature to be able to toggle between Celsius and Fahrenheit. A counter-argument would be that, at this time, we only need to display temperatures in Fahrenheit and it is part of the job of the weather service to be able to convert the units. This argument makes sense as well. The ultimate implementation is to write a custom Angular pipe and apply it in the template. A pipe can easily bind with the planned toggle button as well.

However, at this time, we only need to display temperatures in Fahrenheit, and I would err on the side of *not* over-engineering a solution.

Chapter 3

3. Update `ICurrentWeather.date` to the `number` type

> While writing the transformation function, note that the API returns the date as a number. This number represents the amount of time in seconds since the Unix epoch (timestamp), which is January 1, 1970 00:00:00 UTC. However, `ICurrentWeather` expects a `Date` object. It is easy enough to convert the timestamp by passing it into the constructor of the `Date` object like a new `Date(data.dt)`. This is fine, but also unnecessary since Angular's `DatePipe` can directly work with the timestamp. In the name of relentless simplicity and maximally leveraging the functionality of the frameworks we use, we update `ICurrentWeather` to use number. There's also a performance and memory benefit to this approach if you're transforming massive amounts of data, but that concern is not applicable here. There's one caveat—JavaScript's timestamp is in milliseconds, but the server value is in seconds, so a simple multiplication during the transformation is still required.

4. Import the RxJS `map` operator right below the other `import` statements:

   src/app/weather/weather.service.ts
   ```
   import { map } from 'rxjs/operators'
   ```

> It may seem odd to have to manually import the `map` operator. RxJS is a capable framework with a wide API surface. An `Observable` alone has over 200 methods attached to it. Including all of these methods by default creates development time issues with too many functions to choose from and also negatively impacts the size of the final deliverable, including app performance and memory use. You must add each operator you intend to use individually.

5. Apply the `map` function to the data stream returned by the `httpClient.get` method through a `pipe`
6. Pass the data object into the `transformToICurrentWeather` function:

   src/app/weather/weather.service.ts
   ```
   ...
   return this.httpClient
     .get<ICurrentWeatherData>(
   ```

[119]

Creating a Basic Angular App

```
    `${environment.baseUrl}api.openweathermap.org/data/2.5/
weather`,
    { params: uriParams }
  )
  .pipe(map(data => this.transformToICurrentWeather(data)))
...
```

Now incoming data can be transformed as it flows through the stream, ensuring that the `OpenWeatherMap` Current Weather API data is in the correct shape so that the `CurrentWeather` component can consume it.

7. Ensure that your app compiles successfully
8. Inspect the results in the browser:

Figure 3.11: Displaying live data from OpenWeatherMap

You should see that your app is able to pull live data from `OpenWeatherMap` and correctly transform server data into the format you expect.

> You have completed the development of Feature 1: **Display Current Location weather information for the current day**. Commit your code!

9. Finally, we can move this task to the **Done** column:

Figure 3.12: GitHub project Kanban board status

Great work! You're now familiar with the fundamental architecture of Angular. You also started implementing code in the reactive paradigm by leveraging RxJS.

Now let's increase the resiliency of our app by guarding against null or undefined values that can break your application code.

Null guarding in Angular

In JavaScript, the `undefined` and `null` values are a persistent issue that must be proactively dealt with every step of the way. This is especially critical when dealing with external APIs and other libraries. If we don't deal with `undefined` and `null` values, then your app may present badly rendered views, console errors, issues with business logic, or even a crash of your entire app.

There are multiple strategies to guard against null values in Angular:

- Property initialization
- The safe navigation operator, `?.`
- Null guarding with `*ngIf`

You may use one or more of these strategies. However, in the next few sections I demonstrate why the `*ngIf` strategy is the optimal one to use.

To simulate the scenario of getting an empty response from the server, go ahead and comment out the `getCurrentWeather` call in `ngOnInit` of `CurrentWeatherComponent`:

```
src/app/current-weather/current-weather.component.ts
ngOnInit(): void {
  // this.weatherService
  //   .getCurrentWeather('Bethesda', 'US')
  //   .subscribe(data => (this.current = data))
}
```

Let's start with implementing the property initialization strategy to guard against null values.

Property initialization

In statically-typed languages such as Java, it is drilled into you that proper variable initialization/instantiation is the key to error-free operation. So, let's try that in `CurrentWeatherComponent` by initializing `current` with default values:

src/app/current-weather/current-weather.component.ts
```
constructor(private weatherService: WeatherService) {
  this.current = {
    city: '',
    country: '',
    date: 0,
    image: '',
    temperature: 0,
    description: '',
  }
}
```

The outcome of these changes reduces the number of console errors from two to zero. However, the app itself is not in a presentable state, as you can see here:

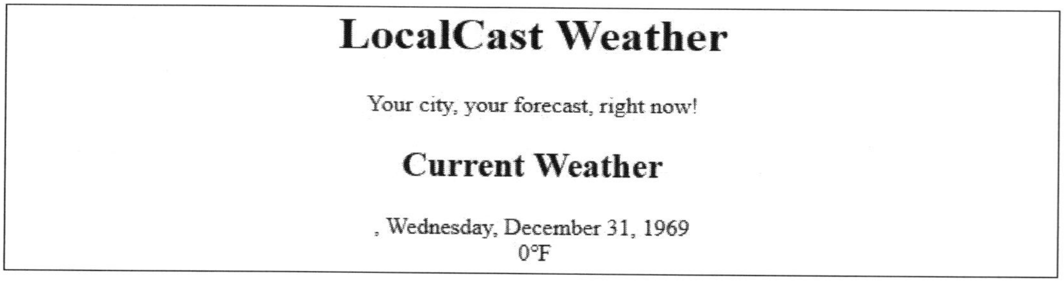

LocalCast Weather

Your city, your forecast, right now!

Current Weather

, Wednesday, December 31, 1969
0°F

Figure 3.13: Results of property initialization

To make this View presentable to the user, we have to code with default values on every property on the template. So, by fixing the null guarding issue with initialization, we created a default value handling issue. Both the initialization and the default value handling are $O(n)$ scale tasks for developers. At its best, this strategy is annoying to implement and at its worst, highly ineffective and error-prone, requiring, at a minimum, $O(2n)$ effort per property.

Next, let's learn about Angular's safe navigation operator, which comes in handy when dealing with objects that are external to our application when we can't control which properties may be null or undefined.

The safe navigation operator

Angular implements the safe navigation operation, ?., to prevent unintended traversals of undefined objects. So, instead of writing initialization code and having to deal with template values, we can just update the template.

Remove the property initialization code from the constructor and instead update the template as shown:

```
src/app/current-weather/current-weather.component.html
<div>
  <div>
    <span>{{current?.city}}, {{current?.country}}</span>
    <span>{{current?.date | date:'fullDate'}}</span>
  </div>
  <div>
    <img [src]='current?.image'>
    <span>{{current?.temperature}}°F</span>
  </div>
  <div>
    {{current?.description}}
  </div>
</div>
```

This time, we didn't have to make up defaults, and we let Angular deal with displaying undefined bindings. The app itself is in somewhat better shape. There's no more confusing data being displayed; however, it still is not in a presentable state, as shown here:

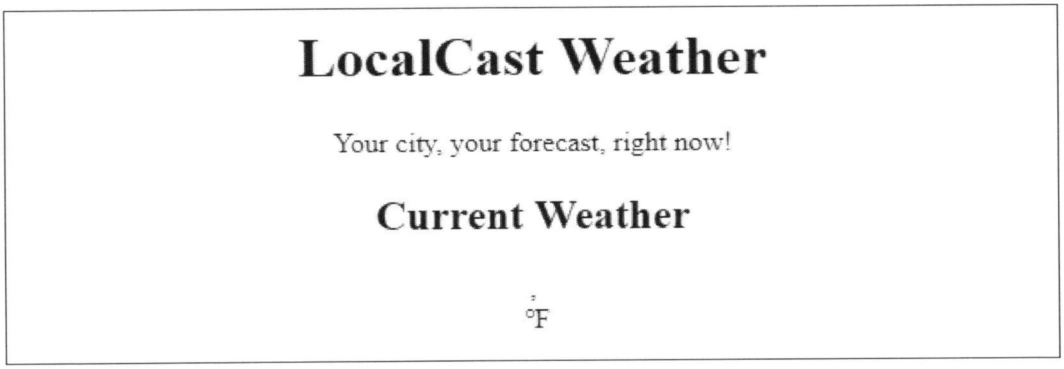

Figure 3.14: Results of using the safe navigation operator

You can probably imagine ways in which the safe navigation operator could come in handy, in far more complicated scenarios. However, when deployed at scale, this type of coding still requires, at a minimum, $O(n)$ level of effort to implement.

When presenting data to the user, we don't want to present empty values. The easiest way to clean up the UI would be to leverage the ngIf directive to hide the entire div.

Null guarding with *ngIf

The ideal strategy is to use *ngIf, which is a structural directive, meaning Angular stops traversing DOM tree elements beyond a falsy statement.

In the CurrentWeather component, we can easily check to see whether the current variable is null or undefined before attempting to render the template:

1. Undo the implementation of the safe navigation operators from the previous section
2. Update the topmost div element with *ngIf to check whether current is an object, as shown:

    src/app/current-weather/current-weather.component.html
    ```
    <div *ngIf="!current">
      no data
    </div>
    <div *ngIf="current">
    ...
    </div>
    ```

    Now observe the console log and that no errors are being reported. You should always ensure that your Angular application reports zero console errors. If you're still seeing errors in the console log, ensure that you have correctly reverted the OpenWeather URL to its correct state or kill and restart your npm start process. I highly recommend that you resolve any console errors before moving on.

3. Observe that the UI will now show that there's no data:

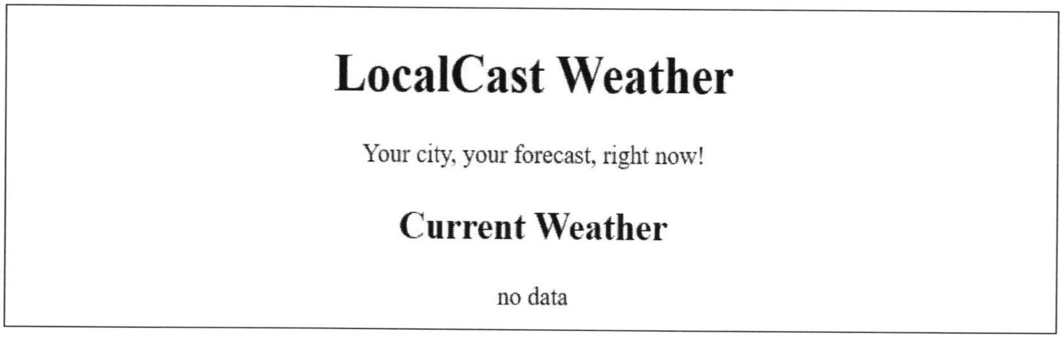

LocalCast Weather

Your city, your forecast, right now!

Current Weather

no data

Figure 3.15: Results of using null guarding with *ngIf

4. Re-enable the `getCurrentWeather` call in `ngOnInit` of `CurrentWeatherComponent`:

    `src/app/current-weather/current-weather.component.ts`
    ```
    ngOnInit(): void {
      this.weatherService
          .getCurrentWeather('Bethesda', 'US')
          .subscribe(data => (this.current = data))
    }
    ```

5. Commit your changes.

With null guarding, you can ensure that your UI always looks professional.

Summary

Congratulations! In this chapter, you created your first Angular application with a flexible architecture while avoiding over-engineering. This was possible because we first built a roadmap and codified it in a Kanban board that is visible to your peers and colleagues. We stayed focused on implementing the first feature we put in progress and didn't deviate from the plan.

You learned how to avoid coding mistakes by proactively declaring the input and return types of functions and working with generic functions. You used the date and decimal pipes to ensure that data is formatted as desired while keeping formatting-related concerns mostly in the template, where this kind of logic belongs.

Finally, you used interfaces to communicate between components and services without leaking the external data structure to internal components. By applying all these techniques in combination, which Angular, RxJS, and TypeScript allowed us to do, you ensured proper separation of concerns and encapsulation. As a result, the `CurrentWeather` component is now truly reusable and composable; this is not an easy feat to achieve.

If you don't ship it, it never happened. In the next chapter, we'll prepare this Angular app for a production release by troubleshooting application errors, ensuring automated unit and e2e tests pass, and containerizing the Angular app with Docker so that it can be published on the web.

Further reading

- *The Back of the Napkin: Solving Problems and Selling Ideas with Pictures*, Dan Roam, 2008.
- *Visual Thinking: Empowering People and Organizations through Visual Collaboration*, Williemien Brand, 2017.
- *The Project Cartoon*, http://projectcartoon.com.
- *Project management, made simple*, GitHub, https://github.com/features/project-management.
- *Creating a project board*, GitHub, https://help.github.com/en/articles/creating-a-project-board.

Questions

Answer the following questions as best as you can to ensure that you've understood the key concepts from this chapter without Googling. Do you need help answering the questions? See *Appendix D, Self-Assessment Answers* online at https://static.packt-cdn.com/downloads/9781838648800_Appendix_D_Self-Assessment_Answers.pdf or visit https://expertlysimple.io/angular-self-assessment.

1. I introduced the concept of a Kanban board. What is it, and what role does a Kanban board play in our software application development?
2. What were the different Angular components we generated using the Angular CLI tool to build out our Local Weather app after we initially created it, and what function and role do each of them serve?
3. What are the different ways of binding data in Angular?
4. Why do we need services in Angular?
5. What is an observable in RxJS?
6. What is the easiest way to present a clean UI if the data behind your template is falsy?

4
Automated Testing, CI, and Release to Production

Ship it, or it never happened! In *Chapter 3*, *Creating a Basic Angular App*, you created a local weather application that could retrieve current weather data. You have created some amount of value in doing this; however, if you don't put your app on the web, you end up creating zero value. This motivation to ship your work is prevalent in many industries. However, delivering a piece of work to someone else or opening it up to public scrutiny can be terrifying. In software engineering, delivering anything is difficult; delivering something to production is even more difficult. This chapter is going to help you implement a **Continuous Integration (CI)** pipeline. A CI pipeline is going to help you achieve frequent, reliable, high-quality, and flexible releases.

Frequent and reliable releases are only possible if we have a set of automated tests that can quickly verify the correctness of our code for us. The app we created in the previous chapter has failing unit and **end-to-end** (**e2e**) tests. We need to fix these unit tests and then ensure that they never break again by leveraging GitHub flow and CircleCI. Then we're going to cover how you can deliver your Angular app to the web. In *Chapter 9*, *DevOps Using Docker*, we are going to cover **Continuous Delivery** (**CD**) pipelines, which can also automate your delivery.

 Check out my 2018 talk, *Ship It or It Never Happened: The Power of Docker, Heroku & CircleCI*, at `https://bit.ly/ship-it-or-it-never-happened`.

This chapter covers:

- Unit testing with test doubles
- Angular unit tests using Jasmine
- Angular e2e tests
- GitHub flow
- Production readiness
- CI using CircleCI
- Deploying an app on the web using Vercel Now

The most up-to-date versions of the sample code for the book are on GitHub at the following linked repository. The repository contains the code in its final and complete state. You can verify your progress at the end of this chapter by looking for the end-of-chapter snapshot of code under the `projects` folder.

For *Chapter 4*:

1. Clone the repo `https://github.com/duluca/local-weather-app`
2. Execute `npm install` on the root folder to install dependencies
3. The code sample for this chapter is in the following sub-folder:
   projects/ch4
4. To run the Angular app for this chapter, execute:
   npx ng serve ch4
5. To run Angular unit tests for this chapter, execute:
   npx ng test ch4 --watch=false
6. To run Angular e2e tests for this chapter, execute:
   npx ng e2e ch4
7. To build a production-ready Angular app for this chapter, execute:
   npx ng build ch4 --prod

> Note that the `dist/ch4` folder at the root of the repository will contain the compiled result.

Beware that the source code in the book or on GitHub may not always match the code generated by the Angular CLI. There may also be slight differences in implementation between the code in the book and what's on GitHub because the ecosystem is ever-evolving. It is natural for the sample code to change over time. Also, on GitHub, expect to find corrections, fixes to support newer versions of libraries, or side-by-side implementations of multiple techniques for the reader to observe. You are only expected to implement the ideal solution recommended in the book. If you find errors or have questions, please create an issue or submit a pull request on GitHub for the benefit of all readers.

You can read more about updating Angular in *Appendix C, Keeping Angular and Tools Evergreen*. You can find this appendix online from `https://static.packt-cdn.com/downloads/9781838648800_Appendix_C_Keeping_Angular_and_Tools_Evergreen.pdf` or at `https://expertlysimple.io/stay-evergreen`.

Throughout this chapter, you need to sign up for accounts at CircleCI and Vercel Now. But before we can deploy our app, we need to ensure we have automated tests in place to ensure the quality of our app over time. First, we will deep dive into unit testing fundamentals to familiarize you with the benefits of test-driven development and cover principles like FIRST and SOLID.

Unit testing

Unit testing is crucial to ensure that the behavior of your application doesn't unintentionally change over time. Unit tests are going to enable you and your team to continue making changes to your application without introducing changes to previously verified functionality. Developers write unit tests, where each test is scoped to test only the code that exists in the **Function Under Test (FUT)** or **Class Under Test (CUT)**. Angular components and services are all classes; however, you are also encouraged to develop reusable functions. Unit tests should be plentiful, automated, and fast. You should write unit tests alongside the original code. If they are separated from the implementation, even by a day or two, you are going to start forgetting the details of your code. Because of that, you may forget to write tests for potential edge cases.

Unit tests should adhere to the FIRST principle:

- **F**ast
- **I**solated
- **R**epeatable
- **S**elf-verifying
- **T**imely

A unit test should be fast, taking only milliseconds to run, so that we can have thousands of them running in just a few minutes. For fast tests to be possible, a unit test should be isolated. It shouldn't talk to a database, make requests over the network, or interact with the DOM. Isolated tests are going to be repeatable, so that every run of the test returns the same result. Predictability means we can assert the correctness of a test without relying on any outside environment, which makes our tests self-verifying. As mentioned earlier, you should write unit tests promptly; otherwise, you lose the benefits of writing unit tests.

It is possible to adhere to the FIRST principle if your tests focus only on a single FUT/CUT. But what about other classes, services, or parameters we must pass into the FUT/CUT? A unit test can isolate the behavior of the FUT/CUT by leveraging test doubles. A test double allows us to control outside dependencies, so instead of injecting an `HttpService` to your component, you may instead inject a fake or mocked `HttpService`. Using test doubles, we can control the effects of outside dependencies and create fast and repeatable tests.

> How much testing is enough testing? You should have at least as much test code as production code. If you don't, then you're nowhere near writing enough tests.

Unit tests aren't the only kind of tests you can create, but they are by far the kind you should create the most of. Let's consider the three major classes of tests you can create: unit, integration, and UI.

As we've said, unit tests only focus on a single FUT/CUT at a time. Integration tests test the integration of various components so that they can include database calls, network requests, and interaction with the DOM. Due to their nature, integration tests are slow to run, and they need to be frequently maintained. Increases in runtime and maintenance mean that over time, integration tests are more expensive than unit tests. UI tests test the application as if a user is using it, filling in fields, clicking on buttons, and observing the expected outcome.

You may imagine that these tests are the slowest and most fragile kind of tests. The UI of an application changes frequently, and it is very tough to create repeatable tests with UI testing.

 We can leverage a mixture of integration and UI testing to create acceptance tests. Acceptance tests are written to automate the business acceptance of the functionality that we deliver. Angular's e2e tests are a way to create acceptance tests.

We can visualize the pros and cons of the three major classes of automated testing with Mike Cohn's Testing Pyramid, shown as following:

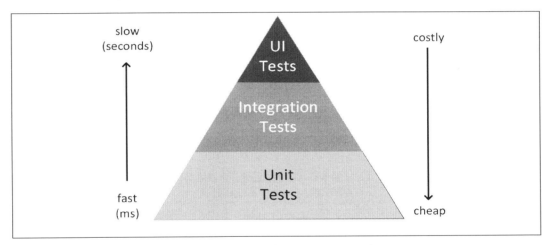

Figure 4.1: Mike Cohn's Testing Pyramid

The testing pyramid effectively summarizes the relative amount of tests of each kind we should create for our applications while considering their speed and cost.

In terms of implementation, unit tests are made up of three parts:

- Arrange – setup
- Act – run the thing you want to test
- Assert – verify the results

During the arrange step, we set up test doubles, expected outcomes, and any other requisite dependencies. During the act step, we execute the line of code we're testing. Finally, in the assert stage, we verify if the outcome of the act step matches the expected results defined in the arrange step. We are going to see how arrange, act, and assert work in practice in the next section.

Let's look into what unit tests mean in Angular.

Angular unit tests

The definition of a unit test in Angular is slightly different from the strict definition of unit testing we defined in the previous section. Angular CLI auto-generates unit tests for us using the Jasmine framework. However, these so-called unit tests include DOM-interactions because they render the view of the component.

Consider the architecture of an Angular component from *Chapter 1, Introduction to Angular and Its Concepts*:

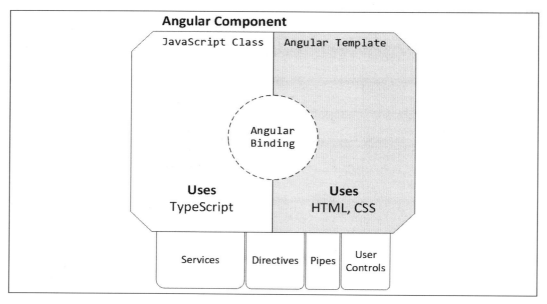

Figure 4.2: Anatomy of a Component

Since Angular uses binding, the component class and its template are inseparable, effectively representing a unit. We can still write pure unit tests by testing individual functions, but otherwise, a component and its template are considered the smallest possible units to test.

> As your application grows, you may find that Angular unit tests are slow to run, because they render views and resolve the dependency tree. There are various ways to deal with this problem, including the parallelization of test runs, opting out of using the Angular TestBed, and more aggressive use of test doubles.

As you may note, we can inject services into the component or use other components in our template. We are going to leverage test double mechanisms provided by Jasmine to isolate our components from such external dependencies.

Let's go over what Jasmine is.

Jasmine

Jasmine is a behavior-driven testing framework for browser and Node.js tests. Jasmine also supports Ruby and Python. Jasmine is a batteries-included framework. It supports elemental unit testing needs, such as test fixtures, asserts, mocks, spies, and reporters.

The naming convention of a Jasmine test file involves using `spec.ts` after the file name, as in `fileUnderTest.spec.ts`. Jasmine tests are organized in `describe` blocks, which can be grouped in levels to reflect the structure of a file, class, or multiple tests that belong to a single function. Individual test cases, or specs, are represented in `it` blocks. The following sample shows a file named `converters.ts` exporting a function that converts Celsius to Fahrenheit:

```
Sample Jasmine Test
describe('Converters', () => {
  describe('convertCtoF', () => {
    it('should convert 0c to 32f', () => {
      ...
    })
  })
})
```

Specs are organized in a manner so that when they execute, they read like a sentence. In this case, the outcome would be *Converters convertCtoF should convert 0c to 32f*.

For more information on Jasmine, visit `https://jasmine.github.io`.

Next, let's cover the major categories of features of Jasmine and most other testing frameworks – fixtures and matches – which help you write coherent unit tests using the act, arrange, and assert structure.

Fixtures

As mentioned earlier, a unit test has three parts: arrange, act, and assert. The arrange part of unit tests can be repetitive as multiple test cases often require the same setup. Jasmine provides fixtures to help reduce the amount of repetition in your score.

Following are the four fixtures:

- `beforeAll()` – runs before all specs in `describe`
- `afterAll()` – runs after all specs in `describe` per test fixtures
- `beforeEach()` – runs before each spec in `describe`
- `afterEach()` – runs after each spec in `describe`

The fixtures execute before and after a spec or a group of specs as scoped with their `describe` block.

Matchers

In the assert part of a unit test, we need to let Jasmine know whether a spec passed or failed. We can do so by writing an assertion. There are two kinds of assertions:

- `fail('message')` – this explicitly fails a spec
- `expect()` – given a matcher, this dynamically asserts if the expected outcome matches the actual outcome

The expect assertion requires matchers to determine the outcome of a test. The combination of expect and matcher is meant to read like a sentence. Following are common matchers that you may use:

```
Jasmine Matchers
expect(expected).toBe(actual)
                .toEqual(actual)
                .toBeDefined()
                .toBeFalsy()
                .toThrow(exception)
                .nothing()
```

For the full extent of Jasmine matchers, see `https://jasmine.github.io/api/edge/matchers.html`.

> Other libraries with richer features exist, such as Jest, Mocha, or testdouble.js. However, when getting started with a new framework like Angular, it's important to keep your toolset minimal. Sticking to defaults is a good idea.

Additionally, Jasmine provides spies, which support stubbing and mocking, with the `spyOn` function. We are going to cover these test doubles in more detail later in the chapter.

Anatomy of auto-generated unit tests

Out of the box, Angular is configured so that you can compose your unit tests with Jasmine. Karma is the test runner, which can continuously monitor changes to your code and automatically re-run your unit tests.

Angular's default configuration leverages `TestBed`, which is an Angular-specific component that facilitates the provision of modules, dependency injection, mocking, the triggering of Angular life-cycle events like `ngOnInit`, and the execution of template logic.

As discussed before, when you leverage `TestBed`, it is not possible to call these tests unit tests in the strictest definition of the term. This is because, by default, `TestBed` injects actual instances of your dependencies. This means when you execute your test, you're also executing code in services or other components, whereas you should be testing only the code that resides in the service or component that is currently under test. We leverage test doubles to help us write isolated and repeatable unit tests.

In *Chapter 3, Creating a Basic Angular App*, the Angular CLI created unit test files as you created new components and services, such as `current-weather.component.spec.ts` and `weather.service.spec.ts`. Take a look at the following spec file and observe the `should create` test. The framework asserts that any component of the `CurrentWeatherComponent` type should not to be null or undefined, but instead should be truthy:

```
src/app/current-weather/current-weather.component.spec.ts
describe('CurrentWeatherComponent', () => {
  let component: CurrentWeatherComponent
  let fixture: ComponentFixture<CurrentWeatherComponent>

  beforeEach(
    async(() => {
      TestBed.configureTestingModule({
        declarations: [CurrentWeatherComponent],
      }).compileComponents()
    })
  )

  beforeEach(() => {
    fixture = TestBed.createComponent(CurrentWeatherComponent)
    component = fixture.componentInstance
    fixture.detectChanges()
  })
```

```
    it('should create', () => {
      expect(component).toBeTruthy()
    })
  })
```

The `WeatherService` spec contains a similar test. However, you'll note that each type of tests is set up slightly differently:

src/app/weather/weather.service.spec.ts
```
describe('WeatherService', () => {
  let service: WeatherService

  beforeEach(() => {
    TestBed.configureTestingModule({})
    service = TestBed.inject(WeatherService);
  })

  it('should be created', () => {
      expect(service).toBeTruthy()
    })
  )
})
```

In the `WeatherService` spec's `beforeEach` function, the CUT is injected into `TestBed`. On the other hand, the `CurrentWeatherComponent` spec has two `beforeEach` functions. The first `beforeEach` function declares and compiles the component's dependent modules asynchronously, while the second `beforeEach` function creates a test fixture and starts listening to changes in the component, ready to run the tests once the compilation is complete.

Next, let's execute our unit tests to see how many are passing or failing.

Unit test execution

The Angular CLI uses the Jasmine unit testing library to define unit tests and the Karma test runner to execute them. Best of all, these testing tools are configured to be run out of the box. You may execute the unit tests with the following command:

`$ npm test`

The tests are run by the Karma test runner in a new Chrome browser window. The main benefit of Karma is that it brings live-reloading capabilities similar to what the Angular CLI achieves with webpack when developing your application.

After the initial execution of the `npm test` command, you're likely to run into compilation errors, because when we implemented our application code we didn't update the corresponding unit test code.

> During the development process, it is normal to run into many errors. So, don't be frustrated! See *Appendix A, Debugging Angular*, to learn how to troubleshoot and debug errors using Chrome/Edge Dev Tools and VS Code.

Let's how you can address these errors.

Compilation errors

It is important to update your unit test code as you develop your application code. Failing to do so usually results in compilation errors.

> Remember that test code is not built when you build your Angular app. You must execute `npm test` to build and run your test code.

When you execute the tests, you should see an error message like the one following:

```
ERROR in src/app/app.component.spec.ts:21:16 - error TS2339:
Property 'title' does not exist on type 'AppComponent'.
21     expect(app.title).toEqual('local-weather-app')
```

The first test we need to correct is under `app.component.spec.ts`, named `'should have as title "local-weather-app"'`. We deleted the app property `title` from `AppComponent` in the previous chapter because we were not using it. So, we don't need this unit test anymore.

1. Delete the `should have as title 'local-weather-app'` unit test.

> As discussed before, Jasmine combines the text provided in the `describe` and `it` functions. As a result, this test is called `'AppComponent should have as title 'local-weather-app''`. This is a convenient convention for quickly locating tests. As you write new tests, it is up to you to maintain readable descriptions of your specs.

The second test to fix is under `AppComponent` and is named `should render title`. We render the words LocalCast Weather as the title now, so let's change the test.

2. Update the `should render title` test as shown:

   `src/app/app.component.spec.ts`
   ```
   it('should render title', () => {
     ...
     expect(compiled.querySelector('h1').textContent)
       .toContain('LocalCast Weather')
   })
   ```

3. Commit your code changes.

We have fixed the logical issues in our unit tests. They should now execute without compilation errors. However, you should expect all of them fail because we haven't yet configured Angular's `TestBed`.

Test results

You should observe the last message on the Terminal to be `TOTAL: 2 FAILED, 2 SUCCESS`. This is normal because we haven't been paying attention to the tests at all, so let's fix them all.

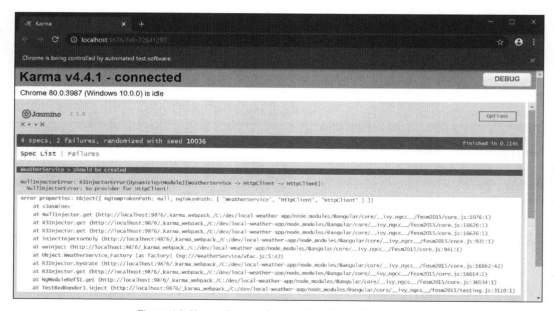

Figure 4.3: Karma Runner showing Jasmine unit test results

Keep the Karma Runner window open side by side with VS Code so that you can instantly see the results of your changes.

Let's now configure TestBed.

Configuring TestBed

TestBed has three major features that assist you in creating unit-testable components:

- Declarations – builds component classes, along with their template logic, to facilitate testing
- Providers – provides component classes without template logic and dependencies that need to be injected
- Imports – imports support modules to be able to render template logic or other platform functionality

 TestBed is not a hard requirement to write unit tests in Angular, a topic covered well at https://angular.io/guide/testing. My colleague and reviewer of this book, Brendon Caulkins, contributed a bed-less spec file to *Chapter 12, Recipes – Master/Detail, Data Tables, and NgRx* code samples, named `current-weather.component.nobed.spec.ts`. He cites significant performance increases in running the tests, with fewer imports and less maintenance, but a higher level of care and expertise required to implement the tests. If you're on a large project, you should seriously consider skipping the TestBed.

You can find the sample code on GitHub at https://github.com/duluca/local-weather-app/tree/master/projects/ch12.

Let's go over these features one by one while fixing the tests at hand so they can run successfully.

Declarations

Declarations allow us to provide all components necessary to render the component under test. Normally, you will only be declaring the component that is under test. So, `app.component.spec.ts` declares `AppComponent` and `current-weather.component.spec.ts` declares `CurrentWeatherComponent` and so forth.

Note that we use `<app-current-weather>` within the template of `AppComponent`; however, this does not mean that we need to also declare `CurrentWeatherComponent` in `app.component.spec.ts`. Previous versions of Angular's TestBed required child components to be declared as part of the parent component's unit tests, causing significant overhead in creating unit tests. Including multiple components in declarations has the side effect of needing to inject all dependencies of all components declared, not just those of the one that is under test. This meant adding unrelated dependencies to our "unit" tests, making them integration tests.

In this case, `CurrentWeatherComponent` is a hard-coded dependency of `AppComponent`. It is possible to decouple the two components further in two ways: one way is to inject the component dynamically using an `ng-container`, and the other would be to leverage the Angular Router and `router-outlet`. The `router-outlet` strategy is how we structure the vast majority of multi-screen Angular apps, which I cover in later chapters. Properly decoupling components using `ng-container` is left as an exercise for the reader.

You may try out declaring `CurrentWeatherComponent` in `app.component.spec.ts`:

src/app/app.component.spec.ts
```
...
TestBed.configureTestingModule({
   declarations: [AppComponent, CurrentWeatherComponent],
}).compileComponents()
...
```

Note that doing so introduces `HttpClient`-related errors for `AppComponent` tests, even though `AppComponent` itself doesn't import `WeatherService`. In fact, `CurrentWeatherComponent` imports `WeatherService`, which itself imports `HttpClient`. You can see how the complexity of the dependencies can quickly get out of hand. Angular unit tests are configured to not require the declaration of the child component, but note that the unit test framework is throwing a warning regarding the unknown element:

WARN: ''app-current-weather' is not a known element

In programming, warnings are almost as serious as errors. Not resolving warnings is bound to cause trouble down the line. We will cover how to properly resolve this issue when we cover mocks later.

> Be sure to undo your change before moving on.

For now, you don't need to declare child components for parent component tests, making it easier to have passing unit tests initially. There are certain cases where you must declare dependent components, such as when you are creating a custom control and you need to test whether your control works properly within the context of a component. An example of creating a custom control is included in *Chapter 11, Recipes – Reusability, Routing, and Caching*.

In the next section, we will look at providers, which help us inject real and fake implementations of dependencies so that we can avoid testing dependencies like `WeatherService` and only test the "unit."

Providers

Providers allow us to provide components without template logic or services that are injected to our component under test. You'll note that our `CurrentWeatherComponent` tests are not passing with an error complaining about the lack of provider for `HttpClient`:

```
CurrentWeatherComponent > should create
NullInjectorError: R3InjectorError(DynamicTestModule)[WeatherService
-> HttpClient -> HttpClient]:
  NullInjectorError: No provider for HttpClient!
```

This is because `WeatherService`, which is injected into `CurrentWeatherComponent`, needs a provider for `HttpClient`. However, `CurrentWeatherComponent` has no knowledge of `HttpClient`. It only knows about `WeatherService`. You may guess that we're perhaps not strictly unit testing but actually integration testing, and you would be right.

However, let's play along and add the provider for `WeatherService` to `current-weather.component.spec.ts`. Provide the `WeatherService` in the declarations in `current-weather.component.spec.ts`, as shown:

src/app/current-weather/current-weather.component.spec.ts
```
...
beforeEach(async(() => {
  TestBed.configureTestingModule({
    declarations: [...],
    providers: [WeatherService],
```

```
    })
    ...
})
...
```

In this example, we have provided the actual implementation of `WeatherService`, which doesn't resolve the issue at hand. The implementation of `WeatherService` still depends on `HttpClient` and the error persists.

 Be sure to undo your change before moving on.

Providers allow us to provide alternative implementations of a dependency, like a fake or a mock of that dependency.

If we define a fake implementation of `WeatherService` named `FakeWeatherService`, we can provide the fake instead of the actual implementation with `useClass` shown as follows:

```
providers: [{ provide: WeatherService, useClass: FakeWeatherService }]
```

A fake implementation would break the dependency on `HttpClient` and resolve our issue. I go over how to implement fakes in the upcoming section on test doubles.

Alternatively, if we create a mock for `WeatherService` named `mockWeatherService`, we can provide the mock with `useValue` shown as follows:

```
providers: [{ provide: WeatherService, useValue: mockWeatherService }]
```

With a mock, we wouldn't even have to implement a fake class and ensure that we're only testing the component under test. The upcoming section on test doubles covers mocks in detail.

Now that we have a good understanding of what providers can and can't do for us, let's see how imports round out `TestBed`.

Imports

Imports help bring in code that can facilitate the rendering of views or other dependencies to the test. Currently, the tests are still failing, because `WeatherService` itself depends on `HttpClient`, so we need to provide `HttpClient`. If we do, then our unit test will attempt to make calls over HTTP. We don't want our tests to depend on other services, as this goes against the FIRST principles covered earlier in the chapter. So, we shouldn't provide the actual `HttpClient`.

Angular provides a test double for `HttpClient` named `HttpClientTestingModule`. To leverage it, you must import it, which automatically provides the test double for you.

Import `HttpClientTestingModule` for `current-weather.component.spec.ts`:

src/app/current-weather/current-weather.component.spec.ts
```
import { HttpClientTestingModule } from '@angular/common/http/testing'
...
  describe(' CurrentWeatherComponent', () => {
    beforeEach(() => {
      TestBed.configureTestingModule({
        imports: [HttpClientTestingModule],
        ...
      })
      ...
  })
...
```

Similar to `HttpClientTestingModule`, there's also a `RouterTestingModule` and a `NoopAnimationsModule`, which are mock versions of the real services, so the unit tests can focus on only testing the component or service code that you write. In later chapters, we also cover how you can write your own mocks.

Phew! Now, all your unit tests should be passing. As you can see, the `CurrentWeatherComponent` tests are not our unit tests, because they are using the actual `WeatherService`, which itself depends on `HttpClient`.

Now, let's look into how test doubles can help us write unit tests that adhere to FIRST principles.

Test doubles

Only the code in the CUT should be exercised. In the case of the `CurrentWeatherComponent`, we need to ensure that the service code is not executed. For this reason, you should *never* provide the actual implementation of the service.

We need to go over two types of test doubles:

- Fakes
- Mocks, stubs, or spies

In general, it is easier to reason about fakes, so we will start with that. Once you're comfortable with unit testing and your existing set of tests are in working order, I highly recommend switching over to exclusively using mocks, as it'll make your tests more robust, efficient, and maintainable.

Fakes

A fake is an alternative, simplified implementation of an existing class. It's like a fake service, where no actual HTTP calls are made, but your service returns pre-baked responses. During unit testing, a fake is instantiated and is used like the real class. In the previous section, we used `HttpClientTestingModule`, which is a fake `HttpClient`. Our custom service is `WeatherService`, so we must provide our implementation of a test double.

We create a test double by creating a fake of the service. Since the fake of the `WeatherService` is used in tests for multiple components, your implementation should be in a separate file. For the sake of the maintainability and discoverability of your codebase, one class per file is a good rule of thumb to follow. Keeping classes in separate files saves you from committing certain coding sins, like mistakenly creating or sharing global state or standalone functions between two classes, keeping your code decoupled in the process.

We also need to ensure that APIs for the actual implementation and the test double don't go out of sync over time. We can accomplish this by creating an interface for the service.

1. Add `IWeatherService` to `weather.service.ts`, as shown:

    src/app/weather/weather.service.ts
    ```
    export interface IWeatherService {
      getCurrentWeather(
      city: string,
      country: string
      ): Observable<ICurrentWeather>
    }
    ```

2. Update `WeatherService` so that it implements the new interface:

    src/app/weather/weather.service.ts
    ```
    export class WeatherService implements IWeatherService
    ```

3. Create a new file `weather/weather.service.fake.ts`

4. Implement a basic fake in `weather.service.fake.ts`, as follows:

    src/app/weather/weather.service.fake.ts
    ```
    import { Observable, of } from 'rxjs'

    import { IWeatherService } from './weather.service'
    import { ICurrentWeather } from '../interfaces'

    export const fakeWeather: ICurrentWeather = {
      city: 'Bethesda',
    ```

```
      country: 'US',
      date: 1485789600,
      image: '',
      temperature: 280.32,
      description: 'light intensity drizzle',
}

export class WeatherServiceFake implements IWeatherService {
  public getCurrentWeather(
    city: string,
    country: string): Observable<ICurrentWeather> {
      return of(fakeWeather)
  }
}
```

We're leveraging the existing `ICurrentWeather` interface that our fake data has correctly shaped, but we must also turn it into an `Observable`. This is easily achieved using `of`, which creates an observable sequence, given the provided arguments.

Now you're ready to provide the fake to `AppComponent` and `CurrentWeatherComponent`.

5. Update the provider in `current-weather.component.spec.ts` to use `WeatherServiceFake` so that the fake is used instead of the actual service:

   src/app/current-weather/current-weather.component.spec.ts

   ```
   ...
   beforeEach(
     async(() => {
       TestBed.configureTestingModule({
         ...
         providers: [{
           provide: WeatherService, useClass: WeatherServiceFake
         }],
         ...
   ```

Note that this alternate implementation is provided under a different file named `current-weather.component.fake.spec`, part of the sub-folder `projects/ch4` on GitHub.

6. Remove `HttpClientTestingModule` from the imports, since it is no longer needed

>  As your services and components get more complicated, it's easy to provide an incomplete or inadequate test double. You may see errors such as `NetworkError: Failed to execute 'send' on 'XMLHttpRequest'`, `Can't resolve all parameters`, or `[object ErrorEvent] thrown`. In case of the latter error, click on the **Debug** button in Karma to discover the view error details, which may look like **Timeout - Async callback was not invoked within timeout specified by jasmine**. Unit tests are designed to run in milliseconds, so it should be impossible to actually hit the default 5-second timeout. The issue is almost always with the test setup or configuration.

7. Verify that all tests are passing

With fakes, we were able to somewhat reduce test complexity and improve isolation. We can do much better with mocks, stubs, and spies.

Mocks, stubs, and spies

A mock, stub, or spy does not contain any implementation whatsoever. Mocks are configured in the unit test file to respond to specific function calls with a set of responses that can be made to vary from test to test with ease.

Earlier in the *Declarations* section, we discussed the need to declare `CurrentWeatherComponent` in `app.component.spec.ts` to resolve the **not a known element** warning. If we declare the real `CurrentWeatherComponent`, then the `AppComponent` test configuration becomes overly complicated with a lot of configuration elements, because we must resolve the dependency tree for the child component, including `WeatherService` and `HttpClient`. In addition, creating a whole fake service just to provide fake weather data is overkill and is not a flexible solution. What if we wanted to test different service responses, given different inputs? We would have to start introducing logic into our fake service, and before you know it, you're dealing with two separate implementations of the `WeatherService`.

An alternative to creating a fake would be to create an empty object that parades as the real thing but contains no implementation. These objects are called mocks. We will leverage two different techniques to create a mock component and a mock service below.

Mock components

If we were to provide a `CurrentWeatherComponent` in `app.component.spec.ts`, we could resolve the **not a known element** warning and not have to worry about all the components and services that `CurrentWeatherComponent` depends on.

If you were to implement it by hand, a mock component would look like this:

```
@Component({
  selector: 'app-current-weather',
  template: ``,
})
class MockCurrentWeatherComponent {}
```

However, this can get tedious really fast, which is why I published a unit test helper library called **angular-unit-test-helper** to make it easier to mock a component. With the library, you can just replace the component in the declaration with this function call:

```
createComponentMock('CurrentWeatherComponent')
```

Let's update `app.component.spec.ts` to use mocked components:

1. Execute `npm i -D angular-unit-test-helper`
2. Update `AppComponent` with the mocked components:

    src/app/app.component.spec.ts
    ```
    import { createComponentMock } from 'angular-unit-test-helper'
      TestBed.configureTestingModule({
        declarations: [ ...,
          createComponentMock('CurrentWeatherComponent')
        ],
        ...
      })
    ```

3. Remove the `providers` property altogether
4. Clean up unused imports

Observe that the unit test file remains lean and the warning is resolved. **angular-unit-test-helper** infers that `CurrentWeatherComponent` represents an HTML tag like `<app-current-weather>` and provides it in the window object of the browser. The `createComponentMock` function then properly decorates the empty class `CurrentWeatherComponent` by assigning the selector `'app-current-weather'` and an empty template. `TestBed` is then able to resolve `<app-current-weather>` as this mocked component. `createComponentMock` also allows you to provide a custom selector or a fake template that you can pass depending on your needs. This is a solution that scales, cutting imports by more than half and adhering to FIRST principles.

The concept of mocks extends to all kinds of objects we can define, including Angular services. By mocking a service, we don't have to worry about any dependencies that may be injected into that service.

Let's see how we can mock a service.

Mock services

Let's write two new unit tests for `CurrentWeatherComponent` to demonstrate the value of mocking a service instead of implementing a fake for it. Mocks allow us to create an empty object and give us the option to supply only the functions that may be needed for a test. We can then stub out the return values of these functions per test or spy on them to see whether our code called them or not. Spying is especially useful if the function in question has no return value. We need to set up our spy in the arrange part of our spec.

1. Let's start by creating a spy `WeatherService`, using `jasmine.createSpyObj`, as shown:

    ```
    src/app/current-weather/current-weather.component.spec.ts
    import {
      ComponentFixture,
      TestBed,
      async
    } from '@angular/core/testing'
    import { injectSpy } from 'angular-unit-test-helper'

    import { WeatherService } from '../weather/weather.service'
    import {
      CurrentWeatherComponent
    } from './current-weather.component'

    describe('CurrentWeatherComponent', () => {
      ...
      let weatherServiceMock: jasmine.SpyObj<WeatherService>

      beforeEach(async(() => {
        const weatherServiceSpy =
          jasmine.createSpyObj(
            'WeatherService',
            ['getCurrentWeather']
          )

        TestBed.configureTestingModule({ ... })
      })
    ```

2. Provide `weatherServiceSpy` as the value of `WeatherService` with `useValue`
3. Finally, get the injected instance from `TestBed` and assign the value to `weatherServiceMock`, using the `injectSpy` method from angular-unit-test-helper as shown:

```
src/app/current-weather/current-weather.component.spec.ts
    beforeEach(async(() => {
      ...
      TestBed.configureTestingModule({
        ...,
        providers: [{
          provide: WeatherService, useValue: weatherServiceSpy
        }]
      }).compileComponents()
      weatherServiceMock = injectSpy(WeatherService)
    }
```

 Note that `injectSpy` is a shorthand for `TestBed.inject(WeatherService) as any`.

In the preceding example, we have a mocked version of `WeatherService`, where declared that it has a function named `getCurrentWeather`. However, note that you're now getting an error:

`TypeError: Cannot read property 'subscribe' of undefined`

This is because `getCurrentWeather` is not returning an observable. Using `weatherServiceMock`, we can spy on whether `getCurrentWeather` is being called or not, but also stub out its return value depending on the test.

In order to manipulate the return value of `getCurrentWeather`, we need to update the **should create** test to reflect the arrange, act, and assert structure. To do this, we need to move `fixture.detectChanges()` from the second `beforeEach`, so we can control its execution order to be after the arrange part.

```
src/app/current-weather/current-weather.component.spec.ts
    import { of } from 'rxjs'
    ...
    beforeEach(() => {
      fixture = TestBed.createComponent(CurrentWeatherComponent)
      component = fixture.componentInstance
    })

    it('should create', () => {
      // Arrange
      weatherServiceMock.getCurrentWeather.and.returnValue(of())

      // Act
      fixture.detectChanges() // triggers ngOnInit

      // Assert
      expect(component).toBeTruthy()
    })
```

[149]

In the arrange part, we configure that `getCurrentWeather` should return an empty observable using the `RxJS\of` function. In the act part, we trigger TestBed's `detectChanges` function, which triggers lifecycle events like `ngOnInit`. Since the code we're testing is in `ngOnInit`, this is the right thing to execute. Finally, in the assert part, we confirm our assertion that the component was successfully created.

In this next test, we can verify that the `getCurrentWeather` function is being called exactly once:

src/app/current-weather/current-weather.component.spec.ts

```
  it('should get currentWeather from weatherService', () => {
    // Arrange
    weatherServiceMock.getCurrentWeather.and.returnValue(of())

    // Act
    fixture.detectChanges() // triggers ngOnInit()

    // Assert
    expect(weatherServiceMock.getCurrentWeather)
      .toHaveBeenCalledTimes(1)

  })
```

And finally, we can test out the fact that the values that are being returned are correctly assigned in the component class, but also that they are correctly rendered on the template:

src/app/current-weather/current-weather.component.spec.ts

```
import { By } from '@angular/platform-browser'
import { fakeWeather } from '../weather/weather.service.fake'
...
  it('should eagerly load currentWeather in Bethesda from weatherService', () => {
    // Arrange
    weatherServiceMock.getCurrentWeather
      .and.returnValue(of(fakeWeather))

    // Act
    fixture.detectChanges() // triggers ngOnInit()

    // Assert
    expect(component.current).toBeDefined()
    expect(component.current.city).toEqual('Bethesda')
```

```
        expect(component.current.temperature).toEqual(280.32)

        // Assert on DOM
        const debugEl = fixture.debugElement
        const titleEl: HTMLElement = debugEl.query(By.css('span'))
          .nativeElement
        expect(titleEl.textContent).toContain('Bethesda')
    })
```

In the preceding example, you can see that we're providing a `fakeWeather` object, where the city name is Bethesda. We are then able to assert that the current property has the correct `city`, and also that the `<div>` element with `class=mat-title` contains the text Bethesda.

You should now have seven passing tests:

TOTAL: 7 SUCCESS

Using mocks, stubs, and spies, we can rapidly test permutations of what outside dependencies can and cannot return and we are able to verify our assertions on the code that resides in the component or service class by observing the DOM.

To learn more about mocks, stubbing, and spies, refer to https://jasmine.github.io. Also, I've found Jasmine 2 Spy Cheat Sheet by Dave Ceddia, located at https://daveceddia.com/jasmine-2-spy-cheat-sheet, to be a useful resource.

In general, your unit tests should be asserting one or two things at most. To achieve adequate unit test coverage, you should focus on testing the correctness of functions that contain business logic: usually wherever you see an `if` or `switch` statement.

To write unit-testable code, be sure to adhere to the Single Responsibility and Open/Closed principles of the SOLID principles.

Check out the **ng-tester** library that my colleague Brendan Sawyer created at https://www.npmjs.com/package/ng-tester. It creates opinionated spec files for your Angular components that leverage **angular-unit-test-helper** to assist with mocking. In addition, the library demonstrates how to mock dependencies and create tests without using `TestBed`.

You may install the library `npm install -D ng-tester` and create a unit test with the command `npx ng generate ng-tester:unit`.

In addition to unit tests, the Angular CLI also generates and configures e2e tests for your application. Next, let's learn about e2e tests.

Angular e2e tests

While unit tests focus on isolating the CUT, e2e tests are about integration testing. The Angular CLI leverages Protractor along with WebDriver so that you can write **Automated Acceptance Tests (AAT)** from the perspective of a user interacting with your application in a browser. As a rule of thumb, you should always write an order of magnitude more unit tests than AATs, because your app changes frequently, and as a result, AATs are vastly more fragile and expensive to maintain compared to unit tests.

If the term web driver sounds familiar, it's because it is an evolution of the canonical Selenium WebDriver. On March 30th, 2017, WebDriver was proposed as an official web standard at the W3C. You read more about it at https://www.w3.org/TR/webdriver. If you're familiar with Selenium, you should feel right at home, since a lot of the patterns and practices are nearly identical.

The CLI provides e2e tests for the initial `AppComponent` and depending on the complexity and the feature set of your application. It's up to you to follow the provided pattern to organize your tests better. There are two files generated per component under the e2e folder:

e2e/src/app.e2e-spec.ts
```
import { browser, logging } from 'protractor'

import { AppPage } from './app.po'

describe('workspace-project App', () => {
  let page: AppPage

  beforeEach(() => {
    page = new AppPage()
  })

  it('should display welcome message', () => {
    page.navigateTo()
    expect(page.getTitleText())
      .toEqual('local-weather-app app is running!')
  })
```

```
    afterEach(async () => {
      // Assert that there are no errors emitted from the browser
      const logs = await browser
        .manage()
        .logs()
        .get(logging.Type.BROWSER)
      expect(logs).not.toContain(
        jasmine.objectContaining({
          level: logging.Level.SEVERE,
        } as logging.Entry)
      )
    })
  })
```

`app.e2e-spec.ts` is written in Jasmine and implements acceptance tests. The spec is dependent upon the page object (po) file, which is defined beside the spec file:

```
e2e/src/app.po.ts
import { browser, by, element } from 'protractor'

export class AppPage {
  navigateTo(): Promise<unknown> {
    return browser.get(browser.baseUrl) as Promise<unknown>
  }

  getTitleText(): Promise<string> {
    return element(by.css('app-root div h1'))
      .getText() as Promise<string>
  }
}
```

Consider the following diagram, which represents the e2e test architecture visually:

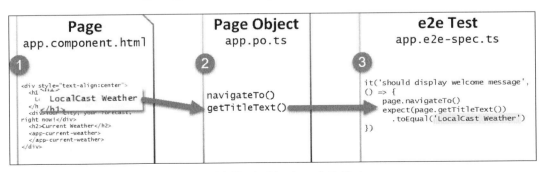

Figure 4.4: The Architecture of e2e Tests

The goal of the **'should display welcome message'** test is to verify that `app.component.html` displays the correct text. The page object file, `app.po.ts`, encapsulates web driver implementation to retrieve the message with the `getTitleText` function. Finally, the test is written as a Jasmine test in the `app.e2e-spec.ts` file. AATs are the most fragile kind of tests. Having a page object layer between the HTML and the spec files results in easy-to-maintain, human-readable tests. By separating concerns at this level, you keep the fragility of AATs to one location. By leveraging class inheritance, you can build a robust collection of page objects that can be easier to maintain over time.

e2e test execution

You can execute e2e tests with the following command in the terminal; ensure that the `npm test` process is not running:

```
$ npm run e2e
```

Note that the test execution is different as compared to unit tests. While you can configure a watcher to continually execute unit tests with Karma, due to the user-driven and stateful nature of e2e tests, it is not a good practice to attempt a similar configuration with e2e tests. Running the tests once and stopping the test harness ensures a clean state with every run.

The e2e page object and spec

After executing the e2e tests, you should see an error message similar to the one here:

```
**************************************************
*                   Failures                     *
**************************************************


1) web-app App should display welcome message
  - Failed: No element found using locator: By(css selector, app-root
.content span)


Executed 1 of 1 spec (1 FAILED) in 0.659 sec.
```

The test is failing because we significantly altered the structure of the HTML in `app.component.html` and the `getTitleText` method in our page object is no longer correct.

Chapter 4

1. Begin by correcting `getTitleText` so it retrieves the correct text:

   e2e/src/app.po.ts
   ```
   getTitleText(): Promise<string> {
     return element(by.css('app-root div h1')).
       getText() as Promise<string>
   }
   ```

   Note that the error message now says:

   ```
   - Expected 'LocalCast Weather' to equal 'local-weather-app app is
   running!'.
   ```

2. Update the `spec` to expect the correct header as follows:

   e2e/src/app.e2e-spec.ts
   ```
   it('should display welcome message', () => {
     page.navigateTo()
     expect(page.getTitleText()).toEqual('LocalCast Weather')
   })
   ```

3. Re-run the tests; they should be passing now:

   ```
   Jasmine started

   web-app App
   √ should display welcome message
   Executed 1 of 1 spec SUCCESS in 0.676 sec.
   ```

4. Commit your code changes.

Our unit tests and e2e tests are now working.

> There are more robust tools for automated acceptance testing, such as https://cypress.io and https://github.com/bigtestjs. Consider using these tools instead of Angular's e2e tests.
>
> You may find a sample implementation of Cypress, integrated with CircleCI, for the LemonMart project, covered in *Chapter 7, Creating a Router-First Line-of-Business App*, at https://github.com/duluca/lemon-mart.
>
> Execute `npm run cypress:run` to see Cypress in action. Cypress can record and replay test runs for easy debugging; it is a robust tool for your next enterprise project.

Automated Testing, CI, and Release to Production

Going forward, make sure that your tests remain in working condition.

Next, we need to ready our app for production deployments, which means building the app in prod mode and setting the appropriate environment variables.

Production readiness

When you run `npm start`, Angular builds in debug mode, which enables faster build times, breakpoint debugging, and live reloading. This also means that the bundle size of a small app balloons to over 7 MB. A 7 MB bundle size results in over two minutes of loading time on a slow 3G connection when we expect our app to load in mere seconds. Additionally, in debug mode, we use environment variables meant for local development. However, in production, we need to use different settings so our application can run in a hosted environment correctly.

Let's start by implementing an `npm` script to help us build in prod mode.

Building for production

Angular ships with a robust build tool that can optimize the size of your bundle by removing redundant, unused, and inefficient code from the debug build and pre-compiling sections of code so browsers can interpret it faster. So, a 7 MB bundle can become 700 KB and load in under 7 seconds even on a slow 3G connection.

By default, the `ng build` command builds your code in debug mode. By adding the `--prod` option to it, we can enable `prod` mode.

1. Add a new script called `build:prod` to `package.json`, as shown:

    package.json
    ```
    "scripts": {
      ...
      "build:prod": "ng build --prod"
    }
    ```

2. Test the script by executing:

    ```
    $ npm run build:prod
    ```

This is a critical configuration for the efficient delivery of Angular apps.

 Do not ship an Angular app without first enabling prod mode.

Next, let's set the environment variables for prod.

Setting environment variables

In *Chapter 3, Creating a Basic Angular App*, we configured the URL for the OpenWeatherMap APIs using environment variables stored in the `src/environment/environment.ts` file. We need to update our variables for production use because the environment that our Angular app lives in is changing. The settings that work in a local or test environment are not necessarily going to work in the hosting environment.

Apply the following changes to `environment.prod.ts`:

1. Set `production` to `true`
2. If necessary, provide a production `appId` variable
3. Update `baseUrl` to `https`:

   src/environments/environment.prod.ts
   ```
   export const environment = {
     production: true,
     appId: 'xxxxxxxxxxxxxxxxxxxxxxxxxxxxxx',
     baseUrl: 'https://',
   }
   ```

Setting `production` to `true` allows the application code to check the mode of the application to adjust its behavior. Also, we changed the `baseUrl` from HTTP to HTTPS, because our app is hosted over HTTPS. Browsers don't allow the serving of mixed content, which weakens the overall security benefits that HTTPS delivers. If we don't switch over to HTTPS, then our calls to the OpenWeatherMap APIs fail.

> You can read more about mixed content at `https://developers.google.com/web/fundamentals/security/prevent-mixed-content/what-is-mixed-content`.

Next, let's set up CI to ensure that our tests are always passing before we deploy the app to production.

Continuous Integration

Before pushing your code to production, you should enable CI. This basic setup helps ensure our application code keeps working even when we make changes to our code, by automating the execution of our unit tests.

CircleCI

CircleCI makes it easy to get started, with a free tier and excellent documentation for beginners and pros alike. If you have unique enterprise needs, CircleCI can be brought on-premises, behind corporate firewalls, or as a private deployment in the cloud.

CircleCI has pre-baked build environments for the virtual configuration of free setups, but it can also run builds using Docker containers, making it a solution that scales to the user's skills and needs, as covered in *Chapter 9, DevOps Using Docker*:

1. Create a CircleCI account at `https://circleci.com/`.
2. Sign up with GitHub:

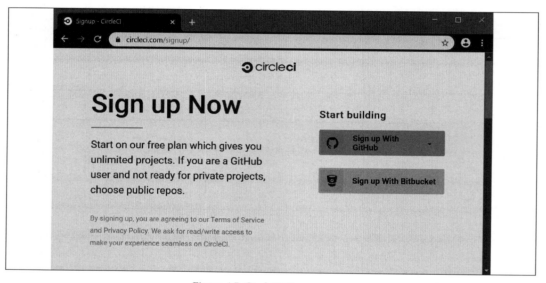

Figure 4.5: CircleCI Sign up page

3. Add a new project:

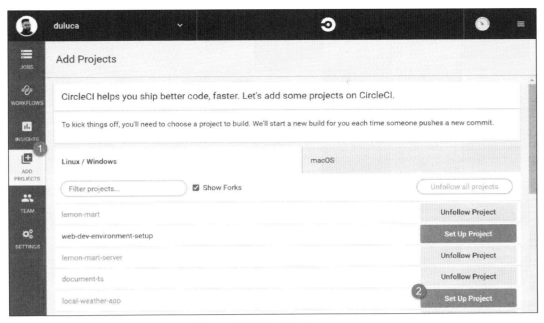

Figure 4.6: CircleCI Projects page

On the next screen, you have an option to select **Linux** or **macOS** build environments. The macOS build environments are good for building iOS or macOS apps. However, there is no free tier for those environments; only Linux instances with 1x parallelism are free.

4. Search for `local-weather-app` and click on **Set Up Project**.
5. Select **Linux**.
6. Select **Language** as **Node**, which provides a sample `.yml` file.

> This section uses the **local-weather-app** repo. The `config.yml` file for this section is named `.circleci/config.ch4.yml`. You can also find a pull request that executes the yml file from this chapter on CircleCI: https://github.com/duluca/local-weatherapp/pull/52 using the `branch build_ch4`. Note that this branch has a modified configuration in `config.yml` and `Dockerfile` to use `projects/ch4` code from **local-weather-app**.

7. In your source code, create a folder named `.circleci` and add a file named config.yml:

.circleci/config.yml
```
version: 2.1
jobs:
  build:
    docker:
      - image: circleci/node:lts-browsers
    working_directory: ~/repo
    steps:
      - checkout

      - restore_cache:
          keys:
            - v1-dependencies-{{ checksum "package-lock.json" }}
      - run: npm ci

      # force update the webdriver
      - run: cd ./node_modules/protractor && npm i webdrivermanager@latest
      # because we use "npm ci" to install NPM dependencies
      # we cache "~/.npm" folder
      - save_cache:
          key: v1-dependencies-{{ checksum "package-lock.json" }}
          paths:
            - ~/.npm

      - run: npm run style
      - run: npm run lint

      - run: npm run build:prod
      - run: npm run test:coverage -- --watch=false
      - run: npm run e2e
      - run:
          name: Tar & Gzip compiled app
          command: tar zcf dist.tar.gz dist/local-weather-app
      - store_artifacts:
          path: dist.tar.gz
workflows:
  version: 2
  build-and-test:
    jobs:
      - build
```

[160]

8. Sync your changes to Github.
9. On CircleCI, click **Start building** to register your project.

If everything goes well, you should have a passing, *green*, build. If not, you see a failed, *red*, build. The following screenshot shows a failed build, **#97**, and a subsequent build, **#98**, which was successful:

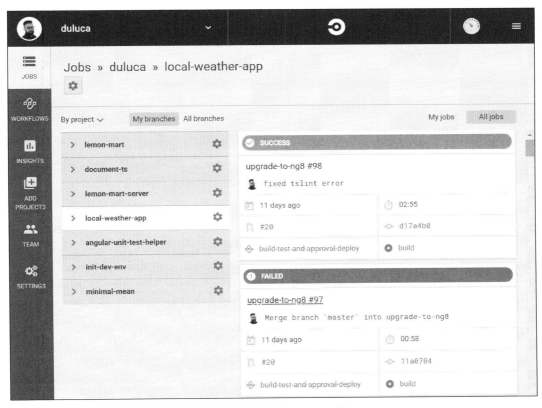

Figure 4.7: Green Build on CircleCI

Now that you have a green build, you can leverage CircleCI to enforce the execution of your automated pipeline with every code push. GitHub flow allows us to control how code flows into our repositories.

GitHub flow

The main reason we're developing software is to deliver value. In automating the way we deliver software, we are creating a value delivery stream. It is easy to deliver broken software; however, to reliably deliver value, each change to the codebase should flow through a stream of checks and balances.

With control gates, we can enforce standards, make our quality control process repeatable for every team member, and have the ability to isolate changes. If something goes wrong or the work doesn't live up to your standards, you can easily discard the proposed changes and restart.

GitHub flow is an essential part of defining a value delivery stream and implement control gates. As GitHub puts it, *"GitHub flow is a lightweight, branch-based workflow that supports teams and projects where deployments are made regularly."*

GitHub flow consists of 6 steps, as shown in the following graphic from GitHub:

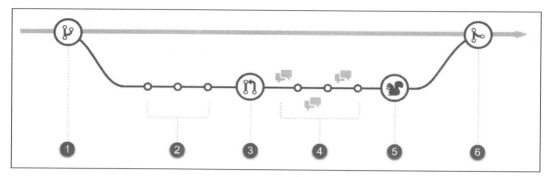

Figure 4.8: GitHub flow diagram

1. **Branch** – always add new code for a bug or a feature in a new branch
2. **Commit** – make multiple commits to your branch
3. **Create a pull request** – signal the readiness of your work to your team members and view CI results in a pull request
4. **Discuss and review** – request a review of your code changes, address general or line-level comments, and make necessary modifications
5. **Deploy** – optionally test your code on a test server or in production with the ability to roll back to the master
6. **Merge** – apply your changes to the master branch

Using GitHub flow, you can ensure that only high-quality code ends up in the master branch. A solid foundation sets other team members up for success when they start making their changes. In order to enforce GitHub flow, you need to restrict push access to the master branch.

Let's enable branch protection for the master branch:

1. Navigate to the GitHub settings tab for your project
2. Select **Branches** from the left navigation pane
3. Click the **Add rule** button
4. Configure your rule as shown in the following image:

Figure 4.9: GitHub Branch protection rule

Automated Testing, CI, and Release to Production

5. After you've saved your changes, you should see your new rule on the **Branches** page as shown:

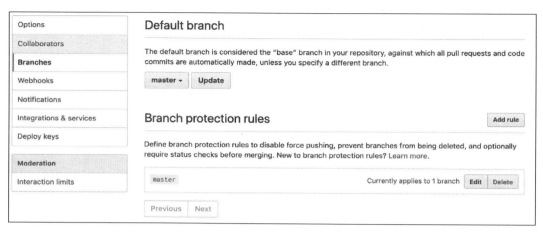

Figure 4.10: GitHub Branches

You are no longer able to commit code to your master branch directly. To commit code, you first need to create a branch from the master, commit your changes to the new branch, and when you're ready, create a pull request using the new branch. If you're not familiar with `git` commands, you can use GitHub Desktop to assist you with these operations. See the handy **Branch** menu in GitHub Desktop here:

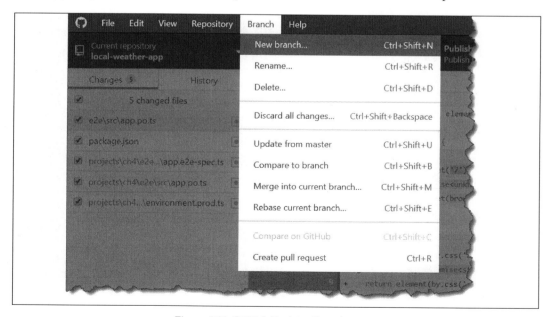

Figure 4.11: GitHub Desktop Branch menu

After creating a pull request, you can now observe checks running against your branch. Now that we have CircleCI configured, if everything went well, you should be able to merge a pull request, as shown:

Figure 4.12: GitHub.com Status Checks Passing

When the checks fail, you are forced to fix any issues before you can merge the new code. Also, you may run into merge conflicts if a team member merged to the master while you were working on your branch. In this case, you may use GitHub Desktop's **Update from master** feature to catch up your branch with the latest branch from the master.

Observe the state of a failing pull request in the following image:

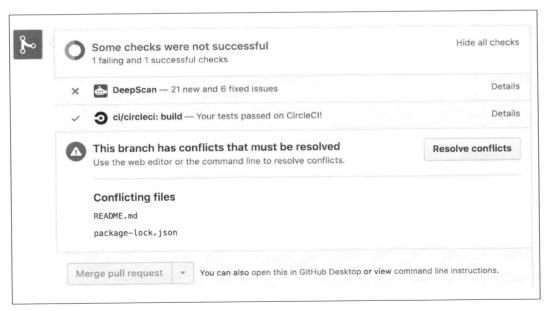

Figure 4.13: GitHub.com status checks failing

> Note that I have an additional check, DeepScan, which runs additional tests against my codebase. You can register your repo with DeepScan at `https://deepscan.io`. In *Chapter 9, DevOps Using Docker*, I demonstrate how you can enforce unit test code coverage using Coveralls.

For more information, refer to `https://guides.github.com/introduction/flow`.

Now that we have ensured that our automated checks are being enforced, we can be reasonably sure that we won't push a broken app to production. Next, let's learn how we can deploy our app to the cloud.

Deploying to the Cloud

If delivering something to production is difficult from a coding perspective, it is very complicated to do it right from an infrastructure perspective. In *Chapter 13, Highly Available Cloud Infrastructure on AWS*, I cover how to provision a world-class AWS **Elastic Container Service (ECS)** infrastructure for your applications, but that won't help if you need to demonstrate an idea quickly or don't need a highly configurable solution. Enter Vercel Now.

Vercel Now

Vercel Now, `https://vercel.com`, is a multi-cloud service that enables real-time global deployments of applications directly from the CLI. Vercel Now works with static files, Node.js, PHP, Go applications, and any custom stack of software you're willing to write a custom builder for, which makes it quite straightforward to work with. Vercel Now, which is currently on version 2, has a free tier that you can use to deploy the `dist` folder of your Angular applications very quickly. In *Chapter 9, DevOps Using Docker*, I demonstrate how you can also deploy a containerized version of your Angular app.

Refer to *Chapter 2, Setting Up Your Development Environment*, for instructions on installing Vercel Now.

With the `now` tool, we're ready to deploy our app to the web.

Deploying static files

After you build an Angular project, the build output resides in the `dist` folder. The files in this folder are considered static files; all a web server needs to do is deliver these files to a client browser, unmodified, and then the browser executes your code dynamically.

This means that any web server is able to serve up your Angular project. However, now makes it exceedingly easy, and free, to pull off.

Let's get started with deploying your Angular app using now's static file hosting capabilities.

1. Add two new scripts to package.json, as shown:

   package.json

   ```
   ...
   "scripts": {
     ...
     "prenow:publish": "npm run build:prod",
     "now:publish": "now --platform-version 2 dist/local-weather-app"
   }
   ```

    To deploy Chapter 4-specific code from https://github.com/duluca/local-weather-app, you need to execute now --platform-version 2 dist/ch4. Accept the default options for the CLI prompts. In my case, the app deployed to https://ch4-dun.now.sh/.

2. Execute npm run now:publish.
3. Accept the default options for the CLI prompts.

   In the terminal window, observe that the Angular project is built first and then uploaded to now:

   ```
   $ npm run now:publish
   > localcast-weather@9.0.0 prenow:publish C:\dev\local-weather-app
   > npm run build:prod

   > localcast-weather@9.0.0 build:prod C:\dev\local-weather-app
   > ng build --prod

   Generating ES5 bundles for differential loading...
   ES5 bundle generation complete.

   chunk {2} polyfills-es2015.ca64e4516afbb1b890d5.js (polyfills) 35.6 kB [initial] [rendered]
   chunk {3} polyfills-es5.1d087d4db6b105875851.js (polyfills-es5) 128 kB [initial] [rendered]
   ```

```
chunk {1} main-es2015.941dc398feac35a1a67d.js (main) 485 kB
[initial] [rendered]
chunk {1} main-es5.941dc398feac35a1a67d.js (main) 577 kB [initial]
[rendered]chunk {0} runtime-es2015.0811dcefd377500b5b1a.js
(runtime) 1.45 kB [entry] [rendered]
chunk {0} runtime-es5.0811dcefd377500b5b1a.js (runtime) 1.45 kB
[entry] [rendered]
chunk {4} styles.1938720bb6985e81892f.css (styles) 62 kB
[initial] [rendered]Date: 2020-03-24T00:14:52.939Z - Hash:
4d78a666345c6761dc95 - Time: 14719ms


> localcast-weather@9.0.0 now:publish C:\dev\local-weather-app
> now --platform-version 2 --prod dist/local-weather-app


> UPDATE AVAILABLE Run `npm i now@latest` to install Now CLI
17.1.1
> Changelog: https://github.com/zeit/now/releases/tag/now@17.1.1
Now CLI 17.0.4
? Set up and deploy "C:\dev\local-weather-app\dist\local-weather-
app"? [Y/n] y
? Which scope do you want to deploy to? Doguhan Uluca
? Found project "duluca/local-weather-app". Link to it? [Y/n] y
◆◎   Linked to duluca/local-weather-app (created .now and added it
to .gitigre)
◆🔍   Inspect: https://zeit.co/duluca/local-weather-app/jy2k1szdi
[2s]
☑    Production: https://local-weather-app.duluca.now.sh [copied to
clipboard] [4s]
```

4. Follow the URL displayed on the screen to see that your app has been successfully deployed, in my case, `https://local-weather-app.duluca.now.sh`.

> Note the warning about a missing `now.json` file. When we run the command, we specify our platform version as version 2 with the option `--platform-version 2`, so a configuration file is not strictly necessary. However, if you wish to customize any aspect of your deployment, perhaps by using a custom domain, selecting a geographical region, or using scaling options, you should configure this file. For further information on how to make the best of now, please refer to `https://vercel.com/docs`.

If your deployment went successfully you should see your app display the current weather from Bethesda, US:

Figure 4.14: Successful deployment

And you're done! Congratulations, your Angular app is live on the internet!

Summary

In this chapter, you learned about the importance of unit testing and mastered Angular unit and e2e test configuration and setup. You learned how to configure Angular's TestBed and how to write unit tests using test doubles. You configured your Angular app for a production deployment. You ensured the quality of your application by creating a value delivery stream using a CI pipeline and GitHub flow. Finally, you successfully deployed a web application to the cloud.

Now you know what it takes to build a production-ready Angular application that is reliable, resilient, and containerized to allow for a flexible deployment strategy. In the next chapter, we go over how you can add Angular Material to your project and make your Local Weather App look great. In the process, you will learn about the negative performance impact that user control or UI component libraries can have on your application, including essential Material components; Angular Flex Layout; accessibility; typography; theming; and how to update Angular Material.

Further reading

- *Succeeding with Agile: Software Development Using Scrum*, Mike Cohn, 2009.
- *TestPyramid*, Martin Fowler, 2012, `https://martinfowler.com/bliki/TestPyramid.html`.
- *Jasmine 2 Spy Cheat Sheet*, Dave Ceddia, 2015, `https://daveceddia.com/jasmine-2-spy-cheat-sheet`.
- *The Practical Test Pyramid*, Ham Vocke, 2018, `https://martinfowler.com/articles/practical-test-pyramid.html`.
- *SOLID Principles*, Wikipedia, 2019, `https://en.wikipedia.org/wiki/SOLID`.

Questions

Answer the following questions as best as you can to ensure that you've understood the key concepts from this chapter without Googling. Do you need help answering the questions? See *Appendix D, Self-Assessment Answers* online at `https://static.packt-cdn.com/downloads/9781838648800_Appendix_D_Self-Assessment_Answers.pdf` or visit `https://expertlysimple.io/angular-self-assessment`.

1. What is the test pyramid?
2. What are fixtures and matchers?
3. What are the differences between a mock, spy, and a stub?
4. What is the benefit of building Angular in prod mode?
5. How does GitHub flow work?
6. Why should we protect the master branch?

5
Delivering High-Quality UX with Material

In *Chapter 4, Automated Testing, CI, and Release to Production*, we mentioned the need to deliver a high-quality application. Currently, the app has a terrible look and feel to it that is only fit for a website created in the late 1990s. The first impression a user or a client gets about your product or your work is very important, so we must be able to create a great-looking application that also delivers a great user experience across mobile and desktop browsers.

As full-stack developers, it is difficult to focus on the polish of your application. This often gets worse as the feature set of an application rapidly grows. It is no fun to write great modular code backing your views, but then revert to CSS hacks and inline styles in a rush to improve the look and feel of your application.

Developed in close coordination with Angular, Angular Material is amazing. If you learn how to leverage Angular Material effectively, the features you create will look and work great from the get-go, whether you're working on small or large applications.

Angular Material will make you a far more effective web developer because it ships with a wide variety of user controls that you can leverage, and you won't have to worry about browser compatibility. As an added bonus, writing custom CSS will become a rarity.

> While this chapter covers how to create an attractive **user interface (UI)** relying on Angular Material for a decent **user experience (UX)** out of the box, it is also important to know what not to do. There's a great website called User Interface, which demonstrates UI/UX worst practices, at `https://userinyerface.com`.

In this chapter, you are going to learn about the following:

- Distinguishing aspects of Angular Material as a UI/UX library
- How to configure Angular Material
- Responsive design using Angular Flex Layout
- Upgrade the UX with Angular Material
- Enforcing accessibility compliance via **command-line interface (CLI)** tools
- Building an interactive prototype

The most up-to-date versions of the sample code for the book are on GitHub at the following repository linked. The repository contains the final and completed state of the code. You can verify your progress at the end of this chapter by looking for the end-of-chapter snapshot of code under the `projects` folder.

For *Chapter 5*:

1. Clone the repo `https://github.com/duluca/local-weather-app`
2. Execute `npm install` on the root folder to install dependencies
3. The code sample for this chapter is under the following sub-folder:
   projects/ch5
4. To run the Angular app for this chapter, execute:
   npx ng serve ch5
5. To run Angular unit tests for this chapter, execute:
   npx ng test ch5 --watch=false
6. To run Angular e2e tests for this chapter, execute:
   npx ng e2e ch5
7. To build a production-ready Angular app for this chapter, execute:
   npx ng build ch5 --prod

Note that the `dist/ch5` folder at the root of the repository will contain the compiled result.

Beware that the source code in the book or on GitHub may not always match the code generated by Angular CLI. There may also be slight differences in implementation between the code in the book and what's on GitHub because the ecosystem is ever-evolving. It is natural for the sample code to change over time. Also on GitHub, expect to find corrections, fixes to support newer versions of libraries, or side-by-side implementations of multiple techniques for you to observe. You are only expected to implement the ideal solution recommended in the book. If you find errors or have questions, please create an issue or submit a pull request on GitHub for the benefit of all readers.

Let's begin by understanding what makes Angular Material an excellent choice as a UI/UX library.

Angular Material

The goal of an Angular Material project is to provide a collection of useful and standard-setting high-quality UI components. The library implements Google's Material Design specification, which is pervasive in Google's mobile apps, web properties, and the Android operating system. Material Design has a particular digital and boxy look and feel, but it is not just another CSS library like Bootstrap. Consider the login experience coded using Bootstrap here:

Figure 5.1: Bootstrap login experience

Note that input fields and their labels are on separate lines, the checkbox is a small target to hit, the error messages are displayed as an ephemeral toast notification, and the **Submit** button just sits in the corner. Now, consider the following Angular Material sample:

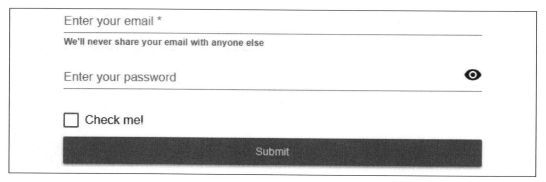

Figure 5.2: Angular Material login experience

The input fields and their labels are initially combined, grabbing the user's attention in a compact form factor. The checkbox is touch-friendly and the **Submit** button stretches to take up the available space for a more responsive UX by default. Once a user clicks on a field, the label tucks away to the top-left corner of the input field, as shown:

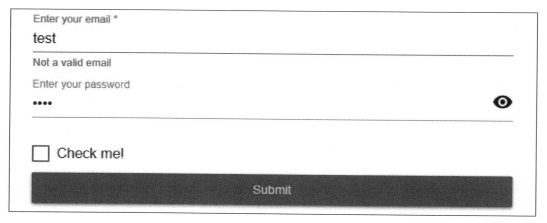

Figure 5.3: Angular Material animations and error

In addition, the validation error messages are shown inline, combined with a color change in the label, keeping the user's attention on the input field.

Material Design helps you design a modular UI with your own branding and styling, while also defining animations that allow the user to have a better UX when using your application. The human brain subconsciously keeps track of objects and their locations. Any kind of animation that aids in transitions or reactions to changes that result from human input results in reduced cognitive load on the user, therefore allowing the user to focus on processing the content instead of trying to figure out the quirks of your particular app.

A combination of modular UI design and fluid motion creates a great UX. Look at how Angular Material implements a simple button:

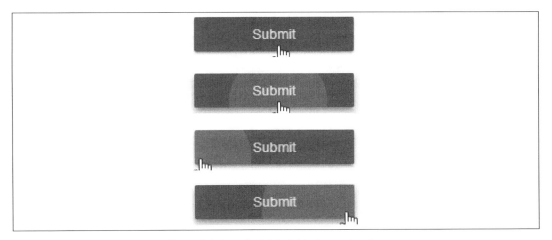

Figure 5.4: Angular Material button animation

In the preceding screenshot, note how the click animation on the button originates from the actual location that the user has clicked on. However subtle, this creates a continuity motion, resulting in an appropriate onscreen reaction to a user's action. This particular effect becomes more pronounced when the button is used on a mobile device, leading to an even more natural human-computer interaction. Most users can't articulate what makes an intuitive UX actually intuitive, and these subtle yet crucial cues in design and experience allow you to make tremendous progress in designing such an experience for your users.

Angular Material also aims to become the reference implementation for high-quality UI components for Angular. If you intend to develop your own custom controls, the source code for Angular Material should be your first and foremost resource. The term high quality is used often, and it's really important to quantify what that means. The Angular Material team puts it well on their website:

What do we mean by "high quality"?

Internationalized and accessible so that all users can use them. Straightforward APIs that don't confuse developers and behave as expected across a wide variety of use cases without bugs. Behavior is well tested with both unit and integration tests. Customizable within the bounds of the Material Design specification. Performance cost is minimized. Code is clean and well documented to serve as an example for Angular devs. Browser and screen reader support.

Angular Material supports the most recent two versions of all major browsers: Chrome (including Android), Firefox, Safari (including iOS), and IE11/Edge.

Building web applications, especially ones that are also mobile-compatible, is really difficult. There are a lot of nuances that you must be aware of. Angular Material abstracts away these nuances, including supporting all major browsers, so that you can focus on creating your application. Angular Material is no fad, and it's not to be taken lightly. If used correctly, you can greatly increase your productivity and the perceived quality of your work.

It won't always be possible to use Angular Material in your projects. I would recommend either PrimeNG, found at `https://www.primefaces.org/primeng`, or Clarity, found at `https://vmware.github.io/clarity`, as component toolkits that can satisfy most, if not all, of your user-control needs. The one thing to avoid here would be to pull dozens of user controls from different sources and end up with a hodgepodge library with hundreds of quirks and bugs to learn, maintain, or work around.

One of the most significant challenges when working with UI components is the amount of bulk they can add to your app's bundle size. Next, let's see how using a cohesive component library can help keep the performance of your app in tip-top shape and configure Angular Material for your app.

Angular Material setup and performance

Angular Material is configured by default to optimize the package size of your final deliverable. In Angular JS and Angular Material 1.x, the entire dependent library would be loaded. However, now with Angular Material, we are able to specify only the components that we intend to use, resulting in dramatic performance improvements.

In the following table, you can see improvement of the performance characteristics of a typical Angular 1.x + Angular Material 1.x versus an Angular 6 + Material 6 application over a fiber connection with high speed and low latency:

Fiber Network	Angular 6 + Material 6	Angular 1.5 + Material 1.1.5	% Diff
First paint (DOMContentLoaded)*	0.61 s	1.69 s**	~2.8x faster
JS bundle size*	113 KB	1,425 KB	12.6x smaller

*Images and other media content have not been included in the results for a fair comparison

**Average value: Lower quality infrastructure causes a wide range of render times from 0.9s to 2.5s

Under the ideal conditions of a high-speed and low-latency connection, Angular 6 + Material 6 apps load under a second. However, when we switch over to a more common moderate-speed and high-latency fast 3G mobile network, the differences become more pronounced, as in the following table:

Fast 3G Mobile Network	Angular 6 + Material 6	Angular 1.5 + Material 1.1.5	% Diff
First paint*	1.94 s	11.02 s	5.7x faster
JS bundle size*	113 KB	1,425 KB	12.6x smaller

*Images or other media content have not been included in the results for a fair comparison

Even though the size differences of the apps remain consistent, you can see that the additional latency introduced by a mobile network results in a dramatic slowdown of the legacy Angular application to an unacceptable level.

Adding all components to Material will result in about ~1.3 MB of additional payload that will need to be delivered to the user. As you can see from the earlier comparison, this must be avoided at all costs. To deliver the smallest app possible, which is crucial in mobile- and sales-related scenarios, where every 100 ms of load time has an impact on user retention, you may load and include modules individually. Webpack's tree-shaking process will divide modules into different files, trimming down the initial download size.

As a real-world example, when you're done building the final version of the LocalCast Weather app, your app's bundle size will come in at around 800 KB, with a first paint happening in just over 2 seconds on a fast 3G connection with Angular 9 + Material 9. A fully-featured multi-page application that leverages lazy loading only loads around ~300 KB of dependencies, while maintaining a sub 2 second first paint.

Note that the sample app contains example code that can be trimmed away to make the app even smaller. This is a testament to how the Angular ecosystem can deliver a rich and optimized UX.

Next, let's set up Angular Material.

Installing Angular Material

There are two ways you can configure Angular Material for your Angular app:

- Automatically using the Angular CLI
- Manually using npm

Let's get started with the task and improve the UX of the weather app with Angular Material. Let's move the **Improve the UX of the app** task to **In Progress** on our GitHub project. Here, you can see the status of my Kanban board:

Figure 5.5: GitHub project Kanban board

Automatically

Since Angular 6, you can automatically add Angular Material to your project, saving a lot of time in the process:

1. Execute the `add` command, as shown:

    ```
    $ npx ng add @angular/material
    ```

2. Choose the prebuilt theme named `indigo-pink`

3. When you get the prompt "Set up global Angular Material typography styles?" enter "no"
4. When you get the prompt "Set up browser animations for Angular Material?" enter "yes"
5. The output should be similar to the following example:

```
Installing packages for tooling via npm.
Installed packages for tooling via npm.
? Choose a prebuilt theme name, or "custom" for a custom
theme: Indigo/Pink         [ Preview: https://material.angular.
io?theme=indigo-pink ]
? Set up global Angular Material typography styles? No
? Set up browser animations for Angular Material? Yes
UPDATE package.json (1348 bytes)
√ Packages installed successfully.
UPDATE src/app/app.module.ts (423 bytes)
UPDATE angular.json (3740 bytes)
UPDATE src/index.html (487 bytes)
UPDATE src/styles.css (181 bytes)
```

Note that the `index.html` file has been modified to add the icons library and the default font, as follows:

src/index.html
```
<head>
  ...
  <link href="https://fonts.googleapis.com/css?family=Roboto:300,4
00,500&display=swap" rel="stylesheet">
  <link href="https://fonts.googleapis.com/
icon?family=Material+Icons" rel="stylesheet">
</head>
```

The `angular.json` file has been updated to set up the default theme:

angular.json
```
...
"styles": [
  "./node_modules/@angular/material/prebuilt-themes/indigo-pink.css",
  "src/styles.css"
],
...
```

`styles.css` has been updated with the default global CSS styles:

src/styles.css

```
html,
body {
  height: 100%;
}
body {
  margin: 0;
  font-family: Roboto, "Helvetica Neue", sans-serif;
}
```

Also note that `app.module.ts` has been updated to import `BrowserAnimationsModule`, as shown:

src/app/app.module.ts
```
import { BrowserAnimationsModule } from '@angular/platform-browser/animations';

@NgModule({
  declarations: [
    AppComponent
  ],
  imports: [
    ...
    BrowserAnimationsModule
  ],
```

6. Start your app and ensure that it works correctly:

   $ npm start

With that, you're done. Your app should be configured with Angular Material. You can now skip over to the *Importing modules* section to see how you can import Material modules in a robust manner.

> I strongly recommend skimming over all the manual installation and configuration steps. The more you know!

It is still important to understand all the various components that make up Angular Material or maybe you dislike automatic things; in the next sections, we will go over the manual installation and configuration steps.

Manually

We will begin by installing all the required libraries. As of Angular 5, the major version of Angular Material should match the version of your Angular installation and with Angular 6, the versions should be synced:

1. In the Terminal, execute `npm install @angular/material @angular/cdk`
2. Observe the `package.json` versions:

   package.json
   ```
   "dependencies": {
       "@angular/cdk": "9.0.0",
       "@angular/material": "9.0.0",
       ...
   ```

In this case, all libraries have the same major and minor versions. If your major and minor versions don't match, you can rerun the `npm install` command to install a specific version or choose to upgrade your version of Angular by appending the server version of the package to the `install` command:

```
$ npm install @angular/material@9.0.0 @angular/cdk@9.0.0
```

> If you are working on a Bash-like shell, you can save some typing by using the bracket syntax to avoid having to repeat portions of the command, in the form of `npm install @angular/{material,cdk}@9.0.0`.

If you need to update your version of Angular, refer to the *Updating Angular* section in *Appendix C, Keeping Angular and Tools Evergreen*. You can find this appendix online from https://static.packt-cdn.com/downloads/9781838648800_Appendix_C_Keeping_Angular_and_Tools_Evergreen.pdf or at https://expertlysimple.io/stay-evergreen.

Understanding Material's components

Let's look at what exactly we are installing:

- `@angular/material` is the official Material library.
- `@angular/cdk` is a peer dependency, not something you use directly unless you intend to build your own components.
- `@angular/animations` enables some of the animations for some Material modules. It can be omitted to keep the app size minimal. You may use `NoopAnimationsModule` to disable animations in the modules that require this dependency. As a result, you will lose some of the UX benefits of Angular Material.

Manually configuring Angular Material

Now that the dependencies are installed, let's configure Angular Material in our Angular app. Note that if you used `ng add @angular/material` to install Angular Material, some of this work will be done for you.

Importing modules

We will start by creating a separate module file to house all of our Material module imports:

1. Execute the following command in the Terminal to generate `material.module.ts`:

   ```
   $ npx ng g m material --flat -m app
   ```

   > Note the use of the `--flat` flag, which indicates that an additional directory shouldn't be created for `material.module.ts`. Also, note that `-m`, an alias for `--module`, is specified so that our new module is automatically imported into `app.module.ts`.

2. Observe the newly created file `material.module.ts` and remove `CommonModule`:

   src/app/material.module.ts
   ```
   import { NgModule } from '@angular/core'

   @NgModule({
     imports: [],
     declarations: [],
   })
   export class MaterialModule {}
   ```

3. Ensure that the module has been imported into `app.module.ts`:

   src/app/app.module.ts
   ```
   import { MaterialModule } from './material.module'
   ...
   @NgModule({
     ...
     imports: [..., MaterialModule],
   }
   ```

4. Add animations and gesture support (if not automatically added):

   src/app/app.module.ts
   ```
   import { BrowserAnimationsModule } from '@angular/platform-
   browser/animations'

   @NgModule({
     ...
     imports: [..., MaterialModule, BrowserAnimationsModule],
   }
   ```

5. Modify `material.module.ts` to import and export basic components for `MatButton`, `MatToolbar`, and `MatIcon`:

   src/app/material.module.ts
   ```
   import { NgModule } from '@angular/core'
   import { MatButtonModule } from '@angular/material/button'
   import { MatIconModule } from '@angular/material/icon'
   import { MatToolbarModule } from '@angular/material/toolbar'

   @NgModule({
     imports: [
       MatButtonModule, MatToolbarModule, MatIconModule
     ],
     exports: [
       MatButtonModule, MatToolbarModule, MatIconModule
     ],
   })
   export class MaterialModule {}
   ```

    The `imports` and `exports` arrays can sometimes become long and duplicative. If you miss an element in one of the arrays, you could be chasing bugs for hours. Consider implementing a single array as a constant that you can assign to `imports` and `exports` properties for a more reliable configuration. Thanks to Brendon Caulkins for the tip.

6. Optimize your code to store your modules in an array and reuse it to import and export:

   src/app/material.module.ts
   ```
   ...
   const modules =
     [MatButtonModule, MatToolbarModule, MatIconModule]
   ```

```
@NgModule({
  declarations: [],
  imports: modules,
  exports: modules,
})
export class MaterialModule {}
```

Material is now imported into the app; let's now configure a theme and add the necessary CSS to our app.

Importing themes

A base theme is necessary in order to use Material components. We already selected a default theme when installing Angular Material. We can define or change the default theme in `angular.json`:

angular.json
```
...
"styles": [
  {
    "input":
      "node_modules/@angular/material/prebuilt-themes/indigo-pink.css"
  },
  "src/styles.css"
],
...
```

Choose a new option from here:

- `deeppurple-amber.css`
- `indigo-pink.css`
- `pink-bluegrey.css`
- `purple-green.css`

Update `angular.json` to use the new Material theme.

> You may create your own themes as well, which is covered in the *Custom themes* section of this chapter. For more information, visit https://material.angular.io/guide/theming.

Note that any CSS implemented in `styles.css` will be globally available throughout the application. That said, do not include view-specific CSS in this file. Every component has its own CSS file for this purpose.

Adding the Material Icon font

You can get access to a good default set of iconography by adding the Material Icon web font to your application. Clocking in at 48 KB in size, this is a very lightweight library.

For icon support, import the font in `index.html`:

src/index.html
```
<head>
  ...
  <link href="https://fonts.googleapis.com/icon?family=Material+Icons" rel="stylesheet">
</head>
```

Discover and search through the icons at `https://material.io/resources/icons`.

> For a richer set of icons, check out `MaterialDesignIcons.com`. This icon set contains the base set of Material icons, plus a rich set of third-party icons that contains useful imagery from social media sites for a rich set of actions that cover a lot of ground. This font is 118 KB in size.

Our UI/UX library for Angular Material is now configured. We also need a layout library that can make life easier when placing components on the page.

Next, let's learn about different layout techniques, from Bootstrap to Flexbox CSS, and why Angular Flex Layout is a great tool to manage your layout. After configuring Angular Flex Layout for our app, we will be ready to implement Material UI components in our app.

Angular Flex Layout

Before you can make effective use of Material, you must be aware of its layout engine. If you have been doing web development for a while, you may have encountered Bootstrap's 12-column layout system. I find it enormously irritating, since it falls foul of a mathematical barrier in my brain, which is wired to divvy things up as parts of 100%. Bootstrap also demands strict adherence to a `div` column and row hierarchy that must be precisely managed from your top-level HTML to the bottom. This can make for a very frustrating development experience.

In the following screenshot, you can see how Bootstrap's 12-column scheme looks:

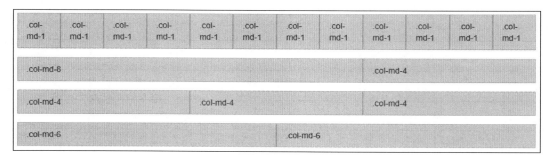

Figure 5.6: Bootstrap's 12-column layout scheme

Bootstrap's custom grid-layout system was revolutionary for its time, but then CSS3 Flexbox arrived on the scene. In combination with media queries, these two technologies allow for the creation of responsive UIs. However, it is very laborious to leverage these technologies effectively. As of Angular v4.1, the Angular team introduced its Flex Layout system that just works.

The Angular Flex Layout documentation on GitHub aptly explains the following:

> *Angular Flex Layout provides a sophisticated layout API using FlexBox CSS and mediaQuery. This module provides Angular (v4.1 and higher) developers with component layout features using a custom Layout API, mediaQuery observables, and injected DOM flexbox-2016 CSS stylings.*

Angular's excellent implementation makes it very easy to use Flexbox. As the documentation further explains:

> *The Layout engine intelligently automates the process of applying appropriate FlexBox CSS to browser view hierarchies. This automation also addresses many of the complexities and workarounds encountered with the traditional, manual, CSS-only application of Flexbox CSS.*

The library is highly capable and can accommodate any kind of grid layout you can imagine, including integration with all CSS features that you would expect, such as the `calc()` function. In the next illustration, you can see how columns can be described using CSS Flexbox:

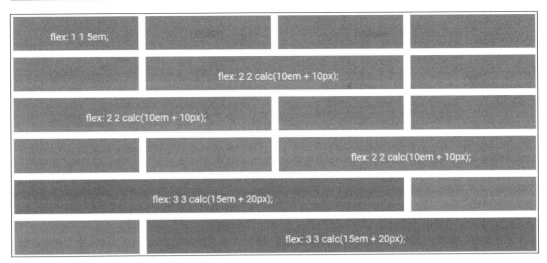

Figure 5.7: Angular Flex Layout scheme

The great news is that Angular Flex Layout is in no way coupled with Angular Material and can be used independently of it. This is a very important decoupling that resolves one of the major pain points of using AngularJS with Material v1, where version updates to Material would often result in bugs in layout.

For more details, check out `https://github.com/angular/flex-layout/wiki`.

 You will notice that `@angular/flex-layout` is installed with a beta tag. This has been the status quo for this library for a very long time. It hasn't been possible for the library to cover every edge case going back to Internet Explorer 11, which prevents it from exiting beta. However, in evergreen browsers, I've found the behavior of the library to reliable and consistent. Further, CSS Grid is poised to supersede CSS Flexbox and as a result, the underlying technology that this library uses may change. My wish is that this library acts as an abstraction layer to the layout engine underneath.

Responsive layouts

All UIs you design and build should be mobile-first UIs. This is not just to serve mobile phone browsers, but also cases where a laptop user may use your application in a window side by side with another one. There are many nuances to getting mobile-first design right.

The following is the *Mozilla Holy Grail Layout,* which demonstrates "the ability to dynamically change the layout for different screen resolutions" while optimizing the display content for mobile devices.

> You can read more about basic concepts of Flexbox at `https://mzl.la/2vvxj25`.

This is a representation of how the UI looks on a large screen:

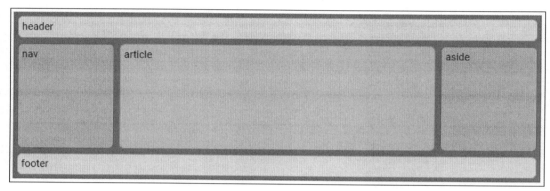

Figure 5.8: Mozilla Holy Grail Layout on a large screen

The same layout is represented on a small screen as follows:

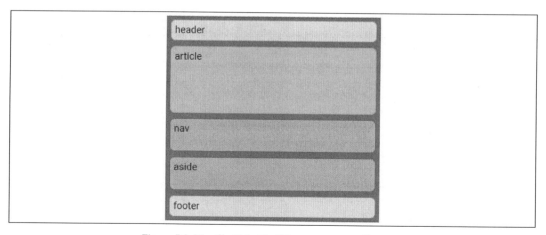

Figure 5.9: Mozilla Holy Grail Layout on a small screen

Mozilla's reference implementation takes 85 lines of code to accomplish this kind of responsive UI. Angular Flex Layout accomplishes the same task with only half the code.

Installing Angular Flex Layout

Let's install and add Angular Flex Layout to our project:

1. In the Terminal, execute `npm i @angular/flex-layout`

> To get around peer dependency errors, execute `npm i @angular/flex-layout@next` or `npm i @angular/flex-layout --force`, as mentioned in *Appendix C, Keeping Angular and Tools Evergreen*. You can find this appendix online from https://static.packt-cdn.com/downloads/9781838648800_Appendix_C_Keeping_Angular_and_Tools_Evergreen.pdf or at https://expertlysimple.io/stay-evergreen.

2. Update `app.module.ts`, as shown:

   src/app.module.ts
   ```
   import { FlexLayoutModule } from '@angular/flex-layout'

   imports: [..., FlexLayoutModule ],
   ```

With Flex Layout installed, let's cover the basics of how the library works.

Layout basics

Bootstrap and CSS Flexbox are different beasts than Angular Flex Layout. If you learn Angular Flex Layout, you will find yourself using a lot less layout code, because Angular Material automatically does the right thing most of the time, but you'll be in for a disappointment once you realize how much more code you have to write to get things working once you leave the protective cocoon of Angular Flex Layout. However, your skills still translate over since the concepts are mostly the same.

Let's review the Flex Layout APIs in the following sections.

> If you're new to CSS or even Flexbox, some of the abbreviations used may not make sense. I recommend that you experiment with the live demo app provided in the documentation to get a better sense of the capabilities of the library at a more intuitive level. For more information and a link to the live demo visit https://github.com/angular/flex-layout/wiki/Declarative-API-Overview.

Flex Layout APIs for DOM containers

These directives can be used on DOM containers such as <div> or <span> to manipulate their layout direction, alignment, or gaps in between elements.

Consider the following example:

```
<div fxLayout="row" fxLayoutAlign="start center"
fxLayoutGap="15px">...</div>
```

The div is laid out as a row, so multiple divs would be rendered on top of each other, versus a column layout where they would render next to each other.

The div is aligned to horizontally left-aligned and vertically centered within its parent container.

The div has a 15-px gap between its surrounding elements.

Consider the following diagram to map fxLayout terminology spatially:

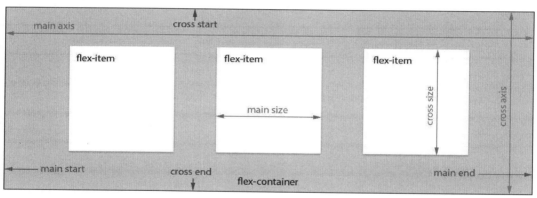

Figure 5.10: Spatial mapping of Angular Flex Layout terminology

The full list of options is presented in the following table:

HTML API	Allowed values
fxLayout	<direction> | <direction> <wrap>
	Use: row | column | row-reverse | column-reverse
fxLayoutAlign	<main-axis> <cross-axis>
	main-axis: start |center | end | space-around | space-between
	cross-axis: start | center | end | stretch
fxLayoutGap	% | px | vw | vh

Flex Layout APIs for DOM elements

These directives influence how DOM elements act within their containers.

Consider the following example:

```
<div fxLayout="column">
  <input fxFlex />
</div>
```

The `input` element will grow to fill all available space that the parent `div` provides. If `fxFlex` was set to `fxFlex="50%"`, it would fill only half of the available space. In this case the `fxFlexAlign` property could be used to left-, right-, or center-align the element within the `div`.

The full list of options is presented in the following table:

HTML API	Allowed values
fxFlex	"" | px | % | vw | vh | <grow> <shrink> <basis>
fxFlexOrder	int
fxFlexOffset	% | px | vw | vh
fxFlexAlign	start | baseline | center | end
fxFlexFill	none

Flex Layout APIs for any element

The following directives can be applied to any HTML element to show, hide, or change the look and feel of these elements.

Consider the following example:

```
<div fxShow fxHide.lt-sm></div>
```

`fxShow`, set to `true` by default, will show the `div` element. Unless the `lt-sm` condition becomes `true`, which occurs when the browser window shrinks below the threshold of *small*. *Small* is defined as a pixel value of 468 px. So, if the width of the browser window shrinks to 467 px or less, `fxHide` would hide the `div` element.

The full list of options is presented in the following table:

HTML API	Allowed values
fxHide	TRUE | FALSE | 0 | ""
fxShow	TRUE | FALSE | 0 | ""
ngClass	@extends ngClass core
ngStyle	@extends ngStyle core

 This section covers the basics of Static Layouts. You can read more about the Static APIs at `https://github.com/angular/flex-layout/wiki/Declarative-API-Overview`. We'll cover the Responsive APIs in *Chapter 11, Recipes – Reusability, Routing, and Caching*. You can read more about the Responsive APIs at `https://github.com/angular/flex-layout/wiki/Responsive-API`.

Now that our layout engine is configured and you have a rudimentary understanding of how it works, we can start building the screens for our app.

Using Material components

Now that we have all the various dependencies installed, we can start modifying our Angular app to add Material components. We will add a toolbar and a Material Design card element, and cover accessibility and typography concerns alongside basic layout techniques.

Angular Material schematics

Since Angular 6 and the introduction of schematics, libraries like Material can provide their own code generators. At the time of publication, Angular Material ships with three rudimentary generators to create Angular components with a side navigation, a dashboard layout, or a data table. You can read more about generator schematics at `https://material.angular.io/guide/schematics`.

For example, you can create a side navigation layout by executing the following command:

```
$ ng generate @angular/material:material-nav --name=side-nav
```

```
CREATE src/app/side-nav/side-nav.component.css (110 bytes) CREATE src/app/side-nav/side-nav.component.html (945 bytes) CREATE src/app/side-nav/side-nav.component.spec.ts (619 bytes) CREATE src/app/side-nav/side-nav.component.ts (489 bytes) UPDATE src/app/app.module.ts (882 bytes)
```

This command updates `app.module.ts`, directly importing Material modules into that file, breaking my suggested `material.module.ts` pattern from earlier. Further, a new `SideNavComponent` is added to the app as a separate component, but as mentioned in the *Side navigation* section in *Chapter 8, Designing Authentication and Authorization*, such a navigation experience needs to be implemented at the very root of your application.

In short, Angular Material Schematics makes it a lot less cumbersome to add various Material modules and components to your Angular app; however, as provided, these schematics are not suitable for creating a flexible, scalable, and well-architected code base, which is the goal pursued by this book.

For the time being, I would recommend using these schematics for rapid prototyping or experimentation purposes.

Now, let's start manually adding some components to our LocalCast Weather app.

Modifying the landing page with Material Toolbar

Before we start making further changes to app.component.ts, let's switch the component to use inline templates and inline styles, so we don't have to switch back and forth between files for a relatively simple component:

1. Update app.component.ts to use an inline template. Cut and paste the contents of app.component.html to app.component.ts and remove the styleUrls property as shown below:

    src/app/app.component.ts
    ```
    import { Component } from '@angular/core'

    @Component({
      selector: 'app-root',
      template: `
        <div style="text-align:center">
          <h1>
            LocalCast Weather
          </h1>
          <div>Your city, your forecast, right now!</div>
          <h2>Current Weather</h2>
          <app-current-weather></app-current-weather>
        </div>
      `,
    })
    export class AppComponent {}
    ```

2. Delete the files app.component.html and app.component.css.

3. Let's start improving our app by implementing an app-wide toolbar. Observe the h1 tag in app.component.ts:

    src/app/app.component.ts
    ```
    <h1>
    ```

```
        LocalCast Weather
    </h1>
```

4. Update the `h1` tag with `mat-toolbar`:

   src/app/app.component.ts
   ```
   <mat-toolbar>
     <span>LocalCast Weather</span>
   </mat-toolbar>
   ```

5. Update `mat-toolbar` with a more attention-grabbing color:

   src/app/app.component.ts
   ```
   <mat-toolbar color="primary">
   ```

> Note that your app will fail to compile if you didn't import `MatToolbarModule` as instructed in the earlier section *Importing modules*.

Note that Material adds the following style as a global style:

src/styles.css
```
body {
  margin: 0;
}
```

Having a `0` margin provides a native app feeling, where the toolbar touches the edges of the browser. This works well both on large- and small-screen formats. When you place clickable elements such as a hamburger menu or a help button on the far-left or far-right side of the toolbar, you'll avoid the potential that the user will click on empty space. This is why Material buttons actually have a larger hit-area than visually represented. This makes a big difference in crafting frustration-free UXs.

Similarly, if you were building an information-dense application, note that your content would go all the way to the edges of the application, making your content more difficult to read, which is not a desirable outcome. In these cases, you should wrap your content area in a `div` and apply the appropriate margins using CSS, as shown here:

example
```
.content-margin {
  margin-left: 8px;
  margin-right: 8px;
}
```

In the next screenshot, you can see the edge-to-edge toolbar with the primary color applied to it:

Figure 5.11: LocalCast Weather with improved toolbar

Now we have the toolbar configured, let's move on to making a container for the weather information.

Material cards

Material cards are a great container to represent the current weather information. The card element is surrounded by a drop-shadow that delineates the content from its surroundings:

1. Import `MatCardModule` in `material.module`:

   src/app/material.module.ts
   ```
   import { MatCardModule } from '@angular/material/card'
   ...
   const modules = [..., MatCardModule]
   ```

2. In AppComponent's template, surround `<app-current-weather>` with `<mat-card>`:

   src/app/app.component.ts
   ```
   ...
     template: `
     ...
     <div style="text-align:center">
   ```

```
<mat-toolbar color="primary">
  <span>LocalCast Weather</span>
</mat-toolbar>
<div>Your city, your forecast, right now!</div>
<mat-card>
  <h2>Current Weather</h2>
  <app-current-weather></app-current-weather>
</mat-card>
</div>
...
`,
...
```

3. Observe the barely distinguishable card element with its shadow near the bottom of the screen below:

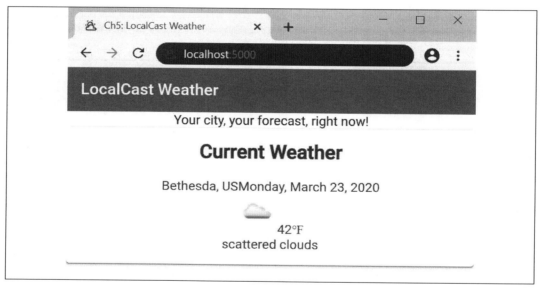

Figure 5.12: LocalCast Weather with indistinguishable card element

To lay out the screen better, we need to switch to the Flex Layout engine. We'll start by removing the training wheels from the component template.

4. Remove `style="text-align:center"` from the outermost `<div>` element.
5. Surround `<mat-card>` with the following HTML, where the contents of `<mat-card>` replaces the ellipses in the middle of the code:

To center an element in a page, we need to create a row, assign a width to the center element, and create two additional columns on either side that can flex to take the empty space, such as this:

src/app/app.component.ts
```
...
<div fxLayout="row">
  <div fxFlex></div>
  <div fxFlex="300px">
      ...
  </div>
  <div fxFlex></div>
</div>
...
```

6. Observe that the `mat-card` element is properly centered, as follows:

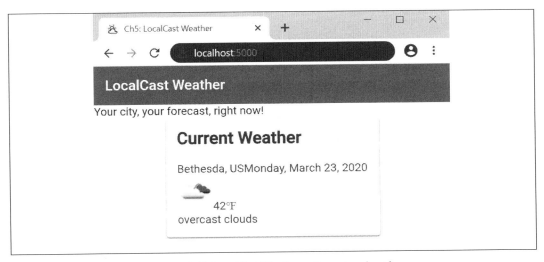

Figure 5.13: LocalCast Weather with centered card

Reading through the card documentation and looking through the examples on Material's documentation site at `https://material.angular.io/components/card/overview`, you'll note that `mat-card` provides elements to house the title and content. We will implement this in the upcoming sections.

 On `material.angular.io`, you can view the source code of any example by clicking on the brackets icons or launch a working example in `StackBlitz.io` by clicking on the arrow icon.

Card header and content

Now, let's implement the title and content elements of mat-card using mat-card-header and mat-card-content, as shown:

```
src/app/app.component.ts
...
<mat-toolbar color="primary">
  <span>LocalCast Weather</span>
</mat-toolbar>
<div>Your city, your forecast, right now!</div>
<div fxLayout="row">
  <div fxFlex></div>
  <div fxFlex="300px">
    <mat-card>
      <mat-card-header>
        <mat-card-title>Current Weather</mat-card-title>
      </mat-card-header>
      <mat-card-content>
        <app-current-weather></app-current-weather>
      </mat-card-content>
    </mat-card>
  </div>
  <div fxFlex></div>
</div>
...
```

All Material elements have native support for the Flex Layout engine. This allows us to optimize our HTML and merge `<div fxFlex="300px">` with `<mat-card>` and simplify the code:

```
src/app/app.component.ts
...
<div fxLayout="row">
  <div fxFlex></div>
  <mat-card fxFlex="300px">
    ...
  </mat-card>
  <div fxFlex></div>
</div>
...
```

This has tremendous positive implications for maintainability in complicated UIs.

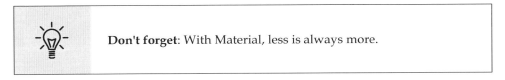

Don't forget: With Material, less is always more.

After we apply `mat-card-header` and `mat-card-content`, you can see this result:

Figure 5.14: LocalCast Weather card with title and content

Note that fonts within the card now match Material's Roboto font. However, **Current Weather** is no longer as attention-grabbing as it was before. If you add back in the h2 tag inside `mat-card-title`, **Current Weather** will visually look bigger; however, the font won't match the rest of your application. To fix this issue, you must understand Material's typography features.

Material typography

Material's documentation aptly puts it as follows:

> *Typography is a way of arranging type to make text legible, readable, and appealing when displayed.*

Material offers a different level of typography that has different `font-size`, `line-height`, and `font-weight` characteristics that you can apply to any HTML element, not just the components provided out of the box.

In the following table are CSS classes that you can use to apply Material's typography.

Consider the following example:

```
<div class="mat-display-4">Hello, Material world!</div>
```

The `display-4` typography is applied to the `div` by prepending it with `"mat-"`.

See the following table for a full list of typographical styles:

Class Name	Usage
`display-4`, `display-3`, `display-2`, and `display-1`	Large, one-off headers, usually at the top of the page (for example, a hero header)
`h1`, `headline`	Section heading corresponding to the `<h1>` tag
`h2`, `title`	Section heading corresponding to the `<h2>` tag
`h3`, `subheading-2`	Section heading corresponding to the `<h3>` tag
`h4`, `subheading-1`	Section heading corresponding to the `<h4>` tag
`body-1`	Base body text
`body-2`	Bolder body text
`Caption`	Smaller body and hint text
`Button`	Buttons and anchors

You can read more about Material typography at https://material.angular.io/guide/typography.

Applying typography

There are multiple ways to apply typography. One way is to leverage the `mat-typography` class and use the corresponding HTML tag, such as `<h2>`:

example
```
<mat-card-header class="mat-typography">
<mat-card-title><h2>Current Weather</h2></mat-card-title>
</mat-card-header>
```

Another way is to apply the specific typography directly on an element, as in `class="mat-title"`:

example
```
<mat-card-title>
  <div class="mat-title">Current Weather</div>
</mat-card-title>
```

> Note that class="mat-title" can be applied to div, span, or an h2 with the same results.

As a rule of thumb, it is usually a better idea to implement the more specific and localized option, which is the second implementation here.

As we implement Material typography in the upcoming sections, we need to ensure the card title stands out from rest of the elements on the screen. In this context, I prefer the look of the mat-headline typography to achieve this goal, so your implementation should look like:

src/app/app.component.ts
```
<mat-card-title>
  <div class="mat-headline">Current Weather</div>
</mat-card-title>
```

Next, let's see how we can align the other elements on the screen.

Flex Layout Align

We can center the tagline of the application using fxLayoutAlign and give it a subdued look using the mat-caption typography:

1. Center the div containing the tagline using fxLayoutAlign:

   src/app/app.component.ts
   ```
   <div fxLayoutAlign="center">
     <div>
       Your city, your forecast, right now!
     </div>
   </div>
   ```

2. Apply the mat-caption typography to the tagline:

   src/app/app.component.ts
   ```
   <div class="mat-caption">
     Your city, your forecast, right now!
   </div>
   ```

3. Observe the results, as shown here:

Delivering High-Quality UX with Material

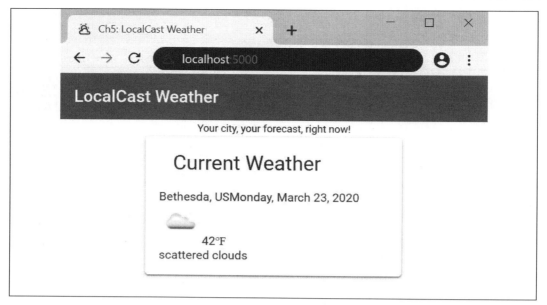

Figure 5.15: LocalCast Weather with centered tagline

Next, we need to work on laying out the elements to match the design.

Flex Layout

There's still more work to do to make the UI look like the design. Observe the following design of the Current Weather card:

Figure 5.16: Lo-fi design of Current Weather

To design the layout, we'll leverage Angular Flex.

You'll be editing `current-weather.component.html`, which uses the `<div>` and `<span>` tags to establish elements that live on separate lines or on the same line, respectively. With the switch over to Angular Flex, we need to switch all elements to `<div>` and specify rows and columns using `fxLayout`.

Implementing layout scaffolding

We need to start by implementing the rough scaffolding. Consider the current state of the template:

```
src/app/current-weather/current-weather.component.html
1   <div *ngIf="!current">
2     no data
3   </div>
4   <div *ngIf="current">
5     <div>
6       <span>{{current.city}}, {{current.country}}</span>
7       <span>{{current.date | date:'fullDate'}}</span>
8     </div>
9     <div>
10      <img [src]='current.image'>
11      <span>{{current.temperature | number:'1.0-0'}}°F</span>
12    </div>
13    <div>
14      {{current.description}}
15    </div>
16  </div>
```

Let's go through the file step by step and update it. First let's make the structural changes to support Flex Layout:

1. On lines 6, 7, and 11, update `<span>` elements to `<div>` elements.
2. On line 10, wrap the `<img>` element with a `<div>` element.
3. On lines 5 and 9, add the `fxLayout="row"` property to the outer `<div>` element that has multiple child elements.

Next, apply the `fxFlex` attribute to `div` elements to determine how much horizontal space elements should take:

1. On line 6, the City and Country column should take roughly ⅔ of the screen, so add `fxFlex="66%"` to the `<div>` element.
2. On line 7, add `fxFlex` to the `<div>` element to ensure that it fills up the rest of the horizontal space.
3. On line 10, add `fxFlex="66%"` to the new `<div>` element, surrounding the `<img>` element.
4. On line 11, add `fxFlex` to the `<div>` element.

The final state of the template should look like this:

```
src/app/current-weather/current-weather.component.html
5      <div fxLayout="row">
6        <div fxFlex="66%">{{current.city}}, ...</div>
7        <div fxFlex>{{current.date | date:'fullDate'}}</div>
8      </div>
9      <div fxLayout="row">
10       <div fxFlex="66%"><img [src]='current.image'></div>
11       <div fxFlex>{{current.temperature | number:'1.0-0'}}°F</div>
12     </div>
13     <div>
14       {{current.description}}
15     </div>
```

You can be more verbose in adding Angular Flex attributes; however, the more code you write, the more you'll need to maintain, making future changes more difficult. For example, on line 13, the `<div>` element doesn't need `fxLayout="row"`, since a `<div>` implicitly gets a new line. Similarly, on lines 7 and 11, the right-hand column doesn't need an explicit `fxFlex` attribute, since the left-hand element automatically squeezes it. However, we are going to keep those `fxFlex` attributes in.

From a grid placement perspective, all your elements are now in the correct *cell*, as shown here:

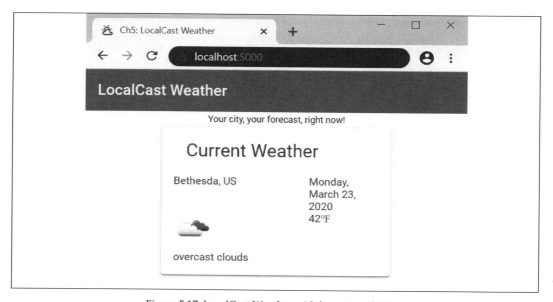

Figure 5.17: LocalCast Weather with layout scaffolding

With a responsive design implemented, next, let's work on alignment of major elements.

Aligning elements with CSS

Now, we need to align and style each cell to match the design. For this purpose, we rely on CSS over `fxLayoutAlign`. The date and temperature need to be right-aligned and the description centered:

1. To right-align the date and temperature, create a new CSS class named `.right` in `current-weather.component.css`:

   `src/app/current-weather/current-weather.component.css`
   ```
   .right {
     text-align: right
   }
   ```

2. Add `class="right"` to the `<div>` element on lines 7 and 11.

3. Center the `<div>` element for the description in the same way you centered the app's tagline earlier in the chapter. Use a surrounding `div` with an `fxLayoutAlign="center"` attribute.

4. Observe that the elements are aligned correctly, as follows:

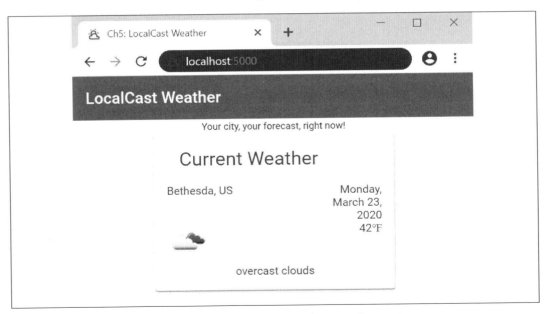

Figure 5.18: LocalCast Weather with correct alignments

After aligning the major elements, let's apply the first layer of styling to every element to match the design.

Individually styling elements

Finalizing the styling of elements is usually the most time-consuming part of front-end development. I recommend doing multiple passes to achieve a close-enough version of the design with minimal effort first and then have your client or team decide whether it's worth the extra resources to spend more time to polish the design:

1. Add a new CSS property:

   `src/app/current-weather/current-weather.component.css`
   ```
   .no-margin {
     margin-bottom: 0
   }
   ```

2. For the city name, add `class="mat-title no-margin"`.
3. For the date, add `"mat-h3 no-margin"` to `class="right"`.
4. Change the display format of the date from `'fullDate'` to `'EEEE MMM d'` so it matches the design.
5. Modify `<img>` to add `style="zoom: 175%"`.
6. For the temperature, add `"mat-display-3 no-margin"` to `class="right"`.
7. For the description, add `class="mat-caption"`.

   This is the final state of the template:

   `src/app/current-weather/current-weather.component.html`
   ```
   <div *ngIf="!current">
     no data
   </div>
   <div *ngIf="current">
     <div fxLayout="row">
       <div fxFlex="66%" class="mat-title no-margin">
         {{current.city}}, {{current.country}}
       </div>
       <div fxFlex class="right mat-h3 no-margin">
         {{current.date | date:'EEEE MMM d'}}
       </div>
     </div>
     <div fxLayout="row">
       <div fxFlex="66%">
         <img style="zoom: 175%" [src]='current.image'>
       </div>
       <div fxFlex class="right mat-display-3 no-margin">
         {{current.temperature | number:'1.0-0'}}°F
   ```

```
      </div>
    </div>
      <div fxLayoutAlign="center">
        <div class="mat-caption">
          {{current.description}}
        </div>
      </div>
    </div>
```

8. Observe that the styled output of your code changes, as illustrated:

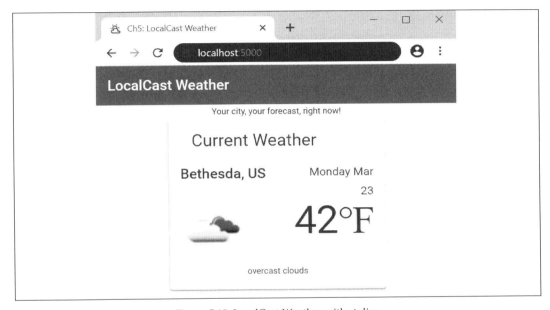

Figure 5.19: LocalCast Weather with styling

We're done with adding the first layer of styles for our design. Next, let's fine-tune the spacing and alignment of elements.

Fine-tuning styles

The tagline can benefit from some top and bottom margins. This is common CSS that we're likely to use across the application, so let's put it in `styles.css`:

1. Implement `vertical-margin` in the global `styles.css`:

    src/styles.css
    ```
    .vertical-margin {
      margin-top: 16px;
      margin-bottom: 16px;
    }
    ```

2. In app.component.ts, apply vertical-margin to the app's tagline:

   src/app/app.component.ts
   ```
   <div class="mat-caption vertical-margin">
     Your city, your forecast, right now!
   </div>
   ```

3. In current-weather.component.html, the image and the temperature aren't centered, so add fxLayoutAlign="center center" to the outer div surrounding these elements:

   src/app/current-weather/current-weather.component.html
   ```
   <div fxLayout="row" fxLayoutAlign="center center">
     ...
   </div>
   ```

4. Observe the finalized layout of your app, which should look like this:

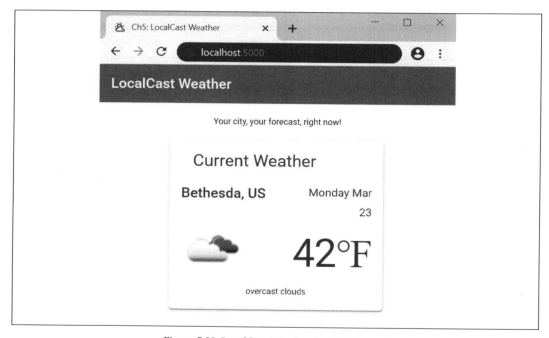

Figure 5.20: LocalCast Weather finalized layout

Finally, let's add some more visual flair by tightening up our design, like fixing the missing line break between the day and the month, and adding some nice-to-have features.

Tweaking to match design

This is an area where you may spend a significant amount of time. If we were following the 80-20 principle, pixel-perfect tweaks usually end up being the last 20% that takes 80% of the time to complete. Let's examine the differences between our implementation in the previous figure, and the original design as shown in the following figure, and what it would take to bridge the gap:

Figure 5.21: LocalCast Weather original design

The date needs further customization. The numeric ordinal *th* is missing in our implementation; to accomplish this, we will need to bring in a third-party library such as `moment` or implement our own solution and bind it next to the date on the template:

1. Implement a `getOrdinal` function in `CurrentWeatherComponent`:

    src/app/current-weather/current-weather.component.ts
    ```
    export class CurrentWeatherComponent implements OnInit {
      ...
      getOrdinal(date: number) {
        const n = new Date(date).getDate()
        return n > 0
          ? ['th', 'st', 'nd', 'rd'][(n > 3 && n < 21) ||
                                      n % 10 > 3 ? 0 : n % 10]
          : ''
      }
      ...
    }
    ```

2. In the template, update `current.date` to append an ordinal to it:

    src/app/current-weather/current-weather.component.html
    ```
    <div fxFlex class="right mat-h3 no-margin">
      {{current.date |
        date:'EEEE MMM d'}}{{getOrdinal(current.date)}}
    </div>
    ```

Note that the implementation of `getOrdinal` boils down to a complicated one-liner that isn't very readable and is very difficult to maintain. Such functions, if critical to your business logic, should be heavily unit tested.

Next, let's fix the missing line break between the day of the week and the month. On certain days like Monday Mar 23rd, Monday and Mar will be on the first line, leaving 23rd by itself on the second line. However, on Tuesday Mar 24th, the issue doesn't exist and Mar and 24th fall on the same line. Angular, at the time of publishing, doesn't support new line breaks in the date template; ideally, we should be able to specify the date format as "EEEE\nMMM d" to ensure that the line break is always consistent. We can, however, throw some inefficient code at the problem and enforce the behavior we desire.

3. Break up the current date into two parts and separate them with the line break tag `<br>`, then remove the class right from the outer `div`:

   src/app/current-weather/current-weather.component.html
   ```
   <div fxFlex class="mat-h3 no-margin">
     {{current.date | date:'EEEE'}}<br>
     {{current.date | date:'MMM d'}}{{getOrdinal(current.date)}}
   </div>
   ```

> Never use `<br>` for layout purposes. It's acceptable in this limited case, because we're breaking up content within a div or a p tag.

Now, let's add some visual flair, when displaying the temperature unit. To accomplish this, the temperature implementation needs to separate the digits from the unit with a `<span>` element, surrounded with a `<p>` element, so a superscript style can be applied to the unit along the lines of `<span class="unit">°F</span>`, where `unit` is a CSS class that makes its content look like a superscript element.

4. Implement a `unit` CSS class:

   src/app/current-weather/current-weather.component.css
   ```
   .unit {
   vertical-align: super;
   }
   ```

5. Reduce the flex on the image to 55%, wrap the temperature and the unit with a p tag and apply `mat-display-3` on the p tag. Then implement a span around the temperature unit with the p tag, and apply the classes `unit` and `mat-display-1` to the span:

```
src/app/current-weather/current-weather.component.html
<div fxFlex="55%">
  <img style="zoom: 175%" [src]='current.image'>
</div>
<div fxFlex class="right no-margin">
  <p class="mat-display-3">
    {{current.temperature | number:'1.0-0'}}
    <span class="mat-display-1 unit">°F</span>
  </p>
</div>
```

You usually need to experiment with how much space the forecast image should have by tweaking the `fxFlex` value on the preceding first line. If it takes too much space, the temperature overflows to the next line. Your settings can further be affected by the size of your browser window. 60% seems to work well, but when I was coding this sample the current weather was 55°F, so for entirely poetic reasons I decided to go with 55%. See the polished version of our app here:

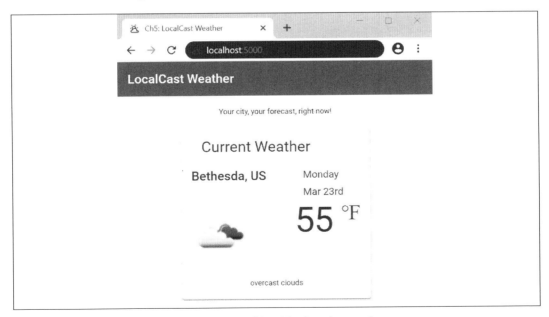

Figure 5.22: LocalCast Weather after tweaks

As always, it is possible to further tweak the margins and paddings to further customize the design. However, each deviation from the library will have maintainability consequences down the line. Unless you're truly building a business around displaying weather data, you should defer any further optimizations to the end of the project, if time permits, and if experience is any guide, you will not be making this optimization.

With two negative margin-bottom hacks, you can attain a design fairly close to the original, but I will not include those hacks here and leave it as an exercise for the reader to discover on the GitHub repository. Such hacks are sometimes necessary evils, but in general, they point to a disconnect between design and implementation realities. The solution leading up to the tweaks section is the sweet spot, where Angular Material thrives. Beyond that you're probably wasting your time. I went ahead and wasted my time for you and here's the result:

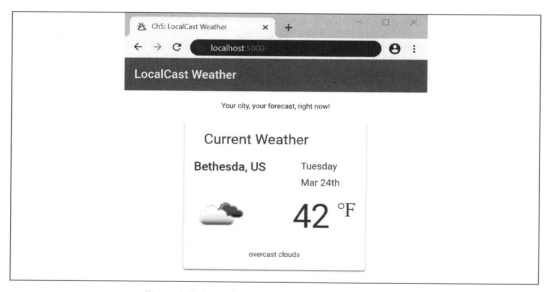

Figure 5.23: LocalCast Weather after tweaks and hacks

Now that our layout and design is in great shape, let's look into creating a custom theme using Angular Material.

Custom themes

As we previously discussed, Material ships with some default themes including `deeppurple-amber`, `indigo-pink`, `pink-blue-grey`, and `purple-green`. However, your company or product may have its own color scheme. For this, you can create a custom theme to change the look of your application.

In order to create a new theme, you must implement a new SCSS file:

1. Remove all definitions of your default theme from `angular.json`.
2. Re-run the command `npx ng add @angular/material`.
3. This time select `Custom` as the theme.
4. After running the command make sure that your `index.html` and `styles.css` files have not been modified. If so, revert the changes.
5. This will create a new file under `src` called `custom-theme.scss`. Rename it to `localcast-theme.scss`, shown as follows:

   src/localcast-theme.scss
   ```
   // Custom Theming for Angular Material
   // For more information: https://material.angular.io/guide/theming
   @import '~@angular/material/theming';
   // Plus imports for other components in your app.

   // Include the common styles for Angular Material.
   // We include this here so that you only have to
   // load a single css file for Angular Material in your app.
   // Be sure that you only ever include this mixin once!
   @include mat-core();
   // Define the palettes for your theme using
   // the Material Design palettes available in palette.scss
   // (imported above). For each palette, you can optionally
   // specify a default, lighter, and darker hue.
   // Available color palettes: https://material.io/design/color/
   $local-weather-app-primary: mat-palette($mat-indigo);
   $local-weather-app-accent: mat-palette(
     $mat-pink,
     A200, A100, A400
   );
   // The warn palette is optional (defaults to red).
   $local-weather-app-warn: mat-palette($mat-red);
   // Create the theme object (a Sass map containing
   // all of the palettes).
   $local-weather-app-theme: mat-light-theme(
     $local-weather-app-primary,
     $local-weather-app-accent,
     $local-weather-app-warn
   );

   // Custom Theming for Angular Material
   // For more information: https://material.angular.io/guide/theming
   ```

```scss
@import '~@angular/material/theming';
// Plus imports for other components in your app.

// Include the common styles for Angular Material.
// We include this here so that you only have to
// load a single css file for Angular Material in your app.
// Be sure that you only ever include this mixin once!
@include mat-core();

// Define the palettes for your theme using
// the Material Design palettes available in palette.scss
// (imported above). For each palette, you can optionally
// specify a default, lighter, and darker hue.
// Available color palettes: https://material.io/design/color/
$local-weather-app-primary: mat-palette($mat-indigo);
$local-weather-app-accent: mat-palette($mat-pink, A200, A100, A400);

// The warn palette is optional (defaults to red).
$local-weather-app-warn: mat-palette($mat-red);

// Create the theme object (a Sass map containing
// all of the palettes).
$local-weather-app-theme: mat-light-theme(
  $local-weather-app-primary,
  $local-weather-app-accent,
  $local-weather-app-warn
);

// Include theme styles for core and each component used in
// your app. Alternatively, you can import and @include the
// theme mixins for each component that you are using.
@include angular-material-theme($local-weather-app-theme);
```

You can find the Material theme guide at `https://material.angular.io/guide/theming` for more detailed information.

Note that `mat-core()` should only be included once in your application; otherwise, you'll introduce unnecessary and duplicated CSS payloads in your application.

`mat-core()` contains the necessary SCSS functions to be able to inject your custom colors into Material, such as `mat-palette`, `mat-light-theme`, and `mat-dark-theme`.

At a minimum, we must define a new primary and an accent color. Defining new colors, however, is not a straightforward process. Material requires a palette to be defined through `mat-palette`, which needs to be seeded by a complicated color object that can't just be overridden by a simple hex value such as `#BFB900`.

To pick your colors, you can use the Material Design Color Tool, located at `https://material.io/resources/color`. Here's a screenshot of the tool:

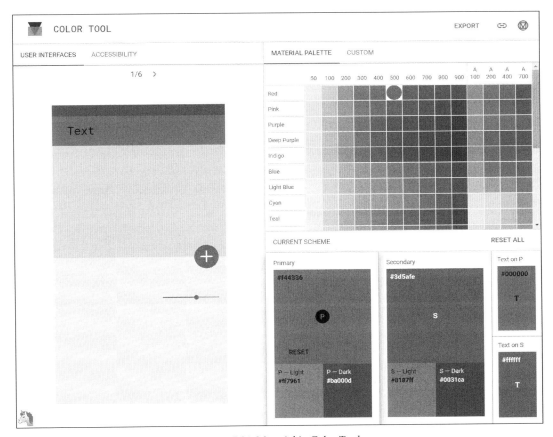

Figure 5.24: Material.io Color Tool

6. Using **Material Palette**, select a **Primary** and a **Secondary** color:
    - My primary selection is red with a hue value of `500`.
    - My secondary selection is indigo with a hue value of `A400`.

7. Observe how your selections would apply to a Material Design app by going through the six prebuilt screens on the left of the page.

8. Evaluate the accessibility implications of your selections, as shown:

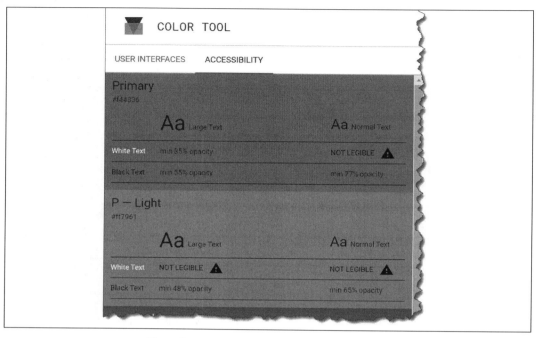

Figure 5.25: Material.io Color Tool Accessibility tab

 The tool is warning us that our selections result in illegible text, when white text is used over the primary color. You should either take care to avoid displaying white text over your primary color or change your selection.

If you want to create your own palette, then the interface for `mat-palette` looks like this:

```
mat-palette($base-palette, $default: 500, $lighter: 100, $darker: 700)
```

9. Define the primary and secondary `mat-palette` objects using the default hue from the tool:

   src/localcast-theme.scss
   ```
   $local-weather-app-primary: mat-palette($mat-red, 500);
   $local-weather-app-accent: mat-palette($mat-indigo, A400);
   ```

Even though your theme is in SCSS, you may continue using CSS in the rest of your application. The Angular CLI supports compiling both SCSS and CSS. If you would like to change the default behavior, you may switch to SCSS altogether by changing the `defaults.styleExt` property in the `angular.json` file from CSS to SCSS.

You may also choose to eliminate `styles.css` and merge its contents with `localcast-theme.scss` or convert `styles.css` to a SASS file by simply renaming it to `styles.scss`. If you do this, don't forget to update `angular.json`.

Congratulations! Your application should now bear your trademark color scheme:

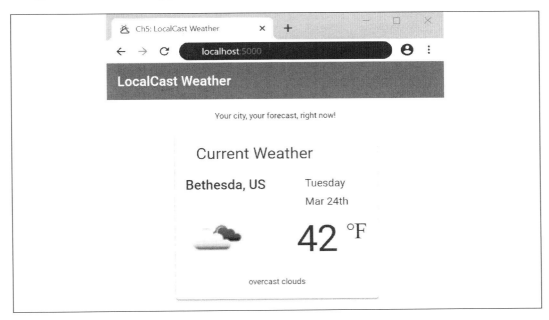

Figure 5.26: LocalCast Weather with custom theme

Push your code to GitHub and check out your CircleCI pipeline.

Unit testing with Material

Once you commit your code, you will notice that your pipeline is now failing due to failed tests. In order to keep your unit tests running, you will need to import `MaterialModule` to any component's `spec` file that uses Angular Material:

```
*.component.spec.ts
```

```
    ...
      beforeEach(async(() => {
        TestBed.configureTestingModule({
          ...
            imports: [..., MaterialModule],
        }).compileComponents()
      })
    )
```

You will also need to update any test, including e2e tests, that search for a particular HTML element.

For example, since the app's title, LocalCast Weather, is not in an `h1` tag anymore, you must update the `spec` file to look for it in a `span` element:

src/app/app.component.spec.ts
```
expect(compiled.querySelector('span').textContent).
    toContain('LocalCast Weather')
```

Another example is in the `CurrentWeather` component, where the surrounding element for `city` is no longer `span`, so you can use the `mat-title` CSS class instead:

src/app/current-weather/current-weather.component.spec.ts
```
import { By } from '@angular/platform-browser'
// Assert on DOM
const debugEl = fixture.debugElement
const titleEl: HTMLElement =
    debugEl.query(By.css('.mat-title')).nativeElement
expect(titleEl.textContent).toContain('Bethesda')
```

Similarly, in e2e tests, you will need to update your page object function to retrieve the text from the correct location:

src/e2e/app.po.ts
```
getParagraphText() {
    return element(by.css('app-root mat-toolbar span'))
      .getText() as Promise<string>
}
```

Once your tests are passing, push your code to GitHub again. When your CircleCI pipeline succeeds, ship your app using Vercel Now. Remember, if you don't ship it, it never happened!

We can now move the UX task to the **Done** column:

Figure 5.27: GitHub project Kanban board status

In *Chapter 7, Creating a Router-First Line-of-Business App*, you will learn about more sophisticated tools to be able to further customize the look and feel of your Material theme to create a truly unique experience that fits the brand you're representing.

Accessibility

It is important to be aware of potential accessibility issues with your app. You may familiarize yourself with accessibility concerns by visiting the A11Y project website at `https://a11yproject.com`. Material itself provides additional tooling to help you improve accessibility; you can read about it at `https://material.angular.io/cdk/a11y/overview`.

Leveraging such Material features may feel unnecessary; however, you must consider responsiveness, styling, spacing, and accessibility concerns when designing your app. The Material team has put in a lot of effort so that your code works correctly under most circumstances and can serve the largest possible user base with a high-quality UX. This can include visually impaired or keyboard-primary users, who must rely on specialized software or keyboard features such as tabs to navigate your app. Leveraging Material elements provides crucial metadata for these users to be able to navigate your app.

Material claims support for the following screen-reader software:

- NVDA and JAWS with Internet Explorer/Firefox/Chrome on Windows
- VoiceOver with Safari on iOS and Safari/Chrome on macOS X
- TalkBack with Chrome on Android

Beyond Material, you may be required or have a desire to support specific accessibility standards, like the US-based Section 508 or the W3C-defined **Web Content Accessibility Guidelines (WCAG)**. Claiming official support for such standards requires expensive certifications and qualified testers to ensure compliance.

Consider pa11y, which is a command-line tool that automates accessibility testing. Since it is a CLI tool, you can easily integrate it with your CI pipeline. Being able to catch accessibility issues automatically and early in the development cycle dramatically decreases the cost of implementing accessibility features in your application.

 A11y is short for **accessibility**, as there are 11 characters between *a* and *y* in the word accessibility. You may read more about why accessibility support matters at https://a11yproject.com/.

You may learn more about pa11y at https://pa11y.org/. Next, let's configure the pa11y CLI tool in our project.

Configuring automated pa11y testing

pa11y is an automated accessibility tool that you can execute from the command line to check your web app against various accessibility rulesets like Section 508 or WCAG 2 AAA. You may configure pa11y to run on your project locally or your CI server. In both cases, you must be running the tests against a deployed version of your application.

Let's start with configuring pa11y for a local run:

1. Install the pa11y and pa11y-ci packages with the following command:
   ```
   npm i -D pa11y pa11y-ci http-server
   ```

2. Add npm scripts to execute pa11y for local runs, checking for Section 508 compliance issues:

   package.json
   ```
   ...
   "scripts": {
     ...
     "test:a11y": "pa11y --standard Section508 http://localhost:5000"
   }
   ```

3. Ensure that the app is running by executing `npm start`.

4. In a new Terminal window, execute `npm run test:a11y`. The output should be as follows:
   ```
   Welcome to Pa11y
   
   > Running Pa11y on URL http://localhost:5000
   ```

```
Results for URL: http://localhost:5000/

  • Error: Img element missing an alt attribute. Use the alt
attribute to specify a short text alternative.
    |── Section508.A.Img.MissingAlt
    |── html > body > app-root > div:nth-child(4) > mat-card >
mat-card-content > app-current-weather > div > div:nth-child(2) >
div:nth-child(1) > img
    └── <img _ngcontent-pbr-c132="" style="margin-bottom:32px;
zoom:175%" src="">

1 Errors
```

Note that we have one error. The error message indicates that under `app-current-weather`, the image we display inside `mat-card-content` is missing an `alt` attribute. Observe the following line of code that caused the error:

src/app/current-weather/current-weather.component.html

```
...
<img style="zoom: 175%" [src]="current.image" />
```

The preceding code refers to the image that we grab from the OpenWeatherMap API. A visually impaired user, relying on a screen reader, would not be able to determine what the image is for without an `alt` attribute present. Since this is a dynamic image, a static `alt` attribute like the **Current weather icon** would be a disservice to our user. However, it would be appropriate to bind the current weather description value as the attribute. We can fix the accessibility issue as shown:

src/app/current-weather/current-weather.component.html

```
...
<img style="zoom: 175%" [src]="current.image"
  [alt]="current.description" />
```

5. Re-run pa11y to confirm that the issue has been fixed.

Now users relying on screen readers quickly figure out that the image on the page reflects the current weather. In this case, we already have the description on our page. This is a very important issue to fix because it is crucial to avoid having mystery elements on our page that an entire class of users is unable to decipher.

Now let's configure pa11y for our CI pipeline.

1. Create a .pallyci configuration file in the root of your project:

   .pallyci
   ```
   {
     "default": {
       "timeout": 1000,
       "page": {
         "viewport": {
           "width": 320,
           "height": 480
         }
       }
     },
     "urls": [
       "https://localcast-weather.duluca.now.sh/"
     ]
   }
   ```

2. Add npm scripts to execute pa11y for local runs, checking for Section 508 compliance issues:

   package.json
   ```
   ...
   "scripts": {
     ...
     "test:a11y:ci": "pa11y-ci"
   }
   ```

Now we can add the command npm run test:a11y:ci to .circleci/config.yml. However, as you may notice, we would be running the test against the already deployed version of our app. To overcome this challenge, you must create an alternative now:publish command that will deploy our branch to a different URL, update .pallyci to check against the new URL, and perform a deployment in your pipeline. Since all actions involved here are CLI commands, you may execute them sequentially. I leave this as an exercise for the user to complete.

More advanced uses for CircleCI are covered in *Chapter 9, DevOps Using Docker*. Next, we are going to go over how you can build an interactive prototype to discover UI/UX issues early in development to reduce your development costs.

Building an interactive prototype

Appearances do matter. Whether you're working in a development team or as a freelancer, your colleagues, bosses, or clients will always take a well-put-together presentation more seriously. In *Chapter 3, Creating a Basic Angular App*, I mentioned the time and information management challenges of being a full-stack developer. We must pick a tool that can achieve the best results with the least amount of work. This usually means going down the paid-tool route, but UI/UX design tools are rarely free or cheap.

A prototyping tool will help you create a better, more professional-looking, mock-up of the app. Whatever tool you choose should also support the UI framework you choose to use, in this case, Material.

If a picture is worth a thousand words, an interactive prototype of your app is worth a thousand lines of code. An interactive mock-up of the app will help you vet ideas before you write a single line of code and save you a lot of code writing.

MockFlow WireframePro

I've picked MockFlow WireframePro, available at `https://mockflow.com`, as an easy-to-use, capable, online tool that supports Material Design UI elements and allows you to create multiple pages, which can then be linked together to create the illusion of a working application.

Most importantly, at the time of publishing, MockFlow allows one free project forever with the full feature set and capabilities available. This will give you a chance to truly vet the usefulness of the tool without artificial limits or a trial period that always seems to go by much quicker than you expect.

> Balsamiq (available at `https://balsamiq.com`) is a better-known wireframing tool; however, it doesn't offer any free usage. If you are looking for a tool without a monthly cost, I would highly recommend Balsamiq's desktop application Mockups, which has a one-time purchase cost.

Building a mock-up

We start by adding a new task to create an interactive prototype and at the end of the task, I'll attach all artifacts to this task so that they're stored on GitHub and are accessible to all team members and can also be linked from the wiki page for persistent documentation.

Let's pull this new task to the **In Progress** column and take a look at the status of our Kanban board from Waffle.io:

Figure 5.28: Current Kanban board status

WireframePro is pretty intuitive as a drag and drop design interface, so I won't go into the details of how the tool works, but I will highlight some tips:

1. Create your project
2. Select a component pack, either **Hand Drawn UI** or **Material Design**
3. Add each screen as a new page, as shown in the following screenshot:

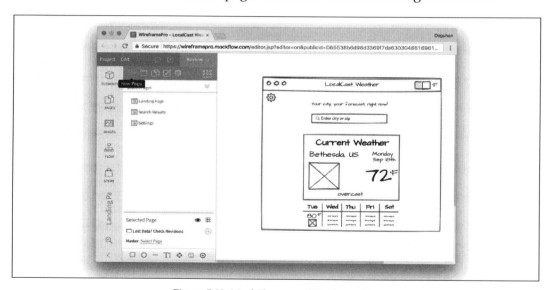

Figure 5.29: MockFlow.com WireFrame Pro

I would recommend sticking to the hand-drawn UI look and feel, because it sets the right expectations for your audience. If you present a very high-quality mock-up on your first meeting with a client, your first demo will be an understatement. You will, at best, merely meet expectations and, at worst, underwhelm your audience.

Home screen

Here's the new mock-up of the home screen that we just created:

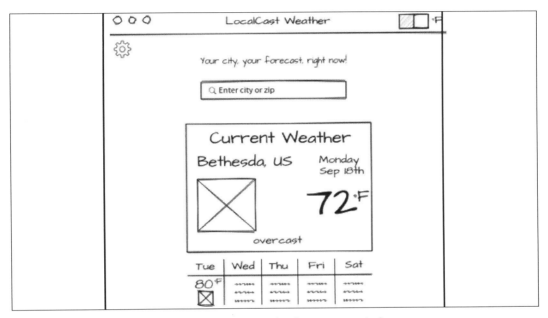

Figure 5.30: LocalCast Weather home screen wireframe

You'll note some differences, such as the app toolbar being conflated with the browser bar and the intentional vagueness of the repeating elements. I have made these choices to reduce the amount of design time I would need to spend on each screen. I simply used horizontal and vertical line objects to create the grid.

Search results

The search screen similarly remains intentionally vague to avoid having to maintain any kind of detailed information. Surprisingly, your audience is far more likely to focus on what your test data is rather than focusing on the design elements.

Delivering High-Quality UX with Material

By being vague, we intentionally keep the audience's attention on what matters. Here's the search screen mock-up:

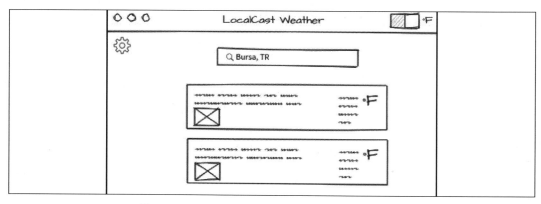

Figure 5.31: LocalCast Weather search screen wireframe

Settings pane

The **Settings** pane is a separate screen with the elements from the home screen copied over and with 85% opacity applied to create a model-like experience. The **Settings** pane itself is just a rectangle with a black border and a solid white background.

Take a look at the following mock-up:

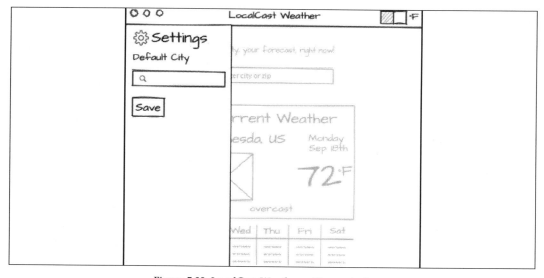

Figure 5.32: LocalCast Weather settings wireframe

Adding interactivity

Being able to click around a mock-up and get a feel for the navigational workflow is an indispensable tool to get early user feedback. This will save you and your clients a lot of frustration, time, and money.

To link elements together, do as follows:

1. Select a clickable element such as the *gear* icon on the home screen
2. Under the **Link** subheading, click on **Select Page**
3. On the pop-over window, select **Settings**
4. Click on **Create Link**, as shown in this screenshot:

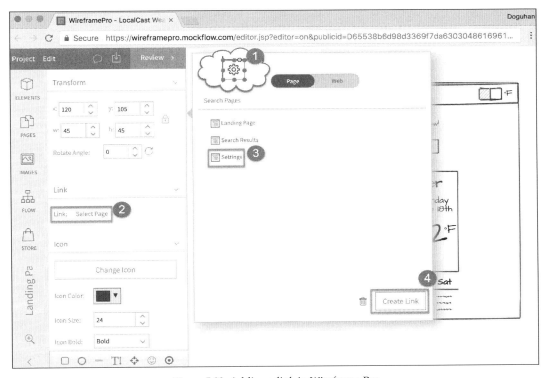

Figure 5.33: Adding a link in Wireframe Pro

Now, when you click on the *gear* icon, the tool will display the **Settings** page, which will create the effect of the sidebar actually being displayed on the same page. To go back to the home screen, you can link the *gear* icon and the section outside of the sidebar back to that page so that the user can navigate back and forth.

Exporting the functional prototype

Once your prototype is completed, you can export it as various formats:

1. Under the **Project** menu, select the **Export Wireframe** button, as shown:

Figure 5.34: Wireframe Pro's Export Wireframe menu option

2. Now select your file format, as follows:

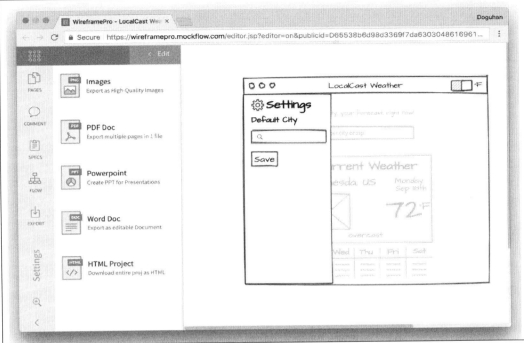

Figure 5.35: File formats in Wireframe Pro

I prefer the HTML format for flexibility; however, your workflow and needs will differ.

3. If you selected HTML, you will get to download a ZIP bundle of all the assets.

4. Unzip the bundle and navigate to it using your browser; you should get an interactive version of your wireframe, as illustrated:

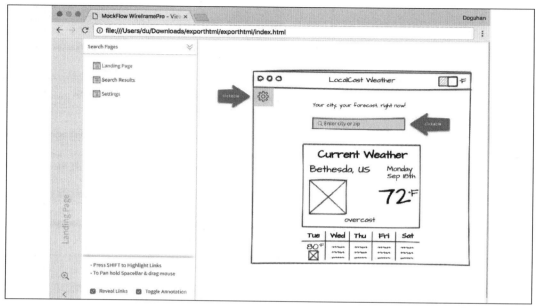

Figure 5.36: Interactive wireframe in Wireframe Pro

 The interactive elements are highlighted in yellow (light gray in print) and pointed out by the fat arrows in the preceding screenshot. You can enable or disable this behavior with the **Reveal Links** option in the bottom-left corner of the screen.

Now add all assets to comment on the GitHub issue, including the ZIP bundle, and we are done.

You can also publish your prototype's HTML project using Vercel Now, as discussed in *Chapter 4, Automated Testing, CI, and Release to Production*.

Summary

In this chapter, you learned what Angular Material is, how to use the Angular Flex Layout engine, the impact of UI libraries on performance, and how to apply specific Angular Material components to your application. You became aware of pitfalls of over-optimized UI design with individual CSS tweaks and how to add a custom theme to your application.

We also went over how you can improve the accessibility of your application and build an interactive prototype to vet your designs before implementing them.

In the next chapter, we will update the weather app to respond to user input with reactive forms and keep our components decoupled, while also enabling data exchange between them using `BehaviorSubject`. After the next chapter, we will be done with the weather app and shift our focus to building larger line-of-business applications.

> See *Appendix C, Keeping Angular and Tools Evergreen*, for information on how you can upgrade Angular Material. You can find this appendix online from `https://static.packt-cdn.com/downloads/9781838648800_Appendix_C_Keeping_Angular_and_Tools_Evergreen.pdf` or at `https://expertlysimple.io/stay-evergreen`.

Further reading

- *Insanely Simple: The Obsession That Drives Apple's Success, Ken Segall*, 2013
- *Material Design, Google*, 2020, at `https://material.io`
- *Pa11y, Team Pa11y*, 2020, at `https://pa11y.org`

Exercises

Implement pa11y in your CI pipeline by implementing an alternative Now deployment so that you can test against the changes in your branch.

Questions

Answer the following questions as best as you can to ensure that you've understood the key concepts from this chapter without Googling. Do you need help answering the questions? See *Appendix D, Self-Assessment Answers* online at `https://static.packt-cdn.com/downloads/9781838648800_Appendix_D_Self-Assessment_Answers.pdf` or visit `https://expertlysimple.io/angular-self-assessment`.

1. What are the benefits of using Angular Material?
2. Which underlying CSS technology does Angular Flex Layout rely on?
3. Why is it important to test for accessibility?
4. Why should you build an interactive prototype?

6
Forms, Observables, and Subjects

So far, you've been working with putting together the essential elements that make up an Angular application, such as modules, components, pipes, services, RxJS, unit testing, and environment variables, and even going a step further by learning how to deliver your web application using Docker and giving it a polished look with Angular Material.

At this point, our app is not interactive. It can only pull weather information for one city. As a result, it is not a very useful app. To build an interactive app, we need to be able to handle user input. Enabling user input in your application opens up possibilities for creating great user experiences. Consider google.com's landing page:

Figure 6.1: Google's landing page

Forms, Observables, and Subjects

In this context, what is Google Search, apart from a simple input field with two buttons? That simple input field unlocks some of the world's most sophisticated and advanced software technologies. It is a deceptively simple and an insanely powerful way to interact with users. You can augment user input by leveraging modern web functionality such as `GeoLocation` and gain new meaning from user input. So, when the user types in `Paris` you don't have to guess if they mean Paris, France, or Paris, Texas, or whether you should show the current temperature in Celsius or Fahrenheit. With `LocalStorage`, you can cache user credentials and remember user preferences so that you can enable dark mode in your app.

By the end of this chapter, we won't be implementing Google, GeoLocation, or dark mode, but will enable users to search for their cities using a city name or postal code (often referred to as "zip codes" in the US). Once you realize how complicated it can get implementing something as seemingly simple as a search by postal code, you may gain a new appreciation for well-designed web apps.

To build a UX driven by an input field, we need to leverage Angular forms with validation messages so that we can create engaging search experiences with search-as-you-type functionality. Behind the scenes, RxJS/BehaviorSubject enables us to build decoupled components that can communicate with one another and a reactive data stream allows us to merge data from multiple web APIs without increasing the complexity of our app.

In this chapter, you are going to learn about:

- Template-driven and reactive forms, including two-way binding and input field validation
- Interactions between components
- Observables and RxJS/BehaviorSubject
- Managing subscriptions, and how to handle memory leaks and unsubscribing
- Handling multiple API calls with the async pipe, including chaining multiple API calls

The most up-to-date versions of the sample code for the book are on GitHub at the repository linked as follows. The repository contains the final and completed state of the code. You can verify your progress at the end of this chapter by looking for the end-of-chapter snapshot of code under the `projects` folder.

For *Chapter 6*:

1. Clone the repo `https://github.com/duluca/local-weather-app`
2. Execute `npm install` on the root folder to install dependencies
3. The code sample for this chapter is under the sub-folder:
   projects/ch6
4. To run the Angular app for this chapter, execute:
   npx ng serve ch6
5. To run Angular unit tests for this chapter, execute:
   npx ng test ch6 --watch=false
6. To run Angular e2e tests for this chapter, execute:
   npx ng e2e ch6
7. To build a production-ready Angular app for this chapter, execute:
   npx ng build ch6 --prod

Note that the `dist/ch6` folder at the root of the repository will contain the compiled result.

Beware that the source code in the book or on GitHub may not always match the code generated by the Angular CLI. There may also be slight differences in implementation between the code in the book and what's on GitHub because the ecosystem is ever-evolving. It is natural for the sample code to change over time. Also on GitHub, expect to find corrections, fixes to support newer versions of libraries, or side-by-side implementations of multiple techniques for the reader to observe. The reader is only expected to implement the ideal solution recommended in the book. If you find errors or have questions, please create an issue or submit a pull request on GitHub for the benefit of all readers.

Next, let's see how we can implement an input field using forms. Forms are the primary mechanism that we need to capture user input. In Angular, there are two kinds of forms: reactive and template-driven. We need to cover both techniques, so that you're familiar with how forms work in Angular.

Forms, Observables, and Subjects

Reactive forms versus template-driven forms

Now, we'll implement the search bar on the home screen of the application. The next user story states **Display forecast information for current location**, which may be taken to imply an inherent GeoLocation functionality. However, as you may note, GeoLocation is listed as a separate task. The challenge is that with native platform features such as GeoLocation, you are never guaranteed to receive the actual location information. This may be due to signal loss issues on mobile devices or the user may simply refuse to give permission to share their location information.

First and foremost, we must deliver a good baseline UX and implement value-added functionality such as GeoLocation only afterward. Instead, let's move **Add city search capability ...** to **In progress**, as shown on our Kanban board:

Figure 6.2: GitHub project Kanban board

As part of this story, we are going to implement a search-as-you-type functionality while providing feedback to the user if the service is unable to retrieve the expected data.

Initially, it may be intuitive to implement a type-search mechanism; however, `OpenWeatherMap` APIs don't provide such an endpoint. Instead, they provide bulk data downloads, which are costly and are in the multiples of megabytes range.

We will need to implement our application server to expose such an endpoint so that our app can effectively query while using minimal amounts of data.

The free endpoints for `OpenWeatherMap` do pose an interesting challenge, where a two-digit country code may accompany either a city name or zip code for the most accurate results. This is an excellent opportunity to implement a feedback mechanism to the user if more than one result is returned for a given query.

We want every iteration of the app to be a potentially releasable increment and avoid doing too much at any given time.

Before you begin working on a story, it is a good idea to break the story out into technical tasks. The following is the task breakdown for this story:

1. Add Angular form control so that we can capture user input events.
2. Use Angular Material input as documented at `https://material.angular.io/components/input` to improve the UX of the input field.
3. Create the search bar as a separate component to enforce separation of concerns and a decoupled component architecture.
4. Extend the existing endpoint to accept a zip code and make the country code optional in `weather.service.ts` in order to make it more intuitive for end users to interact with our app.
5. Throttle requests so that we don't query the API with every keystroke, but at an interval where users still get immediate feedback without having to click on a separate button.

Let's tackle these tasks over the next few sections.

Adding Angular reactive forms

You may wonder why we're adding Angular forms since we are adding just a single input field and not a form with multiple inputs. As a general rule of thumb, any time you add an input field, it should be wrapped in a `<form>` tag. The `Forms` module contains the `FormControl` that enables you to write the backing code behind the input field to respond to user inputs, and provide the appropriate data or the validation or message in response.

There are two types of forms in Angular:

- **Template-driven forms**: These forms are similar to what you may be familiar with in the case of AngularJS, where the form logic is mostly inside the HTML template. I'm personally not a fan of this approach because it is harder to test these behaviors, and fat HTML templates become challenging to maintain quickly.
- **Reactive forms**: The behavior of reactive forms is driven by TypeScript code written in the controller. This means that your validation logic can be unit tested and, better yet, reused across your application. Reactive forms are the core technology that, in the future, will enable the Angular Material team to write automated tools that can autogenerate an input form based on a TypeScript interface.

Read more about reactive forms at https://angular.io/guide/reactive-forms.

Let's start by importing `FormsModule` and `ReactiveFormsModule` into our app:

src/app/app.module.ts
```
...
import { FormsModule, ReactiveFormsModule } from '@angular/forms'
...
@NgModule({
  ...
  imports: [
    ...
    FormsModule,
    ReactiveFormsModule,
  ]
```

Note that in a pure reactive form implementation, you only need the `ReactiveFormsModule`. `FormsModule` supports template-driven forms, and other scenarios, where you may only want to declare a `FormControl` without a `FormGroup`. This is how we implement the input field for this app. `FormGroup` is defined in the next section.

Also, reactive forms allow you to write code in the reactive paradigm, which is a net positive. Next, let's add a city search component to our app.

Adding and verifying components

We will be creating a `citySearch` component using Material form and input modules:

1. Add `MatFormFieldModule` and `MatInputModule` to `material.module.ts` so that it becomes available for use in the app:

   src/app/material.module.ts
   ```
   import { MatFormFieldModule } from '@angular/material/form-field'
   import { MatInputModule } from '@angular/material/input'

   const modules = [..., MatFormFieldModule, MatInputModule]
   ```

   We're adding `MatFormFieldModule` because each input field should be wrapped in a `<mat-form-field>` tag to get the most out of Angular Material functionality.

At a high level, `<form>` encapsulates numerous default behaviors for keyboard, screen-reader, and browser extension users; `<mat-form-field>` enables easy two-way data binding, a technique that should be used in moderation, and also allows for graceful label, validation, and error message displays.

2. Create the new `citySearch` component:

   `$ npx ng g c citySearch --module=app.module`

   Since we added the `material.module.ts` file, ng can't guess what feature module `citySearch` should be added to, resulting in an error such as `More than one module matches`. Therefore, we need to provide the module that we want `citySearch` to be added to, using the `--module` option. Use the `--skip-import` option to skip importing the component into any module.

3. Create a basic template, replacing the existing content:

   src/app/city-search/city-search.component.html
   ```
   <form>
     <mat-form-field appearance="outline">
       <mat-label>City Name or Postal Code</mat-label>
       <mat-icon matPrefix>search</mat-icon>
       <input matInput aria-label="City or Zip" [formControl]="search">
     </mat-form-field>
   </form>
   ```

4. Declare a property named `search` and instantiate it as an instance of `FormControl`:

   src/app/city-search/city-search.component.ts
   ```
   import { FormControl } from '@angular/forms'
   ...
   export class CitySearchComponent implements OnInit {

     search = new FormControl()
     ...
   ```

- Reactive forms have three levels of control:
    - `FormControl` is the most basic element that has a one-to-one relationship with an input field.
    - `FormArray` represents repetitive input fields that represent a collection of objects.

Forms, Observables, and Subjects

- FormGroup is used to register individual FormControl or FormArray objects as you add more input fields to a form.

Finally, the FormBuilder object is used to orchestrate and maintain the actions of a FormGroup object more easily. FormBuilder and FormGroup are first used in *Chapter 8, Designing Authentication and Authorization*, and all controls, including FormArray, are covered in depth in *Chapter 11, Recipes – Reusability, Routing, and Caching*.

5. Add app-city-search to app.component.ts as a new div in between the row that contains the tagline of the app and the row that contains mat-card:

src/app/app.component.ts
```
template: `
  ...
  </div>
  <div fxLayoutAlign="center">
    <app-city-search></app-city-search>
  </div>
  <div fxLayout="row">
  ...
`,
```

6. Test the integration of components by checking out the app in the browser, as shown:

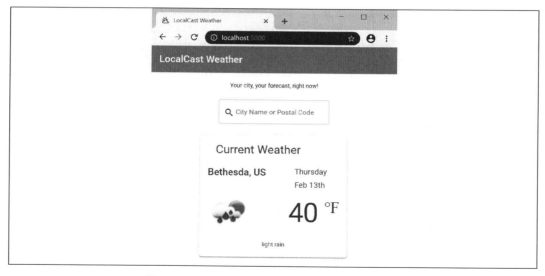

Figure 6.3: LocalCast Weather app with a search field

If no errors occur, now we can start adding the `FormControl` elements and wire them to a search endpoint.

Adding a search option to the weather service

So far, we have been passing parameters to get the weather for a city using its name and country code. By allowing users to enter zip codes, we must make our service more flexible in accepting both types of inputs.

OpenWeatherMap's API accepts URI parameters, so we can refactor the existing `getCurrentWeather` function (introduced in *Chapter 3, Creating a Basic Angular App*) using a TypeScript union type and a type guard. That means we can supply different parameters, while preserving type checking:

1. Refactor the `getCurrentWeather` function in `weather.service.ts` to handle both `zip` and `city` inputs:

    src/app/weather/weather.service.ts
    ```
    getCurrentWeather(
      search: string | number,
      country?: string
    ): Observable<ICurrentWeather> {
      let uriParams = new HttpParams()
      if (typeof search === 'string') {
        uriParams = uriParams.set('q',
          country ? `${search},${country}` : search
        )
      } else {
        uriParams = uriParams.set('zip', 'search')
      }

      uriParams = uriParams.set('appid', environment.appId)
      return this.httpClient
        .get<ICurrentWeatherData>(
          `${environment.baseUrl}api.openweathermap.org/data/2.5/weather`,
          { params: uriParams }
        )
        .pipe(map(data => this.transformToICurrentWeather(data)))
    }
    ```

    We renamed the `city` parameter to `search` since it can either be a city name or a zip code. We then allowed its type to be either a `string` or a `number`, and depending on what the type is at runtime, we will either use `q` or `zip`. We also made `country` optional and only append it to the query if it exists.

getCurrentWeather now has business logic embedded into it and is thus a good target for unit testing. Following the single responsibility principle, from the SOLID principles, we will refactor the HTTP call to its own function, called getCurrentWeatherHelper.

2. Refactor the HTTP call into getCurrentWeatherHelper.

In the next sample, note the use of a backtick character, `` ` ``, instead of a single-quote character, `'`, which leverages the template literals' functionality that allows embedded expressions in JavaScript:

src/app/weather/weather.service.ts
```
  getCurrentWeather(
    search: string | number,
    country?: string
  ): Observable<ICurrentWeather> {
    let uriParams = new HttpParams()
    if (typeof search === 'string') {
      uriParams = uriParams.set('q',
        country ? `${search},${country}` : search
      )
    } else {
      uriParams = uriParams.set('zip', 'search')
    }

    return this.getCurrentWeatherHelper(uriParams)
  }

  private getCurrentWeatherHelper(uriParams: HttpParams):
    Observable<ICurrentWeather> {
    uriParams = uriParams.set('appid', environment.appId)
    return this.httpClient
      .get<ICurrentWeatherData>(
        `${environment.baseUrl}api.openweathermap.org/data/2.5/weather`,
        { params: uriParams }
      )
      .pipe(map(data => this.transformToICurrentWeather(data)))
  }
```

As a positive side effect, getCurrentWeatherHelper adheres to the open/closed principle. After all, it is open to extension by our ability to change the function's behavior by supplying different uriParams and is closed to modification because it won't have to be changed frequently.

To demonstrate the latter point, let's implement a new function to get the current weather by latitude and longitude.

3. Implement `getCurrentWeatherByCoords`:

   src/app/weather/weather.service.ts
   ```
   getCurrentWeatherByCoords(coords: Coordinates):
   Observable<ICurrentWeather> {
     const uriParams = new HttpParams()
         .set('lat', coords.latitude.toString())
         .set('lon', coords.longitude.toString())

     return this.getCurrentWeatherHelper(uriParams)
   }
   ```

   As you can see, `getCurrentWeatherHelper` can easily be extended without any modification.

4. Ensure that you update `IWeatherService` with the changes made earlier:

   src/app/weather/weather.service.ts
   ```
   export interface IWeatherService {
     getCurrentWeather(
       search: string | number,
       country?: string
     ): Observable<ICurrentWeather>
     getCurrentWeatherByCoords(coords: Coordinates):
   Observable<ICurrentWeather>
   }
   ```

As a result of adhering to the SOLID design principles, we make it easier to robustly unit test flow-control logic and ultimately end up writing code that is more resilient to bugs and is cheaper to maintain.

Implementing a search

Now, let's connect the new service method to the input field:

1. Update `citySearch` to inject the `weatherService` and subscribe to input changes:

   src/app/city-search/city-search.component.ts
   ```
   import { WeatherService } from '../weather/weather.service'
   ...

   export class CitySearchComponent implements OnInit {
     search = new FormControl()

     constructor(private weatherService: WeatherService) {}
     ...
   ```

```
ngOnInit(): void {
  this.search.valueChanges
    .subscribe()
}
```

We are treating all input as `string` at this point. The user input can be a city, zip code, or a city and country code, or a zip code and country code, separated by a comma. While a city or zip code is required, a country code is optional. We can use the `String.split` function to parse any potential comma-separated input and then trim any whitespace out from the beginning and the end of the string with `String.trim`. We then ensure that we trim all parts of the string by iterating over them with `Array.map`.

We then deal with the optional parameter with the ternary operator `?:`, only passing in a value if it exists, otherwise leaving it undefined.

2. Implement the search handler:

   src/app/city-search/city-search.component.ts
   ```
   this.search.valueChanges
     .subscribe(
       (searchValue: string) => {
         if (searchValue) {
           const userInput = searchValue.split(',').map(s => s.trim())

           this.weatherService.getCurrentWeather(
             userInput[0],
             userInput.length > 1 ? userInput[1] : undefined
           ).subscribe(data => (console.log(data)))
         }
       })
   ```

3. Add a hint for the user, under the input field, informing them about the optional country functionality:

   src/app/city-search/city-search.component.html
   ```
   ...
     <mat-form-field appearance="outline">
       ...
       <mat-hint>Specify country code like 'Paris, US'</mat-hint>
     </mat-form-field>
   ...
   ```

At this point, the subscribe handler will make calls to the server and log its output to the console.

Observe how this works using Chrome DevTools. Note how often the `search` function is run and that we are not handling service errors.

Limiting user inputs with throttle/debounce

At the moment, we submit a request to the server with every keystroke. This is not desirable behavior, because it can lead to a bad user experience and drain battery life, resulting in wasted network requests and performance issues both on the client and server side. Users make typos; they can change their mind about what they are inputting and rarely ever do the first few characters of information input result in useful results.

We can still listen to every keystroke, but we don't have to react to every keystroke. By leveraging `throttle/debounce`, we can limit the number of events generated to a predetermined interval and still maintain the type-as-you-search functionality.

 Note that `throttle` and `debounce` are not functional equivalents, and their behavior will differ from framework to framework. In addition to throttling, we expect to capture the last input that the user has typed. In the `lodash` framework, the `throttle` function fulfills this requirement, whereas, in RxJS, debounce fulfills it. Beware that this discrepancy may be fixed in future framework updates.

It is very easy to inject throttling into the observable stream using `RxJS/debounceTime`. Implement `debounceTime` with `pipe`:

```
src/app/city-search/city-search.component.ts
import { debounceTime } from 'rxjs/operators'

  this.search.valueChanges
    .pipe(debounceTime(1000))
    .subscribe(...)
```

`debounceTime` will, at a maximum, run a search every second, but also run another search after the user has stopped typing. In comparison, `RxJS/throttleTime` will only run a search every second, on the second, and will not necessarily capture the last few characters the user may have input.

RxJS also has the `throttle` and `debounce` functions, which you can use to implement custom logic to limit input that is not necessarily time-based.

Since this is a time- and event-driven functionality, breakpoint debugging is not feasible. You may monitor the network calls within the **Chrome Dev Tools | Network** tab, but to get a more real-time feel for how often your search handler is actually being invoked, add a `console.log` statement.

> It is not a good practice to check in code with active `console.log` statements. As covered in *Chapter 3, Creating a Basic Angular App*, `console.log` is a poor man's debugging method. The statements make it difficult to read the actual code, which itself bears a high cost of maintainability. So, whether they are commented out or not, do not check in code with `console.log` statements.

Input validation and error messages

`FormControl` is highly customizable. It allows you to set a default initial value, add validators, or listen to changes on `blur`, `change`, and `submit` events, as follows:

```
example
new FormControl('Bethesda', { updateOn: 'submit' })
```

We won't be initializing `FormControl` with a value, but we need to implement a validator to disallow single character inputs:

1. Import `Validators` from `@angular/forms`:

    src/app/city-search/city-search.component.ts
    ```
    import { FormControl, Validators } from '@angular/forms'
    ```

2. Modify `FormControl` to add a minimum length validator:

    src/app/city-search/city-search.component.ts
    ```
    search = new FormControl('', [Validators.minLength(2)])
    ```

3. Modify the template to show a validation error message below the hint text:

    src/app/city-search/city-search.component.html
    ```
    ...
    <form style="margin-bottom: 32px">
      <mat-form-field appearance="outline">
        ...
        <mat-error *ngIf="search.invalid">
          Type more than one character to search
        </mat-error>
      </mat-form-field>
    </form>
    ...
    ```

Note the addition of some extra margin to make room for lengthy error messages.

If you are handling different kinds of errors, the `hasError` syntax in the template can get repetitive. You may want to implement a more scalable solution that can be customized through code, as shown:

example
```
<mat-error *ngIf="search.invalid">
  {{getErrorMessage()}}
</mat-error>

getErrorMessage() {
  return this.search.hasError('minLength') ?
    'Type more than one character to search' : '';
}
```

4. Modify the `search` function to not execute a search with invalid input replacing the condition in the existing `if` statement:

   src/app/city-search/city-search.component.ts
   ```
   this.search.valueChanges
     .pipe(debounceTime(1000))
     .subscribe((search Value: string) => {
       if (!this.search.invalid) {
         ...
   ```

Instead of doing a simple check to see whether `searchValue` is defined and not an empty string, we can tap into the validation engine for a more robust check by calling `this.search.invalid`.

For now, we're done with implementing `search` functionality. Next, let's go over a what-if scenario to see how a template-driven implementation of the form would appear.

Template-driven forms with two-way binding

The alternative to reactive forms is template-driven forms. If you're familiar with `ng-model` from AngularJS, you'll find that the new `ngModel` directive is an API-compatible replacement for it.

> Behind the scenes, ngModel implements a `FormControl` that can automatically attach itself to a `FormGroup`. ngModel can be used at the `<form>` level or individual `<input>` level. You can read more about ngModel at https://angular.io/api/forms/NgModel.

In the *Chapter 6* example code of the Local Weather app repository on GitHub, I have included a template-driven component in app.component.ts named app-city-search-tpldriven rendered under `<div class="example">`. You can experiment with this component to see what the alternate template implementation looks like:

projects/ch6/src/app/city-search-tpldriven/city-search-tpldriven.component.html

```
...
  <input matInput aria-label="City or Zip"
    [(ngModel)]="model.search"
    (ngModelChange)="doSearch($event)" minlength="2"
    name="search" #search="ngModel">
...
  <mat-error *ngIf="search.invalid">
    Type more than one character to search
  </mat-error>
...
```

> Note the [()] "box of bananas" two-way binding syntax in use with ngModel.

The differences in the component are implemented as follows:

projects/ch6/src/app/city-search-tpldriven/city-search-tpldriven.component.ts

```
import { WeatherService } from '../weather/weather.service'

export class CitySearchTpldrivenComponent {
  model = {
    search: '',
  }

  constructor(private weatherService: WeatherService) {}

  doSearch(searchValue) {
    const userInput = searchValue.split(',').map(s => s.trim())
    this.weatherService
```

```
      .getCurrentWeather(userInput[0], userInput.length > 1 ?
        userInput[1] : undefined
      )
      .subscribe(data => console.log(data))
  }
}
```

As you can see, most of the logic is implemented in the template; as such, you are required to maintain an active mental model of the template and the controller. Any changes to event handlers and validation logic require you to switch back and forth between the two files.

Furthermore, we have lost input limiting and the ability to prevent service calls when the input is in an invalid state. It is still possible to implement these features, but they require convoluted solutions and do not neatly fit into the new Angular syntax and concepts.

Overall, I do not recommend the use of template-driven forms. There may be a few instances where it may be very convenient to use the box of bananas syntax. However, this sets a bad precedent for other team members to replicate the same pattern around the application.

Component interaction with BehaviorSubject

To update the current weather information, we need the `city-search` component to interact with the `current-weather` component. There are four main techniques to enable component interaction in Angular:

- Global events
- Parent components listening for information bubbling up from children components
- Sibling, parent, or children components within a module that works off of similar data streams
- Parent components passing information to children components

Global events

This is a technique that's been leveraged since the early days of programming in general. In JavaScript, you may have achieved this with global function delegates or jQuery's event system. In AngularJS, you may have created a service and stored values in it.

In Angular, you can still create a root-level service, store values in it, use Angular's `EventEmitter` class, which is really meant for directives, or use an `rxjs/Subscription` to create a fancy messaging bus for yourself.

As a pattern, global events are open to rampant abuse and rather than helping to maintain a decoupled application architecture, it leads to a global state over time. A global state or even a localized state at the controller level, where functions read and write to variables in any given class, is enemy number one of writing maintainable and unit testable software.

Ultimately, if you're storing all your application data or routing all events in one service to enable component interaction, you're merely inventing a better mousetrap. This is an anti-pattern that should be avoided at all costs. In a later section, you will find that, essentially, we will still be using services to enable component interaction; however, I want to point out that there's a fine line that exists between a flexible architecture that enables decoupling and the global or centralized decoupling approach that does not scale well.

Child-parent relationships with event emitters

Your child component should be completely unaware of its parent. This is key to creating reusable components.

We can implement the communication between the city search component and the current weather component leveraging `AppComponent` as a parent element and let the `app` module controller orchestrate the data.

Commit your code now! In the next two sections you will be making code changes that you will need to discard.

Let's see how this implementation will look:

1. The `city-search` component exposes an `EventEmitter` through an `@Output` property:

    src/app/city-search/city-search.component.ts
    ```
    import { Component, OnInit, Output, EventEmitter } from '@angular/core'

    export class CitySearchComponent implements OnInit {
      @Output() searchEvent = new EventEmitter<string>()
    ```

```
...
this.search.valueChanges
  .pipe(debounceTime(1000))
  .subscribe((search Value: string) => {
    if (!this.search.invalid) {
      this.searchEvent.emit(searchValue)
    }
  })
...
}
```

2. The `app` component consumes that and calls the `weatherService`, setting the `currentWeather` variable:

   src/app/app.component.ts
   ```
   import { WeatherService } from './weather/weather.service'
   import { ICurrentWeather } from './interfaces'

   ...
   template: `
     ...
       <app-city-search (searchEvent)="doSearch($event)">
       </app-city-search>
     ...
   `,

   export class AppComponent {
     currentWeather: ICurrentWeather
     constructor(private weatherService: WeatherService) { }

     doSearch(searchValue) {
       const userInput = searchValue.split(',').map(s => s.trim())
       this.weatherService
         .getCurrentWeather(userInput[0], userInput.length > 1 ?
           userInput[1] : undefined
         )
         .subscribe(data => this.currentWeather = data)
     }
   }
   ```

> Note that we are binding to the `searchEvent` with the parenthesis syntax. The `$event` variable automatically captures the output from the event and passes it into the `doSearch` method.

Forms, Observables, and Subjects

We successfully bubbled the information up to the parent component, but we must also be able to pass it down to the `current-weather` component.

Parent-child relationships with input binding

By definition, your parent component will be aware of what child components it is working with. Since the `currentWeather` property is bound to the `current` property on the `current-weather` component, the results pass down to be displayed. This is achieved by creating an `@Input` property:

src/app/current-weather/current-weather.component.ts
```
import { Component, Input } from '@angular/core'
...
export class CurrentWeatherComponent implements OnInit {
  @Input() current: ICurrentWeather
  ...
}
```

> Note that the ngOnInit function of CurrentWeatherComponent is now superfluous and can be removed.

You can then update the `app` component to bind the data to `current` weather:

src/app/app.component.ts
```
template: `
  ...
  <app-current-weather [current]="currentWeather">
  </app-current-weather>
  ...
`
```

At this point, your code should work! Try searching for a city. If the `current-weather` component updates, then success!

The event emitter and input binding approach is appropriate in cases where you are creating well-coupled components or user controls and no outside data is being consumed. A good example might be adding forecast information to the `current-weather` component, as shown:

Figure 6.4: Weather forecast wireframe

Each day of the week can be implemented as a component that is repeated using *ngFor, and it will be perfectly reasonable for current-weather to retrieve and bind this information to its child component:

```
example
<app-mini-forecast
    *ngFor="let dailyForecast of forecastArray
    [forecast]="dailyForecast"
>
</app-mini-forecast>
```

In general, if you're working with data-driven components, the parent-child or child-parent communication pattern results in an inflexible architecture, making it very difficult to reuse or rearrange your components. A good example of the tight coupling is when we imported the weather service in app.component.ts. AppComponent should have no idea about the weather service; its only job is to layout several components. Given the ever-changing business requirements and design, this is an important lesson to keep in mind.

 Discard the changes you've made in the last two sections before moving on. We will instead be implementing an alternate solution.

Next, we cover a better way for two components to interact with each other without introducing additional coupling with subjects.

Sibling interactions with subjects

The main reason for components to interact is to send or receive updates to data either provided by the user or received from the server. In Angular, your services expose RxJS.Observable endpoints, which are data streams that your components can subscribe to. RxJS.Observer complements RxJS.Observable as a consumer of events emitted by Observable. RxJS.Subject brings the two sets of functionalities together in an easy to work with object.

You can essentially describe a stream that belongs to a particular set of data, such as the current weather data that is being displayed, with subjects:

```
example
import { Subject } from 'rxjs'
...
export class WeatherService implements IWeatherService {
  currentWeather$: Subject<ICurrentWeather>
  ...
}
```

`currentWeather$` is still a data stream and does not simply represent one data point. You can subscribe to changes to `currentWeather$` data using `subscribe`, or you can publish changes to it using `next` as follows:

```
example
currentWeather$.subscribe(data => (this.current = data))
currentWeather$.next(newData)
```

> Note the naming convention for the `currentWeather$` property, which is appended by $. This is the naming convention for properties that are observable.

The default behavior of `Subject` is very much like generic pub/sub mechanisms, such as jQuery events. However, in an asynchronous world where components are loaded or unloaded in unpredictable ways, using the default `Subject` is not very useful.

There are three advanced variants of subjects:

- `ReplaySubject` remembers and caches data points that occurred within the data stream so that a subscriber can replay old events at any given time.
- `BehaviorSubject` remembers only the last data point while continuing to listen for new data points.
- `AsyncSubject` is for one-time-only events that are not expected to reoccur.

`ReplaySubject` can have severe memory and performance implications on your application, so it should be used with care. In the case of `current-weather`, we are only interested in displaying the latest weather data received, but through user input or other events, we are open to receiving new data so that we can keep the `current-weather` component up to date. The `BehaviorSubject` would be the appropriate mechanism to meet these needs:

1. Add currentWeather$ as a read-only property to IWeatherService:

   src/app/weather/weather.service.ts
   ```
   import { BehaviorSubject, Observable } from 'rxjs'

   export interface IWeatherService {
     readonly currentWeather$: BehaviorSubject<ICurrentWeather>
     ...
   }
   ```

   currentWeather$ is declared as read-only because its BehaviorSubject should not be reassigned. Any updates to the value should be sent by calling the .next function on the property.

2. Define BehaviorSubject in WeatherService and set a default value:

   src/app/weather/weather.service.ts
   ```
   ...
   export class WeatherService implements IWeatherService {
     readonly currentWeather$ =
       new BehaviorSubject<ICurrentWeather>({
         city: '--',
         country: '--',
         date: Date.now(),
         image: '',
         temperature: 0,
         description: '',
       })
   ...
   }
   ```

3. Add a new function named updateCurrentWeather, which will trigger getCurrentWeather and update the value of currentWeather$:

   src/app/weather/weather.service.ts
   ```
   ...
   updateCurrentWeather(search: string | number,
     country?: string): void {
     this.getCurrentWeather(search, country)
       .subscribe(weather =>
         this.currentWeather$.next(weather)
       )
   }
   ...
   ```

4. Update `IWeatherService` with the new function so that it appears as follows:

   src/app/weather/weather.service.ts
   ```
   ...
   export interface IWeatherService {
     readonly currentWeather$: BehaviorSubject<ICurrentWeather>
     getCurrentWeather(city: string | number, country?: string):
       Observable<ICurrentWeather>
     getCurrentWeatherByCoords(coords: Coordinates):
       Observable<ICurrentWeather>
     updateCurrentWeather(
       search: string | number,
       country?: string
     ): void
   }
   ```

5. Update the `current-weather` component to subscribe to the new `BehaviorSubject`:

   src/app/current-weather/current-weather.component.ts
   ```
   ...
     ngOnInit() {
       this.weatherService.currentWeather$
         .subscribe(data => (this.current = data))
     }
   ...
   ```

6. In the `city-search` component, update the `getCurrentWeather` function call to utilize the new `updateCurrentWeather` function:

   src/app/city-search/city-search.component.ts
   ```
   ...
     this.weatherService.updateCurrentWeather(
       userInput[0],
       userInput.length > 1 ? userInput[1] : undefined
     )
   ...
   ```

7. Test your app in the browser; it should appear as follows:

Figure 6.5: Weather information for Bursa, Turkey

When you type in a new city, the component should update to include the current weather information for that city. We can move the **Add city search capability...** task to the **Done** column, as shown on our Kanban board:

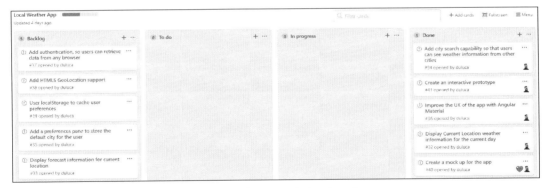

Figure 6.6: GitHub project Kanban board status

We have a functional app. However, we have introduced a memory leak, so let's fix that in the next section.

Managing subscriptions

Subscriptions are a convenient way to read a value from a data stream to be used in your application logic. If unmanaged, they can create memory leaks in your application. A leaky application will end up consuming ever-increasing amounts of RAM, eventually leading the browser tab to become unresponsive, leading to a negative perception of your app and, even worse, potential data loss, which can frustrate end users.

In the `current-weather` component, we inject `weatherSevice` so that we can access the `currentWeather$` component of `BehaviorSubject`. In Angular, services are singletons, meaning when they are first created in memory, they're kept alive as long as the module they're a part of is in memory. From a practical perspective, this will mean that most services in your application will live in the memory for the lifetime of the application. However, the lifetime of a component may be much shorter and there could be multiple instances of the same component created over and over again. If we don't manage the interactions between long-lived and short-lived objects carefully, we can end up with dangling references between objects, leading to memory leaks.

Exposé of a memory leak

When we subscribe to `currentWeather$`, we attach an event handler to it so that our component can react to value changes that are pushed to `BehaviorSubject`. This presents a problem when the `current-weather` component needs to be destroyed.

In managed languages such as JavaScript, memory is managed by the garbage collector, or GC for short, as opposed to having to allocate and deallocate memory by hand in unmanaged languages such as C or C++. At a very high level, the GC works by periodically scanning the stack for objects that are not referenced by other objects.

If an object is found to be dereferenced, then the space it takes up in the stack can be freed up. However, if an unused object still has a reference to another object that is still in use, it can't be garbage collected. The GC is not magical and can't read our minds. When an object is unused and can't be deallocated, the memory taken up by the object can never be used for another purpose so long as your application is running. This is considered a memory leak.

My colleague, Brendon Caulkins, provides a helpful analogy:

> *Imagine the memory space of the browser as a parking lot; every time we assign a value or create a subscription, we park a car in that lot. If we happen to abandon a car, we still leave the parking spot occupied; no one else can use it. If all the applications in the browser do this, or we do it repeatedly, you can imagine how quickly the parking lot is full, and we never get to run our application.*

Next, let's see how we can ensure that we don't abandon our car in the parking lot.

Unsubscribing from a subscription

Subscriptions or event handlers create references to other objects, such as from a short-lived component to a long-lived service. Granted, in our case, the `current-weather` component is also a singleton, but that could change if we added more features to the app, navigating from page to page or displaying weather from multiple cities at once. If we don't unsubscribe from `currentWeather$`, then any instance of `current-weather` would be stuck in memory. We subscribe in `ngOnInit`, so we must unsubscribe in `ngOnDestroy`. `ngOnDestroy` is called when Angular determines that the framework is no longer using the component.

Let's see an example of how you can unsubscribe from a subscription in the sample code in the following:

```
example
import { ..., OnDestroy } from '@angular/core'
import { ..., Subscription } from 'rxjs'

export class CurrentWeatherComponent implements OnInit, OnDestroy {
  currentWeatherSubscription: Subscription
  ...
  ngOnInit() {
    this.currentWeatherSubscription =
      this.weatherService.currentWeather$
        .subscribe((data) => (this.current = data))
  }

  ngOnDestroy(): void {
    this.currentWeatherSubscription.unsubscribe()
  }
...
```

First, we need to implement the `OnDestroy` interface for the component. Then, we update `ngOnInit` to store a reference to the subscription in a property named `currentWeatherSubscription`. Finally, in `ngOnDestroy`, we can call the `unsubscribe` method.

Should our component get destroyed, it will no longer result in a memory leak. However, if we have multiple subscriptions in a given component, this can lead to tedious amounts of coding.

Note that in `city-search`, we subscribe to the `valueChanges` event of a `FormControl` object. We don't need to manage the subscription to this event, because `FormControl` is a child object of our component. When the parent component is dereferenced from all objects, all of its children can be safely collected by the GC.

Let's now look at a better way to manage multiple subscriptions.

Unsubscribing using SubSink

SubSink, published by Ward Bell, is a straightforward library to keep track of all subscriptions in a given class, whether it be a component or a service.

Add the SubSink package to your Angular project:

```
$ npm i subsink
```

Next, update `current-weather` to use SubSink, replacing `currentWeatherSubscription`:

```
src/app/current-weather/current-weather.component.ts
import { ..., OnDestroy } from '@angular/core'
import { SubSink } from 'subsink'

export class CurrentWeatherComponent implements OnInit, OnDestroy {
  private subscriptions = new SubSink()
  ...
  ngOnInit(): void {
    this.subscriptions.add(
      this.weatherService.currentWeather$
        .subscribe((data) => (this.current = data))
    )
  }

  ngOnDestroy(): void {
    this.subscriptions.unsubscribe()
  }
  ...
```

In the preceding code sample, we instantiated a private `subscriptions` object, which will serve as the sink to contain all of the subscriptions. Then, in `ngOnInit`, we simply add the subscription to `currentWeather$` to the sink. In `ngOnDestroy`, we call `unsubscribe` on the sink rather than an individual subscription.

This is a scalable approach, as the amount of boilerplate code we must write remains consistent, as you can add many subscriptions to the sink without additional coding.

Subscribing to values in data streams itself can be considered an anti-pattern because you switch your programming model from reactive to imperative. In addition, you could avoid having to manage subscriptions in the first place. We will cover this topic in the next section.

Implementing the reactive style

As covered in *Chapter 1, Introduction to Angular and Its Concepts*, we should only subscribe to an observable stream to activate it. If we treat a `subscribe` function as an event handler, then we're implementing our code imperatively.

 Seeing anything other than an empty `.subscribe()` call in your code base should be considered a sign of ditching reactive programming.

In reactive programming, when you subscribe to an event in a reactive stream, then you're shifting your coding paradigm from reactive programming to imperative programming. There are two places in our application where we subscribe, once in `current-weather`, and the other in the `city-search` component.

Let's start by fixing `current-weather`, so that we don't drop back into imperative programming.

Binding to an observable with an async pipe

Angular has been designed to be an asynchronous framework from the ground up. You can get the most out of Angular by staying in the reactive programming realm. It can feel unnatural to do so at first, but Angular provides all the tools you need to reflect the current state of your application to the user without having to shift to imperative programming.

You may leverage the `async` pipe in your templates to reflect the current value of an observable. Let's update the `current-weather` component to use the `async` pipe:

1. Start by replacing `current: ICurrentWeather` with an observable property: `current$: Observable<ICurrentWeather>`.
2. In the constructor, assign `weatherService.currentWeather$` to `current$`:

   `src/app/current-weather/current-weather.component.ts`

Forms, Observables, and Subjects

```
import { Observable } from 'rxjs'
export class CurrentWeatherComponent {
  current$: Observable<ICurrentWeather>

  constructor(private weatherService: WeatherService) {
    this.current$ = this.weatherService.currentWeather$
  }
  ...
```

3. Remove all code related to `SubSink`, `ngOnInit`, and `ngOnDestroy`.
4. Update the template to so you can bind to `current$`:

   src/app/current-weather/current-weather.component.html
   ```
   <div *ngIf="current$ | async as current">
   ...
   </div>
   ```

   The `async` pipe automatically subscribes to the current value of `current$` and makes it available to the template to be used in an imperative manner as the variable `current`. The beauty of this approach is that the `async` pipe implicitly manages the subscription, so you don't have to worry about unsubscribing.

5. Remove `<div *ngIf="!current">`. This is no longer needed, because the `BehaviorSubject` is always initialized.

So far, the reactive style allowed us to streamline and clean up our code.

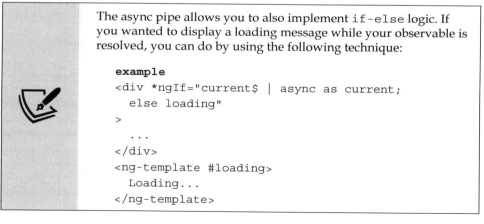

> The async pipe allows you to also implement if-else logic. If you wanted to display a loading message while your observable is resolved, you can do by using the following technique:
>
> **example**
> ```
> <div *ngIf="current$ | async as current;
>   else loading"
> >
>   ...
> </div>
> <ng-template #loading>
>   Loading...
> </ng-template>
> ```

Next, let's further improve our code.

Tapping into an observable stream

The `city-search` component implements a callback within a `subscribe` statement when firing the `search` function. This leads to an imperative style of coding and mindset. The danger with switching programming paradigms is that you can introduce unintentional side effects to your code, making it easier to introduce errors or state into your application.

Let's refactor `city-search.component.ts` to be in the reactive functional programming style, as shown in the following example:

```
src/app/city-search/city-search.component.ts
import { debounceTime, filter, tap } from 'rxjs/operators'

export class CitySearchComponent {
  search = new FormControl('',
    [Validators.required, Validators.minLength(2)])

  constructor(private weatherService: WeatherService) {
    this.search.valueChanges
      .pipe(
        debounceTime(1000),
        filter(() => !this.search.invalid),
        tap((searchValue: string) => this.doSearch(searchValue))
      )
      .subscribe()
  }

  doSearch(searchValue: string) {
    const userInput = searchValue.split(',').map(s => s.trim())
    const searchText = userInput[0]
    const country = userInput.length > 1 ? userInput[1] : undefined
    this.weatherService.updateCurrentWeather(searchText, country)
  }
}
```

In the preceding code, we removed the `OnInit` implementation and implemented our filtering logic reactively. The `tap` operator will only get triggered if `this.search` is valid. In addition, `doSearch` is called in a functional context, making it very difficult to reference any other class property within the function.

Forms, Observables, and Subjects

This reduces the chances of the state of the class impacting the outcome of our function. As a result, `doSearch` is a composable and unit testable function, whereas in the previous implementation, it would have been very challenging to unit test `ngOnInit` in a straightforward manner.

> Note that `.subscribe()` must be called on `valueChanges` to activate the observable data stream, otherwise no event will fire.

The fact that we don't implement `ngOnInit` reflects the truly asynchronous nature of our code, which is independent of the life cycle or state of the application.

With our refactoring complete, the app should function the same as before, but with less boilerplate code. Now, let's look into enhancing our app so that it can handle postal codes from any country.

Multiple API calls

Currently, our app can only handle 5-digit numerical postal or zip codes from the US. A postal code such as `22201` is easy to differentiate from a city name with a simplistic conditional such as `typeof search === 'string'`. However, postal codes can vary widely from country to country, Great Britain being a great example with postal codes such as `EC2R 6AB`. Even if we had a perfect understanding of how postal codes are formatted for every country on earth, we still couldn't ensure that the user didn't fat-finger a slightly incorrect postal code. Today's sophisticated users expect web applications to be resilient toward such mistakes.

> After the first edition of this book was published, I received some passionate reader feedback on their disappointment that the sample app can only support US zip codes. I've decided to implement this feature because it demonstrates the degree to which such seemingly simple requests can introduce unplanned complexity to your apps. As a bonus, the app now works worldwide 😊

Let's add a new item, **Support international zip codes**, to the backlog and move it to **In progress**:

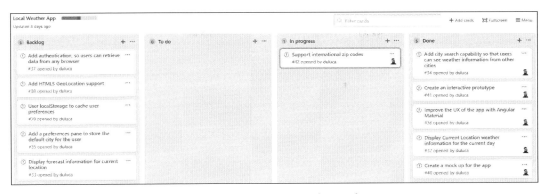

Figure 6.7: Adding an international zip codes story

Implementing a postal code service

To properly understand if the user inputs a valid postal code versus the name of a city, we must rely on a third-party API call provided by geonames.org. Let's see how we can inject a secondary API call into the search logic of our app.

> You need to sign up for a free account on geonames.org. Afterward, store your username as a new parameter in environment.ts and environment.prod.ts.

You may experiment with a postal code API on this page: https://www.geonames.org/postal-codes.

Start by implementing a PostalCodeService, as shown in the following:

> You may generate the service by executing npx ng generate service postalCode --project=local-weather-app --no-flat --lintFix.

src/app/postal-code/postal-code.service.ts
```
import { HttpClient, HttpParams } from '@angular/common/http'
import { Injectable } from '@angular/core'
import { Observable } from 'rxjs'
import { defaultIfEmpty, flatMap } from 'rxjs/operators'
import { environment } from '../../environments/environment'

export interface IPostalCode {
```

Forms, Observables, and Subjects

```
    countryCode: string
    postalCode: string
    placeName: string
    lng: number
    lat: number
}

export interface IPostalCodeData {
  postalCodes: [IPostalCode]
}

export interface IPostalCodeService {
  resolvePostalCode(postalCode: string): Observable<IPostalCode>
}

@Injectable({
  providedIn: 'root',
})
export class PostalCodeService implements IPostalCodeService {
  constructor(private httpClient: HttpClient) {}

  resolvePostalCode(postalCode: string): Observable<IPostalCode> {
    const uriParams = new HttpParams()
      .set('maxRows', '1')
      .set('username', environment.username)
      .set('postalcode', postalCode)

    return this.httpClient
      .get<IPostalCodeData>(
        `${environment.baseUrl}${environment.geonamesApi}.geonames.org/postalCodeSearchJSON`,
        { params: uriParams }
      )
      .pipe(
        flatMap(data => data.postalCodes),
        defaultIfEmpty(null)
      )
  }
}
```

Note the new environment variable, `environment.geonamesApi`. In `environment.ts`, set this value to `api` and, in `environment.prod.ts`, to `secure`, so calls over https work correctly to avoid the mixed-content error, as covered in *Chapter 4, Automated Testing, CI, and Release to Production*.

In the preceding code segment, we implement a `resolvePostalCode` function that makes a call to an API, which is configured to receive the first viable result the API returns. The results are then flattened and piped out to the subscriber. With `defaultIfEmpty`, we ensure that a null value will be provided if we don't receive a result from the API. If the call is successful, we will get back all the information defined in `IPostalCode`, making it possible to leverage `getCurrentWeatherByCoords` using coordinates.

Chaining API calls

Let's update the weather service so that it can call the `postalCode` service to determine whether the user input was a valid postal code:

1. Start by updating the interface, so we only deal with a string:

   src/app/weather/weather.service.ts
   ```
   ...
   export interface IWeatherService {
   ...
     getCurrentWeather(search: string, country?: string):
       Observable<ICurrentWeather>
     updateCurrentWeather(search: string, country?: string)
   }
   ```

2. Inject `PostalCodeService` to the weather service as a private property:

   src/app/weather/weather.service.ts
   ```
   import {
     PostalCodeService
   } from '../postal-code/postal-code.service'
   ...
   constructor(
     private httpClient: HttpClient,
     private postalCodeService: PostalCodeService
   ) {}
   ```

3. Update the method signature for `updateCurrentWeather`

4. Update `getCurrentWeather` to try and resolve `searchText` as a postal code:

   src/app/weather/weather.service.ts
   ```
   import { map, switchMap } from 'rxjs/operators'
   ...
   getCurrentWeather(
     searchText: string,
     country?: string
   ): Observable<ICurrentWeather> {
     return this.postalCodeService.
       resolvePostalCode(searchText)
         .pipe(
   ```

```
      switchMap((postalCode) => {
        if (postalCode) {
          return this.getCurrentWeatherByCoords({
            latitude: postalCode.lat,
            longitude: postalCode.lng,
          } as Coordinates)
        } else {
          const uriParams = new HttpParams().set(
            'q',
            country ? `${searchText},${country}` : searchText
          )
          return this.getCurrentWeatherHelper(uriParams)
        }
      })
    )
  }
```

 If you run into TypeScript issues when passing the latitude and longitude into getCurrentWeatherByCoords, then you may have to cast the object using the as operator. So, your code would look like:
```
return this.getCurrentWeatherByCoords({
    latitude: postalCode.lat,
    longitude: postalCode.lng,
} as Coordinates)
```

In the preceding code segment, our first call is to the postalCode service. We then react to postal codes that are posted on the data stream using switchMap. Inside switchMap, we can observe whether postalCode is null and make the appropriate follow-up call to either get the current weather by coordinates or by city name.

Now, LocalCast weather should work with global postal codes, as shown in the following screenshot:

Figure 6.8: LocalCast Weather with global postal codes

We are done with implementing international zip code support. Move it to the **Done** column on your Kanban board:

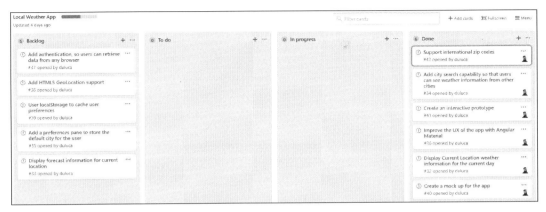

Figure 6.9: International zip code support done

As we complete our implementation of LocalCast Weather, there's still room for improvement. Initially, the app looks broken when it first loads, because of the dashes and empty fields that are shown. There are at least two different ways to handle this. The first is to hide the entire component, at the app component level, if there's no data to display. For this to work, we will have to inject `weatherService` into the app component, ultimately leading to a less flexible solution. Another way is to enhance the `current-weather` component so that it is better able to handle missing data.

You improve the app further by implementing geolocation to get the weather for the user's current location upon launching the app. You can also leverage `window.localStorage` to store the city that was last displayed or the last location that was retrieved from `window.geolocation` upon initial launch.

We are done with the Local Weather app until *Chapter 12, Recipes — Master/Detail, Data Tables, and NgRx*, where I demonstrate how NgRx compares to using RxJS/BehaviorSubject.

Summary

In this chapter, you learned how to create a search-as-you-type functionality using `MatInput`, validators, reactive forms, and data stream-driven handlers. You became aware of two-way binding and template-driven forms. You also learned about different strategies to enable inter-component interactions and data sharing. You dove into understanding how memory leaks can be created and the importance of managing your subscriptions.

You are now better able to differentiate between imperative and reactive programming styles and the importance of sticking with reactive programming where possible. Finally, you learned how you can implement sophisticated functionality by chaining multiple API calls together.

LocalCast Weather is a straightforward application that we used to cover the basic concepts of Angular. As you saw, Angular is great for building such small and dynamic applications, while delivering a minimal amount of framework code to the end user. You should consider leveraging Angular for even quick and dirty projects, which is also a great practice when building larger applications. In the next chapter, you will be creating a far more complicated **line-of-business** (**LOB**) application, using a router-first approach to designing and architecting scalable Angular applications with first-class authentication and authorization, user experience, and numerous recipes that cover a vast majority of requirements that you may find in LOB applications.

Exercises

After completing the **Support international zip codes** feature, did we switch coding paradigms here? Is our implementation above imperative, reactive, or a combination of both? If our implementation is not entirely reactive, how would you implement this function reactively? I leave this as an exercise for the reader.

Don't forget to execute `npm test`, `npm run e2e`, and `npm run test:a11y` before moving on. It is left as an exercise for the reader to fix the unit and end-to-end tests.

Visit GitHub to see the unit tests that I implemented for this chapter at `https://github.com/duluca/local-weather-app/tree/master/projects/ch6`.

Questions

Answer the following questions as best as you can to ensure that you've understood the key concepts from this chapter without Googling. Do you need help answering the questions? See *Appendix D, Self-Assessment Answers* online at `https://static.packt-cdn.com/downloads/9781838648800_Appendix_D_Self-Assessment_Answers.pdf` or visit `https://expertlysimple.io/angular-self-assessment`.

1. What is the `async` pipe?
2. Explain how reactive and imperative programming is different and which technique we should prefer?
3. What is the benefit of a BehaviorSubject, and what is it used for?
4. What are memory leaks and why should they be avoided?

7
Creating a Router-First Line-of-Business App

Line-of-Business (LOB) applications are the bread and butter of the software development world. As defined on Wikipedia, LOB is a general term that refers to a product or a set of related products that serve a particular customer transaction, or business need. LOB apps present an excellent opportunity to demonstrate a variety of features and functionality, without getting into the contorted or specialized scenarios that large enterprise applications usually need to address.

The Pareto principle, also known as the 80-20 rule, states that we can accomplish 80% of our goals with 20% of the overall effort. We will be applying the 80-20 rule to the design and architecture of our LOB app. Given the common use cases LOB apps cover, they are, in a sense, perfect for the 80-20 learning experience. With only 20% of the effort, you can learn about 80% of the things you will need to deliver high-quality experiences to your users.

LOB apps have a curious property to them. If you end up building a semi-useful app, the demand for it grows, uncontrollably, and you quickly become the victim of your success. It's challenging to balance the architectural needs of a project; you want to avoid potentially devastating under-engineering and, on the flip side, also avoid costly over-engineering for an app that will never need it.

In this chapter, I'm going to introduce you to router-first architecture, the 80-20 design solution to address the challenges of delivering a modern web application in an incremental and iterative manner.

As you read in *Chapter 1, Introduction to Angular and Its Concepts*, software architecture doesn't stay static. It's essential to experiment with new ideas by using coding-katas, proofs-of-concept apps, and reference projects, to get better at creating more flexible architectures.

In this and the remaining chapters of the book, we'll set up a new application with rich features that can meet the demands of an LOB application with a scalable architecture and engineering best practices that will help you start small and be able to grow your solution quickly if there's demand. We will follow the Router-first design pattern, relying on reusable components to create a grocery store LOB named LemonMart. We'll discuss the idea of designing around major data entities, and the importance of completing high-level mock-ups for your application before you start to implement various conditional navigation elements, which may change significantly during the design phase.

In this chapter, you will learn to do the following:

- Apply the 80-20 solution to software development
- Learn how to build router-first apps
- Begin your creation of the LemonMart app you'll expand over the remainder of this book
- Create effective branding, as well as custom and material iconography
- Achieve sub-second first-paint with lazy loading
- Create a walking skeleton
- Reduce repetition using a common testing module
- Design around major data entities
- Recognize the importance of high-level UX design

The most up-to-date versions of the sample code for the book are on GitHub at the following linked repository. The repository contains the final and completed state of the code. You can verify your progress at the end of this chapter by looking for the end-of-chapter snapshot of code under the `projects` folder.

For *Chapter 7*:

1. Clone the repo `https://github.com/duluca/lemon-mart`
2. Execute `npm install` on the root folder to install dependencies
3. The code sample for this chapter is under the sub-folder: `projects/ch7`

4. To run the Angular app for this chapter, execute:

   `npx ng serve ch7`

5. To run Angular unit tests for this chapter, execute:

   `npx ng test ch7 --watch=false`

6. To run Angular e2e tests for this chapter, execute:

   `npx ng e2e ch7`

7. To build a production-ready Angular app for this chapter, execute:

   `npx ng build ch7 --prod`

Note that the `dist/ch7` folder at the root of the repository will contain the compiled result.

Beware that the source code in the book or on GitHub may not always match the code generated by the Angular CLI. There may also be slight differences in implementation between the code in the book and what's on GitHub, because the ecosystem is ever-evolving. It is natural for the sample code to change over time.

Also, on GitHub, expect to find corrections, fixes to support newer versions of libraries, or side-by-side implementations of multiple techniques for you to observe. You are only expected to implement the ideal solution recommended in the book. If you find errors or have questions, please create an issue or submit a pull request on GitHub for the benefit of all readers.

You may read more about updating Angular in *Appendix C, Keeping Angular and Tools Evergreen*. You can find this appendix online from `https://static.packt-cdn.com/downloads/9781838648800_Appendix_C_Keeping_Angular_and_Tools_Evergreen.pdf` or at `https://expertlysimple.io/stay-evergreen`.

Let's start by covering the philosophy behind the design and architecture of our apps.

The 80-20 solution

Whether we develop apps at home, for passion projects, or at the office, for work, we must remain mindful of our purpose: to deliver value. If we don't deliver value with our passion projects, then we won't feel fulfilled or happy. If we fail to deliver value at work, we may not get paid.

Delivering a modern web application is difficult. There are numerous challenges that we need to overcome to be successful:

- Deliver iteratively and incrementally
- Be scalable
- Serve dozens of screen and input types
- Be usable
- Be accessible
- Manage a team
- Groom a prioritized backlog
- Ensure acceptance criteria are clear, concise, and concrete

If you've ever led a project or tried to implement and deliver a project on your own, you'll have realized that there's just never enough time and resources to cover the wide variety of stakeholder, team, and technical needs on any given project. Remember that the Pareto principle, also known as the 80-20 rule, implies that we can accomplish 80% of our goals with 20% of the overall effort.

If we apply the 80-20 rule to our work, we can maximize our output, quality, and happiness. Line-of-business applications are the bread and butter of our industry. Applying the 80-20 rule, we can surmise that most of us are likely to earn most of our income by delivering such applications. Therefore, we should keep our engineering overhead to a minimum, and reduce the delivery risk of our project. By limiting experimentation in production code, we create a predictable environment for our team members, and only introduce changes that we had a chance to vet in proof-of-concept or small apps.

Our 80-20 strategy, combined with discipline, can help us deliver the same project in the same time with more features and better quality. By treating our careers as marathons and not a series of sprints, you can find yourself in a position of delivering high-quality solutions, project after project, without feeling burned out.

Understanding Line-of-Business apps

Line-of-business applications are, according to Wikipedia, a "set of critical computer applications perceived as vital to running an enterprise." LOB apps are what most developers end up developing, even though we may think we develop small apps or large enterprise apps. Consider the following illustration, which demonstrates the kinds of apps we might develop, placed on an axis relative to their size and scope:

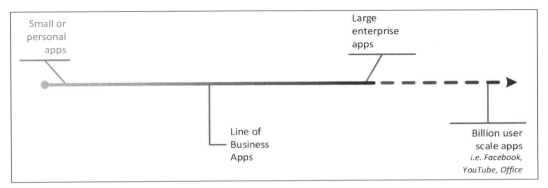

Figure 7.1: Relative size and scope of four kinds of apps

From my perspective, we think about four kinds of apps when we begin developing software:

- Small apps
- LOB apps
- Large enterprise apps
- Billion user scale apps

Billion user scale apps are completely niche implementations that rarely have needs that align with the vast majority of apps that are out there. For this reason, we must classify these apps as outliers.

Small apps start small. Architecturally, they're likely to be initially under-engineered. As you add features and team members to work on a small app, at some point, you're going to run into trouble. As your team size and feature set grow, or the overall complexity of the app increases, the architectural needs of the application grow exponentially.

Once you cross the inflection point of the amount of complexity your architecture can bear, you're left with a costly reengineering effort to get back on track. See the following graph, illustrating this idea:

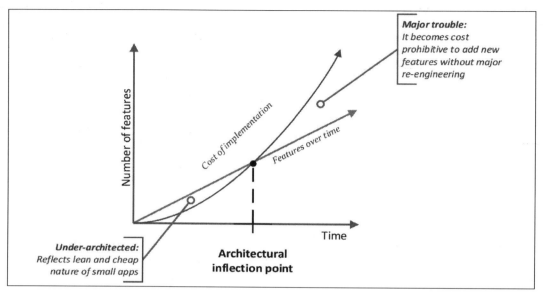

Figure 7.2: Architectural journey of a small app

The area under the feature line represents under-engineering, which introduces risk to your project. The area above the feature line shows the required engineering overhead to support the features needed. In comparison, large enterprise apps start with a massive over-engineering effort, as shown in the following diagram:

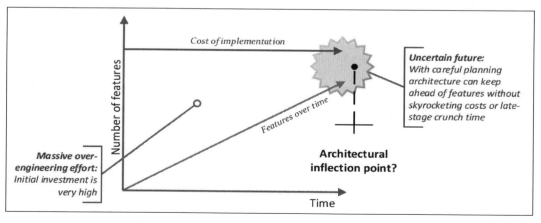

Figure 7.3: Architectural journey of a large enterprise app

As time goes on and the overall complexity of the system increases, large enterprise apps can also face a similar inflection point, where the original architecture can become inadequate. With careful planning and management, you can avoid trouble and protect the significant initial investment made. Such large enterprise apps require hundreds of developers, with multiple levels of managers and architects, to execute successfully. Similar to billion-user scale apps, these apps can also have niche architectural needs. In between the small apps and the large enterprise apps that we develop lie LOB apps.

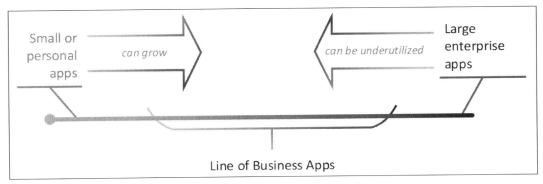

Figure 7.4: Dynamic nature of software evolution

As shown in the preceding diagram, small apps can grow and morph into LOB apps, and large enterprise apps can become under-utilized as users ignore the features that they never need, but keep the app to serve a singular purpose as a LOB app. In either case, despite our best efforts, we ultimately end up delivering an inefficient solution for the problem we're solving. None of us have a crystal ball to see the future, and planning and engineering can only do so much for us in an unpredictable business setting; we need to rely on the 80-20 rule to come up with an architecture that is flexible to change, but adequate to meet most business requirements.

Router-first architecture aims to maintain optimal architectural overhead, so that in the rush to deliver all required features, costly re-engineering or late-stage crunch can be avoided. Let's see how.

Disciplined and balanced approach

We covered the *what* of software development, but we must also consider the *why*, *when*, *where*, and *who*, before we can get to the *how*. When we develop apps for learning or passion projects, we usually end up under-engineering our projects. If your passion project somehow becomes an overnight success, then it becomes costly to maintain or keep adding features to your app. In this case, you're likely to face a choice to either bear the cost of ongoing maintenance, or rewrite your application.

When we develop apps for work, we tend to be more conservative, and we're likely to over-engineer our solution. However, if you only code for work, then you're likely to experiment in production-bound code. It is dangerous to experiment in a codebase with other team members. You may be introducing a new pattern, without your team understanding the consequences of your choices. You're also less likely to be aware of mid-to long-term risks or benefits of the technologies you are introducing.

Reckless experimentation can also have a severe negative impact on your team members. In a team of senior and experienced software engineers, you can likely get away with experimenting in a moving car. However, we are likely to have team members of varying backgrounds and learning styles on our teams. Some of us have computer science degrees, some of us are lone wolves, and some of us depend a bit too much on Stack Overflow. Some of us work at companies that are great at supporting professional growth, but some of us work at places that won't even give you a day to learn something new. So, when we are experimenting, we must consider our environment; otherwise we can cause our colleagues to work overtime or feel helpless and frustrated.

With a disciplined and balanced approach, we can reduce the number of bugs delivered, avoid costly rework, and work with a group of people who are all moving in the same direction. We also need the right architecture, tools, and patterns/practices to deliver successfully. In summary, our approach must consider:

- The size of our app
- The reason we are developing the app
- The skill level of developers
- Iterative and incremental delivery
- Constant forward flow of features
- All the cloud things

Ideally, we need to maintain optimal engineering overhead. Our architecture should support our short-term needs while being extensible, so we can pivot in different directions if our mid-or long-term needs change without having to rewrite large swaths of code. Consider the following diagram, in contrast to the ones about small and large enterprise apps in the previous section:

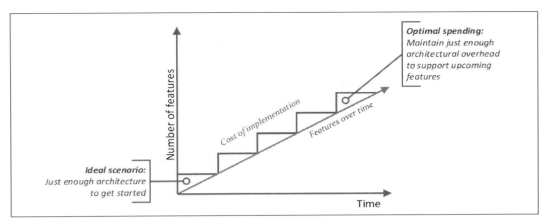

Figure 7.5: Ideal architectural journey of a LOB app

Router-first architecture aims to help you find the balance in the engineering overhead, feature delivery, and flexibility of your codebase. However, you must bring the discipline yourself.

> 守破離 or Shu Ha Ri is a concept that can help bring discipline to your work. It is a way of thinking that instructs you first to master the basics without worrying about the underlying theory, then master the theory, and finally be able to adapt what you mastered to your needs. However, if you skip steps 1 or 2, you are going to find yourself adapting the wrong thing in the wrong way.

Having covered the *what*, *why*, *when*, *where*, and *who*, let's jump into the *how* in the next section.

Router-first architecture

Router-first architecture is a way to:

- **Enforce** high-level thinking
- **Ensure** consensus on features, *before* you start coding
- **Plan** for your codebase/team to grow
- **Introduce** little engineering overhead

There are seven steps to implementing router-first architecture:

1. Develop a roadmap and scope (*Chapter 7*)
2. Design with lazy loading in mind (*Chapter 7*)
3. Implement a walking-skeleton navigation experience (*Chapter 7*)
4. Achieve a stateless, data-driven design (*Chapters 7* and *10*)
5. Enforce a decoupled component architecture (*Chapters 8*, *11*, and *12*)
6. Differentiate between user controls and components (*Chapter 11*)
7. Maximize code reuse with TypeScript and ES features (*Chapters 8*, *10*, *11*, and *12*)

Each step will be covered in more detail in this and coming chapters, as noted previously. Before we go over these steps at a high level, let's first cover feature modules in Angular, which are an important fundamental technical concept.

Feature modules

In *Chapter 1, Introduction to Angular and Its Concepts*, we covered Angular's architecture at a high level and introduced the concepts of lazy loading and routing. Feature modules are a key component in implementing lazy loading. There are two kinds of modules, the root module and feature modules. Modules are implemented by the class `NgModule`. An `NgModule` contains all the necessary metadata to render components and inject services. A component without a module doesn't do much.

An Angular application is defined by an `NgModule` that sits at the root of the application. This is called the root module. The root module is responsible for rendering what appears in the `<app-root>` element in your `index.html` file. Locate the root module in the following diagram:

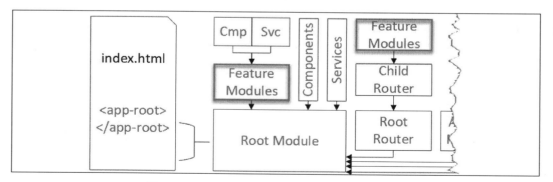

Figure 7.6: Major architectural components of Angular

An NgModule can contain many other NgModules. An Angular app only has one root module, so by definition every other NgModule becomes a feature module. In the preceding diagram, you can see that you can organize a group of components (**Cmp**) and services (**Svc**) into feature modules. Grouping functionality into modules allows us to organize our code into chunks, which can be separated from the initial payload of our application.

This idea of root and feature modules represents a parent/child relationship, which is a concept that extends to other functionality and frameworks. For example, note that the preceding diagram injects a root router into the root module. A root router can have child routes. Child routes can be configured to load feature modules. Similarly, NgRx has root and feature module-level stores to organize the state data of your application.

For all intents and purposes, any mention of a sub-module, child module, or a feature module in this book refers to the same thing: a module that is not the root module.

Feature modules and child routes allows for a separation of concerns between major components of your application. Two teams can work on two different modules without interfering with each other. This separation means that any dependency required by a feature module must be explicitly added to the imports, declarations, or providers of that module. This can seem repetitive and annoying, when sharing code between modules, but it is a necessary evil.

In Angular, by default, services are singletons – one instance per module. Before importing a service that's already imported to the root module into a feature module, consider if this is truly the desired behavior. A service that is provided in the root module is available to be imported in a feature module without needing to be provided again. Providing a service in the root and feature modules will result in having multiple instances of that service in memory, which breaks your expectation that, by default, services are singletons. In *Chapter 8, Designing Authentication and Authorization*, you will see this in action when we implement the `AuthService`.

With the introduction of the Ivy rendering engine in Angular 9, the road is paved to create self-describing components. Self-describing components do not need an NgModule to be useful. With future versions of Angular it will be possible to implement simple apps without the whole ceremony (read: boilerplate code) of modules.

Now, let's go over the seven steps of router-first architecture at a high level.

Developing a roadmap and scope

Developing a roadmap and establishing the scope of your project early on is critical to getting the high-level architecture right. Creating a backlog, wireframes, mock-ups and interactive prototypes will help you define the map before getting on the road and capture the vision concretely. It is important to remember to bring tools only when necessary. Don't start with Photoshop, when a piece of paper and a pencil will do. If stakeholders and team members understand what is being developed, then it will be possible to deliver your solution iteratively and incrementally. However, don't fall into the perfection trap. Save the tweaking and furniture rearranging for after the fundamentals are in place and agreed upon.

Document every artifact you create. Later in the chapter we cover how you can leverage GitHub Wikis to store your artifacts.

Later in this chapter, we will go over how to develop a roadmap and a technique to define your scope, building on the roadmap building techniques covered in *Chapter 3, Creating a Basic Angular App*.

Designing with lazy loading in mind

First-paint matters, a lot! According to Google Analytics data gathered by the Angular Team in 2018, 53% of mobile users abandoned a website when load times exceeded 3 seconds. During the same time period most websites were consumed on mobile devices, around 70%+ in the US and 90%+ in China. As we covered in *Chapter 5, Delivering High-Quality UX with Material*, UI libraries and static assets can add significant size to your application. Given that most content is consumed on mobile, it's very important to defer the loading of non-critical assets.

We defer loading of assets by divvying up the parts of our Angular application into feature modules. This way Angular can load only the assets that are necessary to render the current screen and dynamically download further resources as they are needed. A good way to divide your application into feature modules is by defining the various user roles your application may use. User roles normally indicate the job function of a user, such as a manager or data-entry specialist. In technical terms, they can be thought of as a group of actions that a particular class of user is allowed to execute. After all, a data-entry specialist won't ever see most of the screens that a manager can, so why deliver those assets to those users and slow down their experience?

Lazy loading is critical in creating a scalable application architecture, allowing you to deliver high-quality and efficient products. Lazy loading is a low-hanging fruit that we will tackle as a baseline design goal. It can be costly to implement lazy loading after the fact.

Starting with Angular 9, it is possible to lazy load individual components. Angular 9's Ivy rendering engine enables self-describing and standalone components. Components that do not require all the bootstrapping that an Angular application requires have the potential to revolutionize and simplify how we design applications. However, it is not yet feasible to design apps this way. Expect future versions of Angular to introduce public APIs that make it easy to use the new features, reducing the need to carefully design feature modules early on.

Later in this chapter, you will learn about how to implement lazy loading using feature modules.

Implementing a walking-skeleton

Configuring lazy loading can be tricky, which is why it is essential to nail down a walking-skeleton navigation experience early on. Implementing a clickable version of your app will help you gather feedback from users early on. That way, you'll be able to work out fundamental workflow and integration issues quickly. Additionally, you'll be able to establish a concrete representation of the scope of your current development effort. Developers and stakeholders alike will be able to better visualize how the end product will look.

A walking-skeleton also sets the stage for multiple teams to work in tandem. Multiple people can start developing different feature modules or components at the same time, without worrying about how the puzzle pieces are going to come together later on. By the end of this chapter, you will have completed implementing the walking-skeleton of the sample app LemonMart.

Achieve a stateless, data-driven design

As highlighted in *Chapter 10*, *RESTful APIs and Full-Stack Implementation*, stateless design in full-stack architecture is critical to implementing a maintainable application. As covered in *Chapter 1*, *Introduction to Angular and Its Concepts*, and later in *Chapter 12*, *Recipes – Master/Detail, Data Tables, and NgRx*, the flux pattern and NgRx make it possible to achieve an immutable state for your application. However, the flux pattern is likely to be overkill for most applications. NgRx itself leverages a lot of the core technologies present in RxJS.

We are going to use RxJS and the reactive programming paradigm to implement a minimal, stateless, and data-driven pattern for our application. Identifying major data entities, such as invoices or people, that your users will work with is going to help you avoid over-engineering your application. Designing around major data entities will inform API design early on, and help define `BehaviorSubject` data anchors that you will use to achieve a stateless, data-driven design. That design will, in turn, ensure a decoupled component architecture, as detailed in *Chapter 6, Forms, Observables, and Subjects*.

By defining observable data anchors, you can ensure that data across various components will be kept in sync. By writing functional reactive code, leveraging RxJS features, and not storing state in components, we can implement immutable data streams.

We will cover how to design the data models for your application in *Chapter 10, RESTful APIs and Full-Stack Implementation*, and will continue using these models in the following chapters.

Enforce a decoupled component architecture

As we discussed in *Chapter 1, Introduction to Angular and Its Concepts*, decoupling components of your architecture is critical in ensuring a maintainable codebase. In Angular, you can decouple components by leveraging `@Input` and `@Output` bindings and Router orchestration.

Bindings will help you maintain a simple hierarchy of components, and avoid using dynamic templates in situations where static designs are more effective, such as the creation of multi-page forms.

Router outlets and auxiliary paths allow you to compose your view using the router. Resolvers can help load data by consuming router parameters. Auth guards can help control access to various modules and components. Using router links, you can dynamically customize elements that a user will see in an immutable and predictable way, similar to the way we designed and developed data anchors in the previous step.

If you ensure every component is responsible for loading its own data, then you can compose components via URLs. However, overusing the router can in itself become an anti-pattern. If a parent component logically owns a child component, then the effort to decouple them will be wasted.

In *Chapter 6, Forms, Observables, and Subjects*, you learned how to enable component interactions using `BehaviorSubject`. In *Chapter 11, Recipes – Reusability, Routing, and Caching*, you will learn how to implement `@Input` and `@Output` bindings and in the upcoming chapters you will learn about how to implement router features.

Differentiate between user controls and components

Another important idea is differentiating user controls from components. A user control is like a custom date input, or a custom star rater. It is often highly interactive and dynamic code that ends up being highly coupled, convoluted, and complicated code. Such controls may use Angular features no one has ever heard of before, which are most likely not covered in this book.

A component is more like a form with fields, which may contain simple date inputs or a star rater. Because forms encapsulate business functionality, their code must be easy to read and understand. Your code should stick to Angular basics, so the code is stable and easy to maintain, like most of the code that is presented in this book.

By differentiating between user controls and components you can make better decisions when deciding what kind of code you want to make reusable. Creating reusable code is costly. If you create the right reusable code, you can save time and resources. If you create the wrong reusable code, then you can waste a lot of time and resources.

Wire-framing allows you to identify reusable elements early on. User controls will help keep user interaction code separate from business logic. Well-crafted component reuse will enable you to encapsulate domain-specific behavior, and share it later.

It's important to identify self-contained user controls that encapsulate unique behaviors that you wish to create for your app. User controls will likely be created as directives or components that have data-binding properties and tightly coupled controller logic and templates.

Components, on the other hand, leverage router life cycle events to parse parameters and perform CRUD operations on data. Identifying these component reuses early on will result in creating more flexible components that can be reused in multiple contexts (as orchestrated by the router), maximizing code reuse.

We will cover how to create reusable components and user controls in *Chapter 11, Recipes – Reusability, Routing, and Caching*.

Maximize code reuse with TypeScript and ES

It's essential to remember the underlying features of the language you work with before you consider the features offered by Angular, RxJS, and all the libraries you use. There are decades of software engineering fundamentals that you can leverage to write readable and maintainable code.

First and foremost is the DRY principle. It stands for don't repeat yourself. So, don't copy-paste code. Don't just change a variable or two. Proactively refactor your code to make your functions stateless and reusable. In a few words: don't repeat yourself, don't repeat yourself, and don't repeat yourself.

Leverage object-oriented design. Move behavior to classes; if your person has a `fullName` property, don't re-implement the same logic in a dozen different places, but implement it once in the `person` class. This means you will need to become familiar with hydration, also known as injecting a JSON object into a newly instantiated class, and serialization using `toJSON`. It is important not to abuse OOP. You should still remain stateless, and functional, by avoiding storing state in class parameters.

You can truly unleash the power of OO design by leveraging generics, inheritance, and abstract classes.

TypeScript introduces the concept of interfaces to JavaScript. Interfaces are a concept mostly reserved for statically typed languages. An interface represents an abstract notion of what an object can do, without specifying any implementation details. Furthermore, an interface can be used to document the shape of data. For example, you can write a partial interface of a third-party API to document the fields you're interested in consuming. When other developers read your code, they have an inherent understanding of the structure of the data they're consuming, without having to read documentation on another website.

Interfaces also allow you to morph the shape of your data in a well-defined manner. So, you can write a transform function to transform the shape of external data into internal data. TypeScript will catch any errors you may make. Taking this concept further, you can also use interfaces to flatten data. If the data you receive has a multi-entity relational structure, you can flatten the relationship to decouple the design of the data from your UI code.

Don't overly flatten your data. Arrays and simple shapes for common objects are okay, such as a name object or commonly used domain-specific object.

You should also avoid string literals in your code. Writing business logic where you compare `'apples' !== 'Oranges'` results in unmaintainable code. You should leverage `enums` in TypeScript, so your code isn't subject to the spelling mistakes of coders or changing business requirements. So `'oranges' === Fruit.Organes`.

Beyond TypeScript and ECMAScript, Angular also offers helpful functions for you to reuse logic. Angular validators, pipes, route resolvers, and route guards all allow you to share code across components and templates.

The following chapters will demonstrate the aforementioned concepts:

- *Chapter 8, Designing Authentication and Authorization*
- *Chapter 10, RESTful APIs and Full-Stack Implementation*
- *Chapter 11, Recipes – Reusability, Routing, and Caching*
- *Chapter 12, Recipes – Master/Detail, Data Tables, and NgRx*

Next, let's start by creating, LemonMart™, a fully featured line-of-business app that you can use as a template to kickstart your next professional project. LemonMart is a robust and realistic project that can support feature growth and different backend implementations, and it comes with a complete and configurable authentication and authorization solution out of the box.

Since its introduction, LemonMart has served more than 160,000 lemons to over 14,000 developers. Zesty!

You can always clone the finished project from GitHub, `https://www.github.com/duluca/lemon-mart`, whenever you need it. Let's jump right into it.

Creating LemonMart

LemonMart will be a mid-sized line-of-business application with over 90 code files. We will start our journey by creating a new Angular app, with routing and Angular Material configured from the get-go.

> It is presumed that you have installed all the requisite software mentioned in *Chapter 2, Setting Up Your Development Environment*. If you have not, execute the following commands for your OS to configure your environment.
>
> On Windows PowerShell, execute:
>
> ```
> PS> Install-Script -Name setup-windows-dev-env
> PS> setup-windows-dev-env.ps1
> ```
>
> On macOS Terminal, execute:
>
> ```
> $> bash <(wget -O - https://git.io/JvHi1)
> ```
>
> For more information refer to https://github.com/duluca/web-dev-environment-setup.

Creating a router-first app

With the router-first approach, we want to enable routing early on in our application:

1. You can create the new application, with routing already configured, by executing this command.

   Ensure that `@angular/cli` is not installed globally, or you may run into errors:

   ```
   $ npx @angular/cli new lemon-mart --routing --strict
   (Select CSS as the stylesheet format )
   ```

   > Starting with Angular 9, you may use `--strict` to turn on TypeScript features like `noImplicitAny`, `noImplicitReturns`, `noFallthroughCasesInSwitch`, and `strictNullChecks`. These options will decrease the chances of making coding mistakes, but result in more verbose code. In my opinion, that is a good thing, and this option is highly recommended for production-bound applications.

2. A new `AppRoutingModule` file has been created for us:

   src/app/app-routing.modules.ts
   ```
   import { NgModule } from '@angular/core';
   import { Routes, RouterModule } from '@angular/router';

   const routes: Routes = [];

   @NgModule({
     imports: [RouterModule.forRoot(routes)],
     exports: [RouterModule],
   })
   export class AppRoutingModule { }
   ```

We will be defining routes inside the routes array. Note that the routes array is passed in to be configured as the root routes for the application; the default root route is /.

When configuring your `RouterModule`, you can pass in additional options to customize the default behavior of the Router, such as when you attempt to load a route that you're already on. Normally, if the route you're attempting to navigate to is the same as the current one, the router wouldn't take any action. However, if you wanted the router to refresh the page, you would customize the default behavior of the router, such as with `RouterModule.forRoot(routes, { onSameUrlNavigation: 'reload' })`. With this setting in place, if you navigate to the same URL that you are on, you will force a reload of the current component.

3. Finally, `AppRoutingModule` is registered with `AppModule`, as shown:

   src/app/app.module.ts
   ```
   ...
   import { AppRoutingModule } from './app-routing.module';

   @NgModule({
     ...
     imports: [ AppRoutingModule, ... ],
     ...
   })
   ```

[289]

Configuring Angular and VS Code

To quickly apply configuration steps covered in *Chapters 2-6* run the following commands:

> The following scripts do not require you to use VS Code. If you wish to use another IDE like WebStorm, the npm scripts that are configured will run equally well.

1. Install the Angular VS Code task:

   `npm i -g mrm-task-angular-vscode`

2. Apply the Angular VS Code configuration:

   `npx mrm angular-vscode`

3. Install the npm Scripts for the Docker task:

   `npm i -g mrm-task-npm-docker`

4. Apply the npm Scripts for the Docker configuration:

   `npx mrm npm-docker`

5. Implement an npm script to build your application in production mode named `build:prod`

   ```
   "scripts": {
     ...,
     "build:prod": "ng build --prod",
   }
   ```

> These settings are continually tweaked to adapt to the ever-evolving landscape of extensions, plug-ins, Angular, and VS Code. Always make sure to install a fresh version of the task by re-running the `install` command to get the latest version. Alternatively, you can use the Angular Evergreen extension for VS Code, to run the configuration commands with one click.

Note that if the preceding configuration scripts fail to execute, then the following npm scripts will also fail. In this case, you have two options: revert your changes and ignore these scripts, or manually implement these scripts as covered in earlier chapters (or as demonstrated on GitHub).

6. Execute `npm run style:fix`
7. Execute `npm run lint:fix`
8. Execute `npm start` and ensure you're running on `http://localhost:5000`, instead of the default port `4200`

Refer to *Chapter 2, Setting Up Your Development Environment*, for further configuration details.

 You may optionally setup npm Scripts for AWS ECS, which is used in *Chapter 13, Highly Available Cloud Infrastructure on AWS*, by using `mrm-task-npm-aws`.

For more information on the mrm tasks refer to:

- `https://github.com/expertly-simple/mrm-task-angular-vscode`
- `https://github.com/expertly-simple/mrm-task-npm-docker`
- `https://github.com/expertly-simple/mrm-task-npm-aws`

Configuring Material and Styles

We will also need to set up Angular Material and configure a theme to use, as covered in *Chapter 5, Delivering High-Quality UX with Material*:

1. Install Angular Material:

    `$ npx ng add @angular/material`

    (select Custom, No to global typography, Yes to browser animations)

    `$ npm i @angular/flex-layout`

    `$ npx ng g m material --flat -m app`

2. In `material.module.ts`, define a `const modules` array and export `MatButtonModule`, `MatToolbarModule`, and `MatIconModule`, removing `CommonModule`

3. In `app.modules.ts`, import `FlexLayoutModule` so Angular Flex Layout can be activated

4. Append common CSS to `styles.css` as shown in the following code:

   src/styles.css
   ```
   html,
   body {
     height: 100%;
   }
   body {
     margin: 0;
     font-family: Roboto, "Helvetica Neue", sans-serif;
   }

   .margin-top {
     margin-top: 16px;
   }

   .horizontal-padding {
     margin-left: 16px;
     margin-right: 16px;
   }

   .flex-spacer {
     flex: 1 1 auto;
   }
   ```

5. Update your application's title in `index.html`

Refer to *Chapter 5, Delivering High-Quality UX with Material*, for further configuration details.

We will apply custom branding to the app later in this chapter. Next, let's start designing our line-of-business application.

Designing LemonMart

It is important to build a rudimentary roadmap to follow, from the database to the frontend, while also avoiding over-engineering. This initial design phase is critical to the long-term health and success of your project, where any existing silos between teams must be broken down and an overall technical vision well understood by all members of the team. This is easier said than done, and there are volumes of books written on the topic.

In engineering, there's no one right answer to a problem, so it is important to remember that no one person can ever have all the answers, nor a crystal-clear vision. It is important that technical and non-technical leaders create a safe space with opportunities for open discussion and experimentation as part of the culture. The humility and empathy that comes along with being able to court such uncertainty as a team is as important as any single team member's technical capability. Every team member must be comfortable with checking their egos at the door because our collective goal will be to grow and evolve an application to ever-changing requirements during the development cycle. You will know that you have succeeded if individual parts of the software you created are easily replaceable by anyone.

So, let's start by developing a roadmap and identifying the scope of our application. For this, we will be defining user roles and then building a site map, to create a vision of how our app might work.

Identifying user roles

The first step of our design will be to think about who is using the application and why.

We envision four user states, or roles, for LemonMart:

- Authenticated; any authenticated user would have access to their profile
- Cashier, whose sole role is to check out customers
- Clerk, whose sole role is to perform inventory-related functions
- Manager, who can perform all actions a cashier and a clerk can perform but also have access to administrative functions

With this in mind, we can start to create a high-level design for our app.

Identifying high-level modules with a site map

Develop a high-level site map of your application, as shown:

Figure 7.7: Landing pages for users

I used MockFlow.com's SiteMap tool to create the site map shown: `https://sitemap.mockflow.com`.

Upon first examination, three high-level modules emerge as lazy-loading candidates:

1. **Point of Sale (POS)**
2. **Inventory**
3. **Manager**

The Cashier will only have access to the **POS** module and component. The Clerk will only have access to the **Inventory** module, which will include additional screens for the **Stock Entry**, **Products**, and **Categories** management components:

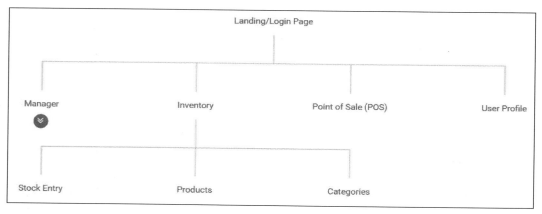

Figure 7.8: Inventory pages

Finally, the **Manager** will be able to access all three modules with the **Manager** module, including user management and receipt lookup components:

Figure 7.9: Manager pages

There'll be great benefits from enabling lazy loading for all three modules; since Cashiers and Clerks will never use components belonging to other user roles, there's no reason to send those bytes down to their devices. This means as the **Manager** module gains more advanced reporting features, or new roles are added to the application, the **POS** module will be unaffected by the bandwidth and memory impact of an otherwise growing application.

This means fewer support calls, and consistent performance on the same hardware for a much longer period of time.

Generating router-enabled modules

Now that we have our high-level components defined as **Manager**, **Inventory**, and **POS**, we can define them as modules. These modules will be different from the ones you've created so far, for routing and Angular Material. We can create the user profile as a component on the app module; however, note that user profile will only ever be used for already-authenticated users, so it makes sense to define a fourth module only meant for authenticated users in general. This way, you will ensure that your app's first payload remains as minimal as possible. In addition, we will create a Home component to contain the landing experience for our app so that we can keep implementation details out of app.component:

1. Generate manager, inventory, pos, and user modules, specifying their target module and routing capabilities:

    ```
    $ npx ng g m manager -m app --routing
    $ npx ng g m inventory -m app --routing
    $ npx ng g m pos -m app --routing
    $ npx ng g m user -m app --routing
    ```

>  As discussed in *Chapter 2, Setting Up Your Development Environment*, if you have configured npx to automatically recognize ng as a command, you can save some more keystrokes because you won't have to append npx to your commands every time. Do not globally install @angular/cli.
>
> Note the abbreviated command structure, where `ng generate module manager` becomes `ng g m manager`, and similarly, `--module` becomes `-m`.

2. Verify that you don't have CLI errors.

   Note that using npx on Windows may throw an error such as `Path must be a string. Received undefined`. This error doesn't seem to have any effect on the successful operation of the command, which is why it is critical to always inspect what the CLI tool generated.

3. Verify that the folder and the files are created:

```
/src/app
    |   app-routing.module.ts
    |   app.component.css
    |   app.component.html
    |   app.component.spec.ts
    |   app.component.ts
    |   app.module.ts
    |   material.module.ts
    ├───inventory
    |       inventory-routing.module.ts
    |       inventory.module.ts
    ├───manager
    |       manager-routing.module.ts
    |       manager.module.ts
    ├───pos
    |       pos-routing.module.ts
    |       pos.module.ts
    └───user
            user-routing.module.ts
            user.module.ts
```

4. Examine how `ManagerModule` has been wired.

A feature module implements an `@NgModule` similar to `app.module`. The biggest difference is that a feature module does not implement the `bootstrap` property, which is required for your root module to initialize your Angular app:

src/app/manager/manager.module.ts
```
import { NgModule } from '@angular/core'
import { CommonModule } from '@angular/common'
import { ManagerRoutingModule } from './manager-routing.module'

@NgModule({
  imports: [CommonModule, ManagerRoutingModule],
  declarations: [],
})
export class ManagerModule {}
```

Since we have specified the `-m` option, the module has been imported into `app.module`:

src/app/app.module.ts
```
...
import { ManagerModule } from './manager/manager.module'
...
@NgModule({
  ...
  imports: [..., ManagerModule],
  ...
})
```

In addition, because we also specified the `--routing` option, a routing module has been created and imported into `ManagerModule`:

src/app/manager/manager-routing.module.ts
```
import { NgModule } from '@angular/core'
import { Routes, RouterModule } from '@angular/router'

const routes: Routes = []

@NgModule({
  imports: [RouterModule.forChild(routes)],
  exports: [RouterModule],
})
export class ManagerRoutingModule {}
```

Note that `RouterModule` is being configured using `forChild`, as opposed to `forRoot`, which was the case for the `AppRouting` module. This way, the router understands the proper relationship between routes defined in different modules' contexts and can correctly prepend `/manager` to all child routes in this example.

 The CLI doesn't respect your `tslint.json` settings. If you have correctly configured your VS Code environment with Prettier, your code styling preferences will be applied as you work on each file or globally when you run the `prettier` command.

Be sure to run your `style:fix` and `lint:fix` commands before moving on. Now, let's design how the landing page for LemonMart will look and work.

Designing the home route

Consider the following mock-up as the landing experience for LemonMart:

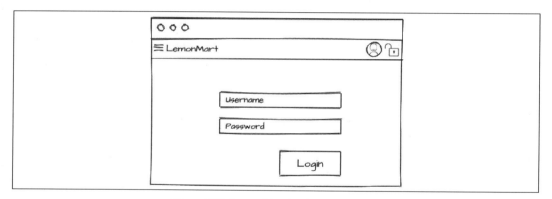

Figure 7.10: LemonMart landing experience

Unlike the `LocalCastWeather` app, we don't want all this markup to be in the `App` component. The `App` component is the root element of your entire application; therefore, it should only contain elements that will persistently appear throughout your application. In the following annotated mock-up, the toolbar marked as **1** will be persistent throughout the app.

The area marked as **2** will house the `home` component, which itself will contain a login user control, marked as **3**:

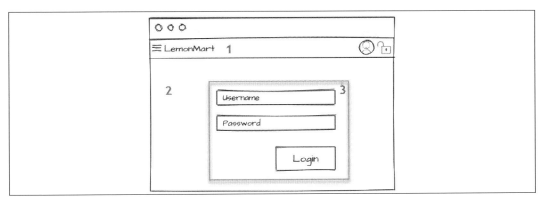

Figure 7.11: LemonMart layout structure

It's best practice to create your default or landing component as a separate element in Angular. This helps reduce the amount of code that must be loaded and logic executed in every page, but it also results in a more flexible architecture when utilizing the router.

Generate the `home` component with inline template and styles:

```
$ npx ng g c home -m app --inline-template --inline-style
```

 Note that a component with an inline template and a style is also referred to as a **Single File Component** or an **SFC**.

Now, you are ready to configure the router.

Setting up default routes

Let's get started with setting up a simple route for LemonMart. We need to set up the / route (also known as the empty route) and the /home routes to display the HomeComponent. We also need a wildcard route to capture all undefined routes and display a PageNotFoundComponent, which also needs to be created:

1. Configure your home route:

   src/app/app-routing.module.ts

   ```
   ...

   import { HomeComponent } from './home/home.component'

   const routes: Routes = [
     { path: '', redirectTo: '/home', pathMatch: 'full' },
     { path: 'home', component: HomeComponent },
   ]
   ...
   ```

   We first define a path for 'home' and inform the router to render HomeComponent by setting the component property. Then, we set the default path of the application '' to be redirected to '/home'. By setting the pathMatch property, we always ensure that this very specific instance of the home route will be rendered as the landing experience.

2. Create a pageNotFound component with an inline template

3. Configure a wildcard route for PageNotFoundComponent:

   src/app/app-routing.module.ts

   ```
   import {
     PageNotFoundComponent
   } from './page-not-found/page-not-found.component'
   ...
   const routes: Routes = [
     ...
       { path: '**', component: PageNotFoundComponent },
   ]
   ...
   ```

This way, any route that is not matched will be directed to the PageNotFoundComponent.

RouterLink

When a user lands on the `PageNotFoundComponent`, we would like them to be redirected to the `HomeComponent` using the `routerLink` direction:

1. On `PageNotFoundComponent`, replace the inline template to link back to home using `routerLink`:

   `src/app/page-not-found/page-not-found.component.ts`

   ```
   ...
     template: `
       <p>
         This page doesn't exist. Go back to
         <a routerLink="/home">home</a>.
       </p>
     `,
   ...
   ```

> This navigation can also be done via an `<a href>` tag implementation; however, in more dynamic and complicated navigation scenarios, you will lose features such as automatic active link tracking or dynamic link generation.

The Angular bootstrap process will ensure that `AppComponent` is inside the `<app-root>` element in your `index.html`. However, we must manually define where we would like `HomeComponent` to render, to finalize the router configuration.

Router outlet

`AppComponent` is considered a root element for the root router defined in `app-routing.module`, which allows us to define outlets within this root element to dynamically load any content we wish using the `<router-outlet>` element:

1. Configure `AppComponent` to use inline template and styles, deleting any existing content in the html and css files
2. Add the toolbar for your application
3. Add the name of your application as a button link so that it takes the user to the home page when clicked on

4. Add `<router-outlet>` for the content to render:

src/app/app.component.ts
```
...
template: `
  <mat-toolbar color="primary">
    <a mat-button routerLink="/home"><h1>LemonMart</h1></a>
  </mat-toolbar>
  <router-outlet></router-outlet>
`,
```

Now, the contents of `home` will render inside `<router-outlet>`.

Branding, customization, and Material icons

In order to construct an attractive and intuitive toolbar, we must introduce some iconography and branding to the app so that the users can easily navigate through the app with the help of familiar icons.

Branding

In terms of branding, you should ensure that your web app has a custom color palette and integrates with desktop and mobile browser features to bring forward your app's name and iconography.

Color palette

Pick a color palette using the Material Color tool, as discussed in *Chapter 5, Delivering High-Quality UX with Material*. Here's the one I picked for LemonMart:

https://material.io/resources/color/#!/?view.left=0&view.right=0&primary.color=2E7D32&secondary.color=C6FF00.

1. Rename `custom-theme.scss` to `lemonmart-theme.scss`
2. Update `angular.json` with the new theme file name
   angular.json
   ```
   "apps": [ {
     ...
     "styles": [
       "src/lemonmart-theme.scss",
       "src/styles.css"
   ```

                ],
                ...
            }]

3. Configure your custom theme with the chosen color palette

 You can also grab LemonMart-related assets from GitHub at `https://github.com/duluca/lemon-mart`.

For the Local Weather app, we replaced the `favicon.ico` file to brand our app in the browser. While this would've been enough ten years ago, today's devices vary wildly, and each platform can leverage optimized assets to better represent your web app within their operating systems. Next, let's implement a more robust favicon.

Implementing browser manifest and icons

You need to ensure that the browser shows the correct title text and icon in a **Browser** tab. Further, a manifest file should be created that implements specific icons for various mobile operating systems, so that if a user pins your website, a desirable icon is displayed similar to other app icons on a phone. This will ensure that if a user favorites or pins your web app on their mobile device's home screen, they'll get a native-looking app icon:

1. Create or obtain an SVG version of your website's logo from a designer or a site like `https://www.flaticon.com`
2. In this case, I will be using the likeness of the Eureka Lemon:

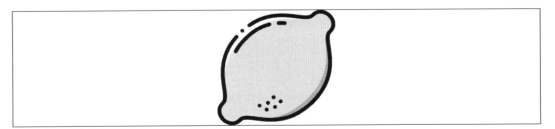

Figure 7.12: LemonMart's signature logo

> When using images you find on the internet, pay attention to applicable copyrights. In this case, I have purchased a license to be able to publish this lemon logo, but you may grab your own copy at the following URL, given that you provide the required attribution to the author of the image: https://www.flaticon.com/free-icon/lemon_605070.

3. Generate the `favicon.ico` and manifest files using a tool such as https://realfavicongenerator.net
4. Adjust settings for iOS, Android, Windows Metro, and macOS Safari to your liking
5. Ensure that you set a version number, as favicons can be notorious with caching; a random version number will ensure that users always get the latest version
6. Download and extract the generated `favicons.zip` file into your `src` folder
7. Edit the `angular.json` file to include the new assets in your app:

angular.json
```
"apps": [
  {
  ...
    "assets": [
      "src/assets",
      "src/favicon.ico",
      "src/android-chrome-192x192.png",
      "src/favicon-16x16.png",
      "src/mstile-310x150.png",
      "src/android-chrome-512x512.png",
      "src/favicon-32x32.png",
      "src/mstile-310x310.png",
      "src/apple-touch-icon.png",
      "src/manifest.json",
      "src/mstile-70x70.png",
      "src/browserconfig.xml",
      "src/mstile-144x144.png",
      "src/safari-pinned-tab.svg",
      "src/mstile-150x150.png"
    ]
```

8. Insert the generated code in the `<head>` section of your `index.html`:

src/index.html
```
<link rel="apple-touch-icon" sizes="180x180" href="/apple-touch-icon.png?v=rMlKOnvxlK">
<link rel="icon" type="image/png" sizes="32x32" href="/favicon-32x32.png?v=rMlKOnvxlK">
<link rel="icon" type="image/png" sizes="16x16" href="/favicon-16x16.png?v=rMlKOnvxlK">
<link rel="manifest" href="/manifest.json?v=rMlKOnvxlK">
<link rel="mask-icon" href="/safari-pinned-tab.svg?v=rMlKOnvxlK" color="#b3ad2d">
<link rel="shortcut icon" href="/favicon.ico?v=rMlKOnvxlK">
<meta name="theme-color" content="#ffffff">
```

> Please put the preceding HTML after your favicon declaration, but before your style imports. The order does matter. Browsers load data top down. You want your application's icon to be parsed before the user has to wait for CSS files to be downloaded.

9. Ensure that your new favicon displays correctly

Once your basic branding work has been completed, consider if you'd like to establish a more unique look and feel with theming.

Custom themes

You may further customize Material's look and feel, to achieve a unique experience for your app, by leveraging tools listed on `https://material.io/tools` and some other tools that I have discovered, which are listed as follows:

- Material Theme Editor (retired as of March 2020) is a plugin for the popular design app Sketch on macOS to create a theme that is more than skin deep. An alternative tool is yet to be announced, but you can find resources you can continue to use in the meantime on the blog post linked at `https://material.io/tools/theme-editor`

- Material Theme Builder is an alternative to build custom themes that work in the browser on Glitch.com at `https://material-theme-builder.glitch.me`

- Material Design Theme Palette Generator will generate the necessary code to define your custom color palette to create truly unique themes at `http://mcg.mbitson.com`

- Color Blender helps with finding midway points between two colors, which is useful when defining in-between colors for the color swatches, located at https://meyerweb.com/eric/tools/color-blend

There is a wealth of information on https://material.io on the in-depth philosophy behind Material design, with great sections on things like the color system, https://material.io/design/color/the-color-system.html, which dives deep into selecting the right color palette for your brand and other topics such as creating a dark theme for your app.

It is very important to distinguish your brand from other apps or your competitors. Creating a high-quality custom theme will be a time-consuming process; however, the benefits of creating a great first impression with your users are considerable.

Next, we will show you how you can add custom icons to your Angular apps.

Custom icons

Now, let's add your custom branding inside your Angular app. You will need the svg icon you used to create your favicon:

1. Place the image under `src/assets/img/icons`, named `lemon.svg`
2. In `app.module.ts`, import `HttpClientModule` to `AppComponent` so that the `.svg` file can be requested over HTTP
3. Update `AppComponent` to register the new svg file as an icon:

```
src/app/app.component.ts
import { MatIconRegistry } from '@angular/material/icon'
import { DomSanitizer } from '@angular/platform-browser'
...
export class AppComponent {
  constructor(
    iconRegistry: MatIconRegistry,
    sanitizer: DomSanitizer
  ) {
    iconRegistry.addSvgIcon(
      'lemon',
      sanitizer.bypassSecurityTrustResourceUrl(
        'assets/img/icons/ lemon.svg'
      )
    )
  }
}
```

4. Add the icon to the toolbar:

`src/app/app.component.ts`
```
template: `
  <mat-toolbar color="primary">
    <mat-icon svgIcon="lemon"></mat-icon>
    <a mat-button routerLink="/home"><h1>LemonMart</h1></a>
  </mat-toolbar>
  <router-outlet></router-outlet>
`,
```

Now let's add the remaining icons for menu, user profile, and logout.

Material icons

Angular Material works out of the box with the Material Design icon font, which is automatically imported into your app as a web font in your `index.html`. It is possible to self-host the font; however, if you go down that path, you don't get the benefit if the user's browser has already cached the font from when they visited another website, which could save the speed and latency of downloading a 42-56 KB file in the process. The complete list of icons can be found at `https://material.io/icons/`.

Now let's update the toolbar with some icons and set up the home page with a minimal template for a fake login button:

1. Ensure that the Material icons `<link>` tag has been added to `index.html`:

`src/index.html`
```
<head>
  ...
  <link href="https://fonts.googleapis.com/icon?family=Material+Icons" rel="stylesheet">
</head>
```

Instructions on how to self-host can be found under the **Self Hosting** section at `http://google.github.io/material-design-icons/#getting-icons`.

Creating a Router-First Line-of-Business App

Once configured, working with Material icons is easy.

2. On `AppComponent`, update the toolbar to place a **Menu** button to the left of the title.
3. Add the `fxFlex` directive so that the remaining icons are right aligned.
4. Add user profile and logout icons:

   src/app/app.component.ts
   ```
   template: `
     <mat-toolbar color="primary">
       <button mat-icon-button><mat-icon>menu</mat-icon></button>
       <mat-icon svgIcon="lemon"></mat-icon>
       <a mat-button routerLink="/home"><h1>LemonMart</h1></a>
       <span class="flex-spacer"></span>
       <button mat-icon-button>
         <mat-icon>account_circle</mat-icon>
       </button>
       <button mat-icon-button>
         <mat-icon>lock_open</mat-icon>
       </button>
     </mat-toolbar>
     <router-outlet></router-outlet>
   `,
   ```

5. On `HomeComponent`, add a minimal template for a login experience, replacing any existing content:

   src/app/home/home.component.ts
   ```
   styles: [`
     div[fxLayout] {margin-top: 32px;}
   `],
   template: `
     <div fxLayout="column" fxLayoutAlign="center center">
       <span class="mat-display-2">Hello, Limoncu!</span>
       <button mat-raised-button color="primary">Login</button>
     </div>
   `
   ```

Your app should look similar to this screenshot:

Figure 7.13: LemonMart with minimal login

There's still some work to be done, in terms of implementing and showing/hiding the menu, profile, and logout icons, given the user's authentication status. We will cover this functionality in *Chapter 8, Designing Authentication and Authorization*.

 In order to debug the router, get a visualization of your routers, and tightly integrate Chrome debugging features using Angular Augury, see *Appendix A, Debugging Angular*.

Now that you've set up basic routing for your app, we can move on to setting up lazily loaded modules with subcomponents. If you're not familiar with troubleshooting and debugging Angular, please refer to the *Appendix A, Debugging Angular*, before moving forward.

Feature modules with lazy loading

There are two ways resources are loaded: eagerly or lazily. When the browser loads up the `index.html` for your app, it starts processing it top to bottom. First the `<head>` element is processed, then the `<body>`. For example, the CSS resources we defined in the `<head>` of our app will be downloaded before our app is rendered, because our Angular app is defined as a `<script>` in the `<body>` of the HTML file.

When you use the command `ng build`, Angular leverages the webpack module bundler to combine all the JavaScript, HTML, and CSS into minified and optimized JavaScript bundles.

Creating a Router-First Line-of-Business App

If you don't leverage lazy loading in Angular, the entire contents of your app will be eagerly loaded. The user won't see the first screen of your app until all screens are downloaded and loaded.

Lazy loading allows the Angular build process, working in tandem with webpack, to separate your web application into different JavaScript files called chunks. We can enable this chunking by separating out portions of the application into feature modules. Feature modules and their dependencies can be bundled into separate chunks. Remember that the root module and its dependencies will always be in the first chunk that is downloaded. So, by chunking our application's JavaScript bundle size, we keep the size of the initial chunk at a minimum. With a minimal first chunk, no matter how big your application grows, the time to first meaningful paint remains constant. Otherwise, your app would take longer and longer to download and render as you add more features and functionality to it. Lazy loading is critical to achieving a scalable application architecture.

Consider the following graphic to determine which routes are eagerly loaded and which ones are lazily loaded:

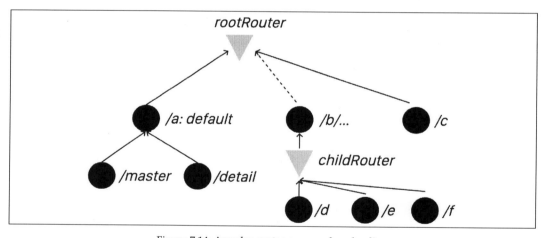

Figure 7.14: Angular router eager vs lazy loading

The `rootRouter` defines three routes: a, b, and c. `/master` and `/detail` represent named router outlets, which are covered in *Chapter 12, Recipes – Master/Detail, Data Tables, and NgRx*. Route a is the default route for the app. Routes a and c are connected to the `rootRouter` with a solid line, whereas route b is connected using a dashed line. In this context, route b is configured as a lazy-loaded route. This means that route b will dynamically load a feature module, called **BModule**, that contains its `childRouter`. This `childRouter` can define any number of components, even reusing route names that were reused elsewhere. In this case, b defines three additional routes: d, e, and f.

Consider the example router definition for the `rootRouter`:

rootRouter example
```
const routes: Routes = [
  { path: '', redirectTo: '/a', pathMatch: 'full' },
  {
    path: 'a',
    component: AComponent,
    children: [
      { path: '', component: MasterComponent, outlet: 'master' },
      { path: '', component: DetailComponent, outlet: 'detail' },
    ],
  },
  {
    path: 'b',
    loadChildren:
      () => import('./b/b.module')
        .then((module) => module.BModule),
    canLoad: [AuthGuard],
  },
  { path: 'c', component: CComponent },
  { path: '**', component: PageNotFoundComponent },
]
```

Note that the definitions for routes d, e, and f do not exist in the `rootRouter`. See the example router definition for the `childRouter`:

childRouter example
```
const routes: Routes = [
  { path: '', redirectTo: '/b/d', pathMatch: 'full' },
  { path: 'd', component: DComponent },
  { path: 'e', component: EComponent },
  { path: 'f', component: FComponent },
]
```

As you can see the routes defined in the `childRouter` are independent of the ones defined in the `rootRouter`. Child routes exist in a hierarchy, where /b is the parent path. To navigate to the `DComponent`, you must use the path /b/d, whereas, to navigate to `CComponent`, you can just use /c.

Given this example configuration, every component defined in the `rootRouter` and their dependencies would be in the first chunk of our app, and thus eagerly loaded. The first chunk would include the components A, Master, Detail, C, and PageNotFound. The second chunk would contain the components D, E, and F. This second chunk would not be downloaded or loaded until the user navigated to a path starting with /b; thus, it's lazily loaded.

> In the book I only cover the well-established method of lazily loaded feature modules. Check out John Papa's blog post on creating lazily loading components at `https://johnpapa.net/angular-9-lazy-loading-components/`.

We will now go over how to set up a feature module with components and routes. We will also use Augury to observe the effects of our various router configurations.

Configuring feature modules with components and routes

The manager module needs a landing page, as shown in this mock-up:

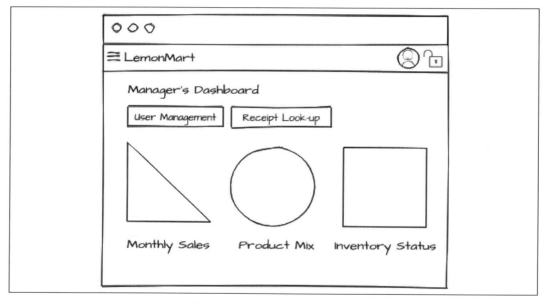

Figure 7.15: Manager's dashboard

Let's start by creating the home screen for the `ManagerModule`:

1. Create the `ManagerHome` component:

   ```
   $ npx ng g c manager/managerHome -m manager -s -t
   ```

> In order to create the new component under the `manager` folder, we must prefix `manager/` in front of the component name. In addition, we specify that the component should be imported and declared with the `ManagerModule`. Since this is another landing page, it is unlikely to be complicated enough to require separate HTML and CSS files. You can use `--inline-style` (alias `-s`) and/or `--inline-template` (alias `-t`) to avoid creating additional files.

2. Verify that your folder structure looks as follows:

```
/src
├───app
│   │
│   ├───manager
│   │   │   manager-routing.module.ts
│   │   │   manager.module.ts
│   │   │
│   │   └───manager-home
│   │           manager-home.component.spec.ts
│   │           manager-home.component.ts
```

3. Configure the `ManagerHome` component's route with `manager-routing.module`, similar to how we configured the `Home` component with `app-route.module`:

   src/app/manager/manager-routing.module.ts
   ```
   import {
     ManagerHomeComponent
   } from './manager-home/manager-home.component'

   const routes: Routes = [
     { path: '', redirectTo: '/manager/home', pathMatch: 'full' },
     { path: 'home', component: ManagerHomeComponent },
   ]
   ```

Note that `http://localhost:5000/manager` doesn't actually resolve to a component yet, because our Angular app isn't aware that `ManagerModule` exists. Let's first try the brute-force, eager-loading approach to import `ManagerModule` and register the manager route with our app.

Eager loading

Let's start by eagerly loading the `ManagerModule`, so we can see how importing and registering routes in the root module doesn't result in a scalable solution:

1. Import the `ManagerModule` in `app.module.ts`:

    src/app/app.module.ts
    ```
    import { ManagerModule } from './manager/manager.module'
    ...
    @NgModule({
      imports: [..., ManagerModule],
      ...
    })
    ```

    You will note that `http://localhost:5000/manager` still doesn't render its `home` component.

2. Use **Augury** to debug the router state, as shown:

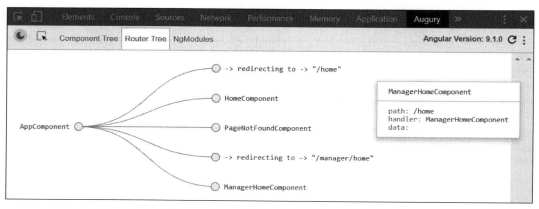

Figure 7.16: Router tree with eager loading

> Note that at the time of publishing, Augury's support for the Ivy rendering engine is not great. In order to reliably view the **Router Tree** tab, you need to disable Ivy. You can do so by adding the following setting to the `tsconfig.app.json` file in your project:
>
>   "angularCompilerOptions": {
>   "enableIvy": false
>   }
>
> You will need to restart your Angular app and reload Augury for changes to take effect. However, getting the pretty diagram is not worth accidentally shipping your app with Ivy disabled. Be careful with this one!

3. It seems as if the /manager path is correctly registered and pointed at the correct component, ManagerHomeComponent. The issue here is that the rootRouter configured in app-routing.module isn't aware of the /manager path, so the ** path is taking precedence and rendering the PageNotFoundComponent instead.

4. Implement the 'manager' path in app-routing.module.ts and assign ManagerHomeComponent to it, so we can see what happens:

```
src/app/app-routing.module.ts
import {
  ManagerHomeComponent
} from './manager/manager-home/ manager-home.component'
...
const routes: Routes = [
  ...
  { path: 'manager', component: ManagerHomeComponent },
  { path: '**', component: PageNotFoundComponent },
]
```

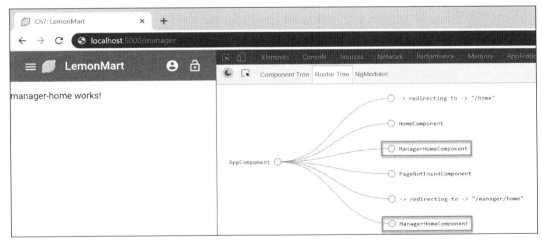

Figure 7.17: Manager home renders with duplicate path registration

As shown in the image above, `http://localhost:5000/manager` renders correctly, by displaying manager-home works! However, when you debug the router state through Augury, note that the `ManagerHomeComponent` is registered twice. This is because both the `rootRouter` and the `childRouter` registrations are being picked up. To avoid this issue, we would have to centralize all path creation in the `rootRouter` and not use child routers.

Centralizing all paths in the `rootRouter` doesn't scale well, because it forces all developers to maintain a single master file to import and configure every module. It is ripe for merge conflicts and frustrating exchanges between team members. As a file grows larger, the chances of introducing a bug increase exponentially, where the same route could unintentionally be registered multiple times.

It is possible to engineer a solution to divide up the modules into multiple files. Instead of the standard `*-routing.module`, you could implement a new routes array in `ManagerModule` and import it to the `rootRouter`. Let's fix the duplicate registration issue.

5. In `manager.module.ts`, remove `ManagerRoutingModule` from the imports array.

6. In `manager.module.ts`, implement a `Routes` array and set an empty path for the component `ManagerHomeComponent` as shown:

   src/app/manager/manager.module.ts
   ```
   import { Routes } from '@angular/router'
   export const managerModuleRoutes: Routes = [
     { path: '', component: ManagerHomeComponent }
   ]
   ```

7. In `app-routing.module.ts`, import the array you just created and assign it to the `children` property of the `'manager'` path:

   src/app/app-routing.module.ts
   ```
   import { managerModuleRoutes } from './manager/manager.module'
   ...
   { path: 'manager', children: managerModuleRoutes },
   ```

> Don't forget to remove the `component` property and the import for `ManagerHomeModule`.

Let's inspect the **Router Tree** on Augury again to see if we resolved the duplicate registration issue:

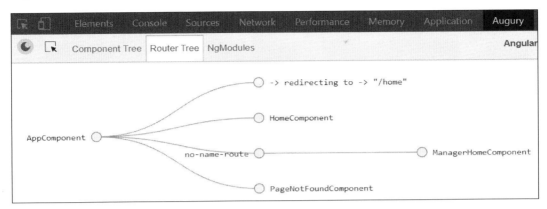

Figure 7.18: Router Tree with children routes

The provided solution works. There are no duplicate registrations, because we stopped using the `childRouters` in `manager-routing.module.ts`. In addition, we maintained some separation of concerns, by not importing `ManagerHomeComponent` outside of `ManagerModule`, resulting in a more scalable solution. However, as the app grows, we must still register all modules with `app.module.ts`. As a result, feature modules are still tightly coupled to the root module in potentially unpredictable ways. Further, this code can't be chunked, because the feature module is directly imported in `app.module.ts`, so the TypeScript compiler sees it as a required dependency.

Next, let's transform our configuration into a lazily loading one.

Lazy loading

Now that you understand how eager loading of modules works, you will be able to better understand the code we are about to write, which may otherwise seem like black magic, and magical (also known as misunderstood) code always leads to spaghetti architectures.

We will now evolve the eager loading solution to be a lazy loading one. In order to load routes from a different module, we know we can't simply import them, otherwise they will be eagerly loaded. The answer lies in configuring a route using the `loadChildren` attribute with an inline import statement informing the router how to load a feature module in `app-routing.module.ts`:

1. Ensure that any module you intend to lazy load is not imported in `app.module.ts`, so remove the `ManagerModule` from the `imports`.
2. Remove the `Routes` array added to `ManagerModule`.
3. Add back the `ManagerRoutingModule` to `imports` in `ManagerModule`.
4. In `app-routing.module.ts`, implement or update the `'manager'` path with the `loadChildren` attribute:

   src/app/app-routing.module.ts
   ```
   import { NgModule } from '@angular/core'
   import { RouterModule, Routes } from '@angular/router'

   import { HomeComponent } from './home/home.component'
   import { PageNotFoundComponent } from './page-not-found/page-not-found.component'
   ...
     const routes: Routes = [
       ...,
       {
         path: 'manager',
         loadChildren:
           () => import('./manager/manager.module')
             .then(m=> m.ManagerModule),
       },
       { path: '**', component: PageNotFoundComponent },
     ]
   ...
   ```

   Lazy loading is achieved via a clever trick that avoids using an import statement at the file level. A function delegate is set to the `loadChildren` property, which contains an inline import statement defining the location of the feature module file, such as `./manager/manager.module`, allowing us to refer to `ManagerModule` in a type-safe manner without actually fully loading it. The inline import statement can be interpreted during the build process to create a separate JavaScript chunk that can be downloaded only when needed. `ManagerModule` then acts as if its own Angular app and manages all its children dependencies and routes.

5. Update the `manager-routing.module` routes, considering that `manager` is now their root route:

```
src/app/manager/manager-routing.module.ts
const routes: Routes = [
  { path: '', redirectTo: '/manager/home', pathMatch: 'full' },
  { path: 'home', component: ManagerHomeComponent },
]
```

We can now update the route for `ManagerHomeComponent` to a more meaningful `'home'` path. This path won't clash with the one found in `app-routing.module`, because in this context, `'home'` resolves to `'manager/home'` and, similarly, where `path` is empty, the URL will look like `http://localhost:5000/manager`.

6. Restart your `ng serve` or `npm start` command, so Angular can chunk the app properly.
7. Navigate to `http://localhost:5000/manager`.
8. Confirm that lazy loading is working by looking at Augury, as follows:

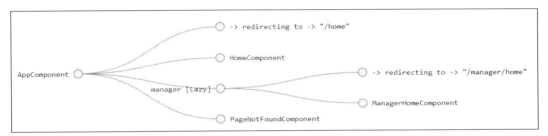

Figure 7.19: Router tree with lazy loading

 The root node for `ManagerHomeComponent` is now named **manager [Lazy]**.

We have successfully set up a feature module with lazy loading. Next, let's implement the walking skeleton for LemonMart.

Completing the walking skeleton

Using the site map we created for LemonMart earlier in the chapter, we need to complete the walking skeleton navigation experience for the app. In order to create this experience, we will need to create some buttons to link all modules and components together. We will go at this module by module.

Before we start, update the login button on the `HomeComponent` to navigate to the `'manager'` path using the `routerLink` attribute and rename the button:

```
src/app/home/home.component.ts
...
  <button mat-raised-button color="primary" routerLink="/manager">
    Login as Manager
  </button>
...
```

Now, we can navigate to the `ManagerHome` component by clicking on the **Login** button.

The manager module

Since we already enabled lazy loading for `ManagerModule`, let's go ahead and complete the rest of the navigational elements for it.

In the current setup, `ManagerHomeComponent` renders in the `<router-outlet>` defined in `AppComponent`'s template, so when the user navigates from `HomeComponent` to `ManagerHomeComponent`, the toolbar implemented in `AppComponent` remains in place. See the following mock-up for **Manager's Dashboard**:

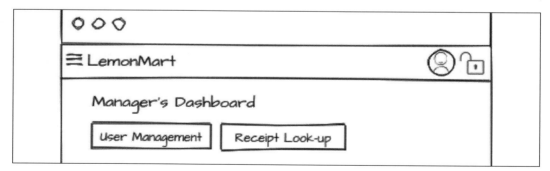

Figure 7.20: App-wide and feature module toolbars

Chapter 7

The app-wide toolbar remains in place no matter where we navigate to. You can imagine that we can implement a similar toolbar for the feature module that persists throughout `ManagerModule`. So, the navigational buttons **User Management** and **Receipt Look-up** would always be visible. This allows us to create a consistent UX for navigating subpages across modules.

To implement a secondary toolbar, we need to replicate the parent-child relationship between `AppComponent` and `HomeComponent`, where the parent implements the toolbar and a `<router-outlet>` so that children elements can be rendered in there:

1. Start by creating the base `manager` component:

   ```
   $ npx ng g c manager/manager -m manager --flat -s -t
   ```

    The `--flat` option skips directory creation and places the component directly under the `manager` folder, just like `app.component` residing directly under the app folder.

2. In `ManagerComponent`, implement a navigational toolbar with `activeLink` tracking:

   src/app/manager/manager.component.ts
   ```
   styles: [
     `
       div[fxLayout] {
         margin-top: 32px;
       }
     `,
     `
       .active-link {
         font-weight: bold;
         border-bottom: 2px solid #005005;
       }
     `,
   ],
   template: `
   <mat-toolbar color="accent">
     <a mat-button
       routerLink="/manager/home"
       routerLinkActive="active-link"
     >
         Manager's Dashboard
     </a>
     <a mat-button
       routerLink="/manager/users"
       routerLinkActive="active-link"
     >
   ```

```
      User Management
    </a>
    <a mat-button
       routerLink="/manager/receipts"
       routerLinkActive="active-link"
     >
       Receipt Lookup
    </a>
</mat-toolbar>
<router-outlet></router-outlet>
```

> It must be noted that feature modules don't automatically have access to services or components created in parent modules. This is an important default behavior to preserve a decoupled architecture. However, there are certain cases where it is desirable to share some amount of code. In this case, mat-toolbar needs to be reimported. Since the MatToolbarModule is already loaded in src/app/material.module.ts, we can just import this module into manager.module.ts and there will not be a performance or memory penalty for doing so.

3. Ensure `ManagerComponent` is declared and `MaterialModule` is imported in `ManagerModule`:

   src/app/manager/manager.module.ts
   ```
   import { MaterialModule } from '../material.module'
   import { ManagerComponent } from './manager.component'
   ...

   declarations: [..., ManagerComponent],
   imports: [..., MaterialModule],
   ```

4. Create components for the subpages:

   ```
   $ npx ng g c manager/userManagement -m manager
   $ npx ng g c manager/receiptLookup -m manager
   ```

5. Create the parent-children routing. We know that we need the following routes to be able to navigate to our subpages, as follows:

   example
   ```
   { path: '', redirectTo: '/manager/home', pathMatch: 'full' },
   { path: 'home', component: ManagerHomeComponent },
   { path: 'users', component: UserManagementComponent },
   { path: 'receipts', component: ReceiptLookupComponent },
   ```

In order to target the `<router-outlet>` defined in `ManagerComponent`, we need to create a parent route first and then specify routes for the subpages:

```
src/app/manager/manager-routing.module.ts
...
import { NgModule } from '@angular/core'
import { RouterModule, Routes } from '@angular/router'

import { ManagerHomeComponent } from './manager-home/manager-home.component'
import { ManagerComponent } from './manager.component'
import { ReceiptLookupComponent } from './receipt-lookup/receipt-lookup.component'
import { UserManagementComponent } from './user-management/user-management.component'
const routes: Routes = [
  {
    path: '',
    component: ManagerComponent,
    children: [
      { path: '', redirectTo: '/manager/home', pathMatch: 'full' },
      { path: 'home', component: ManagerHomeComponent },
      { path: 'users', component: UserManagementComponent },
      { path: 'receipts', component: ReceiptLookupComponent },
    ],
  },
]
```

You should now be able to navigate through the app. When you click on the **Login as Manager** button, you will be taken to the page shown here. The clickable targets are highlighted, as shown:

Figure 7.21: Manager's Dashboard with all router links highlighted

If you click on **LemonMart**, you will be taken to the home page. If you click on **Manager's Dashboard**, **User Management**, or **Receipt Lookup**, you will be navigated to the corresponding subpage, while the active link will be bold and underlined on the toolbar.

User module

Upon login, users will be able to access their profiles and view a list of actions they can access in the LemonMart app through a side navigation menu. In *Chapter 8, Designing Authentication and Authorization*, when we implement authentication and authorization, we will be receiving the role of the user from the server. Based on the role of the user, we will be able to automatically navigate or limit the options users can see. We will implement these components in this module so that they will only be loaded once a user is logged in. For the purpose of completing the walking skeleton, we will ignore authentication-related concerns:

1. Create the necessary components:

   ```
   $ npx ng g c user/profile -m user
   $ npx ng g c user/logout -m user -t -s
   $ npx ng g c user/navigationMenu -m user -t -s
   ```

2. Implement routing.

   Start with implementing the lazy loading in `app-routing.module.ts`:

   src/app/app-routing.module.ts
   ```
   ...
   {
     path: 'user',
     loadChildren:
       () => import('./user/user.module')
         .then(m => m.UserModule),
   },
   ```

    Ensure that the `PageNotFoundComponent` route is always the last route in `app-routing.module`.

   Now implement the child routes in `user-routing.module.ts`:

   src/app/user/user-routing.module.ts
   ```
   ...
   const routes: Routes = [
     { path: 'profile', component: ProfileComponent },
     { path: 'logout', component: LogoutComponent },
   ]
   ```

We are implementing routing for `NavigationMenuComponent`, because it'll be directly used as an HTML element. In addition, since `UserModule` doesn't have a landing page, there's no default path defined.

3. In `AppComponent`, wire up the user and logout icons:

   src/app/app.component.ts
   ```
   ...
   <mat-toolbar>
     ...
     <button
       mat-mini-fab routerLink="/user/profile"
       matTooltip="Profile" aria-label="User Profile"
     >
       <mat-icon>account_circle</mat-icon>
     </button>
     <button
       mat-mini-fab routerLink="/user/logout"
       matTooltip="Logout" aria-label="Logout"
     >
       <mat-icon>lock_open</mat-icon>
     </button>
   </mat-toolbar>
   ```

 Icon buttons can be cryptic, so it's a good idea to add tooltips to them. In order for tooltips to work, switch from the `mat-icon-button` directive to the `mat-mini-fab` directive and ensure that you import `MatTooltipModule` in `material.module.ts`. In addition, ensure that you add `aria-label` for icon-only buttons so that users with disabilities relying on screen readers can still navigate your web application.

4. Ensure that the app works.

   You'll note that the two buttons are too close to each other, as follows:

Figure 7.22: Toolbar with icons

5. You can fix the icon layout issue by adding `fxLayoutGap="8px"` to `<mat-toolbar>`; however, now the lemon logo is too far apart from the app name, as shown:

Figure 7.23: Toolbar with padded icons

6. The logo layout issue can be fixed by merging the icon and the button:

src/app/app.component.ts
```
...
<mat-toolbar>
  ...
  <a mat-icon-button routerLink="/home">
    <mat-icon svgIcon="lemon"></mat-icon>
    <span class="mat-h2">LemonMart</span>
  </a>
  ...
</mat-toolbar>
```

As shown in the following screenshot, the grouping fixes the layout issue:

Figure 7.24: Toolbar with grouped and padded elements

This is more desirable from a UX perspective also; now users can go back to the home page by clicking on the lemon as well.

POS and inventory modules

Our walking skeleton presumes the role of the manager. To be able to access all components we are about to create, we need to enable the manager to be able to access POS and inventory modules.

Update `ManagerComponent` with two new buttons:

src/app/manager/manager.component.ts
```
<mat-toolbar color="accent" fxLayoutGap="8px">
  ...
  <span class="flex-spacer"></span>
  <button
    mat-mini-fab routerLink="/inventory"
    matTooltip="Inventory" aria-label="Inventory"
  >
    <mat-icon>list</mat-icon>
  </button>
  <button
    mat-mini-fab routerLink="/pos"
    matTooltip="POS" aria-label="POS"
  >
    <mat-icon>shopping_cart</mat-icon>
  </button>
</mat-toolbar>
```

Note that these router links will navigate us out of the realm of the `ManagerModule`, so it is normal for the manager-specific secondary toolbar to disappear.

Now, it'll be up to you to implement the last two remaining modules. For the two new modules, I provide high-level steps and refer you to a previous module you can model the new one on. If you get stuck refer to the `projects/ch7` folder on the GitHub project at https://github.com/duluca/lemon-mart.

POS module

`PosModule` is very similar to the `UserModule`, except that `PosModule` was a default path. The `PosComponent` will be the default component. This has the potential to be a complicated component with some subcomponents, so don't use inline templates or styles:

1. Create the `PosComponent`
2. Register `PosComponent` as the default path
3. Configure lazy loading for `PosModule`
4. Ensure that the app works

Now let's implement the inventory module.

Inventory module

`InventoryModule` is very similar to `ManagerModule`, as shown:

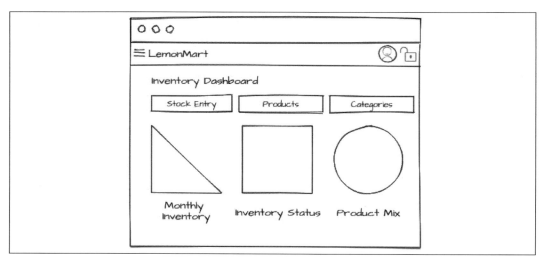

Figure 7.25: Inventory Dashboard mock-up

1. Create a base `Inventory` component
2. Register the `MaterialModule`
3. Create **Inventory Home**, **Stock Entry**, **Products**, and **Categories** components
4. Configure parent-children routes in `inventory-routing.module.ts`
5. Configure lazy loading for `InventoryModule`
6. Implement a secondary toolbar for internal `InventoryModule` navigation in `InventoryComponent`
7. Ensure that the app works, as shown:

Figure 7.26: LemonMart Inventory Dashboard

Now that the walking skeleton of the app is completed, it is important to inspect the router tree to ensure that lazy loading has been configured correctly and modules aren't unintentionally being eagerly loaded.

Inspect the router tree

Navigate to the base route of the app and use Augury to inspect the router tree, as illustrated:

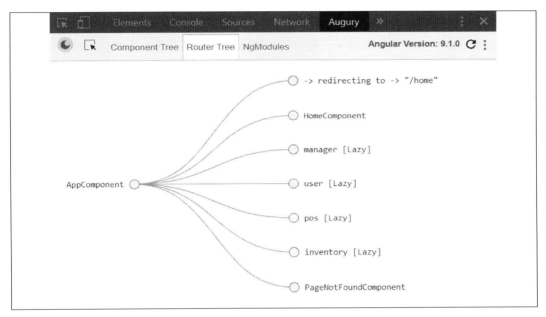

Figure 7.27: Router tree with lazy loading

Everything but the initially required components should be denoted with the **[Lazy]** attribute. If, for some reason, routes are not denoted with **[Lazy]**, chances are that they are mistakenly being imported in `app.module.ts` or some other component.

In your router tree, you may notice that `ProfileComponent` and `LogoutComponent` are eagerly loaded, whereas the `UserModule` is correctly labeled as **[Lazy]**. Even multiple visual inspections through the tooling and the codebase may leave you searching for the culprit. However, if you run a global search for `UserModule`, you'll quickly discover that it was being imported into `app.module.ts`. When running CLI commands, your module may inadvertently get re-imported into `app.module.ts`, so keep an eye out for this!

Creating a Router-First Line-of-Business App

To be on the safe side, inspect your `app.module.ts` file and be sure to remove any import statements for modules or components that are not at the root level. Your file should look like the following one:

src/app/app.module.ts
```
import { HttpClientModule } from '@angular/common/http'
import { NgModule } from '@angular/core'
import { FlexLayoutModule } from '@angular/flex-layout'
import { BrowserModule } from '@angular/platform-browser'
import {
  BrowserAnimationsModule
} from '@angular/platform-browser/ animations'

import { AppRoutingModule } from './app-routing.module'
import { AppComponent } from './app.component'
import { HomeComponent } from './home/home.component'
import { MaterialModule } from './material.module'
import {
  PageNotFoundComponent
} from './page-not-found/page-not-found.component'

@NgModule({
  declarations: [AppComponent, HomeComponent, PageNotFoundComponent],
  imports: [
    BrowserModule,
    AppRoutingModule,
    BrowserAnimationsModule,
    MaterialModule,
    HttpClientModule,
    FlexLayoutModule,
  ],
  providers: [],
  bootstrap: [AppComponent],
})
export class AppModule {}
```

 If you disabled Ivy while debugging your routes with Augury, now's the time to re-enable it.

It is expected that the reader resolves any testing errors before moving on. Ensure that `npm test` and `npm run e2e` execute without errors.

Common testing module

Now that we have a lot of modules to deal with, it becomes tedious to configure the imports and providers for each spec file individually. For this purpose, I recommend creating a common testing module to contain generic configuration that you can reuse across the board.

First start by creating a new .ts file

1. Create common/common.testing.ts.
2. Populate it with common testing providers, fakes, and modules.

    I have provided fake implementations of ObservableMedia, MatIconRegistry, and DomSanitizer, along with arrays for commonTestingProviders and commonTestingModules:

    src/app/common/common.testing.ts
    ```
    import {
      HttpClientTestingModule
    } from '@angular/common/http/ testing'
    import { SecurityContext } from '@angular/core'
    import { MediaChange } from '@angular/flex-layout'
    import { ReactiveFormsModule } from '@angular/forms'
    import {
      SafeResourceUrl,
      SafeValue
    } from '@angular/platform-browser'
    import {
      NoopAnimationsModule
    } from '@angular/platform-browser/animations'
    import { RouterTestingModule } from '@angular/router/testing'
    import { Observable, Subscription, of } from 'rxjs'

    import { MaterialModule } from '../material.module'

    const FAKE_SVGS = {
      lemon: '<svg><path id="lemon" name="lemon"></path></svg>',
    }

    export class MediaObserverFake {
      isActive(query: string): boolean {
        return false
      }

      asObservable(): Observable<MediaChange> {
        return of({} as MediaChange)
      }
    ```

```typescript
    subscribe(
      next?: (value: MediaChange) => void,
      error?: (error: any) => void,
      complete?: () => void
    ): Subscription {
      return new Subscription()
    }
  }

  export class MatIconRegistryFake {
    // tslint:disable-next-line: variable-name
    _document = document
    addSvgIcon(iconName: string, url: SafeResourceUrl): this {
      // this.addSvgIcon('lemon', 'lemon.svg')
      return this
    }

    getNamedSvgIcon(name: string, namespace: string = ''):
  Observable<SVGElement> {
      return of(this._svgElementFromString(FAKE_SVGS.lemon))
    }

    private _svgElementFromString(str: string): SVGElement {
      const div = (this._document || document)
        .createElement('DIV')
      div.innerHTML = str
      const svg = div.querySelector('svg') as SVGElement
      if (!svg) {
        throw Error('<svg> tag not found')
      }
      return svg
    }
  }

  export class DomSanitizerFake {
    bypassSecurityTrustResourceUrl(url: string): SafeResourceUrl {
      return {} as SafeResourceUrl
    }
    sanitize(
      context: SecurityContext,
      value: SafeValue | string | null):
        string | null
    {
      return value?.toString() || null
    }
```

```
    }

    export const commonTestingProviders: any[] = [
      // Intentionally Left Blank!!!
    ]

    export const commonTestingModules: any[] = [
      ReactiveFormsModule,
      MaterialModule,
      NoopAnimationsModule,
      HttpClientTestingModule,
      RouterTestingModule,
    ]
```

Now let's see a sample use of this shared configuration file:

src/app/app.component.spec.ts
```
import { MediaObserver } from '@angular/flex-layout'
import { MatIconRegistry } from '@angular/material/icon'
import { DomSanitizer } from '@angular/platform-browser'
...

import {
  DomSanitizerFake,
  MatIconRegistryFake,
  MediaObserverFake,
  commonTestingModules,
} from './common/common.testing'

...
  TestBed.configureTestingModule({
    imports: commonTestingModules,
    providers: commonTestingProviders.concat([
      { provide: MediaObserver, useClass: MediaObserverFake },
      { provide: MatIconRegistry, useClass: MatIconRegistryFake },
      { provide: DomSanitizer, useClass: DomSanitizerFake },
    ]),
    declarations: [AppComponent],
...
```

Most other modules will just need commonTestingModules to be imported.

> Stop! Did you ensure all your unit tests are passing? To ensure that your tests are always passing implement a CI pipeline in CircleCI, as demonstrated in *Chapter 4, Automated Testing, CI, and Releasing to Production*.

With your tests up and running, the walking skeleton for LemonMart is completed. Now, let's look ahead and start thinking about what kinds of data entities we might be working with.

Designing around major data entities

The fourth step in router-first architecture is achieving a stateless, data-driven design. To achieve this, it helps a lot to organize your APIs around major data components. This will roughly match how you consume data in various components in your Angular application. We will start off by defining our major data components by creating a rough data **entity relationship diagram** (**ERD**). In *Chapter 10, RESTful APIs and Full-Stack Implementation*, we will design and implement an API for the user data entity using Swagger.io and Express.js.

Defining entities

Let's start by taking a stab at what kind of entities you would like to store and how these entities might relate to one another.

Here's a sample design for LemonMart, created using `draw.io`:

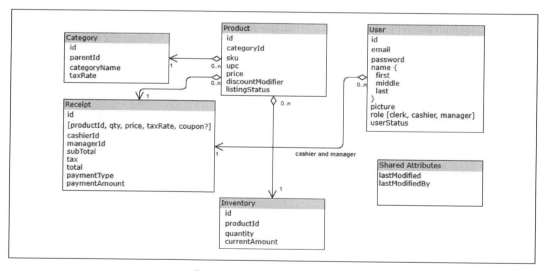

Figure 7.28: ERD for LemonMart

At this moment, whether your entities are stored in a SQL or NoSQL database is inconsequential. My suggestion is to stick to what you know, but if you're starting from scratch, a NoSQL database like MongoDB will offer the most flexibility as your implementation and requirements evolve.

Generally speaking, you will need CRUD APIs for each entity. Considering these data elements, we can also imagine some user interfaces around these CRUD APIs. Let's do that next.

High-level UX design

Mock-ups are important in determining what kind of components and user controls we will need throughout the app. Any user control or component that will be used across components will need to be defined at the root level and others scoped with their own modules.

Earlier in this chapter, we identified the sub modules and designed landing pages for them to complete the walking skeleton. Now that we have defined the major data components, we can complete mock-ups for the rest of the app. When designing screens at a high level, keep several things in mind:

- Can a user complete common tasks required for their role with as little navigation as possible?
- Can users readily access all information and functionality of the app through visible elements on the screen?
- Can a user search for the data they need easily?
- Once a user finds a record of interest, can they drill down into detail records or view related records with ease?
- Is that pop-up alert really necessary? You know users won't read it, right?

Keep in mind that there's no one right way to design any user experience, which is why when designing screens, you should always keep modularity and reusability in mind.

Creating an artifacts Wiki

As mentioned earlier in the chapter, it is important to document every artifact you create. Wikis offer a way to create living documentation that can be collaboratively updated or edited. While Slack, Teams, email, and whiteboards offer good collaboration opportunities, their ephemeral nature leaves a lot to be desired.

So, as you generate various design artifacts, such as mock-ups or design decisions, take care to post them on a wiki reachable by all team members:

1. On GitHub, switch over to the **Wiki** tab
2. You may check out my sample wiki at `https://github.com/duluca/lemon-mart/wiki`, as shown:

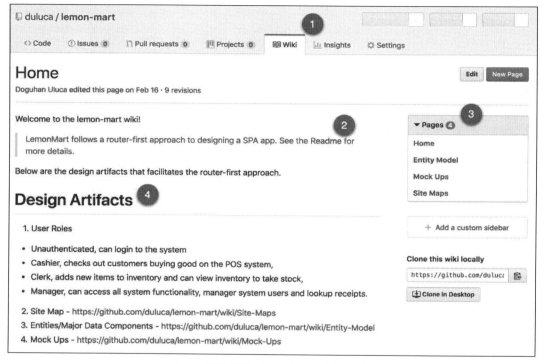

Figure 7.29: GitHub.com LemonMart wiki

3. When creating a wiki page, ensure that you cross-link between any other documentation available, such as **Readme**
4. Note that GitHub shows subpages on the wiki under **Pages**
5. However, an additional summary is helpful, such as the **Design Artifacts** section, since some people may miss the navigational element on the right
6. As you complete mock-ups, post them on the wiki

You can see a summary view of the wiki here:

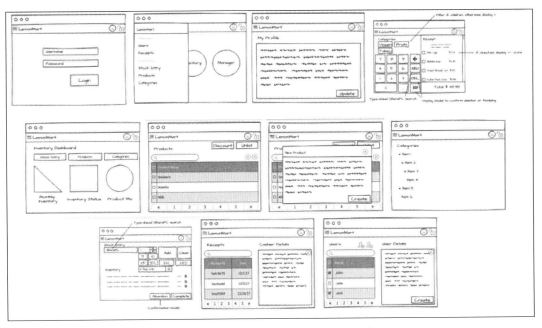

Figure 7.30: Summary view of LemonMart mock-ups

Now that your artifacts are in a centralized place, it is accessible by all team members. They can add, edit, update, or groom the content. This way your wiki becomes useful, living documentation of the information that your team needs, as opposed to a piece of documentation you feel like you're being forced to create. Raise your hand if you've ever found yourself in that situation!

Next, integrate your mock-ups into your app, so you can collect early feedback from your stakeholders and test out the flow of your application.

Leveraging mock-ups in your app

Place the mock-ups in the walking skeleton app so that testers can better envision the functionality that is yet to be developed. See an example of this idea in action here:

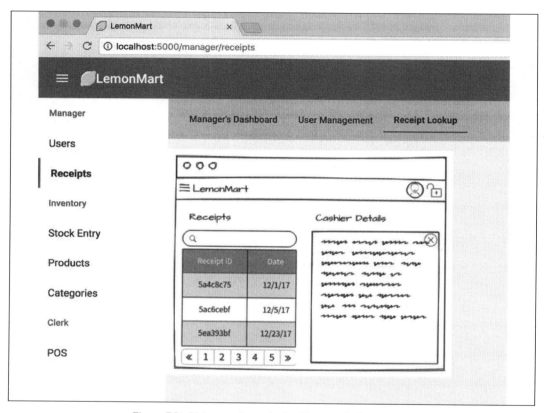

Figure 7.31: Using mock-ups in the UI to verify flow of app

This will also be helpful when designing and implementing your authentication and authorization workflow. With the mock-ups completed, we can now continue the implementation of LemonMart's authentication and authorization workflow in *Chapter 8, Designing Authentication and Authorization*.

Summary

In this chapter, you mastered how to effectively use the Angular CLI to create major Angular components and scaffolds. You became familiar with the 80-20 rule. You created the branding of your app, leveraging custom and built-in Material iconography. You learned how to debug complicated router configurations with Augury. Finally, you began building router-first apps, defining user roles early on, designing with lazy loading in mind, and nailing down a walking-skeleton navigation experience early on. We went over designing around major data entities. We also covered the importance of completing and documenting high-level UX design of our entire app so that we can properly design a great conditional navigation experience.

To recap, in order to pull off a router-first implementation, you need to do this:

1. Develop a roadmap and scope
2. Design with lazy loading in mind
3. Implement a walking-skeleton navigation experience
4. Achieve a stateless, data-driven design
5. Enforce a decoupled component architecture
6. Differentiate between user controls and components
7. Maximize code reuse with TypeScript and ES6

In this chapter, you executed steps 1-3; in the next four chapters, you will execute steps 4-7. In *Chapter 8, Designing Authentication and Authorization*, we will tap into OOP design and inheritance and abstraction, along with a deep dive into security considerations and designing a conditional navigation experience. In *Chapter 10, RESTful APIs and Full-Stack Implementation*, you will see a concrete full-stack implementation using the Minimal MEAN stack. *Chapter 11, Recipes – Reusability, Routing, and Caching*, and *Chapter 12, Recipes – Master/Detail, Data Tables, and NgRx*, we will tie everything together by sticking to a decoupled component architecture, smartly choosing between creating user controls and components, and maximizing code reuse with various TypeScript, RxJS, and Angular coding techniques.

Further reading

- *Ha, Not Ready to Ri: The Shu Ha Ri Approach to Agile Development*, Brian Sjoberg, Ken Furlong, July 29, 2015, https://www.excella.com/insights/ha-not-ready-to-ri-the-shu-ha-ri-approach-to-agile-development.
- *Angular 9: Lazy Loading Components*, John Papa, February 16, 2020, https://johnpapa.net/angular-9-lazy-loading-components/.
- Webpack module bundler, https://webpack.js.org/.

Questions

Answer the following questions as best as you can to ensure that you've understood the key concepts from this chapter without Googling. Do you need help answering the questions? See *Appendix D, Self-Assessment Answers* online at https://static.packt-cdn.com/downloads/9781838648800_Appendix_D_Self-Assessment_Answers.pdf or visit https://expertlysimple.io/angular-self-assessment.

1. What is the Pareto principle?
2. What are the main goals of router-first architecture?
3. What is the difference between the root module and a feature module?
4. What are the benefits of lazy loading?
5. Why create a walking skeleton of your application?

8
Designing Authentication and Authorization

Designing a high-quality authentication and authorization system without frustrating the end user is a difficult problem to solve. Authentication is the act of verifying the identity of a user, and authorization specifies the privileges that a user must have to access a resource. Both processes, auth for short, must seamlessly work in tandem to address the needs of users with varying roles, needs, and job functions.

On today's web, users have a high baseline level of expectations from any auth system they encounter through the browser, so this is an important part of your application to get absolutely right the first time. The user should always be aware of what they can and can't do in your application. If there are errors, failures, or mistakes, the user should be clearly informed about why they occurred. As your application grows, it will be easy to miss all the ways that an error condition could be triggered. Your implementation should be easy to extend or maintain, otherwise this basic backbone of your application will require a lot of maintenance. In this chapter, we will walk through the various challenges of creating a great auth UX and implement a solid baseline experience.

We will continue the router-first approach to designing SPAs by implementing the auth experience of LemonMart. In *Chapter 7, Creating a Router-First Line-of-Business App*, we defined user roles, finished our build-out of all major routing, and completed a rough walking-skeleton navigation experience of LemonMart. This means that we are well prepared to implement a role-based conditional navigation experience that captures the nuances of a seamless auth experience.

Designing Authentication and Authorization

In this chapter, we will implement a token-based auth scheme around the User entity that we defined in the last chapter. For a robust and maintainable implementation, we will deep dive into **object-oriented programming (OOP)** with abstraction, inheritance, and factories, along with implementing a cache service, a UI service, and two different auth schemes: an in-memory fake auth service for educational purposes and a Google Firebase auth service that you can leverage in real-world applications.

In this chapter, you will learn about the following topics:

- Designing an auth workflow
- TypeScript operators for safe data handling
- Reusable services leveraging OOP concepts
- Dynamic UI components and navigation
- Role-based routing using guards
- Firebase authentication recipe
- Providing a service using a factory

The most up-to-date versions of the sample code for the book are on GitHub at the linked repository that follows. The repository contains the final and completed state of the code. You can verify your progress at the end of this chapter by looking for the end-of-chapter snapshot of code under the `projects` folder.

For *Chapter 8*:

1. Clone the repository `https://github.com/duluca/lemon-mart`
2. Execute `npm install` on the root folder to install dependencies
3. The code sample for this chapter is under the sub-folder `projects/ch8`
4. To run the Angular application for this chapter, execute
   `npx ng serve ch8`
5. To run the Angular unit tests for this chapter, execute
   `npx ng test ch8 --watch=false`
6. To run Angular e2e tests for this chapter, execute
   `npx ng e2e ch8`
7. To build a production-ready Angular application for this chapter, execute
   `npx ng build ch8 --prod`

Note that the `dist/ch8` folder at the root of the repository will contain the compiled result.

Be aware that the source code in the book or on GitHub may not always match the code generated by Angular CLI. There may also be slight differences in implementation between the code in the book and what's on GitHub because the ecosystem is ever-evolving. It is natural for the sample code to change over time. Also, on GitHub, expect to find corrections, fixes to support newer versions of libraries, or side-by-side implementations of multiple techniques for you to observe. You are only expected to implement the ideal solution recommended in the book. If you find errors or have questions, please create an issue or submit a pull request on GitHub for the benefit of all readers.

Let's start with going over how a token-based auth workflow functions.

Designing an auth workflow

A well-designed authentication workflow is stateless so that there's no concept of an expiring session. Users are free to interact with your stateless REST APIs from as many devices and tabs as they wish, simultaneously or over time. **JSON Web Token (JWT)** implements distributed claims-based authentication that can be digitally signed or integration that is protected and/or encrypted using a **Message Authentication Code (MAC)**. This means that once a user's identity is authenticated (that is, a password challenge on a login form), they receive an encoded claim ticket or a token, which can then be used to make future requests to the system without having to reauthenticate the identity of the user.

The server can independently verify the validity of this claim and process the requests without requiring any prior knowledge of having interacted with this user. Thus, we don't have to store session information regarding a user, making our solution stateless and easy to scale. Each token will expire after a predefined period and due to their distributed nature, they can't be remotely or individually revoked; however, we can bolster real-time security by interjecting custom account and user role status checks to ensure that the authenticated user is authorized to access server-side resources.

> JWTs implement the **Internet Engineering Task Force (IETF)** industry standard RFC 7519, found at `https://tools.ietf.org/html/rfc7519`.

A good authorization workflow enables conditional navigation based on a user's role so that users are automatically taken to the optimal landing screen; they are not shown routes or elements that are not suitable for their roles and if, by mistake, they try to access a restricted path, they are prevented from doing so. You must remember that any client-side role-based navigation is merely a convenience and is not meant for security. This means that every call made to the server should contain the necessary header information, with the secure token, so that the user can be reauthenticated by the server and their role independently verified. Only then will they be allowed to retrieve secured data. Client-side authentication can't be trusted, which is why password reset screens must be built with a server-side rendering technology so that both the user and the server can verify that the intended user is interacting with the system.

JWT life cycle

JWTs complement a stateless REST API architecture with an encrypted token mechanism that allows convenient, distributed, and high-performance authentication and authorization of requests sent by clients. There are three main components of a token-based authentication scheme:

- **Client-side**: Captures login information and hides disallowed actions for a good UX
- **Server-side**: Validates that every request is both authenticated and has the proper authorization
- **Auth service**: Generates and validates encrypted tokens, and independently verifies the auth status of user requests from a data store

A secure system presumes that data sent/received between clients (applications and browsers), systems (servers and services), and databases is encrypted using **transport layer security** (**TLS**), which is essentially a newer version of **secure sockets layer** (**SSL**). This means that your REST API must be hosted with a properly configured SSL certificate, serving all API calls over HTTPS, so that user credentials are never exposed between the client and the server. Similarly, any database or third-party service call should happen over TLS. This ensures the security of the data in transit.

At-rest (when the data is sitting in the database) passwords should be stored using a secure one-way hashing algorithm with good salting practices.

> Did all the talk of hashing and salting make you think of breakfast? Unfortunately, they're cryptography-related terms. If you're interested in learning more, check out this article: `https://crackstation.net/hashing-security.htm`.

Sensitive user information, such as **personally identifiable information** (**PII**), should be encrypted at rest with a secure two-way encryption algorithm, unlike passwords. Passwords are hashed, so we verify that the user is providing the same password without the system knowing what the password is. With PII, we must be able to decrypt the data so that we can display it to the user. But since the data is encrypted at rest, if the database is compromised then the hacked data is worthless.

Following a layered approach to security is critical, because attackers will need to accomplish the unlikely feat of compromising all layers of your security at the same time to cause meaningful harm to your business.

> **Fun fact**: When you hear about massive data breaches from major corporations, most of the time the root cause is a lack of proper implementation of in-transit or at-rest security. Sometimes this is because it is too computationally expensive to continually encrypt/decrypt data, so engineers rely on being behind firewalls. In that case, once the outer perimeter is breached, as they say, the fox has access to the hen house.

Consider the following sequence diagram, which highlights the life cycle of JWT-based authentication:

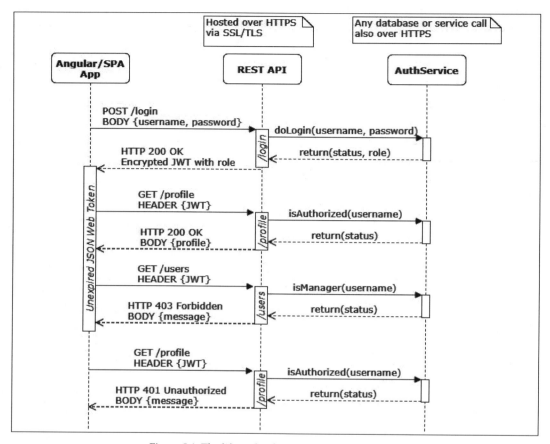

Figure 8.1: The life cycle of JWT-based authentication

Initially, a user logs in by providing their username and password. Once validated, the user's authentication status and role are encrypted in a JWT with an expiration date and time, and it is sent back to the browser.

Our Angular (or any other) application can cache this token in local or session storage securely so that the user isn't forced to log in with every request. This way, we don't resort to insecure practices like storing user credentials in cookies to provide a good UX.

You will get a better understanding of the JWT life cycle when you implement your own auth service later in this chapter. In the following sections, we will design a fully featured auth workflow around the **User** data entity, as follows:

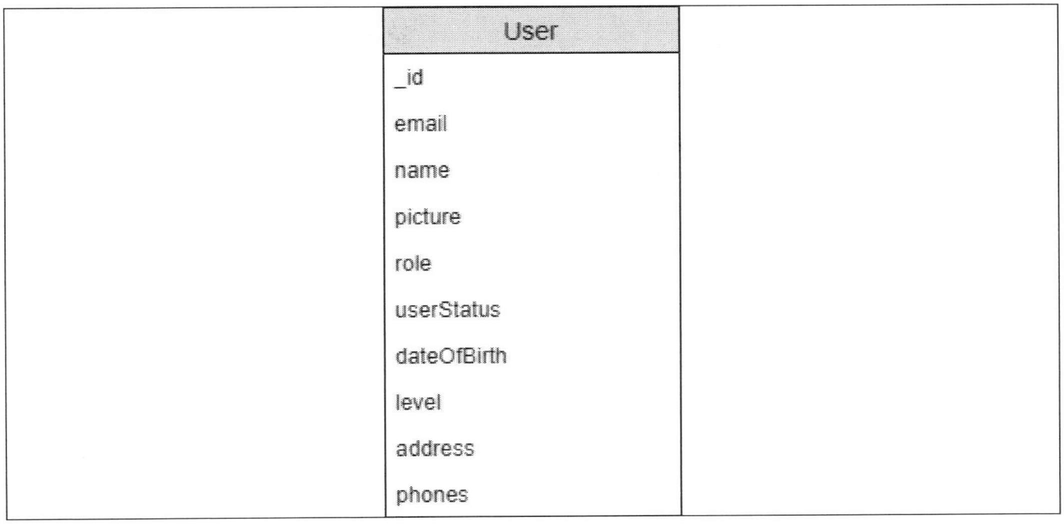

```
                    ┌─────────────────┐
                    │      User       │
                    ├─────────────────┤
                    │ _id             │
                    │ email           │
                    │ name            │
                    │ picture         │
                    │ role            │
                    │ userStatus      │
                    │ dateOfBirth     │
                    │ level           │
                    │ address         │
                    │ phones          │
                    └─────────────────┘
```

Figure 8.2: The User entity

The User entity described is slightly different to our initial entity model. The entity model reflects how data is stored in the database. The entity is a flattened (or simplified) representation of the user record. Even a flattened entity has complex objects, like **name**, which has properties for first, middle, and last. Furthermore, not all properties are required. Additionally, when interacting with auth systems and other APIs, we may receive incomplete, incorrect, or maliciously formed data, so our code will have to effectively deal with `null` and `undefined` variables.

Next, let's see how we can leverage TypeScript operators to effectively deal with unexpected data.

TypeScript operators for safe data handling

JavaScript is a dynamically typed language. At runtime, the JavaScript engine executing our code, like Chrome's V8, doesn't know the type of the variable we're using. As a result, the engine must infer the type. We can have basic types like `boolean`, `number`, `array`, or `string`, or we can have a complex type, which is essentially a JSON object. In addition, variables can be `null` or `undefined`. In broad terms, `undefined` represents something that hasn't been initialized and `null` represents something that isn't currently available.

In strongly typed languages, the concept of undefined doesn't exist. Basic types have default values, like a number is a zero or a string is an empty string. However, complex types can be null. A null reference means that the variable is defined, but there's no value behind it.

> The inventor of the null reference, Tony Hoare, called it his "billion-dollar mistake."

TypeScript brings the concepts of strongly typed languages to JavaScript, so it must bridge the gap between the two worlds. As a result, TypeScript defines types like null, undefined, any, and never to make sense of JavaScript's type semantics. I've added links to relevant TypeScript documentation in the *Further reading* section for a deeper dive into TypeScript types.

As the TypeScript documentation puts it, TypeScript treats null and undefined differently in order to match the JavaScript semantics. For example, the union type string | null is a different type than string | undefined and string | undefined | null.

There's another nuance: checking to see whether a value equals null using == versus ===. Using the double equals operator, checking that foo != null means that foo is defined and not null. However, using the triple equals operator, foo !== null means that foo is not null, but could be undefined. However, these two operators don't consider the truthiness of the variable, which includes the case of an empty string.

These subtle differences have a great impact on how you write code, especially when using the strict TypeScript rules that are applied when you create your Angular application using the --strict option. It is important to remember that TypeScript is a development time tool and not a runtime tool. At runtime, we're still dealing with the realities of a dynamically typed language. Just because we declared a type to be a string, it doesn't mean that we will receive a string.

Next, let's see how we can deal with issues related to working with unexpected values.

Null and undefined checking

When working with other libraries or dealing with information sent or received outside of your application, you must deal with the fact that the variable you receive might be null or undefined.

Outside of your application means dealing with user input, reading from a cookie or `localStorage`, URL parameters from the router, or an API call over HTTP, to name a few examples.

In our code, we mostly care about the truthiness of a variable. This means that a variable is defined, not null, and if it's a basic type, it has a non-default value. Given a `string`, we can check whether the `string` is truthy with a simple `if` statement:

```
example
const foo: string = undefined

if(foo) {
  console.log('truthy')
} else {
  console.log('falsy')
}
```

If `foo` is `null`, `undefined`, or an empty string, the variable will be evaluated as `falsy`. For certain situations, you may want to use the conditional or ternary operator instead of `if-else`.

The conditional or ternary operator

The conditional or ternary operator has the `?:` syntax. On the left-hand side of the question mark, the operator takes a conditional statement. On the right-hand side, we provide the outcomes for true and false around the colon: `conditional ? true-outcome : false-outcome`. The conditional or ternary operator is a compact way to represent `if-else` conditions, and can be very useful for increasing the readability of your code base. This operator is not a replacement for an `if-else` block, but it is great when you're using the output of the `if-else` condition.

Consider the following example:

```
example
const foo: string = undefined
let result = ''
if(foo) {
  result = 'truthy'
} else {
  result = 'falsy'
}
console.log(result)
```

The preceding `if-else` block can be re-written as:

```
example
const foo: string = undefined
console.log(foo ? 'truthy' : 'falsy')
```

In this case, the conditional or ternary operator makes the code more compact and easier to understand at a glance. Another common scenario is returning a default value, where the variable is `falsy`.

We will consider the null coalescing operator next.

The null coalescing operator

The null coalescing operator is `||`. This operator saves us from repetition, when the truthy result of the conditional is the same as the conditional itself.

Consider the example where if `foo` is defined, we would like to use the value of `foo`, but if it is `undefined`, we need a default value of `'bar'`:

```
example
const foo: string = undefined
console.log(foo ? foo : 'bar')
```

As you can see, `foo` is repeated twice. We can avoid the duplication by using the null coalescing operator:

```
example
const foo: string = undefined
console.log(foo || 'bar')
```

So, if `foo` is `undefined`, `null` or an empty string, `bar` will be output. Otherwise, the value of `foo` will be used. But in some cases, we need to only use the default value if the value is `undefined` or `null`. We will consider the nullish coalescing operator next.

The nullish coalescing operator

The nullish coalescing operator is `??`. This operator is like the null coalescing operator, with one crucial difference. Checking the truthiness of a variable is not enough when dealing with data received from an API or user input, where an empty string may be a valid value. As we covered earlier in this section, checking for `null` and `undefined` is not as straightforward as it seems. But we know that by using the double equals operator, we can ensure that `foo` is defined and not null:

example
```
const foo: string = undefined
console.log(foo != null ? foo : 'bar')
```

In the preceding case, if `foo` is an empty string or another value, we will get the value of `foo` output. If it is `null` or `undefined`, we will get `'bar'`. A more compact way to do this is by using the nullish coalescing operator:

example
```
const foo: string = undefined
console.log(foo ?? 'bar')
```

The preceding code will yield the same result as the previous example. However, when dealing with complex objects, we need to consider whether their properties are `null` or `undefined` as well. For this, we will consider the optional chaining operator.

Optional chaining

The optional chaining operator is `?`. It is like Angular's safe navigation operator, which was covered in *Chapter 3, Creating a Basic Angular App*. Optional chaining ensures that a variable or property is defined and not `null` before attempting to access a child property or invoke a function. So the statement `foo?.bar?.callMe()` executes without throwing an error, even if `foo` or `bar` is `null` or `undefined`.

Consider the **User** entity, which has a `name` object with properties for `first`, `middle`, and `last`. Let's see what it would take to safely provide a default value of an empty string for a middle name using the nullish coalescing operator:

example
```
const user = {
  name: {
    first: 'Doguhan',
    middle: null,
    last: 'Uluca'
  }
}
console.log((user && user.name && user.name.middle) ?? '')
```

As you can see, we need to check whether a parent object is truthy before accessing a child property. If `middle` is `null`, an empty string is output. Optional chaining makes this task simpler:

example
```
console.log(user?.name?.middle ?? '')
```

Using optional chaining and the nullish coalescing operator together, we can eliminate repetition and deliver robust code that can effectively deal with the realities of JavaScript's dynamic runtime.

So, when designing your code, you have to make decisions on whether to introduce the concept of null to your logic or work with default values like empty strings. In the next section, as we implement the User entity, you will see how these choices play out. So far, we have only used interfaces to define the shape of our data. Next, let's build the User entity, leveraging OOP concepts like classes, enums, and abstraction to implement it, along with an auth service.

Reusable services leveraging OOP concepts

As mentioned, we have only worked with interfaces to represent data. We still want to continue using interfaces when passing data around various components and services. Interfaces are great for describing the kind of properties or functions an implementation has, but they suggest nothing about the behavior of these properties or functions.

With ES2015 (ES6), JavaScript gained native support for classes, which is a crucial concept of the OOP paradigm. Classes are actual implementations of behavior. As opposed to just having a collection of functions in a file, a class can properly encapsulate behavior. A class can then be instantiated as an object using the new keyword.

TypeScript takes the ES2015 (and beyond) implementation of classes and introduces necessary concepts like abstract classes, private, protected, and public properties, and interfaces to make it possible to implement OOP patterns.

OOP is an imperative programming style, compared to the reactive programming style that RxJS enables. Classes form the bedrock of OOP, whereas observables do the same for reactive programming using RxJS.

I encourage you to become familiar with OOP terminology. Please see the *Further reading* section for some useful resources. You should become familiar with:

1. Classes versus objects
2. Composition (interfaces)

3. Encapsulation (private, protected, and public properties, and property getters and setters)
4. Polymorphism (inheritance, abstract classes, and method overriding)

As you know, Angular uses OOP patterns to implement components and services. For example, interfaces are used to implement life cycle hooks such as `OnInit`. Let's see how these patterns are implemented within the context of JavaScript classes.

JavaScript classes

In this section, I will demonstrate how you can use classes in your own code design to define and encapsulate the behavior of your models, such as the `User` class. Later in this chapter, you will see examples of class inheritance with abstract base classes, which allows us to standardize our implementation and reuse base functionality in a clean and easy-to-maintain manner.

> I must point out that OOP has very useful patterns that can increase the quality of your code; however, if you overuse it then you will start losing the benefits of the dynamic, flexible, and functional nature of JavaScript.
>
> Sometimes all you need are a bunch of functions in a file, and you'll see examples of that throughout the book.

A great way to demonstrate the value of classes would be to standardize the creation of a default `User` object. We need this because a `BehaviorSubject` object needs to be initialized with a default object. It is best to do this in one place, rather than copy-paste the same implementation in multiple places. It makes a lot of sense for the `User` object to own this functionality instead of an Angular service creating default `User` objects. So, let's implement a `User` class to achieve this goal.

Let's begin by defining our interfaces and enums:

1. Define user roles as an `enum` at the location `src/app/auth/auth.enum.ts`:

    src/app/auth/auth.enum.ts
    ```
    export enum Role {
      None = 'none',
      Clerk = 'clerk',
      Cashier = 'cashier',
      Manager = 'manager',
    }
    ```

Designing Authentication and Authorization

2. Create a `user.ts` file under the `src/app/user/user` folder.
3. Define a new interface named `IUser` in the `user.ts` file:

   src/app/user/user/user.ts
   ```
   import { Role } from '../../auth/auth.enum'

   export interface IUser {
     _id: string
     email: string
     name: IName
     picture: string
     role: Role | string
     userStatus: boolean
     dateOfBirth: Date | null | string
     level: number
     address: {
       line1: string
       line2?: string
       city: string
       state: string
       zip: string
     }
     phones: IPhone[]
   }
   ```

Note that every complex property that is defined on the interface can also be represented as a `string`. In transit, all objects are converted to strings using `JSON.stringify()`. No type information is included. We also leverage interfaces to represent `Class` objects in-memory, which can have complex types. So, our interface properties must reflect both cases using union types. For example, `role` can either be of type `Role` or `string`. Similarly, `dateOfBirth` can be a `Date` or a `string`.

We define `address` as an inline type, because we don't use the concept of an address outside of this class. In contrast, we define `IName` as its own interface, because in *Chapter 11, Recipes – Reusability, Routing, and Caching*, we will implement a separate component for names. We also define a separate interface for phones, because they are represented as an array. When developing a form, we need to be able to address individual array elements, like `IPhone`, in the template code.

It is the norm to insert a capital `I` in front of interface names so they are easy to identify. Don't worry, there are no compatibility issues with using the `IPhone` interface on Android phones!

4. In user.ts, define the IName and IPhone interfaces, and implement the PhoneType enum:

   src/app/user/user/user.ts

   ```
   export interface IName {
     first: string
     middle?: string
     last: string
   }

   export enum PhoneType {
     None = 'none',
     Mobile = 'mobile',
     Home = 'home',
     Work = 'work',
   }

   export interface IPhone {
     type: PhoneType
     digits: string
     id: number
   }
   ```

   Note that in the PhoneType enum, we explicitly defined string values. By default, enum values are converted into strings as they're typed, which can lead to issues with values stored in a database falling out of sync with how a developer chooses to spell a variable name. With explicit and all lowercase values, we reduce the risk of bugs.

5. Finally, define the User class, which implements the IUser interface:

   src/app/user/user/user.ts

   ```
   export class User implements IUser {
     constructor(
       // tslint:disable-next-line: variable-name
       public _id = '',
       public email = '',
       public name = { first: '', middle: '', last: '' } as IName,
       public picture = '',
       public role = Role.None,
       public dateOfBirth: Date | null = null,
       public userStatus = false,
       public level = 0,
       public address = {
   ```

```
      line1: '',
      city: '',
      state: '',
      zip: '',
    },
    public phones: IPhone[] = []
  ) {}

  static Build(user: IUser) {
    if (!user) {
      return new User()
    }

    if (typeof user.dateOfBirth === 'string') {
      user.dateOfBirth = new Date(user.dateOfBirth)
    }

    return new User(
      user._id,
      user.email,
      user.name,
      user.picture,
      user.role as Role,
      user.dateOfBirth,
      user.userStatus,
      user.level,
      user.address,
      user.phones
    )
  }
}
```

Note that by defining all properties with default values in the constructors as `public` properties, we hit two birds with one stone; otherwise, we would need to define properties and initialize them separately. This way, we achieve a concise implementation.

Using a static `Build` function, we can quickly hydrate the object with data received from the server. We can also implement the `toJSON()` function to customize the serialization behavior of our object before sending the data up to the server. But before that, let's add a calculated property.

We can use calculated properties in templates or in toast messages to conveniently display values assembled from multiple parts. A great example is extracting a full name from the `name` object as a property in the `User` class.

Chapter 8

 A calculated property for assembling a full name encapsulates the logic for combining a first, middle, and last name, so you don't have to rewrite this logic in multiple places, adhering to the DRY principle!

6. Implement a `fullName` property getter in the `User` class:

    src/app/user/user/user.ts
    ```
    export class User implements IUser {
      ...
      public get fullName(): string {
        if (!this.name) {
          return ''
        }

        if (this.name.middle) {
          return `${this.name.first} ${this.name.middle} ${this.name.last}`
        }
        return `${this.name.first} ${this.name.last}`
      }
    }
    ```

7. Add `fullName` `IUser` as `readonly` and an optional property:

    src/app/user/user/user.ts
    ```
    export interface IUser {
      ...
      readonly fullName?: string
    }
    ```

    You can now use the `fullName` property through the `IUser` interface.

8. Implement the `toJSON` function:

    src/app/user/user/user.ts
    ```
    export class User implements IUser {
      ...

      toJSON(): object {
          const serialized = Object.assign(this)
          delete serialized._id
          delete serialized.fullName
          return serialized
        }
    }
    ```

[357]

Note that when serializing the object, we delete the `_id` and `fullName` fields. These are values that we don't want to be stored in the database. The `fullName` field is a calculated property, so it doesn't need to be stored. The `_id` is normally passed as a parameter in a `GET` or a `PUT` call to locate the record. This avoids mistakes that may result in overwriting the `id` fields of existing objects.

Now that we have the `User data` entity implemented, next let's implement the auth service.

Abstraction and inheritance

We aim to design a flexible auth service that can implement multiple auth providers. In this chapter, we will implement an in-memory provider and a Google Firebase provider. In *Chapter 10, RESTful APIs and Full-Stack Implementation*, we will implement a custom provider to interact with our backend.

By declaring an abstract base class, we can describe the common login and logout behavior of our application, so when we implement another auth provider, we don't have to re-engineer our application.

In addition, we can declare abstract functions, which the implementors of our base class would have to implement, enforcing our design. Any class that implements the base class would also get the benefit of the code implemented in the base class, so we wouldn't need to repeat the same logic in two different places.

The following class diagram reflects the architecture and inheritance hierarchy of our abstract `AuthService`:

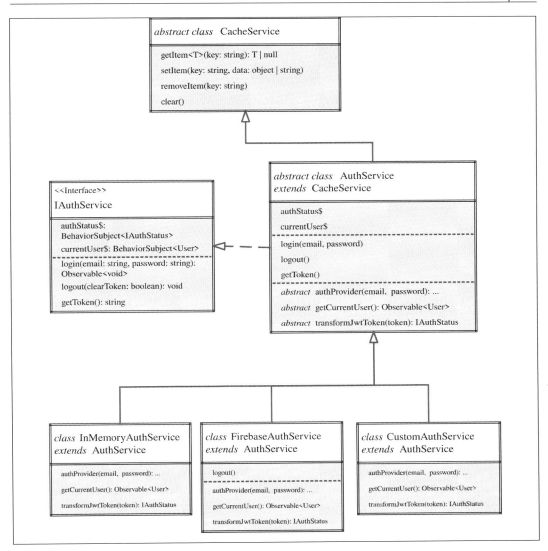

Figure 8.3: The AuthService inheritance structure

Designing Authentication and Authorization

`AuthService` implements the interface `IAuthService`, as shown:

```
export interface IAuthService {
  readonly authStatus$: BehaviorSubject<IAuthStatus>
  readonly currentUser$: BehaviorSubject<IUser>
  login(email: string, password: string): Observable<void>
  logout(clearToken?: boolean): void
  getToken(): string
}
```

The interface reflects the public properties that the service exposes. The service provides the authentication status as the `authStatus$` observable and the current user as `currentUser$`, and it provides three functions to `login`, `logout`, and `getToken`.

`AuthService` inherits caching functionality from another abstract class called `CacheService`. Since `AuthService` is an abstract class, it can't be used on its own, so we implement three auth providers, `InMemoryAuthService`, `FirebaseAuthService`, and `CustomAuthService`, as seen at the bottom of the diagram.

Note that all three auth services implement all abstract functions. In addition, the `FirebaseAuthService` overrides the base `logout` function to implement its own behavior. All three classes inherit from the same abstract class and expose the same public interface. All three will execute the same auth workflow against different auth servers.

The in-memory auth service doesn't communicate with a server. The service is for demonstration purposes only. It implements fake JWT encoding, so we can demonstrate how the JWT life cycle works.

Let's start by creating the auth service.

Create the auth service

We will start by creating the abstract auth service and the in-memory service:

1. Add an auth service:

   ```
   $ npx ng g s auth --flat false --lintFix
   $ npx ng g s auth/inMemoryAuth --lintFix --skipTests
   ```

2. Rename `in-memory-auth.service.ts` to `auth.inmemory.service.ts` so the different auth providers visually group together in File Explorer.

3. Remove the config object `{ providedIn: 'root' }` from the `@Injectable()` decorator of `auth.service.ts` and `auth.inmemory.service.ts`.

4. Ensure that `authService` is provided in `app.module.ts`, but the `InMemoryAuthService` is actually used and not the abstract class:

```
src/app/app.module.ts
import { AuthService } from './auth/auth.service'
import { InMemoryAuthService } from './auth/auth.inmemory.service'
...
  providers: [
    {
      provide: AuthService,
      useClass: InMemoryAuthService
    },
    ...
  ]
```

Creating a separate folder for the service organizes various components related to auth, such as the `enum` definition for the user role. Additionally, we will be able to add an `authService` fake to the same folder for automated testing.

Implement an abstract auth service

Now, let's build an abstract auth service that will orchestrate logins and logouts, while encapsulating the logic of how to manage JWTs, auth status, and information regarding the current user. By leveraging the abstract class, we should be able to implement our own auth service against any auth provider without modifying the internal behavior of our application.

The abstract auth service that is being demonstrated enables rich and intricate workflows. It is a solution that you can drop into your applications without modifying the internal logic. As a result, it is a complicated solution.

This auth service will enable us to demonstrate logging in with an email and password, caching, and conditional navigation concepts based on authentication status and a user's role:

1. Start by installing a JWT decoding library, and, for faking authentication, a JWT encoding library:

   ```
   $ npm install jwt-decode
   $ npm install -D @types/jwt-decode
   ```

2. Implement an `IAuthStatus` interface to store decoded user information, a helper interface, and the secure by default `defaultAuthStatus`:

   src/app/auth/auth.service.ts
   ```
   import { Role } from './auth.enum'
   ...
   export interface IAuthStatus {
     isAuthenticated: boolean
     userRole: Role
     userId: string
   }

   export interface IServerAuthResponse {
     accessToken: string
   }

   export const defaultAuthStatus: IAuthStatus = {
     isAuthenticated: false,
     userRole: Role.None,
     userId: '',
   }
   ...
   ```

`IAuthStatus` is an interface that represents the shape of a typical JWT that you may receive from your authentication service. It contains minimal information about the user and the user's role. The auth status object can be attached to the header of every REST call to APIs to verify the user's identity. The auth status can be optionally cached in `localStorage` to remember the user's login state; otherwise, they would have to re-enter their password with every page refresh.

In the preceding implementation, we're assuming the default role of `None`, as defined in the `Role` enum. By not giving any role to the user by default, we're following a least-privileged access model. The user's correct role will be set after they log in successfully with the information received from the auth API.

3. Define the `IAuthService` interface in `auth.service.ts`:

   src/app/auth/auth.service.ts
   ```
   export interface IAuthService {
     readonly authStatus$: BehaviorSubject<IAuthStatus>
     readonly currentUser$: BehaviorSubject<IUser>
     login(email: string, password: string): Observable<void>
     logout(clearToken?: boolean): void
     getToken(): string
   }
   ```

4. Make `AuthService` an `abstract` class, as shown:

   ```
   export abstract class AuthService
   ```

5. Implement the interface, `IAuthService`, using VS Code's quick fix functionality:

   src/app/auth/auth.service.ts

   ```
   @Injectable()
   export abstract class AuthService implements IAuthService {
     authStatus$: BehaviorSubject<IAuthStatus>
     currentUser$: BehaviorSubject<IUser>

     constructor() {}

     login(email: string, password: string): Observable<void> {
       throw new Error('Method not implemented.')
     }
     logout(clearToken?: boolean): void {
       throw new Error('Method not implemented.')
     }
     getToken(): string {
       throw new Error('Method not implemented.')
     }
   }
   ```

6. Implement the `authStatus$` and `currentUser$` properties as `readonly` and initialize our data anchors with their default values:

   src/app/auth/auth.service.ts
   ```
   import { IUser, User } from '../user/user/user'
   ...
   @Injectable()
   export abstract class AuthService implements IAuthService {
     readonly authStatus$ =
   ```

```
        new BehaviorSubject<IAuthStatus>(defaultAuthStatus)
    readonly currentUser$ =
        new BehaviorSubject<IUser>(new User())
        ...
}
```

Note that we removed the type definitions of the properties. Instead, we're letting TypeScript infer the type from the initialization.

You must always declare your data anchors as `readonly`, so you don't accidentally overwrite the data stream by re-initializing a data anchor as a new `BehaviorSubject`. Doing so would render any prior subscribers orphaned, leading to memory leaks, and have many unintended consequences.

All implementors of `IAuthService` need to be able to log the user in, transform the token we get back from the server so we can read it and store it, support access to the current user, and the auth status, and provide a way to log the user out. We have successfully put in the functions for our public methods and implemented default values for our data anchors to create hooks for the rest of our application to use. But so far, we have only defined what our service can do, and not how it can do it.

As always, the devil is in the details, and the hard part is the "how." Abstract functions can help us to complete the implementation of a workflow in a service within our application, while leaving the portions of the service that must implement external APIs undefined.

Abstract functions

Auth services that implement the abstract class should be able to support any kind of auth provider, and any kind of token transformation, while being able to modify behaviors like user retrieval logic. We must be able to implement login, logout, token, and auth status management without implementing calls to specific services.

By defining abstract functions, we can declare a series of methods that must implement a given set of inputs and outputs—a signature without an implementation. We can then use these abstract functions to orchestrate the implementation of our auth workflow.

Chapter 8

 Our design goal here is driven by the Open/Closed principle. The `AuthService` will be open to extension through its ability to be extended to work with any kind of token-based auth provider, but closed to modification. Once we're done implementing the `AuthService`, we won't need to modify its code to add additional auth providers.

Now we need to define the abstract functions that our auth providers must implement, as shown in *Figure 8.3* from earlier in the chapter:

- `authProvider(email, password): Observable<IServerAuthResponse>` can log us in via a provider and return a standardized `IServerAuthResponse`
- `transformJwtToken(token): IAuthStatus` can normalize the token a provider returns to the interface of `IAuthStatus`
- `getCurrentUser(): Observable<User>` can retrieve the user profile of the logged-in user

We can then use these functions in our `login`, `logout`, and `getToken` methods to implement the auth workflow:

1. Define the abstract methods that the derived classes should implement as protected properties, so they're accessible in the derived class, but not publicly:

    `src/app/auth/auth.service.ts`

    ```
    ...
    export abstract class AuthService implements IAuthService {
        protected abstract authProvider(
          email: string,
          password: string
        ): Observable<IServerAuthResponse>
        protected abstract transformJwtToken(token: unknown):
          IAuthStatus
        protected abstract getCurrentUser(): Observable<User>
        ...
    }
    ```

    Leveraging these stubbed out methods, we can now implement a `login` method that performs a login and retrieves the currently logged-in user, making sure to update the `authStatus$` and `currentUser$` data streams.

2. Before we move on, implement a `transformError` function to handle errors of different types like `HttpErrorResponse` and `string`, providing them in an observable stream. In a new file named `common.ts` under `src/app/common` create the `transformError` function:

   src/app/common/common.ts
   ```
   import { HttpErrorResponse } from '@angular/common/http'
   import { throwError } from 'rxjs'

   export function transformError(error: HttpErrorResponse | string) {
     let errorMessage = 'An unknown error has occurred'
     if (typeof error === 'string') {
       errorMessage = error
     } else if (error.error instanceof ErrorEvent) {
       errorMessage = `Error! ${error.error.message}`
     } else if (error.status) {
       errorMessage =
          `Request failed with ${error.status} ${error.statusText}`
     } else if (error instanceof Error) {
       errorMessage = error.message
     }
     return throwError(errorMessage)
   }
   ```

3. In `auth.service.ts`, implement the `login` method:

   src/app/auth/auth.service.ts
   ```
   import * as decode from 'jwt-decode'
   import { transformError } from '../common/common'
   ...
     login(email: string, password: string): Observable<void> {
       const loginResponse$ = this.authProvider(email, password)
         .pipe(
           map((value) => {
             const token = decode(value.accessToken)
             return this.transformJwtToken(token)
           }),
           tap((status) => this.authStatus$.next(status)),
           filter((status: IAuthStatus) => status.isAuthenticated),
           flatMap(() => this.getCurrentUser()),
           map(user => this.currentUser$.next(user)),
           catchError(transformError)
         )
   ```

```
    loginResponse$.subscribe({
      error: err => {
        this.logout()
        return throwError(err)
      },
    })

    return loginResponse$
}
```

The `login` method encapsulates the correct order of operations by calling the `authProvider` with the `email` and `password` information, then decoding the received JWT, transforming it, and updating `authStatus$`. Then `getCurrentUser()` is called only if `status.isAuthenticated` is `true`. Later, `currentUser$` is updated and, finally, we catch any errors using our custom `transformError` function.

We activate the observable stream by calling `subscribe` on it. In the case of an error, we call `logout()` to maintain the correct status of our application and bubble up errors to consumers of `login` by re-throwing the error using `throwError`.

Now, the corresponding `logout` function needs to be implemented. Logout is triggered by the **Logout** button from the application toolbar in the case of a failed login attempt, as shown earlier, or if an unauthorized access attempt is detected. We can detect unauthorized access attempts by using a router auth guard as the user is navigating the application, which is a topic covered later in the chapter.

4. Implement the `logout` method:

   src/app/auth/auth.service.ts
   ```
   ...
   logout(clearToken?: boolean): void {
     setTimeout(() => this.authStatus$.next(defaultAuthStatus), 0)
   }
   ```

We log out by pushing out the `defaultAuthStatus` as the next value in the `authStatus$` stream. Note the use of `setTimeout`, which allows us to avoid timing issues when core elements of the application are all changing statuses at once.

Designing Authentication and Authorization

Think about how the `login` method adheres to the Open/Closed principle. The method is open to extension through the abstract functions `authProvider`, `transformJwtToken`, and `getCurrentUser`. By implementing these functions in a derived class, we maintain the ability to externally supply different auth providers without having to modify the `login` method. As a result, the implementation of the method remains closed to modification, thus adhering to the Open/Closed principle.

The true value of creating abstract classes is the ability to encapsulate common functionality in an extensible way.

You may ignore the `getToken` function for now, as we are not yet caching our JWT. Without caching, the user would have to log in with every page refresh. Let's implement caching next.

Abstract caching service using localStorage

We must be able to cache the authentication status of the logged-in user. As mentioned, otherwise, with every page refresh, the user will have to go through the login routine. We need to update `AuthService` so that it persists the auth status.

There are three main ways to store data:

- `cookie`
- `localStorage`
- `sessionStorage`

Cookies should not be used to store secure data because they can be sniffed or stolen by bad actors. In addition, cookies can store only 4 KB of data and can be set to expire.

`localStorage` and `sessionStorage` are similar to each other. They are protected and isolated browser-side stores that allow the storage of larger amounts of data for your application. Unlike cookies, you can't set an expiration date-time on values stored in either store. Values stored in either store survive page reloads and restores, making them better candidates than cookies for caching information.

The major difference between `localStorage` and `sessionStorage` is that the values are removed when the browser window is closed. In most cases, user logins are cached anywhere from minutes to a month or more depending on your business, so relying on whether the user closes the browser window isn't very useful. Through this process of elimination, I prefer `localStorage` because of the isolation it provides and long-term storage capabilities.

JWTs can be encrypted and include a timestamp for expiration. In theory, this counters the weaknesses of both cookies and `localStorage`. If implemented correctly, either option should be secure for use with JWTs, but `localStorage` is still preferred.

Let's start by implementing a caching service that can abstract away our method of caching. We can then derive from this service to cache our authentication information:

1. Start by creating an abstract `cacheService` that encapsulates the method of caching:

   src/app/auth/cache.service.ts
   ```
   export abstract class CacheService {
     protected getItem<T>(key: string): T | null {
       const data = localStorage.getItem(key)
       if (data != null) {
         return JSON.parse(data)
       }
       return null
     }

     protected setItem(key: string, data: object | string) {
       if (typeof data === 'string') {
         localStorage.setItem(key, data)
       }
       localStorage.setItem(key, JSON.stringify(data))
     }

     protected removeItem(key: string) {
       localStorage.removeItem(key)
     }

     protected clear() {
       localStorage.clear()
     }
   }
   ```

This cache service base class can be used to give caching capabilities to any service. It is not the same as creating a centralized cache service that you inject into another service. By avoiding a centralized value store, we avoid interdependencies between various services.

2. Update `AuthService` to extend the `CacheService`, which will enable us to implement caching of the JWT in the next section:

    src/app/auth/auth.service.ts
    ```
    ...
    export abstract class AuthService
      extends CacheService implements IAuthService {
      constructor() {
        super()
      }
      ...
    }
    ```

Note that we must call the constructor of the base class from the derived class's constructor using the `super` method.

Let's go over an example of how to use the base class's functionality by caching the value of the `authStatus` object:

```
example
authStatus$ = new BehaviorSubject<IAuthStatus>(
  this.getItem('authStatus') ?? defaultAuthStatus
)

constructor() {
  super()
  this.authStatus$.pipe(
    tap(authStatus => this.setItem('authStatus', authStatus))
  )
}
```

The technique demonstrated in the example leverages RxJS observable streams to update the cache whenever the value of `authStatus$` changes. You can use this pattern to persist any kind of data without having to litter your business logic with caching code. In this case, we wouldn't need to update the `login` function to call `setItem`, because it already calls `this.authStatus.next`, and we can just tap into the data stream. This helps with staying stateless and avoiding side effects by decoupling functions from each other.

Chapter 8

Note that we also initialize the `BehaviorSubject` using the `getItem` function. Using the nullish coalescing operator, we only use cached data if it is not `undefined` or `null`. Otherwise, we provide the default value.

You can implement your own custom cache expiration scheme in the `setItem` and `getItem` functions, or leverage a service created by a third party.

However, for an additional layer of security, we won't cache the `authStatus` object. Instead, we will only cache the encoded JWT, which contains just enough information, so we can authenticate requests sent to the server. It is important to understand how token-based authentication works to avoid revealing compromising secrets. Review the JWT life cycle from earlier in this chapter to improve your understanding.

Next, let's cache the token.

Caching the JWT

Let's update the authentication service so that it can cache the token.

1. Update `AuthService` to be able to set, get, and clear the token, as shown:

   src/app/auth/auth.service.ts

   ```
   ...
     protected setToken(jwt: string) {
       this.setItem('jwt', jwt)
     }

     getToken(): string {
       return this.getItem('jwt') ?? ''
     }

     protected clearToken() {
       this.removeItem('jwt')
     }
   ```

2. Call `clearToken` and `setToken` during `login`, and `clearToken` during `logout`, as shown:

   src/app/auth/auth.service.ts
   ```
   ...
     login(email: string, password: string): Observable<void> {
       this.clearToken()

       const loginResponse$ = this.authProvider(email, password)
         .pipe(
           map(value => {
             this.setToken(value.accessToken)
             const token = decode(value.accessToken)
             return this.transformJwtToken(token)
           }),
           tap((status) => this.authStatus$.next(status)),
           ...
     }

     logout(clearToken?: boolean) {
       if (clearToken) {
         this.clearToken()
       }
       setTimeout(() => this.authStatus$.next(defaultAuthStatus), 0)
     }
   ```

Every subsequent request will contain the JWT in the request header. You should secure every API to check for and validate the token received. For example, if a user wants to access their profile, the `AuthService` will validate the token to check whether the user is authenticated or not; however, a further database call will still be required to check whether the user is also authorized to view the data. This ensures an independent confirmation of the user's access to the system and prevents any abuse of an unexpired token.

If an authenticated user makes a call to an API where they don't have the proper authorization, say if a clerk wants to get access to a list of all users, then the `AuthService` will return a `falsy` status, and the client will receive a **403 Forbidden** response, which will be displayed as an error message to the user.

A user can make a request with an expired token; when this happens, a **401 Unauthorized** response is sent to the client. As a good UX practice, we should automatically prompt the user to log in again and let them resume their workflow without any data loss.

In summary, true security is achieved with robust server-side implementation. Any client-side implementation is largely there to enable a good UX around good security practices.

Implement an in-memory auth service

Now, let's implement a concrete version of the auth service that we can actually use:

1. Start by installing a JWT decoding library and, for faking authentication, a JWT encoding library:

   ```
   $ npm install fake-jwt-sign
   ```

2. Extend the abstract `AuthService`:

   src/app/auth/auth.inmemory.service.ts
   ```
   import { AuthService } from './auth.service'

   @Injectable()
   export class InMemoryAuthService extends AuthService {
     constructor() {
       super()
       console.warn(
         "You're using the InMemoryAuthService. Do not use this service in production."
       )
     }
     ...
   }
   ```

3. Implement a fake `authProvider` function that simulates the authentication process, including creating a fake JWT on the fly:

   src/app/auth/auth.inmemory.service.ts
   ```
     import { sign } from 'fake-jwt-sign'//For InMemoryAuthService only

   ...
     protected authProvider(
       email: string,
       password: string
     ): Observable<IServerAuthResponse> {
       email = email.toLowerCase()

       if (!email.endsWith('@test.com')) {
         return throwError('Failed to login! Email needs to end with
   ```

```
      @test.com.')
    }

    const authStatus = {
      isAuthenticated: true,
      userId: this.defaultUser._id,
      userRole: email.includes('cashier')
        ? Role.Cashier
        : email.includes('clerk')
        ? Role.Clerk
        : email.includes('manager')
        ? Role.Manager
        : Role.None,
    } as IAuthStatus

    this.defaultUser.role = authStatus.userRole

    const authResponse = {
      accessToken: sign(authStatus, 'secret', {
        expiresIn: '1h',
        algorithm: 'none',
      }),
    } as IServerAuthResponse

    return of(authResponse)
  }
...
```

The `authProvider` implements what would otherwise be a server-side method right in the service, so we can conveniently experiment with the code while fine-tuning our auth workflow. The provider creates and signs a JWT with the temporary `fake-jwt-sign` library so that I can also demonstrate how to handle a properly formed JWT.

Do not ship your Angular application with the `fake-jwt-sign` dependency, since it is meant to be server-side code.

In contrast, a real auth provider would include a POST call to a server. See the example code that follows:

example
```
private exampleAuthProvider(
```

```
    email: string,
    password: string
): Observable<IServerAuthResponse> { return this.httpClient.
post<IServerAuthResponse>(
    `${environment.baseUrl}/v1/login`,
    { email: email, password: password }
  )
}
```

It is pretty straightforward, since the hard work is done on the server side. This call can also be made to a third-party auth provider, which I cover in the Firebase authentication recipe later in this chapter.

 Note that the API version, v1, in the URL path is defined at the service and not as part of the baseUrl. This is because each API can change versions independently. Login may remain v1 for a long time, while other APIs may be upgraded to v2, v3, and so on.

4. Implementing transformJwtToken will be trivial, because the login function provides us with a token that adheres to IAuthStatus:

    src/app/auth/auth.inmemory.service.ts
    ```
    protected transformJwtToken(token: IAuthStatus):
      IAuthStatus {
        return token
      }
    ```

5. Finally, implement getCurrentUser, which should return some default user:

    src/app/auth/auth.inmemory.service.ts

    ```
    protected getCurrentUser(): Observable<User> {
      return of(this.defaultUser)
    }
    ```

    Next, provide a defaultUser as a private property to the class; what follows is one that I've created.

6. Add a private defaultUser property to the InMemoryAuthService class:

    src/app/auth/auth.inmemory.service.ts
    ```
    import { PhoneType, User } from '../user/user/user'
    ...
    private defaultUser = User.Build({
      _id: '5da01751da27cc462d265913',
      email: 'duluca@gmail.com',
      name: { first: 'Doguhan', last: 'Uluca' },
    ```

```
      picture: 'https://secure.gravatar.com/avatar/7cbaa9afb5ca78d97f3
c689f8ce6c985',
      role: Role.Manager,
      dateOfBirth: new Date(1980, 1, 1),
      userStatus: true,
      address: {
        line1: '101 Sesame St.',
        city: 'Bethesda',
        state: 'Maryland',
        zip: '20810',
      },
      level: 2,
      phones: [
        {
          id: 0,
          type: PhoneType.Mobile,
          digits: '5555550717',
        },
      ],
    })
```

Congratulations, you've implemented a concrete, but still fake, auth service. Now that you have the in-memory auth service in place, be sure to run your Angular application and ensure that there are no errors.

Let's test our auth service by implementing a simple login and logout functionality accessible through the UI.

Simple login

Before we implement a fully-featured `login` component, let's wire up pre-baked login behavior to the **Login as manager** button we have in the `HomeComponent`. We can test the behavior of our auth service before getting into the details of delivering a rich UI component.

Our goal is to simulate logging in as a manager. To accomplish this, we need to hard code an e mail address and a password to log in, and upon successful login, maintain the functionality of navigating to the `/manager` route.

Note that on GitHub the code sample for this section resides in a file named `home.component.simple.ts` under the folder structure of `projects/ch8`. The alternate file exists for reference purposes only, since the code from this section dramatically changes later in the chapter. Ignore the file name difference, as it will not impact your coding for this section.

Let's implement a simple login mechanism:

1. In the `HomeComponent`, implement a `login` function that uses the `AuthService`:

   src/app/home/home.component.ts
   ```
   import { AuthService } from '../auth/auth.service'

   export class HomeComponent implements OnInit {
     constructor(private authService: AuthService) {}

     ngOnInit(): void {}

     login() {
       this.authService.login('manager@test.com', '12345678')
     }
   }
   ```

2. Update the template to remove the `routerLink` and instead call the `login` function:

   src/app/home/home.component.ts
   ```
   template: `
       <div fxLayout="column" fxLayoutAlign="center center">
         <span class="mat-display-2">Hello, Limoncu!</span>
         <button mat-raised-button color="primary" (click)="login()">
           Login as Manager
         </button>
       </div>
     `,
   ```

   On successful login, we need to navigate to the `/manager` route. We can verify that we're successfully logged in by listening to the `authStatus$` and `currentUser$` observables exposed by the `AuthService`. If `authStatus$.isAuthenticated` is `true` and `currentUser$._id` is a non-empty string, that means that we have a valid login. We can listen to both observables by using RxJS's `combineLatest` operator. Given a valid login condition, we can then use the `filter` operator to reactively navigate to the `/manager` route.

3. Update the `login()` function to implement the login conditional and upon success, navigate to the `/manager` route:

   src/app/home/home.component.ts
   ```
   constructor(
     private authService: AuthService,
     private router: Router
   ) {}
   ```

[377]

```
login() {
  this.authService.login('manager@test.com', '12345678')

  combineLatest([
    this.authService.authStatus$, this.authService.currentUser$
  ])
    .pipe(
      filter(([authStatus, user]) =>
        authStatus.isAuthenticated && user?._id !== ''
      ),
      tap(([authStatus, user]) => {
        this.router.navigate(['/manager'])
      })
    )
    .subscribe()
}
```

Note that we subscribe to the `combineLatest` operator at the end, which is critical in activating the observable streams. Otherwise, our login action will remain dormant unless some other component subscribes to the stream. You only need to activate a stream once.

4. Now test out the new `login` functionality. Verify that the JWT is created and stored in `localStorage` using the **Chrome DevTools | Application** tab, as shown here:

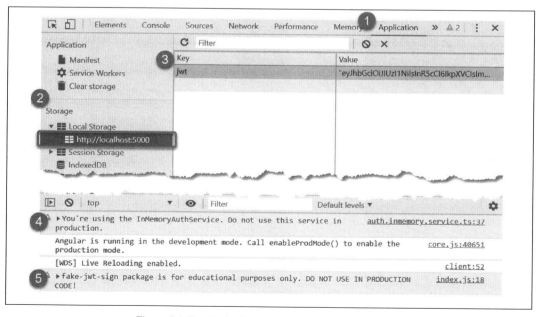

Figure 8.4: DevTools showing Application Local Storage

You can view **Local Storage** under the **Application** tab. Make sure that the URL of your application is highlighted. In step 3, you can see that we have a key named jwt with a valid-looking token.

Note steps 4 and 5 highlighting two warnings, which advise us not to use the InMemoryAuthService and the fake-jwt-sign package in production code.

Use breakpoints to debug and step through the code to get a more concrete understanding of how HomeComponent, InMemoryAuthService, and AuthService work together to log the user in.

When you refresh the page, note that you're still logged in, because we're caching the token in local storage.

Since we're caching the login status, we also need to implement a logout experience to complete the auth workflow.

Logout

The logout button on the application toolbar is already wired up to navigate to the logout component we created before. Let's update this component so it can log the user out when navigated to:

1. Implement the logout component:

    src/app/user/logout/logout.component.ts
    ```
    import { Component, OnInit } from '@angular/core'
    import { Router } from '@angular/router'
    import { AuthService } from '../../auth/auth.service'

    @Component({
      selector: 'app-logout',
      template: `<p>Logging out...</p>`,
    })
    export class LogoutComponent implements OnInit {
      constructor(private router: Router, private authService:
    AuthService) {}

      ngOnInit() {
        this.authService.logout(true)
        this.router.navigate(['/'])
    ```

}
     }

Note that we are explicitly clearing the JWT by passing in `true` to the `logout` function. After we call `logout`, we navigate the user back to the home page.

2. Test out the `logout` button.
3. Verify that local storage is cleared after logout.

We have nailed a solid login and logout implementation. However, we're not yet done with the fundamentals of our auth workflow.

Next, we need to consider the expiration status of our JWT.

Resuming a JWT session

It wouldn't be a great UX if you had to log in to Gmail or Amazon every single time you visited the site. This is why we cache the JWT, but it would be an equally bad UX to keep you logged in forever. A JWT has an expiration date policy, where the provider can select a number of minutes or even months to allow your token to be valid for depending on security needs. The in-memory service creates tokens that expire in one hour, so if a user refreshes their browser window within that frame, we should honor the valid token and let the user continue using the application without asking them to log back in.

On the flip side, if the token is expired, we should automatically navigate the user to the login screen for a smooth UX.

Let's get started:

1. Update the `AuthService` class to implement a function named `hasExpiredToken` to check whether the token is expired, and a helper function named `getAuthStatusFromToken` to decode the token, as shown:

    src/app/auth/auth.service.ts
    ```
    ...
      protected hasExpiredToken(): boolean {
        const jwt = this.getToken()

        if (jwt) {
          const payload = decode(jwt) as any
          return Date.now() >= payload.exp * 1000
        }

        return true
      }
    ```

[380]

```
protected getAuthStatusFromToken(): IAuthStatus {
  return this.transformJwtToken(decode(this.getToken()))
}
```

 Keep your code DRY! Update the `login()` function to use `getAuthStatusFromToken()` instead.

2. Update the constructor of `AuthService` to check the status of the token:

   src/app/auth/auth.service.ts

   ```
   ...
   constructor() {
       super()
       if (this.hasExpiredToken()) {
         this.logout(true)
       } else {
         this.authStatus$.next(this.getAuthStatusFromToken())
       }
   }
   ```

   If the token has expired, we log the user out and clear the token from `localStorage`. Otherwise, we decode the token and push the auth status to the data stream.

   A corner case to consider here is to also trigger the reloading of the current user in the event of a resumption. We can do this by implementing a new pipe that reloads the current user if activated.

3. First, let's refactor the existing user update logic in the `login()` function to a private property named `getAndUpdateUserIfAuthenticated` so we can reuse it:

   src/app/auth/auth.service.ts

   ```
   ...
     @Injectable()
   export abstract class AuthService extends CacheService implements
   IAuthService {
     private getAndUpdateUserIfAuthenticated = pipe(
       filter((status: IAuthStatus) => status.isAuthenticated),
       flatMap(() => this.getCurrentUser()),
       map((user: IUser) => this.currentUser$.next(user)),
       catchError(transformError)
     )
   ```

```
...
login(email: string, password: string): Observable<void> {
  this.clearToken()

  const loginResponse$ = this.authProvider(email, password)
    .pipe(
      map((value) => {
        this.setToken(value.accessToken)
        const token = decode(value.accessToken)
        return this.transformJwtToken(token)
      }),
      tap((status) => this.authStatus$.next(status)),
      this.getAndUpdateUserIfAuthenticated
    )
  ...
}
...
}
```

4. In `AuthService`, define an observable property named `resumeCurrentUser$` as a fork of `authStatus$`, and use the `getAndUpdateUserIfAuthenticated` logic:

   src/app/auth/auth.service.ts

   ```
   ...
     protected readonly resumeCurrentUser$ = this.authStatus$.pipe(
       this.getAndUpdateUserIfAuthenticated
     )
   ```

   Once `resumeCurrentUser$` is activated and `status.isAuthenticated` is true, then `this.getCurrentUser()` will be invoked and `currentUser$` will be updated.

5. Update the constructor of `AuthService` to activate the pipeline if the token is unexpired:

   src/app/auth/auth.service.ts

   ```
   ...
   constructor() {
     super()

     if (this.hasExpiredToken()) {
       this.logout(true)
     } else {
       this.authStatus$.next(this.getAuthStatusFromToken())
       // To load user on browser refresh,
   ```

```
          // resume pipeline must activate on the next cycle
          // Which allows for all services to constructed properly
          setTimeout(() => this.resumeCurrentUser$.subscribe(), 0)
      }
    }
```

Using the preceding technique, we can retrieve the latest user profile data without having to deal with caching issues.

> To experiment with token expiration, I recommend that you create a faster-expiring token in `InMemoryAuthService`.

> As demonstrated earlier in the caching section, it is possible to cache the user profile data using `this.setItem` and the profile data from cache on first launch. This would provide a faster UX and cover cases where users may be offline. After the application launches, you could then asynchronously fetch fresh user data and update `currentUser$` when new data comes in. You would need to add additional caching and tweak the `getCurrentUser()` logic to get such functionality working. Oh, and you would need a whole lot of testing! It takes a lot of testing to create a high-quality auth experience.

Congratulations, we're done implementing a robust auth workflow! Next, we need to integrate auth with Angular's HTTP client so we can attach the token to the HTTP header of every request.

HTTP interceptor

Implement an HTTP interceptor to inject the JWT into the header of every request sent to the user and gracefully handle authentication failures by asking the user to log back in:

1. Create an `AuthHttpInterceptor` under auth:

    src/app/auth/auth-http-interceptor.ts
    ```
    import {
      HttpEvent,
      HttpHandler,
      HttpInterceptor,
      HttpRequest,
    ```

Designing Authentication and Authorization

```
    } from '@angular/common/http'
import { Injectable } from '@angular/core'
import { Router } from '@angular/router'
import { Observable, throwError } from 'rxjs'
import { catchError } from 'rxjs/operators'

import { AuthService } from './auth.service'

@Injectable()
export class AuthHttpInterceptor implements HttpInterceptor {
  constructor(private authService: AuthService, private router:
Router) {}
    intercept(req: HttpRequest<any>, next: HttpHandler):
Observable<HttpEvent<any>> {
    const jwt = this.authService.getToken()
    const authRequest = req.clone({ setHeaders: { authorization:
`Bearer ${jwt}` } })
    return next.handle(authRequest).pipe(
      catchError((err, caught) => {
        if (err.status === 401) {
          this.router.navigate(
            ['/login'], { queryParams: {
              redirectUrl: this.router.routerState.snapshot.url},}
          )
        }
        return throwError(err)
      })
    )
  }
}
```

Note that `AuthService` is leveraged to retrieve the token, and the `redirectUrl` is set for the `login` component after a `401` error.

2. Update `app.module.ts` to provide the interceptor:

   src/app/app.module.ts
   ```
     providers: [
       ...
       {
         provide: HTTP_INTERCEPTORS,
         useClass: AuthHttpInterceptor,
         multi: true,
       },
     ],
   ```

3. Ensure that the interceptor is adding the token to requests. To do this, open the **Chrome DevTools | Network** tab, log in, and then refresh the page:

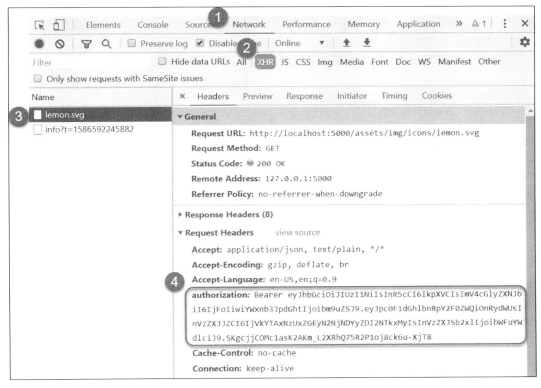

Figure 8.5: The request header for lemon.svg

In step **4**, you can now observe the interceptor in action. The request for the `lemon.svg` file has the bearer token in the request header.

Now that we have our auth mechanisms in place, let's take advantage of all the supporting code we have written with dynamic UI components and a conditional navigation system for a role-based UX.

Dynamic UI components and navigation

`AuthService` provides asynchronous auth status and user information, including a user's name and role. We can use all this information to create a friendly and personalized experience for users. In this next section, we will implement the `LoginComponent` so that users can enter their username and password information and attempt a login.

Implementing the login component

The `login` component leverages the `AuthService` that we just created and implements validation errors using reactive forms.

> Remember that in `app.module.ts` we provided `AuthService` using the class `InMemoryAuthService`. So, during run time, when `AuthService` is injected into the `login` component, the in-memory service will be the one in use.

The `login` component should be designed to be rendered independently of any other component, because during a routing event, if we discover that the user is not properly authenticated or authorized, we will navigate them to this component. We can capture this origination URL as a `redirectUrl` so that once a user logs in successfully, we can navigate them back to it.

Let's begin:

1. Install the `SubSink` package.
2. Create a new component named `login` in the root of your application with inline styles.
3. Let's start with implementing the routes to the `login` component:

   src/app/app-routing.modules.ts
   ```
   ...
     { path: 'login', component: LoginComponent },
     { path: 'login/:redirectUrl', component: LoginComponent },
   ...
   ```

   > Remember that the `'**'` path must be the last one defined.

4. Using a similar `login` logic to the one we implemented in `HomeComponent`, now implement the `LoginComponent` with some styles:

   > Don't forget to import the requisite dependent modules into your Angular application for the upcoming steps. This is intentionally left as an exercise for you to locate and import the missing modules.

src/app/login/login.component.ts
...
```
import { AuthService } from '../auth/auth.service'
import { Role } from '../auth/role.enum'

@Component({
  selector: 'app-login',
  templateUrl: 'login.component.html',
  styles: [
    `
      .error {
        color: red
      }
    `,
    `
      div[fxLayout] {
        margin-top: 32px;
      }
    `,
  ],
})
export class LoginComponent implements OnInit {
  private subs = new SubSink()
  loginForm: FormGroup
  loginError = ''
  redirectUrl: string
  constructor(
    private formBuilder: FormBuilder,
    private authService: AuthService,
    private router: Router,
    private route: ActivatedRoute
  ) {
    this.subs.sink = route.paramMap.subscribe(
      params => (this.redirectUrl =
        params.get('redirectUrl') ?? ''
      )
    )
  }

  ngOnInit() {
    this.authService.logout()
    this.buildLoginForm()
  }

  buildLoginForm() {
```

```typescript
    this.loginForm = this.formBuilder.group({
      email: ['', [Validators.required, Validators.email]],
      password: ['', [
        Validators.required,
        Validators.minLength(8),
        Validators.maxLength(50),
      ]],
    })
  }

  async login(submittedForm: FormGroup) {
    this.authService
      .login(
        submittedForm.value.email,
        submittedForm.value.password
      )
      .pipe(catchError(err => (this.loginError = err)))

    this.subs.sink = combineLatest([
      this.authService.authStatus$,
      this.authService.currentUser$,
    ])
      .pipe(
        filter(
          ([authStatus, user]) =>
            authStatus.isAuthenticated && user?._id !== ''
        ),
        tap(([authStatus, user]) => {
          this.router.navigate([this.redirectUrl || '/manager'])
        })
      )
      .subscribe()
  }
}
```

We are using `SubSink` to manage our subscriptions. We ensure that we are logged out when `ngOnInit` is called. We build the reactive form in a standard manner. Finally, the `login` method calls `this.authService.login` to initiate the login process.

We listen to the `authStatus$` and `currentUser$` data streams simultaneously using `combineLatest`. Every time there's a change in each stream, our pipe gets executed. We filter out unsuccessful login attempts. As the result of a successful login attempt, we leverage the router to navigate an authenticated user to their profile. In the case of an error sent from the server via the service, we assign that error to `loginError`.

5. Here's an implementation for a login form to capture and validate a user's `email` and `password`, and if there are any server errors, display them:

 Don't forget to import `ReactiveFormsModule` in `app.modules.ts`.

src/app/login/login.component.html
```html
<div fxLayout="row" fxLayoutAlign="center">
  <mat-card fxFlex="400px">
    <mat-card-header>
      <mat-card-title>
        <div class="mat-headline">Hello, Limoncu!</div>
      </mat-card-title>
    </mat-card-header>
    <mat-card-content>
      <form [formGroup]="loginForm" (ngSubmit)="login(loginForm)" fxLayout="column">
        <div fxLayout="row" fxLayoutAlign="start center" fxLayoutGap="10px">
          <mat-icon>email</mat-icon>
          <mat-form-field fxFlex>
            <input matInput placeholder="E-mail" aria-label="E-mail" formControlName="email">
            <mat-error *ngIf="loginForm.get('email')?.hasError('required')">
              E-mail is required
            </mat-error>
            <mat-error *ngIf="loginForm.get('email')?.hasError('email')">
              E-mail is not valid
            </mat-error>
          </mat-form-field>
        </div>
        <div fxLayout="row" fxLayoutAlign="start center" fxLayoutGap="10px">
          <mat-icon matPrefix>vpn_key</mat-icon>
          <mat-form-field fxFlex>
            <input matInput placeholder="Password" aria-label="Password" type="password" formControlName="password">
            <mat-hint>Minimum 8 characters</mat-hint>
            <mat-error *ngIf="loginForm.get('password')?.hasError('required')">
```

```
                    Password is required
                </mat-error>
                <mat-error *ngIf="loginForm.get('password')?.
hasError('minlength')">
                    Password is at least 8 characters long
                </mat-error>
                <mat-error *ngIf="loginForm.get('password')?.
hasError('maxlength')">
                    Password cannot be longer than 50 characters
                </mat-error>
            </mat-form-field>
        </div>
        <div fxLayout="row" class="margin-top">
          <div *ngIf="loginError" class="mat-caption
error">{{loginError}}</div>
          <div class="flex-spacer"></div>
          <button mat-raised-button type="submit" color="primary"
[disabled]="loginForm.invalid">Login</button>
        </div>
      </form>
    </mat-card-content>
  </mat-card>
</div>
```

> The **Login** button is disabled until the email and password meet client site validation rules. Additionally, `<mat-form-field>` will only display one `mat-error` at a time, unless you create more space for more errors, so be sure to place your error conditions in the correct order.

Once you're done implementing the `login` component, you can now update the home screen to conditionally display or hide the new component we created.

6. Update the `HomeComponent` to clean up the code we added previously, so we can display the `LoginComponent` when users land on the home page of the app:

src/app/home/home.component.ts

```
...
  template: `
    <div *ngIf="displayLogin">
      <app-login></app-login>
    </div>
    <div *ngIf="!displayLogin">
```

```
      <span class="mat-display-3">You get a lemon, you get a
lemon, you get a lemon...</span>
    </div>
  `,
})
export class HomeComponent {
  displayLogin = true
  constructor() {
  }
}
```

Your application should look similar to this screenshot:

Figure 8.6: LemonMart with login

There's still some work to be done in terms of implementing and showing/hiding the `sidenav` menu, profile, and logout icons given the user's authentication status.

Conditional navigation

Conditional navigation is necessary for creating a frustration-free UX. By selectively showing the elements that the user has access to and hiding the ones they don't have access to, we allow the user to confidently navigate through the application.

Let's start by hiding the `login` component after a user logs in to the application:

Designing Authentication and Authorization

1. On the `HomeComponent`, inject the `AuthService` into the constructor as a `public` variable:

   src/app/home/home.component.simple.ts
   ```
   ...
   import { AuthService } from '../auth/auth.service'
   ...
   export class HomeComponent {
     constructor(public authService: AuthService) {}
   }
   ```

2. Remove the local variable `displayLogin`, because we can directly tap into the auth status in the template using the `async` pipe.

3. Implement a new template using the `ngIf; else` syntax, along with the `async` pipe, as shown here:

   src/app/home/home.component.ts
   ```
   ...
     template: `
       <div *ngIf=
   "(authService.authStatus$ | async)?.isAuthenticated; else doLogin">
         <div class="mat-display-4">
           This is LemonMart! The place where
         </div>
         <div class="mat-display-4">
           You get a lemon, you get a lemon, you get a lemon...
         </div>
         <div class="mat-display-4">
           Everybody gets a lemon.
         </div>
       </div>
       <ng-template #doLogin>
         <app-login></app-login>
       </ng-template>
     `,
   ```

    Using the `async` pipe avoids errors like `Error: ExpressionChangedAfterItHasBeenCheckedError: Expression has changed after it was checked.` Whenever you see this error, stop using local variables and instead use the `async` pipe. It is the reactive thing to do!

4. On the `AppComponent`, we will follow a similar pattern by injecting `AuthService` as a `public` variable:

src/app/app.component.ts

```
import { Component, OnInit } from '@angular/core'
import { AuthService } from './auth/auth.service'
...
export class AppComponent implements OnInit {
  constructor(..., public authService: AuthService) {
  }
  ngOnInit(): void {}
  ...
}
```

5. Update `mat-toolbar` in the template, so that we monitor both `authStatus$` and `currentUser$` using the `async` pipe:

```
<mat-toolbar ...
  *ngIf="{
    status: authService.authStatus$ | async,
    user: authService.currentUser$ | async
  } as auth;">
```

6. Use `*ngIf` to hide all buttons meant for logged-in users:

src/app/app.component.ts
```
<button *ngIf="auth?.status?.isAuthenticated" ... >
```

Now, when a user is logged out, your toolbar should look all clean, with no buttons, as shown here:

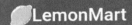

Figure 8.7: The LemonMart toolbar before a user logs in

7. We can also swap out the generic `account_circle` icon in the `profile` button if the user has a picture:

src/app/app.component.ts

```
styles: [
`
  .image-cropper {
    width: 40px;
    height: 40px;
    position: relative;
    overflow: hidden;
```

```
      border-radius: 50%;
      margin-top: -8px;
    }
  `],
  template: `
    ...
    <button
      *ngIf="auth?.status?.isAuthenticated"
      mat-mini-fab
      routerLink="/user/profile"
      matTooltip="Profile"
      aria-label="User Profile"
    >
      <img *ngIf="auth?.user?.picture" class="image-cropper"
        [src]="auth?.user?.picture" />
      <mat-icon *ngIf="!auth?.user?.picture">account_circle</mat-icon>
    </button>
```

We now have a highly functional toolbar that reacts to the auth status of the application and is additionally able to display information that belongs to the logged-in user.

Common validations for forms

Before we move on, we need to refactor the validations for `LoginComponent`. As we implement more forms in *Chapter 11, Recipes – Reusability, Routing, and Caching*, you will realize that it gets tedious, fast, to repeatedly type out form validations in either template or reactive forms. Part of the allure of reactive forms is that they are driven by code, so we can easily extract the validations to a shared class, unit test, and reuse them, as follows:

1. Create a `validations.ts` file under the `common` folder.
2. Implement email and password validations:

   src/app/common/validations.ts
   ```
   import { Validators } from '@angular/forms'

   export const EmailValidation = [
     Validators.required, Validators.email
   ]

   export const PasswordValidation = [
     Validators.required,
     Validators.minLength(8),
     Validators.maxLength(50),
   ]
   ```

Depending on your password validation needs, you can use a RegEx pattern with the Validations.pattern() function to enforce password complexity rules or leverage the OWASP npm package, owasp-password-strength-test, to enable pass-phrases, as well as set more flexible password requirements. See the link to the OWASP authentication general guidelines in the *Further reading* section.

3. Update the login component with the new validations:

   src/app/login/login.component.ts
   ```
   import { EmailValidation, PasswordValidation } from '../common/validations'
   ...
      this.loginForm = this.formBuilder.group({
        email: ['', EmailValidation],
        password: ['', PasswordValidation],
      })
   ```

Next, let's encapsulate some common UI behavior in an Angular service.

UI service

As we start dealing with complicated workflows, such as the auth workflow, it is important to be able to programmatically display a toast notification for the user. In other cases, we may want to ask for a confirmation before executing a destructive action with a more intrusive pop-up notification.

No matter what component library you use, it gets tedious to recode the same boilerplate just to display a quick notification. A UI service can neatly encapsulate a default implementation that can also be customized as needed.

In the UI service, we will implement a showToast and a showDialog function that can trigger notifications or prompt users for a decision, in such a manner that we can use it within the code that implements our business logic.

Let's get started:

1. Create a new service named ui under common.
2. Implement a showToast function using MatSnackBar:

[395]

Designing Authentication and Authorization

Check out the documentation for `MatSnackBar` at https://material.angular.io.

Don't forget to update `app.module.ts` and `material.module.ts` with the various dependencies as they are introduced.

src/app/common/ui.service.ts

```
@Injectable({
  providedIn: 'root',
})
export class UiService {
  constructor(private snackBar: MatSnackBar, private dialog: MatDialog) {}

  showToast(message: string, action = 'Close', config?: MatSnackBarConfig) {
    this.snackBar.open( message,
    action,
    config || { duration: 7000}
    )
  }
  ...
}
```

For a `showDialog` function using `MatDialog`, we must implement a basic `dialog` component.

Check out the documentation for `MatDialog` at https://material.angular.io.

3. Add a new component named `simpleDialog` under the `common` folder provided in `app.module.ts` with inline templates and styling, skip testing, and a flat folder structure:

app/common/simple-dialog.component.ts
```
import { Component, Inject } from '@angular/core'
import { MAT_DIALOG_DATA, MatDialogRef } from '@angular/material/
```

```
dialog'

@Component({
  // prettier-ignore
  template: `
    <h2 mat-dialog-title>{{ data.title }}</h2>
    <mat-dialog-content>
      <p>{{ data.content }}</p>
    </mat-dialog-content>
    <mat-dialog-actions>
      <span class="flex-spacer"></span>
      <button mat-button mat-dialog-close *ngIf="data.cancelText">
        {{ data.cancelText }}
      </button>
      <button mat-button mat-button-raised color="primary" [mat-dialog-close]="true"
        cdkFocusInitial>
        {{ data.okText }}
      </button>
    </mat-dialog-actions>
  `
})
export class SimpleDialogComponent {
  constructor(
    public dialogRef: MatDialogRef<SimpleDialogComponent, boolean>,
    @Inject(MAT_DIALOG_DATA) public data: any
  ) {}
}
```

 Note that `SimpleDialogComponent` should not have an application selector like `selector: 'app-simple-dialog'` since we only plan to use it with `UiService`. Remove this property from your component.

4. Then, implement a `showDialog` function using `MatDialog` to display the `SimpleDialogComponent`:

   app/common/ui.service.ts
   ```
   ...
   showDialog(
     title: string,
     content: string,
     okText = 'OK',
   ```

```
      cancelText?: string,
      customConfig?: MatDialogConfig
): Observable<boolean> {
    const dialogRef = this.dialog.open(
      SimpleDialogComponent,
      customConfig || {
        width: '300px',
        data: { title, content, okText, cancelText },
      }
    )

    return dialogRef.afterClosed()
}
```

ShowDialog returns an Observable<boolean>, so you can implement a follow-on action, depending on what selection the user makes. Clicking on **OK** will return true, and **Cancel** will return false.

In SimpleDialogComponent, using @Inject, we're able to use all variables sent by showDialog to customize the content of the dialog.

5. In app.module.ts, declare SimpleDialogComponent as an entry component:

   src/app/app.module.ts
   ```
   @NgModule({
     ...
     bootstrap: [AppComponent],
     entryComponents: [SimpleDialogComponent],
   })
   Export class AppModule {}
   ```

    Note that with the Ivy rendering engine, entryComponents should be unnecessary and is deprecated in Angular 9. However, at the time of publishing, it is still required to declare this component as an entry component.

6. Update the login() function on the LoginComponent to display a toast message after login:

   src/app/login/login.component.ts
   ```
   import { UiService } from '../common/ui.service'
   ...
   constructor(... , private uiService: UiService)
     ...
   ```

```
async login(submittedForm: FormGroup) {
  ...
  tap(([authStatus, user]) => {
    this.uiService.showToast(
      `Welcome ${user.fullName}! Role: ${user.role}`
    )
    ...
  })
  ...
```

Now, a toast message will appear after a user logs in, as shown:

Figure 8.8: Material snackbar

 The `snackBar` will either take up the full width of the screen or a portion, depending on the size of the browser.

7. Experiment with displaying a dialog instead:

src/app/login/login.component.ts

```
this.uiService.showDialog(
  `Welcome ${user.fullName}!`, `Role: ${user.role}`
)
```

Now that you've verified that both `showToast` and `showDialog` work, which one do you prefer? My rule of thumb is that unless the user is about to take an irreversible action, you should choose toast messages over dialogs, so you don't interrupt the user's workflow.

Next, let's implement an application-wide side navigation experience as an alternative to the toolbar-based navigation we already have, so that users can switch between modules with ease.

Side navigation

Enable mobile-first workflows and provide an easy navigation mechanism to quickly jump to the desired functionality. Using the authentication service, given a user's current role, only display the links for features they can access. We will be implementing the side navigation mock-up as follows:

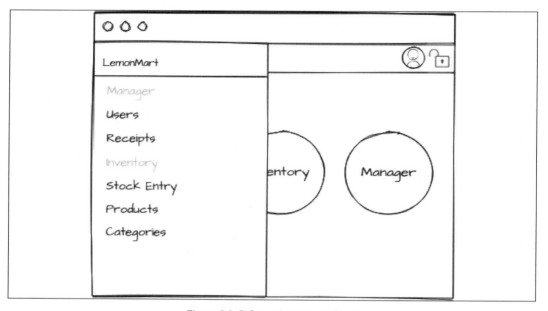

Figure 8.9: Side navigation mock-up

Let's implement the code for the side navigation as a separate component, so that it is easier to maintain:

1. In the root of the application, create a component named `NavigationMenu` with inline templates and styles.

   > The side navigation isn't technically required until after a user is logged in. However, in order to be able to launch the side navigation menu from the toolbar, we need to be able to trigger it from `AppComponent`. Since this component will be simple, we will eagerly load it. To do this lazily, Angular does have a Dynamic Component Loader pattern, which has a high implementation overhead that will only make sense if multi-hundred kilobyte savings are made.

SideNav will be triggered from the toolbar, and it comes with a `<mat-sidenav-container>` parent container that hosts the SideNav itself and the content of the application. So, we will need to render all application content by placing the `<router-outlet>` inside `<mat-sidenav-content>`.

2. In AppComponent, define some styles that will ensure that the web application will expand to fill the entire page and remain properly scrollable for desktop and mobile scenarios:

   src/app/app.component.ts
   ```
   styles: [
       `
       .app-container {
         display: flex;
         flex-direction: column;
         position: absolute;
         top: 0;
         bottom: 0;
         left: 0;
         right: 0;
       }
       .app-is-mobile .app-toolbar {
         position: fixed;
         z-index: 2;
       }
       .app-sidenav-container {
         flex: 1;
       }
       .app-is-mobile .app-sidenav-container {
         flex: 1 0 auto;
       }
       mat-sidenav {
         width: 200px;
       }
       .image-cropper {
         width: 40px;
         height: 40px;
         position: relative;
         overflow: hidden;
         border-radius: 50%;
         margin-top: -8px;
       }
       `,
   ],
   ```

3. Inject the `MediaObserver` service from Angular Flex Layout in `AppComponent`. Also, implement `OnInit` and `OnDestory`, initialize `SubSink`, and add a Boolean property named `opened`:

src/app/app.component.ts

```
import { MediaObserver } from '@angular/flex-layout'

export class AppComponent implements OnInit, OnDestroy {
  private subs = new SubSink()
  opened: boolean

  constructor(
    ...
    public media: MediaObserver
  ) {
    ...
  }

  ngOnDestroy() {
    this.subs.unsubscribe()
  }

  ngOnInit(): void {
    throw new Error('Method not implemented.')
  }
}
```

To automatically determine the open/closed status of the side navigation, we need to monitor the media observer and the auth status. When the user logs in, we would like to show the side navigation, and hide it when the user logs out. We can do this with settings `opened` to the value of `authStatus$.isAuthenticated`. However, if we only consider `isAuthenticated`, and the user is on a mobile device, we will create a less than ideal UX. Watching for the media observer's `mediaValue`, we can check to see whether the screen size is set to extra small, or `xs`; if so, we can keep the side navigation closed.

4. Update `ngOnInit` to implement the dynamic side navigation open/closed logic:

src/app/app.component.ts

```
ngOnInit() {
  this.subs.sink = combineLatest([
    this.media.asObservable(),
    this.authService.authStatus$,
  ])
    .pipe(
      tap(([mediaValue, authStatus]) => {
        if (!authStatus?.isAuthenticated) {
          this.opened = false
```

```
          } else {
            if (mediaValue[0].mqAlias === 'xs') {
              this.opened = false
            } else {
              this.opened = true
            }
          }
        })
      )
      .subscribe()
  }
```

By monitoring both the media and `authStatus$` streams, we can consider unauthenticated scenarios where the side navigation should not be opened even if there's enough screen space.

5. Update the template with a responsive `SideNav` that will slide over the content in mobile or push the content aside in desktop scenarios:

src/app/app.component.ts
```
...
// prettier-ignore
template: `
  <div class="app-container">
  <mat-toolbar color="primary" fxLayoutGap="8px"
    class="app-toolbar"
    [class.app-is-mobile]="media.isActive('xs')"
    *ngIf="{
      status: authService.authStatus$ | async,
      user: authService.currentUser$ | async
    } as auth;"
  >
    <button *ngIf="auth?.status?.isAuthenticated"
      mat-icon-button (click)="sidenav.toggle()"
    >
      <mat-icon>menu</mat-icon>
    </button>
    ...
  </mat-toolbar>
  <mat-sidenav-container class="app-sidenav-container">
    <mat-sidenav #sidenav
      [mode]="media.isActive('xs') ? 'over' : 'side'"
      [fixedInViewport]="media.isActive('xs')"
      fixedTopGap="56" [(opened)]="opened"
    >
      <app-navigation-menu></app-navigation-menu>
    </mat-sidenav>
    <mat-sidenav-content>
      <router-outlet></router-outlet>
    </mat-sidenav-content>
```

```
      </mat-sidenav-container>
    </div>
  `,
```

The preceding template leverages the Angular Flex Layout media observer that was injected earlier for a responsive implementation.

You can use the `// prettier-ignore` directive above your template to prevent Prettier from breaking up your template into too many lines, which can hurt readability in certain conditions similar to this one.

We will implement navigational links in `NavigationMenuComponent`. The number of links in our application will likely grow over time and be subject to various role-based business rules. Therefore, if we were to implement these links in `app.component.ts`, we would risk that file getting too large. In addition, we don't want `app.component.ts` to change very often, since changes made there can impact the entire application. It is a good practice to implement the links in a separate component.

6. Implement navigational links in `NavigationMenuComponent`:

    `src/app/navigation-menu/navigation-menu.component.ts`
    ```
    ...
      styles: [
        `
          .active-link {
            font-weight: bold;
            border-left: 3px solid green;
          }
        `,
      ],
      template: `
        <mat-nav-list>
          <h3 matSubheader>Manager</h3>
          <a mat-list-item
            routerLinkActive="active-link"
            routerLink="/manager/users">
              Users
          </a>
          <a mat-list-item
            routerLinkActive="active-link"
            routerLink="/manager/receipts">
              Receipts
          </a>
    ```

```html
        <h3 matSubheader>Inventory</h3>
        <a mat-list-item
          routerLinkActive="active-link"
          routerLink="/inventory/stockEntry">
            Stock Entry
        </a>
        <a mat-list-item
          routerLinkActive="active-link"
          routerLink="/inventory/products">
            Products
        </a>
        <a mat-list-item
          routerLinkActive="active-link"
          routerLink="/inventory/categories">
            Categories
        </a>
        <h3 matSubheader>Clerk</h3>
        <a mat-list-item
          routerLinkActive="active-link"
          routerLink="/pos">
            POS
        </a>
      </mat-nav-list>
    `,
...
```

`<mat-nav-list>` is functionally equivalent to `<mat-list>`, so you can use the documentation of `MatList` for layout purposes. Observe the `subheaders` for **Manager**, **Inventory**, and **Clerk** here:

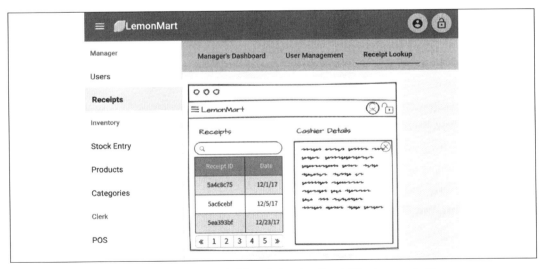

Figure 8.10: The Manager dashboard showing Receipt Lookup on desktop

Designing Authentication and Authorization

`routerLinkActive="active-link"` highlights the selected **Receipts** route, as shown in the preceding screenshot.

Additionally, you can see the difference in appearance and behavior on mobile devices as follows:

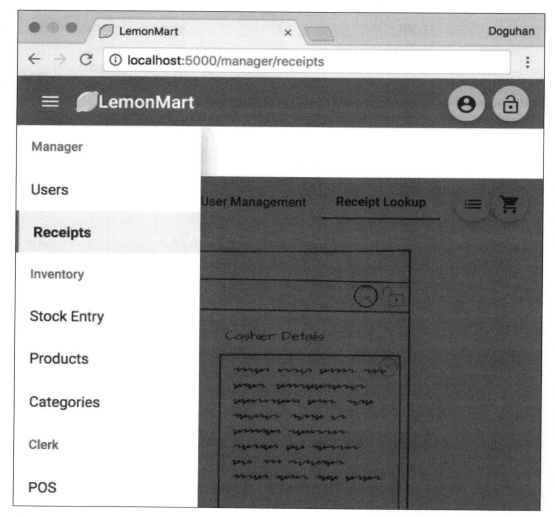

Figure 8.11: The Manager dashboard showing Receipt Lookup on mobile

Next, let's implement role-based routing.

Role-based routing using guards

This is the most elemental and important part of your application. With lazy loading, we have ensured that only the bare minimum number of assets will be loaded to enable a user to log in.

Once a user logs in, they should be routed to the appropriate landing screen as per their user role, so they're not guessing how they need to use the application. For example, a cashier needs to only access the point of sale (POS) to check out customers, so they can automatically be routed to that screen.

The following is a mock-up of the POS screen:

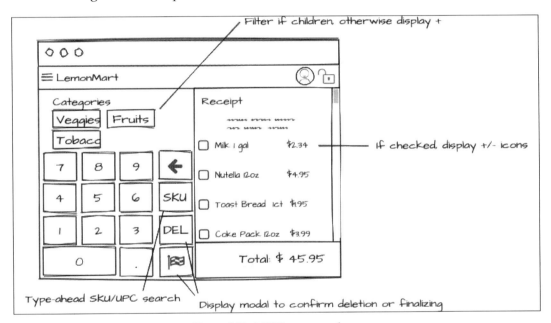

Figure 8.12: A POS screen mock-up

Let's ensure that users get routed to the appropriate page after logging in by updating the `LoginComponent`.

Update the `login` logic to route per role in the function named `homeRoutePerRole`:

`app/src/login/login.component.ts`

```
async login(submittedForm: FormGroup) {
  ...
    this.router.navigate([
      this.redirectUrl ||
```

```
            this.homeRoutePerRole(user.role as Role)
      ])
      ...
}

    private homeRoutePerRole(role: Role) {
      switch (role) {
        case Role.Cashier:
          return '/pos'
        case Role.Clerk:
          return '/inventory'
        case Role.Manager:
          return '/manager'
        default:
          return '/user/profile'
      }
    }
```

Similarly, clerks and managers are routed to their landing screens to access the features they need to accomplish their tasks, as shown earlier. Since we have implemented a default manager role, the corresponding landing experience will be launched automatically. The other side of the coin is intentional and unintentional attempts to access routes that a user isn't meant to have access to. In the next section, you will learn about router guards that can help to check authentication and even load requisite data before the form is rendered.

Router guards

Router guards enable the further decoupling and reuse of logic, and greater control over the component life cycle.

Here are the four major guards you will most likely use:

1. `CanActivate` and `CanActivateChild`: Used for checking auth access to a route
2. `CanDeactivate`: Used to ask permission before navigating away from a route
3. `Resolve`: Allows the pre-fetching of data from route parameters
4. `CanLoad`: Allows custom logic to execute before loading feature module assets

Refer to the following sections to discover how to leverage `CanActivate` and `CanLoad`. The `Resolve` guard will be covered in *Chapter 11, Recipes – Reusability, Routing, and Caching*.

Auth guards

Auth guards enable a good UX by allowing or disallowing accidental navigation to a feature module or a component before the module has loaded or before any improper data requests have been made to the server. For example, when a manager logs in, they're automatically routed to the /manager/home path. The browser will cache this URL, and it would be completely plausible for a clerk to accidentally navigate to the same URL. Angular doesn't know whether a particular route is accessible to a user or not and, without an AuthGuard, it will happily render the manager's home page and trigger server requests that will end up failing.

> Regardless of the robustness of your frontend implementation, every REST API you implement should be properly secured server-side.

Let's update the router so that ProfileComponent can't be activated without an authenticated user and the ManagerModule won't load unless a manager is logging in using an AuthGuard:

1. Implement an AuthGuard service:

    src/app/auth/auth-guard.service.ts
    ```
    import { Injectable } from '@angular/core'
    import {
      ActivatedRouteSnapshot,
      CanActivate,
      CanActivateChild,
      CanLoad,
      Route,
      Router,
      RouterStateSnapshot,
    } from '@angular/router'
    import { Observable } from 'rxjs'
    import { map, take } from 'rxjs/operators'

    import { UiService } from '../common/ui.service'
    import { Role } from './auth.enum'
    import { AuthService } from './auth.service'

    @Injectable({
      providedIn: 'root',
    })
    export class AuthGuard implements CanActivate, CanActivateChild, CanLoad {
      constructor(
    ```

```typescript
    protected authService: AuthService,
    protected router: Router,
    private uiService: UiService
  ) {}

  canLoad(route: Route):
    boolean | Observable<boolean> | Promise<boolean> {
      return this.checkLogin()
  }

  canActivate(
    route: ActivatedRouteSnapshot,
    state: RouterStateSnapshot
  ): boolean | Observable<boolean> | Promise<boolean> {
    return this.checkLogin(route)
  }

  canActivateChild(
    childRoute: ActivatedRouteSnapshot,
    state: RouterStateSnapshot
  ): boolean | Observable<boolean> | Promise<boolean> {
    return this.checkLogin(childRoute)
  }

  protected checkLogin(route?: ActivatedRouteSnapshot):
    Observable<boolean> {
    return this.authService.authStatus$.pipe(
      map((authStatus) => {
        const roleMatch = this.checkRoleMatch(
          authStatus.userRole, route
        )
        const allowLogin = authStatus.isAuthenticated && roleMatch
        if (!allowLogin) {
          this.showAlert(authStatus.isAuthenticated, roleMatch)
          this.router.navigate(['login'], {
            queryParams: {
              redirectUrl: this.getResolvedUrl(route),
            },
          })
        }
        return allowLogin
      }),
      take(1) // complete the observable for the guard to work
    )
  }

  private checkRoleMatch(
```

```
      role: Role,
      route?: ActivatedRouteSnapshot
  ) {
    if (!route?.data?.expectedRole) {
      return true
    }
    return role === route.data.expectedRole
  }

  private showAlert(isAuth: boolean, roleMatch: boolean) {
    if (!isAuth) {
      this.uiService.showToast('You must login to continue')
    }

    if (!roleMatch) {
      this.uiService.showToast(
        'You do not have the permissions to view this resource'
      )
    }
  }

  getResolvedUrl(route?: ActivatedRouteSnapshot): string {
    if (!route) {
      return ''
    }

    return route.pathFromRoot
      .map((r) => r.url.map((segment) => segment.toString()))
      .join('/'))
      .join('/')
      .replace('//', '/')
  }
}
```

2. Use the `CanLoad` guard to prevent the loading of a lazily loaded module, such as the manager's module:

src/app/app-routing.module.ts

```
...
{
  path: 'manager',
  loadChildren: () => import('./manager/manager.module')
    .then((m) => m.ManagerModule),
  canLoad: [AuthGuard],
},
...
```

In this instance, when the `ManagerModule` is being loaded, `AuthGuard` will be activated during the `canLoad` event, and the `checkLogin` function will verify the authentication status of the user. If the guard returns `false`, the module will not be loaded. At this point, we don't have the metadata to check the role of the user.

3. Use the `CanActivate` guard to prevent the activation of individual components, such as the user's `profile`:

   src/app/user/user-routing.module.ts
   ```
   ...
   {
     path: 'profile', component: ProfileComponent,
     canActivate: [AuthGuard]
   },
   ...
   ```

   In the case of `user-routing.module.ts`, `AuthGuard` is activated during the `canActivate` event, and the `checkLogin` function controls where this route can be navigated to. Since the user is viewing their own profile, there's no need to check the user's role here.

4. Use `CanActivate` or `CanActivateChild` with an `expectedRole` property to prevent the activation of components by other users, such as `ManagerHomeComponent`:

   src/app/mananger/manager-routing.module.ts
   ```
   ...
   {
     path: 'home',
     component: ManagerHomeComponent,
     canActivate: [AuthGuard],
     data: {
       expectedRole: Role.Manager,
     },
   },
   {
     path: 'users',
     component: UserManagementComponent,
     canActivate: [AuthGuard],
     data: {
       expectedRole: Role.Manager,
     },
   },
   {
     path: 'receipts',
   ```

```
      component: ReceiptLookupComponent,
      canActivate: [AuthGuard],
      data: {
        expectedRole: Role.Manager,
      },
    },
  ...
```

Inside `ManagerModule`, we can verify whether the user is authorized to access a particular route. We can do this by defining some metadata in the route definition, like `expectedRole`, which will be passed into the `checkLogin` function by the `canActivate` event. If a user is authenticated but their role doesn't match `Role.Manager`, `AuthGuard` will return `false` and the navigation will be prevented.

Next, we will go over some techniques to get our tests passing.

Auth service fake and common testing providers

We need to provide mocked versions of services like `AuthService` or `UiService` using the `commonTestingProviders` function in `common.testing.ts`, using a pattern similar to `commonTestingModules`, which was mentioned in *Chapter 7, Creating a Router-First Line-of-Business App*. This way, we won't have to mock the same objects over and over again.

Let's create the spy objects using the `autoSpyObj` function from `angular-unit-test-helper` and go over some less obvious changes we need to implement to get our tests passing:

1. Update `commonTestingProviders` in `common.testing.ts`:

    src/app/common/common.testing.ts

    ```
    import { autoSpyObj } from 'angular-unit-test-helper'

    export const commonTestingProviders: any[] = [
      { provide: AuthService, useValue: autoSpyObj(AuthService) },
      { provide: UiService, useValue: autoSpyObj(UiService) },
    ]
    ```

2. Observe the fake being provided for the `MediaObserver` in `app.component.spec.ts` and update it to use `commonTestingModules`:

    src/app/app.component.spec.ts
    ```
    ...
      TestBed.configureTestingModule({
    ```

```
    imports: commonTestingModules,
    providers: commonTestingProviders.concat([
      { provide: MediaObserver, useClass: MediaObserverFake },
...
```

See how the `commonTestingProviders` array is being concatenated with fakes that are specific to `app.component.ts`; our new mocks should apply automatically.

3. Update the spec file for `LoginComponent` to leverage `commonTestingModules` and `commonTestingProviders`:

   src/app/login/login.component.spec.ts
   ```
   ...
     TestBed.configureTestingModule({
       imports: commonTestingModules,
       providers: commonTestingProviders,
       declarations: [LoginComponent],
     }).compileComponents()
   ```

4. Go ahead and apply this technique to all spec files that have a dependency on `AuthService` and `UiService`.

5. The notable exception is services, as in `auth.service.spec.ts`, where you do *not* want to use a test double. Since `AuthService` is the class under test, make sure it is configured as follows:

   src/app/auth/auth.service.spec.ts
   ```
   ...
   TestBed.configureTestingModule({
     imports: [HttpClientTestingModule],
     providers: [AuthService,
       { provide: UiService, useValue: autoSpyObj(UiService) }],
   })
   ```

6. Update `ui.service.spec.ts` with similar considerations.

Remember, don't move on until all your tests are passed!

Firebase authentication recipe

We can leverage our current authentication setup and integrate it with a real authentication service. For this section, you need a free Google and Firebase account. Firebase is Google's comprehensive mobile development platform: https://firebase.google.com. You can create a free account to host your application and leverage the Firebase authentication system.

The Firebase console, found at `https://console.firebase.google.com`, allows you to manage users and send a password reset email without having to implement a backend for your application. Later on, you can leverage Firebase functions to implement APIs in a serverless manner.

Start by adding your project to Firebase using the Firebase console:

Figure 8.13: The Firebase console

1. Click on **Add project**
2. Provide your project name
3. Enable Google Analytics for your project

It helps to create a Google Analytics account before attempting this, but it should still work. Once your project is created, you should see your project dashboard:

Figure 8.14: The Firebase project overview

On the left-hand side, marked with step **1**, you can see a menu of tools and services that you can add to your project. At the top, marked with step **2**, you can quickly jump between your projects. First, you need to add an application to your project.

Add an application

Your project can include multiple distributions of your application, like web, iOS, and Android versions. In this chapter, we're only interested in adding a web application.

Let's get started:

1. On your project dashboard, click on the web application button to add an application, which is marked with step **3** in *Figure 8.14*
2. Provide an application nickname
3. Select the option to set up **Firebase Hosting**
4. Continue by hitting the **Register app** button
5. Skip over the **Add Firebase SDK** section
6. Install the Firebase CLI as instructed:

   ```
   $ npm install -g firebase-tools
   ```

7. Sign in:

   ```
   $ firebase login
   ```

    Make sure your current directory is your project's root folder.

8. Initialize your project:

   ```
   $ firebase init
   ```

9. Select the **Hosting** option; don't worry, you can add more features later
10. Select the project you created as the default, that is, **lemon-mart-007**
11. For the public directory enter `dist/lemon-mart` or the `outputPath` defined in your `angular.json` file
12. Say **yes** to configure it as a single-page application.

    This will create two new files: `firebase.json` and `.firebaserc`.
13. Build your project for production:

    `$ npx ng build --prod`

    or

    `$ npm run build:prod`
14. Now you can deploy your Angular application by executing the following command:

    `$ firebase deploy`

Your website should be available on a URL similar to `https://lemon-mart-007.firebaseapp.com`, as shown in the terminal.

> Add the `.firebase` folder to `.gitignore` so you don't check in your cache files. The other two files, `firebase.json` and `.firebaserc`, are safe to commit.

Optionally, connect a custom domain name that you own to the account using the Firebase console.

Configure authentication

Now, let's configure authentication.

In the Firebase console:

1. Select **Authentication** from the side navigation:

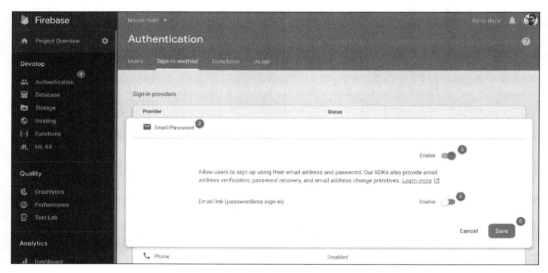

Figure 8.15: The Firebase Authentication page

2. Select **Email/Password** as the provider
3. Enable it
4. Do not enable the email link
5. Save your configuration

You can now see the user management console:

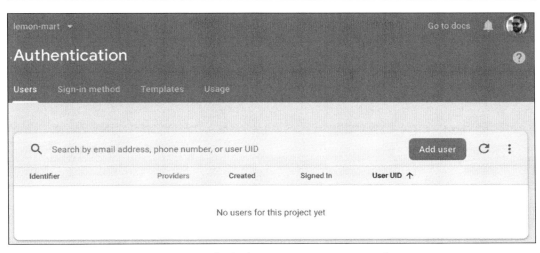

Figure 8.16: The Firebase user management console

It is fairly straightforward and intuitive to operate, so I will leave the configuration of it as an exercise for you.

Implement Firebase authentication

Let's start by adding Angular Fire, the official Firebase library for Angular, to our application:

`$ npx ng add @angular/fire`

 Follow Angular Fire's quickstart guide to finish setting up the library with your Angular project, which you can find linked from the readme file on GitHub at https://github.com/angular/angularfire2.

1. Ensure Firebase modules are provided in `app.module.ts` as per the documentation.
2. Ensure your Firebase config object is in all your `environment.ts` files.

> Note that any information provided in `environment.ts` is public information. So, when you place your Firebase API key in this file, it will be publicly available. There's a small chance that another developer could abuse your API key and run up your bill. To protect yourself from any such attack, check out this blog post by paachu: *How to secure your Firebase project even when your API key is publicly available* at https://medium.com/@impaachu/how-to-secure-your-firebase-project-even-when-your-api-key-is-publicly-available-a462a2a58843.

3. Create a new `FirebaseAuthService`:

   ```
   $ npx ng g s auth/firebaseAuth --lintFix
   ```

4. Rename the service file to `auth.firebase.service.ts`.
5. Be sure to remove `{ providedIn: 'root' }`.
6. Implement Firebase auth by extending the abstract auth service:

   src/app/auth/auth.firebase.service.ts

   ```
   import { Injectable } from '@angular/core'
   import { AngularFireAuth } from '@angular/fire/auth'
   import { User as FirebaseUser } from 'firebase'
   import { Observable, Subject } from 'rxjs'
   import { map } from 'rxjs/operators'

   import { IUser, User } from '../user/user/user'
   import { Role } from './auth.enum'
   import {
     AuthService,
     IAuthStatus,
     IServerAuthResponse,
     defaultAuthStatus,
   } from './auth.service'

   interface IJwtToken {
     email: string
     iat: number
   ```

```
  exp: number
  sub: string
}

@Injectable()
export class FirebaseAuthService extends AuthService {
  constructor(private afAuth: AngularFireAuth) {
    super()
  }

  protected authProvider(
    email: string,
    password: string
  ): Observable<IServerAuthResponse> {
    const serverResponse$ = new Subject<IServerAuthResponse>()

    this.afAuth.signInWithEmailAndPassword(email, password).then(
      (res) => {
        const firebaseUser: FirebaseUser | null = res.user
        firebaseUser?.getIdToken().then(
          (token) => serverResponse$.next(
            { accessToken: token } as IServerAuthResponse
          ),
          (err) => serverResponse$.error(err)
        )
      },
      (err) => serverResponse$.error(err)
    )

    return serverResponse$
  }

  protected transformJwtToken(token: IJwtToken): IAuthStatus {
    if (!token) {
      return defaultAuthStatus
    }

    return {
      isAuthenticated: token.email ? true : false,
      userId: token.sub,
      userRole: Role.None,
    }
  }
```

```
  protected getCurrentUser(): Observable<User> {
    return this.afAuth.user.pipe(map(this.transformFirebaseUser))
  }

  private transformFirebaseUser(firebaseUser: FirebaseUser): User
  {
    if (!firebaseUser) {
      return new User()
    }

    return User.Build({
      name: {
        first: firebaseUser?.displayName?.split(' ')[0] ||
          'Firebase',
        last: firebaseUser?.displayName?.split(' ')[1] || 'User',
      },
      picture: firebaseUser.photoURL,
      email: firebaseUser.email,
      _id: firebaseUser.uid,
      role: Role.None,
    } as IUser)
  }

  logout() {
    if (this.afAuth) {
      this.afAuth.signOut()
    }
    this.clearToken()
    this.authStatus$.next(defaultAuthStatus)
  }
}
```

As you can see, we only had to implement the delta between our already established authentication code and Firebase's authentication methods. We didn't have to duplicate any code and we even transformed a Firebase `user` object into our application's internal user object.

7. To use Firebase authentication instead of in-memory authentication, update the `AuthService` provider in `app.module.ts`:

src/app/app.module.ts

```
{
  provide: AuthService,
  useClass: FirebaseAuthService,
},
```

Once you've completed the steps, add a new user from the Firebase authentication console and you should be able to log in using real authentication.

> Always make sure that you're using HTTPS when transmitting any kind of **personally identifiable information** (**PII**) or sensitive information (like passwords) over the Internet. Otherwise, your information will get logged on third-party servers or captured by bad actors.

8. Once again, be sure to update your unit tests before moving on:

    `src/app/auth/auth.firebase.service.spec.ts`

    ```
    import { AngularFireAuth } from '@angular/fire/auth'

    import { UiService } from '../common/ui.service'
    import { FirebaseAuthService } from './auth.firebase.service'

    TestBed.configureTestingModule({
      imports: [HttpClientTestingModule],
      providers: [
        FirebaseAuthService,
        { provide: UiService, useValue: autoSpyObj(UiService) },
        { provide: AngularFireAuth,
          useValue: autoSpyObj(AngularFireAuth)
        },
      ],
    })
    ```

> Stop! Remove the `fake-jwt-sign` package from your project before deploying a real authentication method.

Congratulations, your application is integrated with Firebase! Next, let's cover service factories, which can help you to switch the providers of your abstract classes dynamically.

Designing Authentication and Authorization

Providing a service using a factory

You can dynamically choose providers during load time, so instead of having to change code to switch between authentication methods, you can parametrize environment variables, so different kinds of builds can have different authentication methods. This is especially useful when writing automated UI tests against your application, where real authentication can be difficult, if not impossible, to deal with.

First, we will create an `enum` in `environment.ts` to help define our options, and then we will use that `enum` to choose an auth provider during our application's bootstrap process.

Let's get started:

1. Create a new `enum` called `AuthMode`:

    src/app/auth/auth.enum.ts

    ```
    export enum AuthMode {
      InMemory = 'In Memory',
      CustomServer = 'Custom Server',
      Firebase = 'Firebase',
    }
    ```

2. Add an `authMode` property in `environment.ts`:

    src/environments/environment.ts

    ```
    ...
      authMode: AuthMode.InMemory,
    ...
    ```

    src/environments/environment.prod.ts

    ```
    ...
      authMode: AuthMode.Firebase,
    ...
    ```

3. Create an `authFactory` function in a new file under `auth/auth.factory.ts`:

    src/app/auth/auth.factory.ts

    ```
    export function authFactory(afAuth: AngularFireAuth) {
      switch (environment.authMode) {
        case AuthMode.InMemory:
          return new InMemoryAuthService()
        case AuthMode.Firebase:
          return new FirebaseAuthService(afAuth)
        case AuthMode.CustomServer:
    ```

[424]

```
            throw new Error('Not yet implemented')
        }
    }
```

Note that the factory has to import any dependent service.

4. Update the `AuthService` provider in `app.module.ts` to use the factory instead:

src/app/app.module.ts

```
providers: [
  {
    provide: AuthService,
    useFactory: authFactory,
    deps: [AngularFireAuth],
  },
```

Note that you can remove imports of `InMemoryAuthService` and `FirebaseAuthService` from `AppModule`.

With this configuration in place, whenever you build your application for local development, you will be using the in-memory auth service and production (or prod) builds will use the Firebase auth service.

Summary

You should now be familiar with how to create high-quality auth experiences. In this chapter, we defined a User object that we can hydrate from or serialize to JSON objects, applying object-oriented class design and TypeScript operators for safe data handling.

We leveraged OOP design principals, using inheritance and abstract classes to implement a base auth service that demonstrates the Open/Closed principle.

We covered the fundamentals of token-based authentication and JWTs so that you don't leak any critical user information. You learned that caching and HTTP interceptors are necessary so that users don't have to input their login information with every request. Following that, we implemented two distinct auth providers, one in-memory and one with Firebase.

We then designed a great conditional navigation experience that you can use in your own applications by copying the base elements to your project and implementing your own auth provider. We created a reusable UI service so that you can conveniently inject alerts into the flow-control logic of your application.

Finally, we covered router guards to prevent users from stumbling onto screens they are not authorized to use, and we reaffirmed the point that the real security of your application should be implemented on the server side. You saw how you can use a factory to dynamically provide different auth providers for different environments.

In the next chapter, we will shift gears a bit and learn about containerization using Docker. Docker allows powerful workflows that can greatly improve development experiences, while allowing you to implement your server configuration as code, putting a final nail in the coffin of the developer's favorite excuse when their software breaks: "But it works on my machine!"

Further reading

- *Salted Password Hashing - Doing it Right, Defuse Security*, 2019, `https://crackstation.net/hashing-security.htm`.
- *Object-oriented programming*, `https://en.wikipedia.org/wiki/Object-oriented_programming`.
- *TypeScript Classes*, `https://www.typescriptlang.org/docs/handbook/classes.html`.
- *TypeScript Basic Types*, `https://www.typescriptlang.org/docs/handbook/basic-types.html`.
- *TypeScript Advanced Types*, `https://www.typescriptlang.org/docs/handbook/advanced-types.html`.
- *TypeScript 3.7 Features*, `https://www.typescriptlang.org/docs/handbook/release-notes/typescript-3-7.html`.
- *Angular NgIf Directive*, `https://angular.io/api/common/NgIf`.
- *Authentication General Guidelines*, `https://github.com/OWASP/CheatSheetSeries/blob/master/cheatsheets/Authentication_Cheat_Sheet.md`.
- *How to secure your Firebase project even when your API key is publicly available*, paachu, 2019, `https://medium.com/@impaachu/how-to-secure-your-firebase-project-even-when-your-api-key-is-publicly-available-a462a2a58843`.

Questions

Answer the following questions as best as you can to ensure that you've understood the key concepts from this chapter without Googling. Do you need help answering the questions? See *Appendix D, Self-Assessment Answers* online at https://static.packt-cdn.com/downloads/9781838648800_Appendix_D_Self-Assessment_Answers.pdf or visit https://expertlysimple.io/angular-self-assessment.

1. What's in-transit and at-rest security?
2. What's the difference between authentication and authorization?
3. Explain inheritance and polymorphism.
4. What is an abstract class?
5. What is an abstract method?
6. Explain how the `AuthService` adheres to the Open/Closed principle.
7. How does JWT verify your identity?
8. What is the difference between RxJS's `combineLatest` and `merge` operators?
9. What is a router guard?
10. What does a service factory allow you to do?

9
DevOps Using Docker

By the end of *Chapter 8*, *Designing Authentication and Authorization*, we had a fairly sophisticated app. In *Chapter 4*, *Automated Testing, CI, and Release to Production*, I emphasized the need to ensure that every code push we create has passing tests, adheres to the coding standards, and is an executable artifact that team members can run tests against as we develop our application. By the end of *Chapter 7*, *Creating a Router-First Line-of-Business App*, you should have replicated the same CircleCI setup we implemented for the Local Weather app for LemonMart. If not, before we start building more complicated features for our **Line-of-Business** (**LOB**) app, go ahead and do this.

We live in an era of moving fast and breaking things. However, the latter part of that statement rarely works in an enterprise. You can choose to live on the edge and adopt the YOLO lifestyle, but this doesn't make good business sense.

```
--yolo          Skips cleanup and testing
```

Figure 9.1: A creative CLI option for a tool

Continuous Integration (**CI**) is critical to ensuring a quality deliverable by building and executing tests on every code push. Setting up a CI environment can be time-consuming and requires specialized knowledge of the tool being used. In *Chapter 4*, *Automated Testing, CI, and Release to Production*, we implemented GitHub flow with CircleCI integration. However, we manually deployed our app. To move fast without breaking things, we need to implement **Continuous Deployment** (**CD**) using DevOps best practices such as **Infrastructure-as-Code** (**IaC**), so we can verify the correctness of our running code more often.

In this chapter, we will go over a Docker-based approach to implement IaC that can be run on most CI services and cloud providers, allowing you to achieve repeatable builds and deployments from any CI environment to any cloud provider. Working with flexible tools, you will avoid overspecializing in one service and keep your configuration management skills relevant across different CI services.

This book leverages CircleCI as the CI server. Other notable CI servers are Jenkins, Azure DevOps, and the built-in mechanisms within GitLab and GitHub.

In this chapter, you will learn the following:

- DevOps and IaC
- Containerizing web apps using Docker
- Deploying containerized apps using Google Cloud Run
- CD to multiple cloud providers
- Advanced CI
- Code coverage reports

The following software is required to follow along with this chapter:

- Docker Desktop Community version 2+
- Docker Engine CE version 18+
- A Google Cloud Engine account
- A Coveralls account

The most up-to-date versions of the sample code for the book are on GitHub at the repository linked in the following list. The repository contains the final and completed version of the code. Each section contains information boxes to help direct you to the correct filename or branch on GitHub so that you can use them to verify your progress.

For the *Chapter 9* examples based on **local-weather-app**, do the following:

1. Clone the repo at `https://github.com/duluca/local-weather-app`.
2. Execute `npm install` on the root folder to install dependencies.
3. Use `.circleci/config.ch9.yml` to verify your `config.yml` implementation.
4. To run the CircleCI Vercel Now configuration, execute
   `git checkout deploy_Vercelnow`

   Refer to the pull request at `https://github.com/duluca/local-weather-app/pull/50`.

5. To run the CircleCI GCloud configuration, execute

   `git checkout deploy_cloudrun`

   Refer to the pull request at https://github.com/duluca/local-weather-app/pull/51.

> Note that both branches leverage modified code to use the projects/ch6 code from the **local-weather-app** repo.

For the *Chapter 9* examples based on **lemon-mart**, do the following:

1. Clone the repo at https://github.com/duluca/lemon-mart.
2. Use .circleci/config.ch9.yml and config.docker-integration.yml to verify your config.yml implementation.
3. Execute npm install on the root folder to install dependencies.
4. To run the CircleCI Docker integration configuration, execute

   `git checkout docker-integration`

   Refer to the pull request at https://github.com/duluca/lemon-mart/pull/25.

> Note that the docker-integration branch is slightly modified to use code from the projects/ch8 folder on the **lemon-mart** repo.

> Beware that there may be slight differences in implementation between the code in the book and what's on GitHub because the ecosystem is ever-evolving. It is natural for the sample code to change over time. Also, on GitHub, expect to find corrections, fixes to support newer versions of libraries, or side-by-side implementations of multiple techniques for the reader to observe. The reader is only expected to implement the ideal solution recommended in the book. If you find errors or have questions, please create an issue or submit a pull request on GitHub for the benefit of all readers.

> You can read more about updating Angular in *Appendix C, Keeping Angular and Tools Evergreen*. You can find this appendix online from `https://static.packt-cdn.com/downloads/9781838648800_Appendix_C_Keeping_Angular_and_Tools_Evergreen.pdf` or at `https://expertlysimple.io/stay-evergreen`.

Let's start by understanding what DevOps is.

DevOps

DevOps is the marriage of development and operations. In development, it is well established that code repositories like Git track every code change. In operations, there has long been a wide variety of techniques to track changes to environments, including scripts and various tools that aim to automate the provisioning of operating systems and servers.

Still, how many times have you heard the saying, "it works on my machine"? Developers often use that line as a joke. Still, it is often the case that software that works perfectly well on a test server ends up running into issues on a production server due to minor differences in configuration.

In *Chapter 4, Automated Testing, CI, and Release to Production*, we discussed how GitHub flow can enable us to create a value delivery stream. We always branch from the master before making a change. Enforce that change to go through our CI pipeline, and once we're reasonably sure that our code works, we can merge back to the master branch. See the following diagram:

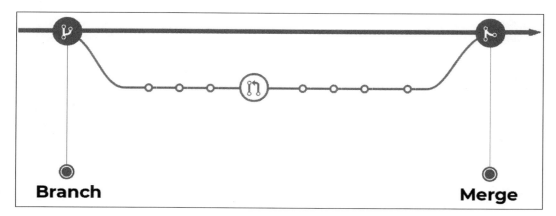

Figure 9.2: Branching and merging

Remember, your master branch should always be deployable, and you should frequently merge your work to the master branch.

Docker allows us to define the software and the specific configuration parameters that our code depends on in a declarative manner using a special file named a `Dockerfile`. Similarly, CircleCI allows us to define the configuration of our CI environment in a `config.yml` file. By storing our configuration in files, we are able to check the files in alongside our code. We can track changes using Git and enforce them to be verified by our CI pipeline. By storing the definition of our infrastructure in code, we achieve IaC. With IaC, we also achieve repeatable integration, so no matter what environment we run our infrastructure in, we should be able to stand up our full-stack app with a one-line command.

You may remember that in *Chapter 1, Introduction to Angular and Its Concepts*, we covered how TypeScript covers the JavaScript Feature Gap. Similar to TypeScript, Docker covers the configuration gap, as demonstrated in the following diagram:

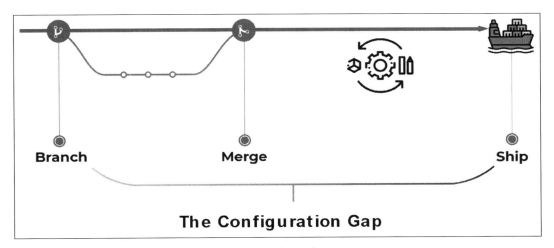

Figure 9.3: Covering the configuration gap

By using Docker, we can be reasonably sure that our code, which worked on our machine during testing, will work exactly the same way when we ship it.

In summary, with DevOps, we bring operations closer to development, where it is cheaper to make changes and resolve issues. So, DevOps is primarily a developer's responsibility, but it is also a way of thinking that the operations team must be willing to support. Let's dive deeper into Docker.

Containerizing web apps using Docker

Docker, which can be found at `https://docker.io`, is an open platform for developing, shipping, and running applications. Docker combines a lightweight container virtualization platform with workflows and tooling that help manage and deploy applications. The most obvious difference between **Virtual Machines** (**VMs**) and Docker containers is that VMs are usually dozens of gigabytes in size and require gigabytes of memory, whereas containers take up megabytes in terms of disk and memory size requirements. Furthermore, the Docker platform abstracts away host **operating system** (**OS**) - level configuration settings, so every piece of configuration that is needed to successfully run an application is encoded within a human-readable format.

Anatomy of a Dockerfile

A `Dockerfile` consists of four main parts:

- **FROM** – where we can inherit from Docker's minimal "scratch" image or a pre-existing image
- **SETUP** – where we configure software dependencies to our requirements
- **COPY** – where we copy our built code into the operating environment
- **CMD** – where we specify the commands that will bootstrap the operating environment

Bootstrap refers to a set of initial instructions that describe how a program loads or starts up.

Consider the following visualization of the anatomy of a `Dockerfile`:

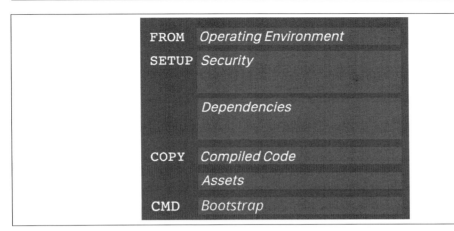

Figure 9.4: Anatomy of a Dockerfile

A concrete representation of a `Dockerfile` is demonstrated in the following code:

```
Dockerfile
FROM duluca/minimal-nginx-web-server:1-alpine
COPY /dist/local-weather-app /var/www
CMD 'nginx'
```

You can map the FROM, COPY, and CMD parts of the script to the visualization. We inherit from the `duluca/minimal-nginx-web-server` image using the FROM command. Then, we copy the compiled result of our app from our development machine or build environment into the image using the COPY (or, alternatively, the ADD) command. Finally, we instruct the container to execute the nginx web server using the CMD (or, alternatively, the ENTRYPOINT) command.

Note that the preceding `Dockerfile` doesn't have a distinct SETUP part. SETUP doesn't map to an actual `Dockerfile` command but represents a collection of commands you can execute to set up your container. In this case, all the necessary setup was done by the base image, so there are no additional commands to run.

Common `Dockerfile` commands are FROM, COPY, ADD, RUN, CMD, ENTRYPOINT, ENV, and EXPOSE. For the full `Dockerfile` reference, refer to https://docs.docker.com/engine/reference/builder/.

The `Dockerfile` describes a new container that inherits from a container named `duluca/minimal-nginx-web-server`. This is a container that I published on Docker Hub, which inherits from the `nginx:alpine` image, which itself inherits from the `alpine` image. The `alpine` image is a minimal Linux operating environment that is only 5 MB in size. The `alpine` image itself inherits from `scratch`, which is an empty image. See the inheritance hierarchy demonstrated in the following diagram:

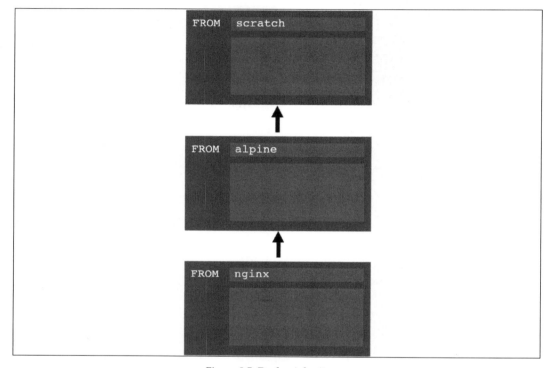

Figure 9.5: Docker inheritance

The `Dockerfile` then copies the contents of the `dist` folder from your development environment into the container's www folder, as shown in the following diagram:

Chapter 9

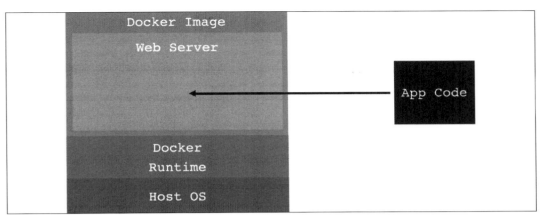

Figure 9.6: Copying code into a containerized web server

In this case, the parent image is configured with an nginx server to act as a web server to serve the content inside the www folder. At this point, our source code is accessible from the internet but lives inside layers of secure environments. Even if our app has a vulnerability of some kind, it would be tough for an attacker to harm the systems we are operating on. The following diagram demonstrates the layers of security that Docker provides:

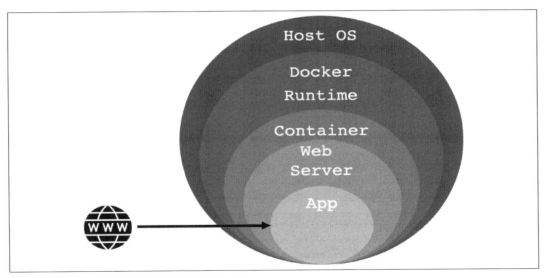

Figure 9.7: Docker security

In summary, at the base layer we have our host OS, such as Windows or macOS, that runs the Docker runtime, which will be installed in the next section. The Docker runtime is capable of running self-contained Docker images, which are defined by the aforementioned `Dockerfile`. `duluca/minimal-nginx-web-server` is based on the lightweight Linux operating system, Alpine. Alpine is a completely pared-down version of Linux that doesn't come with any GUI, drivers, or even most of the sCLI tools you may expect from a Linux system. As a result, the OS is around only ~5 MB in size. We then inherit from the nginx image, which installs the web server, which itself is around a few megabytes in size. Finally, our custom nginx configuration is layered over the default image, resulting in a tiny ~7 MB image. The nginx server is configured to serve the contents of the `/var/www` folder. In the `Dockerfile`, we merely copy the contents of the `/dist` folder in our development environment and place it into the `/var/www` folder. We will later build and execute this image, which will run our Nginx web server containing the output of our `dist` folder. I have published a similar image named `duluca/minimal-node-web-server`, which clocks in at ~15 MB.

`duluca/minimal-node-web-server` can be more straightforward to work with, especially if you're not familiar with Nginx. It relies on an `Express.js` server to serve static content. Most cloud providers provide concrete examples using Node and Express, which can help you narrow down any errors. In addition, `duluca/minimal-node-web-server` has HTTPS redirection support baked into it. You can spend a lot of time trying to set up a nginx proxy to do the same thing, when all you need to do is set the environment variable `ENFORCE_HTTPS` in your `Dockerfile`. See the following sample Dockerfile:

Dockerfile
```
FROM duluca/minimal-node-web-server:lts-alpine

WORKDIR /usr/src/app

COPY dist/local-weather-app public

ENTRYPOINT [ "npm", "start" ]

ENV ENFORCE_HTTPS=xProto
```

> You can read more about the options `minimal-node-web-server` provides at `https://github.com/duluca/minimal-node-web-server`.

As we've now seen, the beauty of Docker is that you can navigate to https://hub.docker.com, search for duluca/minimal-nginx-web-server or duluca/minimal-node-web-server, read its Dockerfile, and trace its origins all the way back to the original base image that is the foundation of the web server. I encourage you to vet every Docker image you use in this manner to understand what exactly it brings to the table for your needs. You may find it either overkill, or that it has features you never knew about that can make your life a lot easier.

Note that the parent images should pull a specific tag of duluca/minimal-nginx-web-server, which is 1-alpine. Similarly, duluca/minimal-node-web-server pulls from lts-alpine. These are evergreen base packages that always contain the latest release of version 1 of Nginx and Alpine or an LTS release of Node. I have pipelines set up to automatically update both images when a new base image is published. So, whenever you pull these images, you will get the latest bug fixes and security patches.

Having an evergreen dependency tree removes the burden on you as the developer to go hunting down the latest available version of a Docker image. Alternatively, if you specify a version number, your images will not be subject to any potential breaking changes. However, it is better to remember to test your images after a new build, than never update your image and potentially deploy compromised software. After all, the web is ever-changing and will not slow down for you to keep your images up to date.

Just like npm packages, Docker can bring great convenience and value, but you must take care to understand the tools you are working with.

In *Chapter 13, Highly Available Cloud Infrastructure on AWS*, we are going to leverage the lower-footprint Docker image based on Nginx, duluca/minimal-nginx-web-server. If you're comfortable configuring nginx, this is the ideal choice.

Installing Docker

In order to be able to build and run containers, you must first install the Docker execution environment on your computer. Refer back to *Chapter 2, Setting Up Your Development Environment*, for instructions on installing Docker.

Setting up npm scripts for Docker

Now, let's configure some Docker scripts for your Angular apps that you can use to automate the building, testing, and publishing of your container. I have developed a set of scripts called **npm scripts for Docker** that work on Windows 10 and macOS. You can get the latest version of these scripts and automatically configure them in your project by executing the following code:

Run the following commands on both the **local-weather-app** and **lemon-mart** projects now!

1. Install the npm scripts for Docker task:

   ```
   $ npm i -g mrm-task-npm-docker
   ```

2. Apply the npm scripts for Docker configuration:

   ```
   $ npx mrm npm-docker
   ```

After you execute the `mrm` scripts, we're ready to take a deep dive into the configuration settings using the Local Weather app as an example.

Build and publish an image to Docker Hub

Next, let's make sure that your project is configured correctly so we can containerize it, build an executable image, and publish it to Docker Hub, thereby allowing us to access it from any build environment. We will be using the Local Weather app for this section that we last updated in *Chapter 6, Forms, Observables, and Subjects*:

This section uses the **local-weather-app** repo.

1. Sign up for a Docker Hub account on `https://hub.docker.com/`.
2. Create a public (free) repository for your application.

   Later in this chapter, we use Google Cloud's container registry as a private repository. Additionally, in *Chapter 13, Highly Available Cloud Infrastructure on AWS*, I cover how to set up a private container repository using **AWS Elastic Container Service (AWS ECS)**.

3. In `package.json`, add or update the `config` property with the following configuration properties:

   package.json

   ```
   ...
   "config": {
     "imageRepo": "[namespace]/[repository]",
   ```

```
    "imageName": "custom_app_name",
    "imagePort": "0000",
    "internalContainerPort": "3000"
},
...
```

The `namespace` will be your Docker Hub username. You will define what your repository will be called during creation. An example image `repository` variable should look like `duluca/localcast-weather`. The image name is for easy identification of your container while using Docker commands such as `docker ps`. I will just call mine `localcast-weather`. The `imagePort` property will define which port should be used to expose your application from inside the container. Since we use port `5000` for development, pick a different one, like `8080`. The `internalContainerPort` defines the port that your web server is mapped to. For Node servers, this will mostly be port `3000`, and for Nginx servers, `80`. Refer to the documentation of the base container you're using.

4. Let's review the Docker scripts that were added to `package.json` by the `mrm` task from earlier. The following snippet is an annotated version of the scripts that explains each function.

   Note that with npm scripts, the `pre` and `post` keywords are used to execute helper scripts, respectively, before or after the execution of a given script. Scripts are intentionally broken into smaller pieces to make it easier to read and maintain them.

   The `build` script is as follows:

    Note that the following `cross-conf-env` command ensures that the script executes equally well in macOS, Linux, and Windows environments.

package.json
```
...
  "scripts": {
    ...
    "predocker:build": "npm run build",
    "docker:build": "cross-conf-env docker image build . -t $npm_package_config_imageRepo:$npm_package_version",
    "postdocker:build": "npm run docker:tag",
    ...
```

`npm run docker:build` will build your Angular application in the `pre` script, then build the Docker image using the `docker image build` command, and tag the image with a version number in the `post` script:

DevOps Using Docker

In my project, the `pre` command builds my Angular application in prod mode and also runs a test to make sure that I have an optimized build with no failing tests.

My pre command looks like:

`"predocker:build": "npm run build:prod && npm test -- --watch=false"`

The `tag` script is as follows:

package.json

```
...
    "docker:tag": " cross-conf-env docker image tag $npm_package_config_imageRepo:$npm_package_version $npm_package_config_imageRepo:latest",
...
```

`npm run docker:tag` will tag an already built Docker image using the version number from the `version` property in `package.json` and the latest tag.

The `stop` script is as follows:

package.json

```
...
    "docker:stop": "cross-conf-env docker stop $npm_package_config_imageName || true",
...
```

`npm run docker:stop` will stop the image if it's currently running, so the `run` script can execute without errors.

The `run` script is as follows:

Note that the `run-s` and `run-p` commands ship with the `npm-run-all` package to synchronize or parallelize the execution of npm scripts.

package.json

```
...
    "docker:run": "run-s -c docker:stop docker:runHelper",
    "docker:runHelper": "cross-conf-env docker run -e NODE_ENV=local --rm --name $npm_package_config_imageName -d -p $npm_package_config_imagePort:$npm_package_config_internalContainerPort $npm_package_config_imageRepo",
...
```

npm run docker:run will stop if the image is already running, and then run the newly built version of the image using the docker run command. Note that the imagePort property is used as the external port of the Docker image, which is mapped to the internal port of the image that the Node.js server listens to, port 3000.

The publish script is as follows:

package.json

```
    ...
    "predocker:publish": "echo Attention! Ensure `docker login` is correct.",
    "docker:publish": "cross-conf-env docker image push $npm_package_config_imageRepo:$npm_package_version",
    "postdocker:publish": "cross-conf-env docker image push $npm_package_config_imageRepo:latest",
    ...
```

npm run docker:publish will publish a built image to the configured repository, in this case, Docker Hub, using the docker image push command.

First, the versioned image is published, followed by one tagged with latest in post. The taillogs script is as follows:

package.json

```
    ...
    "docker:taillogs": "cross-conf-env docker logs -f $npm_package_config_imageName",
    ...
```

npm run docker:taillogs will display the internal console logs of a running Docker instance using the docker log -f command, a very useful tool when debugging your Docker instance.

The open script is as follows:

package.json

```
    ...
    "docker:open": "sleep 2 && cross-conf-env open-cli http://localhost:$npm_package_config_imagePort",
    ...
```

npm run docker:open will wait for 2 seconds and then launch the browser with the correct URL for your application using the imagePort property.

The `debug` script is as follows:

package.json

```
...
    "predocker:debug": "run-s docker:build docker:run",
    "docker:debug": "run-s -cs docker:open:win docker:open:mac docker:taillogs"
  },
...
```

`npm run docker:debug` will build your image and run an instance of it in `pre`, open the browser, and then start displaying the internal logs of the container.

5. Customize the pre-build script to build your angular app in production mode and execute unit tests before building the image:

package.json

```
    "build": "ng build",
    "build:prod": "ng build --prod",
    "predocker:build": "npm run build:prod && npm test ----watch=false",
```

> Note that `ng build` is provided with the `--prod` argument, which achieves two things: the size of the app is optimized to be significantly smaller with **Ahead-of-Time (AOT)** compilation to increase runtime performance, and the configuration items defined in `src/environments/environment.prod.ts` are used.

6. Update `src/environments/environment.prod.ts` to look like you're using your own `appId` from `OpenWeather`:

```
export const environment = {
  production: true,
  appId: '01ff1xxxxxxxxxxxxxxxxxxxxx',
  username: 'localcast',
  baseUrl: 'https://',
  geonamesApi: 'secure',
}
```

> We are modifying how `npm test` is executed, so the tests are run only once and the tool stops executing. The `--watch=false` option is provided to achieve this behavior, as opposed to the development-friendly default continuous execution behavior.

Chapter 9

7. Create a new file named `Dockerfile` with no file extensions in the project root.

8. Implement or replace the contents of the `Dockerfile`, as shown here:

   Dockerfile
   ```
   FROM duluca/minimal-node-web-server:lts-alpine

   WORKDIR /usr/src/app

   COPY dist/local-weather-app public
   ```

    Be sure to inspect the contents of your `dist` folder to ensure you're copying the correct folder, which contains the `index.html` file at its root.

9. Execute `npm run predocker:build` and make sure it runs without errors in the Terminal to ensure that your application changes have been successful.

10. Execute `npm run docker:build` and make sure it runs without errors in the Terminal to ensure that your image builds successfully.

    While you can run any of the provided scripts individually, you really only need to remember two of them going forward:

    - `npm run docker:debug` will test, build, tag, run, tail, and launch your containerized app in a new browser window for testing.
    - `npm run docker:publish` will publish the image you just built and test to the online Docker repository.

11. Execute `docker:debug` in your Terminal:

    ```
    $ npm run docker:debug
    ```

    A successful `docker:debug` run should result in a new in-focus browser window with your application and the server logs being tailed in the Terminal, as follows:

    ```
    Current Environment: local.
    Server listening on port 3000 inside the container
    Attention: To access server, use http://localhost:EXTERNAL_PORT
    EXTERNAL_PORT is specified with 'docker run -p EXTERNAL_PORT:3000'. See 'package.json->imagePort' for the default port.
    GET / 304 2.194 ms - -
    GET /runtime-es2015.js 304 0.371 ms - -
    GET /polyfills-es2015.js 304 0.359 ms - -
    ```

```
GET /styles-es2015.js 304 0.839 ms - -
GET /vendor-es2015.js 304 0.789 ms - -
GET /main-es2015.js 304 0.331 ms - -
```

> You should always run `docker ps` to check whether your image is running, when it was last updated, and whether it is clashing with any existing images claiming the same port.

12. Execute `docker:publish` in your Terminal:

    ```
    $ npm run docker:publish
    ```

    You should observe a successful run in the Terminal window like this:

    ```
    The push refers to a repository [docker.io/duluca/localcast-weather]
    60f66aaaaa50: Pushed
    ...
    latest: digest: sha256:b680970d76769cf12cc48f37391d8a542fe226b66d9a6f8a7ac81ad77be4 f58b size: 2827
    ```

> Over time, your local Docker cache may grow to a significant size; for example, on my laptop, it's reached roughly 40 GB over two years. You can use the `docker image prune` and `docker container prune` commands to reduce the size of your cache. For more detailed information, refer to the documentation at https://docs.docker.com/config/pruning.

By defining a `Dockerfile` and scripting our use of it, we created living documentation in our code base. We have achieved DevOps and closed the configuration gap.

> Make sure to containerize **lemon-mart** in the same way you've done with **local-weather-app** and verify your work by executing `npm run docker:debug`.

You may find it confusing to interact with npm scripts in general through the CLI. Let's look at VS Code's npm script support next.

NPM scripts in VS Code

VS Code provides support for npm scripts out of the box. In order to enable npm script explorer, open VS Code settings and ensure that the `"npm.enableScriptExplorer": true` property is present. Once you do, you will see an expandable title named **NPM SCRIPTS** in the **Explorer** pane, as highlighted with an arrow in the following screenshot:

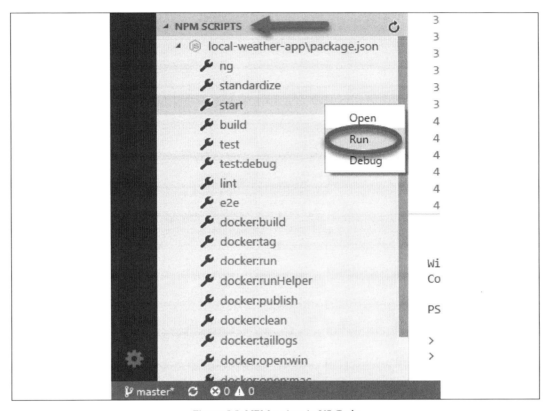

Figure 9.8: NPM scripts in VS Code

You can click on any script to launch the line that contains the script in `package.json` or right-click and select **Run** to execute the script.

Let's look at an easier way to interact with Docker next.

Docker extensions in VS Code

Another way to interact with Docker images and containers is through VS Code. If you have installed the `ms-azuretools.vscode-docker` Docker extension from Microsoft, as suggested in *Chapter 2, Setting Up Your Development Environment*, you can identify the extension by the Docker logo on the left-hand navigation menu VS Code, as circled in white in the following screenshot:

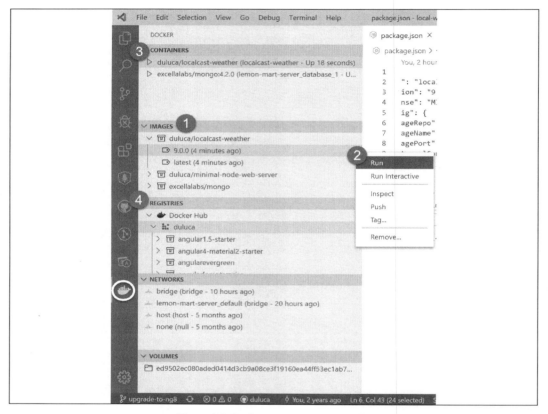

Figure 9.9: Docker extension in VS Code

Let's go through some of the functionality provided by the extension. Refer to the preceding screenshot and the numbered steps in the following list for a quick explanation:

1. **Images** contain a list of all the container snapshots that exist on your system.
2. Right-clicking on a Docker image brings up a context menu to run various operations on it, like **Run**, **Push**, and **Tag**.

3. **Containers** list all executable Docker containers that exist on your system, which you can start, stop, or attach to.
4. **Registries** display the registries that you're configured to connect to, such as Docker Hub or **AWS Elastic Container Registry (AWS ECR)**.

While the extension makes it easier to interact with Docker, the **npm scripts for Docker** (which you configured using the `mrm` task) automate a lot of the chores related to building, tagging, and testing an image. They are both cross-platform and will work equally well in a CI environment.

The `npm run docker:debug` script automates a lot of chores to verify that you have a good image build!

Now let's see how we can deploy our containers to the cloud and later achieve CD.

Deploying a Dockerfile to the cloud

One of the advantages of using Docker is that we can deploy it on any number of operating environments, from personal PCs to servers and cloud providers. In any case, we would expect our container to function the same way. Let's deploy the LocalCast Weather app to Google Cloud Run.

Google Cloud Run

Google Cloud Run allows you to deploy arbitrary Docker containers and execute them on the Google Cloud Platform without any onerous overhead. Fully managed instances offer some free time; however, there's no free-forever version here. Please be mindful of any costs you may incur. Refer to `https://cloud.google.com/run/pricing?hl=en_US for pricing`.

Refer to *Chapter 2, Setting Up Your Development Environment*, for instructions on how to install glcoud.

This section uses the **local-weather-app** repo.

Let's configure glcoud so we can deploy a `Dockerfile`:

1. Update your `Dockerfile` to override the `ENTRYPOINT` command:

   Dockerfile
   ```
   FROM duluca/minimal-node-web-server:lts-alpine

   WORKDIR /usr/src/app

   COPY dist/local-weather-app public

   ENTRYPOINT [ "npm", "start" ]
   ```

    The `ENTRYPOINT` command in `minimal-node-web-server` runs a process called `dumb-init` to force the process ID for your Node process to be randomized. However, gcloud fails to execute this command, which is why we're overriding it.

2. Create a new gcloud project:

   ```
   $ gcloud projects create localcast-weather
   ```

    Remember to use your own project name!

3. Navigate to `https://console.cloud.google.com/`
4. Locate your new project and select the **Billing** option from the sidebar, as shown in the following screenshot:

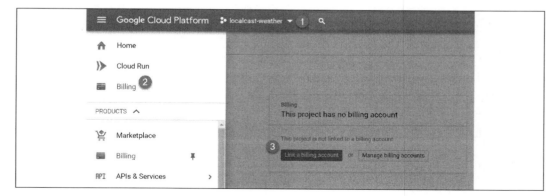

Figure 9.10: Billing options

5. Follow the instructions to set up a billing account.

> If you see it, the Freemium account option will also work. Otherwise, you may choose to take advantage of free trial offers. However, it is a good idea to set a budget alert to be notified if you get charged over a certain amount per month. Find more info at https://cloud.google.com/billing/docs/how-to/modify-project.

6. Create a .gcloudignore file and ignore everything but your Dockerfile and dist folder:

.gcloudignore
```
/*
!Dockerfile
!dist/
```

7. Add a new npm script to build your Dockerfile in the cloud:

package.json
```
scripts: {
  "gcloud:build": "gcloud builds submit --tag gcr.io/localcast-weather/localcast-weather --project localcast-weather",
}
```

> Remember to use your own project name!

8. Add another npm script to deploy your published container:

package.json
```
scripts: {
  "gcloud:deploy": "gcloud run deploy --image gcr.io/localcast-weather/localcast-weather --platform managed --project localcast-weather --region us-east1"
}
```

Note that you should provide the region closest to your geographical location for the best possible experience.

9. Build your Dockerfile as follows:

```
$ npm run gcloud:build
```

Before running this command, remember to build your application for prod. Whatever you have in your dist folder will get deployed.

> Note that on the initial run, you will be prompted to answer questions to configure your account for initial use. Select your account and project name correctly, otherwise, take the default options. The `build` command may fail during the first run. Sometimes it takes multiple runs for gcloud to warm up and successfully build your container.

10. Once your container is published, deploy it using the following command:

    ```
    $ npm run gcloud:deploy
    ```

A successful deployment will look like the following:

```
Service name (localcast-weather):
Deploying container to Cloud Run service [localcast-weather] in project [localcast-weather] region [us-east1]
Deploying...
  Creating Revision...done
  Routing traffic...done
Done.
Service [localcast-weather] revision [localcast-weather-00011-yup] has been deployed and is serving 100 percent of traffic at https://localcast-weather-sgzmgloslq-ue.a.run.app
```

Figure 9.11: A successful deployment

Congrats, you've just deployed your container on Google Cloud. You should be able to access your app using the URL in the Terminal output.

>  As always, consider adding CLI commands as npm scripts to your project so that you can maintain a living documentation of your scripts. These scripts will also allow you to leverage pre and post scripts in npm, allowing you to automate the building of your application, your container, and the tagging process. So, the next time you need to deploy, you only need to run one command. I encourage the reader to seek inspiration from the npm scripts for Docker utility we set up earlier to create your own set of scripts for gcloud.

For more information and some sample projects, refer to `https://cloud.google.com/run/docs/quickstarts/prebuilt-deploy` and `https://cloud.google.com/run/docs/quickstarts/build-and-deploy`.

Configuring Docker with Cloud Run

In the previous section, we submitted our `Dockerfile` and `dist` folder to gcloud so that it can build our container for us. This is a convenient option that avoids some of the additional configuration steps. However, you can still leverage your Docker-based workflow to build and publish your container.

Let's configure Docker with gcloud:

1. Set your default region:

   ```
   $ gcloud config set run/region us-east1
   ```

2. Configure Docker with the gcloud container registry:

   ```
   $ gcloud auth configure-docker
   ```

3. Tag your already built container with a gcloud hostname:

   ```
   $ docker tag duluca/localcast-weather:latest gcr.io/localcast-weather/localcast-weather:latest
   ```

    For detailed instructions on how to tag your image, refer to https://cloud.google.com/container-registry/docs/pushing-and-pulling.

4. Publish your container to gcloud using Docker:

   ```
   $ docker push gcr.io/localcast-weather/localcast-weather:latest
   ```

5. Execute the `deploy` command:

   ```
   $ gcloud run deploy --image gcr.io/localcast-weather/localcast-weather --platform managed --project localcast-weather
   ```

    During initial deployment, this command may appear to be stuck. Try again in 15 minutes or so.

6. Follow the onscreen instructions to complete your deployment.
7. Follow the URL displayed on screen to check that your app has been successfully deployed.

The preceding steps demonstrate a deployment technique that is similar to the one we leveraged when deploying to AWS ECS in *Chapter 13, Highly Available Cloud Infrastructure on AWS*.

For more information, refer to `https://cloud.google.com/sdk/gcloud/reference/run/deploy`. For the following few sections, we will be switching back to LemonMart.

Troubleshooting Cloud Run

In order to troubleshoot your glcoud commands, you may utilize the Google Cloud Platform Console at `https://console.cloud.google.com/`.

Under the Cloud Run menu, you can keep track of the containers you are running. If errors occur during your deployment, you may want to check the logs to see the messages created by your container. Refer to the following screenshot, which shows the logs from my `localcast-weather` deployment:

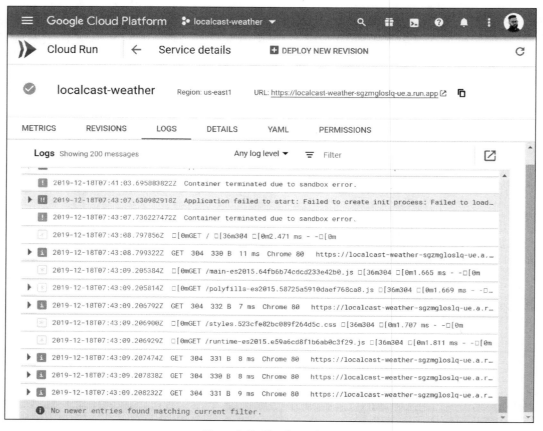

Figure 9.12: Cloud Run logs

To learn more about troubleshooting Cloud Run, refer to `https://cloud.google.com/run/docs/troubleshooting`.

Congratulations! You have mastered the fundamentals of working with Docker containers in your local development environment and pushing them to multiple registries and runtime environments in the cloud.

Continuous deployment

CD is the idea that code changes that successfully pass through your pipeline can be automatically deployed to a target environment. Although there are examples of continuously deploying to production, most enterprises prefer to target a dev environment. A gated approach is adopted to move the changes through the various stages of dev, test, staging, and finally production. CircleCI can facilitate gated deployment with approval workflows, which is covered later in this section.

In CircleCI, to deploy your image, we need to implement a `deploy` job. In this job, you can deploy to a multitude of targets such as Google Cloud Run, Docker Hub, Heroku, Azure, or AWS ECS. Integration with these targets will involve multiple steps. At a high level, these steps are as follows:

1. Configure an orb for your target environment, which provides the CLI tools required to deploy your software.
2. Store login credentials or access keys specific to the target environment as CircleCI environment variables.
3. Build a container in the CI pipeline, if not using a platform-specific `build` command. Then use `docker push` to submit the resulting Docker image to the target platform's Docker registry.
4. Execute a platform-specific `deploy` command to instruct the target to run the Docker image that was just pushed.

By using a Docker-based workflow, we achieve great amounts of flexibility in terms of systems and target environments we can use. The following diagram illustrates this point by highlighting the possible permutation of choices that are available to us:

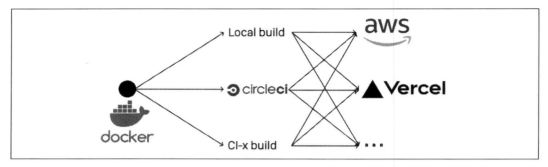

Figure 9.13: n-to-n deployment

As you can see, in a containerized world, the possibilities are limitless. I will demonstrate how you can deploy to Google Cloud Run using containers and CI later in this chapter. Outside of Docker-based workflows, you can use purpose-built CLI tools to quickly deploy your app. Next, let's see how you can deploy your app to Vercel Now using CircleCI.

Deploying to Vercel Now using CircleCI

In *Chapter 4*, *Automated Testing, CI, and Release to Production*, we configured the LocalCast Weather app to build using CircleCI. We can enhance our CI pipeline to take the build output and optionally deploy it to Vercel Now.

Note that ZEIT Now has rebranded to Vercel Now in 2020.

This section uses the **local-weather-app** repo. The `config.yml` file for this section is named `.circleci/config.ch9.yml`. You can also find a pull request that executes the `.yml` file from this chapter on CircleCI at `https://github.com/duluca/local-weather-app/pull/50` using the branch `deploy_Vercelnow`.

Note that this branch has a modified configuration in `config.yml` and `Dockerfile` to use the `projects/ch6` code from **local-weather-app**.

Let's update the `config.yml` file to add a new job named `deploy`. In the upcoming Workflows section, we will use this job to deploy a pipeline when approved:

1. Create a token from your Vercel Now account.
2. Add an environment variable to your CircleCI project named `NOW_TOKEN` and store your Vercel Now token as the value.
3. In `config.yml`, update the `build` job with the new steps and add a new job named `deploy`:

.circleci/config.yml

```
...
jobs:
  build:
    ...
    - run:
        name: Move compiled app to workspace
        command: |
          set -exu
          mkdir -p /tmp/workspace/dist
          mv dist/local-weather-app /tmp/workspace/dist/
    - persist_to_workspace:
        root: /tmp/workspace
        paths:
          - dist/local-weather-app
  deploy:
    docker:
      - image: circleci/node:lts
    working_directory: ~/repo
    steps:
      - attach_workspace:
          at: /tmp/workspace
      - run: npx now --token $NOW_TOKEN --platform-version 2 --prod /tmp/workspace/dist/local-weather-app --confirm
```

In the `build` job, after the build is complete, we add two new steps. First, we move the compiled app that's in the `dist` folder to a workspace and persist that workspace so we can use it later in another job. In a new job, named `deploy`, we attach the workspace and use npx to run the `now` command to deploy the `dist` folder. This is a straightforward process.

Note that $NOW_TOKEN is the environment variable we stored on the CircleCI project.

4. Implement a simple CircleCI workflow to continuously deploy the outcome of your `build` job:

   `.circleci/config.yml`
   ```
   ...
   workflows:
     version: 2
     build-test-and-deploy:
       jobs:
         - build
         - deploy:
             requires:
               - build
   ```

    Note that the `deploy` job waits for the `build` job to complete before it can execute.

5. Ensure that your CI pipeline executed successfully by inspecting the test results:

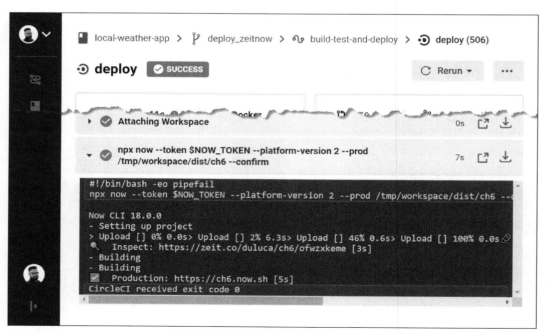

Figure 9.14: Successful Vercel Now deployment of local-weather-app on the deploy_Vercelnow branch

Most CLI commands for cloud providers need to be installed in your pipeline to function. Since Vercel Now has an npm package, this is easy to do. CLI tools for AWS, Google Cloud, or Microsoft Azure need to be installed using tools such as `brew` or `choco`. Doing this manually in a CI environment is tedious. Next, we will cover orbs, which helps to solve the problem.

Deploying to GCloud using orbs

Orbs contain a set of configuration elements to encapsulate shareable behavior between CircleCI projects. CircleCI provides orbs that are developed by the maintainers of CLI tools. These orbs make it easy for you to add a CLI tool to your pipeline without having to set it up manually, with minimal configuration.

To work with orbs, your `config.yml` version number must be set to `2.1` and, in your CircleCI security settings, you must select the option to allow uncertified orbs.

The following are some orbs that you can use in your projects:

- `circleci/aws-cli` and `circleci/aws-ecr` provide you with the AWS CLI tool and help you to interact with **AWS Elastic Container Service** (**AWS ECS**), performing tasks such as deploying your containers to AWS ECR.
- `circleci/aws-ecs` streamlines your CircleCI config to deploy your containers to AWS ECS.
- `circleci/gcp-cli` and `circleci/gcp-gcr` provide you with the GCloud CLI tool and access to **Google Container Registry** (**GCR**).
- `circleci/gcp-cloud-run` streamlines your CircleCI config to deploy your containers to Cloud Run.
- `circleci/azure-cli` and `circleci/azure-acr` provide you with the Azure CLI tools and access to **Azure Container Registry** (**ACR**).

Check out the Orb registry for more information on how to use these orbs at `https://circleci.com/orbs/registry`.

Now, let's configure the `circleci/gcp-cloud-run` orb with the Local Weather app so we can continuously deploy our app to GCloud, without having to manually install and configure the gcloud CLI tool on our CI server.

DevOps Using Docker

On the **local-weather-app** repo, you can find a pull request that executes the Cloud Run configuration from this step on CircleCI, at `https://github.com/duluca/local-weather-app/pull/51`, using the `deploy_cloudrun` branch.

Note that this branch has a modified configuration in `config.yml` and `Dockerfile` to use the `projects/ch6` code from **local-weather-app**.

First, configure your CircleCI and GCloud accounts so you can deploy from a CI server. This is markedly different from deploying from your development machine, because the gcloud CLI tools automatically set up the necessary authentication configuration for you. Here, you will have to do this manually:

1. In your CircleCI account settings, under the security section, ensure you allow execution of uncertified/unsigned orbs.

2. In the CircleCI project settings, add an environment variable named GOOGLE_PROJECT_ID.

   If you used the same project ID as I did, this should be `localcast-weather`.

3. Create a GCloud service account key for your project's existing service account.

   Creating a service account key will result in a JSON file. Do not check this file into your code repository. Do not share the contents of it over insecure communication channels such as email or SMS. Exposing the contents of this file means that any third party can access your GCloud resources permitted by the key permissions.

4. Copy the contents of the JSON file to a CircleCI environment variable named GCLOUD_SERVICE_KEY.

5. Add another environment variable named GOOGLE_COMPUTE_ZONE and set it to your preferred zone.

   I used `us-east1`.

[460]

6. Update your `config.yml` file to add an orb named `circleci/gcp-cloud-run`:

   .circleci/config.yml
   ```
   version: 2.1
   orbs:
     cloudrun: circleci/gcp-cloud-run@1.0.2
     ...
   ```

7. Next, implement a new job named `deploy_cloudrun`, leveraging orb features to initialize, build, deploy, and test our deployment:

   .circleci/config.yml
   ```
   ...
   deploy_cloudrun:
     docker:
       - image: 'cimg/base:stable'
     working_directory: ~/repo
     steps:
       - attach_workspace:
           at: /tmp/workspace
       - checkout
       - run:
           name: Copy built app to dist folder
           command: cp -avR /tmp/workspace/dist/ .
       - cloudrun/init
       - cloudrun/build:
           tag: 'gcr.io/${GOOGLE_PROJECT_ID}/test-${CIRCLE_SHA1}'
           source: ~/repo
       - cloudrun/deploy:
           image: 'gcr.io/${GOOGLE_PROJECT_ID}/test-${CIRCLE_SHA1}'
           platform: managed
           region: us-east1
           service-name: localcast-weather
           unauthenticated: true
       - run:
           command: >
             GCP_API_RESULTS=$(curl -s "$GCP_DEPLOY_ENDPOINT")
             if ! echo "$GCP_API_RESULTS" | grep -nwo "LocalCast Weather"; then
                 echo "Result is unexpected"
                 echo 'Result: '
                 curl -s "$GCP_DEPLOY_ENDPOINT"
                 exit 1;
             fi
           name: Test managed deployed service.
   ```

We first load the dist folder from the build job. We then run cloudrun/init, so that the CLI tool can be initialized. With cloudrun/build, we build the Dockerfile at the root of our project, which automatically stores the result of our build in GCR. Then, cloudrun/deploy deploys the image we just built, taking our code live. In the last command, using the curl tool, we retrieve the index.html file of our website and check to see that it's properly deployed by searching for the LocalCast Weather string.

8. Update your workflow to continuously deploy to gcloud:

   .circleci/config.yml

   ```
   ...
   workflows:
    version: 2
     build-test-and-deploy:
       jobs:
         - build
         - deploy_cloudrun:
             requires:
               - build
   ```

    Note that you can have multiple deploy jobs that simultaneously deploy to multiple targets.

9. Ensure that your CI pipeline executed successfully by inspecting the test results:

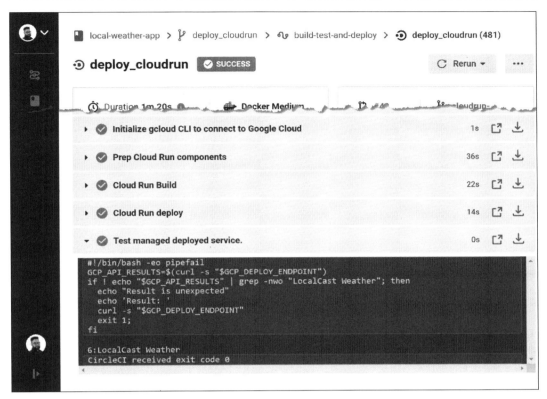

Figure 9.15: Successful gcloud deployment of local-weather-app on the deploy_cloudrun branch

CD works great for development and testing environments. However, it is usually desirable to have gated deployments, where a person must approve a deployment before it reaches a production environment. Next, let's see how you can implement this with CircleCI.

Gated CI workflows

In CircleCI, you can define a workflow to control how and when your jobs are executed. Consider the following configuration, given the jobs `build` and `deploy`:

```yaml
.circleci/config.yml
workflows:
  version: 2
  build-and-deploy:
    jobs:
      - build
      - hold:
          type: approval
          requires:
            - build
      - deploy:
          requires:
            - hold
```

First, the `build` job gets executed. Then, we introduce a special job named `hold` with type `approval`, which requires the `build` job to be successfully completed. Once this happens, the pipeline is put on hold. If or when a decision-maker approves the `hold`, then the `deploy` step can execute. Refer to the following screenshot to see what a `hold` looks like:

Figure 9.16: A hold in the pipeline

Consider a more sophisticated workflow, shown in the following code snippet, where the `build` and `test` steps are broken out into two separate jobs:

```yaml
workflows:
  version: 2
  build-test-and-approval-deploy:
```

```
jobs:
- build
- test
- hold:
    type: approval
    requires:
      - build
      - test
    filters:
      branches:
        only: master
- deploy:
    requires:
      - hold
```

In this case, the `build` and `test` jobs are executed in parallel. If we're on a branch, this is where the pipeline stops. Once the branch is merged with `master`, then the pipeline is put on hold and a decision-maker has the option to deploy a particular build or not. This type of branch filtering ensures that only code that's been merged to `master` can be deployed, which is in line with GitHub flow.

Next, we dive deeper into how you can customize Docker to fit your workflow and environments.

Advanced continuous integration

In *Chapter 4*, *Automated Testing, CI, and Release to Production*, we covered a basic CircleCI pipeline leveraging default features. Beyond the basic automation of unit test execution, one of the other goals of CI is to enable a consistent and repeatable environment to build, test, and generate deployable artifacts of your application with every code push. Before pushing some code, a developer should have a reasonable expectation that their build will pass; therefore, creating a reliable CI environment that automates commands that developers can also run in their local machines is paramount. To achieve this goal, we will build a custom build pipeline that can run on any OS without configuration or any variation in behavior.

This section uses the **lemon-mart** repo. Ensure that your project has been properly configured by executing `npm run docker:debug` as described earlier in the chapter.

Containerizing build environments

In order to ensure a consistent build environment across various OS platforms, developer machines, and CI environments, you may containerize your build environment. Note that there are at least half a dozen common CI tools currently in use. Learning the ins and outs of every tool is an almost impossible task to achieve.

Containerization of your build environment is an advanced concept that goes above and beyond what is currently expected of CI tools. However, containerization is a great way to standardize over 90% of your build infrastructure and can be executed in almost any CI environment. With this approach, the skills you learn and the build configuration you create become far more valuable, because both your knowledge and the tools you create become transferable and reusable.

There are many strategies to containerize your build environment with different levels of granularity and performance expectations. For the purpose of this book, we will focus on reusability and ease of use. Instead of creating a complicated, interdependent set of Docker images that may allow for more efficient fail-first and recovery paths, we will focus on a single and straightforward workflow. Newer versions of Docker have a great feature called multi-stage builds, which allow you to define a multi-image process in an easy-to-read manner and maintain a singular Dockerfile.

At the end of the process, you can extract an optimized container image as our deliverable artifact, shedding the complexity of the images used previously in the process.

As a reminder, your single Dockerfile would look like the following sample:

```
Dockerfile
FROM duluca/minimal-node-web-server:lts-alpine
WORKDIR /usr/src/app
COPY dist/lemon-mart public
```

Multi-stage Dockerfiles

Multi-stage builds work by using multiple FROM statements in a single Dockerfile, where each stage can perform a task and make any resources within its instance available to other stages. In a build environment, we can implement various build-related tasks as their own stages, and then copy the end result, such as the dist folder of an Angular build, to the final image, which contains a web server. In this case, we will implement three stages of images:

- **Builder**: Used to build a production version of your Angular app
- **Tester**: Used to run unit and e2e tests against headless Chrome instances
- **Web server**: The final result containing only the optimized production bits

Multi-stage builds require Docker version 17.05 or higher. To read more about multi-stage builds, read the documentation at https://docs.docker.com/develop/develop-images/multistage-build.

As the following diagram shows, the builder will build the application and the tester will execute the tests:

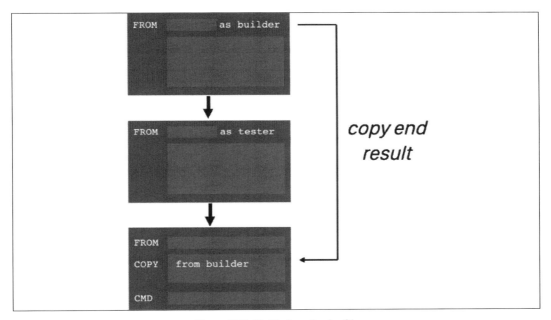

Figure 9.17: Multi-stage Dockerfile

The final image will be built using the outcome of the builder step.

Start by creating a new file to implement the multi-stage configuration, named integration.Dockerfile, at the root of your project.

Builder

The first stage is builder. We need a lightweight build environment that can ensure consistent builds across the board. For this purpose, I've created a sample Alpine-based Node build environment complete with the npm, bash, and Git tools. This minimal container is called duluca/minimal-node-build-env, which is based on node-alpine and can be found on Docker Hub at https://hub.docker.com/r/duluca/minimal-node-build-env. This image is about 10 times smaller than node.

The size of Docker images has a real impact on build times, since the CI server or your team members will spend extra time pulling a larger image. Choose the environment that best fits your needs.

Let's create a builder using a suitable base image:

1. Ensure that you have the `build:prod` command in place in `package.json`:

   package.json
   ```
   "scripts": {
     "build:prod": "ng build --prod",
   }
   ```

2. Inherit from a Node.js-based build environment, such as `node:lts-alpine` or `duluca/minimal-node-build-env:lts-alpine`.

3. Implement your environment-specific build script in a new `Dockerfile`, named `integration.Dockerfile`, as shown:

   integration.Dockerfile
   ```
   FROM duluca/minimal-node-build-env:lts-alpine as builder

   ENV BUILDER_SRC_DIR=/usr/src

   # setup source code directory and copy source code
   WORKDIR $BUILDER_SRC_DIR
   COPY . .

   # install dependencies and build
   RUN npm ci

   RUN npm run style
   RUN npm run lint

   RUN npm run build:prod
   ```

> CI environments will check out your source code from GitHub and place it in the current directory. So, copying the source code from the **current working directory** (**CWD**) using the dot notation should work, as it does in your local development environment. If you run into issues, refer to your CI provider's documentation.

Next, let's see how you can debug your Docker build.

Debugging build environments

Depending on your particular needs, your initial setup of the builder portion of the Dockerfile may be frustrating. To test out new commands or debug errors, you may need to directly interact with the build environment.

To interactively experiment and/or debug within the build environment, execute the following command:

```
$ docker run -it duluca/minimal-node-build-env:lts-alpine /bin/bash
```

You can test or debug commands within this temporary environment before baking them into your `Dockerfile`.

Tester

The second stage is `tester`. By default, the Angular CLI generates a testing requirement that is geared toward a development environment. This will not work in a CI environment; we must configure Angular to work against a headless browser that can execute without the assistance of a GPU and, furthermore, a containerized environment to execute the tests against.

Angular testing tools are covered in *Chapter 4, Automated Testing, CI, and Release to Production*.

Configuring a headless browser for Angular

The protractor testing tool officially supports running against Chrome in headless mode. In order to execute Angular tests in a CI environment, you will need to configure your test runner, Karma, to run with a headless Chrome instance:

1. Update `karma.conf.js` to include a new headless browser option:

    Karma.conf.js
    ```
    ...
        browsers: ['Chrome', 'ChromiumHeadless', 'ChromiumNoSandbox'],
        customLaunchers: {
          ChromiumHeadless: {
            base: 'Chrome',
            flags: [
              '--headless',
              '--disable-gpu',
              // Without a remote debugging port, Google Chrome exits immediately.
              '--remote-debugging-port=9222',
            ],
            debug: true,
    ```

```
      },
      ChromiumNoSandbox: {
        base: 'ChromiumHeadless',
        flags: ['--no-sandbox', '--disable-translate', '--disable-extensions']
      },
    },
```

The `ChromiumNoSandbox` custom launcher encapsulates all the configuration elements needed for a good default setup.

2. Update the `protractor` configuration to run in headless mode:

   e2e/protractor.conf.js
```
...
  capabilities: {
    browserName: 'chrome',
    chromeOptions: {
      args: [
        '--headless',
        '--disable-gpu',
        '--no-sandbox',
        '--disable-translate',
        '--disable-extensions',
        '--window-size=800,600',
      ],
    },
  },
...
```

> In order to test your application for responsive scenarios, you can use the `--window-size` option, as shown earlier, to change the browser settings.

3. Update the `package.json` scripts to select the new browser option in the production build scenarios:

   package.json
```
"scripts": {
  ...
  "test": "ng test lemon-mart --browsers Chrome",
  "test:prod": "npm test -- --browsers ChromiumNoSandbox -- watch=false"
  ...
}
```

Note that test:prod doesn't include npm run e2e. e2e tests are integration tests that take longer to execute, so think twice about including them as part of your critical build pipeline. e2e tests will not run on the lightweight testing environment mentioned in the next section, as they require more resources and time to execute.

Now, let's define the containerized testing environment.

Configuring our testing environment

For a lightweight testing environment, we will be leveraging an Alpine-based installation of the Chromium browser:

1. Inherit from `duluca/minimal-node-chromium:lts-alpine`.
2. Append the following configuration to `integration.Dockerfile`:

   integration.Dockerfile
   ```
   ...
   FROM duluca/minimal-node-chromium:lts-alpine as tester

   ENV BUILDER_SRC_DIR=/usr/src
   ENV TESTER_SRC_DIR=/usr/src

   WORKDIR $TESTER_SRC_DIR
   COPY --from=builder $BUILDER_SRC_DIR .

   # force update the webdriver, so it runs with latest version of Chrome
   RUN cd ./node_modules/protractor && npm i webdriver-manager@latest

   WORKDIR $TESTER_SRC_DIR

   RUN npm run test:prod
   ```

The preceding script will copy the production build from the `builder` stage and execute your test scripts in a predictable manner.

Web server

The third and final stage generates the container that will be your web server. Once this stage is complete, the prior stages will be discarded, and the end result will be an optimized sub-10 MB container:

1. Append the following FROM statement at the end of the file to build the web server, but this time, COPY the production-ready code from builder, as shown in the following code snippet:

   integration.Dockerfile
   ```
   ...
   FROM duluca/minimal-nginx-web-server:1-alpine as webserver

   ENV BUILDER_SRC_DIR=/usr/src

   COPY --from=builder $BUILDER_SRC_DIR/dist/lemon-mart /var/www
   CMD 'nginx'
   ```

2. Build and test your multi-stage Dockerfile:
   ```
   $ docker build -f integration.Dockerfile .
   ```

    Depending on your operating system, you may see Terminal errors. So long as the Docker image successfully builds in the end, then you can safely ignore these errors. For reference purposes, when we later build this image on CircleCI, no errors are logged on the CI server.

3. Save your script as a new npm script named build:integration, as shown:

   package.json
   ```
   "scripts": {
   ...
     "build:integration": "cross-conf-env docker image build -f integration.Dockerfile . -t $npm_package_config_imageRepo:latest",
   ...
   }
   ```

Great work! You've defined a custom build and test environment. Let's visualize the end result of our efforts as follows:

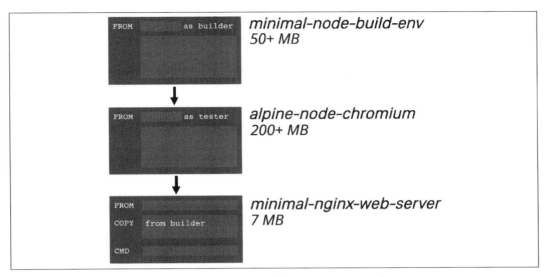

Figure 9.18: Multi-stage build environment results

By leveraging a multi-stage `Dockerfile`, we can define a customized build environment, and only ship the necessary bytes at the end of the process. In the preceding example, we are avoiding shipping 250+ MB of development dependencies to our production server and only delivering a 7 MB container that has a minimal memory footprint.

Now, let's execute this containerized pipeline on CircleCI.

CircleCI container-in-container

In *Chapter 4, Automated Testing, CI, and Release to Production*, we created a relatively simple CircleCI file. Later on, we will repeat the same configuration for this project as well, but for now, we will be using a container-within-a-container setup leveraging the multi-stage `Dockerfile` we just created.

> On the **lemon-mart** repo, the `config.yml` file for this section is named `.circleci/config.docker-integration.yml`. You can also find a pull request that executes the `.yml` file from this chapter on CircleCI at https://github.com/duluca/lemon-mart/pull/25 using the `docker-integration` branch.
>
> Note that this build uses a modified `integration.Dockerfile` to use the `projects/ch8` code from **lemon-mart**.

In your source code, create a folder named `.circleci` and add a file named `config.yml`:

```yml
.circleci/config.yml
version: 2.1
jobs:
  build:
    docker:
      - image: circleci/node:lts
    working_directory: ~/repo
    steps:
      - checkout
      - setup_remote_docker
      - run:
          name: Execute Pipeline (Build Source -> Test -> Build Web Server)
          command: |
            docker build -f integration.Dockerfile . -t lemon-mart:$CIRCLE_BRANCH
            mkdir -p docker-cache
            docker save lemon-mart:$CIRCLE_BRANCH | gzip > docker-cache/built-image.tar.gz
      - save_cache:
          key: built-image-{{ .BuildNum }}
          paths:
            - docker-cache
      - store_artifacts:
          path: docker-cache/built-image.tar.gz
          destination: built-image.tar.gz
workflows:
  version: 2
  build-and-deploy:
    jobs:
      - build
```

In the preceding `config.yml` file, a workflow named `build-and-deploy` is defined, which contains a job named `build`. The job uses CircleCI's pre-built `circleci/node:lts` image.

The `build` job has five steps:

1. `checkout` checks out the source code from GitHub.
2. `setup_remote_docker` informs CircleCI to set up a Docker-within-Docker environment, so we can run containers within our pipeline.

3. `run` executes the `docker build -f integration.Dockerfile .` command to initiate our custom build process, caches the resulting Alpine-based image, and tags it with `$CIRCLE_BRANCH`.
4. `save_cache` saves the image we created in the cache, so it can be consumed by the next step.
5. `store_artifacts` reads the created image from the cache and publishes the image as a build artifact, which can be downloaded from the web interface or used by another job to deploy it to a cloud environment.

After you sync your changes to GitHub, if everything goes well, you will have a passing *green* build. As shown in the following screenshot, this build was successful:

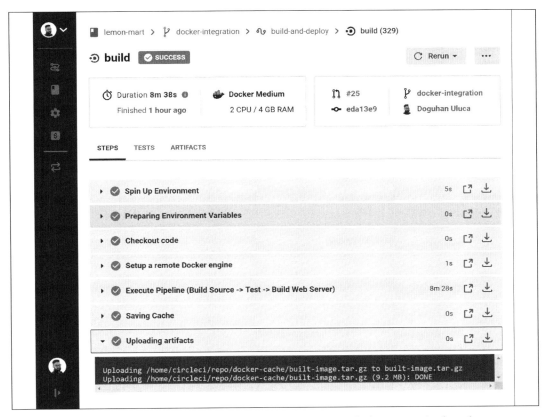

Figure 9.19: Green build on CircleCI using the lemon-mart docker-integration branch

Note that the tarred and gzipped image file size is 9.2 MB, which includes our web applications on top of the roughly 7 MB base image size.

At the moment, the CI server is running and executing our three-step pipeline. As you can see in the preceding screenshot, the build is producing a tarred and gzipped file of the web server image, named `built-image.tar.gz`. You can download this file from the **Artifacts** tab. However, we're not deploying the resulting image to a server.

You have now adequately mastered working with CircleCI. We will revisit this multi-stage `Dockerfile` to perform a deployment on AWS in *Chapter 13, Highly Available Cloud Infrastructure on AWS*.

Next, let's see how you can get a code coverage report from your Angular app and record the result in CircleCI.

Code coverage reports

A good way to understand the amount and the trends of unit test coverage for your Angular project is through a code coverage report.

In order to generate the report for your app, execute the following command from your `project` folder:

```
$ npx ng test --browsers ChromiumNoSandbox --watch=false --code-coverage
```

The resulting report will be created as an HTML file under a folder named `coverage`; execute the following command to view it in your browser:

```
$ npx http-server -c-1 -o -p 9875 ./coverage
```

Install `http-server` as a development dependency in your project.

Here's the folder-level sample coverage report generated by `istanbul/nyc` for LemonMart:

Chapter 9

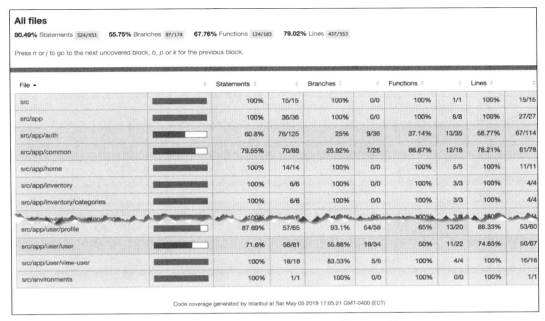

Figure 9.20: Istanbul code coverage report for LemonMart

You can drill down on a particular folder, such as `src/app/auth`, and get a file-level report, as shown here:

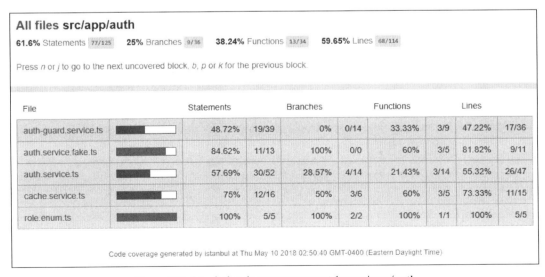

Figure 9.21: Istanbul code coverage report for src/app/auth

You can drill down further to get line-level coverage for a given file, such as `cache.service.ts`, as shown here:

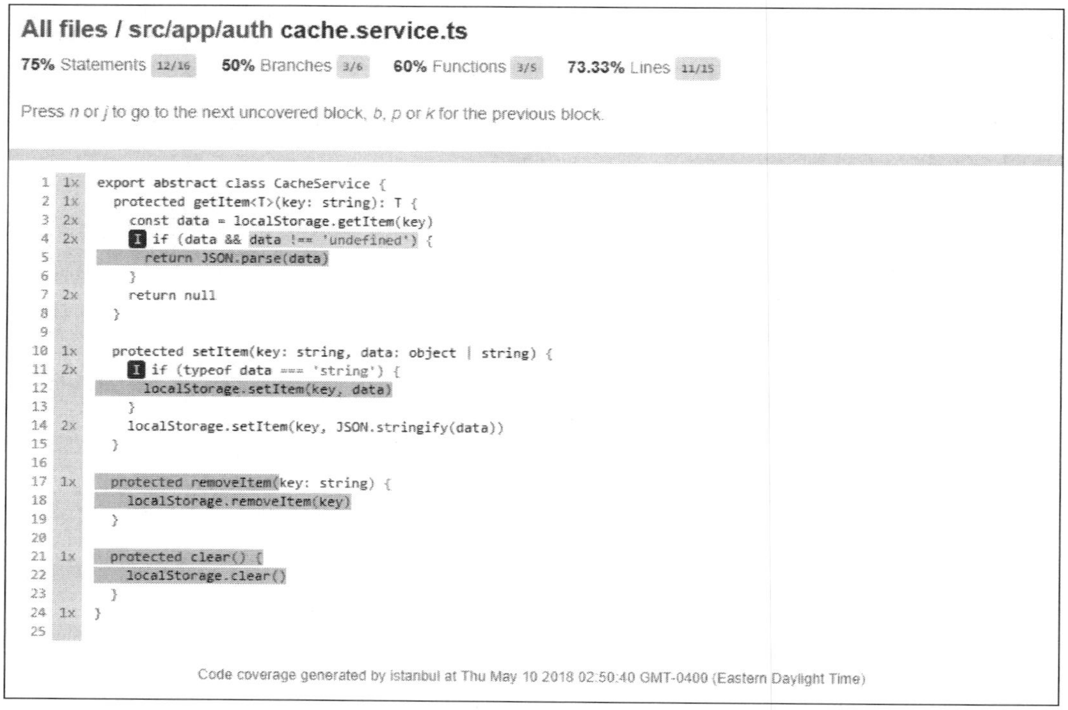

Figure 9.22: Istanbul code coverage report for cache.service.ts

In the preceding screenshot, you can see that lines **5**, **12**, **17-18**, and **21-22** are not covered by any test. The **I** icon denotes that the `if` path was not taken. We can increase our code coverage by implementing unit tests that exercise the functions that are contained within `CacheService`. As an exercise, the reader should attempt to at least cover one of these functions with a new unit test and observe the code coverage report change.

Code coverage in CI

Ideally, your CI server configuration should generate and host the code coverage report with every test run. You can then use code coverage as another code quality gate to prevent pull requests being merged if the new code is bringing down the overall code coverage percentage. This is a great way to reinforce the **test-driven development (TDD)** mindset.

You can use a service such as Coveralls, found at https://coveralls.io/, to implement your code coverage checks, which can embed your code coverage levels directly on a GitHub pull request.

Let's configure Coveralls for LemonMart:

 On the **lemon-mart** repo, the config.yml file for this section is named .circleci/config.ch9.yml.

1. In your CircleCI account settings, under the SECURITY section, ensure that you allow execution of uncertified/unsigned orbs.
2. Register your GitHub project at https://coveralls.io/.
3. Copy the repo token and store it as an environment variable in CircleCI named COVERALLS_REPO_TOKEN.
4. Create a new branch before you make any code changes.
5. Update karma.conf.js so it stores code coverage results under the coverage folder:

   karma.conf.js
   ```
   ...
       coverageIstanbulReporter: {
         dir: require('path').join(__dirname, 'coverage'),
         reports: ['html', 'lcovonly'],
         fixWebpackSourcePaths: true,
       },
   ...
   ```

6. Update the .circleci/config.yml file with the Coveralls orb as shown:

   .circleci/config.yml
   ```
   version: 2.1
   orbs:
     coveralls: coveralls/coveralls@1.0.4
   ```

7. Update the build job to store code coverage results and upload them to Coveralls:

   .circleci/config.yml
   ```
   jobs:
     build:
       ...
         - run: npm test -- --watch=false --code-coverage
         - run: npm run e2e
   ```

```
      - store_test_results:
          path: ./test_results
      - store_artifacts:
          path: ./coverage

      - coveralls/upload

      - run:
          name: Tar & Gzip compiled app
          command: tar zcf dist.tar.gz dist/lemon-mart
      - store_artifacts:
          path: dist.tar.gz
```

Note that the orb automatically configures Coveralls for your account, so the `coveralls/upload` command can upload your code coverage results.

8. Commit your changes to the branch and publish it.
9. Create a pull request on GitHub using the branch.
10. On the pull request, verify that you can see that Coveralls is reporting your project's code coverage, as shown:

Figure 9.23: Coveralls reporting code coverage

11. Merge the pull request to your master branch.

Congratulations! Now, you can modify your branch protection rules to require that code coverage levels must be above a certain percentage before a pull request can be merged to master.

The LemonMart project at https://github.com/duluca/lemon-mart implements a full-featured config.yml file. This file also implements Cypress.io, a far more robust solution compared to Angular's e2e tool, in CircleCI as well. The Cypress orb can record test results and allow you to view them from your CircleCI pipeline.

Leveraging what you have learned in this chapter, you can incorporate the deploy scripts from LocalCast Weather for LemonMart and implement a gated deployment workflow.

Summary

In this chapter, you learned about DevOps and Docker. You containerized your web app, deployed a container to Google Cloud Run using CLI tools, and learned how to implement gated CI workflows. You leveraged advanced CI techniques to build a container-based CI environment leveraging a multi-stage Dockerfile. Also, you became familiar with orbs, workflows, and code coverage tools.

We leveraged CircleCI as a cloud-based CI service and highlighted the fact that you can deploy the outcome of your builds to all major cloud hosting providers. You have seen how you can achieve CD. We covered example deployments to Vercel Now and Google Cloud Run via CircleCI, allowing you to implement automated deployments.

With a robust CI/CD pipeline, you can share every iteration of your app with clients and team members and quickly deliver bug fixes or new features to your end users.

Exercise

1. Add CircleCI and Coveralls badges to the README.md file on your code repository.
2. Implement Cypress for e2e testing and run it in your CircleCI pipeline using the Cypress orb.
3. Implement a Vercel Now deployment and a conditional workflow for the Lemon Mart app. You can find the resulting config.yml file on the lemon-mart repo, named .circleci/config.ch9.yml.

Further reading

- *Dockerfile reference*, 2020, `https://docs.docker.com/engine/reference/builder/`
- *CircleCI orbs*, 2020, `https://circleci.com/orbs/`
- *Deploying container images*, 2020, `https://cloud.google.com/run/docs/deploying`
- *Creating and managing service account keys*, 2020, `https://cloud.google.com/iam/docs/creating-managing-service-account-keys#iam-service-account-keys-create-console`

Questions

Answer the following questions as best as you can to ensure that you've understood the key concepts from this chapter without Googling. Do you need help answering the questions? See *Appendix D, Self-Assessment Answers* online at `https://static.packt-cdn.com/downloads/9781838648800_Appendix_D_Self-Assessment_Answers.pdf` or visit `https://expertlysimple.io/angular-self-assessment`.

1. Explain the difference between a Docker image and a Docker container.
2. What is the purpose of a CD pipeline?
3. What is the benefit of CD?
4. How do we cover the configuration gap?
5. What does a CircleCI orb do?
6. What are the benefits of using a multi-stage `Dockerfile`?
7. How does a code coverage report help maintain the quality of your app?

10
RESTful APIs and Full-Stack Implementation

In *Chapter 1*, *Introduction to Angular and Its Concepts*, I introduced you to the wider architecture in which web applications exist. The choices that are made in full-stack architecture can profoundly impact the success of your web application. You simply cannot afford to be ignorant of how the APIs you interact with are designed. In this chapter, we are going to cover how to implement a backend for your frontend using Node, Express, and Mongo. Combined with Angular, this stack of software is referred to as the MEAN stack.

My take on the MEAN stack is minimal MEAN, which prioritizes ease of use, happiness, and effectiveness, the main ingredients for a great **developer experience** (**DX**). To keep up with the theme, we'll implement the LemonMart server. This server will round out JWT auth from *Chapter 8*, *Designing Authentication and Authorization*. In addition, the server will support recipes that I am going to cover in *Chapter 11*, *Recipes – Reusability, Routing, and Caching*, and *Chapter 12*, *Recipes – Master/Detail, Data Tables, and NgRx*.

This chapter covers a lot of ground. It is designed to serve as a roadmap to the GitHub repository (`https://github.com/duluca/lemon-mart-server`). I cover the architecture, design, and major components of the implementation. I highlight important pieces of code to explain how the solution comes together. However, unlike prior chapters, you cannot solely rely on the code sample provided in the text to complete your implementation. For the purposes of this book, it is more important that you understand why we are implementing various functionality over having a strong grasp of the implementation details. So, for this chapter, I recommend that you read and understand the server code versus trying to recreate it on your own.

RESTful APIs and Full-Stack Implementation

You will need to take action towards the end of the chapter to implement a custom auth provider in your Angular app to authenticate against **lemon-mart-server** and also leverage Postman to generate test data, which will be useful in later chapters.

We begin by covering full-stack architecture, covering lemon-mart-server's monorepo design and how you can use Docker Compose to run a three-tier application with a web app, server, and a database. Then, we go over RESTful API design and documentation, leveraging the OpenAPI specification using `Swagger.io`, and implementation using Express.js. Then, we cover the implementation of a MongoDB **object document mapper (ODM)** using my DocumentTS library to store users with login credentials. We implement a token-based auth function and use it to secure our APIs. Finally, we leverage Postman to generate test data in our database using the APIs we have developed.

In this chapter, you will learn about the following:

- Full-stack architecture
- Docker Compose
- RESTful APIs
- MongoDB ODM with DocumentTS
- Implementing JWT auth
- Generating users with Postman

The most up-to-date versions of the sample code for the book can be found on GitHub at the repository linked below. The repository contains the final and completed state of the code. This chapter requires Docker and Postman applications.

It is critical that you get **lemon-mart-server** up and running on your development environment and have **lemon-mart** communicate with it. Refer to the instructions documented here or in the README on GitHub to get your server up and running.

In the case of this *chapter*:

1. Clone the **lemon-mart-server** repository using the `--recurse-submodules` option: `git clone --recurse-submodules https://github.com/duluca/lemon-mart-server`

2. In the VS Code terminal, execute `cd web-app; git checkout master` to ensure that the submodule from https://github.com/duluca/lemon-mart is on the master branch.

Later, in the *Git submodules* section, you can configure the web-app folder to pull from your lemon-mart server.

3. Execute `npm install` on the root folder to install dependencies.

Note that running the `npm install` command on the root folder triggers a script, which also installs dependencies under the server and web-app folders.

4. Execute `npm run init:env` on the root folder to configure environment variables in .env files.

This command will create two .env files, one on the root folder and the other under the server folder, to contain your private configuration information. The initial files are generated based on the example.env file. You can modify these files later and set your own secure secrets.

5. Execute `npm run build` on the root folder, which builds both the server and the web app.

Note that the web app is built using a new configuration named `--configuration=lemon-mart-server`, which uses src/environments/environment.lemon-mart-server.ts.

6. Execute `docker-compose up --build` to run containerized versions of the server, web app, and a MongoDB database.

Note that the web app is containerized using a new file named nginx.Dockerfile.

[485]

7. Navigate to `http://localhost:8080` to view the web app.

> To log in, click on the **Fill** button to populate the email and password fields with the default demo credentials.

8. Navigate to `http://localhost:3000` to view the server landing page.
9. Navigate to `http://localhost:3000/api-docs` to view interactive API documentation.
10. You can use `npm run start:database` to only start the database, and `npm start` on the `server` folder for debugging.
11. You can use `npm run start:backend` to only start the database and the server, and `npm start` on the `web-app` folder for debugging.

In the case of examples from this *chapter* that are based on **lemon-mart**:

1. Clone the repository: `https://github.com/duluca/lemon-mart`
2. Execute `npm install` on the root folder to install dependencies.
3. The code sample for this chapter is available under the sub-folder: `projects/ch10`
4. To run the Angular app for this chapter, execute the following command:
   `npx ng serve ch10`
5. To run Angular unit tests for this chapter, execute the following command:
   `npx ng test ch10 --watch=false`
6. To run Angular e2e tests for this chapter, execute the following command:
   `npx ng e2e ch10`
7. To build a production-ready Angular app for this chapter, execute the following command:
   `npx ng build ch10 --prod`

> Note that the `dist/ch10` folder at the root of the repository will contain the compiled result.

Beware that the source code in the book or on GitHub may not always match the code generated by the Angular CLI. There may also be slight differences in implementation between the code in the book and what's on GitHub because the ecosystem is ever-evolving. It is natural for the sample code to change over time. Also, on GitHub, expect to find corrections, fixes to support newer versions of libraries, or side-by-side implementations of multiple techniques for the reader to observe. The reader is only expected to implement the ideal solution recommended in the book. If you find errors or have questions, please create an issue or submit a pull request on GitHub for the benefit of all readers.

You can read more about updating Angular in the *Appendix C, Keeping Angular and Tools Evergreen*. You can find this appendix online from `https://static.packt-cdn.com/downloads/9781838648800_Appendix_C_Keeping_Angular_and_Tools_Evergreen.pdf` or at `https://expertlysimple.io/stay-evergreen`.

With your LemonMart server up and running, we are ready to explore the architecture of the MEAN stack. By the end of this section, you should have your own version of LemonMart communicating with the server.

Full-stack architecture

Full-stack refers to the entire stack of software that makes an application work, all the way from databases to servers, APIs, and the web and/or mobile apps that leverage them. The mythical full-stack developer is all-knowing and can comfortably operate in all verticals of the profession. It is next to impossible to specialize in all things software-related and to be considered an expert in relation to every given topic. However, to be considered an expert in a single topic, you must also be well-versed in related topics. When learning a new topic, it is very helpful to keep your tooling and language consistent so that you can absorb the new information without additional noise. For these reasons, I opted to introduce you to the MEAN stack over Spring Boot using Java or ASP.NET using C#. By sticking to familiar tools and languages such as TypeScript, VS Code, npm, GitHub, Jasmine, Docker, and CircleCI, you can better understand how a full-stack implementation comes together and become a better web developer as a result.

Minimal MEAN

Choosing the Correct-Stack™ for your project is difficult. First and foremost, your technical architecture should be adequate to meet business needs. For example, if you're trying to deliver an artificial intelligence project with Node.js, you're likely using the wrong stack. Our focus will be on delivering web applications, but beyond that, we have other parameters to consider, including the following:

- Ease of use
- Happiness
- Effectiveness

If your development team will be working on your application for an extended period of time, then it is very important to consider factors beyond compatibility. Your stack, choice of tool, and coding style can have a significant impact if your code base is easy to use, keeps your developers happy, or makes them feel like effective contributors to the project.

A well configured stack is key for a great DX. This can be the difference between a towering stack of dried-out pancakes, or a delicious short stack with the right amount of butter and syrup over it.

By introducing too many libraries and dependencies, you can slow down your progress, make your code difficult to maintain, and find yourself in a feedback loop of introducing more libraries to resolve the issues of other libraries. The only way to win this game is to simply not play it.

If you take your time to learn how to work with a few fundamental libraries, you can become a far more effective developer. In essence, you can do more with less. My advice would be to:

- **Think** before you write a single line of code, and apply the 80-20 rule.
- **Wait** for libraries and tools to mature, skipping the betas.
- **Fast** by reducing your gluttony for new packages and tools, mastering the fundamentals instead.

 Watch my 2017 Ng conference talk entitled *Do More with Less JavaScript* on YouTube at `https://www.youtube.com/watch?v=Sd1aM8l8lkc`.

This minimalist mindset is the design philosophy behind minimal MEAN. You can review a reference implementation on GitHub at `https://github.com/duluca/minimal-mean`. Refer to the following diagram for the overall architecture:

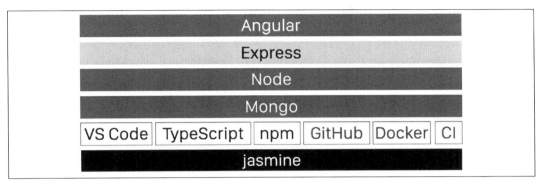

Figure 10.1: Minimal MEAN software stack and tooling

Let's go over the components of the architecture one by one.

Angular

Angular is the presentation layer. Angular is a capable and reliable development platform. It is well understood and has a great community. You should definitely take the time to master the fundamentals of Angular before considering another option.

Libraries such as Angular Material, Angular Evergreen, and `angular-unit-test-helper` help you deliver optimal and great-looking solutions with minimal effort.

You may containerize your Angular (or any other web app) using the minimal Docker container, `duluca/minimal-nginx-web-server` or `duluca/minimal-node-web-server`.

Express

Express.js will be our API layer. Express is a fast, unopinionated, and minimalist web framework for Node.js. Express has a vast plugin ecosystem that is almost guaranteed to meet every need. In minimal MEAN, we only leverage two packages:

- `cors`: To configure cross-origin resource sharing settings
- `morgan`: To log HTTP requests

In addition, we use express parsers to parse incoming HTTP requests in `req.body` and the `express.static` function to serve the content of the `public` folder.

You can read more about Express.js at `https://expressjs.com/`.

Node

Express.js runs on Node.js. We will be implementing the business layer in Node. Node is a lightweight and efficient JavaScript runtime, using an event-driven, non-blocking I/O model that makes it suitable for high-performance and real-time applications. Node runs everywhere, from fridges to smart watches. You can increase the reliability of your Node applications by using TypeScript to develop your application.

 Refer to the blog post by Frank Rosner on non-blocking I/O for a more in-depth explanation of the topic at `https://blog.codecentric.de/en/2019/04/explain-non-blocking-i-o-like-im-five/`.

Later in this chapter, you're going to learn how to configure Node projects using TypeScript.

Mongo

MongoDB represents the persistence layer. MongoDB is a document-oriented database with dynamic JSON-like schemas. The major benefit of using a JSON-based database is the fact that you don't need to transform your data from one format to another. You can retrieve, display, edit, and then update the data solely using JSON.

In addition, the MongoDB native driver for Node is mature, performant, and capable. I have developed a library called `document-ts`, which aims to simplify interacting with MongoDB by introducing rich document objects that are easy to code. DocumentTS is a very thin TypeScript-based MongoDB helper with optional, rich ODM convenience features.

You can read more about MongoDB at `https://www.mongodb.com/`, and the DocumentTS library at `https://github.com/duluca/document-ts`.

Tooling

The tooling that supports your development is as important as your choice of software stack. Minimal MEAN leverages the following:

- **VS Code**: Great extension support, lightweight, fast, and cross-platform
- **TypeScript**: Fast and easy-to-use transpiler with great linting support using tslint
- **Npm**: Multi-platform scripting and dependency management with a rich ecosystem of packages
- **GitHub**: Flexible, free, and well supported Git host. GitHub flow enables gated code check-ins in tandem with a CI server
- **Docker**: Lightweight virtualization technology that encapsulates your environment configuration and settings
- **Continuous Integration (CI)**: Critical to ensuring the delivery of quality code
- **Jasmine**: Batteries-included unit testing framework that works with nyc/istanbul.js to deliver code coverage metrics

Note that the tooling and language of choice we are using is the same as the ones we use for Angular development. This enables developers to be able to switch between frontend and backend development with minimal context switching.

Now that we have covered all major components and tooling for delivering a minimal MEAN stack app, let's start by creating a Git repository that can house our frontend and backend code.

Configuring a monorepo

You can optimize your development experience by creating a monorepo, which contains your frontend and backend code. A monorepo allows developers to be able to jump between projects within the same IDE window. Developers can reference code more easily across projects, such as sharing TypeScript interfaces between the frontend and the backend, thereby ensuring that data objects line up every time. The CI server can build all projects at once to ensure that all components of the full-stack application remain in working order.

> Note that a monorepo is different to multi-root workspaces in VS Code, where you can add multiple projects to show in the same IDE windows. A monorepo combines projects at the source control level. Read more about multi-root workspaces at https://code.visualstudio.com/docs/editor/multi-root-workspaces.

Let's take a quick tour of the code base.

Monorepo structure

Under the `lemon-mart-server` project, you are going to have three main folders, as shown here:

```
lemon-mart-server
├──bin
├──web-app (default Angular setup)
├──server
│   ├──src
│   │   ├──models
│   │   ├──public
│   │   ├──services
│   │   ├──v1
│   │   │   └──routes
│   │   └──v2
│   │       └──routes
│   └──tests
│   package.json
│   README.md
```

The `bin` folder contains helper scripts or tools, the `web-app` folder represents your frontend, and `server` contains the source code for the backend. In our case, the `web-app` folder is the `lemon-mart` project. Instead of copying and pasting the code from the existing project, we leverage Git submodules to link two repositories together.

Git submodules

Git submodules help you share code between multiple repositories, while keeping the commits separate. Frontend developers may choose to only work using the frontend repository, whereas full-stack developers will prefer access to all code. Git submodules also provide a convenient way for existing projects to be combined.

Let's start by seeing how you can add your own `lemon-mart` project as a submodule of `lemon-mart-server`, leveraging the scripts that reside in the `package.json` file in the root folder of our monorepo:

I recommend that you perform this action on the version of **lemon-mart-server** that you cloned from GitHub. Otherwise, you will need to create a new project and execute `npm init -y` to get things started.

1. Observe the following `package.json` scripts that assist in the initialization, updating, and cleaning up of Git submodules:

   package.json

   ```
     "config": {
     ...
       "webAppGitUrl": "https://github.com/duluca/lemon-mart.git"
     },

     "scripts": {
       "webapp:clean": "cross-conf-env rimraf web-app && git rm -r --cached web-app",
       "webapp:init": "cross-conf-env git submodule add $npm_package_config_webAppGitUrl web-app",
       "postwebapp:init": "git submodule status web-app",
       "modules:init": "git submodule update --init --recursive",
       "modules:update": "git submodule update --recursive --remote"
     },
   ```

2. Update `webAppGitUrl` with the URL to your own project.
3. Execute `webapp:clean` to remove the existing `web-app` folder.
4. Finally, execute the `webapp:init` command to initialize your project in the `web-app` folder:

   ```
   $ npm run webapp:init
   ```

Going forward, execute the `modules:update` command to update the code in the submodule. To pull the submodules after cloning the repo in another environment, execute `npm modules:init`. If you ever need to reset the environment and restart, then execute `webapp:clean` to clean Git's cache and remove the folder.

 Note that you can have multiple submodules in your repository. The `modules:update` command will update all the submodules.

Your web application code is now available in the folder named `web-app`. Additionally, you should be able to see both projects under VS Code's **Source Control** pane, as shown:

Figure 10.2: VS Code Source Control Providers

Using VS Code's source control, you can independently perform Git actions on either repository.

 If things get messy with your submodule, simply `cd` into the submodule directory and execute `git pull` and then `git checkout master` to restore the master branch. Using this technique, you may checkout any branch from your project and submit PRs.

Now that we have our submodule ready, let's see how the server project is configured.

Configuring a Node project with TypeScript

To create a new Node.js application using TypeScript, perform the following steps:

 The following steps are only relevant if you are creating a new server project. I recommend that you use the one already provided in the `lemon-mart-server` project that you cloned from GitHub.

1. Create a sub-folder `server`:

   ```
   $ mkdir server
   ```

2. Change your current directory to the `server` folder:

   ```
   $ cd server
   ```

3. Initialize npm to set up `package.json` in the `server` folder:

   `$ npm init -y`

    Note that the top-level `package.json` will be utilized for scripts that are relevant to the full-stack project. `server/package.json` will contain scripts and dependencies for the backend project.

4. Configure your repository using `mrm-task-typescript-vscode`:

   `$ npm i -g mrm-task-typescript-vscode`

   `$ npx mrm typescript-vscode`

The `mrm` task configures VS Code for an optimized TypeScript development experience, similar to the way we did using `mrm-task-angular-vscode` in *Chapter 2, Setting Up Your Development Environment*.

When the command has finished executing, the `project` folder appears as shown here:

```
server
|    .gitignore
|    .nycrc
|    .prettierignore
|    .prettierrc
|    example.env
|    jasmine.json
|    package-lock.json
|    package.json
|    pull_request_template.md
|    tsconfig.json
|    tsconfig.src.json
|    tslint.json
|
├───.vscode
|        extensions.json
|        launch.json
|        settings.json
|
├───src
|        index.ts
```

```
|
└──tests
|       index.spec.ts
|       tsconfig.spec.json
```

The task configures the following:

- Common npm packages used for scripting: cross-conf-env (https://www.npmjs.com/package/cross-conf-env), npm-run-all (https://www.npmjs.com/package/npm-run-all), dev-norms (https://www.npmjs.com/package/dev-norms), and rimraf (https://www.npmjs.com/package/rimraf)
- Npm scripts for styling, linting, building, and testing:
    - `style` and `lint`: Check compliance in code styling and linting errors. They are intended for CI server usage.
    - `style:fix` and `lint:fix`: Apply code styling and linting rules to the code. Not all linting errors can be fixed automatically. You will need to address each error by hand.
    - `build`: Transpiles the code into the `dist` folder.
    - `start`: Runs the transpiled code in Node.js.

> `prepublishOnly` and `prepare` scripts are only relevant if you're developing an npm package. In that case, you should also implement a `.npmignore` file, which excludes the `src` and `tests` folders.

- `ImportSort`: Maintains the order of the `import` statements:
    - Settings are added to `package.json`
    - Supporting npm packages are installed: import-sort, import-sort-cli, import-sort-parser-typescript, and import-sort-style-module
- TypeScript with tslint:
    - `tsconfig.json`: Common TypeScript settings
    - `tsconfig.src.json`: Settings that are specific to the source code under the `src` folder
    - `tslint.json`: Linting rules
- The Prettier plugin, which automatically formats the styling of our code:
    - `.prettierrc`: Prettier settings
    - `.prettierignore`: Files to ignore

- Jasmine and nyc for unit testing and code coverage:
    - jasmine.json: Testing settings.
    - .nycrc: Code coverage settings.
    - The tests folder: Contains spec.ts files, which include your tests and tsconfig.spec.json, which configures more relaxed settings that make it easier to write tests quickly.
    - In package.json: Test scripts are created to build your tests using build:test and execute them with npm test. The test:ci command is intended for CI servers and test:nyc provides the code coverage report.
- example.env: Used to document required environment variables that would be present in your private .env file
    - .env is added to .gitignore
- PR template: A pull request template that requests additional information from developers
- VS Code extensions, settings, and debugging configurations, respectively, in three files:
    - .vscode/extensions.json
    - .vscode/settings.json
    - .vscode/launch.json

Once you are comfortable with the changes introduced to your project, verify that your project is in working order.

Verify the project by executing the tests:

$ npm test

Before the test command is run, npm run build && npm run build:test is executed to transpile our TypeScript code to JavaScript. The output is placed in the dist folder, as shown:

```
server
|
├──dist
|       index.js
|       index.js.map
```

Note that on your filesystem, `.js` and `.js.map` files are created alongside every `.ts` file. In `.vscode/settings.json`, we configure the `files.exclude` property to hide these files in the IDE so that they don't distract developers during development. Additionally, in `.gitignore`, we also ignore `.js` and `.js.map` files, so they don't get checked into our repository.

Now that we have a barebones monorepo, we can configure our CI server.

CircleCI config

One of the benefits of using Git submodules is that we can verify that our frontend and backend works in the same pipeline. We will implement two jobs:

1. `build_server`
2. `build_webapp`

These jobs will follow the workflow shown here:

```
.circleci/config.yml
...
workflows:
  version: 2
  build-and-test-compose:
    jobs:
      - build_server
      - build_webapp
```

The CI pipeline will build the server and the web app simultaneously, with an option to run the `deploy` job if the jobs succeed on the master branch. Refer to the `config.yml` file on GitHub on how to implement the `build_webapp` job, which is similar to the one you implemented in *Chapter 9, DevOps Using Docker*, but that includes a number of subtle differences to handle working with submodules and the folder structure changes. The pipeline for building the server is not too dissimilar to the web app one, as shown here:

```
.circleci/config.yml
version: 2.1
orbs:
  coveralls: coveralls/coveralls@1.0.4
jobs:
  build_server:
    docker:
      - image: circleci/node:lts
```

```yaml
working_directory: ~/repo/server
steps:
  - checkout:
      path: ~/repo
  - restore_cache:
      keys:
        - web-modules-{{ checksum "package-lock.json" }}

  # check npm dependencies for security risks - 'npm audit' to fix
  - run: npx audit-ci --high --report-type full

  - run: npm ci

  - save_cache:
      key: web-modules-{{ checksum "package-lock.json" }}
      paths:
        - ~/.npm

  - run: npm run style
  - run: npm run lint

  # run tests and store test results
  - run: npm run pretest
  - run: npm run test:ci
  - store_test_results:
      path: ./test_results

  # run code coverage and store coverage report
  - run: npm run test:nyc
  - store_artifacts:
      path: ./coverage

  - coveralls/upload

  - run:
      name: Move compiled app to workspace
      command: |
        set -exu
        mkdir -p /tmp/workspace/server
        mv dist /tmp/workspace/server
  - persist_to_workspace:
      root: /tmp/workspace
      paths:
        - server
```

The pipeline checks out the code, verifies the security of the packages we're using with `audit-ci`, installs dependencies, checks for styling and linting errors, runs tests, and checks for code coverage levels.

The test commands implicitly build the server code, which is stored under the `dist` folder. In the final step, we move the `dist` folder into the workspace so that we can use it at a later stage.

Next, let's see how we can bring together all tiers of our app and run it using Docker Compose.

Docker Compose

Since we have a three-tiered architecture, we need a convenient way to set up the infrastructure for our full-stack application. You can create scripts to start various Docker containers individually, but there's a purpose-built tool that runs multi-container applications called Docker Compose. Compose uses a YAML file format, named `docker-compose.yml`, so you declaratively define the configuration of your application. Compose allows you to adhere to infrastructure-as-code principles. Compose will also allow us to conveniently start a database instance without having to install a permanent and always-on database solution in our development environments.

You can use Compose to deploy your application on cloud services, scale the number of container instances you're running, and even run integration tests of your application on your CI server. Later in this section, we go over how you can run Docker Compose on CircleCI.

Consider the architecture of the following application with the communication port of each tier:

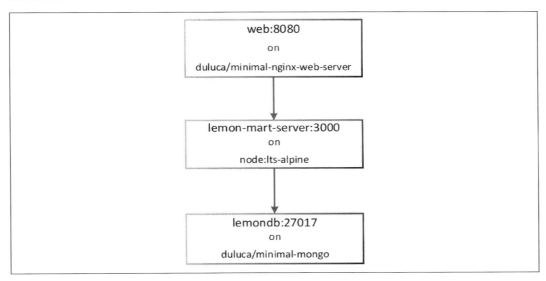

Figure 10.3: Lemon Mart three-tier architecture

Using Docker Compose, we are able to describe the architecture shown here precisely. You can read more about Compose at https://docs.docker.com/compose/.

Next, let's implement a more efficient web server for Lemon Mart.

Using Nginx as the web server

Our web app is already containerized as covered in *Chapter 9*, *DevOps Using Docker*. For this exercise, we will use the nginx-based container.

Add a new Dockerfile named nginx.Dockerfile to the root of your web-app. This image will be smaller than the Node-based one we have, since we're using nginx as the web server:

web-app/nginx.Dockerfile

```
FROM duluca/minimal-nginx-web-server:1-alpine

COPY dist/lemon-mart /var/www

CMD 'nginx'
```

Now, let's containerize our server.

Containerizing the server

So far, we have been using mostly preconfigured Docker images to deploy our web app. The following is a more detailed implementation of a Node.js-based server:

 If you need it, refer to the *Containerizing the app using Docker* section in *Chapter 9, DevOps Using Docker*, as a refresher on Docker.

1. Let's begin by defining the `Dockerfile`:

   server/Dockerfile
   ```
   FROM node:lts-alpine

   RUN apk add --update --no-progress make python bash
   ENV NPM_CONFIG_LOGLEVEL error

   ADD https://github.com/Yelp/dumb-init/releases/download/v1.2.2/dumb-init_1.2.2_amd64 /usr/local/bin/dumb-init
   RUN chmod +x /usr/local/bin/dumb-init

   RUN mkdir -p /usr/src/app

   RUN chown node: /usr/src/app
   USER node

   WORKDIR /usr/src/app

   COPY package*.json ./
   RUN NODE_ENV=production

   RUN npm install --only=production

   ENV HOST "0.0.0.0"
   ENV PORT 3000
   EXPOSE 3000

   ADD dist dist

   ENTRYPOINT ["dumb-init", "--"]
   CMD ["node", "dist/src/index"]
   ```

Note that we ADD the dist folder to our server and then run it using nodes with CMD.

 You can read more about how our server container is configured by checking out README.md on the similarly configured minimal-node-web-server repo at https://github.com/duluca/minimal-node-web-server.

Now, set up the cross-environment, **npm scripts for Docker**, which works on Windows 10 and macOS for our server.

2. Install the npm scripts for the Docker task:

```
$ npm i -g mrm-task-npm-docker
```

3. Apply the npm scripts for Docker configuration, making sure to execute the command in the server folder:

```
$ npx mrm npm-docker
```

4. Configure your package.json with the configuration parameters:

server/package.json
```
"config": {
  "imageRepo": "duluca/lemon-mart-server",
  "imageName": "lemon-mart-server",
  "imagePort": "3000",
  "internalContainerPort": "3000"
}
```

Be sure to build your app before building your Docker container.

Configuring environment variables with DotEnv

DotEnv files are widely supported to store secrets conveniently in a .env file that is not checked in to your code repository. Docker and Compose natively support .env files.

Let's start by understanding the environment variables at the heart of the monorepo:

1. Refer to the example.env file at the root of the project:

example.env
```
# Root database admin credentials
MONGO_INITDB_ROOT_USERNAME=admin
MONGO_INITDB_ROOT_PASSWORD=anAdminPasswordThatIsNotThis
# Your application's database connection information.
# Corresponds to MONGO_URI on server-example.env
MONGODB_APPLICATION_DATABASE=lemon-mart
```

```
MONGODB_APPLICATION_USER=john.smith
MONGODB_APPLICATION_PASS=g00fy
# Needed for AWS deployments
AWS_ACCESS_KEY_ID=xxxxxx
AWS_SECRET_ACCESS_KEY=xxxxxx
# See server-example.env for server environment variables
```

> Don't store any real secrets in example.env. Store them in the .env file. example.env is there to document the environment variables that are required for your project. In this case, I've populated my example.env file with sample values so that readers can run the example without having to configure all these parameters.

2. Ensure that init-dev-env is installed in the root of the project by executing:

   ```
   $ npm i -D init-dev-env
   ```

3. The npm run init:env script generates .env files based on the example.env file using the init-dev-env package:

   > In **lemon-mart-server** the example.env file for the server exists in two places. First in the root of the project as server-example.env and second under server/example.env. This is done to increase the visibility of the sample configuration settings.

   ```
   $ npx init-dev-env generate-dot-env example.env -f &&
   init-dev-env generate-dot-env server-example.env --source=.
   --target=server -f
   ```

4. The second .env file is generated for the server as shown:

   server/.env
   ```
   # MongoDB connection string as defined in example.env
   MONGO_URI=mongodb://john.smith:g00fy@localhost:27017/lemon-mart
   # Secret used to generate a secure JWT
   JWT_SECRET=aSecureStringThatIsNotThis
   # DEMO User Login Credentials
   DEMO_EMAIL=duluca@gmail.com
   DEMO_PASSWORD=l0l1pop!!
   DEMO_USERID=5da01751da27cc462d265913
   ```

Note that this file contains the connection string to MongoDB, the secret we will use to encrypt our JWTs, and a seed user so that we can log in to the application. Normally, you wouldn't configure a password or a user ID for your seed users. These are only here to support repeatable demo code.

Now, we're ready to define the YAML file for Compose.

Define Docker-Compose YAML

Let's define a `docker-compose.yml` file in the root of the monorepo to reflect our architecture:

```yaml
docker-compose.yml
version: '3.7'
services:
  web-app:
    container_name: web
    build:
      context: ./web-app
      dockerfile: nginx.Dockerfile
    ports:
      - '8080:80'
    links:
      - server
    depends_on:
      - server

  server:
    container_name: lemon-mart-server
    build: server
    env_file: ./server/.env
    environment:
      - MONGO_URI=mongodb://john.smith:g00fy@lemondb:27017/lemon-mart
    ports:
      - '3000:3000'
    links:
      - database
    depends_on:
      - database

  database:
    container_name: lemondb
    image: duluca/minimal-mongo:4.2.2
    restart: always
    env_file: .env
    ports:
```

```
      - '27017:27017'
    volumes:
      - 'dbdata:/data/db'

volumes:
  dbdata:
```

At the top, we build the `web-app` service using the nginx-based container. The `build` property automatically builds the `Dockerfile` for us. We are exposing the `web-app` on port `8080` and linking it to the `server` service. The `links` property creates an isolated Docker network to ensure that our containers can communicate with each other. By using the `depends_on` property, we ensure that the server is started before the `web-app` is started.

The `server` also uses the `build` property for an automatic `Dockerfile` build. It also uses the `env_file` property to load environment variables from the `.env` file under the `server` folder. Using the `environment` property, we override the `MONGO_URI` variable to use the internal Docker network name for the database container. The server both `links` and `depends_on` the database, which is named `lemondb`.

The `database` service pulls the `duluca/minimal-mongo` image from Docker Hub. Using the `restart` property, we ensure that the database will automatically restart if it crashes. We use the setup parameters within the `.env` file to configure and password-protect the database. Using the `volumes` property, we mount the database's storage directory to a local directory so that your data can persist across container reboots.

In a cloud environment, you can mount the volume of your database to your cloud provider's persistence solution, including AWS **Elastic File System** (**EFS**) or Azure File Storage.

Additionally, we define a Docker volume named `dbdata` for data storage.

Occasionally, your database may stop working correctly. This can happen if you upgrade your container, use a different container, or use the same volume in another project. In this instance, you can reset the state of your Docker setup by executing the following command:

```
$ docker image prune
$ docker container prune
$ docker volume prune
```

or

```
$ docker system prune --volumes (this will delete everything)
```

To run your infrastructure, you will be executing the `docker-compose up` command. You can also use the `-d` option to your infrastructure in detached mode. You stop it with the `down` command and remove the containers it creates by means of the `rm` command.

Before you can run your infrastructure, you will need to build your application, which is covered in the next section.

Orchestrating the Compose launch

Running `docker-compose up` is a convenient and simple way to start your infrastructure. However, you need your code to be built before building your containers. It is an easy step to overlook. Refer to some npm scripts that you can use to orchestrate the launch of your infrastructure:

package.json
```
scripts: {
  "build": "npm run build --prefix ./server && npm run build --prefix ./web-app -- --configuration=lemon-mart-server",
  "test": "npm test --prefix ./server && npm test --prefix ./web-app -- --watch=false",
  "prestart": "npm run build && docker-compose build",
  "start": "docker-compose up",
  "stop": "docker-compose down",
  "clean": "docker-compose rm",
  "clean:all": "docker system prune --volumes",
  "start:backend": "docker-compose -f docker-compose.backend.yml up --build",
  "start:database": "docker-compose -f docker-compose.database.yml up --build",
```

We implemented a `build` script that runs the `build` commands for the server and the web app. A `test` script can do the same for executing tests. We implemented an `npm start` command that can automatically run the `build` command and run `compose up`. As a bonus, we also implemented `start:backend` and `start:database` scripts that can run alternate `docker-compose` files to stand up just the server or the database. You may create these files by removing the unnecessary parts of the master `docker-compose.yml` file. Refer to the GitHub repo for examples.

RESTful APIs and Full-Stack Implementation

> When coding on the server, I normally execute `npm run start:database` to stand up the database and, in a separate terminal window, I launch the server using `npm start` from the server folder. This way, I can see logs being generated by both systems side by side.

Execute `npm start` to verify that your `docker-compose` configuration is working. Hit *Ctrl + C* to stop the infrastructure.

Compose on CircleCI

You can execute your Compose infrastructure on CircleCI to verify the correctness of your configuration and run a quick integration test. Refer to the following updated workflow:

```
.circleci/config.yml
workflows:
  version: 2
  build-and-test-compose:
    jobs:
      - build_server
      - build_webapp
      - test_compose:
          requires:
            - build_server
            - build_webapp
```

We ensure that both `server` and `web-app` are built before running a new job named `test_compose`, which checks out the code, initializes the submodule, and copies the `dist` folders of both builds, as shown here:

```
.circleci/config.yml
  test_compose:
    docker:
      - image: circleci/node:lts-browsers
    working_directory: ~/repo
    steps:
      - setup_remote_docker
      - attach_workspace:
          at: /tmp/workspace
      - checkout:
          path: ~/repo
      - run: npm run modules:init
      - run:
```

```
              name: Copy built server to server/dist folder
              command: cp -avR /tmp/workspace/server/dist/ ./server
        - run:
              name: Copy built web-app to web-app/dist folder
              command: cp -avR /tmp/workspace/dist/ ./web-app
        - run:
              name: Restore .env files
              command: |
                set +H
                echo -e $PROJECT_DOT_ENV > .env
                echo -e $SERVER_DOT_ENV > server/.env
        - run:
              name: Compose up
              command: |
                set -x
                docker-compose up -d
        - run:
              name: Verify web app
              command: |
                set -x
                docker run --network container:web jwilder/dockerize -wait http://localhost:80
                docker run --network container:web appropriate/curl http://localhost:80
          - run:
              name: Verify db login with api
              command: |
                set -x
                docker run --network container:lemon-mart-server jwilder/dockerize -wait http://localhost:3000
                docker run --network container:lemon-mart-server appropriate/curl \
                    -H "accept: application/json" -H "Content-Type: application/json" \
                    -d "$LOGIN_JSON" http://localhost:3000/v1/auth/login
```

After copying the `dist` files, the job then lays down the `.env` files from the CircleCI environment variables. Then, we run `docker-compose up` to stand up our server. Next, we test the `web-app` by running a `curl` command to retrieve its `index.html` file. We run `curl` after waiting for the server to become available using `dockerize -wait`. Similarly, we test the integration of our API server and the database by logging in using our demo user.

Congratulations! Now, you have a pretty good understanding of how our full stack architecture is pieced together at a high level. In the latter half of this chapter, we will go over how the API is implemented, how it integrates with the database, and see how JWT auth works in tandem with the API and database.

Let's continue by diving into API design.

RESTful APIs

In full stack development, nailing down the API design early on is important. The API design itself is closely correlated with how your data contract will look. You may create RESTful endpoints or use the next-gen GraphQL technology. In designing your API, frontend and backend developers should collaborate closely to achieve shared design goals. Some high-level goals are listed as follows:

- Minimize data transmitted between the client and server
- Stick to well-established design patterns (in other words, data pagination)
- Design to reduce business logic present in the client
- Flatten data structures
- Do not expose database keys or relationships
- Version endpoints from the get-go
- Design around major data entities

You should aim to implement the business logic in your RESTful API. Ideally, your frontend shouldn't contain anything more than presentation logic. Any `if` statement implemented by the frontend should also be verified in your backend.

As discussed in *Chapter 1, Introduction to Angular and Its Concepts*, it is critical to aim for a stateless design in both the backend and frontend. Every request should utilize non-blocking I/O methods and should not rely on any existing session. This is the key to infinitely scaling your web application using cloud hosting providers.

Whenever you're implementing a project, it is important to limit, if not eliminate, experimentation. This is especially true in full stack projects. The downstream effect of missteps in API design can be profound and impossible to correct once your application goes live.

Next, let's look into designing an API around major data entities. In this case, we'll review the implementation of an API surrounding users, including authentication. First we'll explore how we can define an endpoint using Swagger, so we can concretely communicate the intent of our design to team members.

Remember that only significant pieces of code that are conceptually significant are covered in this chapter. While you may choose to implement this code from scratch, it is not necessary to get an understanding of how it works. If you choose to implement it from scratch, refer to the complete source code at https://github.com/duluca/lemon-mart-server to follow along and bridge the gaps in your implementation.

Later on, Swagger will become a documentation tool, reflecting the capability of our APIs.

API design with Swagger

Swagger will allow you to design and document your web API. For teams, it can act as a great communication tool between frontend and backend developers, thereby reducing a lot of friction. Additionally, defining your API surface early on allows implementation to begin without worrying about late-stage integration challenges.

We will implement a users API as we move on, so as to demonstrate how Swagger works.

I highly recommend installing the Swagger Viewer VS Code extension, which allows us to preview the YAML file without running any additional tools.

Let's begin by exploring the `swagger.yaml` file at the root of the monorepo:

1. Open `swagger.yaml` in VS Code.
2. Install the VS Code extension called Swagger Preview.
3. Hit *Ctrl + Shift + P*, or ⌘ + ⇧ +*P*, to bring up the command palette and run **Preview Swagger**.

RESTful APIs and Full-Stack Implementation

4. See the preview, as shown here:

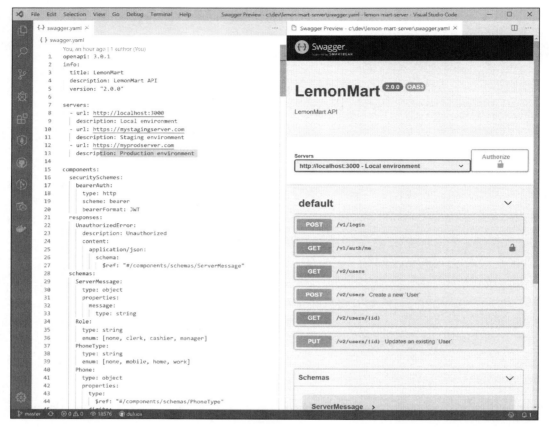

Figure 10.4: Swagger.yaml preview

Using the Swagger UI view, you are going to be able to try out commands and execute them against your server environment.

Defining a Swagger YAML file

We'll use Swagger spec version `openapi: 3.0.1`, which implements the OpenAPI standard. Let's go over the major components of the `swagger.yaml` file here:

> For more information about how a Swagger file is defined, refer to https://swagger.io/specification/.

1. The YAML file starts with general information and target servers:

   swagger.yaml
   ```
   openapi: 3.0.1
   info:
     title: LemonMart
     description: LemonMart API
     version: "2.0.0"

   servers:
     - url: http://localhost:3000
       description: Local environment
     - url: https://mystagingserver.com
       description: Staging environment
     - url: https://myprodserver.com
       description: Production environment
   ```

2. Under `components`, we define common `securitySchemes` and responses, which define the authentication scheme we intend to implement and how the shape of our error message response will appear:

   swagger.yaml
   ```
   ...
   components:
     securitySchemes:
       bearerAuth:
         type: http
         scheme: bearer
         bearerFormat: JWT
     responses:
       UnauthorizedError:
         description: Unauthorized
         content:
           application/json:
             schema:
               $ref: "#/components/schemas/ServerMessage"
             type: string
   ```

    Note the usage of `$ref` to reuse repeating elements. You can see `ServerMessage` being defined here.

RESTful APIs and Full-Stack Implementation

3. Under `components`, we define shared data `schemas`, which declares the data entities that we either take in as input or return to the client:

   swagger.yaml
   ```
   ...
     schemas:
       ServerMessage:
         type: object
         properties:
           message:
             type: string
       Role:
         type: string
         enum: [none, clerk, cashier, manager]
     ...
   ```

4. Under `components`, we add shared `parameters`, making it easy to reuse common patterns such as paginated endpoints:

   swagger.yaml
   ```
   ...
     parameters:
       filterParam:
         in: query
         name: filter
         required: false
         schema:
           type: string
         description: Search text to filter the result set by
   ...
   ```

5. Under `paths`, we begin defining REST endpoints, such as a `post` endpoint for the `/login` path:

   swagger.yaml
   ```
   ...
   paths:
     /v1/login:
       post:
         description: |
           Generates a JWT, given correct credentials.
         requestBody:
           required: true
           content:
             application/json:
               schema:
                 type: object
   ```

```
              properties:
                email:
                  type: string
                password:
                  type: string
              required:
                - email
                - password
      responses:
        '200': # Response
          description: OK
          content:
            application/json:
              schema:
                type: object
                properties:
                  accessToken:
                    type: string
                    description: JWT token that contains userId as
subject, email and role as data payload.
        '401':
          $ref: '#/components/responses/UnauthorizedError'
```

> Note that `requestBody` defines input variables that are required with a type of `string`. Under `responses`, we can define how a successful `200` response and an unsuccessful `401` response to a request appear. In the former case, we return an `accessToken`, while in the latter case, we return an `UnauthorizedError`, as defined in Step 2.

6. Under `paths`, we continue by adding the following paths:

   swagger.yaml
   ```
   ...
   paths:
     /v1/auth/me:
     get: ...
   /v2/users:
       get: ...
       post: ...
   /v2/users/{id}:
       get: ...
       put: ...
   ```

RESTful APIs and Full-Stack Implementation

The OpenAPI spec is powerful, allowing you to define intricate requirements on how users should be able to interact with your API. The specification document at `https://swagger.io/docs/specification` is an invaluable resource while developing your own API definition.

Preview Swagger file

You can validate your Swagger file at `https://swaggerhub.com` for free. After you sign up for a free account, create a new project and define your YAML file. SwaggerHub will highlight any errors you made. It will also give you a preview of the web view, which is the same one you get with the Swagger Preview VS Code extension.

Refer to the following screenshot to see how a valid Swagger YAML definition looks on SwaggerHub:

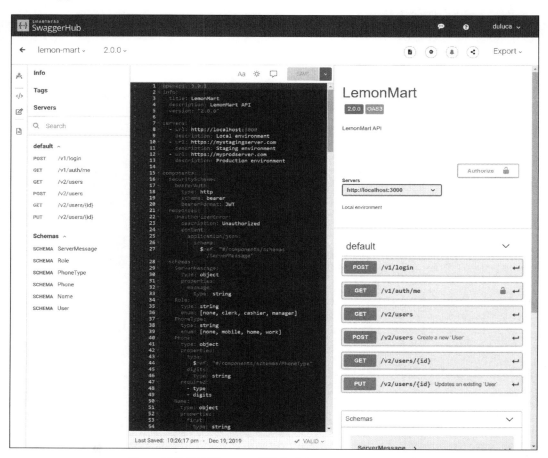

Figure 10.5: Valid Swagger YAML definition on SwaggerHub

Our goal is to integrate this interactive documentation with our Express.js APIs.

Now, let's see how you can implement such an API.

Implementing APIs with Express.js

Before we begin implementing our APIs, let's review the target file structure of our backend in sections, so we get an understanding of how the server is bootstrapped, how routing is configured for API endpoints, how public resources are served, and how services are configured. Minimal MEAN intentionally sticks to the basics, so you can learn more about the underlying technologies. While I have delivered production systems using minimal MEAN, you may not enjoy the barebones development experience as much as I do. In this case, you may consider Nest.js, which is a popular framework for implementing full stack Node.js apps. Nest.js has a rich feature set with an architecture and coding style that closely resemble Angular. I recommend using such a library after you have mastered the basics of the MEAN stack.

 Kudos to Kamil Mysliwiec and Mark Pieszak for creating a great tool and vibrant community around Nest.js. You can read more about Nest.js at https://nestjs.com/ and solicit consulting services at https://trilon.io/.

Now, let's review the file structure of our Express server:

```
server/src
|    api.ts
|    app.ts
|    config.ts
|    docs-config.ts
|    index.ts
|
|————models
|       enums.ts
|       phone.ts
|       user.ts
|
|————public
|       favicon.ico
|       index.html
|
|————services
```

```
|       authService.ts
|       userService.ts
|
├───v1
|   |   index.ts
|   |
|   └───routes
|           authRouter.ts
|
└───v2
    |   index.ts
    |
    └───routes
            userRouter.ts
```

Let's review the purpose and the interaction between these files by looking at a component diagram, giving us an overview of the architecture and the dependency tree:

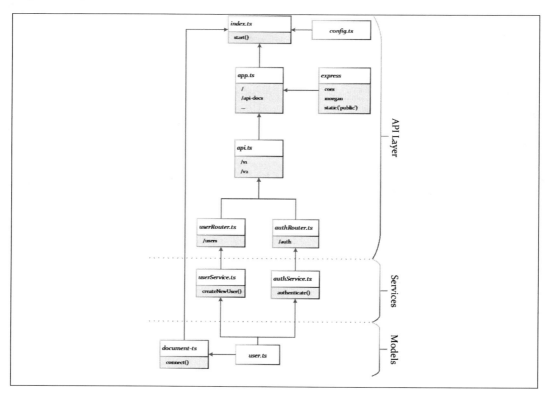

Figure 10.6: Express server architecture

index.ts contains a start function, which bootstraps the application leveraging three major helpers:

1. config.ts: Manages environment variables and settings.
2. app.ts: Configures Express.js, defines all API paths, and then routers implement the paths and leverage services that contain the business logic. Services use models, such as user.ts, to access the database.
3. document-ts: Establishes a connection to the database and configures it, and leverages user.ts to configure a seed user during startup.

You can see that the components at the top of the diagram are responsible for start up and configuration chores, including configuring API paths, which represent the **API** layer. The **Services** layer should contain most of the business logic for the app, while persistence is handled in the **Models** layer.

Refer to the following implementation of index.ts without any database features:

server/src/index.ts

```
import * as http from 'http'

import app from './app'

import * as config from './config'

export let Instance: http.Server
async function start() {
  console.log('Starting server: ')
  console.log(`isProd: ${config.IsProd}`)
  console.log(`port: ${config.Port}`)

  Instance = http.createServer(app)

  Instance.listen(config.Port, async () => {
    console.log(`Server listening on port ${config.Port}...`)
  })
}

start()
```

Note that the last line of code shown, `start()`, is the function call that triggers the initialization of the server.

Now, let's look into how the Express server is set up.

Bootstrapping the server

`App.ts` configures Express.js, along with serving static assets, routing, and versioning. Express.js leverages middleware functions to integrate with libraries or your own code, such as an authenticate method:

server/src/app.ts
```
import * as path from 'path'

import * as cors from 'cors'
import * as express from 'express'
import * as logger from 'morgan'

import api from './api'

const app = express()

app.use(cors())
app.use(express.json())
app.use(express.urlencoded({ extended: true }))
app.use(logger('dev'))

app.use('/', express.static(path.join(__dirname, '../public'), { redirect: false }))

app.use(api)

export default app
```

In the preceding code, note that configuring Express is straightforward with the `use()` method. First, we configure `cors`, and then express parsers and `logger`.

Next, using the `express.static` function, we serve the `public` folder at the root's route, /, so we can display some useful information about our server, as shown:

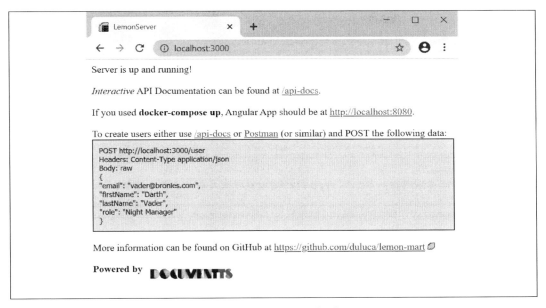

Figure 10.7: LemonMart server landing page

We will cover how to configure the /api-docs endpoint, which is referenced above, in the next section.

Finally, we configure the router, which is defined in api.ts.

Routes and versioning

Api.ts configures the Express router. Refer to the following implementation:

```
server/src/api.ts
import { Router } from 'express'

import api_v1 from './v1'
import api_v2 from './v2'

const api = Router()

// Configure all routes here
api.use('/v1', api_v1)
api.use('/v2', api_v2)

export default api
```

RESTful APIs and Full-Stack Implementation

In this case, we have two child routes for v1 and v2. It is critical to always version the APIs you implement. Once an API becomes public, it can be very tricky, even impossible sometimes, to simply phase out an API for a newer version. Even minor code changes or slight differences in the API can cause clients to break. You must pay careful attention to only making backward-compatible changes to your API.

At some point, you will have a need to completely rewrite the endpoint to meet new requirements, performance, and business needs, at which point you can simply implement a v2 version of your endpoint, while leaving the v1 implementation unchanged. This allows you to innovate at the pace you need to, while keeping legacy consumers of your app functional.

In short, you should version every API you create. By doing this, you force your consumers to version their HTTP calls to your API. As time goes on, you may transition, duplicate, and retire APIs under different versions. Consumers then have a choice to call whichever version of the API works for them.

Configuring a route is trivial. Let's see the configuration for v2, as shown:

```
server/src/v2/index.ts
import { Router } from 'express'

import userRouter from './routes/userRouter'

const router = Router()

// Configure all v2 routers here
router.use('/users?', userRouter)

export default router
```

 The question mark at the end of /users? means that both /user and /users will work against operations implemented in userRouter. This is a great way to avoid typos, while allowing the developer to choose the plurality that makes sense for the operation.

In userRouter, you can then implement GET, POST, PUT, and DELETE operations. Refer to the following implementation:

```
server/src/v2/routes/userRouter.ts
const router = Router()
router.get('/', async (req: Request, res: Response) => {
})
```

```
router.post('/', async (req: Request, res: Response) => {
})

router.get('/:userId', async (req: Request, res: Response) => {
})

router.put('/:userId', async (req: Request, res: Response) => {
})

export default router
```

In the preceding code, you can observe the use of route parameters. You can consume route parameters through a request object, such as `req.params.userId`.

> Note that all routes in the sample code are tagged as `async` because they will all be making a database call, which we are going to `await`. If your route is synchronous, then you don't require the `async` keyword.

Next, let's look into services.

Services

We don't want to implement our business logic in the router files, which represents our API layer. The API layer should largely consist of transforming data and making calls to the business logic layer.

You can implement services using Node.js and TypeScript features. No fancy dependency injection is necessary. The sample application implements two services – `authService` and `userService`.

For example, in `userService.ts`, you can implement a function called `createNewUser`:

server/src/services/userService.ts
```
import { IUser, User } from '../models/user'
export async function createNewUser(userData: IUser): Promise<User | boolean> {
  // create user
}
```

`createNewUser` accepts `userData` in the shape of `IUser` and, when it is done creating the user, it returns an instance of `User`. We can then use this function in our router as follows:

server/src/v2/routes/userRouter.ts
```
import { createNewUser } from '../../services/userService'

router.post('/', async (req: Request, res: Response) => {
  const userData = req.body as IUser
  const success = await createNewUser(userData)
  if (success instanceof User) {
    res.send(success)
  } else {
    res.status(400).send({ message: 'Failed to create user.' })
  }
})
```

We can await the result of `createNewUser` and, if successful, return the created object as a response to the POST request.

> Note that even though we are casting `req.body` as `IUser`, this is only a development time comfort feature. At runtime, the consumer may pass any number of properties to the body. Careless handling of request parameters is one of the primary ways in which your code can be maliciously exploited.

Now that we have an understanding of the skeleton of our Express server, let's see how you can configure Swagger so that you can use it as a guide to implementation and create living documentation for your API.

Configuring Swagger with Express

Configuring Swagger with Express is a manual process. Forcing yourself to manually document the endpoints has a great side effect. By slowing down, you will get the opportunity to consider your implementation from the consumer's perspective as well as the implementor's perspective. This perspective will help you to resolve potential issues with your endpoints during development, thereby avoiding costly reworking.

The major benefit of integrating Swagger with your server is that you will get the same interactive Swagger UI that was covered earlier in this chapter, so your testers and developers can discover or test your API directly from a web interface.

Chapter 10

We are going to use two helper libraries to help us integrate Swagger into our server:

- swagger-jsdoc: This allows you to implement OpenAPI specs right on top of the relevant code by using the @swagger identifier in a JSDoc comment block, generating a swagger.json file as output.
- swagger-ui-express: This consumes the swagger.json file to display the interactive Swagger UI web interface.

Let's go over how Swagger is configured to work with Express.js:

1. The dependencies and type information for TypeScript are shown here:
    ```
    $ npm i swagger-jsdoc swagger-ui-express
    $ npm i -D @types/swagger-jsdoc @types/swagger-ui-express
    ```

2. Let's go over the docs-config.ts file, which configures the base OpenAPI definition:

    server/src/docs-config.ts

    ```
    import * as swaggerJsdoc from 'swagger-jsdoc'
    import { Options } from 'swagger-jsdoc'

    import * as packageJson from '../package.json'

    const options: Options = {
      swaggerDefinition: {
        openapi: '3.0.1',
        components: {},
        info: {
          title: packageJson.name,
          version: packageJson.version,
          description: packageJson.description,
        },
        servers: [
          {
            url: 'http://localhost:3000',
            description: 'Local environment',
          },
          {
            url: 'https://mystagingserver.com',
            description: 'Staging environment',
          },
          {
            url: 'https://myprodserver.com',
            description: 'Production environment',
    ```

```
      },
    ],
  },
  apis: [
    '**/models/*.js',
    '**/v1/routes/*.js',
    '**/v2/routes/*. js'
  ],
}

export const specs = swaggerJsdoc(options)
```

Modify the `servers` property to include the location of your testing, staging, or production environments. This allows consumers of your API to test the API using the web interface without additional tooling. Note that the `apis` property informs the code files that `swaggerJsdoc` should parse when constructing the `swagger.json` file. This routine runs during the bootstrapping of the server, which is why we reference the transpiled `.js` files instead of `.ts` files.

3. Bootstrap the swagger config in `app.ts`:

   server/src/app.ts

   ```
   import * as swaggerUi from 'swagger-ui-express'
   import { specs } from './docs-config'

   const app = express()

   app.use(cors())
   ...
   app.use('/api-docs', swaggerUi.serve, swaggerUi.setup(specs))
   ...

   export default app
   ```

Specs contain the content of the `swagger.json` file, which is then passed to `swaggerUi`. Then, using the server middleware, we can configure `swaggerUi` to host the web interface at `/api-docs`.

> You already have the OpenAPI definitions that need to be used to complete the implementation of the application from the beginning of this chapter. Refer to the complete source code at https://github.com/duluca/lemon-mart-server for additional help.

Congratulations! Now you have a good understanding of how our Express server works. Next, let's look at how to connect to MongoDB.

MongoDB ODM with DocumentTS

DocumentTS acts as an ODM, implementing a layer of models to enable rich and customizable interaction with database objects. ODM is the document-based database equivalent of an **Object Relational Mapper (ORM)** in relational databases. Think Hibernate or Entity Framework. If you're not familiar with these concepts, I recommend that you do further research before moving on.

At its core, DocumentTS leverages the Node.js driver for MongoDB. This driver is implemented by the makers of MongoDB. It guarantees to offer the best performance and feature parity with new MongoDB releases, whereas third-party libraries often lag in supporting new features. Using the `database.getDbInstance` method, you can get access to the native driver directly. Otherwise, you will be accessing Mongo through models that you implement. Refer to the following diagram for an overview:

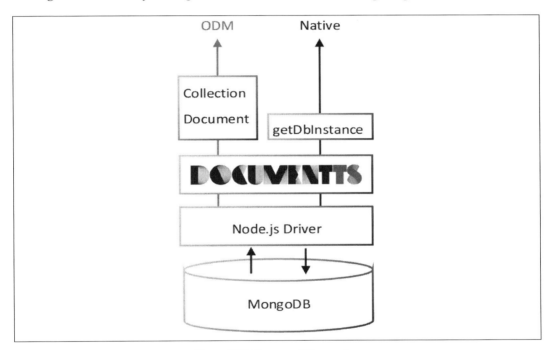

Figure 10.8: DocumentTS overview

 You can read more about MongoDB's Node.js driver at `https://mongodb.github.io/node-mongodb-native/`.

About DocumentTS

DocumentTS provides three major features:

- `connect()`: A MongoDB async connection harness
- `Document` and `IDocument`: A base class and interface to help define your own models
- `CollectionFactory`: Defines collections, organizes indexes, and aggregates queries alongside collection implementations

Here are the convenience features that a DocumentTS collection provides:

- `get collection` returns the native MongoDB collection, so you can operate on it directly:

  ```
  get collection(): ICollectionProvider<TDocument>
  ```

- `aggregate` allows you to run a MongoDB aggregation pipeline:

  ```
  aggregate(pipeline: object[]): AggregationCursor<TDocument>
  ```

- `findOne` and `findOneAndUpdate` simplify the operation of commonly used database functionality, automatically hydrating the models returned:

  ```
  async findOne(
     filter: FilterQuery<TDocument>,
     options?: FindOneOptions
  ): Promise<TDocument | null>
  async findOneAndUpdate(
     filter: FilterQuery<TDocument>,
     update: TDocument | UpdateQuery<TDocument>,
     options?: FindOneAndReplaceOption
   ): Promise<TDocument | null>
  ```

- `findWithPagination` is by far the best feature of DocumentTS, allowing you to filter, sort, and paginate large collections of data. This function is geared toward use with data tables, so you specify searchable properties, turn off hydration, and use a debug feature to fine-tune your queries:

  ```
  async findWithPagination<TReturnType extends IDbRecord>(
     queryParams: Partial<IQueryParameters> & object,
     aggregationCursorFunc?: Func<AggregationCursor<TReturnType>>,
     query?: string | object,
     searchableProperties?: string[],
     hydrate = true,
     debugQuery = false
  ): Promise<IPaginationResult<TReturnType>>
  ```

DocumentTS aims to be reliable, optional, and convenient to use. DocumentTS directly exposes the developer to the native Node.js driver, so you learn how to work with MongoDB instead of some library. Developers can optionally leverage the library's convenience features, including the following:

- Define your own models through simple interfaces.
- Choose fields that you want to automatically hydrate, such as child or related objects.
- Serialize calculated fields with every request.
- Protect certain fields (such as passwords) from serialization so that they aren't accidently sent across the wire.

By being optional, DocumentTS allows developers to transition to new features in their own time. If performance becomes a concern, you can easily switch to native MongoDB calls to get the best performance. Using DocumentTS, you will spend more time reading MongoDB documentation than DocumentTS documentation.

> Mongoose is a popular library for interacting with MongoDB. However, it is a wrapper around MongoDB, requiring a full buy-in. Furthermore, the library abstracts away the native driver, so it is very sensitive to changes and updates in the ecosystem. You can read more about Mongoose at https://mongoosejs.com/.

Install MongoDB dependencies and type information for TypeScript with the following commands:

```
$ npm i mongodb document-ts
$ npm i -D @types/mongodb
```

Next, let's see how we connect to the database.

Connecting to the database

It can be a challenge to ensure that database connectivity exists when writing a fully async web application. `connect()` makes it easy to connect to a MongoDB instance and makes it safe to be called simultaneously from multiple threads starting up at the same time.

Let's start by configuring your environment variables:

1. Remember that the MONGO_URI connection string resides in server/.env:

    server/.env
    MONGO_URI=mongodb://john.smith:g00fy@localhost:27017/lemon-mart

In order to update the username, password, and database name, you'll need to edit the following variables in the top level `.env` file:

.env
```
MONGODB_APPLICATION_DATABASE=lemon-mart
MONGODB_APPLICATION_USER=john.smith
MONGODB_APPLICATION_PASS=g00fy
```

> Remember that `.env` changes only take effect when you restart your servers.

2. Let's see how `document-ts` integrates with `index.ts`:

   server/src/index.ts
   ```
   ...
   import * as document from 'document-ts'
   import { UserCollection } from './models/user'
   ...
   async function start() {
     ...
     console.log(`mongoUri: ${config.MongoUri}`)

     try {
       await document.connect(config.MongoUri, config.IsProd)
       console.log('Connected to database!')
     } catch (ex) {
       console.log(`Couldn't connect to a database: ${ex}`)
     }
   ...

     Instance.listen(config.Port, async () => {
       console.log(`Server listening on port ${config.Port}...`)
       await createIndexes()
       console.log('Done.')
     })
   }

   async function createIndexes() {
     console.log('Create indexes...')
     await UserCollection.createIndexes()
   }

   start()
   ```

We attempt to connect to the database using a `try/catch` block. Once the Express server is up and running, we call `createIndexes`, which, in turn, calls a function with the same name on `UserCollection`. Beyond performance considerations, MongoDB indexes are necessary to enable fields to become searchable.

Models with IDocument

You may implement an `IUser` interface similar to the one in LemonMart. However, this one will be extending the `IDocument` defined in DocumentTS:

1. Here is the `IUser` interface:

   server/src/models/user.ts
   ```
   export interface IUser extends IDocument {
     email: string
     name: IName
     picture: string
     role: Role
     userStatus: boolean
     dateOfBirth: Date
     level: number
     address: {
       line1: string
       line2?: string
       city: string
       state: string
       zip: string
     }
     phones?: IPhone[]
   }
   ```

    The interfaces and base classes provided by DocumentTS aim to help you develop your business logic and database queries in a consistent manner. I encourage you to explore the base classes and interfaces by *Ctrl* + clicking on them so that you can see the source code behind them.

2. Now, here is the `User` class extending `Document<T>` and implementing Swagger documentation:

   server/src/models/user.ts
   ```
   import { v4 as uuid } from 'uuid'

   /**
    * @swagger
   ```

```
 *   components:
 *     schemas:
 *       Name:
 *         type: object
 *         ...
 *       User:
 *         type: object
 *         ...
 */
export class User extends Document<IUser> implements IUser {
  static collectionName = 'users'
  private password: string
  public email: string
  public name: IName
  public picture: string
  public role: Role
  public dateOfBirth: Date
  public userStatus: boolean
  public level: number
  public address: {
    line1: string
    city: string
    state: string
    zip: string
  }

  public phones?: IPhone[]

  constructor(user?: Partial<IUser>) {
    super(User.collectionName, user)
  }

  fillData(data?: Partial<IUser>) {
    if (data) {
      Object.assign(this, data)
    }

    if (this.phones) {
      this.phones = this.hydrateInterfaceArray(
        Phone, Phone.Build, this.phones
      )
    }
  }

  getCalculatedPropertiesToInclude(): string[] {
```

```
    return ['fullName']
  }

  getPropertiesToExclude(): string[] {
    return ['password']
  }

  public get fullName(): string {
    if (this.name.middle) {
      return `${this.name.first} ${this.name.middle} ${this.name.last}`
    }
    return `${this.name.first} ${this.name.last}`
  }

  async create(id?: string, password?: string, upsert = false) {
    if (id) {
      this._id = new ObjectID(id)
    }

    if (!password) {
      password = uuid()
    }

    this.password = await this.setPassword(password)
    await this.save({ upsert })
  }

  hasSameId(id: ObjectID): boolean {
    return this._id.toHexString() === id.toHexString()
  }
}
```

Note the properties, getCalculatedPropertiesToInclude and getPropertiesToExclude. These define whether a field should be serialized by the client or allowed to be written to the database.

> Serialization and deserialization of data is the concept of transforming data into a format that can be stored or transported. Refer to the *Further reading* section for links to articles regarding serialization and the JSON data format.

`fullName` is a calculated property, so we don't want to write this value to the database. However, `fullName` is useful for the client. On the other hand, the `password` property should never be transmitted back to the client, but obviously we need to be able to save it to the database for password comparison and changes. Upon saving, we pass in the `{ upsert }` object to instruct the database to update records even if partial information is provided.

Remember to provide the complete Swagger definition.

3. And finally, let's go over `UserCollectionFactory`, which implements `CollectionFactory<T>`:

server/src/models/user.ts

```
class UserCollectionFactory extends CollectionFactory<User> {
  constructor(docType: typeof User) {
    super(User.collectionName, docType, ['name.first', 'name.last', 'email'])
  }

  async createIndexes() {
    await this.collection().createIndexes([
      {
        key: {
          email: 1,
        },
        unique: true,
      },
      {
        key: {
          'name.first': 'text',
          'name.last': 'text',
          email: 'text',
        },
        weights: {
          'name.last': 4,
          'name.first': 2,
          email: 1,
        },
        name: 'TextIndex',
      },
    ])
  }

  userSearchQuery(
    searchText: string
```

```
        ): AggregationCursor<{ _id: ObjectID; email: string }> {
          const aggregateQuery = [
            {
              $match: {
                $text: { $search: searchText },
              },
            },
            {
              $project: {
                email: 1,
              },
            },
          ]

          if (searchText === undefined || searchText === '') {
            delete (aggregateQuery[0] as any).$match.$text
          }

          return this.collection().aggregate(aggregateQuery)
        }
    }

    export let UserCollection = new UserCollectionFactory(User)
```

Here, we create a unique index, so another user with the same email won't be able to register. We also create a weighted index, which can assist in writing filter queries. We apply the indexes right after we connect to the database in `index.ts`.

`userSearchQuery` is a somewhat contrived example to demonstrate aggregate queries in MongoDB. It is possible to execute far more sophisticated and high-performance queries using aggregation in MongoDB. You can read more about aggregation in MongoDB at https://docs.mongodb.com/manual/aggregation.

At the bottom of the file, we instantiate a `UserCollection` and export it, so it can be referenced from anywhere in the application:

server/src/models/user.ts
```
export let UserCollection = new UserCollectionFactory(User)
```

Note that `UserCollectionFactory` is not exported, as it is only needed in the `user.ts` file.

Let's see how you can fetch data using the new user model.

Implementing JWT auth

In *Chapter 8, Designing Authentication and Authorization*, we discussed how to implement a JWT-based authentication mechanism. In LemonMart, you implemented a base auth service that can be extended for custom authentication services.

We'll leverage three packages for our implementation:

- `jsonwebtoken`: Used to create and encode JWTs
- `bcryptjs`: Used to hash and salt a user's password before saving it in the database, so we never store a user's password in plain text
- `uuid`: A generated universally unique identifier that is useful when resetting a user's password to a random value

 A hash function is a consistently repeatable, one-way encryption method, which means you get the same output every time you provide the same input, but even if you have access to the hashed value, you cannot readily figure out what information it stores. We can, however, compare whether the user has entered the correct password by hashing the user's input and comparing the hash of their input to that of the stored hash of their password.

1. Let's see the JWT auth-related dependencies and type information for TypeScript:

   ```
   $ npm i bcryptjs jsonwebtoken uuid
   $ npm i -D @types/bcryptjs @types/jsonwebtoken @types/uuid
   ```

2. Observe the `User` model with password hashing functionality:

   server/src/models/user.ts

   ```
   import * as bcrypt from 'bcryptjs'

     async create(id?: string, password?: string, upsert = false) {
         ...

         this.password = await this.setPassword(password)
         await this.save({ upsert })
     }

     async resetPassword(newPassword: string) {
       this.password = await this.setPassword(newPassword)
       await this.save()
   ```

```
    }

    private setPassword(newPassword: string): Promise<string> {
      return new Promise<string>((resolve, reject) => {
        bcrypt.genSalt(10, (err, salt) => {
          if (err) {
            return reject(err)
          }
          bcrypt.hash(newPassword, salt, (hashError, hash) => {
            if (hashError) {
              return reject(hashError)
            }
            resolve(hash)
          })
        })
      })
    }

    comparePassword(password: string): Promise<boolean> {
      const user = this
      return new Promise((resolve, reject) => {
        bcrypt.compare(password, user.password, (err, isMatch) => {
          if (err) {
            return reject(err)
          }
          resolve(isMatch)
        })
      })
    }
```

Using the `setPassword` method, you can hash the user-provided password and safely save it to the database. Later, we will use the `comparePassword` function to compare the user-provided value to the hashed password. We never store the user-provided value, so the system can never reproduce the user's password, making it a safe implementation.

Login API

The following is the login method implementation in `authService` for `lemon-mart-server`:

```
server/src/services/authService.ts
import * as jwt from 'jsonwebtoken'
```

```
import { JwtSecret } from '../config'

export const IncorrectEmailPasswordMessage = 'Incorrect email and/or
password'
export const AuthenticationRequiredMessage = 'Request has not been
authenticated'

export function createJwt(user: IUser): Promise<string> {
  return new Promise<string>((resolve, reject) => {
    const payload = {
      email: user.email,
      role: user.role,
      picture: user.picture,
    }

    jwt.sign(
      payload,
      JwtSecret(),
      {
        subject: user._id.toHexString(),
        expiresIn: '1d',
      },
      (err: Error, encoded: string) => {
        if (err) {
          reject(err.message)
        }
        resolve(encoded)
      }
    )
  })
}
```

The preceding code sample implements a `createJwt` function to create a JWT per user. We also defined canned responses for auth failures. Note the vagueness of the incorrect email/password message, meaning that bad actors cannot fish the system to exploit the authentication system.

Let's implement the login API at `/v1/auth/login`:

server/src/v1/routes/authRouter.ts
```
import { Request, Response, Router } from 'express'

import { UserCollection } from '../../models/user'
import {
  AuthenticationRequiredMessage,
```

```
    IncorrectEmailPasswordMessage,
    authenticate,
    createJwt,
} from '../../services/authService'

const router = Router()

/**
 * @swagger
 * /v1/auth/login:
 *   post:
 *   ...
 */
router.post('/login', async (req: Request, res: Response) => {
  const userEmail = req.body.email?.toLowerCase()
  const user = await UserCollection.findOne({ email: userEmail })

  if (user && (await user.comparePassword(req.body.password))) {
    return res.send({ accessToken: await createJwt(user) })
  }

  return res.status(401).send({
    message: IncorrectEmailPasswordMessage
  })
})
```

> Note that when retrieving a user by email, keep in mind that emails are case-insensitive. So, you should always convert the input to lowercase. You can improve this implementation further by validating the email, and stripping any white space, script tags, or even rogue Unicode characters. Consider using libraries such as `express-validator` or `express-sanitizer`.

The `login` method leverages the `user.comparePassword` function to confirm the correctness of the password provided. The `createJwt` function then creates the `accessToken` to be returned to the client.

Authenticating middleware

The `authenticate` function is a middleware that we can use in our API implementations to ensure that only authenticated users with appropriate permissions can access an endpoint. Remember that real security is achieved in your backend implementation and this authenticate function is your gate keeper.

`authenticate` takes an optional `options` object to verify the current user's role with the `requiredRole` property, so if an API is configured as shown below, only a manager can access that API:

```
authenticate({ requiredRole: Role.Manager })
```

In certain cases, we want a user to be able to update their own records, but also allow managers to update everyone else's records. In this case, we leverage the `permitIfSelf` property, as shown:

```
authenticate({
    requiredRole: Role.Manager,
    permitIfSelf: {
      idGetter: (req: Request) => req.body._id,
      requiredRoleCanOverride: true,
    },
}),
```

In this case, if the `_id` of the record being updated matches the current user's `_id`, then the user can update their own record. Since, `requiredRoleCanOverride` is set to `true` a manager can update any record. If it were set to `false`, this wouldn't be allowed. By mixing and matching these properties you can cover a vast majority of your gate keeping needs.

> Note that `idGetter` is a function delegate, so that you can specify how the `_id` property should be accessed, when the `authenticate` middleware executes.

See the following implementation of `authenticate` and `authenticateHelper`:

server/src/services/authService.ts
```
import { NextFunction, Request, Response } from 'express'

import { ObjectID } from 'mongodb'
import { IUser, UserCollection } from '../models/user'

interface IJwtPayload {
  email: string
  role: string
  picture: string
  iat: number
  exp: number
  sub: string
}
```

```
export function authenticate(options?: {
  requiredRole?: Role
  permitIfSelf?: {
    idGetter: (req: Request) => string
    requiredRoleCanOverride: boolean
  }
}) {
  return async (req: Request, res: Response, next: NextFunction) => {
    try {
      res.locals.currentUser =
        await authenticateHelper(
          req.headers.authorization, {
            requiredRole: options?.requiredRole,
            permitIfSelf: options?.permitIfSelf
              ? {
                  id: options?.permitIfSelf.idGetter(req),
                  requiredRoleCanOverride:
                    options?.permitIfSelf.requiredRoleCanOverride,
                }
              : undefined,
          }
        )
      return next()
    } catch (ex) {
      return res.status(401).send({ message: ex.message })
    }
  }
}

export async function authenticateHelper(
  authorizationHeader?: string,
  options?: {
    requiredRole?: Role
    permitIfSelf?: {
      id: string
      requiredRoleCanOverride: boolean
    }
  }
): Promise<User> {
  if (!authorizationHeader) {
    throw new Error('Request is missing authorization header')
  }
```

```
    const payload = jwt.verify(
      sanitizeToken(authorizationHeader),
      JwtSecret()
    ) as IJwtPayload
    const currentUser = await UserCollection.findOne({
      _id: new ObjectID(payload?.sub),
    })
    if (!currentUser) {
      throw new Error("User doesn't exist")
    }

    if (
      options?.permitIfSelf &&
      !currentUser._id.equals(options.permitIfSelf.id) &&
      !options.permitIfSelf.requiredRoleCanOverride
    ) {
      throw new Error(`You can only edit your own records`)
    }

    if (
      options?.requiredRole &&
      currentUser.role !== options.requiredRole
    ) {
      throw new Error(`You must have role: ${options.requiredRole}`)
    }

    return currentUser
  }

  function sanitizeToken(authorization: string | undefined) {
    const authString = authorization || ''
    const authParts = authString.split(' ')
    return authParts.length === 2 ? authParts[1] : authParts[0]
  }
```

The `authenticate` method is implemented as an Express.js middleware. It can read the request header for an authorization token, verify the validity of the JWT provided, load the current user, and inject it into the response stream, so an authenticated API endpoint can conveniently access the current user's information. This will be demonstrated by the `me` API. If successful, the middleware calls the `next()` function to yield control back to Express. If unsuccessful, then the API can't be called.

Note that `authenticateHelper` returns useful error messages, so users aren't confused if they try to execute an action they're not permitted to execute.

Consider the implementation of the me API, which returns the currently logged-in user to the client via `/v1/auth/me`, as shown here:

```
server/src/v1/routes/authRouter.ts
/**
 * @swagger
 * /v1/auth/me:
 *   get:
 *     ...
 */
// tslint:disable-next-line: variable-name
router.get('/me', authenticate(),
  async (_req: Request, res: Response) => {
    if (res.locals.currentUser) {
      return res.send(res.locals.currentUser)
    }
    return res.status(401)
      .send({ message: AuthenticationRequiredMessage })
  }
)
```

Note that the `/v1/auth/me` method uses the `authenticate` middleware and simply returns the user who was loaded into the response stream.

Custom server auth provider

Now that we have a functional auth implementation in our server, we can implement a custom auth provider in LemonMart, as covered in *Chapter 8, Designing Authentication and Authorization*:

You must implement this custom auth provider in your Angular app.

> The code sample for this section is in the projects/ch10 folder on the **lemon-mart** repo. Note that the sample is also accessible under the web-app folder.

1. In environment.ts and environment.prod.ts, implement a baseUrl variable.

2. Also select authMode as AuthMode.CustomServer:

   web-app/src/environments/environment.ts
   web-app/src/environments/environment.prod.ts

   ```
   export const environment = {
     ...
     baseUrl: 'http://localhost:3000',
     authMode: AuthMode.CustomServer,
   ```

3. Install a helper library to programmatically access TypeScript enum values:

   ```
   $ npm i ts-enum-util
   ```

4. Implement the custom authentication provider as shown here:

   web-app/src/app/auth/auth.custom.service.ts
   ```
   import { $enum } from 'ts-enum-util'

   interface IJwtToken {
     email: string
     role: string
     picture: string
     iat: number
     exp: number
     sub: string
   }

   @Injectable()
   export class CustomAuthService extends AuthService {
     constructor(private httpClient: HttpClient) {
       super()
     }

     protected authProvider(
       email: string,
       password: string
     ): Observable<IServerAuthResponse> {
       return this.httpClient.post<IServerAuthResponse>(
   ```

```
      `${environment.baseUrl}/v1/auth/login`,
      {
        email,
        password,
      }
    )
  }

  protected transformJwtToken(token: IJwtToken): IAuthStatus {
    return {
      isAuthenticated: token.email ? true : false,
      userId: token.sub,
      userRole: $enum(Role)
        .asValueOrDefault(token.role, Role.None),
      userEmail: token.email,
      userPicture: token.picture,
    } as IAuthStatus
  }

  protected getCurrentUser(): Observable<User> {
    return this.httpClient
      .get<IUser>(`${environment.baseUrl}/v1/auth/me`)
      .pipe(map(User.Build, catchError(transformError)))
  }
}
```

The `authProvider` method calls our `/v1/auth/login` method and `getCurrentUser` calls `/v1/auth/me` to retrieve the current user.

> Ensure that calls to `login` methods always happen on HTTPS, otherwise you will be sending user credentials on the open internet. This is ripe for eavesdroppers on public Wi-Fi networks to steal user credentials.

5. Update `authFactory` to return the new provider for the `AuthMode.CustomServer` option:

web-app/src/app/auth/auth.factory.ts
```
export function authFactory(
  afAuth: AngularFireAuth,
  httpClient: HttpClient
) {
  ...
  case AuthMode.CustomServer:
    return new CustomAuthService(httpClient)
}
```

6. In app.modules.ts, update the AuthService provider's deps property to inject HttpClient into authFactory:

web-app/src/app/app.module.ts
```
...
  {
    provide: AuthService,
    useFactory: authFactory,
    deps: [AngularFireAuth, HttpClient],
  },
...
```

7. Start your web app to make sure that things are working.

Next, let's implement the get user endpoint, so our auth provider can get the current user.

GET User by ID

Let's implement the GET User by ID API endpoint, at /v2/users/{id}, in userRouter:

server/src/v2/routes/userRouter.ts
```
import { ObjectID } from 'mongodb'

import { authenticate } from '../../services/authService'
import { IUser, User, UserCollection } from '../../models/user'
/**
 * @swagger
 * /v2/users/{id}:
 *   get: …
 */
router.get(
  '/:userId',
  authenticate({
    requiredRole: Role.Manager,
    permitIfSelf: {
      idGetter: (req: Request) => req.body._id,
      requiredRoleCanOverride: true,
    },
  }),
```

```
    async (req: Request, res: Response) => {
      const user = await UserCollection
        .findOne({ _id: new ObjectID(req.params.userId) })
      if (!user) {
        res.status(404).send({ message: 'User not found.' })
      } else {
        res.send(user)
      }
    }
)
```

In the preceding code sample, we query the database by user ID to find the record we're looking for. We import `UserCollection` and call the `findOne` method to get a `User` object back. Note that we are not leveraging the `userService`. Since we're only retrieving a single record and immediately sending the result back, the additional layer of abstraction is cumbersome. However, if you start adding any business logic to the retrieval of a user, then refactor the code to leverage `userService`.

We secure the endpoint using the `authenticate` middleware, allowing users to retrieve their records and managers to retrieve any record.

Generating users with Postman

Earlier in this chapter, we covered how to create a POST method to create a new user in the *Services* subsection of the *Implementing APIs with Express.js* section. Using this POST endpoint and the Postman API client, we can quickly generate user records for testing purposes.

You must generate test data in **lemon-mart-server** following the instructions below, which will be required in later chapters.

Let's install and configure Postman.

Go to `https://www.getpostman.com` to download and install Postman.

Configuring Postman for authenticated calls

First, we need to configure Postman so that we can access our authenticated endpoints:

 Bring up your server and database using either `docker-compose up` or `npm run start:backend`. Remember, make sure that, first and foremost, you're able to execute the sample server provided on GitHub at https://github.com/duluca/lemon-mart-server. Getting your own version of the server going is a secondary goal.

1. Create a new collection named `LemonMart`.
2. Add a POST request with the URL `http://localhost:3000/v1/auth/login`.
3. In the headers, set the key-value pair, Content-Type: `application/json`.
4. In the body section, provide the email and password for the demo user login that we defined in the top-level `.env` file:

    ```
    http://localhost:3000/v1/auth/login - Body
    {
        "email": "duluca@gmail.com",
        "password": "l0l1pop!!"
    }
    ```

5. Hit **Send** to log in.
6. Copy the `accessToken`, as shown here:

Chapter 10

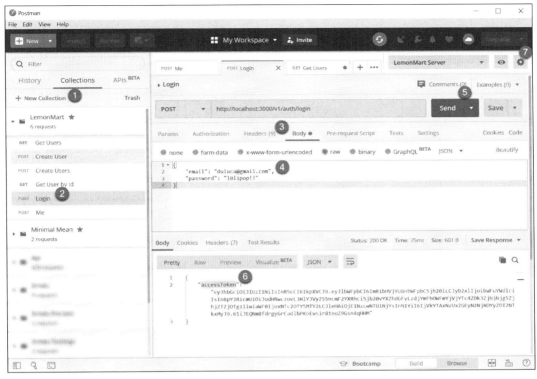

Figure 10.9: Setting up Postman

7. Click on the settings icon in the top-right corner to manage environments.
8. Add a new environment called LemonMart Server.
9. Create a variable named `token`.
10. Paste the `accessToken` value you have as the current value (no parentheses).
11. Click on **Add/Update**.

Going forward, when you add a new request in Postman, you must provide the token variable as an authorization header, as shown:

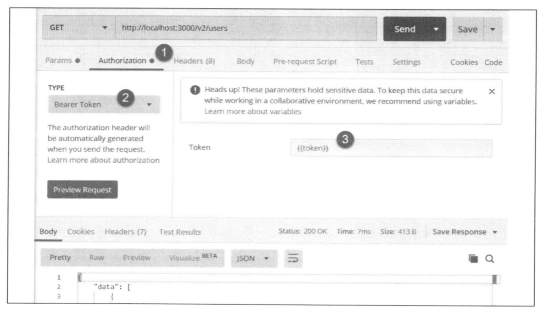

Figure 10.10: Providing a token in Postman

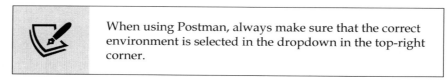

When using Postman, always make sure that the correct environment is selected in the dropdown in the top-right corner.

1. Switch over to the **Authorization** tab.
2. Select **Bearer Token** as the type.
3. Provide the token variable as `{{token}}`.

When you **Send** your request, you should see the results. Be mindful that when your token expires, you will need to repeat this process.

Postman automation

Using Postman, we can automate the execution of requests. In order to create sample users in our system, we can leverage this functionality:

1. Create a new POST request for `http://localhost:3000/v2/user` named **Create Users**.

2. Set the `token` in the **Authorization** tab
3. In the **Body** tab, provide a templated JSON object, as shown here:

```
{
  "email": "{{email}}",
  "name": {
    "first": "{{first}}",
    "last": "{{last}}"
  },
  "picture": "https://en.wikipedia.org/wiki/Bugs_Bunny#/media/File:Bugs_Bunny.svg",
  "role": "clerk",
  "userStatus": true,
  "dateOfBirth": "1940-07-27",
  "address": {
    "line1": "123 Acme St",
    "city": "LooneyVille",
    "state": "Virginia",
    "zip": "22201"
  },
  "phones": [
    {
      "type": "mobile",
      "digits": "5551234567"
    }
  ]
}
```

For the purposes of this example, I'm only templating the email and the first and last name fields. You may template all properties.

4. Implement a Postman **Pre-request Script**, which executes arbitrary logic before sending a request. The script will define an array of people, and one by one set the current environment variable to be the next row as requests are executed:

 For more information on pre-request scripts, check out https://learning.postman.com/docs/postman/scripts/pre-request-scripts/.

5. Switch to the **Pre-request Script** tab and implement the script:

```
var people = pm.environment.get('people')

if (!people) {
  people = [
    {email: 'efg@gmail.com', first: 'Ali', last: 'Smith'},
    {email: 'veli@gmail.com', first: 'Veli', last: 'Tepeli'},
```

```
        {email: 'thunderdome@hotmail.com', first: 'Justin', last:
'Thunderclaps'},
        {email: 'jt23@hotmail.com', first: 'Tim', last: 'John'},
        {email: 'apple@smith.com', first: 'Obladi', last: 'Oblada'},
        {email: 'jones.smith@icloud.com', first: 'Smith', last: 'Jones'},
        {email: 'bugs@bunnylove.com', first: 'Bugs', last: 'Bunny'},
    ]
}

var person = people.shift()
pm.environment.set('email', person.email)
pm.environment.set('first', person.first)
pm.environment.set('last', person.last)

pm.environment.set('people', people)
```

 pm is a global variable that stands for **PostMan**.

In the first line, we get the `people` array from the environment. During the first request, this won't exist, which allows us to initialize the array with our test data. Next, we shift to the next record, and set the individual variables we used in our templated request body. Then, we save the current state of the array back to the environment, so, during the next execution, we can shift to the next record, until such time as we run out of records.

6. Implement a `test` script in the **Tests** tab:

```
var people = pm.environment.get('people')

if (people && people.length > 0) {
  postman.setNextRequest('Create Users')
} else {
  postman.setNextRequest(null)
}
```

7. Make sure to save your request.

Here, we define a `test` script, which will continue to execute until `people.length` reaches zero. With each iteration, we call the **Create Users** request. When there are no people left, we call `null` to terminate the test.

 As you may imagine, you can combine multiple requests and multiple environment variables to execute sophisticated tests.

8. Now, execute the script using **Runner**, located in the top-left corner of the screen:

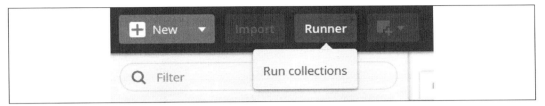

Figure 10.11: Runner button in the top-left corner of the Postman UI

9. Update your `login` token before moving on.
10. Configure the runner as shown:

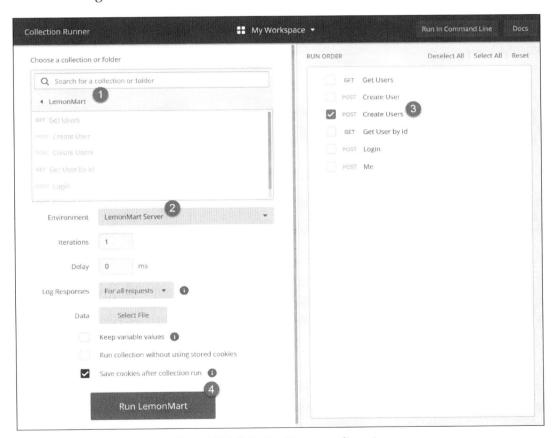

Figure 10.12: Collection Runner configuration

RESTful APIs and Full-Stack Implementation

11. Select the **LemonMart** collection.
12. Select the **LemonMart Server** environment, which contains the `token` variable.
13. Only select the **Create Users** request.
14. Click on **Run LemonMart** to execute.

If your run succeeded, you should see the following output:

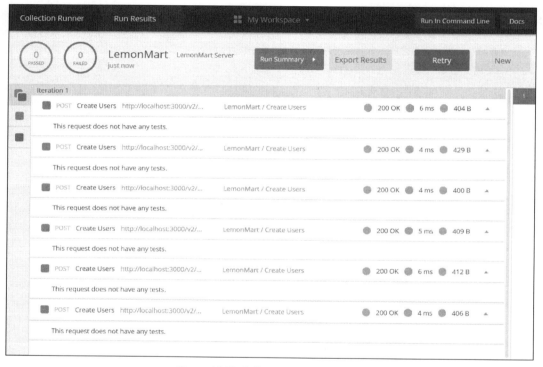

Figure 10.13: Collection Runner results

If you use Studio 3T as a MongoDB explorer, you can observe that all records have been created or you can check them out with Postman, when we implement the `/v2/users` endpoint.

 Note that since we have a unique email index, your run partially succeeds on the next run. POST requests for already created records will return a `400 Bad Request`.

You can read more about Studio 3T at `https://studio3t.com/`.

Put User

We have already covered how to create a POST request in the *Services* section earlier in the chapter. Now, let's see how you can update an existing user record:

server/src/v2/routes/userRouter.ts

```
/**
 * @swagger
 * /v2/users/{id}:
 *   put:
 */
router.put(
  '/:userId',
  authenticate({
    requiredRole: Role.Manager,
    permitIfSelf: {
      idGetter: (req: Request) => req.body._id,
      requiredRoleCanOverride: true,
    },
  }),
  async (req: Request, res: Response) => {
    const userData = req.body as User
    delete userData._id
    await UserCollection.findOneAndUpdate(
      { _id: new ObjectID(req.params.userId) },
      {
        $set: userData,
      }
    )

    const user = await UserCollection
```

```
      .findOne({ _id: new ObjectID(req.params.userId) })

    if (!user) {
      res.status(404).send({ message: 'User not found.' })
    } else {
      res.send(user)
    }
  }
)
```

We set `userData` from the request body. We then `delete` the `_id` property that's in the body, since the URL parameter is the authoritative source of information. Additionally, this prevents a user's ID from being accidentally changed to a different value.

We then leverage the `findOneAndUpdate` method to locate and update the record. We query for the record using the ID. We update the record by using MongoDB's `$set` operator.

Finally, we load the saved record from the database and return it back to the client.

 POST and PUT methods should always respond with the updated state of the record.

For our last piece of implementation, let's review API endpoints that can support paginated data tables.

Pagination and filtering with DocumentTS

By far the most useful functionality of DocumentTS is `findWithPagination`, as mentioned in the *About DocumentTS* section. Let's leverage `findWithPagination` to implement the `/v2/users` endpoint, which can return all users:

server/src/v2/routes/userRouter.ts

```
/**
 * @swagger
 * components:
 *   parameters:
 *     filterParam: …
 *     skipParam: …
 *     limitParam: …
```

```
 *        sortKeyParam: ...
 */

/**
 * @swagger
 * /v2/users:
 *    get:
 */
router.get(
  '/',
  authenticate({ requiredRole: Role.Manager }),
  async (req: Request, res: Response) => {
    const query: Partial<IQueryParameters> = {
      filter: req.query.filter,
      limit: req.query.limit,
      skip: req.query.skip,
      sortKeyOrList: req.query.sortKey,
      projectionKeyOrList: ['email', 'role', '_id', 'name'],
    }

    const users = await UserCollection.findWithPagination<User>(query)
    res.send(users)
  }
)
```

We copy all the parameters from the URL using the `req.query` object as local variables. We define an additional property named `projectionKeyOrList` to limit the properties of a record that can be returned to the client. In this case, only the `email`, `role`, `_id`, and `name` properties will be returned. This minimizes the amount of data that is sent over the wire.

Finally, we simply pass the new `query` object to the `findWithPagination` function and return the results to the client.

You can create a new request in Postman to verify the correct functionality of your new endpoint, as shown in the following screenshot:

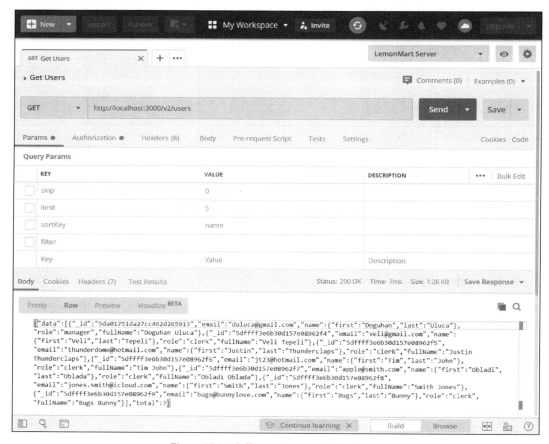

Figure 10.14: Calling get users with Postman

In *Chapter 12, Recipes – Master/Detail, Data Tables, and NgRx*, we will implement a paginated data table that takes advantage of the filtering, sorting, and data limiting features.

Congratulations! You now have a grasp on how code works across the entire stack of software, from the database to the frontend and back.

Summary

In this chapter, we covered full-stack architecture. You learned about building a minimal MEAN stack. You now know how to create a monorepo for a full-stack application and configure a Node.js server with TypeScript. You containerized your Node.js server and declaratively defined your infrastructure with Docker Compose. Using Docker Compose with CircleCI, you verified your infrastructure in a CI environment.

You designed a RESTful API using Swagger and the OpenAPI spec, set up an Express.js app and configured it such that you can integrate your Swagger definition as documentation for your APIs. You configured MongoDB with the DocumentTS ODM so you can easily connect and query documents. You defined a user model with password hashing features.

You then implemented a JWT-based authentication service. You implemented an `authenticate` middleware to secure API endpoints and allow role-based access. You learned how to interact with RESTful APIs using Postman. Using Postman's automation features, you generated test data. Finally, you implemented RESTful APIs for authentication functions and CRUD operations for users.

In the next two chapters, we will go over Angular recipes to create forms and data tables. You will want your Lemon Mart Server up and running to verify the correct functionality of your forms and tables as you implement them.

Exercise

You secured your endpoints using the `authenticate` middleware. You configured Postman to send a valid token so that you can communicate with your secured endpoints. By way of an exercise, try removing the `authenticate` middleware and call the same endpoint with and without a valid token. Re-add the middleware and try the same thing again. Observe the different responses you get from the server.

Further reading

- *What is DX? (Developer Experience)*, Albert Cavalcante, 2019: `https://medium.com/@albertcavalcante/what-is-dx-developer-experience-401a0e44a9d9`
- *Overview of Blocking versus Non-Blocking*, 2020: `https://nodejs.org/en/docs/guides/blocking-vs-non-blocking/`
- *Explain Non-Blocking I/O like I'm Five*, Frank Rosner, 2019: `https://blog.codecentric.de/en/2019/04/explain-non-blocking-i-o-like-im-five/`
- *OpenAPI Specification*, 2020: `https://swagger.io/docs/specification`
- *Serialization*, 2020: `https://en.wikipedia.org/wiki/Serialization`
- *JSON*, 2020: `https://en.wikipedia.org/wiki/JSON`
- *Aggregation in MongoDB*, 2020: `https://docs.mongodb.com/manual/aggregation`

Questions

Answer the following questions as best as you can to ensure that you've understood the key concepts from this chapter without Googling. Do you need help answering the questions? See *Appendix D, Self-Assessment Answers* online at `https://static.packt-cdn.com/downloads/9781838648800_Appendix_D_Self-Assessment_Answers.pdf` or visit `https://expertlysimple.io/angular-self-assessment`.

1. What are the main components that make for a great developer experience?
2. What is a `.env` file?
3. What is the purpose of the `authenticate` middleware?
4. How does Docker Compose differ from using the `Dockerfile`?
5. What is an ODM? How does it differ from an ORM?
6. What is middleware?
7. What are the uses of Swagger?
8. How would you refactor the code for the `/v2/users/{id}` PUT endpoint in `userRouter.ts`, so the code is reusable?

11
Recipes – Reusability, Routing, and Caching

In the next two chapters, we will complete the majority of the implementation of LemonMart and round out our coverage of the router-first approach. In this chapter, I will reinforce the idea of a decoupled component architecture through the creation of a reusable and routable component that also supports data binding. We use Angular directives to reduce boilerplate code and leverage classes, interfaces, enums, validators, and pipes to maximize code reuse with TypeScript and ES features.

In addition, we will create a multi-step form that architecturally scales well and supports a responsive design. Then, we will differentiate between user controls and components by introducing a lemon rater and a reusable form part that encapsulates the name object.

Make sure to have your **lemon-mart-server** up and running as you implement the recipes mentioned in this chapter. Refer to *Chapter 10, RESTful APIs and Full-Stack Implementation*, for more information.

This chapter covers a lot of ground. It is organized in recipe format, so you can quickly refer to a particular implementation when you are working on your projects. I will cover the architecture, design, and major components of the implementations. I will highlight important pieces of code to explain how the solution comes together. Leveraging what you've learned so far, I expect the reader to fill in routine implementation and configuration details. However, you can always refer to the GitHub project if you get stuck.

In this chapter, you will learn about the following topics:

- HTTP PUT requests with caching service responses
- Multi-step responsive forms
- Reusing repeating template behavior with directives
- Scalable form architecture with reusable form parts
- Input masking
- Custom controls with `ControlValueAccessor`
- Layouts using grid list

The most up-to-date versions of the sample code for the book are on GitHub at the repository linked shortly. The repository contains the final and completed state of the code. You can verify your progress at the end of this chapter by looking at the end-of-chapter snapshot of the code under the `projects` folder.

To get set up for this chapter, do the following:

1. Clone the repo at `https://github.com/duluca/lemon-mart`.
2. Execute `npm install` on the root folder to install the dependencies.
3. The code sample for this chapter is available under the following subfolder: `projects/ch11`
4. To run the Angular app for this chapter, execute the following command:
   `npx ng serve ch11`
5. To run Angular unit tests for this chapter, execute the following command:
   `npx ng test ch11 --watch=false`
6. To run Angular e2e tests for this chapter, execute the following command:
   `npx ng e2e ch11`
7. To build a production-ready Angular app for this chapter, execute the following command:
   `npx ng build ch11 --prod`

> Note that the `dist/ch11` folder at the root of the repository will contain the compiled result.

> Beware that the source code in the book or on GitHub may not always match the code generated by the Angular CLI. There may also be slight differences in implementation between the code in the book and what's on GitHub because the ecosystem is ever-evolving. It is natural for the sample code to change over time. Also on GitHub, expect to find corrections, fixes to support newer versions of libraries, or side-by-side implementations of multiple techniques for the reader to observe. The reader is only expected to implement the ideal solution recommended in the book. If you find errors or have questions, please create an issue or submit a pull request on GitHub for the benefit of all readers.

> You can read more about updating Angular in *Appendix C, Keeping Angular and Tools Evergreen*. You can find this appendix online from `https://static.packt-cdn.com/downloads/9781838648800_Appendix_C_Keeping_Angular_and_Tools_Evergreen.pdf` or at `https://expertlysimple.io/stay-evergreen`.

Let's start with implementing a user service to retrieve data, so we can build out a form to display and edit profile information. Later, we will refactor this form to abstract out its reusable parts.

Implementing a user service with GET

In order to implement a user profile, we need a service that can perform CRUD operations on `IUser`. We will be creating a user service that implements the following interface:

```
export interface IUserService {
  getUser(id: string): Observable<IUser>
  updateUser(id: string, user: IUser): Observable<IUser>
  getUsers(
    pageSize: number,
    searchText: string,
    pagesToSkip: number
  ): Observable<IUsers>
}
```

> Before creating the service, make sure to start the **lemon-mart-server** and set your application's `AuthMode` to `CustomServer`.

In this section, we will implement the `getUser` and `updateUser` functions. We will implement `getUsers` in *Chapter 12, Recipes – Master/Detail, Data Tables, and NgRx*, to support pagination with a data table.

Start by creating the user service:

1. Create a `UserService` under `src/app/user/user`
2. Declare the `IUserService` interface from the preceding snippet, excluding the `getUsers` function.
3. Extend the `UserService` class with `CacheService` and implement `IUserService`.
4. Inject the `HttpClient` in the constructor as shown:

   `src/app/user/user/user.service.ts`
   ```
   export interface IUserService {
     getUser(id: string): Observable<IUser>
     updateUser(id: string, user: IUser): Observable<IUser>
   }

   @Injectable({
     providedIn: 'root',
   })
   export class UserService extends CacheService implements IUserService {
     constructor() {
       super()
     }

     getUser(id: string): Observable<IUser> {
       throw new Error('Method not implemented.')
     }
     updateUser(id: string, user: IUser): Observable<IUser> {
       throw new Error('Method not implemented.')
     }
   }
   ```

5. Implement the `getUser` function as shown:

   `src/app/user/user/user.service.ts`
   ```
   getUser(id: string | null): Observable<IUser> {
     if (id === null) {
       return throwError('User id is not set')
     }

     return this.httpClient.get<IUser>(
       `${environment.baseUrl}/v2/user/${id}`
     )
   }
   ```

We provide a getUser function that can load any user's profile information. Note that the security for this function is provided in the server implementation with the authenticate middleware. The requestor can either get their own profile or they'll need to be a manager. We use getUser with a resolve guard later in the chapter.

Implementing PUT with caching

Implement updateUser, which accepts an object that implements the IUser interface, so the data can be sent to a PUT endpoint:

```
src/app/user/user/user.service.ts
  updateUser(id: string, user: IUser): Observable<IUser> {
    if (id === '') {
      return throwError('User id is not set')
    }

    // cache user data in case of errors
    this.setItem('draft-user', Object.assign(user, { _id: id }))
    const updateResponse$ = this.httpClient
      .put<IUser>(`${environment.baseUrl}/v2/user/${id}`, user)
      .pipe(map(User.Build), catchError(transformError))

    updateResponse$.subscribe(
      (res) => {
        this.authService.currentUser$.next(res)
        this.removeItem('draft-user')
      },
      (err) => throwError(err)
    )

    return updateResponse$
  }
```

Note the use of the cache service with setItem to save user-entered data in case the put call fails. When the call succeeds, we remove the cached data using removeItem. Also note how we hydrate a user coming from the server as a User object with map(User.Build), which calls the constructor of class User.

Hydrate is a common term that refers to populating an object with data from a database or a network request. For example, the User JSON object we pass between components or receive from the server fits the IUser interface, but it is not of the class User type. We serialize objects to JSON using the toJSON method. When we hydrate and then instantiate a new object from JSON, we do the reverse and deserialize the data.

> It is important to highlight that you should always stick to interfaces, and not concrete implementations like User, when passing data around. This is the **D** in **SOLID** – the Dependency Inversion Principle. Depending on concrete implementations creates a lot of risk, because they change a lot, whereas an abstraction such as IUser will seldom change. After all, you wouldn't solder a lamp directly to the electrical wiring in the wall. Instead, you would first solder the lamp to a plug and then use the plug to get the electricity you need.

With this code completed, UserService can now be used for basic CRUD operations.

Multi-step responsive forms

Overall forms are a different beast than the rest of your application and they require special architectural considerations. I don't recommend over-engineering your form solution with dynamic templates or route-enabled components. By definition, the different parts of a form are tightly coupled. From the perspectives of maintainability and ease of implementation, creating one giant component is a better strategy than using some of the aforementioned strategies and over-engineering.

We will be implementing a multi-step input form to capture user profile information in a single component. I will be covering my recommended technique to split forms up into multiple components later in the chapter in the *Reusable form parts and scalability* section.

> Since the implementation of the form changes dramatically between this section and later in the chapter, you can find the code for the initial version on GitHub at projects/ch11/src/app/user/profile/profile.initial.component.ts and projects/ch11/src/app/user/profile/profile.initial.component.html.

We will also make this multi-step form responsive for mobile devices using media queries:

1. Let's start by adding some helper data that will help us display an input form with options:

    src/app/user/profile/data.ts
    ```
    export interface IUSState {
      code: string
    ```

```
    name: string
  }

  export function USStateFilter(value: string): IUSState[] {
    return USStates.filter((state) => {
      return (
        (state.code.length === 2 &&
          state.code.toLowerCase() === value.toLowerCase()) ||
          state.name.toLowerCase().indexOf(value.toLowerCase()) === 0
      )
    })
  }

  const USStates = [
    { code: 'AK', name: 'Alaska' },
    { code: 'AL', name: 'Alabama' },
    ...
    { code: 'WY', name: 'Wyoming' },
  ]
```

2. Add new validation rules to `common/validations.ts`:

   src/app/common/validations.ts
   ```
   ...

   export const OptionalTextValidation = [Validators.minLength(2),
   Validators.maxLength(50)]
   export const RequiredTextValidation = OptionalTextValidation.
   concat([Validators.required])
   export const OneCharValidation = [Validators.minLength(1),
   Validators.maxLength(1)]
   export const USAZipCodeValidation = [
     Validators.required,
     Validators.pattern(/^\d{5}(?:[-\s]\d{4})?$/),
   ]
   export const USAPhoneNumberValidation = [
     Validators.required,
     Validators.pattern(/^\D?(\d{3})\D?\D?(\d{3})\D?(\d{4})$/),
   ]
   ```

3. Now, implement `profile.component.ts` as follows:

   src/app/user/profile/profile.component.ts
   ```
   import { Role } from '../../auth/auth.enum'
   import { $enum } from 'ts-enum-util'
   import { IName, IPhone, IUser, PhoneType }
     from '../user/user'
   ```

```typescript
...
@Component({
  selector: 'app-profile',
  templateUrl: './profile.component.html',
  styleUrls: ['./profile.component.css'],
})
export class ProfileComponent implements OnInit {
  Role = Role
  PhoneType = PhoneType
  PhoneTypes = $enum(PhoneType).getKeys()
  formGroup: FormGroup
  states$: Observable<IUSState[]> userError = ''

  currentUserId: string

constructor(
  private formBuilder: FormBuilder,
  private uiService: UiService,
  private userService: UserService,
  private authService: AuthService
) {}

ngOnInit() {
  this.buildForm()
  this.authService.currentUser$
        .pipe(
          filter((user) => user !== null),
          tap((user) => {
            this.currentUserId = user._id
            this.buildForm(user)
          })
        )
        .subscribe()
}

  private get currentUserRole() {
    return this.authService.authStatus$.value.userRole
  }

buildForm(user?: IUser) {}
...
}
```

Upon load, we request the current user from `authService`, but this might take a while, so we first build an empty form with `this.buildForm()` as the first statement. We also store the user's ID in the `currentUserId` property, which we will need later when implementing the `save` functionality.

Note that we filter out users that are `null` or `undefined`.

Later in this chapter, we will implement a resolve guard to load a user based on their `userId` provided on a route to increase the reusability of this component.

Form controls and form groups

As you may recall, `FormControl` objects are the most elemental parts of a form, usually representing a single input field. We can use `FormGroup` to group together a collection of related `FormControl` objects, such as the individual first, middle, and last parts of a person's name. `FormGroup` objects can also group together a mix of `FormControl`, `FormGroup`, and `FormArray` objects, the latter of which allows us to have dynamically repeating elements. `FormArray` is covered later in the chapter in the *Dynamic form arrays* section.

Our form has many input fields, so we will use a `FormGroup` created by `this.formBuilder.group` to house our various `FormControl` objects. Additionally, children `FormGroup` objects will allow us to maintain the correct shape of the data structure.

Since the implementation of the form changes dramatically between this section and later in the chapter, you can find the code for the initial version on GitHub at `projects/ch11/src/app/user/profile/profile.initial.component.ts` and `projects/ch11/src/app/user/profile/profile.initial.component.html`.

Start building the `buildForm` function, as follows:

```
src/app/user/profile/profile.component.ts
...
  buildForm(user?: IUser) {
    this.formGroup =
    this.formBuilder.group({
      email: [
```

```
      {
        value: user?.email || '',
        disabled: this.currentUserRole !== Role.Manager,
      },
      EmailValidation,
    ],
    name: this.formBuilder.group({
      first: [user?.name?.first || '', RequiredTextValidation],
      middle: [user?.name?.middle || '', OneCharValidation],
      last: [user?.name?.last || '', RequiredTextValidation],
    }),
    role: [
      {
        value: user?.role || '',
        disabled: this.currentUserRole !== Role.Manager,
      },
      [Validators.required],
    ],
    dateOfBirth: [user?.dateOfBirth || '', Validators.required],
    address: this.formBuilder.group({
      line1: [user?.address?.line1 || '', RequiredTextValidation],
      line2: [user?.address?.line2 || '', OptionalTextValidation],
      city: [user?.address?.city || '', RequiredTextValidation],
      state: [user?.address?.state || '', RequiredTextValidation],
      zip: [user?.address?.zip || '', USAZipCodeValidation],
    }),
  })
}
```

`buildForm` optionally accepts an `IUser` to prefill the form, otherwise, all fields are set to their default values. The `formGroup` property itself is the top-level `FormGroup`. Various `FormControls` are added to it, such as `email`, with validators attached to them as needed. Note how `name` and `address` are their own `FormGroup` objects. This parent-child relationship ensures the proper structure of the form data, when serialized to JSON, which fits the structure of `IUser` in a manner that the rest of our application and server-side code can utilize.

You will be completing the implementation of the `formGroup` independently by following the sample code provided for the chapter. I will be going over sections of the code piece by piece over the next few sections to explain certain key capabilities.

Stepper and responsive layout

Angular Material's stepper ships with the `MatStepperModule`. The stepper allows for form inputs to be broken up into multiple steps so that the user is not overwhelmed with processing dozens of input fields all at once. The user can still track their place in the process and, as a side effect, as the developer, we break up our `<form>` implementation and enforce validation rules on a step-by-step basis or create optional workflows where certain steps can be skipped or required. As with all Material user controls, the stepper has been designed with a responsive UX in mind. In the next few sections, we will implement three steps covering different form-input techniques in the process:

1. Account information
    - Input validation
    - Responsive layout with media queries
    - Calculated properties
    - DatePicker
2. Contact information
    - Typeahead support
    - Dynamic form arrays
3. Review
    - Read-only views
    - Saving and clearing data

Let's prep the `UserModule` for some new Material modules:

> As we start adding sub-Material modules, it makes sense to rename our root `material.module.ts` file to `app-material.modules.ts` in line with how `app-routing.module.ts` is named. Going forward, I will be using the latter convention.

1. Rename the `src/app/material.modules.ts` file to `app-material.module.ts`, and then rename the `MaterialModule` class to `AppMaterialModule`.
2. Create a `user-material.module.ts` file containing the following Material modules:

    ```
    MatAutocompleteModule,
    MatDatepickerModule,
    MatDividerModule,
    ```

```
MatLineModule,
MatNativeDateModule,
MatRadioModule,
MatSelectModule,
MatStepperModule,
```

3. Ensure `user.module.ts` correctly imports the following:
   - The new `user-material.module`
   - The baseline `app-material.module`
   - The required `ReactiveFormsModule` and `FlexLayoutModule`

4. Implement a horizontal stepper with a form containing the first step:

> Since the implementation of the form changes dramatically between this section and later in the chapter, you can find the code for the initial version on GitHub at `projects/ch11/src/app/user/profile/profile.initial.component.ts` and `projects/ch11/src/app/user/profile/profile.initial.component.html`.

src/app/user/profile/profile.component.html
```html
<mat-toolbar color="accent">
<h5>User Profile</h5>
</mat-toolbar>
<mat-horizontal-stepper #stepper="matHorizontalStepper">
  <mat-step [stepControl]="formGroup">
    <form [formGroup]="formGroup">
      <ng-template matStepLabel>Account Information</ng-template>
      <div class="stepContent">
        ...
      </div>
    </form>
  </mat-step>
</mat-horizontal-stepper>
```

5. Now, start implementing the `name` row of the `Account Information` step in place of the ellipses in the preceding step:

src/app/user/profile/profile.component.html
```html
<div fxLayout="row" fxLayout.lt-sm="column"
[formGroup]="formGroup.get('name')"
      fxLayoutGap="10px">
  <mat-form-field appearance="outline" fxFlex="40%">
    <input matInput placeholder="First Name"
```

```html
      aria-label="First Name" formControlName="first">
    <mat-error
       *ngIf="formGroup.get('name.first')?.hasError('required')">
      First Name is required
    </mat-error>
    <mat-error
       *ngIf="formGroup.get('name.first')?.hasError('minLength')">
      Must be at least 2 characters
    </mat-error>
    <mat-error
       *ngIf="formGroup.get('name.first')?.hasError('maxLength')">
      Can't exceed 50 characters
    </mat-error>
  </mat-form-field>
  <mat-form-field appearance="outline" fxFlex="20%">
    <input matInput placeholder="MI" aria-label="Middle Initial"
           formControlName="middle">
    <mat-error *ngIf="formGroup.get('name.middle')?.invalid">
      Only initial
    </mat-error>
  </mat-form-field>
  <mat-form-field appearance="outline" fxFlex="40%">
    <input matInput placeholder="Last Name" aria-label="Last Name"
           formControlName="last">
    <mat-error
       *ngIf="formGroup.get('name.last')?.hasError('required')">
      Last Name is required
    </mat-error>
    <mat-error
       *ngIf="formGroup.get('name.last')?.hasError('minLength')">
      Must be at least 2 characters
    </mat-error>
    <mat-error
       *ngIf="formGroup.get('name.last')?.hasError('maxLength')">
      Can't exceed 50 characters
    </mat-error>
  </mat-form-field>
</div>
```

6. Take care to understand how the stepper and the form configuration work so far. You should see the first row render, pulling in data from **lemon-mart-server**:

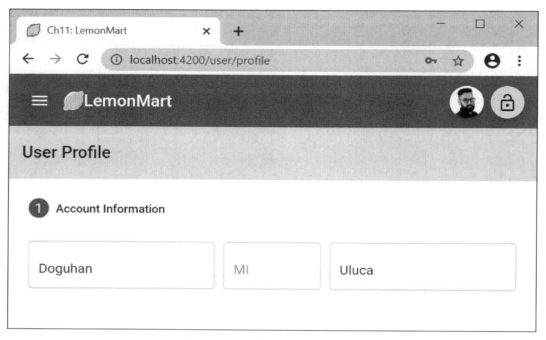

Figure 11.1: Multi-step form – Step 1

Note that adding `fxLayout.lt-sm="column"` to a row with `fxLayout="row"` enables a responsive layout of the form, as shown:

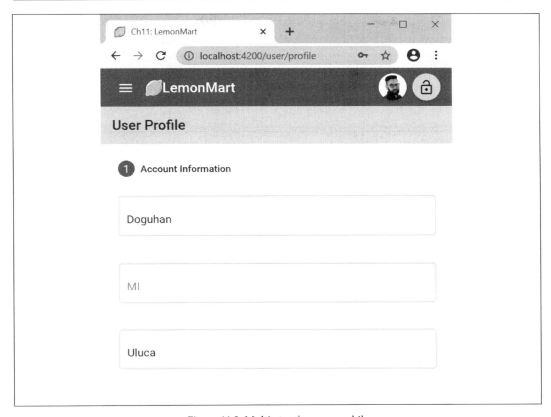

Figure 11.2: Multi-step form on mobile

Before we move on to how to implement the **Date of Birth** field, let's reevaluate our strategy by implementing error messages.

Reusing repeating template behavior with directives

In the previous section, we implemented a `mat-error` element for every validation error for every field part of the `name` object. This quickly adds up to seven elements for three fields. In *Chapter 8, Designing Authentication and Authorization*, we implemented `common/validations.ts` to reuse validation rules. We can reuse the behavior we implement within `mat-error`, or any other `div` for that matter, using an attribute directive.

Attribute directives

In *Chapter 1, Introduction to Angular and Its Concepts*, I mentioned that Angular components represent the most basic unit of an Angular app. With components, we define our own HTML elements that can reuse features and functionality represented by a template and some TypeScript code. On the other hand, a directive augments the capabilities of an existing element or component. In a sense, a component is a super directive that augments basic HTML capabilities.

With this view in mind, we can define three kinds of directives:

- Components
- Structural directives
- Attribute directives

Basically, components are directives with templates, and this is the most common type of directive you will use. Structural directives modify the DOM by adding or removing elements, `*ngIf` and `*ngFor` being the canonical examples. Finally, attribute directives allow you to define new attributes that you can add to HTML elements or components to add new behavior to them.

Let's implement an attribute directive that can encapsulate field-level error behavior.

Field error attribute directive

Imagine how we could use a directive to reduce repetitive elements to display field errors. Consider the following example using the first name field as an example:

```
example
<mat-form-field appearance="outline" fxFlex="40%">
  <mat-label>First Name</mat-label>
  <input matInput aria-label="First Name"
         formControlName="first" #name />
  <mat-error [input]="name" [group]="formGroup.get('name')"
```

```
      [appFieldError]="ErrorSets.RequiredText">
  </mat-error>
</mat-form-field>
```

We have the standard layout structure for a material form field, but there's only a single `mat-error` element. There are three new properties on `mat-error`:

- `input` binds to the HTML input element that was tagged with #name using a template reference variable, so that we can tap into the blur event of the input element and be able to read the `placeholder`, `aria-label`, and `formControlName` properties.

- `group` binds to the parent form group object that contains the form control, so using the `formControlName` property from input, we can retrieve the `formControl` object, while avoiding extra code.

- `appFieldError` binds to an array of validation errors that need to be checked against the `formControl` object, such as `required`, `minlength`, `maxlength`, and `invalid`.

Using the preceding information, we can craft a directive that can render one or more lines of error messages inside the `mat-error` element, effectively replicating the verbose method we used in the previous section.

Let's go ahead and create an attribute directive named `FieldErrorDirective`:

1. Create `FieldErrorDirective` under `src/app/user-controls`.

2. Define the directive's selector as a bindable attribute named `appFieldError`:

   src/app/user-controls/field-error/field-error.directive.ts
   ```
   @Directive({
     selector: '[appFieldError]',
   })
   ```

3. Outside of the directive, define a new type named `ValidationError`, which defines the kinds of error conditions we will deal with:

   src/app/user-controls/field-error/field-error.directive.ts
   ```
   export type ValidationError =
       'required' | 'minlength' | 'maxlength' | 'invalid'
   ```

4. Similar to the way we grouped validations, let's define two sets of commonly occurring error conditions, so we don't have to type them out over and over again:

   src/app/user-controls/field-error/field-error.directive.ts
   ```
   export const ErrorSets: { [key: string]: ValidationError[] } = {
     OptionalText: ['minlength', 'maxlength'],
     RequiredText: ['minlength', 'maxlength', 'required'],
   }
   ```

5. Next, let's define the `@Input` targets for the directive:

   `src/app/user-controls/field-error/field-error.directive.ts`
   ```
   export class FieldErrorDirective implements OnDestroy, OnChanges {
     @Input() appFieldError:
       | ValidationError
       | ValidationError[]
       | { error: ValidationError; message: string }
       | { error: ValidationError; message: string }[]
     @Input() input: HTMLInputElement | undefined
     @Input() group: FormGroup

     @Input() fieldControl: AbstractControl | null
     @Input() fieldLabel: string | undefined
   ```

    Note that we already went over the purpose of the top three attributes. `fieldControl` and `fieldLabel` are optional attributes. If `input` and `group` are specified, the optional attributes can be auto-populated. Since they are class-wide variables, it made sense to expose them, in case the user wants to override the default behavior of the directive. This is an easy win for creating flexible and reusable controls.

6. Import the element reference in the `constructor`, which can be later used by a `renderErrors` function display error in the inner HTML of the `mat-error` element:

   `src/app/user-controls/field-error/field-error.directive.ts`
   ```
     private readonly nativeElement: HTMLElement

     constructor(private el: ElementRef) {
       this.nativeElement = this.el.nativeElement
     }
     renderErrors(errors: string) {
       this.nativeElement.innerHTML = errors
     }
   ```

7. Implement a function that can return canned error messages depending on the error type:

   `src/app/user-controls/field-error/field-error.directive.ts`
   ```
     getStandardErrorMessage(error: ValidationError): string {
       const label = this.fieldLabel || 'Input'

       switch (error) {
   ```

```
      case 'required':
        return `${label} is required`
      case 'minlength':
        return `${label} must be at least ${
          this.fieldControl?.getError(error)?.requiredLength ?? 2
        } characters`
      case 'maxlength':
        return `${label} can\'t exceed ${
          this.fieldControl?.getError(error)?.requiredLength ?? 50
        } characters`
      case 'invalid':
        return `A valid ${label} is required`
  }
}
```

Note that we can extract the required `minlength` or `maxlength` amount dynamically from the `fieldControl`, greatly reducing the number of custom messages we need to generate.

8. Implement the algorithm that can loop through all the elements in `appFieldError` and the errors that need to be displayed in an array using the `getStandardErrorMessage` method:

src/app/user-controls/field-error/field-error.directive.ts
```
updateErrorMessage() {
    const errorsToDisplay: string[] = []

    const errors = Array.isArray(this.appFieldError)
      ? this.appFieldError
      : [this.appFieldError]

    errors.forEach(
      (error: ValidationError
          | { error: ValidationError; message: string }) => {
        const errorCode =
          typeof error === 'object' ? error.error : error
        const message =
          typeof error === 'object'
            ? () => error.message
            : () => this.getStandardErrorMessage(errorCode)
        const errorChecker =
          errorCode === 'invalid'
            ? () => this.fieldControl?.invalid
```

```
          : () => this.fieldControl?.hasError(errorCode)
      if (errorChecker()) {
        errorsToDisplay.push(message())
      }
    }
  )

  this.renderErrors(errorsToDisplay.join('<br>'))
}
```

At the end, we can display the error messages using the `renderErrors` method.

> Note the use of function delegates. Since this piece of code will execute hundreds of times a minute, it is important to avoid unnecessary invocations. Function delegates help organize our code better, while deferring the execution of their logic unless absolutely necessary.

9. Now, initialize the `fieldControl` property, which represents a `formControl`. We will listen to the `valueChanges` events of the control and, if the validation status is invalid, then we execute our custom `updateErrorMessage` logic to display error messages:

   src/app/user-controls/field-error/field-error.directive.ts
   ```
   private controlSubscription: Subscription | undefined

   ngOnDestroy(): void {
     this.unsubscribe()
   }

   unsubscribe(): void {
     this.controlSubscription?.unsubscribe()
   }

   initFieldControl() {
      if (this.input && this.group) {
        const controlName = this.input.
          getAttribute('formControlName') ?? ''

        this.fieldControl =
          this.fieldControl || this.group.get(controlName)

        if (!this.fieldControl) {
   ```

```
    throw new Error(
      `[appFieldError] couldn't bind to control ${controlName}`
    )
  }

  this.unsubscribe()

  this.controlSubscription = this.fieldControl?.valueChanges
    .pipe(
      filter(() => this.fieldControl?.status === 'INVALID'),
      tap(() => this.updateErrorMessage())
    )
    .subscribe()
  }
}
```

> Note that, since we're subscribing to `valueChanges`, we must also unsubscribe. We unsubscribe once with `ngOnDestroy` and again right before subscribing. This is because `initFieldControl` may be called multiple times. If we don't clear the prior subscription, it will result in a memory leak and related performance issues.
>
> Additionally, if we can't bind to a `fieldControl`, we throw an error message, since this usually points to a coding error.

10. Finally, we configure all major attributes with the `ngOnChanges` event, which triggers any time an `@Input` attribute is updated. This ensures that in the case where form elements could be dynamically added or removed, we will always consider the newest values. We call `initFieldControl` to start listening to value changes, we implement an `onblur` event handler that triggers `updateErrorMessage()` for the HTML input element, and we assign the value of `fieldLabel`:

src/app/user-controls/field-error/field-error.directive.ts
```
  ngOnChanges(changes: SimpleChanges): void {
    this.initFieldControl()

    if (changes.input.firstChange) {
      if (this.input) {
        this.input.onblur = () => this.updateErrorMessage()
        this.fieldLabel =
          this.fieldLabel ||
          this.input.placeholder ||
```

```
                    this.input.getAttribute('aria-label') ||
                    ''
            } else {
                throw new Error(
                    `appFieldError.[input] couldn't bind to any input
    element`
                )
            }
        }
    }
```

Note that if we can't bind to an HTML `input` element, this usually means that the developer simply forgot to wire things up correctly. In this case, we throw a new `Error` object, which generates a helpful stack trace in the console, so you can pinpoint the location in the template where the error is happening.

This wraps up the implementation of the directive. Now, we need to package the directive in a module named `field-error.module.ts`:

src/app/user-controls/field-error/field-error.directive.ts
```
@NgModule({
    imports: [CommonModule, ReactiveFormsModule],
    declarations: [FieldErrorDirective],
    exports: [FieldErrorDirective],
})
export class FieldErrorModule {}
```

Now go ahead and use the directive in our existing forms:

1. Import the module in `app.module.ts` and `user.module.ts`.
2. Update `profile.component.html` with the new directive.
3. Update `login.component.html` with the new directive.

Be sure to define `ErrorSets` as a public property variable in the `component` class so that you can use it in the template.

Test your forms to ensure that our validation messages are being displayed as expected and that there are no console errors.

Congratulations! You've learned how you can inject new behavior into other elements and components using directives. By doing this, we are able to avoid a lot of repeated code and standardize error messages across our app.

>
> Before moving on, finish implementation of the form by looking at the implementation on GitHub. You can find the code for the form template at `projects/ch11/src/app/user/profile/profile.initial.component.html` and the `component` class at `projects/ch11/src/app/user/profile/profile.initial.component.ts`.
>
> Do not include the `app-lemon-rater` and `app-view-user` elements, and remove the `mask` attribute from the phone number, which we will implement later in the chapter.

Here, you can see the User Profile as it will appear on LemonMart:

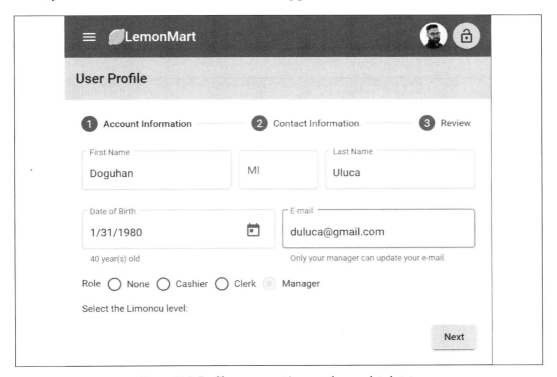

Figure 11.3: Profile component in a mostly completed state

Next, let's continue going over the `profile` component and see how the **Date of Birth** field works.

Calculated properties and DatePicker

We can display calculated properties based on user input. For example, to display a person's age based on their date of birth, introduce class properties that calculate the age and display it as follows:

src/app/user/profile/profile.component.ts
```
now = new Date()
get dateOfBirth() {
  return this.formGroup.get('dateOfBirth')?.value || this.now
}

get age() {
  return this.now.getFullYear() - this.dateOfBirth.getFullYear()
}
```

To validate a date within the last hundred years, implement a `minDate` class property:

src/app/user/profile/profile.component.ts
```
minDate = new Date(
  this.now.getFullYear() - 100,
  this.now.getMonth(),
  this.now.getDate()
)
```

The usage of the calculated properties in the template looks like this:

src/app/user/profile/profile.component.html
```
<mat-form-field appearance="outline" fxFlex="50%">
  <mat-label>Date of Birth</mat-label>
  <input matInput aria-label="Date of Birth" formControlName="dateOfBirth"
    [min]="minDate" [max]="now" [matDatepicker]="dateOfBirthPicker" #dob />
  <mat-hint *ngIf="formGroup.get('dateOfBirth')?.value">
    {{ age }} year(s) old
  </mat-hint>
  <mat-datepicker-toggle matSuffix [for]="dateOfBirthPicker">
  </mat-datepicker-toggle>
  <mat-datepicker #dateOfBirthPicker></mat-datepicker>
  <mat-error [input]="dob" [group]="formGroup"
    [appFieldError]="{error: 'invalid', message: 'Date must be within the last 100 years'}">
  </mat-error>
</mat-form-field>
```

Refer to the highlighted [min] and [max] attributes in the preceding snippet for the application of the hundred-year date range.

The DatePicker in action looks as follows:

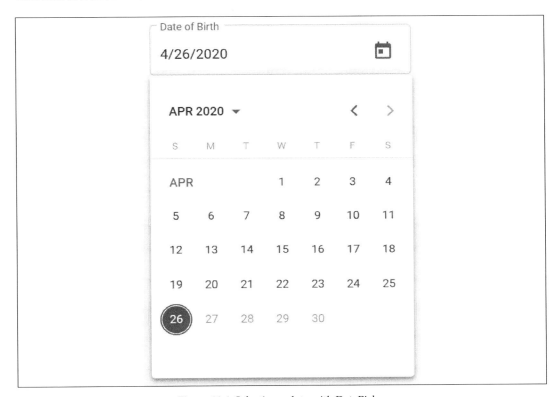

Figure 11.4: Selecting a date with DatePicker

Note that dates beyond April 26, 2020 are grayed out. After the date is selected, the calculated age is displayed as follows:

Figure 11.5: Calculated age property

Now, let's move on to the next step, **Contact Information**, and see how we can enable a convenient way to display and input the state portion of the address field.

Typeahead support

In `buildForm`, we set a listener on `address.state` to support a typeahead filtering drop-down experience:

```
src/app/user/profile/profile.component.ts
const state = this.formGroup.get('address.state')
if (state != null) {
  this.states$ = state.valueChanges.pipe(
    startWith(''),
    map((value) => USStateFilter(value))
  )
}
```

On the template, implement `mat-autocomplete`, bound to the filtered states array with an `async` pipe:

```
src/app/user/profile/profile.component.html
...
<mat-form-field appearance="outline" fxFlex="30%">
  <mat-label>State</mat-label>
  <input type="text" aria-label="State" matInput formControlName="state"
    [matAutocomplete]="stateAuto" #state />
  <mat-autocomplete #stateAuto="matAutocomplete">
    <mat-option *ngFor="let state of (states$ | async)" [value]="state.name">
      {{ state.name }}
    </mat-option>
  </mat-autocomplete>
  <mat-error [input]="state" [group]="formGroup.get('address')"
    appFieldError="required">
  </mat-error>
</mat-form-field>
...
```

Here's how it looks when a user enters the v character:

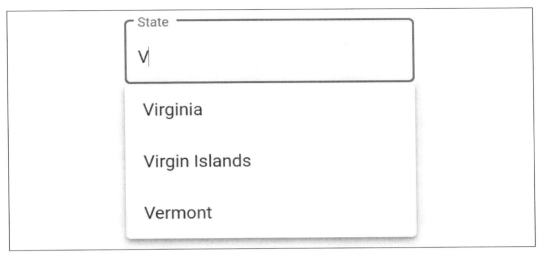

Figure 11.6: Dropdown with typeahead support

In the next section, let's enable the input of multiple phone numbers.

Dynamic form arrays

Note that `phones` is an array, potentially allowing for many inputs. We can implement this by building a `FormArray` with the `this.formBuilder.array` function. We also define several helper functions to make it easier to build the `FormArray`:

- `buildPhoneFormControl` helps to build `FormGroup` objects of individual entries.
- `buildPhoneArray` creates as many `FormGroup` objects as needed or, if the form is empty, it creates an empty entry.
- `addPhone` adds a new empty `FromGroup` object to the `FormArray`.
- `get phonesArray()` is a convenient property to get the `phones` control from the form.

Let's see how the implementation comes together:

`src/app/user/profile/profile.component.ts`
```
...
phones: this.formBuilder.array(this.buildPhoneArray(user?.phones ||
[])),
...
  private buildPhoneArray(phones: IPhone[]) {
    const groups = []

    if (phones?.length === 0) {
      groups.push(this.buildPhoneFormControl(1))
    } else {
      phones.forEach((p) => {
        groups.push(
          this.buildPhoneFormControl(p.id, p.type, p.digits)
        )
      })
    }
    return groups
  }

private buildPhoneFormControl(
  id: number, type?: string, phoneNumber?: string
) {
    return this.formBuilder.group({
      id: [id],
      type: [type || '', Validators.required],
      digits: [phoneNumber || '', USAPhoneNumberValidation],
    })
  }
...
```

`buildPhoneArray` supports initialization of a form with a single phone input or filling it with the existing data, working in tandem with `buildPhoneFormControl`. The latter function comes in handy when a user clicks on an **Add** button to create a new row for the entry:

`src/app/user/profile/profile.component.ts`
```
...
addPhone() { this.phonesArray.push(
this.buildPhoneFormControl(
  this.formGroup.get('phones').value.length + 1)
)
}

get phonesArray(): FormArray {
```

```
    return this.formGroup.get('phones') as FormArray
  }
...
```

The `phonesArray` property getter is a common pattern to make it easier to access certain form properties. However, in this case, it is also necessary because `get('phones')` must be typecast to `FormArray` so that we can access the `length` property on it on the template:

src/app/user/profile/profile.component.html
```
...
<mat-list formArrayName="phones">
  <h2 mat-subheader>Phone Number(s)
    <button mat-button (click)="addPhone()">
      <mat-icon>add</mat-icon>
      Add Phone
    </button>
  </h2>
  <mat-list-item style="margin-top: 36px;"
    *ngFor="let position of phonesArray.controls; let i = index"
      [formGroupName]="i">
    <mat-form-field appearance="outline" fxFlex="100px">
      <mat-label>Type</mat-label>
      <mat-select formControlName="type">
        <mat-option *ngFor="let type of PhoneTypes"
             [value]="convertTypeToPhoneType(type)">
          {{ type }}
        </mat-option>
      </mat-select>
    </mat-form-field>
    <mat-form-field appearance="outline" fxFlex fxFlexOffset="10px">
      <mat-label>Number</mat-label>
      <input matInput type="text" formControlName="digits"
        aria-label="Phone number" prefix="+1" />
      <mat-error
        *ngIf="phonesArray.controls[i].invalid &&
             phonesArray.controls[i].touched">
        A valid phone number is required
      </mat-error>
    </mat-form-field>
    <button fxFlex="33px" mat-icon-button
      (click)="phonesArray.removeAt(i)">
      <mat-icon>delete</mat-icon>
    </button>
  </mat-list-item>
</mat-list>
...
```

> Note the highlighted `convertTypeToPhoneType` function, which converts a `string` to `enum PhoneType`.
>
> Also highlighted in the preceding code block, note how the `remove` function is implemented inline in the template, making it easier to read and maintain.

Let's see how the dynamic array should be working:

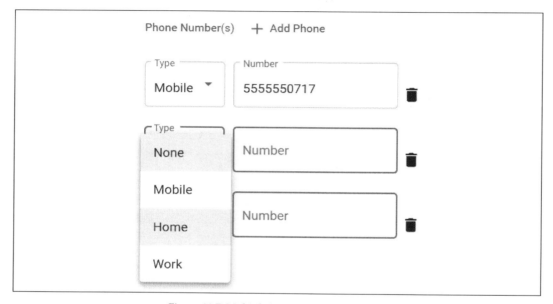

Figure 11.7: Multiple inputs using FormArray

Now that we're done with inputting data, we can move on to the last step of the stepper, **Review**. However, as was mentioned earlier, the **Review** step uses the `<app-view-user>` directive to display its data. Let's build that view first.

Creating shared components

Here's a minimal implementation of the `<app-view-user>` directive that is a prerequisite for the **Review** step.

Create a new `viewUser` component under the `user` module, as follows:

```
src/app/user/view-user/view-user.component.ts
import { Component, Input, OnChanges, SimpleChanges } from '@angular/core'
```

```
import { Router } from '@angular/router'
import { BehaviorSubject } from 'rxjs'

import { IUser, User } from '../user/user'

@Component({
  selector: 'app-view-user',
  template: `
    <div *ngIf="currentUser$ | async as currentUser">
      <mat-card>
        <mat-card-header>
          <div mat-card-avatar>
            <mat-icon>account_circle</mat-icon>
          </div>
          <mat-card-title>
            {{ currentUser.fullName }}
          </mat-card-title>
          <mat-card-subtitle>
            {{ currentUser.role }}
          </mat-card-subtitle>
        </mat-card-header>
        <mat-card-content>
          <p><span class="mat-input bold">E-mail</span></p>
          <p>{{ currentUser.email }}</p>
          <p><span class="mat-input bold">Date of Birth</span></p>
          <p>{{ currentUser.dateOfBirth | date: 'mediumDate' }}</p>
        </mat-card-content>
        <mat-card-actions *ngIf="editMode">
          <button mat-button mat-raised-button
                  (click)="editUser(currentUser._id)">
            Edit
          </button>
        </mat-card-actions>
      </mat-card>
    </div>
  `,
  styles: [
    `
      .bold {
        font-weight: bold;
      }
    `,
  ],
})
export class ViewUserComponent implements OnChanges {
```

```
    @Input() user: IUser
    readonly currentUser$ = new BehaviorSubject(new User())

    get editMode() {
      return !this.user
    }

    constructor(private router: Router) {}

    ngOnChanges(changes: SimpleChanges): void {
      this.currentUser$.next(User.Build(changes.user.currentValue))
    }

    editUser(id: string) {
      this.router.navigate(['/user/profile', id])
    }
}
```

The preceding component uses input binding with `@Input` to get user data, compliant with the `IUser` interface, from an outside component. We implement the `ngOnChanges` event, which fires whenever the bound data changes. In this event, we hydrate the simple JSON object stored in the `user` property as an instance of the `User` class with `User.Build`.

We then define a read-only `BehaviorSubject`, named `this.currentUser$`, so we can asynchronously push updates to it using the next function. This flexibility will come in handy when we later make this component reusable in multiple contexts. Even if we wanted to, we couldn't directly bind to `user`, because calculated properties such as `fullName` will only work if the data is hydrated into an instance of the `User` class.

Now, we are ready to complete the multi-step form.

Reviewing and saving form data

On the last step of the multistep form, users should be able to review and then save the form data. As a good practice, a successful POST request will return the data that was saved back to the browser. We can then reload the form with the information received back from the server:

src/app/user/profile/profile.component.ts
```
...
  async save(form: FormGroup) {
    this.subs.add(
      this.userService
```

```
      .updateUser(this.currentUserId, form.value)
      .subscribe(
        (res: IUser) => {
          this.formGroup.patchValue(res)
          this.uiService.showToast('Updated user')
        },
        (err: string) => (this.userError = err)
      )
    )
  }
  ...
```

 Note that `updateUser` returns the saved value of the user. It is possible that the database returns a different version of `user` than what we had before, so we use `formGroup.patchValue` to update the data powering the form. The form automatically updates to reflect any changes.

If there are errors when saving the data, they'll be set to `userError` to be displayed on the form. And before saving the data, we present it in a compact format with the reusable `app-view-user` component that we can bind the form data to:

src/app/user/profile/profile.component.html
```
...
<mat-step [stepControl]="formGroup">
  <form [formGroup]="formGroup" (ngSubmit)="save(formGroup)">
    <ng-template matStepLabel>Review</ng-template>
    <div class="stepContent">
      Review and update your user profile.
      <app-view-user [user]="formGroup.getRawValue()"></app-view-user>
    </div>
    <div fxLayout="row" class="margin-top">
      <button mat-button matStepperPrevious>Back</button>
      <div class="flex-spacer"></div>
      <div *ngIf="userError" class="mat-caption error">
        {{ userError }}
      </div>
      <button mat-button color="warn" (click)="stepper.reset()">
        Reset
      </button>
      <button mat-raised-button matStepperNext color="primary"
        type="submit" [disabled]="formGroup.invalid">
        Update
      </button>
```

```
        </div>
      </form>
</mat-step>
    ...
```

 Note that we use `formGroup.getRawValue()` to extract the JSON of the form data. See how we bind `userError` to display error messages. Also, the **Reset** button uses `stepper.reset()`, which can conveniently reset all the user input.

This is how the final product should appear:

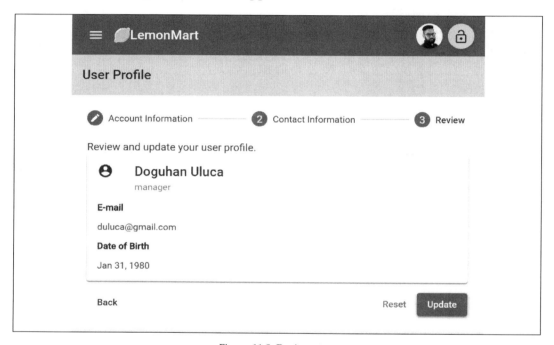

Figure 11.8: Review step

Now that the user profile input is done, we are about halfway to our eventual goal of creating a master/detail view where a **Manager** can click on a user and view their profile details. We still have a lot more code to add, and along the way, we have fallen into a pattern of adding lots of boilerplate code to load the requisite data for a component.

Next, let's refactor our form to make our code reusable and scalable, so even if our form has dozens of fields, the code is still maintainable and we don't introduce an exponential cost increase to make changes.

Scaling architecture with reusable form parts

As mentioned in the introduction to the *Multi-step responsive forms* section, forms are tightly coupled beasts that can grow large, and using the wrong architectural pattern to scale your implementation can cause significant issues when implementing new features or maintaining existing ones.

To demonstrate how you can break up your form into multiple parts, we will refactor the form to extract the highlighted section in the following screenshot, the name form group, as its own component. The technique to accomplish this is the same as you'd use when you want to put each step of your form into a separate component:

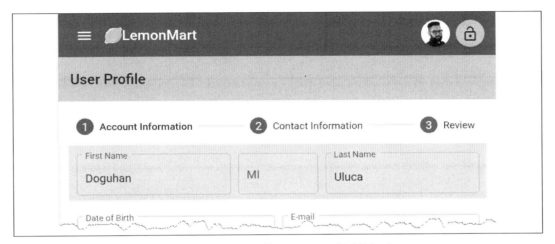

Figure 11.9: User profile's name part highlighted

By making the name form group reusable, you will also learn about how you can reuse the business logic that you build into that form group in other forms. We will extract the name form group logic into a new component named `NameInputComponent`. In doing so, we also have an opportunity to extract some reusable form functionality to a `BaseFormComponent` as an abstract class.

There are going to be several components that are working together here, including `ProfileComponent`, `ViewUserComponent`, and `NameInputComponent`. We need all the values in these three components to be up to date as the user enters them.

`ProfileComponent` will own the master form to which we'll need to register any child form. Once we do this, all the form validation techniques you've learned so far will still apply.

This is a key way to make your form able to scale across many components and continue to be easy to work with, without introducing unnecessary validation overhead. Hence, it is useful to review the different interactions between these objects to solidify your understanding of the asynchronous and decoupled nature of their behavior:

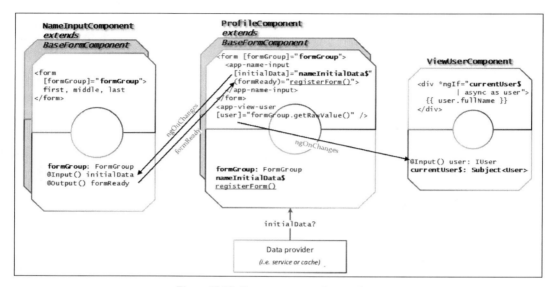

Figure 11.10: Form component interactions

In this section, we bring together a lot of the different concepts that you've learned over the course of the book. Utilize the preceding diagram to understand how the various form components interact with each other.

In the preceding diagram, properties in bold indicate data binding. Underlined function elements indicate event registrations. Arrows show the points of connection between the components.

The workflow begins with the instantiation of `ProfileComponent`. The `OnInit` event of the component begins building the `formGroup` object, while asynchronously loading any potential `initialData` that may need to be patched into the forms. Refer to the preceding diagram for a visual representation of `initialData` coming in from a service or cache.

`NameInputComponent` is used in the `ProfileComponent` form as `<app-name-input>`. In order to synchronize `initialData` with the `NameInputComponent`, we bind a `nameInitialData$` subject using the `async` pipe, since `initialData` is coming in asynchronously.

`NameInputComponent` implements the `OnChanges` life cycle hook, so whenever `nameInitialData$` updates, its value is patched into the `NameInputComponent` form.

Like `ProfileComponent`, `NameInputComponent` also implements the `OnInit` event to construct its `formGroup` object. Since this is an asynchronous event, `NameInputComponent` needs to expose a `formReady` event that `ProfileComponent` can subscribe to. Once the `formGroup` object is ready, we emit the event, and the `registerForm` function on `ProfileComponent` triggers. `registerForm` adds the `formGroup` object of `NameInputComponent` as a child element to the parent `formGroup` on `ProfileComponent`.

`ViewUserComponent` is used in the `ProfileComponent` form as `<app-view-user>`. When the values in the parent form change, we need `<app-view-user>` to stay up to date. We bind to the `user` property on `ViewUserComponent`, which implements `OnChanges` to receive updates. Every time there is an update, the `User` object is hydrated from the `IUser` object, so that calculated fields such as `fullName` can continue to work. The updated `User` is pushed to `currentUser$`, which is bound to the template with an `async`.

We will begin by building a `BaseFormComponent`, which `NameInputComponent` and `ProfileComponent` will then implement.

Base form component as an abstract class

We can share common functionality and standardize the implementation of all components that implement a form by implementing a base abstract class. An abstract class cannot be instantiated on its own because it wouldn't make sense to do so, since it will not have a template, making it useless on its own.

 Note that `BaseFormComponent` is just a `class` and not an Angular component.

`BaseFormComponent` will standardize the following:

- `@Input initialData`, and disable as binding targets
- The `@Output formReady` event
- `formGroup`, the `FormGroup` to be used in the template's `buildForm` function to build the `formGroup`

With the preceding assumptions, the base class can provide some generic functionality:

- `patchUpdatedData`, which can update the data (partially or fully) in the `formGroup` without having to rebuild it.
- `registerForm` and `deregisterForm` can register or deregister child forms.
- `deregisterAllForms` can automatically deregister any registered child form.
- `hasChanged` can determine whether `initialData` has changed given a `SimpleChange` object provided by the `ngOnChange` event handler.
- `patchUpdatedDataIfChanged` leverages `hasChanged` and uses `patchUpdatedData` to update the data if, and only if, there has been an update to `initialData` and `formGroup` is already initialized.

Create a new class, `BaseFormComponent`, under `src/common` as follows:

src/app/common/base-form.class.ts

```typescript
import { EventEmitter, Input, Output, SimpleChange, SimpleChanges }
    from '@angular/core'
import { AbstractControl, FormGroup } from '@angular/forms'

export abstract class BaseFormComponent<TFormData extends object> {
  @Input() initialData: TFormData
  @Input() disable: boolean
  @Output() formReady: EventEmitter<AbstractControl>
  formGroup: FormGroup

  private registeredForms: string[] = []

  constructor() {
    this.formReady = new EventEmitter<AbstractControl>(true)
  }

  abstract buildForm(initialData?: TFormData): FormGroup

  patchUpdatedData(data: object) {
    this.formGroup.patchValue(data, { onlySelf: false })
  }

  patchUpdatedDataIfChanged(changes: SimpleChanges) {
    if (this.formGroup && this.hasChanged(changes.initialData)) {
      this.patchUpdatedData(this.initialData)
    }
```

```typescript
  }

  emitFormReady(control: AbstractControl | null = null) {
    this.formReady.emit(control || this.formGroup)
  }

  registerForm(name: string, control: AbstractControl) {
    this.formGroup.setControl(name, control)
    this.registeredForms.push(name)
  }

  deregisterForm(name: string) {
    if (this.formGroup.contains(name)) {
      this.formGroup.removeControl(name)
    }
  }

  protected deregisterAllForms() {
    this.registeredForms.forEach(() => this.deregisterForm(name))
  }

  protected hasChanged(change: SimpleChange): boolean {
    return change?.previousValue !== change?.currentValue
  }
}
```

Let's implement `NameInputComponent` using the `BaseFormComponent`.

Implementing a reusable form part

Start by identifying the name form group in the `profile` component code and template files:

1. The following is the name form group implementation:

    src/app/user/profile/profile.component.ts

    ```typescript
    ...
    name: this.formBuilder.group({
      first: [user?.name?.first || '', RequiredTextValidation],
      middle: [user?.name?.middle || '', OneCharValidation],
      last: [user?.name?.last || '', RequiredTextValidation],
    }),
    ...
    ```

> Note that when we move these validation rules to a new component, we still want them to be in effect when determining the overall validation status of the parent form. We achieve this by using the `registerForm` function we implemented in the previous section. Once our new `FormGroup` is registered with the existing one, they work exactly the same way before our refactor.

2. Next is the name form group template:

   src/app/user/profile/profile.component.html

   ```
   ...
   <div fxLayout="row" fxLayout.lt-sm="column"
   [formGroup]="formGroup.get('name')" fxLayoutGap="10px">
     <mat-form-field appearance="outline" fxFlex="40%">
       <mat-label>First Name</mat-label>
       <input matInput aria-label="First Name"
              formControlName="first" #name />
       ...
   </div>
   ...
   ```

   You will be moving most of this code to the new component.

3. Create a new `NameInputComponent` under the `user` folder.
4. Extend the class from `BaseFormComponent`.
5. Inject `FormBuilder` in the `constructor`:

> For components with small or limited pieces of functionality, I prefer creating them with an inline template and styling, so it is easier to change the code from one place.

src/app/user/name-input/name-input.component.ts

```
export class NameInputComponent extends BaseFormComponent<IName> {
  constructor(private formBuilder: FormBuilder) {
    super()
  }

  buildForm(initialData?: IName): FormGroup {
    throw new Error("Method not implemented.");
  }
```

```
    ...
}
```

Remember that the base class already implements `formGroup`, `initialData`, `disable`, and `formReady` properties, so you don't need to redefine them.

Note that we are forced to implement the `buildForm` function since it was defined as abstract. This is a great way to enforce standards across developers. Also, note that any base function provided can be overridden by the implementing class by simply redefining the function. You'll see this in action when we refactor the `ProfileComponent`.

6. Implement the `buildForm` function.
7. Set the `name` property part of the `formGroup` in `ProfileComponent` to null:

   src/app/user/name-input/name-input.component.ts

   ```
   export class NameInputComponent implements OnInit {
     ...

     buildForm(initialData?: IName): FormGroup {
       const name = initialData
       return this.formBuilder.group({
         first: [name?.first : '', RequiredTextValidation],
         middle: [name?.middle : '', OneCharValidation],
         last: [name?.last : '', RequiredTextValidation],
       })
     }
   ```

8. Implement the template by bringing over the content from `ProfileComponent`:

   src/app/user/name-input/name-input.component.ts

   ```
   template: `
     <form [formGroup]="formGroup">
       <div fxLayout="row" fxLayout.lt-sm="column"
         fxLayoutGap="10px">
         ...
       </div>
   ```

[601]

Recipes – Reusability, Routing, and Caching

```
  </form>
`,
```

9. Implement the `ngOnInit` event handler:

   src/app/user/name-input/name-input.component.ts

   ```
   ngOnInit() {
     this.formGroup = this.buildForm(this.initialData)

     if (this.disable) {
       this.formGroup.disable()
     }

     this.formReady.emit(this.formGroup)
   }
   ```

   > It is critical to get the implementation of the `ngOnInit` event handler right in every implementation of `BaseFormComponent`. The preceding example is fairly standard behavior for any child component you may implement.
   >
   > Note that the implementation in `ProfileComponent` will be a bit different.

10. Implement the `ngOnChanges` event handler, leveraging the base `patchUpdatedDataIfChanged` behavior:

    src/app/user/name-input/name-input.component.ts

    ```
    ngOnChanges(changes: SimpleChanges) {
      this.patchUpdatedDataIfChanged(changes)
    }
    ```

    > Note that in `patchUpdatedDataIfChanged`, setting `onlySelf` to `false` will cause the parent form to also update. If you'd like to optimize this behavior, you may override the function.

Now you have a fully implemented `NameInputComponent` that you can integrate into `ProfileComponent`.

[602]

Chapter 11

To verify your `ProfileComponent` code going forward, refer to `projects/ch11/src/app/user/profile/profile.component.ts` and `projects/ch11/src/app/user/profile/profile.component.html`.

Before you begin using `NameInputComponent`, perform the following refactors:

11. Refactor `ProfileComponent` to extend `BaseFormComponent` and conform to its default values as needed.
12. Define a readonly `nameInitialData$` property with the `BehaviorSubject<IName>` type and initialize it with empty strings.
13. Replace the content in `ProfileComponent` with the new `<app-name-input>` component:

    src/app/user/profile/profile.component.html

    ```
    <mat-horizontal-stepper #stepper="matHorizontalStepper">
      <mat-step [stepControl]="formGroup">
        <form [formGroup]="formGroup">
          <ng-template matStepLabel>Account Information</ng-template>
          <div class="stepContent">
            <app-name-input [initialData]="nameInitialData$ | async"
              (formReady)="registerForm('name', $event)">
            </app-name-input>
          </div>
          ...
        </ng-template>
        </form>
      </mat-step>
      ...
    </mat-horizontal-stepper>
    ```

    Note that the base form component function, `registerForm`, is leveraged here.

14. Ensure that your `ngOnInit` is implemented correctly:

    Note that there are some additional refactors present on the updated `ProfileComponent`, such as the `patchUser` function seen in the following snippet. Don't miss these updates when you update your component.

[603]

src/app/user/profile/profile.component.ts

```
ngOnInit() {
  this.formGroup = this.buildForm()

  this.subs.sink = this.authService.currentUser$
    .pipe(
      filter((user) => user != null),
      tap((user) => this.patchUser(user))
    )
    .subscribe()
}
```

It is important to update the current form's data with `pathUpdatedData`, as well as `nameInitialData$`, when there's an update to `initialData`.

15. Ensure that `ngOnDestroy` is implemented correctly:

src/app/user/profile/profile.component.ts

```
ngOnDestroy() {
  this.subs.unsubscribe()
  this.deregisterAllForms()
}
```

Always remember to unsubscribe from subscriptions, which you can do so easily with the `SubSink` package. You can also leverage the base class functionality to automatically deregister from all child forms.

Next, let's learn about masking user input to increase the quality of our data.

Input masking

Masking user input is an input UX tool, as well as a data quality one. I'm a fan of the **ngx-mask** library, which makes it really easy to implement input masking in Angular. We will demonstrate input masking by updating the phone number input field so we can ensure that users input a valid phone number, as shown in the following screenshot:

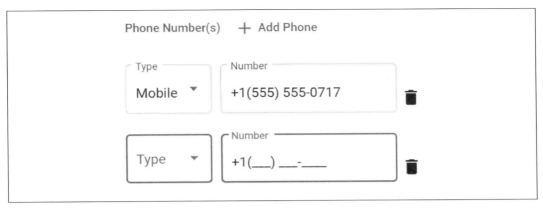

Figure 11.11: Phone number field with input masking

Set up your input masking as follows:

1. Install the library via npm with `npm i ngx-mask`.
2. Import the `forRoot` module:

   src/app/app.module.ts

   ```
   export const options: Partial<IConfig> | (() => Partial<IConfig>)
   = {
     showMaskTyped: true,
   }

   @NgModule({
     imports: [
       ...
       NgxMaskModule.forRoot(options),
     ]
   })
   ```

3. Import the module in the `user` feature module as well:

   src/app/user/user.module.ts

   ```
   @NgModule({
     imports: [

       ...
       NgxMaskModule.forChild(),
     ]
   })
   ```

[605]

4. Update the `number` field in `ProfileComponent` as follows:

   `src/app/user/profile/profile.component.html`

   ```
   <mat-form-field appearance="outline" fxFlex fxFlexOffset="10px">
     <mat-label>Number</mat-label>
     <input matInput type="text" formControlName="number"
       prefix="+1" mask="(000) 000-0000" [showMaskTyped]="true" />
     <mat-error *ngIf="this.phonesArray.controls[i].invalid">
       A valid phone number is required
     </mat-error>
   </mat-form-field>
   ```

And it's that simple. You can learn more about the module and its capabilities on GitHub at https://github.com/JsDaddy/ngx-mask.

Custom controls with ControlValueAccessor

So far, we've learned about forms using standard form controls and input controls provided by Angular Material. However, it is possible for you to create custom user controls. If you implement the `ControlValueAccessor` interface, then your custom controls will play nicely with forms and the `ControlValueAccessor` interface's validation engine.

We will be creating the custom rater control shown in the following screenshot, and will place it as a control on the first step of `ProfileComponent`:

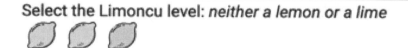

Figure 11.12: The lemon rater user control

User controls are inherently highly reusable, tightly coupled, and customized components to enable rich user interactions. Let's implement one.

Implementing a custom rating control

The lemon rater will highlight the number of lemons selected dynamically as the user interacts with the control in real time. As such, creating a high-quality custom control is an expensive endeavor.

> The Lemon Rater is a modified version of Jennifer Wadella's Galaxy Rating App sample found at https://github.com/tehfedaykin/galaxy-rating-app. I highly recommend that you watch Jennifer's Ng-Conf 2019 talk on `ControlValueAccessor`, linked in the *Further reading* section.

Set up your custom rating control as follows:

1. Generate a new component called `LemonRater` under the `user-controls` folder.
2. Create a `LemonRaterModule` in the same folder.
3. Declare and export the component.
4. In `LemonRater`, implement the `ControlValueAccess` interface:

    `src/app/user-controls/lemon-rater/lemon-rater.component.ts`

    ```
    export class LemonRaterComponent implements ControlValueAccessor {
      disabled = false
      private internalValue: number

      get value() {
        return this.internalValue
      }

      onChanged: any = () => {}
      onTouched: any = () => {}

      writeValue(obj: any): void {
        this.internalValue = obj
      }
      registerOnChange(fn: any): void {
        this.onChanged = fn
      }

      registerOnTouched(fn: any): void {
        this.onTouched = fn
      }
      setDisabledState?(isDisabled: boolean): void {
        this.disabled = isDisabled
      }
    }
    ```

5. Add the NG_VALUE_ACCESSOR provider with the `multi` property set to `true`. This will register our component with the form's change events, so form values can be updated when the user interacts with the rater:

   src/app/user-controls/lemon-rater/lemon-rater.component.ts

   ```
   @Component({
     selector: 'app-lemon-rater',
     templateUrl: 'lemon-rater.component.html',
     styleUrls: ['lemon-rater.component.css'],
     providers: [
       {
         provide: NG_VALUE_ACCESSOR,
         useExisting: forwardRef(() => LemonRaterComponent),
         multi: true,
       },
     ],
   ```

6. Implement a custom rating scheme with a function to allow for setting the selected rating based on user input:

   src/app/user-controls/lemon-rater/lemon-rater.component.ts

   ```
   export class LemonRaterComponent implements ControlValueAccessor {
     @ViewChild('displayText', { static: false }) displayTextRef: ElementRef

     ratings = Object.freeze([
       {
         value: 1,
         text: 'no zest',
       },
       {
         value: 2,
         text: 'neither a lemon or a lime ',
       },
       {
         value: 3,
         text: 'a true lemon',
       },
     ])

     setRating(lemon: any) {
       if (!this.disabled) {
         this.internalValue = lemon.value
         this.ratingText = lemon.text
         this.onChanged(lemon.value)
         this.onTouched()
       }
     }
   ```

```
  setDisplayText() {
    this.setSelectedText(this.internalValue)
  }

  private setSelectedText(value: number) {
    this.displayTextRef.nativeElement.textContent =
      this.getSelectedText(value)
  }

  private getSelectedText(value: number) {
    let text = ''

    if (value) {
      text = this.ratings
        .find((i) => i.value === value)?.text || ''
    }

    return text
  }
}
```

Note that by using @ViewChild, we're getting the HTML element named #displayText (highlighted in the following template). Using setSelectText, we replace the textContent of the element.

7. Implement the template, referring to the sample code for the contents of the svg tag:

src/app/user-controls/lemon-rater/lemon-rater.component.html

```html
<i #displayText></i>
<div class="lemons" [ngClass]="{'disabled': disabled}">
  <ng-container *ngFor="let lemon of ratings">
    <svg width="24px" height="24px" viewBox="0 0 513 513"
         [attr.title]="lemon.text" class="lemon rating"
         [ngClass]="{'selected': lemon.value <= value}"
         (mouseover)=
           "displayText.textContent = !disabled ? lemon.text : ''"
         (mouseout)="setDisplayText()"
         (click)="setRating(lemon)"
    >
      ...
    </svg>
  </ng-container>
</div>
```

[609]

The three most important attributes in the template are `mouseover`, `mouseout`, and `click`. `mouseover` displays the text for the rating that the user is currently hovering over, `mouseout` resets the display text to the selected value, and `click` calls the `setRating` method we implemented to record the user's selection. However, the control can have even richer user interactivity by highlighting the number of lemons when the user hovers over a rating or selects it. We will accomplish this via some CSS magic.

8. Implement the `css` for the user control:

   `src/app/user-controls/lemon-rater/lemon-rater.component.css`

   ```css
   .lemons {
     cursor: pointer;
   }

   .lemons:hover .lemon #fill-area {
     fill: #ffe200 !important;
   }

   .lemons.disabled:hover {
     cursor: not-allowed;
   }

   .lemons.disabled:hover .lemon #fill-area {
     fill: #d8d8d8 !important;
   }

   .lemons .lemon {
     float: left; margin: 0px 5px;
   }

   .lemons .lemon #fill-area {
     fill: #d8d8d8;
   }

   .lemons .lemon:hover~.lemon #fill-area {
     fill: #d8d8d8 !important;
   }

   .lemons .lemon.selected #fill-area {
     fill: #ffe200 !important;
   }

   .lemons .dad.heart #ada
       {
          fill: #6a0dad !important;
   }
   ```

The most interesting bit is with `.lemons .lemon:hover~.lemon #fill-area`. Note that the operator `~` or the general sibling combinator is used to select a range of elements so that a dynamic number of lemons will be highlighted as the user hovers over them.

`#fill-area` refers to a `<path>` defined within the lemon svg, which allows for the lemon's color to be adjusted dynamically. I had to manually inject this ID field into the svg file.

Now, let's see how you can use this new user control in a form.

Using custom controls in forms

We will use the lemon rater in the `profile` component to record the Limoncu level of the employee.

Limoncu, meaning a person who grows or sells lemons in Turkish, is Lemon Mart's proprietary employee engagement and performance measurement system.

Let's integrate the lemon rater:

1. Start by importing the `LemonRaterModule` in `UserModule`.
2. Ensure that the level form control is initialized in `buildForm`:

   src/app/user/profile/profile.component.ts

   ```
   buildForm(initialData?: IUser): FormGroup {
   ...
     level: [user?.level || 0, Validators.required],
   ...
   }
   ```

3. Insert the lemon rater as the last element of the first `mat-step`, inside the `form` element:

   src/app/user/profile/profile.component.html

   ```
   <div fxLayout="row" fxLayout.lt-sm="column" class="margin-top"
   fxLayoutGap="10px">
     <mat-label class="mat-body-1">Select the Limoncu level:
       <app-lemon-rater formControlName="level">
   ```

```
      </app-lemon-rater>
    </mat-label>
</div>
```

We simply integrate with the custom control by implementing `formControlName` as you would with any other control.

Congratulations! You should have a working custom control that is integrated with your form.

Layouts using grid list

The Angular Flex Layout library is great for laying out content using CSS Flexbox. Angular Material provides another mechanism to lay out content by using CSS Grid with its Grid List functionality. A good way to demonstrate this functionality is by implementing a helpful list for fake login information in the `LoginComponent`, demonstrated here:

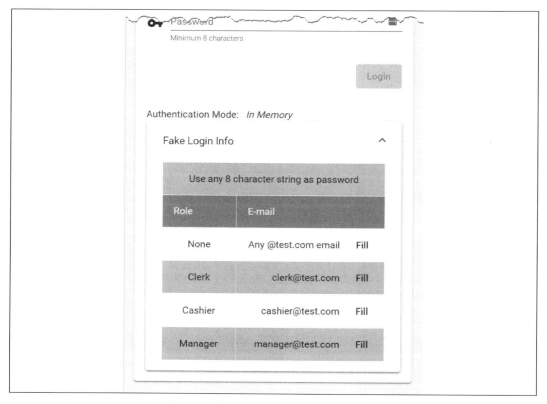

Figure 11.13: Login helper with the grid list

Implement your list as follows:

1. Start by defining a `roles` property that is an array of all the roles:

    src/app/login/login.component.ts
    ```
    roles = Object.keys(Role)
    ```

2. Import `MatExpansionModule` and `MatGridListModule` into `AppMaterialModule`.

3. Implement a new `mat-card-content` below the existing one:

    src/app/login/login.component.html
    ```
    <div fxLayout="row" fxLayoutAlign="center">
      <mat-card fxFlex="400px">
        <mat-card-header>
          <mat-card-title>
            <div class="mat-headline">Hello, Limoncu!</div>
          </mat-card-title>
        </mat-card-header>
        <mat-card-content>
          ...
        </mat-card-content>
        <mat-card-content>
        </mat-card-content>
      </mat-card>
    </div>
    ```

4. Inside the new `mat-card-content`, put in a label to display the authentication mode:

    src/app/login/login.component.html
    ```
    <div fxLayout="row" fxLayoutAlign="start center"
    fxLayoutGap="10px">
      <span>Authentication Mode: </span><i>{{ authMode }}</i>
    </div>
    ```

5. Beneath the label, implement an expansion list:

    src/app/login/login.component.html
    ```
    <mat-accordion>
      <mat-expansion-panel>
        <mat-expansion-panel-header>
            <mat-panel-title>
              Fake Login Info
            </mat-panel-title>
        </mat-expansion-panel-header>
        ...
      </mat-expansion-panel>
    </mat-accordion>
    ```

6. After `mat-expansion-panel-header`, in the area marked with ellipses in the preceding step, implement a table of roles and email addresses, along with some hint text regarding password length using `mat-grid-list`, shown in the following code block:

`src/app/login/login.component.html`
```html
<mat-grid-list cols="3" rowHeight="48px" role="list">
  <mat-grid-tile [colspan]="3" role="listitem"
                 style="background: pink">
    Use any 8 character string as password
  </mat-grid-tile>
  <mat-grid-tile>
    <mat-grid-tile-header>Role</mat-grid-tile-header>
  </mat-grid-tile>
  <mat-grid-tile [colspan]="2">
    <mat-grid-tile-header>E-mail</mat-grid-tile-header>
  </mat-grid-tile>
  <div *ngFor="let role of roles; odd as oddRow">
    <mat-grid-tile role="listitem"
          [style.background]="oddRow ? 'lightGray': 'white'">
      {{role}}
    </mat-grid-tile>
    <mat-grid-tile [colspan]="2" role="listitem"
          [style.background]="oddRow ? 'lightGray': 'white'">
      <div fxFlex fxLayoutAlign="end center">
        <div
          *ngIf="role.toLowerCase() === 'none'; else otherRoles"
        >
          Any @test.com email
        </div>
        <ng-template #otherRoles>
          {{role.toLowerCase()}}@test.com
        </ng-template>
        <button mat-button (click)="
            this.loginForm.patchValue(
              { email: role.toLowerCase() + '@test.com',
                password: 'whatever' }
            )">
          Fill
        </button>
      </div>
    </mat-grid-tile>
  </div>
</mat-grid-list>
```

We use `colspan` to control the width of each row and cell. We leverage `fxLayoutAlign` to right-align the contents of the **E-mail** column. We use `*ngIf; else` to selectively display content. Finally, a **Fill** button helps us to populate the login form with fake login information.

In your application, you can use an expansion panel to communicate password complexity requirements to your users.

You can read more about expansion panels at https://material.angular.io/components/expansion and Grid List at https://material.angular.io/components/grid-list/overview.

Restoring cached data

At the beginning of the chapter, when implementing the `updateUser` method in `UserService`, we cached the `user` object in case of any errors that may wipe out user-provided data:

```
src/app/user/user/user.service.ts
updateUser(id: string, user: IUser): Observable<IUser> {
  ...
  this.setItem('draft-user', user)
  ...
}
```

Consider a scenario where the user may be temporarily offline when they attempt to save their data. In this case, our `updateUser` function will save the data.

Let's see how we can restore this data in `ProfileComponent` when loading the user profile:

1. Start by adding functions named `loadFromCache` and `clearCache` to the `ProfileComponent` class:

   ```
   src/app/user/profile.component.ts
   private loadFromCache(): Observable<User | null> {
     let user = null
     try {
       const draftUser = localStorage.getItem('draft-user')
       if (draftUser != null) {
         user = User.Build(JSON.parse(draftUser))
       }
   ```

```
      if (user) {
        this.uiService.showToast('Loaded data from cache')
      }
    } catch (err) {
      localStorage.removeItem('draft-user')
    }

    return of(user)
  }

  clearCache() {
    localStorage.removeItem('draft-user')
  }
```

 After loading the data, we parse the data into a JSON object, using `JSON.parse`, and then hydrate the `User` object with `User.Build`.

2. Update the template to call the `clearCache` function, so when the user resets the form, we also clear the cache:

   src/app/user/profile.component.html
   ```
   <button mat-button color="warn"
       (click)="stepper.reset(); clearCache()">
     Reset
   </button>
   ```

3. Update `ngOnInit` to conditionally load data from cache or the latest `currentUser$` from `authService`:

   src/app/user/profile.component.ts
   ```
   ngOnInit() {
     this.formGroup = this.buildForm()

     this.subs.sink = combineLatest([
         this.loadFromCache(),
         this.authService.currentUser$,
       ])
         .pipe(
           filter(
             ([cachedUser, me]) =>
               cachedUser != null || me != null
           ),
           tap(
   ```

```
        ([cachedUser, me]) =>
          this.patchUser(cachedUser || me)
      )
    )
    .subscribe()
}
```

We leverage the `combineLatest` operator to combine the outputs of `loadFromCache` and `currentUser$`. We check to see that one of the streams is returning a non-null value. If a cached user exists, it takes precedence over the value received from `currentUser$`.

You can test your cache by setting the network status of your browser to be offline, as shown:

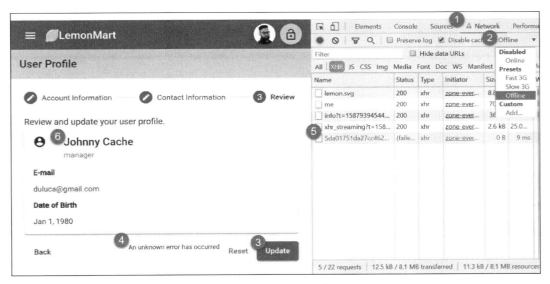

Figure 11.14: Offline network status

Set the network status of your browser to offline as follows:

1. In Chrome DevTools, navigate to the **Network** tab.
2. Select **Offline** in the dropdown marked as **2** in the preceding screenshot.
3. Make a change to your form, such as the name, and hit **Update**.
4. You'll see an error reading **An unknown error has occurred** displayed at the bottom of the form.
5. In the **Network** tab, you'll see that your PUT request has failed.
6. Now, refresh your browser window and observe that the new name you entered is still present.

Refer to the following screenshot, which shows the toast notification you get after loading data from the cache:

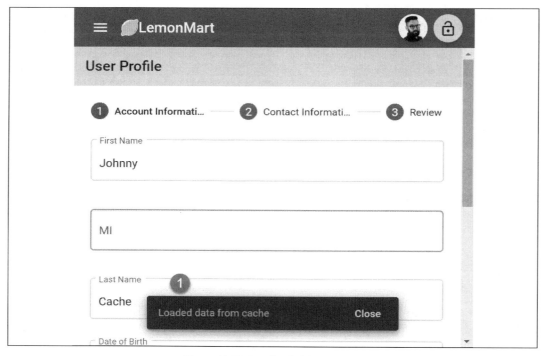

Figure 11.15: Data loaded from cache

Implementing a great UX around caching is incredibly challenging. I provided a rudimentary method to show what is possible. However, there are many edge cases that can impact how caching in your application works.

In my case, the cache stubbornly sticks around until we successfully save the data to the server. This may be frustrating for some users.

Congratulations! You've successfully implemented a sophisticated form to capture data from your users!

Exercise

Further enhance the `login` component to add a login helper for `AuthMode.CustomServer`.

Summary

In this chapter, we covered forms, directives, and user control-related functionality for LemonMart. We created reusable components that can be embedded within another component using data binding. We showed that you can use PUT to send data to the server and cache data input by the user. We also created a multistep input form that is responsive to changing screen sizes. We removed the boilerplate code from our components by leveraging reusable form parts, a base form class to house common functionality, and an attribute directive to encapsulate field-level error behavior and messages.

We created dynamic form elements with a date picker, typeahead support, and form arrays. We implemented interactive controls with input masking and the lemon rater. Using the `ControlValueAccessor` interface, we integrated the lemon rater seamlessly with our form. We showed that we can scale the size and complexity of our forms linearly by extracting the name as its own form section. Additionally, we covered building layouts using grid list.

In the next chapter, we will further enhance our components so that we can orchestrate them using the router. We will also implement a master/detail view and a data table, and explore NgRx as an alternative to using RxJS/BehaviorSubject.

Further reading

- *Reactive forms*, 2020, available at `https://angular.io/guide/reactive-forms`
- *Attribute directives*, 2020, available at `https://angular.io/guide/attribute-directives`
- *rxweb: Good way to show the error messages in Angular Reactive Forms*, Ajay Ojha, 2019, available at `https://medium.com/@oojhaajay/rxweb-good-way-to-show-the-error-messages-in-angular-reactive-forms-c27429f51278`
- *The Control Value Accessor*, Jennifer Wadella, 2019, available at `https://www.youtube.com/watch?v=kVbLSN0AW-Y`
- *CSS Combinators*, 2020, available at `https://developer.mozilla.org/en-US/docs/Web/CSS/CSS_Selectors#Combinators`

Questions

Answer the following questions as best as you can to ensure that you've understood the key concepts from this chapter without Googling. Do you need help answering the questions? See *Appendix D, Self-Assessment Answers* online at `https://static.packt-cdn.com/downloads/9781838648800_Appendix_D_Self-Assessment_Answers.pdf` or visit `https://expertlysimple.io/angular-self-assessment`.

1. What is the difference between a component and a user control?
2. What is an attribute directive?
3. What is the purpose of the `ControlValueAccessor` interface?
4. What are serialization, deserialization, and hydration?
5. What does it mean to patch values on a form?
6. How do you associate two independent `FormGroup` objects with each other?

12
Recipes – Master/Detail, Data Tables, and NgRx

In this chapter, we complete the router-first architecture implementation on LemonMart by implementing the top two most used features in business applications: master/detail views and data tables. I demonstrate data tables with server-side pagination, highlighting the integration between the frontend and backend using LemonMart and LemonMart Server.

> Make sure to have your **lemon-mart-server** up and running as you implement the recipes outlined in this chapter. Refer to *Chapter 10, RESTful APIs and Full-Stack Implementation*, for more information.

We leverage the concept of router orchestration to orchestrate how our components load data or render. We use resolve guards to reduce boilerplate code when loading data before navigating to a component. We use auxiliary routes to lay out components through the router configuration. We reuse the same component in multiple contexts.

We then dive into NgRx using the LocalCast Weather app and explore NgRx Data with LemonMart, so you can become familiar with more advanced application architecture concepts in Angular. By the end of this chapter, we will have touched upon most of the major functionality that Angular and Angular Material have to offer.

This chapter covers a lot of ground. It is organized in a recipe format, so you can quickly refer to a particular implementation when you are working on your projects. I cover the architecture, design, and major components of the implementation. I highlight important pieces of code to explain how the solution comes together. Leveraging what you've learned so far, I expect the reader to fill in routine implementation and configuration details. However, you can always refer to the GitHub repo if you get stuck.

In this chapter, you will learn about the following topics:

- Loading data with resolve guards
- Reusable components with route data
- Master/detail views using auxiliary routes
- Data tables with pagination
- NgRx Store and Effects
- NgRx Data Library

The most up-to-date versions of the sample code for the book are on GitHub at the repository linked in the following list. The repository contains the final and completed state of the code. You can verify your progress at the end of this chapter by looking for the end-of-chapter snapshot of code under the `projects` folder.

To get set up for this chapter's examples based on **lemon-mart**, do the following:

1. Clone the repo at `https://github.com/duluca/lemon-mart`
2. Execute `npm install` on the root folder to install dependencies
3. The code sample for this chapter is under the following subfolder: `projects/ch12`
4. To run the Angular app for this chapter, execute the following command:
   `npx ng serve ch12`
5. To run Angular unit tests for this chapter, execute the following command:
   `npx ng test ch12 --watch=false`
6. To run Angular e2e tests for this chapter, execute the following command:
   `npx ng e2e ch12`
7. To build a production-ready Angular app for this chapter, execute the following command:
   `npx ng build ch12 --prod`

> Note that the `dist/ch12` folder at the root of the repository will contain the compiled result.

To prepare for this chapter's examples based on **local-weather-app**, implement these steps:

1. Clone the repo at `https://github.com/duluca/local-weather-app`
2. Execute `npm install` on the root folder to install dependencies
3. The code sample for this chapter is under the following subfolder: **projects/ch12**
4. To run the Angular app for this chapter, execute the following command:
   `npx ng serve ch12`
5. To run Angular unit tests for this chapter, execute the following command:
   `npx ng test ch12 --watch=false`
6. To run Angular e2e tests for this chapter, execute the following command:
   `npx ng e2e ch12`
7. To build a production-ready Angular app for this chapter, execute the following command:
   `npx ng build ch12 --prod`

> Remember that the `dist/ch12` folder at the root of the repository will contain the compiled result.

> Beware that the source code in the book or on GitHub may not always match the code generated by Angular CLI. There may also be slight differences in implementation between the code in the book and what's on GitHub because the ecosystem is ever-evolving. It is natural for the sample code to change over time. Also on GitHub, expect to find corrections, fixes to support newer versions of libraries, or side-by-side implementations of multiple techniques for the reader to observe. The reader is only expected to implement the ideal solution recommended in the book. If you find errors or have questions, please create an issue or submit a pull request on GitHub for the benefit of all readers.

> You can read more about updating Angular in the *Appendix C, Keeping Angular and Tools Evergreen*. You can find this appendix online from `https://static.packt-cdn.com/downloads/9781838648800_Appendix_C_Keeping_Angular_and_Tools_Evergreen.pdf` or at `https://expertlysimple.io/stay-evergreen`.

In the next section, we will learn about resolve guards so that we can simplify our code and reduce the amount of boilerplate.

Editing existing users

In *Chapter 11, Recipes – Reusability, Routing, and Caching*, we created a `ViewUserComponent` with an `editUser` function. We need this functionality later in the chapter when implementing a master/detail view in the system, where a manager can see all users in the system and have the ability to edit them. Before we can enable the `editUser` functionality, we need to make sure that the `ViewUserComponent` component alongside the `ProfileComponent` can load any user given their ID.

Let's start by implementing a resolve guard we can use for both components.

Loading data with resolve guard

A resolve guard is a type of router guard, as mentioned in *Chapter 8, Designing Authentication and Authorization*. A resolve guard can load necessary data for a component by reading record IDs from `route` parameters, asynchronously load the data, and have it ready by the time the component activates and initializes.

The major advantages of a resolve guard include reusability of the loading logic, a reduction of boilerplate code, and the shedding of dependencies because the component can receive the data it needs without having to import any service:

1. Create a new `user.resolve.ts` class under `user/user`:

    ```
    src/app/user/user/user.resolve.ts
    import { Injectable } from '@angular/core'
    import { ActivatedRouteSnapshot, Resolve } from '@angular/router'
    import { catchError, map } from 'rxjs/operators'

    import { transformError } from '../../common/common'
    import { IUser, User } from './user'
    import { UserService } from './user.service'
    ```

```
@Injectable()
export class UserResolve implements Resolve<IUser> {
constructor(private userService: UserService) {}

  resolve(route: ActivatedRouteSnapshot) {
    return this.userService
      .getUser(route.paramMap.get('userId'))
      .pipe(map(User.Build), catchError(transformError))
  }
}
```

Note that similar to the updateUser method in UserService, we use map(User.Build) to hydrate the user object, so it is ready to be used when a component loads data from the route snapshot, as we'll see next.

2. Provide the resolver in user.module.ts.

   Next, let's configure the router and ProfileComponent to be able to load an existing user.

3. Modify user-routing.module.ts to add a new path, profile/:userId, with a route resolver and the canActivate AuthGuard:

   src/app/user/user-routing.module.ts
   ```
   ...
   {
       path: 'profile/:userId',
       component: ProfileComponent,
       resolve: {
         user: UserResolve,
       },
       canActivate: [AuthGuard],
   },
   ...
   ```

Remember to provide UserResolve and AuthGuard in user.module.ts.

4. Update the profile component to load the data from the route if it exists:

   src/app/user/profile/profile.component.ts
   ...

```
constructor(
  ...
  private route: ActivatedRoute
) {
  super()
}

ngOnInit() {
  this.formGroup = this.buildForm()

  if (this.route.snapshot.data.user) {
    this.patchUser(this.route.snapshot.data.user)
  } else {
    this.subs.sink = combineLatest(
      [this.loadFromCache(),
        this.authService.currentUser$]
    )
    .pipe(
      filter(
        ([cachedUser, me]) =>
          cachedUser != null || me != null
      ),
      tap(
        ([cachedUser, me]) =>
          this.patchUser(cachedUser || me)
      )
    )
    .subscribe()
  }
}
```

We first check to see whether a user is present in the route snapshot. If so, we call patchUser to load this user. Otherwise, we fall back to our conditional cache-loading logic.

Note that the patchUser method also sets the currentUserId and nameInitialDate$ observables, as well as calling the patchUpdateData base to update the form data.

You can verify that the resolver is working by navigating to the profile with your user ID. Using the out-of-the-box settings, this URL will look something like http://localhost:5000/user/profile/5da01751da27cc462d265913.

Reusing components with binding and route data

Now, let's refactor the `viewUser` component so that we can reuse it in multiple contexts. User information is displayed in two places in the app as per the mock-ups that were created.

The first place is the **Review** step of the user profile that we implemented in the previous chapter. The second place is on the user management screen on the `/manager/users` route, as follows:

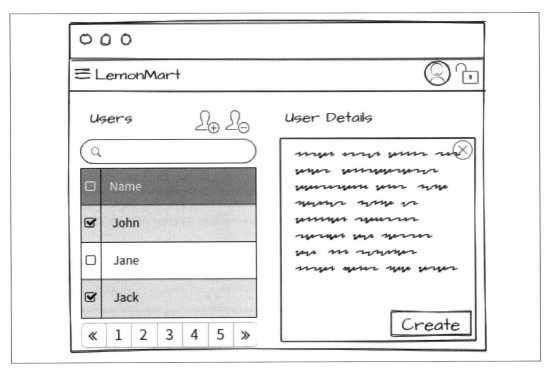

Figure 12.1: Manager user management mock-up

To maximize code reuse, we need to ensure that our shared `ViewUser` component can be used in both contexts.

For the **Review** step of the multi-step input form, we simply bind the current user to it. In the second use case, the component will need to load its own data using a resolve guard, so we don't need to implement additional logic to achieve our goal:

1. Update the `viewUser` component to inject the `ActivatedRoute` object and set `currentUser$` from the route in `ngOnInit()`:

   src/app/user/view-user/view-user.component.ts
   ```
   ...
   import { ActivatedRoute } from '@angular/router'

   export class ViewUserComponent implements OnChanges, OnInit {
     ...
     constructor(
       private route: ActivatedRoute, private router: Router
     ) {}

     ngOnInit() {
       if (this.route.snapshot.data.user) {
         this.currentUser$.next(this.route.snapshot.data.user)
       }
     }
     ...
   }
   ```

   `ngOnInit` will only fire once when the component is first initialized or has been routed to. In this case, if any data for the route has been resolved, then it'll be pushed to `this.currentUser$` with the `next()` function.

   We now have two independent events to update data; one for `ngOnChanges`, which handles updates to the `@Input` value and pushes to it to `BehaviorSubject` `currentUser$` if `this.user` has been bound to.

   To be able to use this component across multiple lazy loaded modules, we must wrap it in its own module:

2. Create a new `shared-components.module.ts` under `src/app`:

   src/app/shared-components.module.ts
   ```
   import { CommonModule } from '@angular/common'
   import { NgModule } from '@angular/core'
   import { FlexLayoutModule } from '@angular/flex-layout'
   import { ReactiveFormsModule } from '@angular/forms'

   import { AppMaterialModule } from './app-material.module'
   import {
     ViewUserComponent
   } from './user/view-user/view-user.component'
   ```

```
@NgModule({
  imports: [
    CommonModule,
    ReactiveFormsModule,
    FlexLayoutModule,
    AppMaterialModule,
  ],
  declarations: [ViewUserComponent],
  exports: [ViewUserComponent],
})
export class SharedComponentsModule {}
```

Ensure that you import the `SharedComponentsModule` module into each feature module you intended to use `ViewUserComponent` in. In our case, these will be `UserModule` and `ManagerModule`.

3. Remove `ViewUserComponent` from the `User` module declarations
4. Similarly declare and export `NameInputComponent` in `SharedComponentsModule`, and then clean up its other declarations
5. Import the modules necessary to support `ViewUserComponent` and `NameInputComponent` in `SharedComponentsModule` as well, such as `FieldErrorModule`

We now have the key pieces in place to begin implementation of the master/detail view. Let's go over this next.

Master/detail view auxiliary routes

The true power of router-first architecture comes to fruition with the use of auxiliary routes, where we can influence the layout of components solely through router configuration, allowing for rich scenarios where we can remix the existing components into different layouts. Auxiliary routes are routes that are independent of each other where they can render content in named outlets that have been defined in the markup, such as `<router-outlet name="master">` or `<router-outlet name="detail">`. Furthermore, auxiliary routes can have their own parameters, browser history, children, and nested auxiliaries.

In the following example, we will implement a basic master/detail view using auxiliary routes:

1. Implement a simple component with two named outlets defined:

   `src/app/manager/user-management/user-management.component.ts`
   ```
   template: `
     <div class="horizontal-padding">
   ```

```
            <router-outlet name="master"></router-outlet>
            <div style="min-height: 10px"></div>
            <router-outlet name="detail"></router-outlet>
        </div>
```

2. Add a new `userTable` component under manager
3. Update `manager-routing.module.ts` to define the auxiliary routes:

   src/app/manager/manager-routing.module.ts
   ```
   ...
     {
       path: 'users',
       component: UserManagementComponent,
       children: [
         {
           path: '', component: UserTableComponent,
            outlet: 'master'
         },
         {
           path: 'user',
           component: ViewUserComponent,
           outlet: 'detail',
           resolve: {
             user: UserResolve,
           },
         },
       ],
       canActivate: [AuthGuard],
       canActivateChild: [AuthGuard],

       data: {
         expectedRole: Role.Manager,
       },
     },
   ...
   ```

   This means that when a user navigates to `/manager/users`, they'll see the `UserTableComponent`, because it is implemented with the default path.

4. Provide `UserResolve` in `manager.module.ts` since `viewUser` depends on it
5. Implement a temporary button in `userTable`:

   src/app/manager/user-table/user-table.component.html
   ```
   <a mat-button mat-icon-button [routerLink]="['/manager/users',
       { outlets: { detail: ['user', { userId: row._id}] } }]"
   ```

```
      skipLocationChange>
  <mat-icon>visibility</mat-icon>
</a>
```

> The `skipLocationChange` directive navigates without pushing a new record into history. So if the user views multiple records and hits the **Back** button, they will be taken back to the previous screen, instead of having to scroll through the records they viewed first.

Imagine that a user clicks on a **View detail** button like the one defined previously – then, `ViewUserComponent` will be rendered for the user with the given `userId`. In the next screenshot, you can see what the **View Details** button will look like after we implement the data table in the next section:

Figure 12.2: View Details button

> You can have as many combinations and alternative components defined for the master and detail, allowing for the infinite possibilities of dynamic layouts. However, setting up the `routerLink` can be a frustrating experience. Depending on the exact condition, you have to either supply or not supply all or some outlets in the link. For example, for the preceding scenario, if the link was `['/manager/users', { outlets: { master: [''], detail: ['user', {userId: row.id}] } }]`, the route will silently fail to load. Expect these quirks to be ironed out in future Angular releases.

Now that we've completed the implementation of the resolve guard for `ViewUserComponent`, you can use Chrome DevTools to see the data being loaded correctly.

> Before debugging, ensure that the **lemon-mart-server** we created in *Chapter 10, RESTful APIs and Full-Stack Implementation*, is running.

6. In Chrome DevTools, set a break point right after `this.currentUser` is assigned, as shown:

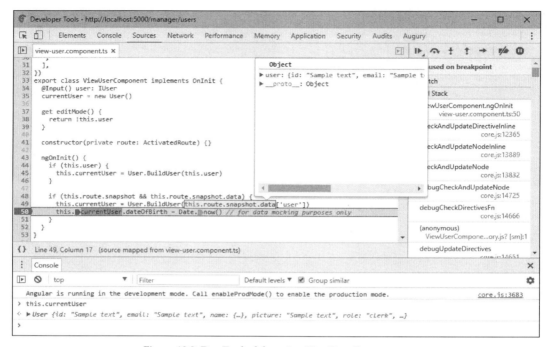

Figure 12.3: Dev Tools debugging ViewUserComponent

You will observe that `this.currentUser` is correctly set without any boilerplate code for loading data inside the `ngOnInit` function, showing the true benefit of a resolve guard. `ViewUserComponent` is the detail view; now let's implement the master view as a data table with pagination.

Data table with pagination

We have created the scaffolding to lay out our master/detail view. In the master outlet, we will have a paginated data table of users, so let's implement `UserTableComponent`, which will contain a `MatTableDataSource` property named `dataSource`. We will need to be able to fetch user data in bulk using standard pagination controls such as `pageSize` and `pagesToSkip` and be able to further narrow down the selection with user-provided `searchText`.

Let's start by adding the necessary functionality to the `UserService`:

1. Implement a new `IUsers` interface to describe the data structure of the paginated data:

   src/app/user/user/user.service.ts
   ```
   ...
   export interface IUsers {
     data: IUser[]
     total: number
   }
   ```

2. Update the interface for `UserService` with a `getUsers` function:

   src/app/user/user/user.service.ts
   ```
   ...
   export interface IUserService {
     getUser(id: string): Observable<IUser>
     updateUser(id: string, user: IUser): Observable<IUser>
     getUsers(pageSize: number, searchText: string,
       pagesToSkip: number): Observable<IUsers>
   }

   export class UserService extends CacheService implements
   IUserService {
   ...
   ```

3. Add `getUsers` to `UserService`:

   src/app/user/user/user.service.ts
   ```
   ...
   getUsers(
       pageSize: number,
       searchText = '',
       pagesToSkip = 0,
       sortColumn = '',
       sortDirection: '' | 'asc' | 'desc' = 'asc'
   ): Observable<IUsers> {
       const recordsToSkip = pageSize * pagesToSkip
       if (sortColumn) {
         sortColumn =
           sortDirection === 'desc' ? `-${sortColumn}` : sortColumn
       }
       return this.httpClient.get<IUsers>(
         `${environment.baseUrl}/v2/users`, {
           params: {
             filter: searchText,
   ```

```
        skip: recordsToSkip.toString(),
        limit: pageSize.toString(),
        sortKey: sortColumn,
      },
    })
  }
...
```

> Note that the sort direction is represented by the keywords asc for ascending and desc for descending. When we want to sort a column in ascending order, we pass the column name as a parameter to the server. To sort a column in descending order, we prepend the column name with a minus sign.

4. Set up `UserTable` with pagination, sorting, and filtering:

   src/app/manager/user-table/user-table.component.ts

```
...
@Component({
  selector: 'app-user-table',
  templateUrl: './user-table.component.html',
  styleUrls: ['./user-table.component.css'],
})
export class UserTableComponent implements OnDestroy,
AfterViewInit {
  displayedColumns = ['name', 'email', 'role', '_id']
  items$: Observable<IUser[]>
  resultsLength = 0
  hasError = false
  errorText = ''
  private skipLoading = false
  private subs = new SubSink()
  readonly isLoadingResults$ = new BehaviorSubject(true)
  loading$: Observable<boolean>
  refresh$ = new Subject()

  search = new FormControl('', OptionalTextValidation)

  @ViewChild(MatPaginator, { static: false })
    paginator: MatPaginator
  @ViewChild(MatSort, { static: false }) sort: MatSort
  constructor(
    private userService: UserService
  ) {
    this.loading$ = this.isLoadingResults$
  }
```

```
  getUsers(
    pageSize: number,
    searchText: string,
    pagesToSkip: number,
    sortColumn: string,
    sortDirection: SortDirection
  ): Observable<IUsers> {
    return this.userService.getUsers(
      pageSize,
      searchText,
      pagesToSkip,
      sortColumn,
      sortDirection
    )
  }

  ngOnDestroy(): void {
    this.subs.unsubscribe()
  }

  ngAfterViewInit() {
    this.subs.sink = this.sort.sortChange
      .subscribe(() => this.paginator.firstPage())

    if (this.skipLoading) {
      return
    }

    this.items$ = merge(
      this.refresh$,
      this.sort.sortChange,
      this.paginator.page,
      this.search.valueChanges.pipe(debounceTime(1000))
    ).pipe(
      startWith({}),
      switchMap(() => {
        this.isLoadingResults$.next(true)
        return this.getUsers(
          this.paginator.pageSize,
          this.search.value,
          this.paginator.pageIndex,
          this.sort.active,
          this.sort.direction
        )
      }),
```

```
      map((results: { total: number; data: IUser[] }) => {
        this.isLoadingResults$.next(false)
        this.hasError = false
        this.resultsLength = results.total

        return results.data
      }),
      catchError((err) => {
        this.isLoadingResults$.next(false)
        this.hasError = true
        this.errorText = err
        return of([])
      })
    )
    this.items$.subscribe()
  }
}
```

We define and initialize various properties to support loading paginated data. `items$` stores the user records, `displayedColumns` defines the columns of data we intend to display, `paginator` and `sort` provide pagination and sorting preferences, and `search` provides the text we need to filter our results by.

In `ngAfterViewInit`, we use the `merge` method, as highlighted in the preceding snippet, to listen for changes in pagination, sorting, and filter properties. If one property changes, the whole pipeline is triggered. This is similar to how we implemented the login routine in `AuthService`. The pipeline contains a call to `this.userService.getUsers`, which will retrieve users based on the pagination, sorting, and filter preferences passed in. Results are then piped into the `this.items$` observable, which the data table subscribes to with an `async` pipe, so it can display the data.

5. Create a `ManagerMaterialModule` containing the following Material modules:

   `src/app/manager/manager-material.module.ts`

   ```
   MatTableModule,
   MatSortModule,
   MatPaginatorModule,
   MatProgressSpinnerModule,
   MatSlideToggleModule,
   ```

6. Ensure that `manager.module.ts` correctly imports the following:
   - The new `ManageMaterialModule`
   - The baseline `AppMaterialModule`
   - The following required modules: `FormsModule`, `ReactiveFormsModule`, and `FlexLayoutModule`

7. Implement the CSS for `userTable`:

   src/app/manager/user-table/user-table.component.css
   ```css
   .loading-shade {
     position: absolute;
     top: 0;
     left: 0;
     bottom: 56px;
     right: 0;
     background: rgba(0, 0, 0, 0.15);
     z-index: 1;
     display: flex;
     align-items: center;
     justify-content: center;
   }

   .filter-row {
     min-height: 64px;
     padding: 8px 24px 0;
   }

   .full-width {
     width: 100%;
   }

   .mat-paginator {
     background: transparent;
   }
   ```

8. Finally, implement the `userTable` template:

   src/app/manager/user-table/user-table.component.html
   ```html
   <div class="filter-row">
     <form style="margin-bottom: 32px">
       <div fxLayout="row">
         <mat-form-field class="full-width">
           <mat-icon matPrefix>search</mat-icon>
           <input matInput placeholder="Search" aria-label="Search" [formControl]="search" />
   ```

```html
            <mat-hint>Search by e-mail or name</mat-hint>
            <mat-error *ngIf="search.invalid">
              Type more than one character to search
            </mat-error>
          </mat-form-field>
        </div>
      </form>
    </div>
    <div class="mat-elevation-z8">
      <div class="loading-shade" *ngIf="loading$ | async as loading">
        <mat-spinner *ngIf="loading"></mat-spinner>
        <div class="error" *ngIf="hasError">
          {{ errorText }}
        </div>
      </div>
      <table mat-table class="full-width" [dataSource]="items$ | async" matSort
        matSortActive="name" matSortDirection="asc" matSortDisableClear>
        <ng-container matColumnDef="name">
          <th mat-header-cell *matHeaderCellDef mat-sort-header> Name </th>
          <td mat-cell *matCellDef="let row">
            {{ row.fullName }}
          </td>
        </ng-container>
        <ng-container matColumnDef="email">
          <th mat-header-cell *matHeaderCellDef mat-sort-header> E-mail </th>
          <td mat-cell *matCellDef="let row"> {{ row.email }} </td>
        </ng-container>
        <ng-container matColumnDef="role">
          <th mat-header-cell *matHeaderCellDef mat-sort-header> Role </th>
          <td mat-cell *matCellDef="let row"> {{ row.role }} </td>
        </ng-container>
        <ng-container matColumnDef="_id">
          <th mat-header-cell *matHeaderCellDef>View Details
          </th>
          <td mat-cell *matCellDef="let row" style="margin-right: 8px">
            <a mat-button mat-icon-button [routerLink]="[
              '/manager/users',
              { outlets: { detail: ['user', { userId: row._id }] } }
            ]" skipLocationChange>
              <mat-icon>visibility</mat-icon>
            </a>
```

```
        </td>
      </ng-container>
      <tr mat-header-row *matHeaderRowDef="displayedColumns"></tr>
      <tr mat-row *matRowDef="let row; columns: displayedColumns">
</tr>
    </table>

    <mat-toolbar>
      <mat-toolbar-row>
        <button mat-icon-button (click)="refresh$.next()">
          <mat-icon title="Refresh">refresh</mat-icon>
        </button>
        <span class="flex-spacer"></span>
        <mat-paginator [pageSizeOptions]="[5, 10, 25, 100]"
                       [length]="resultsLength">
        </mat-paginator>
      </mat-toolbar-row>
    </mat-toolbar>
</div>
```

With just the master view in place, the table is as shown in the following screenshot (make sure you've updated to the latest version of Angular!):

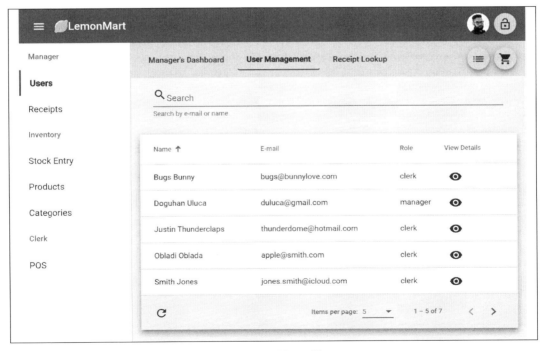

Figure 12.4: User table

Recipes – Master/Detail, Data Tables, and NgRx

If you click on the **View** icon, `ViewUserComponent` will get rendered in the detail outlet, as shown:

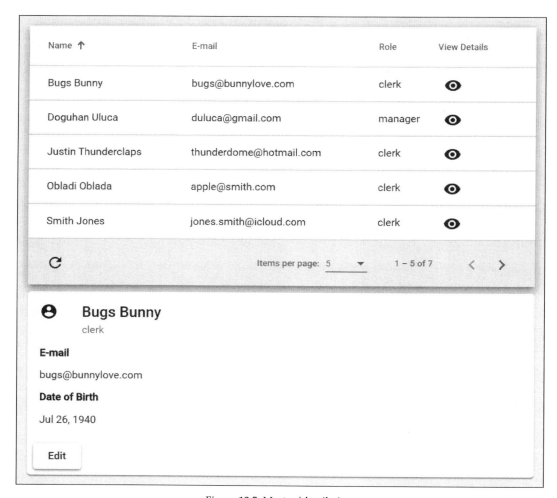

Figure 12.5: Master/detail view

In the previous chapter, we implemented the **Edit** button, passing the `userId` to the `UserProfile` so that the data can be edited and updated.

9. Click on the **Edit** button to be taken to the `ProfileComponent`, edit the user record, and verify that you can update another user's record
10. Confirm that you can view the updated user record in the data table

This demonstration of data tables with pagination completes the major functionality of LemonMart for the purpose of this book. Now, before we move on, let's make sure that all of our tests pass.

Updating unit tests

Let's go over some unit tests for `ProfileComponent` and `UserTableComponent` to see how we can leverage different techniques to test the components:

1. Observe the unit test file for `ProfileComponent` and identify the use of the `authServiceMock` object to provide initial data for the component:

    src/app/user/profile/profile.component.spec.ts
    ```
    describe('ProfileComponent', () => {
      let component: ProfileComponent
      let fixture: ComponentFixture<ProfileComponent>
      let authServiceMock: jasmine.SpyObj<AuthService>

      beforeEach(async(() => {
        const authServiceSpy = autoSpyObj(
          AuthService,
          ['currentUser$', 'authStatus$'],
          ObservablePropertyStrategy.BehaviorSubject
        )

        TestBed.configureTestingModule({
          providers: commonTestingProviders.concat({
            provide: AuthService,
            useValue: authServiceSpy,
          }),
          imports: commonTestingModules.concat([
            UserMaterialModule,
            FieldErrorModule,
            LemonRaterModule,
          ]),
          declarations: [ProfileComponent, NameInputComponent, ViewUserComponent],
        }).compileComponents()

        authServiceMock = injectSpy(AuthService)

        fixture = TestBed.createComponent(ProfileComponent)
        component = fixture.debugElement.componentInstance
      }))

      it('should create', () => {
        authServiceMock.currentUser$.next(new User())
        authServiceMock.authStatus$.next(defaultAuthStatus)
    ```

```
      fixture.detectChanges()
      expect(component).toBeTruthy()
    })
  })
```

 Note that instead of using the `createComponentMock` function from `angular-unit-test-helper` to import `NameInputComponent` or `ViewUserComponent`, I import their actual implementations. This is because `createComponentMock` is not yet sophisticated enough to deal with binding data to child components. In the *Further reading* section, I've included a blog post by Aiko Klostermann that covers testing Angular components with `@Input()` properties.

2. Open the spec file for `UserTableComponent`:

   After fixing up its providers and imports, you will notice that `UserTableComponent` is throwing an `ExpressionChangedAfterItHasBeenCheckedError` error. This is because the component initialization logic requires `dataSource` to be defined. If undefined, the component can't be created. However, we can easily modify component properties in the second `beforeEach` method, which executes after `TestBed` has injected real, mocked, or fake dependencies into the component class. See the highlighted changes in the following snippet for the test data setup:

   src/app/manager/user-table/user-table.component.spec.ts

```
...
beforeEach(() => {
    fixture = TestBed.createComponent(UserTableComponent)
    component = fixture.componentInstance
    component.items$ = of([new User()])
    Object.assign(component, { skipLoading: true })
    fixture.detectChanges()
})
...
```

By now, you may have noticed that just by updating some of our central configuration files, such as `commonTestingProviders` and `commonTestingModules`, some tests are passing, and the rest of the tests can be resolved by applying the various patterns we have been using throughout the book. For example, `user-management.component.spec.ts` uses the common testing modules and providers we have created:

```
src/app/manager/user-management/user-management.component.spec.ts
providers: commonTestingProviders,
imports: commonTestingModules.concat([ManagerMaterialModule]),
```

When you are mocking providers, keep in mind what module, component, service, or class is under test and take care only to mock dependencies.

> `ViewUserComponent` is a special case where we can't use our common testing modules and providers, otherwise, we would end up creating a circular dependency. In this case, manually specify the modules that need to be imported.

3. Fix the unit test configurations so all of them are passing and no warnings are generated.

With the heavy lifting of the implementation completed, we can now explore alternative architectures, tools, and libraries to better understand the best ways to architect Angular apps for various needs. Next, let's explore NgRx.

NgRx Store and Effects

As covered in *Chapter 1, Introduction to Angular and Its Concepts*, the NgRx library brings reactive state management to Angular based on RxJS. State management with NgRx allows developers to write atomic, self-contained, and composable pieces of code, creating actions, reducers, and selectors. This kind of reactive programming allows side effects in state changes to be isolated. In essence, NgRx is an abstraction layer over RxJS to fit the Flux pattern.

There are four major elements of NgRx:

- **Store**: The central location where state information is persisted. You implement a reducer to store a state transition in the store and a selector to read data out of the store. These are atomic and composable pieces of code.

> A view (or user interface) displays data from the store by using a selector.

- **Action**: Unique events that happen throughout your app.

Actions are triggered from a view with the purpose of dispatching them to the store.

- **Dispatcher**: This is a method to send actions to the store.

Reducers on the store listen for dispatched actions.

- **Effect**: This is a combination of an action and a dispatcher. Effects are usually used for actions that are not triggered from a view.

Let's revisit the following Flux pattern diagram, which now highlights an **Effect**:

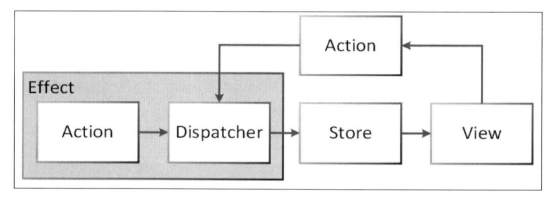

Figure 12.6: Flux pattern diagram

Let's demonstrate how NgRx works by going over a concrete example. In order to keep it simple, we will be leveraging the LocalCast Weather app.

Implementing NgRx for LocalCast Weather

We will be implementing NgRx to execute the search functionality in the LocalCast Weather app. Consider the following architecture diagram:

Chapter 12

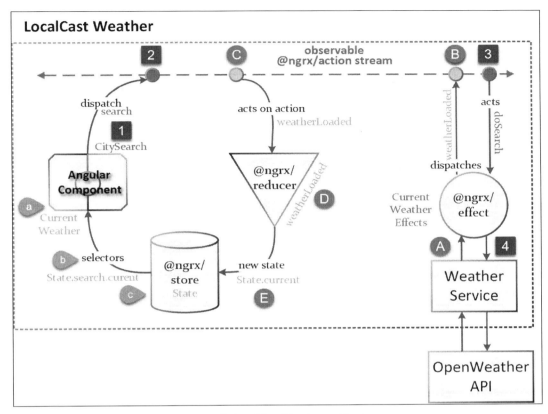

Figure 12.7: LocalCast Weather architecture

In order to achieve our implementation, we will use both the NgRx store and effects libraries. NgRx store actions are reflected in the diagram in light gray with a WeatherLoaded reducer and the app state. At the top, actions are represented as a stream of various data objects either dispatching actions or acting on dispatched actions, enabling us to implement the Flux pattern. The NgRx effects library extends the Flux pattern by isolating side effects in its own model without littering the store with temporary data.

The effects workflow, represented in dark gray, begins with **Step 1**:

1. CitySearchComponent dispatches the search action
2. The search action appears on the observable @ngrx/action stream (or data stream)
3. CurrentWeatherEffects acts on the search action to perform a search
4. WeatherService performs the search to retrieve current weather information from the **OpenWeather API**

Store actions, represented in light gray, begin with **Step A**:

A. `CurrentWeatherEffects` dispatches the `weatherLoaded` action
B. The `weatherLoaded` action appears on the data stream
C. The `weatherLoaded` reducer acts on the `weatherLoaded` action
D. The `weatherLoaded` reducer transforms the weather information to be stored as a new state
E. The new state is a persisted `search` state, part of the `appStore` state

> Note that there's a parent-level `appStore` state, which contains a child `search` state. I intentionally retained this setup to demonstrate how the parent-level state scales as you add different kinds of data elements to the store.

Finally, a view reads from the store, beginning with **step a**:

a. The `CurrentWeather` component subscribes to the `selectCurrentWeather` selector using the `async` pipe
b. The `selectCurrentWeather` selector listens for changes to the `store.search.current` property in the `appStore` state
c. The `appStore` state retrieves the persisted data

Using NgRx, when a user searches for a city, the actions to retrieve, persist, and display that information on the `CurrentWeatherComponent` happens automatically via individual composable and immutable elements.

Comparing BehaviorSubject and NgRx

We will be implementing NgRx side by side with `BehaviorSubjects`, so you can see the differences in the implementation of the same feature. To do this, we will need a slide toggle to switch between the two strategies:

> This section uses the **local-weather-app** repo. You can find the code samples for this chapter under the `projects/ch12` folder.

1. Start by implementing a `<mat-slide-toggle>` element on `CitySearchComponent`, as shown in the following screenshot:

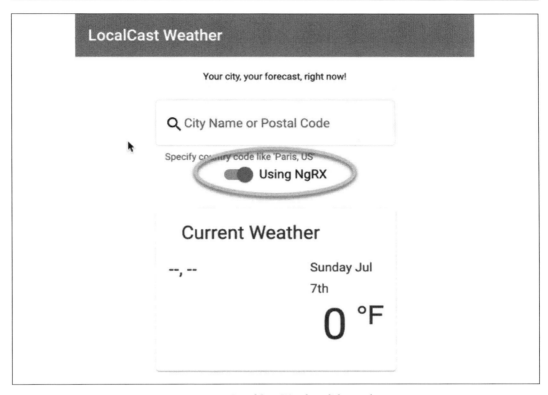

Figure 12.8: LocalCast Weather slide toggle

Ensure that the field is backed by a property on your component named useNgRx.

2. Refactor the doSearch method to extract the BehaviorSubject code as its own function named behaviorSubjectBasedSearch

3. Stub out a function called ngRxBasedSearch:

src/app/city-search/city-search.component.ts

```
doSearch(searchValue: string) {
  const userInput = searchValue.split(',').map((s) => s.trim())
  const searchText = userInput[0]
  const country = userInput.length > 1 ? userInput[1] : undefined

  if (this.useNgRx) {
    this.ngRxBasedSearch(searchText, country)
  } else {
    this.behaviorSubjectBasedSearch(searchText, country)
  }
}
```

We will be dispatching an action from the `ngRxBasedSearch` function that you just created.

Setting up NgRx

You may add the NgRx Store package with the following command:

`$ npx ng add @ngrx/store`

This will create a reducers folder with an `index.ts` file in it. Now add the NgRx effects package:

`$ npx ng add @ngrx/effects --minimal`

> We use the `--minimal` option here to avoid creating unnecessary boilerplate.

Next, install the NgRx schematics library so you can take advantage of generators to create the boilerplate code for you:

`$ npm i -D @ngrx/schematics`

Implementing NgRx can be confusing due to its highly decoupled nature, which may necessitate some insight into the inner workings of the library.

> The sample project under `projects/ch12` configures `@ngrx/store-devtools` for debugging.

If you would like to be able to `console.log` NgRx actions for debugging or instrumentation during runtime, refer to the *Appendix A, Debugging Angular*.

Defining NgRx actions

Before we can implement effects or reducers, we first need to define the actions our app is going to be able to execute. For LocalCast Weather, there are two types of actions:

- `search`: Fetches the current weather for the city or zip code that's being searched

- **weatherLoaded**: Indicates that new current weather information has been fetched

Create an action named `search` by running the following command:

```
$ npx ng generate @ngrx/schematics:action search --group --creators
```

Take the default options when prompted.

The `--group` option groups actions under a folder named `action`. The `--creators` option uses creator functions to implement actions and reducers, which is a more familiar and straightforward way to implement these components.

Now, let's implement the two actions using the `createAction` function, providing a name and an expected list of input parameters:

src/app/action/search.actions.ts

```
import { createAction, props, union } from '@ngrx/store'
import { ICurrentWeather } from '../interfaces'
export const SearchActions = {
  search: createAction(
    '[Search] Search',
    props<{ searchText: string; country?: string }>()
  ),
  weatherLoaded: createAction(
    '[Search] CurrentWeather loaded',
    props<{ current: ICurrentWeather }>()
  ),
}

const all = union(SearchActions)
export type SearchActions = typeof all
```

The search action has the name `'[Search] Search'` and has `searchText` and an optional `country` parameter as inputs. The `weatherLoaded` action follows a similar pattern. At the end of the file, we create a union type of our actions, so we can group them under one parent type to use in the rest of the application.

Notice that action names are prepended by `[Search]`. This is a convention that helps developers visually group related actions together during debugging.

Now that our actions are defined, we can implement the effect to handle the search action and dispatch a `weatherLoaded` action.

Implementing NgRx Effects

As mentioned earlier, effects let us change the stored state without necessarily storing the event data that is causing the change. For example, we want our state to only have weather data, not the search text itself. Effects allow us to do this in one step, rather than forcing us to use an intermediate store for the `searchText` and a far more complicated chain of events to just turn that into weather data.

Otherwise, we would have to implement a reducer in between, to first store this value in the store, and then later retrieve it from a service and dispatch a `weatherLoaded` action. The effect will make it simpler to retrieve data from our service.

Now let's add `CurrentWeatherEffects` to our app:

```
$ npx ng generate @ngrx/schematics:effect currentWeather --module=app.module.ts --root --group --creators
```

Take the default options when prompted.

You will have a new `current-weather.effects.ts` file under the `effects` folder.

Once again, `--group` is used to group effects under a folder of the same name. `--root` registers the effect in `app.module.ts` and we use creator functions with the `--creators` option.

In the `CurrentWeatherEffects` file, start by implementing a private `doSearch` method:

`src/app/effects/current-weather.effects.ts`

Chapter 12

```
private doSearch(action: { searchText: string; country?: string }) {
  return this.weatherService.getCurrentWeather(
    action.searchText,
    action.country
  ).pipe(
    map((weather) =>
      SearchActions.weatherLoaded({ current: weather })
    ),
    catchError(() => EMPTY)
  )
}
```

Note that we're choosing to ignore errors thrown with the
EMPTY function. You can surface these errors to the user with a
UiService like the one you've implemented for LemonMart.

This function takes an action with search parameters, calls `getCurrentWeather`, and upon receiving a response, dispatches the `weatherLoaded` action, passing in the current weather property.

Now let's create the effect itself, so we can trigger the `doSearch` function:

src/app/effects/current-weather.effects.ts

```
getCurrentWeather$ = createEffect(() =>
  this.actions$.pipe(
    ofType(SearchActions.search),
    exhaustMap((action) => this.doSearch(action))
  )
)
```

This is where we tap into the observable action stream, `this.actions$`, and listen to actions of the `SearchAction.search` type. We then use the `exhaustMap` operator to register for the emitted event. Due to its unique nature, `exhaustMap` won't allow another search action to be processed until the `doSearch` function completes dispatching its `weatherLoaded` action.

Confused by all the different kinds of RxJS operators and worried
you'll never remember them? See the *Appendix B, Angular Cheat
Sheet*, for a quick reference.

[651]

Implementing reducers

With the `weatherLoaded` action triggered, we need a way to ingest the current weather information and store it in our `appStore` state. Reducers will help us handle specific actions, creating an isolated and immutable pipeline to store our data in a predictable way.

Let's create a search reducer:

```
$ npx ng generate @ngrx/schematics:reducer search
    --reducers=reducers/index.ts --group --creators
```

 Take the default options. Here, we use `--group` to keep files organized under the `reducers` folder and `--creators` to leverage the creator style of creating NgRx components. We also specify the location of our parent `appStore` state at `reducers/index.ts` with `--reducers`, so our new reducer can be registered with it.

You may observe that `reducers.index.ts` has been updated to register the new `search.reducer.ts`. Let's implement it step by step.

In the `search` state, we will be storing the current weather, so implement the interface to reflect this:

src/app/reducers/search.reducer.ts

```
export interface State {
  current: ICurrentWeather
}
```

Now let's specify the `initialState`. This is similar to how we need to define a default value of a `BehaviorSubject`. Refactor the `WeatherService` to export a `const defaultWeather: ICurrentWeather` object that you can use to initialize `BehaviorSubject` and `initialState`.

src/app/reducers/search.reducer.ts

```
export const initialState:
  State = { current:
  defaultWeather,
}
```

Finally, implement `searchReducer` to handle the `weatherLoaded` action using the `on` operator:

src/app/reducers/search.reducer.ts

```
const searchReducer = createReducer(
  initialState,
  on(SearchActions.weatherLoaded, (state, action) => {
    return {
      ...state,
      current: action.current,
    }
  })
)
```

We simply register for the `weatherLoaded` action and unwrap the data stored in it and pass it into the `search` state.

This is, of course, a very simplistic case. However, it is easy to imagine a more complicated scenario, where we may need to flatten or process a piece of data received and store it in an easy-to-consume manner. Isolating such logic in an immutable way is the key value proposition of utilizing a library like NgRx.

Registering with Store using selector

We need `CurrentWeatherComponent` to register with the `appStore` state for updated current weather data.

Start by dependency injecting the `appStore` state and registering the selector to pluck current weather from the `State` object:

src/app/current-weather/current-weather.component.ts

```
import * as appStore from '../reducers'

export class CurrentWeatherComponent {
  current$: Observable<ICurrentWeather>

  constructor(private store: Store<appStore.State>) {
    this.current$ =
      this.store.pipe(select((state: State) => state.search.current))
  }
  ...
}
```

We simply listen to state change events that flow through the store. Using the `select` function, we can implement an inline select to get the piece of data we need.

We can refactor this a bit and make our selector reusable by using a `createSelector` to create a `selectCurrentWeather` property on `reducers/index.ts`:

src/app/reducers/index.ts

```
export const selectCurrentWeather = createSelector(
  (state: State) => state.search.current,
  current => current
)
```

In addition, since we want to maintain the continued operation of the `BehaviorSubject`, we can implement a `merge` operator in `CurrentWeatherComponent` to listen to both `WeatherService` updates and `appStore` state updates:

src/app/current-weather/current-weather.component.ts

```
import * as appStore from '../reducers'

constructor(
  private weatherService: WeatherService,
  private store: Store<appStore.State>
) {
  this.current$ = merge(
    this.store.pipe(select(appStore.selectCurrentWeather)),
    this.weatherService.currentWeather$
  )
}
```

Now that we are able to listen to store updates, let's implement the final piece of the puzzle: dispatching the search action.

Dispatching store actions

We need to dispatch the search action so that our search effect can fetch current weather data and update the store. Earlier in this chapter, you implemented a stubbed function called `ngRxBasedSearch` in the `CitySearchComponent`.

Let's implement `ngRxBasedSearch`:

src/app/city-search/city-search.component.ts

```
ngRxBasedSearch(searchText: string, country?: string) {
  this.store.dispatch(SearchActions.search({ searchText, country }))
}
```

Don't forget to inject the `appState` store into the component!

And that's it! Now you should be able to run your code and test to see whether it all works.

As you can see, NgRx brings a lot of sophisticated techniques to the table to create ways to make data transformations immutable, well defined, and predictable. However, this comes with considerable implementation overhead. Use your best judgment to determine whether you really need the Flux pattern in your Angular app. Often, the frontend application code can be made much simpler by implementing RESTful APIs that return flat data objects, with complicated data manipulations handled server side.

Unit testing reducers and selectors

You can implement unit tests for the `weatherLoaded` reducer and the `selectCurrentWeather` selector in `search.reducer.spec.ts`:

src/app/reducers/search.reducer.spec.ts

```
import { SearchActions } from '../actions/search.actions'
import { defaultWeather } from '../weather/weather.service'
import { fakeWeather } from '../weather/weather.service.fake'
import { selectCurrentWeather } from './index'
import { initialState, reducer } from './search.reducer'

describe('Search Reducer', () => {
  describe('weatherLoaded', () => {
    it('should return current weather', () => {
      const action = SearchActions.weatherLoaded({ current: fakeWeather })
      const result = reducer(initialState, action)
      expect(result).toEqual({ current: fakeWeather })
    })
  })
})

describe('Search Selectors', () => {
  it('should selectCurrentWeather', () => {
    const expectedWeather = defaultWeather
```

```
      expect(selectCurrentWeather({ search: { current: defaultWeather }
})).toEqual(
        expectedWeather
      )
    })

  })
```

These unit tests are fairly straightforward and will ensure that no unintentional changes to the data structure can happen within the store.

Unit testing components with MockStore

You need to update the tests for `CurrentWeatherComponent` so that we can inject a mock `Store` into the component to test the value of the `current$` property.

Let's look at the delta of what needs to be added to the spec file to configure the mock store:

```
src/app/current-weather/current-weather.component.spec.ts
import { MockStore, provideMockStore } from '@ngrx/store/testing'
describe('CurrentWeatherComponent', () => {
  ...
  let store: MockStore<{ search: { current: ICurrentWeather } }>
  const initialState = { search: { current: defaultWeather } }

  beforeEach(async(() => {
    ...
    TestBed.configureTestingModule({
      imports: [AppMaterialModule],
      providers: [
        ...
        provideMockStore({ initialState }),
      ],
    }).compileComponents()

    ...
    store = TestBed.inject(Store) as any
  }))
  ...
})
```

We can now update the `'should get currentWeather from weatherService'` test to see whether `CurrentWeatherComponent` works with a mock store:

Chapter 12

src/app/current-weather/current-weather.component.spec.ts

```
it('should get currentWeather from weatherService', (done) => {
  // Arrange
  store.setState({ search: { current: fakeWeather } })
  weatherServiceMock.currentWeather$.next(fakeWeather)

  // Act
  fixture.detectChanges() // triggers ngOnInit()

  // Assert
  expect(component.current$).toBeDefined()

  component.current$.subscribe(current => {
    expect(current.city).toEqual('Bethesda')
    expect(current.temperature).toEqual(280.32)

    // Assert on DOM
    const debugEl = fixture.debugElement
    const titleEl: HTMLElement =
      debugEl.query(By.css('.mat-title')).nativeElement
    expect(titleEl.textContent).toContain('Bethesda')
    done()
  })
})
```

The mock store allows us to set the current state of the store, which in turn allows the selector call in the constructor to fire and grab the provided fake weather data.

TestBed is not a hard requirement for writing unit tests in Angular, a topic covered well at https://angular.io/guide/testing. My colleague and reviewer of this book, Brendon Caulkins, contributed a bed-less spec file for this chapter, named current-weather.component.nobed.spec.ts. He cites significant performance increases when running the tests, with fewer imports and less maintenance, but a higher level of care and expertise required to implement the tests. If you're on a large project, you should seriously consider skipping the TestBed.

You can find the sample code on GitHub under the projects/ch12 folder.

Go ahead and update the remainder of your tests and do not move on until they all start passing.

[657]

NgRx Data

If NgRx is a configuration-based framework, NgRx Data is a convention-based sibling of NgRx. NgRx Data automates the creation of stores, effects, actions, reducers, dispatches, and selectors. If most of your application actions are **CRUD** (**Create**, **Retrieve**, **Update**, and **Delete**) operations, then NgRx Data can achieve the same result as NgRx with a lot less code needing to be written.

NgRx Data may be a much better introduction to the Flux pattern for you and your team. Then you can go on to NgRx itself.

@ngrx/data works in tandem with the @ngrx/entity library. Together they offer a rich feature set, including transactional data management. Read more about it at https://ngrx.io/guide/data.

For this example, we will be switching back over to the LemonMart project.

Add NgRx Data to your project by executing the following commands:

```
$ npx ng add @ngrx/store --minimal

$ npx ng add @ngrx/effects --minimal

$ npx ng add @ngrx/entity

$ npx ng add @ngrx/data
```

The sample project under projects/ch12 configures @ngrx/store-devtools for debugging.

If you would like to be able to console.log NgRx actions for debugging or instrumentation during runtime, refer to the *Appendix A, Debugging Angular*.

Implementing NgRx/Data in LemonMart

In LemonMart, we have a great use case for the @ngrx/data library with the User class and the UserService. It neatly represents an entity that could support CRUD operations. With a few modifications and the least amount of effort, you can see the library in action.

Chapter 12

 This section uses the **lemon-mart** repo. You can find the code samples for this chapter under the `projects/ch12` folder.

1. Let's start by defining the `User` entity in `entity-metadata.ts`:

   src/app/entity-metadata.ts
   ```
   import { EntityMetadataMap } from '@ngrx/data'
   const entityMetadata: EntityMetadataMap = {
     User: {},
   }

   export const entityConfig = {
     entityMetadata,
   }
   ```

2. Ensure that the `entityConfig` object is registered with `EntityDataModule`:

   src/app/app.module.ts

   ```
   imports: [
     ...
     StoreModule.forRoot({}),
     EffectsModule.forRoot([]),
     EntityDataModule.forRoot(entityConfig),
   ]
   ```

3. Create a `User` entity service:

   src/app/user/user/user.entity.service.ts

   ```
   import { Injectable } from '@angular/core'
   import {
     EntityCollectionServiceBase,
     EntityCollectionServiceElementsFactory,
   } from '@ngrx/data'
   import { User } from './user'
   @Injectable({ providedIn: 'root' })
   export class UserEntityService
     extends EntityCollectionServiceBase<User> {
     constructor(
       serviceElementsFactory: EntityCollectionServiceElementsFactory
     ) {
       super('User', serviceElementsFactory)
     }
   }
   ```

You now have all the basic elements in place to integrate the entity service with a component. In a sense, it is this easy to set up NgRx Data. However, we'll have to customize it somewhat to fit into our existing REST API structure, which will be covered in detail in the next section. If you were to follow the API implementation pattern that NgRx Data expects, then no changes would be necessary.

NgRx Data wants to access the REST API via the `/api` path, hosted on the same port as your Angular app. To accomplish this during development, we need to leverage Angular CLI's proxy feature.

Configuring proxy in Angular CLI

Normally, HTTP requests sent to our web server and our API server should have exactly the same URL. However, during development, we usually host both applications on two different ports of `http://localhost`. Certain libraries, including NgRx Data, require that HTTP calls be on the same port. This creates a challenge for creating a frictionless development experience. For this reason, Angular CLI ships with a proxy feature with which you can direct the `/api` path to a different endpoint on your localhost. This way, you can use one port to serve your web app and your API requests.

1. Create a `proxy.conf.json` file under `src`, as shown:

    If you're working in the **lemon-mart-server** monorepo, this will be `web-app/src`.

   proxy.conf.json
   ```
   {
     "/api": {
       "target": "http://localhost:3000",
       "secure": false,
       "pathRewrite": {
           "^/api": ""
       }
     }
   }
   ```

2. Register the proxy with `angular.json`:

   angular.json
   ```
   ...

   "serve": {
   ```

```
    "builder": "@angular-devkit/build-angular:dev-server",
    "options": {
      "browserTarget": "lemon-mart:build",
      "proxyConfig": "proxy.conf.json"
    },
    ...
}
```

Now the server that is started when you run `npm start` or `ng serve` can rewrite the URLs of any call made to the `/api` route with `http://localhost:3000`. This is the port that **lemon-mart-server** runs by default.

> If your API is running a different port, then use the correct port number and child route.

Next, let's use the `UserEntityService`.

Using Entity Service

We will be updating the User Management master view, so we can optionally use `BehaviorSubject` or the `UserEntityService` we just created.

1. Start by implementing a toggle switch in `user-table.component.ts`, similar to the way we did for LocalCast Weather and NgRx earlier in the chapter:

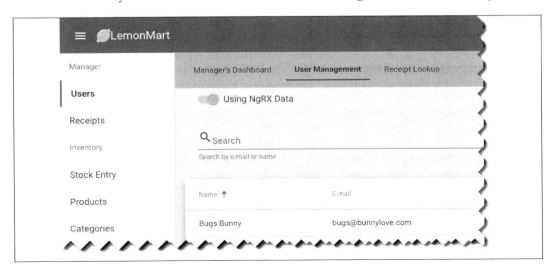

Figure 12.9: UserTableComponent with the NgRx slide toggle

2. Inject the new service into `UserTableComponent` and merge its loading observable with the one that's present on the component:

src/app/manager/user-table/user-table.component.ts

```
useNgRxData = true
readonly isLoadingResults$ = new BehaviorSubject(true) loading$:
Observable<boolean>
constructor(
  private userService: UserService,
  private userEntityService: UserEntityService
) {
  this.loading$ = merge(
    this.userEntityService.loading$,
    this.isLoadingResults$
  )
}
```

 Since `EntityDataModule` is registered in `app.module.ts` at the root of our application, we need to provide `UserService` in `app.module.ts` as well, so we can consume data from it in `UserEntityService`. Even though `UserEntityService` is provided in `UserModule`, the order of operations within NgRx Data doesn't lend itself to properly working with feature modules. This will probably be fixed at some point.

3. You can add CRUD methods to the component, as shown in the following code. However, we will be focused on just updating the `getUsers` function so there is no need to add the others:

src/app/manager/user-table/user-table.component.ts

```
getUsers() {
  return this.userEntityService.getAll().pipe(
    map((value) => {
      return { total: value.length, data: value }
    })
  )
}

add(user: User) {
  this.userEntityService.add(user)
}

delete(user: User) {
  this.userEntityService.delete(user._id)
}
```

```
  update(user: User) {
    this.userEntityService.update(user)
  }
```

4. In ngAfterViewInit, refactor the call to this.userService.getUsers so that it is called from a method named getUsers
5. Then implement a conditional call to this.userEntityService.getAll() and map out the return value so that it fits the IUsers interface:

src/app/manager/user-table/user-table.component.ts

```
...
  getUsers(pageSize: number, searchText = '', pagesToSkip = 0)
      : Observable<IUsers> {
    if (this.useNgRxData) {
      return this.userEntityService.getAll().pipe(
        map((value) => {
          return { total: value.length, data: value }
        })
      )
    } else {
      return this.userService.getUsers(
        pageSize,
        searchText,
        pagesToSkip,
        sortColumn,
        sortDirection
      )
    }
```

Now your component can attempt to get data from either source by toggling the slide toggle and entering some new search text. However, our endpoint does not provide the data in the shape that NgRx Data expects, so we need to customize the entity service to overcome this issue.

Customizing Entity Service

You can customize the behavior of NgRx Data in numerous places. We are interested in overriding the behavior of the getAll() function, so the data we're receiving is properly hydrated and the data can be extracted from the item's object.

 For this example, we will not attempt to restore the full pagination functionality using NgRx Data. To keep it simple, we focus on just getting an array of data into the data table.

Update User Entity Service to inject `UserService` and implement a `getAll` function that uses it:

`src/app/user/user/user.entity.service.ts`

```
...
getAll(options?: EntityActionOptions): Observable<User[]> {
  return this.userService
    .getUsers(10)
    .pipe(map((users) => users.data.map(User.Build)))
}
...
```

As you can see, we're iterating through the item's object and hydrating objects with our builder function, thus flattening and transforming `Observable<IUsers>` to `Observable<User[]>`.

After implementing this change, you should be able to see data flow into the user table as follows:

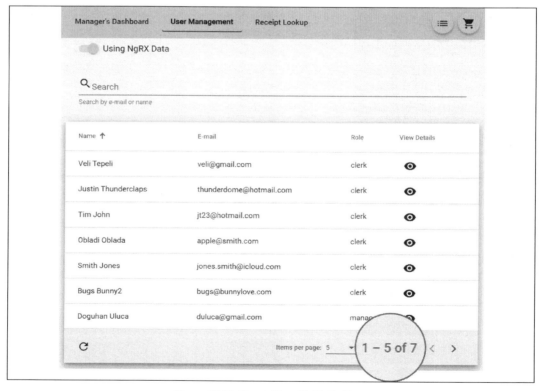

Figure 12.10: User table with NgRx Data

Note that all seven users are displayed at once, and as magnified in the preceding screenshot, the pagination functionality is not working. However, this implementation is adequate enough to demonstrate what NgRx Data brings to the table.

So, should you implement NgRx Data in your next app? It depends. Since the library is an abstraction layer on top of NgRx, you may find yourself lost and restricted if you don't have a good understanding of the internals of NgRx. However, the library holds a lot of promise for reducing boilerplate code regarding entity data management and CRUD operations. If you're doing lots of CRUD operations in your app, you may save time, but be careful to keep the scope of your implementation only to the areas that need it. Either way, you should keep an eye out for the evolution of this great library.

Summary

In this chapter, we completed going over all major Angular app design considerations using router-first architecture, along with our recipes, to implement a line-of-business app with ease. We went over how to edit existing users, leverage a resolve guard to load user data, and hydrate and reuse a component in different contexts.

We implemented a master/detail view using auxiliary routes and demonstrated how to build data tables with pagination. We then learned about NgRx and the `@ngrx/data` libraries and their impact on our code base using the **local-weather-app** and **lemon-mart** projects.

Overall, by using the router-first design, architecture, and implementation approach, we tackled our application's design with a good high-level understanding of what we wanted to achieve. By identifying code reuse opportunities early on, we were able to optimize our implementation strategy to implement reusable components ahead of time, without running the risk of grossly over-engineering our solution.

In the next chapter, we will set up a highly available infrastructure on AWS to host LemonMart. We will update the project with new scripts to enable no-downtime blue-green deployments. Finally, in the last chapter, we will update LemonMart with Google Analytics and go over advanced Cloud Ops concerns.

Further reading

- *Testing Angular Components With @Input()*, Aiko Klostermann, 2017, available at https://medium.com/better-programming/testing-angular-components-with-input-3bd6c07cfaf6
- *What is NgRx?*, 2020, available at https://ngrx.io/docs
- *NgRx Testing*, 2020, available at https://ngrx.io/guide/store/testing
- *@ngrx/data*, 2020, available at https://ngrx.io/guide/data
- *NgRx: Action Creators redesigned*, Alex Okrushko, 2019, available at https://medium.com/angular-in-depth/ngrx-action-creators-redesigned-d396960e46da
- *Simplifying Frontend State Management with Observable Store*, Dan Wahlin, 2019, available at https://blog.codewithdan.com/simplifying-front-end-state-management-with-observable-store/

Questions

Answer the following questions as best as you can to ensure that you've understood the key concepts from this chapter without Googling. Do you need help answering the questions? See *Appendix D, Self-Assessment Answers* online at https://static.packt-cdn.com/downloads/9781838648800_Appendix_D_Self-Assessment_Answers.pdf or visit https://expertlysimple.io/angular-self-assessment.

1. What is a resolve guard?
2. What are the benefits of router orchestration?
3. What is an auxiliary route?
4. How does NgRx differ from using RxJS/Subject?
5. What's the value of NgRx data?
6. In `UserTableComponent`, why do we use `readonly isLoadingResults$: BehaviorSubject<Boolean>` over a simple Boolean to drive the loading spinner?

13
Highly Available Cloud Infrastructure on AWS

The web is a hostile environment. There are good and bad actors. Bad actors can try to poke holes in your security or try to bring down your website with a **Distributed Denial-of-Service (DDoS)** attack. Good actors, if you're lucky, will love your website and won't stop using it. They'll shower you with recommendations to improve your site, but they may also run into bugs and may be so enthusiastic that your site may slow down to a crawl due to high traffic. Real-world deployments on the web require a lot of expertise to get them right. As a full-stack developer, you can only know about so many nuances of hardware, software, and networking. Luckily, with the advent of cloud service providers, a lot of this expertise has been translated into software configurations, with the difficult hardware and networking concerns taken care of by the provider.

One of the best features of a cloud service provider is cloud scalability, which refers to your server automatically scaling out to respond to high volumes of unexpected traffic and scaling down to save costs when the traffic returns back to normal levels. **Amazon Web Services (AWS)** goes beyond basic cloud scalability and introduces high-availability and fault-tolerant concepts, allowing resilient local and global deployments. I have chosen to introduce you to AWS because of its vast capabilities, which go way beyond what I will touch on in this book. With Route 53, you can get free DDoS protection; with API Gateway, you create API keys; with AWS Lambda, you can handle millions of transactions for only a few dollars a month; and with CloudFront, you can cache your content at secret edge locations that are scattered around major cities of the world. In addition, blue-green deployments allow you to achieve no-downtime deployments of your software.

Overall, the tools and techniques you will learn about in this chapter are adaptable to any cloud provider and are fast becoming critical knowledge for any full-stack developer. We will be going over the following topics:

- Creating and protecting AWS accounts
- Right-sizing infrastructure, including simple load testing to optimize instances
- Configuring and deploying to AWS
    - ECS Fargate scripted blue-green deployments
    - Billing

The most up-to-date versions of the sample code for the book are on GitHub at the following repository link. The repository contains the final and complete state of the code. Each section contains information boxes to help direct you to the correct filename or branch on GitHub that you can use to verify your progress.

> The sample code for *Chapter 13* removes all optional and alternate implementations from previous chapters and only enables auth with **lemon-mart-server**. This is so that readers can reference a clean implementation of the **lemon-mart** project.

For *Chapter 13* examples based on **lemon-mart**:

1. Clone the repo at `https://github.com/duluca/lemon-mart`.
2. Use `config.docker-integration.yml` to verify your `config.yml` implementation.
3. Execute `npm install` on the root folder to install dependencies.
4. To run the CircleCI Docker integration configuration, execute `git checkout deploy_aws`. Refer to the pull request at `https://github.com/duluca/lemon-mart/pull/27`.
5. The code sample for this chapter is under the sub-folder:
   `projects/ch13`
6. To run the Angular app for this chapter, execute:
   `npx ng serve ch13`

7. To run Angular unit tests for this chapter, execute:

   `npx ng test ch13 --watch=false`

8. To run Angular e2e tests for this chapter, execute:

   `npx ng e2e ch13`

9. To build a production-ready Angular app for this chapter, execute:

   `npx ng build ch13 --prod`

Note that the `dist/ch13` folder at the root of the repository will contain the compiled result.

Beware that the source code in the book or on GitHub may not always match the code generated by the Angular CLI. There may also be slight differences in implementation between the code in the book and what's on GitHub because the ecosystem is ever-evolving. It is natural for the sample code to change over time. Also on GitHub, expect to find corrections, fixes to support newer versions of libraries, or side-by-side implementations of multiple techniques for you to observe. You are only expected to implement the ideal solution recommended in the book. If you find errors or have questions, please create an issue or submit a pull request on GitHub for the benefit of all readers.

You can read more about updating Angular in *Appendix C, Keeping Angular and Tools Evergreen*. You can find this appendix online from `https://static.packt-cdn.com/downloads/9781838648800_Appendix_C_Keeping_Angular_and_Tools_Evergreen.pdf` or at `https://expertlysimple.io/stay-evergreen`.

AWS is an extremely popular service and AWS accounts are even more popular targets for hacking attempts. Let's begin by creating a secure AWS account.

Creating a secure AWS account

Account access and control is of paramount importance in any cloud service, and this includes AWS as well. After initial account creation, you will have your root credentials, which is your email and password combination.

Let's start by creating an AWS account:

1. Start by navigating to `https://console.aws.amazon.com`.
2. If you don't have one, create a new account.
3. If you are new to AWS, you can get 12 months of free tier access to various services, as shown on the sign-up screen here:

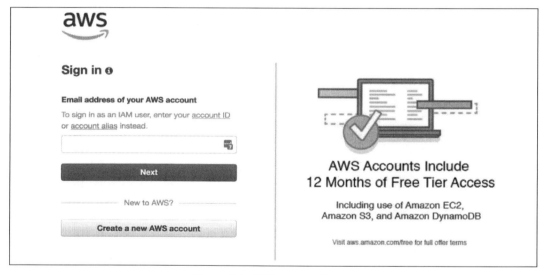

Figure 13.1: AWS account sign up

Your AWS billing is tied to your root credentials. If compromised, a lot of damage can be done on your account before you can regain access.

4. Ensure that you enable 2FA on your root credentials.

 To add another layer of security, going forward, you need to stop logging in to your AWS account using your root credentials. You can create user accounts using the AWS **Identity and Access Management (IAM)** module. If these accounts get compromised, unlike your root account, you can easily and quickly delete or replace them.

5. Navigate to the **IAM module**.
6. Create a new user account with global admin rights.
7. Log in to the AWS console using these credentials.
8. You should enable 2FA for these credentials as well.
9. A secure account setup looks as follows, with every status reported as green:

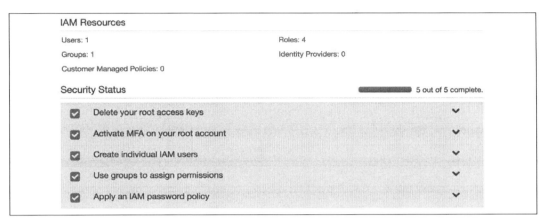

Figure 13.2: AWS IAM module after secure setup

The major benefit of working with user accounts is programmatic access. For each user account, you can create a public access ID and private access key pair. When you're working with third parties, such as hosted continuous integration services, your own application code, or CLI tools, you use your programmatic access keys to connect to your AWS resources. When, inevitably, the access keys leak, it is quick and convenient to disable access to the old keys and create new ones.

Furthermore, user account access can be tightly controlled by very granular permissions. You can also create roles with a group of permissions and further control communication between AWS services and some external services.

When creating user accounts and roles, always err on the side of minimal permissions. This can be an exercise in frustration when working with clients, contractors, or colleagues who are unfamiliar with AWS; however, it is a worthwhile exercise.

You're only as secure and reliable as your weakest link, so you must plan for failures and, most importantly, practice recovery plans on a regular basis.

Securing secrets

Password and private key leaks occur more commonly than you may think. Your keys may be compromised on unsecured public Wi-Fi networks; you may accidentally check them into your code repository or use superbly insecure communication methods like email.

Accidental code check-ins, however, are the biggest issue, since most junior developers don't realize that deletion isn't an option in source control systems.

As a developer, there are a few noteworthy best practices to follow to safeguard your secrets:

1. Always use a VPN service on public Wi-Fi, such as `tunnelbear.com`.
2. Leverage the `.aws/credentials` file located under your user's home folder, to create profiles and store access keys.
3. As a team norm, create an `.env` file in the root of your project that is in `.gitignore` to store any secrets that your CI server may later inject.
4. Always review commits before pushing them.
5. Consider signing up for a service that can monitor your repos for secrets, like GitGurdian at `https://gitguardian.com/`, which is free for open source projects.

Note that GitGuardian flags Firebase and OpenWeather API keys as leaks. This is a false positive, because the keys in question are public keys and must be published for your app to function correctly.

Following these conventions every single time will get you into the good habit of never checking in your secrets to a code repository. In the next section, we will delve into resource considerations for your cloud environment.

Right-sizing infrastructure

The point of optimizing your infrastructure is to protect your company's revenue while minimizing the cost of operating your infrastructure. Your goal should be to ensure that users don't encounter high latency, otherwise known as bad performance or, worse, unfulfilled or dropped requests, all the while making your venture a sustainable endeavor.

The three pillars of web application performance are as follows:

1. CPU utilization
2. Memory usage
3. Network bandwidth

I have intentionally left disk access out of the key consideration metrics, since only particular workloads executed on an application server or data store are affected by it. Disk access would rarely ever impact the performance of serving a web application as long as application assets are delivered by a **Content Delivery Network (CDN)**. That said, still keep an eye on any unexpected runaway disk access, such as the high-frequency creation of temp and log files. Docker, for example, can spit out logs that can easily fill up a drive.

In an ideal scenario, CPU, memory, and network bandwidth use should be utilized evenly at around 60-80% of available capacity. If you encounter performance issues due to various other factors, such as disk I/O, a slow third-party service, or inefficient code, most likely one of your metrics will peak at or near maximum capacity, while the other two are idling or severely underutilized. This is an opportunity to use more CPU, memory, or bandwidth to compensate for the performance issue and also evenly utilize available resources.

The reason behind targeting 60-80% utilization is to allow some time for a new instance (server or container) to be provisioned and ready to serve users. After your predefined threshold has been crossed, while a new instance is provisioned, you can continue serving an increasing number of users, thus minimizing unfulfilled requests.

Throughout this book, I have discouraged over-engineering or perfect solutions. In today's complicated IT landscape, it is nearly impossible to predict where you will encounter performance bottlenecks. Your engineering may, very easily, take $100,000+ worth of engineering hours, where the solution to your problem may be a few hundred dollars of new hardware, whether it be a network switch, solid state drive, CPU, or more memory.

If your CPU is too busy, you may want to introduce more bookkeeping logic to your code, via indexes, hash tables, or dictionaries that you can cache in memory to speed up subsequent or intermediary steps of your logic. For example, if you are constantly running array lookup operations to locate particular properties of a record, you can perform an operation on that record, saving the ID and/or the property of the record in a hash table that you keep in memory, reducing your runtime cost from $O(n)$ down to $O(1)$.

Following the preceding example, you may end up using too much memory with hash tables. In this case, you may want to more aggressively offload or transfer caches to slower but more plentiful data stores using your spare network bandwidth, such as a Redis instance.

If your network utilization is too high, you may want to investigate the use of CDNs with expiring links, client-side caching, throttling requests, and API access limits for customers abusing their quotas, or optimize your instances to have disproportionately more network capacity compared to their CPU or memory capacity.

Optimizing instances

In an earlier example, I demonstrated the use of my `duluca/minimal-node-web-server` Docker image to host our Angular apps. Even though Node.js is a very lightweight server, it is simply not optimized to just be a web server. In addition, Node.js has a single-threaded execution environment, making it a poor choice for serving static content to many concurrent users at once.

You can observe the resource that a Docker image is utilizing by executing `docker stats`:

```
$ docker stats
CONTAINER ID   CPU %   MEM USAGE / LIMIT   MEM %   NET I/O         BLOCK I/O   PIDS
27d431e289c9   0.00%   1.797MiB / 1.9GiB   0.09%   13.7kB / 285kB  0B / 0B     2
```

Here are comparative results of the system resources that Node and NGINX-based servers utilize at rest:

Server	Image Size	Memory Usage
`duluca/minimal-nginx-web-server`	16.8 MB	1.8 MB
`duluca/minimal-node-web-server`	71.8 MB	37.0 MB

However, at rest values only tell a portion of the story. To get a better understanding, we must perform a simple load test to see memory and CPU utilization under load.

Simple load testing

To get a better understanding of the performance characteristics of our server, let's put them under some load and stress them:

1. Start your container using `docker run`:

   ```
   $ docker run --name <imageName> -d -p 8080:<internal_port> <imageRepo>
   ```

   If you're using npm scripts for Docker, execute the following command to start your container:

   ```
   $ npm run docker:debug
   ```

2. Execute the following bash script to start the load test:

   ```
   $ curl -L http://bit.ly/load-test-bash | bash -s 100 "http://localhost:8080"
   ```

   This script will send `100` requests per second to the server until you terminate it.

3. Execute `docker stats` to observe the performance characteristics.

Here are high-level observations of CPU and memory utilization:

CPU utilization statistics	Low	Mid	High	Max memory
duluca/minimal-nginx-web-server	2%	15%	60%	2.4 MB
duluca/minimal-node-web-server	20%	45%	130%	75 MB

As you can see, there's a significant performance difference between the two servers serving the exact same content. Note that this kind of testing based on requests per second is good for comparative analysis and does not necessarily reflect real-world usage.

It is clear that our NGINX server will give us the best bang for our buck. Armed with an optimal solution, let's deploy the application on AWS.

Deploying to AWS ECS Fargate

AWS **Elastic Container Service** (**ECS**) Fargate is a cost-effective and easy-to-configure way to deploy your container in the cloud.

ECS consists of four major parts:

1. A container repository, **Elastic Container Registry** (**ECR**), where you publish your Docker images.

2. Services, tasks, and task definitions, where you define runtime parameters and port mappings for your container as a task definition that a service runs as tasks.
3. A cluster, a collection of EC2 instances, where tasks can be provisioned and scaled out or in.
4. Fargate, a managed cluster service that abstracts away EC2 instances, load balancer, and security group concerns.

In the top right corner of the AWS console, be sure to select the region that is closest to your users. For me, this is the us-east-1 region.

Our goal is to create a highly available blue-green deployment, meaning that at least one instance of our application will be up and running in the event of a server failure or even during a deployment. These concepts are explored in detail in *Chapter 14, Google Analytics and Advanced Cloud Ops*, in the *Cost per user in a scalable environment* section.

Configuring ECS Fargate

You can access ECS functions under the AWS **Services** menu, selecting the **Elastic Container Service** link.

If this is your first time logging in, you must go through a tutorial, where you will be forced to create a sample app. I would recommend going through the tutorial and deleting your sample app afterward. In order to delete a service, you need to update your service's number of tasks to 0. In addition, delete the default cluster to avoid any unforeseen charges.

Creating a Fargate cluster

Let's start by configuring a Fargate cluster, which acts as an anchor point when configuring other AWS services. Our cluster will eventually run a cluster service, which we will gradually build up in the following sections.

Chapter 13

 AWS Fargate is great choice to implement a scalable container orchestration solution in the cloud. In recent years, Kubernetes has gained prevalence as a go-to solution. Kubernetes is an open source alternative to AWS ECS with richer capabilities for container orchestration with on-premises, cloud, and cloud-hybrid deployments. AWS does offer Amazon Elastic Container Service for Kubernetes (Amazon EKS), however RedHat's open source OpenShift platform is easier to use and comes with batteries included compared to vanilla Kubernetes.

Let's create the cluster:

1. Navigate to **Elastic Container Service**.
2. Click on **Clusters | Create Cluster**.
3. Select the **Networking only... Powered by AWS Fargate** template.
4. Click on the **Next step** and you'll see the **Create Cluster** step, as shown:

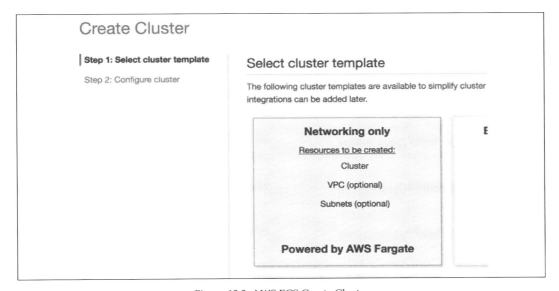

Figure 13.3: AWS ECS Create Cluster

5. Enter **Cluster name** as `fargate-cluster`.
6. Create a **VPC** to isolate your resources from other AWS resources.
7. Click on **Create Cluster** to finish the setup.

You will see the summary of your actions, as follows:

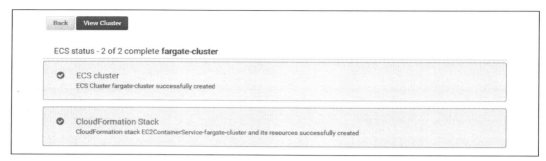

Figure 13.4: AWS ECS Fargate cluster

Now that you have created a cluster within its own **Virtual Private Cloud (VPC)**, you can view it under **Elastic Container Service | Clusters**.

Creating a container repository

Next, we need to set up a repository where we can publish the container images we build in our local or CI environment:

 This section presumes that you have set up Docker and npm scripts for Docker as detailed in *Chapter 9, DevOps Using Docker*. You can get the latest version of these scripts by executing `npm i -g mrm-task-npm-docker` and applying them with `npx mrm npm-docker`.

1. Navigate to **Elastic Container Service**.
2. Click on **Repositories | Create Repository**.
3. Enter the repository name as `lemon-mart`.
4. Copy the **Repository URI** generated on the screen.
5. Paste the URI in the `package.json` file of your application as the new `imageRepo` variable:

   package.json
   ```
   ...
   "config": {
   ```

```
    "imageRepo": "000000000000.dkr.ecr.us-east-1.amazonaws.com/
lemon-mart",
    ...
}
```

6. Click on **Create Repository**.
7. Click on **Next step** and then on **Done** to finish the setup.

On the summary screen, you will get further instructions on how to use your repository with Docker. Later in the chapter, we will go over scripts that will take care of this for us:

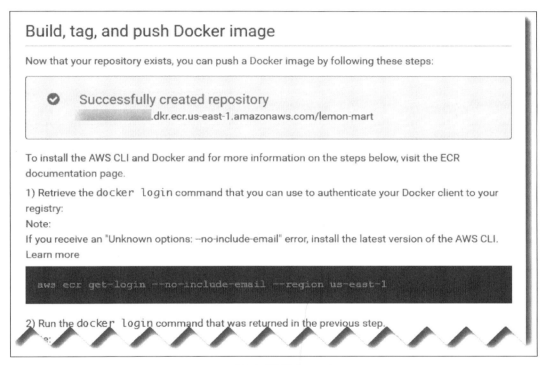

Figure 13.5: AWS ECS repository

You can view your new repository under **Elastic Container Service | Repositories**.

> We will go over how to publish your image in the upcoming *npm scripts for AWS* section.

Let's continue with the setup of ECS.

Creating a task definition

With a container target defined in our repository, we can define a task definition, which contains the necessary metadata to run our container, such as port mappings, reserved CPU, and memory allocations:

1. Navigate to **Elastic Container Service**.
2. Click on **Task Definitions | Create new Task Definition**.
3. Select **Fargate** launch type compatibility.
4. Enter **Task Definition Name** as `lemon-mart-task`.
5. Select **Task role** as none (you can add one later to enable access to other AWS services).
6. Enter **Task Memory** as `0.5 GB`.
7. Enter **Task CPU** as `0.25 CPU`.
8. Click on **Add Container**:
   - Enter **Container name** as `lemon-mart`.
   - For **Image**, paste the image repo URI from earlier, but append the `:latest` tag to it so that it always pulls the latest image in the repository, such as `000000000000.dkr.ecr.us-east-1.amazonaws.com/lemon-mart:latest`.
   - Set a **Soft limit** of `128 MB` for NGINX or `256 MB` for Node.js.
   - Under **Port mappings**, specify **Container port** as `80` for NGINX or `3000` for Node.js.
9. Accept the remaining defaults.
10. Click on **Add**; this is how your task definition will look before creating it:

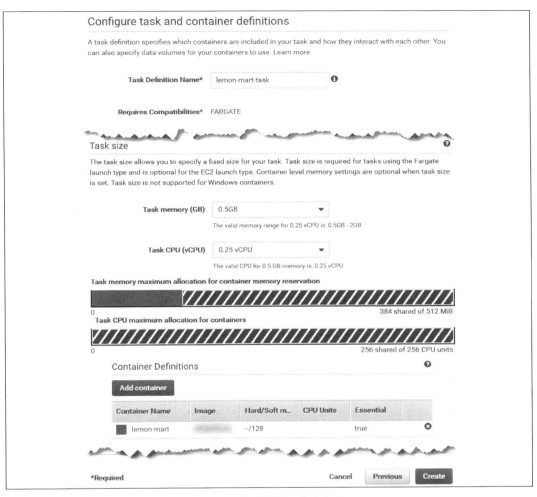

Figure 13.6: AWS ECS task definition

11. Click on **Create** to finish the setup.

View your new **Task Definition** under **Elastic Container Service | Task Definitions**.

Note that the default settings will enable AWS CloudWatch logging, which is a way you can retroactively access the console logs of your container instance. In this example, a CloudWatch log group named /ecs/lemon-mart-task will be created.

View your new log group under **Cloud Watch | Logs**.

If you're adding a container that needs to persist data, the task definition allows you to define a volume and mount a folder to your Docker container. I've published a guide for configuring AWS **Elastic File System (EFS)** with your ECS container at https://bit.ly/mount-aws-efs-ecs-container.

Creating an elastic load balancer

In a highly available deployment, you want to be running two instances of your container, as defined by the task definition we just created, across two different **Availability Zones (AZs)**. For this kind of dynamic scaling out and scaling in, we need to configure an **Application Load Balancer (ALB)** to handle request routing and draining:

1. On a separate tab, navigate to **EC2 | Load Balancers | Create Load Balancer**.
2. Create an **Application Load Balancer**.
3. Enter **Name** as lemon-mart-alb.

In order to support SSL traffic under listeners, you can add a new listener for HTTPS on port 443. An SSL setup can be achieved conveniently via AWS services and wizards. During the ALB configuration process, AWS offers links to these wizards to create your certificates. However, it is an involved process and one that can vary depending on your existing domain hosting and SSL certification setup. I will be skipping over SSL-related configuration in this book. You can find SSL related steps in the guide I've published at https://bit.ly/setupAWSECSCluster.

4. Under **Availability Zones**, select the **VPC** that was created for your **fargate-cluster**.
5. Select all AZs listed.
6. Expand **Tags** and add a key/value pair to be able to identify the ALB, like `"App": "LemonMart"`.
7. Click on **Next: Configure Security Settings**.

> If you added an HTTPS listener, you will see options to configure a certificate.
>
> If configuring a certificate, click on **Choose a certificate from ACM** (AWS Certificate Manager) and select the **Default ELB security policy**.
>
> If you never created a certificate, click on the **Request a new certificate from ACM** link to create one. If you have created a certificate before, then go to **Certificate Manager** to create a new one. Then, refresh and select your certificate.

8. Click on **Next: Configure Security Groups**.
9. Create a new cluster-specific security group, `lemon-mart-sg`, only allowing port `80` inbound or `443` if using HTTPS.

> When creating your cluster service in the next section, ensure that the security group created here is the one selected during service creation. Otherwise, your ALB won't be able to connect to your instances.

10. Click on **Next: Configure Routing**.
11. Name a new **Target group** as `lemon-mart-target-group`.
12. Change the protocol type from `instance` to `ip`.
13. Under **Health check**, keep the default route, /, if serving a website on HTTP.

    Health checks are critical for scaling and deployment operations to work. This is the mechanism that AWS can use to check whether an instance has been created successfully or not.

> If deploying an API and/or redirecting all HTTP calls to HTTPS, ensure that your app defines a custom route that is not redirected to HTTPS. On an HTTP server, `GET /healthCheck` returns a simple 200 message saying `I'm healthy` and verifying that this does not redirect to HTTPS. Otherwise, you will go through a lot of pain and suffering trying to figure out what's wrong, as all health checks fail and deployments inexplicably fail. `duluca/minimal-node-web-server` provides HTTPS redirection, along with an HTTP-only `/healthCheck` endpoint out of the box. With `duluca/minimal-nginx-web-server`, you will need to provide your own configuration.

14. Click on **Next: Register Targets**.
15. Do *not* register any **Targets** or **IP Ranges**. ECS Fargate will magically manage this for you. If you do so yourself, you will provision a semi-broken infrastructure.
16. Click on **Next: Review**; your ALB settings should look similar to the ones shown:

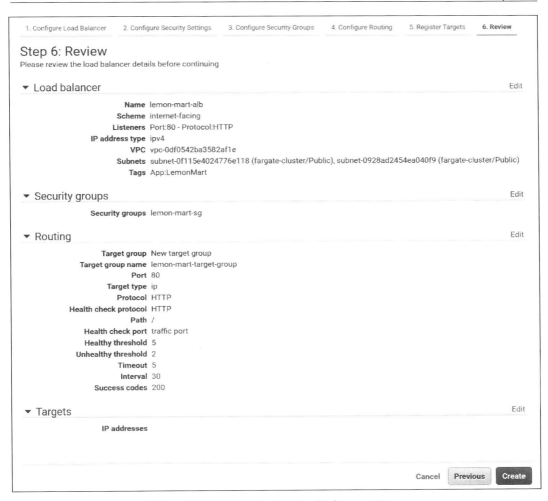

Figure 13.7: AWS Application Load Balancer settings

17. Click on **Create** to finish the setup.

You will be using `lemon-mart-alb` when creating your cluster service in the next section.

Creating a cluster service

Now, we will bring it all together by creating a service in our cluster using the task definition and the ALB we created:

1. Navigate to **Elastic Container Service**.
2. Click on **Clusters | fargate-cluster**.
3. Under the **Services** tab, click on **Create**.
4. Select `Fargate` for **Launch type**.
5. Select the task definition you created earlier.

   Note that task definitions are versioned, such as `lemon-mart-task:1`. If you were to make a change to the task definition, AWS would create `lemon-mart-task:2`. You would need to update the service with this new version for your changes to take effect.

6. Enter **Service name** as `lemon-mart-service`.
7. For **Number of tasks**, select `2`.
8. For **Minimum healthy percent**, select `50`.
9. For **Maximum percent**, select `200`.

   Stick with the **Rolling update** deployment type, as we'll implement our own blue/green deployment strategy.

10. Click on **Next step**.

Chapter 13

Set **Minimum healthy percent** to 100 for high availability even during deployment. Fargate pricing is based on usage per second, so while deploying your application, you will be charged extra for the additional instances, while the old ones are being deprovisioned.

11. Under **Configure network**, select the same VPC as your cluster from earlier.
12. Select all subnets that are available; there should be at least two for high availability.
13. Select the security group you created in the previous section, named `lemon-mart-sg`. (If you can't see it, refresh the page.)
14. Select the **Load Balancer** type as **Application Load Balancer**.
15. Select the **lemon-mart-alb** option.
16. Add **Container port** to the ALB, such as 80 or 3000, by clicking on the **Add to Load Balancer** button.
17. Select the **Production listener port** that you have already defined.
18. Select the **Target group** you have already defined, `lemon-mart-target-group`.
19. Uncheck **Enable service discovery integration**.
20. Click on **Next step**.
21. If you'd like your instances to scale out and in automatically, when their capacities reach a certain limit, then set **Auto Scaling**.

    I would recommend skipping the setup of auto scaling during the initial setup of your service to make it easier to troubleshoot any potential configuration issues. You can come back and set it up later. Automatic task scaling policies rely on alarms, such as CPU utilization. In *Chapter 14, Google Analytics and Advanced Cloud Ops*, in the *Cost per user in scalable environment* section, you can read about calculating your optimum target server utilization and set your alarms based on this number.

22. Click on **Next step** and review your changes, as illustrated:

Figure 13.8: AWS Fargate cluster service settings

23. Finally, click on **Create Service** to finish the setup.

Observe your new service under **Elastic Container Service | Clusters | fargate-cluster | lemon-mart-service**. Until you publish an image to your container repository, your AWS service won't be able to provision an instance, since the health check will continually fail. After you publish an image, you will want to ensure that there are no errors present in the **Events** tab for your service.

AWS is a complicated beast and with Fargate, you can avoid a lot of complexity. However, if you're interested in setting up your own ECS cluster using your own EC2 instances, you can get significant discounts with reserved instances of 1-3 years. I have a 75+ step setup guide available at `https://bit.ly/setupAWSECSCluster`.

We have executed a lot of steps manually to create our cluster. AWS CloudFormation resolves this issue by offering configuration templates that you can customize to your needs or script your own templates from scratch. If you would like to get serious about AWS, this kind of code-as-infrastructure setup is definitely the way to go.

For production deployments, ensure that your configuration is defined by a CloudFormation template, so it can be easily re-provisioned not if, but when a deployment-related faux pas occurs.

Configuring the DNS

To connect a domain or a subdomain name to your app, you must configure your DNS to point to the ALB. AWS offers the Route 53 service to manage your domain.

Route 53 makes it easy to assign a domain or a subdomain to an ALB dynamically:

1. Navigate to **Route 53** | **Hosted Zones**.
2. If you already have a domain registered, select it; otherwise, register it with **Create Hosted Zone**.

   Note that you would need to re-assign the nameservers of your domain to the AWS one for this to take effect.
3. Click on **Create record set**.
4. Enter **Name** as `lemonmart`.
5. Set **Alias** to `yes`.
6. Select **lemon-mart-alb** from the load balancer list.

7. Click on **Create** to finish the setup:

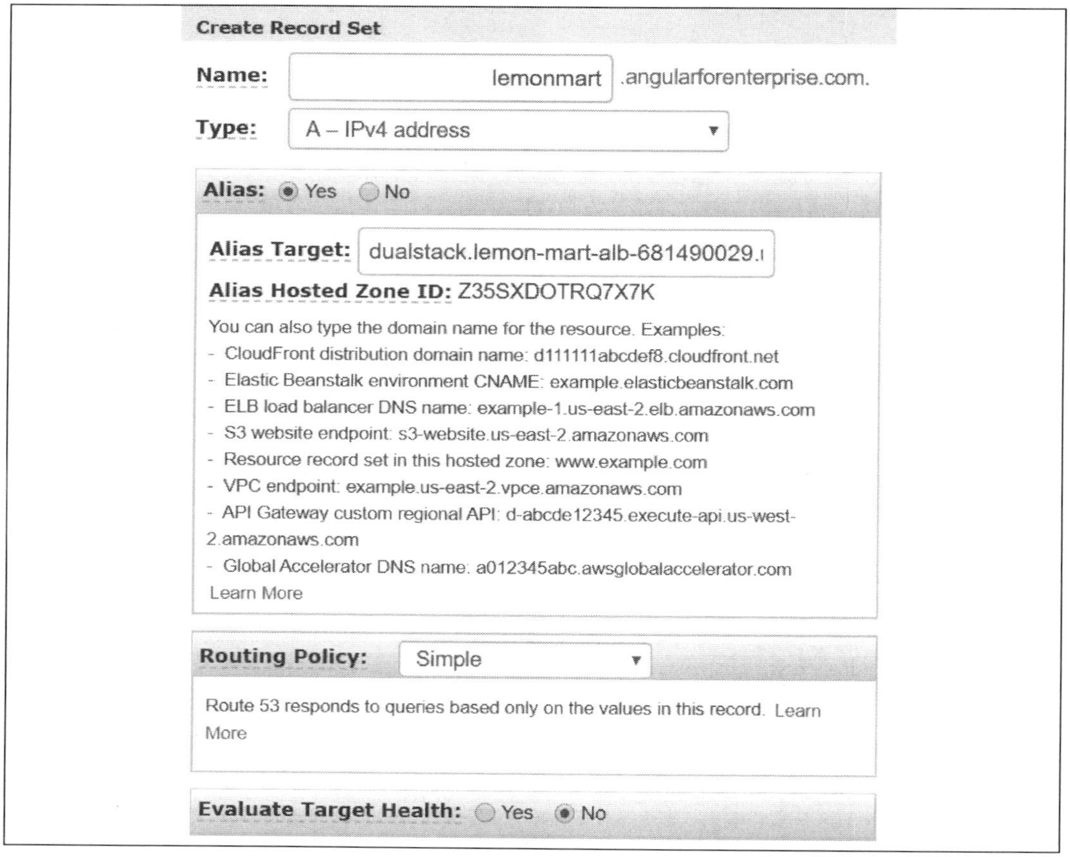

Figure 13.9: Route 53 – Create Record Set

Now, your site will be reachable on the subdomain you just defined, for example, `http://lemonmart.angularforenterprise.com`.

If you don't use Route 53, don't panic. On your domain provider's website, edit the `Zone` file to create an A record to the ALB's DNS address and you're done.

Getting the ALB DNS name

In order to get your load balancer's DNS address, perform these steps:

1. Navigate to **EC2 | Load Balancers**.
2. Select **lemon-mart-alb**.

3. In the **Description** tab, note the DNS name; consider this example:

   DNS name:
   lemon-mart-alb-1871778644.us-east-1.elb.amazonaws.com (A Record)

Now that we configured AWS ECS Fargate, let's prep our Angular app to be deployed to AWS.

Adding npm scripts for AWS

Just like npm scripts for Docker, I have developed a set of scripts, called **npm scripts for AWS**, that work on Windows 10 and macOS. These scripts will allow you to upload and release your Docker images in spectacular, no-downtime, blue/green fashion. You can get the latest version of these scripts and automatically configure them in your project by executing the following steps:

We are configuring these settings on the **lemon-mart** project.

1. Install the npm scripts for the AWS ECS task:

   npm i -g mrm-task-npm-aws

2. Apply the npm scripts for Docker configuration:

   npx mrm npm-aws

Now let's configure the scripts:

1. Ensure that mrm-task-npm-docker scripts are set up in your project.
2. Create a .env file and set AWS_ACCESS_KEY_ID and AWS_SECRET_ACCESS_KEY:

   .env
   AWS_ACCESS_KEY_ID=your_own_key_id
   AWS_SECRET_ACCESS_KEY=your_own_secret_key

3. Ensure that your .env file is in your .gitignore file to protect your secrets.

4. Install or upgrade to the latest AWS CLI:
   - On macOS, `brew install awscli`
   - On Windows, `choco install awscli`

5. Log in to the AWS CLI with your credentials:
   1. Run `aws configure`.
   2. You'll need your **Access Key ID** and **Secret Access Key** from when you configured your IAM account.
   3. Set **Default region name** as `us-east-1`.

6. Update `package.json` to add a new `config` property with the following configuration properties:

   package.json
   ```
   ...
   "config": {
     ...
     "awsRegion": "us-east-1",
     "awsEcsCluster": "fargate-cluster",
     "awsService": "lemon-mart-service"
   },
   ...
   ```

Ensure that you update `package.json` from when you configured npm scripts for Docker so that the `imageRepo` property has the address of your new ECS repository.

7. Ensure AWS scripts have been added to `package.json`, as illustrated:

   package.json
   ```
   ...
   "scripts": {
     ...
     "aws:login:win": "cross-conf-env
        aws ecr get-login --no-include-email --region
        $npm_package_config_awsRegion >
        dockerLogin.cmd && call dockerLogin.cmd &&
        del dockerLogin.cmd",
     "aws:login:mac": "eval $(aws ecr get-login
        --no-include-email --region $npm_package_config_awsRegion)",
     "aws:login": "run-p -cs aws:login:win aws:login:mac",
   }
   ```

> Check your AWS CLI version by executing `aws --version`. Depending on your version, your `aws:login` needs to be different. The preceding script shows login scripts for AWS CLI v1. If you have v2, your login commands will look like the following scripts:
>
> **On macOS / Linux**:
>
> `aws ecr get-login-password --region $npm_package_config_awsRegion | docker login --username AWS --password-stdin $npm_package_config_imageRepo`
>
> **On Windows**:
>
> `(Get-ECRLoginCommand).Password | docker login --username AWS --password-stdin $npm_package_config_imageRepo:latest`

`npm run aws:login` calls platform-specific commands that automate an otherwise multi-step action to get a `docker login` command from the AWS CLI tool, as shown:

example

```
$ npm run aws:login
docker login -u AWS -p eyJwYXl...3ODk1fQ== https://00000000000.dkr.ecr.us-east-1.amazonaws.com


$ docker login -u AWS -p eyJwYXl...3ODk1fQ== https://00000000000.dkr.ecr.us-east-1.amazonaws.com
WARNING! Using --password via the CLI is insecure. Use --password-stdin.
Login Succeeded
```

You first execute `aws ecr get-login` and then copy-paste the resulting `docker login` command and execute it so that your local Docker instance is pointed to AWS ECR. Now let's see how we can deploy a built container:

```
package.json
...
"scripts": {
...
"aws:deploy": "cross-conf-env docker run
    --env-file ./.env silintl/ecs-deploy
    -c $npm_package_config_awsEcsCluster
    -n $npm_package_config_awsService
    -i $npm_package_config_imageRepo:latest
    -r $npm_package_config_awsRegion --timeout 1000",
}
```

...

example
```
$ docker image build . -f nginx.Dockerfile
  -t 000000000.dkr.ecr.us-east-1.amazonaws.com/lemon-mart:latest
$ npm run docker:publish
$ npm run aws:deploy
```

Using image name: 0000000.dkr.ecr.us-east-1.amazonaws.com/lemon-mart:latest

Current task definition: arn:aws:ecs:us-east-1: 0000000:task-definition/lemon-mart-task:7

New task definition: arn:aws:ecs:us-east-1: 0000000:task-definition/lemon-mart-task:8

Service updated successfully, new task definition running.

Waiting for service deployment to complete...

Service deployment successful.

We first build the NGINX version of the Docker image for our web app because we're listening to port `80` on ECS. Then, publish the container to ECR and finally execute `npm run aws:deploy`, which uses the `silintl/ecs-deploy` Docker container that runs a blue/green deployment.

> The details of how blue/green deployment works using ECS commands are beyond the scope of this book. To see more examples using native AWS ECS commands, refer to the `aws-samples` repository at https://github.com/aws-samples/ecs-blue-green-deployment.

We can group our commands together to execute them as a singular `release` command, as shown here:

package.json
```
...
"scripts": {
  ...
  "aws:release": "run-s -cs aws:login docker:publish aws:deploy"
}
...
```

Finally, `npm run aws:release` simply runs `aws:login`, `docker:publish` from the npm scripts for Docker and `aws:deploy` commands in the right order.

Publish

Your project is configured to be deployed on AWS. You mostly need to use two of the commands we created to build and publish an image:

1. Execute `docker:debug` to test, build, tag, run, tail, and launch your app in a browser to test the image:

    `$ npm run docker:debug`

2. Execute `aws:release` to configure Docker login with AWS, publish your latest image build, and release it on ECS:

    `$ npm run aws:release`

     Note that when running multiple commands back to back and one of the commands exits with status 1, then npm considers this a failure. However, this doesn't necessarily mean that your action failed. Always scroll through the terminal outputs to see if any real errors were thrown.

3. Verify that your tasks are up and running at the **Service** level:

Figure 13.10: AWS ECS service

Highly Available Cloud Infrastructure on AWS

 Ensure that **Running count** and **Desired count** are the same. A mismatch or a deploy taking a very long time usually means that the health check on your new container is failing. Check out the **Events** tab for more information. Your container is either failing to start up or you're likely listening to the wrong port.

4. Verify that your instances are running at the **Task** level:

Figure 13.11: AWS ECS task instance

Note the **Public IP** address and navigate to it; for example, `http://54.164.92.137`, and you should see your application or LemonMart running.

5. Verify that the **Load Balancer** setup is correct at the DNS level.
6. Navigate to the **ALB DNS address**, for example `http://lemon-mart-alb-681490029.us-east-1.elb.amazonaws.com`, and confirm that the app renders as follows:

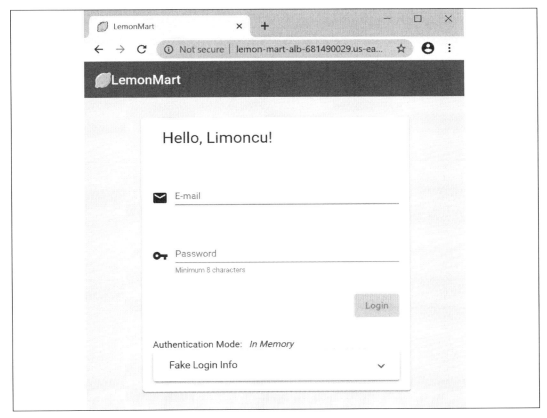

Figure 13.12: LemonMart running on AWS Fargate

Et voilà! Your site should be up and running.

In subsequent releases, following your first, you will be able to observe blue-green deployment in action, as shown:

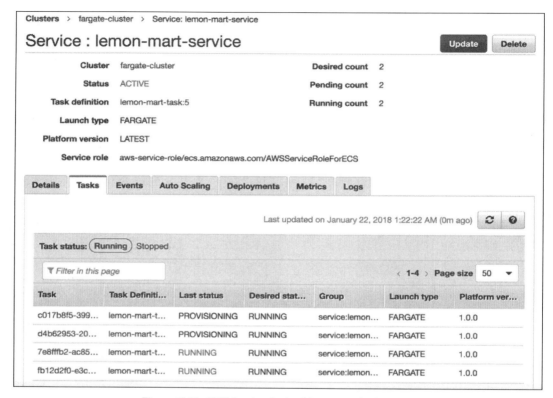

Figure 13.13: AWS Service during blue-green deployment

There are two tasks running, with two new ones being provisioned. While the new tasks are being verified, **Running count** will rise up to four tasks. After the new tasks are verified and the connections from old ones are drained, **Running count** will return to two.

You can automate your deployments by configuring CircleCI with your AWS credentials, using a container that has the `awscli` tool installed and running npm scripts for AWS. With this technique, you can achieve continuous deployment to a staging environment or continuous delivery to a production environment.

Deploying to AWS using CircleCI

In *Chapter 9*, *DevOps Using Docker*, we implemented a CircleCI pipeline based on a multi-stage `Dockerfile`, which resulted in a tar and gzipped Docker image. We also covered how to implement a deploy step using CircleCI. Leveraging what we learned in this chapter, we can combine the two strategies so we can deploy to AWS using CircleCI.

For an AWS deployment, you can use the `aws-cli` orb and a `deploy` job. The `deploy` job will have steps to restore the built Docker image from the cache, log in to AWS, and push the image to your AWS ECS container repository.

On the **lemon-mart** repo, the `config.yml` file for this section is named `.circleci/config.docker-integration.yml`. You can also find a pull request that executes the YML file from this chapter on CircleCI at `https://github.com/duluca/lemon-mart/pull/27` using the branch `deploy_aws`.

For pushing the containers, we then deploy by running `npm run aws:deploy`. Let's add a new `deploy` job to our `config.yml` file.

Under **CircleCI Account Settings** or **Organization Settings**, add a new **context** named aws. Set the `AWS_ACCOUNT_ID`, `AWS_ACCESS_KEY_ID`, `AWS_SECRET_ACCESS_KEY`, and `AWS_DEFAULT_REGION` environment variables as a part of the context.

See the configuration changes here:

```
.circleci/config.yml
version: 2.1
orbs:
  aws-cli: circleci/aws-cli@1.0.0
...
jobs:
  ...
  deploy:
    executor: aws-cli/default
    working_directory: ~/repo
    steps:
      - attach_workspace:
          at: /tmp/workspace
      - checkout
      - setup_remote_docker
      - aws-cli/setup
```

```
          - run: npm ci
          - run:
              name: Restore .env files
              command: |
                set +H
                DOT_ENV=AWS_ACCESS_KEY_ID=$AWS_ACCESS_KEY_ID\\nAWS_SECRET_ACCESS_KEY=$AWS_SECRET_ACCESS_KEY
                echo -e $DOT_ENV > .env
          - run:
              name: Sign Docker into AWS ECR
              command: |
                aws ecr get-login-password --region us-east-1 | docker login --username AWS --password-stdin $AWS_ACCOUNT_ID.dkr.ecr.us-east-1.amazonaws.com/lemon-mart
          - run:
              name: Push it to ECR
              command: |
                docker load < /tmp/workspace/built-image.tar.gz
                ECR_URI=$AWS_ACCOUNT_ID.dkr.ecr.us-east-1.amazonaws.com/lemon-mart
                docker image tag lemon-mart:$CIRCLE_BRANCH $ECR_URI:$CIRCLE_BRANCH
                docker image tag $ECR_URI:$CIRCLE_BRANCH $ECR_URI:latest
                docker image push $ECR_URI:$CIRCLE_BRANCH
                docker image push $ECR_URI:latest
          - run:
              name: Deploy
              command: npm run aws:deploy
```

We configure the `aws-cli` orb with the `aws-cli/setup` job. We then execute `npm ci`, so we can run our npm script later on. We restore the `.env` file using CircleCI environment variables. We configure Docker with our AWS ECR login information, so we can push containers to it. We store `built-image.tar.gz` from the prior step and load it using the `docker load` comment. We tag and push the image to ECR. Finally, we execute `npm run aws:deploy`, which triggers our blue/green deployment.

Last, but not least, we update `workflows` to include the `deploy` job and configure the `aws context` we defined earlier:

```
.circleci/config.yml
...
workflows:
  version: 2
  build-and-deploy:
```

```
jobs:
  - build
  - deploy:
      context: aws
      requires:
        - build
```

 Getting the context configured in CircleCI correctly is critically important. If misconfigured, you will find yourself in a Kafkaesque labyrinth of errors, bad documentation, and misery. Don't say that I didn't warn you.

See the screenshot of a successful deployment here:

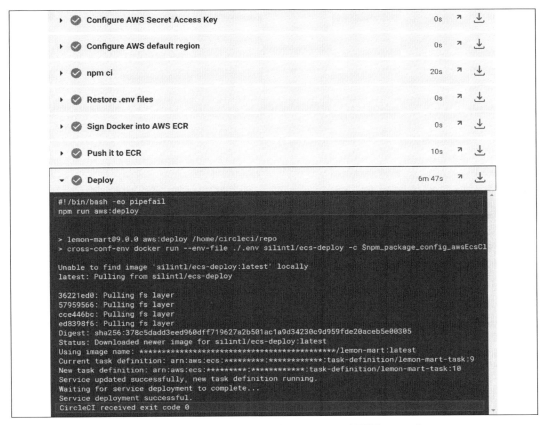

Figure 13.14: Successful CircleCI deployment to an AWS Fargate cluster

> Note that the deploy step takes nearly 7 minutes. This is because the blue/green deployment makes sure that our new deployment is healthy and then it drains connections from existing containers to the new ones, which with the default settings takes 5 minutes. If the new deployment is not healthy, the deploy step will timeout and fail after 10 minutes.

Congratulations! Now we can continuously deploy to AWS in spectacular no-downtime, blue/green fashion. This is all great, but how much does a basic highly available configuration cost?

> To avoid charges, delete `lemon-mart-service`. To do this, you need to update your service's number of tasks to 0 first. In addition, delete the default cluster created for you to avoid any unforeseen charges.

Let's examine the costs in the next section.

AWS billing

My highly-available deployment of LemonMart on AWS Fargate costs roughly $45 a month. Here's the breakdown:

Description	Cost
Amazon Simple Storage Service (S3)	$0.01
AWS Data Transfer	$0.02
Amazon CloudWatch	$0.00
Amazon EC2 Container Service (ECS Fargate)	$27.35
Amazon Elastic Compute Cloud (EC2 Load Balancer instances)	$16.21
Amazon EC2 Container Registry (ECR)	$0.01
Amazon Route 53	$0.50
Total	$44.10

Note that the bill is very detailed, but it does accurately break down all the AWS services we end up using. The major costs are running two instances of our web server on **EC2 Container Service (ECS)** and running load balancers on **Elastic Compute Cloud (EC2)**. Objectively speaking, $45/month may seem like a lot of money to host one web application. It is possible to get a lot more for your money if you're willing to set up your own cluster with dedicated EC2 servers where you can pay in 1 or 3-year increments and get cost savings of up to 50%. A similar, highly available deployment with two instances on Heroku starts at $50/month with other rich features you can get access to. Similarly, two instances on Vercel Now will cost $30/month. Note that both Heroku and Vercel Now don't give you access to physically diverse availability zones. Digital Ocean, on the other hand, allows you to provision servers in different data centers; however, you must code your own infrastructure. For $15/month, you can set up your own highly available cluster across three servers and be able to host multiple sites on it.

Summary

In this chapter, you learned about the nuances and various security considerations in properly protecting your AWS account. We went over the concepts of right-sizing your infrastructure. You conducted simple load testing in an isolated manner to find out relative differences in performance between two web servers. Armed with an optimized web server, you configured an AWS ECS Fargate cluster to achieve a highly available cloud infrastructure. Using npm scripts for AWS, you learned how to script repeatable and reliable no-downtime blue/green deployments. Finally, you became aware of the basic costs of running your infrastructure on AWS and other cloud providers such as Heroku, Vercel Now, and Digital Ocean.

In the next and final chapter, we will complete our coverage of the breadth of topics that a full-stack web developer should know about when deploying applications on the web. We will add Google Analytics to LemonMart to measure user behavior, leverage advanced load testing to understand the financial impact of deploying a well-configured scalable infrastructure, and measure the actual use of important application features with custom analytics events.

Exercise

Deploy LemonMart's server infrastructure, using its `docker-compse.yml` file, to AWS ECS. As a bonus, configure AWS ECS with AWS **Elastic Filesystem (EFS)** to persist your MongoDB data:

1. Install the ECS CLI from `https://docs.aws.amazon.com/AmazonECS/latest/developerguide/ECS_CLI_installation.html`.
2. Add `mrm-task-npm-aws` scripts to the root of `lemon-mart-server`.
3. Create a new `docker-compose.aws.yml` at version 3.0 and update it to refer to already published versions of your containers.
4. Using the `npm run aws:publish:compose` command, deploy your app.

You can use the Minimal MEAN project and the linked GitHub gists as a guide at `https://github.com/duluca/minimal-mean#continuous-integration-and-hosting`.

Further reading

- *AWS Certified Solutions Architect Official Study Guide*, Joe Baron, Hisham Baz, et al. 2016, ISBN-13: 978-1119138556.
- *Configuring AWS ECS to have access to AWS EFS*, 2018, Doguhan Uluca, `https://bit.ly/mount-aws-efs-ecs-container`.
- *BlueGreenDeployment*, Martin Fowler, 2010, `https://martinfowler.com/bliki/BlueGreenDeployment.html`.

Questions

Answer the following questions as best as you can to ensure that you've understood the key concepts from this chapter without Googling. Do you need help answering the questions? See *Appendix D, Self-Assessment Answers* online at `https://static.packt-cdn.com/downloads/9781838648800_Appendix_D_Self-Assessment_Answers.pdf` or visit `https://expertlysimple.io/angular-self-assessment`.

1. What are the benefits of right-sizing your infrastructure?
2. What is the benefit of using AWS ECS Fargate over AWS ECS?
3. Did you remember to turn off your AWS infrastructure to avoid getting billed extra?
4. What is blue/green deployment?

14
Google Analytics and Advanced Cloud Ops

You have designed, developed, and deployed a world-class web application; however, that is only the beginning of the story of your app. The web is an ever-evolving, living, breathing environment that demands attention in order to continue to succeed as a business. In *Chapter 13, Highly Available Cloud Infrastructure on AWS*, we went over the basic concepts and costs of ownership of a cloud infrastructure.

In this chapter, we will dig deeper in to truly understanding how users actually use our application with Google Analytics. We will then use that information to create realistic load tests to simulate actual user behavior to understand the true capacity of a single instance of our server. Knowing the capacity of a single server, we can fine-tune how our infrastructure scales out to reduce waste and discuss the implications of various scaling strategies.

Finally, we will go over advanced analytics concepts, such as custom events, to gain a more granular understanding and tracking of user behavior.

In this chapter, you will learn about the following topics:

- Collecting analytics
- Budgeting and scaling
- Advanced load testing to predict capacity
- Reliable cloud scaling
- Measuring actual use with custom analytics events

Google Analytics and Advanced Cloud Ops

Throughout the chapter, you will be setting up Google Analytics, Google Tag Manager, and OctoPerf accounts.

The most up-to-date versions of the sample code for this book can be found on GitHub at the following repository link. The repository contains the final and completed state of the code. You can verify your progress at the end of this chapter by looking for the end-of-chapter snapshot of code under the `projects` folder.

In the case of *Chapter 14*:

1. Clone the repo: `https://github.com/duluca/lemon-mart`.

   Execute `npm install` on the root folder to install dependencies.

2. The code sample for this chapter can be found under the following subfolder: `projects/ch14`

3. To run the Angular app for this chapter, execute the following command:

   `npx ng serve ch14`

4. To run Angular unit tests for this chapter, execute the following command:

   `npx ng test ch14 --watch=false`

5. To run Angular e2e tests for this chapter, execute the following command:

   `npx ng e2e ch14`

6. To build a production-ready Angular app for this chapter, execute the following command:

   `npx ng build ch14 --prod`

Note that the `dist/ch14` folder at the root of the repository will contain the compiled result.

Beware that the source code in the book or on GitHub may not always match the code generated by the Angular CLI. There may also be slight differences in implementation between the code in the book and what's on GitHub because the ecosystem is ever-evolving. It is natural for the sample code to change over time. Also, on GitHub, expect to find corrections, fixes to support newer versions of libraries, or side-by-side implementations of multiple techniques for the reader to observe. The reader is only expected to implement the ideal solution recommended in the book. If you find errors or have questions, please create an issue or submit a pull request on GitHub for the benefit of all readers.

You can read more about updating Angular in *Appendix C, Keeping Angular and Tools Evergreen*. You can find this appendix online from `https://static.packt-cdn.com/downloads/9781838648800_Appendix_C_Keeping_Angular_and_Tools_Evergreen.pdf` or at `https://expertlysimple.io/stay-evergreen`.

Let's begin by covering the basics of web analytics.

Collecting analytics

Now that our site is up and running, we need to start collecting metrics to understand how it is being used. Metrics are key to operating a web application.

Google Analytics has many facets. The main three are as follows:

1. Acquisition, which measures how visitors arrive at your website
2. Behavior, which measures how visitors interact with your website
3. Conversions, which measure how visitors completed various goals on your website

Here's a look at the **BEHAVIOR | Overview** page from my website `https://thejavascriptpromise.com/`:

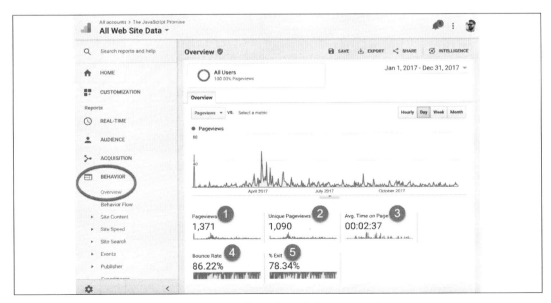

Figure 14.1: Google Analytics behavior overview

Google Analytics and Advanced Cloud Ops

`https://thejavascriptpromise.com/` is a simple single-page HTML site, hence the metrics are quite simple. Let's go over the various metrics on the screen:

1. **Pageviews** shows the number of visitors.
2. **Unique Pageviews** shows the number of unique visitors.
3. **Avg. Time on Page** shows the amount of time each user spent on the site.
4. **Bounce Rate** shows that users left the site without navigating to a subpage or interacting with the site in any manner, such as clicking on a link or button with a custom event.
5. **% Exit** indicates how often users leave the site after viewing a particular page or set of pages.

At a high level, in 2017, the site had about 1,090 unique visitors and, on average, each visitor spent about 2.5 minutes, or 157 seconds, on the site. Given that this is just a single-page site, bounce rate and % exit metrics do not apply in any meaningful manner. Later, we use the number of unique visitors to calculate the cost per user.

As a point of comparison, the LemonMart app from the book served 162,396 lemons between April 2018 and April 2020:

Figure 14.2: LemonMart behavior overview

In addition to page views, Google Analytics can also capture specific events, such as clicking on a button that triggers a server request. These events can then be viewed on the **Events | Overview** page, as shown:

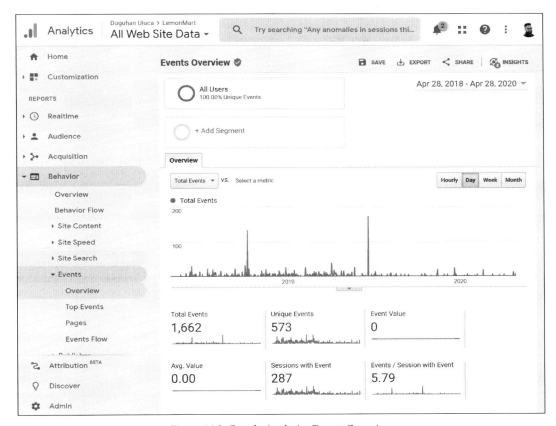

Figure 14.3: Google Analytics Events Overview

It is possible to capture metrics on the server side as well, but this will give requests-over-time statistics. You will require additional code and state management to track the behavior of a particular user so that you can calculate users-over-time statistics. By implementing such tracking on the client side with Google Analytics, you gain a far more detailed understanding as to where the user came from, what they did, whether they succeeded or not, and when they left your app without adding unnecessary code complexity and infrastructure load to your backend.

Adding Google Tag Manager to your Angular app

Let's start capturing analytics in your Angular app. Google is in the process of phasing out the legacy `ga.js` and `analytics.js` products that are shipped with Google Analytics, replacing these with its new, more flexible global site tag, `gtag.js`, that ships with Google Tag Manager. This is by no means an end to Google Analytics; instead, it represents a shift toward an easier-to-configure and manage analytics tool. The global site tag can be configured and managed remotely via Google Tag Manager. Tags are snippets of JavaScript tracking code that is delivered to the client, and they can enable tracking of new metrics and integration with multiple analytics tools without having to change code that has already been deployed. You can still continue to use Google Analytics to analyze and view your analytics data. Another major advantage of Google Tag Manager is that it is version controlled, meaning that you can experiment with different kinds of tags that are triggered under various kinds of conditions without fear of doing any irreversible damage to your analytics configuration.

Setting up Google Tag Manager

Let's begin by setting up a Google Tag Manager account for your application:

1. Sign in to Google Tag Manager at `https://tagmanager.google.com/`.
2. Add a new account with a **Web** container, as follows:

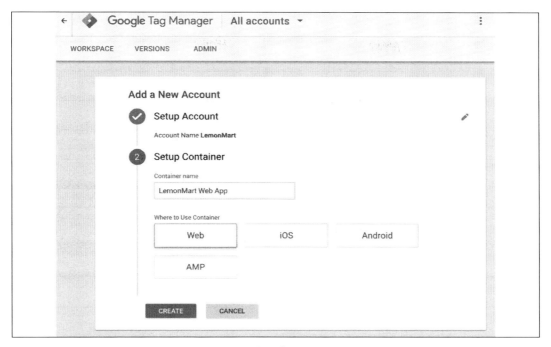

Figure 14.4: Google Tag Manager

3. Paste the generated scripts at or near the top <head> and <body> sections of your index.html file, as instructed on the website:

   src/index.html
   ```
   <head>
   <!-- Google Tag Manager -->
   <script>(function(w,d,s,l,i){w[l]=w[l]||[];w[l].push({'gtm.
   start': new Date().getTime(),event:'gtm.js'});var f=d.
   getElementsByTagName(s)[0], j=d.createElement(s),dl=l!='dataLayer'
   ?'&l='+l:'';j.async=true;j.src='https://www.googletagmanager.com/
   gtm.js?id='+i+dl;f.parentNode.insertBefore(j,f);
   })(window,document,'script','dataLayer','GTM-56D4F6K');</script>
   ```

```
<!-- End Google Tag Manager -->
...
</head>
<body>
<!-- Google Tag Manager (noscript) -->
<noscript><iframe src="https://www.googletagmanager.com/
ns.html?id=GTM-56D4F6K" height="0" width="0" style="display:none;v
isibility:hidden"></iframe></noscript>
<!-- End Google Tag Manager (noscript) -->
<app-root></app-root>
</body>
```

Note that the `<noscript>` tag will only execute if the user has disabled JavaScript execution in their browser. This way, we can collect metrics from such users, rather than being blind to their presence.

4. Submit and publish your tag manager container.
5. You should see the initial setup of your tag manager completed, as shown in the following screenshot:

Figure 14.5: Published tag

6. Verify that your Angular app runs without any errors.

> Note that if you don't publish your tag manager container, you will see a `404` error when loading `gtm.js` in the dev console or the **Network** tab.

Setting up Google Analytics

Now, let's generate a tracking ID through Google Analytics. This is a universally unique identifier for your app to correlate your analytics data:

1. Log in to Google Analytics at `https://analytics.google.com`.
2. Open the **Admin console**, using the gear icon in the bottom-left corner of the screen, as shown in the following screenshot:

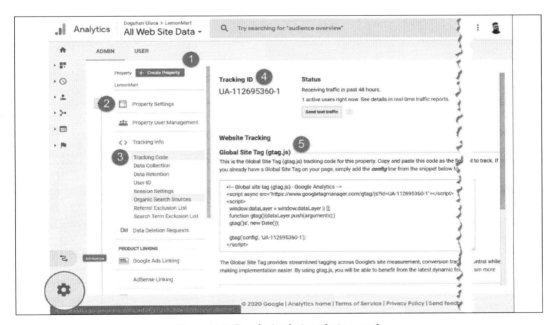

Figure 14.6: Google Analytics admin console

3. Create a new analytics account.
4. Using the steps from the preceding screenshot as a guide, perform the following steps:
    1. Add a new **Property**, `LemonMart`.
    2. Configure the property to your preferences.

3. Click on **Tracking Code**.
4. Copy the **Tracking ID** that starts with UA-xxxxxxxxxx-1.
5. Ignore the gtag.js code provided.

With your tracking ID on hand, we can configure Google Tag Manager so that it can collect analytics.

Configuring Google Analytics Tag in Tag Manager

Now, let's connect our Google Analytics ID to Google Tag Manager:

1. At https://tagmanager.google.com, open the **Workspace** tab.
2. Click on **Add a new tag**.
3. Name it Google Analytics.
4. Click on **Tag Configuration** and select **Universal Analytics**.
5. Under **Google Analytics Settings**, add a new variable.
6. Paste the tracking ID you copied in the previous section.
7. Click on **Triggers** and add the **All Pages** trigger.
8. Click on **Save**, as shown in the following screenshot:

Chapter 14

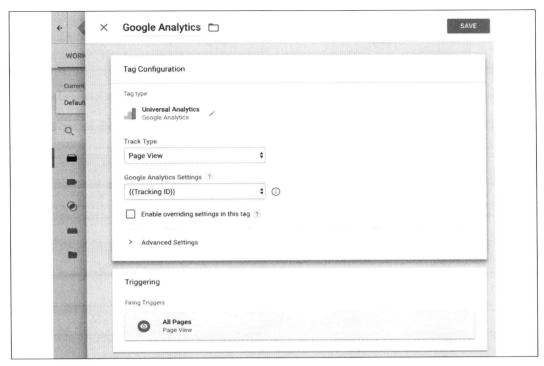

Figure 14.7: Creating a Google Analytics tag

9. Submit and publish your changes, and observe the version summary with one tag, as shown:

Figure 14.8: Version Summary showing one tag

10. Now refresh your Angular app, where you'll be on the /home route.

11. In a private window, open a new instance of your Angular app and navigate to the /manager/home route.

12. At https://analytics.google.com/, open the **REAL-TIME | Overview** pane, as shown in the following screenshot:

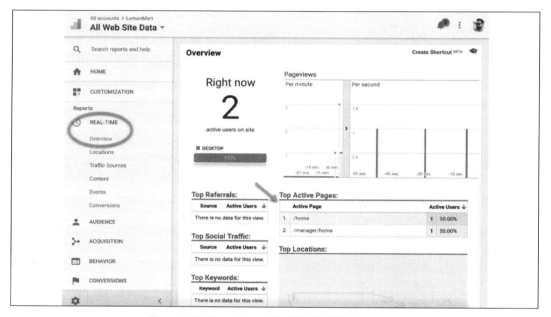

Figure 14.9: Google Analytics REAL-TIME Overview

13. Note that the two active users are being tracked.

14. Under **Top Active Pages**, you should see the pages that the users are on.

By leveraging Google Tag Manager and Google Analytics together, we have been able to accomplish page tracking without changing any code inside our Angular app.

> **Search engine optimization (SEO)** is an important part of analytics. To gain a better understanding of how crawlers perceive your Angular site, use the Google Search Console dashboard, found at https://www.google.com/webmasters/tools, to identify optimizations. In addition, consider using Angular Universal to render certain dynamic content on the server-side so that crawlers can index your dynamic data sources and drive more traffic to your site.

Budgeting and scaling

In the *AWS Billing* section of *Chapter 13*, *Highly Available Cloud Infrastructure on AWS*, we covered the monthly costs of operating a web server, ranging from $5/month to $45/month, from a single-server instance scenario to a highly available infrastructure. For most needs, budgeting discussions will begin and end with this monthly number. You can execute load tests, as suggested in the *Advanced load testing* section, to predict your per-server user capacity and get a general idea of how many servers you may require. In a dynamically scaling cloud environment with dozens of servers running 24/7, this is an overly simplistic way to calculate a budget.

If you operate a web property of any significant scale, things invariably get complicated. You will be operating multiple servers on different tech stacks, serving different purposes. It can be difficult to gauge or justify how much of a budget to spare for seemingly excess capacity or unnecessarily high-performance servers. Somehow, you need to be able to communicate the efficiency of your infrastructure given the number of users you serve and ensure that your infrastructure is fine-tuned so that you don't lose users due to an unresponsive application or overpay because you're using more capacity than you require.

For this reason, we will take a user-centered approach and translate our IT infrastructure costs to a per-user cost metric that the business and the marketing side of your organization can make sense of.

In the next section, we will investigate what it means to calculate the per-user cost of your infrastructure and how these calculations change when cloud scaling comes in to play using one of my websites as an example.

Calculating the per-user cost

We will be leveraging behavior metrics from Google Analytics with the goal of calculating the per-user cost over a given period of time:

Per-user cost is calculated as follows:

$$perUserCost/time = \frac{infrastructureCost/time}{users/time}$$

Using the `https://thejavascriptpromise.com/` data from earlier, let's plug in the data to the formula to calculate *perUserCost/month*.

This website is deployed on an Ubuntu server on DigitalOcean, so the monthly infrastructure cost, including weekly backups, is $6 a month. From Google Analytics, we know there were 1,090 unique visitors in 2017:

$$\frac{\$6/mo}{1{,}090\ users/year \div 12/mo} = \$0.07/user$$

In 2017, I have paid 7 cents per user. Money well spent? At $6/month, I don't mind it. In 2017, `https://thejavascriptpromise.com/` was deployed on a traditional server setup as a static site that doesn't scale out or in. These conditions make it very straightforward to use the unique visitor metric and find the per-user cost. The very same simplicity that allows for an easy calculation also leads to a suboptimal infrastructure. If I were to serve 1,000,000 users on the same infrastructure, my costs would add up to $70,000 a year. If I were to earn $100 for every 1,000 users through Google ads, my site would make $100,000 per year. After taxes, development expenses, and our unreasonable hosting expenses, the operation would likely lose money.

If you were to take advantage of cloud scaling, where instances can scale out or in dynamically based on current user demand, the preceding formula becomes useless pretty quickly because you must take provisioning time and target server utilization into account.

Provisioning time is the amount of time it takes your cloud provider to start a new server from scratch. Target server utilization is the maximum usage metric of a given server, where a scale-out alert must be sent out so that a new server is ready before your current servers max out their capacity. In order to calculate these variables, we must execute a series of load tests against our servers.

Page views are an overly simplistic way to determine user behavior in SPAs such as Angular, where page views do not necessarily correlate to a request, or vice versa. If we execute load tests simply based on page views, we won't get a realistic simulation of how your platform may perform under load.

User behavior, or how users actually use your app, can drastically impact your performance forecasts and wildly fluctuate budget numbers. You can use Google Analytics custom events to capture complicated sets of actions that result in various types of requests served by your platform. Later in this chapter, we will explore how you can measure actual use in the *Measuring actual use* section.

Initially, you won't have any of the aforementioned metrics, and any metrics you may have will be invalidated any time you make a meaningful change to your software or hardware stack. Therefore, it is imperative to execute load tests on a regular basis to simulate realistic user loads.

Advanced load testing

In order to be able to predict capacity, we need to run load tests. In *Chapter 13*, *Highly Available Cloud Infrastructure on AWS*, I discussed a simple load testing technique of just sending a bunch of web requests to a server. In a relative comparison scenario, this works fine for testing raw power. However, actual users generate dozens of requests at varying intervals while they navigate your website, resulting in a wide variety of API calls to your backend server.

We must be able to model virtual users and unleash a whole bunch of them on our servers to find the breaking point of our server. OctoPerf is an easy-to-use service to execute such load tests, and it's located at `https://octoperf.com`. OctoPerf offers a free tier that allows for 50 concurrent users/test over unlimited test runs with two load generators.

OctoPerf is the ideal tool to get us quickly started with advanced testing capability. Let's create an account and see what it can do for us:

1. Create an OctoPerf account.
2. Log in and add a new project for LemonMart, as shown:

Figure 14.10: Adding a project in OctoPerf

OctoPerf allows you to create multiple virtual users with different usage characteristics. Since it is a URL-based setup, any click-based user action can also be simulated by directly calling the application server URL with test parameters.

3. Create two virtual users, one as a `Manager` who navigates to manager-based pages, and a second as a `POS` user who sticks to POS functions.
4. Click on **Create scenario**:

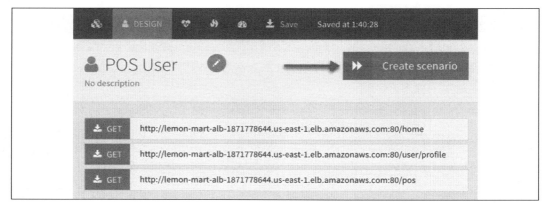

Figure 14.11: POS User scenario

5. Name the scenario `Evening Rush`.
6. You can add a mixture of **Manager** and **POS User** types, as shown:

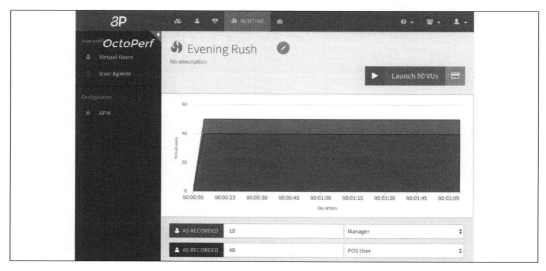

Figure 14.12: Evening Rush scenario

7. Click on the **Launch 50 VUs** button to start the load test.

   You can observe the number of **users** and **hits/sec** being achieved in real-time, as shown in the following screenshot:

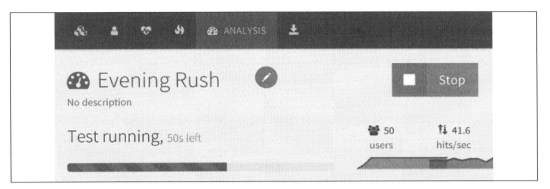

Figure 14.13: Evening Rush load test underway

8. ECS service metrics also give us a high-level idea of real-time utilization, as shown in the following screenshot:

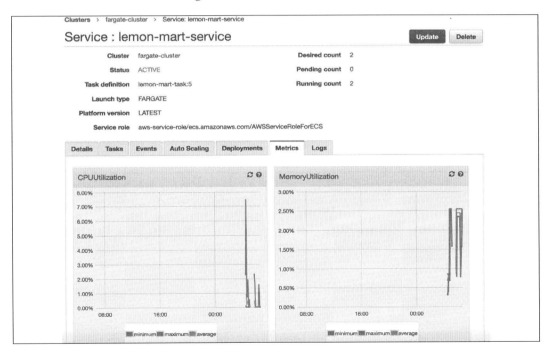

Figure 14.14: ECS real-time metrics

9. Analyze the load test results.

You can get more accurate results from ECS by clicking on the **CPUUtilization** link from **ECS Service Metrics** or by navigating to the **CloudWatch | Metrics** section, as follows:

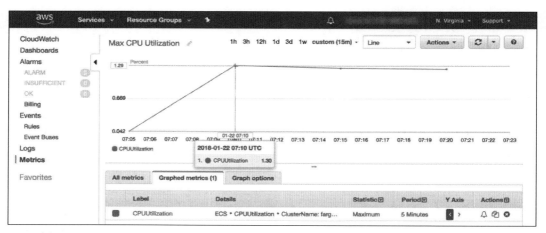

Figure 14.15: AWS CloudWatch Metrics

As you can see in the preceding graph, CPU utilization was fairly consistent, at around 1.3%, given a sustained user load of 50 over a period of 10 minutes. During this period, there were no request errors, as shown in the statistics summary from OctoPerf:

Figure 14.16: OctoPerf Statistics summary

Ideally, we would measure maximum users/second until the moment errors were being generated. However, given only 50 virtual users and the information we already have, we can predict how many users could be handled at 100% utilization:

$$\frac{100\ percent}{1.3\ percent} \times 50\ users/sec = 3{,}846\ users/sec$$

Our load test results reveal that our infrastructure can handle 3,846 users/second. Given this information, we can calculate cost per user in a scalable environment in the next section. However, performance and reliability go hand in hand. How you choose to architect your infrastructure will also provide important information in terms of budgeting, because the level of reliability you need will dictate the minimum number of instances you must keep around at all times.

Reliable cloud scaling

Reliability can be expressed in terms of your organization's **recovery point objective** (**RPO**) and **recovery time objective** (**RTO**). RPO represents how much data you're willing to lose, while RTO represents how fast you can rebuild your infrastructure in the event of a failure.

Let's suppose that you run an e-commerce site. Around noon every weekday, you reach peak sales. Every time a user adds an item to their shopping cart, you store the items on a server-side cache so that users can resume their shopping spree later at home. In addition, you process hundreds of transactions per minute. Business is good, your infrastructure is scaling out beautifully, and everything is going smoothly. Meanwhile, a hungry rat or an overly charged lightning cloud decides to strike your data center. Initially, a seemingly harmless power unit goes down, but it's fine, because nearby power units can pick up the slack. However, this is the lunch rush; other websites on the data center are also facing a high traffic volume. As a result, several power units overheat and fail. There aren't enough power units to pick up the slack, so in quick succession, power units overheat one by one and start failing, triggering a cascade of failures that end up taking down the entire data center. Meanwhile, some of your users just clicked on **Add to cart**, others on the **Pay** button, and some others are just about to arrive on your site. If your RPO is 1 hour, meaning you persisted your shopping cart cache every hour, then you can say goodbye to valuable data and potential sales by those night-time shoppers. If your RTO is 1 hour, it will take you up to 1 hour to get your site back up and running again, and you can rest assured that most of those customers who just clicked on the buy button or arrived to an unresponsive site won't be making a purchase on your site that day.

A well-thought-out RPO and RTO is a critical business need, but they must also be paired with the right infrastructure that makes it possible to implement your objectives in a cost-effective manner. AWS is made up of more than two dozen regions around the world, each region containing at least their **availability zones** (**AZs**). Each AZ is a physically separated infrastructure that is not affected by a failure in another AZ.

A highly available configuration on AWS means that your application is up and running on at least two AZs, so if a server instance fails, or even if the entire data center fails, you have another instance already live in a physically separate data center that is able to pick up incoming requests seamlessly.

A fault-tolerant architecture means that your application is deployed across multiple regions. Even if an entire region goes down due to a natural disaster, a **distributed denial-of-service** (**DDoS**) attack, or a bad software update, your infrastructure remains standing and is able to respond to user requests. Your data is protected by layer upon layer of security and via staggered backups of backups.

AWS offers great services, including **Shield** to protect against DDoS attacks targeted against your website, a **Pilot Light** service to keep a minimal infrastructure waiting dormant in another region that can scale to full capacity if needed, while keeping operational costs down, and a **Glacier** service to store large amounts for data for long periods of time in an affordable manner.

A highly available configuration will require a minimum of two instances in a multi-AZ setup at all times. For a fault-tolerant setup, you require two highly available configurations in at least two regions. Most AWS cloud services, such as DynamoDB for data storage or Redis for caching, are highly available by default, including serverless technologies such as Lambda. Lambda charges on a per-use basis and can scale to match any need you can throw at it in a cost-effective manner. If you can move heavy compute tasks to Lambda, you can reduce your server utilization and your scaling needs dramatically in the process. When planning your infrastructure, you should consider all these variables to set up the right scalable environment for your needs.

Cost per user in a scalable environment

In a scalable environment, you cannot plan on 100% utilization. It takes time to provision a new server. A server that is at 100% utilization can't process additional incoming requests in a timely manner, which results in dropped or erroneous requests from the users' perspective. So, the server in question must send a trigger well before it reaches 100% utilization so that no requests are dropped. Earlier in the chapter, I suggested a 60-80% target utilization before scaling. The exact number will largely depend on your specific choice of software and hardware stack.

Given your custom utilization target, we can calculate the number of users your infrastructure is expected to serve on average per instance. Using this information, you can calculate a more accurate cost per user, which should allow the correct sizing of your IT budget, given your specific needs. It is equally as bad to underspend as it is to overspend. You may be forgoing more growth, security, data, reliability, and resilience than may be considered acceptable.

In the next section, we will walk through the calculation of an optimal target server utilization metric so that you can calculate a more accurate per-user cost. Then, we will explore scaling that can occur during preplanned time frames and software deployments.

Calculating target server utilization

First, calculate your custom server utilization target, which is the point where your server is experiencing increased volumes of traffic and triggers a new server to provision with enough time so that the original server does not reach 100% utilization and drops requests. Consider this formula:

Target utilization:

$$targetUtilization = 1 - \frac{provisioningSpeed \times requests/time}{maxRequestCapacity/time}$$

Let's demonstrate how the formula works with the help of a concrete example:

1. Load test your instances to establish user capacity per instance:

    Load test results: 3,846 users/second.

     Requests/sec and users/sec are not the same, since a user makes multiple requests to complete an action and may execute multiple requests/sec. Advanced load testing tools such as OctoPerf are necessary to execute realistic and varied workloads and measure user capacity over request capacity.

2. Measure instance provisioning speed, from creation/cold boot to the request fulfilled first:

    Measured instance provisioning speed: 60 seconds.

    In order to measure this speed, you can put the stopwatch away. Depending on your exact setup, AWS provides event and application logs in the ECS Service Events tab, CloudWatch, and CloudTrail to correlate enough information to figure out when a new instance was requested and how long it took for the instance to be ready to fulfill requests.

For example, in the **ECS Service Events** tab, take the target registration event as the beginning time. Once the task has been initiated, click on the task ID to see the creation time. Using the task ID, check the task's logs in CloudWatch to see the time at which the task served its first web request as the end time and then calculate the duration.

3. Measure the 95th percentile user growth rate, excluding known capacity increases:

   95th percentile user growth rate: 10 users/second.

The 95th percentile is a common metric to calculate overall network usage. It means that 95% of the time, usage will be below the stated amount, making it a good number to use for planning, as explained by Barb Dijker in her article entitled *What the heck is this 95th Percentile number?*, available at http://www2.arnes.si/~gljsentvid10/pct.html.

If you don't have prior metrics, initially defining user growth rate will be an educated guess at best. However, once you start collecting data, you can update your assumptions. In addition, it is impossible to operate an infrastructure that can respond to any imaginable outlier without dropping a request in a cost-effective manner. Given your metrics, a business decision should be consciously made as to what percentile of outliers should be ignored as an acceptable business risk.

4. Let's plug in the numbers to the formula:

$$1 - \frac{60s \times 10\ users/s}{3{,}846\ /s} = 0.8439$$

The custom target utilization rate, rounded down, would be 84%. Setting your scale-out trigger at 84% will avoid instances from being over provisioned, while preventing user requests from being dropped.

With this custom target utilization in mind, let's update the per-user cost formula with scaling in mind:

Per-user cost with scaling:

$$perUserCost/time = \frac{infrastructureCost/time}{users/time \times targetUtilization}$$

So, if our infrastructure cost was $100 per month serving 150 users, at 100% utilization, you calculate the per-user cost to be $0.67/user/month. If you were to take scaling into account, the cost would be as follows:

$$\frac{\$100/mo}{150 \ users/mo \times 0.84 \ utilization} = \$0.79/user/mo$$

Scaling without dropping requests would cost 16% more of the original $0.67 at $0.79 per user per month. However, it is important to keep in mind that your infrastructure won't always be so efficient. At lower utilization targets, or when these are misconfigured with scaling triggers, costs can easily double, triple, or quadruple the original cost. The ultimate goal here is to find the sweet spot, meaning that you will be paying the right amount per user.

There's no prescriptive per-user cost you should be targeting for. However, if you are running a service where you charge users $5 per month after all other operational costs and profit margins are accounted for, and you're still left with a surplus budget *and* your users complaining about poor performance, then you're underspending. However, if you're eating into your profit margins or, even worse, only breaking even, then you may be overspending or you may need to reconsider your business model.

There are several other factors that can impact your per-user cost, including blue/green deployments, which we'll cover in a moment. You can also increase the efficiency of your scaling by leveraging prescheduled provisioning.

Prescheduled provisioning

Dynamic scaling out and then back in is what defines cloud computing. However, the algorithms currently available still require some planning if you know that certain days, weeks, or months of a year will require uncharacteristically higher resource capacity. Given a sudden deluge of new traffic, your infrastructure will attempt to dynamically scale out, but if the rate of increase in traffic is logarithmic, even an optimized server utilization target won't help. Servers will frequently reach and operate at 100% utilization, resulting in dropped or erroneous requests. To prevent this from happening, you should proactively provision additional capacity during such predictable periods of high demand.

Blue/green deployments

In *Chapter 13, Highly Available Cloud Infrastructure on AWS*, you configured no-downtime blue/green deployments. Blue/green deployments are reliable code deployments that ensure continuous uptime of your site, while minimizing the risk of bad deployments.

Let's presume that you have a highly available deployment, meaning you have two instances active at any given time. During a blue/green deployment, two additional instances would be provisioned. Once these additional instances are ready to fulfill requests, their health is determined using your predefined health metric.

If your new instances are found to be healthy, this means they're in working order. There will be a period of time, say 5 minutes, during which connections in the original instance are drained and rerouted to the new instances. At this time, the original instances are deprovisioned.

If the new instances are found to be unhealthy, then these new instances will be deprovisioned, resulting in a failed deployment. However, a service will remain available without interruption because the original instance will remain intact and keep serving users during the entire process.

Revising estimates with metrics

Load testing and predicting user growth rates give you an idea of how your system may behave in production. Collecting more granular metrics and data is critical in revising your estimates and nailing down a more accurate IT budget.

Measuring actual use

As we discussed earlier, keeping track of page views alone isn't reflective of the number of requests that a user sends to the server. With Google Tag Manager and Google Analytics, you can keep track of more than just page views with ease.

As of the time of publication, here are some of the default events you can configure across various categories. This list will grow over time:

- Page View: Used to track whether a user is sticking around as page resources load and the page is fully rendered:
    - Page View; fired at the first opportunity
    - DOM Ready; when the DOM structure is loaded

- Window Loaded; when all elements are finished loading
- Click: Used to track a user's click interactions with the page:
    - All Elements
    - Just Links
- User Engagement: Tracks user behavior:
    - Element Visibility; whether elements have been shown
    - Form Submission; whether a form was submitted
    - Scroll Depth; how far they scrolled down the page
    - YouTube Video; if they played an embedded YouTube Video
- Other event tracking:
    - Custom Event; defined by a programmer to track a single or multistep event, such as a user going through the steps of a checkout process
    - History Change; whether the user navigates back in the browser's history
    - JavaScript Error; whether JavaScript errors have been generated
    - Timer; to trigger or delay time-based analytics events

Most of these events don't require any extra coding to implement, so we will implement a custom event to demonstrate how you can capture any single event or series of events you want with custom coding. Capturing workflows with a series of events can reveal where you should be focusing your development efforts.

For more information on Google Tag Manager events, triggers, or tips and tricks, I recommend that you check out the blog by Simo Ahava at `https://www.simoahava.com/`.

Creating a custom event

For this example, we will capture the event for when a customer is successfully checked out and a sale is completed. We will implement two events, one for checkout initiation, and the other for when the transaction has been completed successfully:

1. Log on to your Google Tag Manager workspace at `https://tagmanager.google.com`.

2. Under the **Triggers** menu, click on **NEW**, as indicated here:

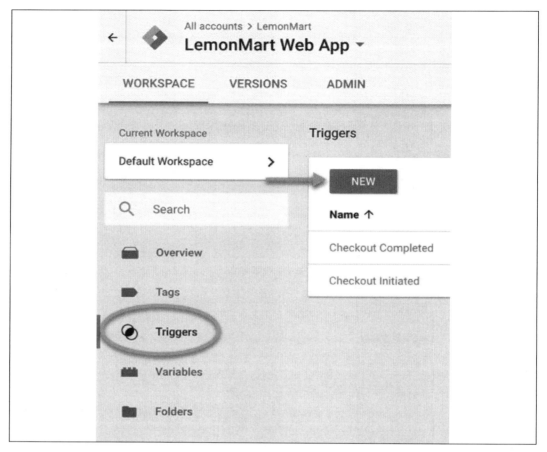

Figure 14.17: Tag Manager workspace

3. Name your trigger.
4. Click on the empty trigger card to select the event type.
5. Select **Custom Event**.

6. Create a custom event named `checkoutCompleted`, as illustrated:

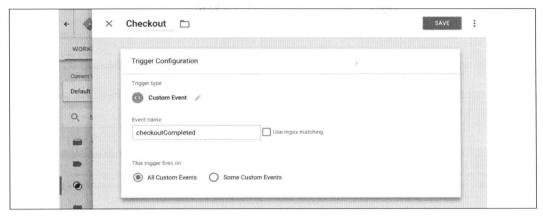

Figure 14.18: Custom Checkout event

By selecting the **Some Custom Events** option, you can limit or control the collection of a particular event, that is, only when on a particular page or a domain, such as on `lemonmart.com`. In the following screenshot, you can see a custom rule that would filter out any checkout event that didn't happen on `lemonmart.com` to weed out development or test data:

Figure 14.19: Some Custom Events

7. **Save** your new event.
8. Repeat the process for an event named `Checkout Initiated`.

9. Add two new Google Analytics event tags, as highlighted here:

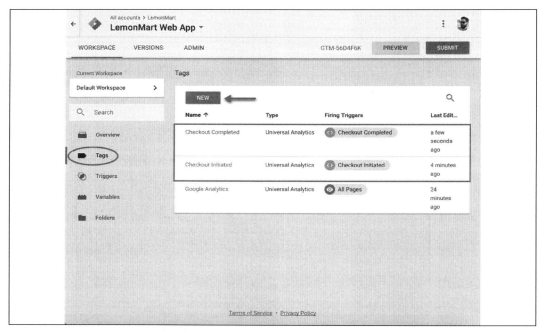

Figure 14.20: New custom event tags

10. Configure the event and attach the relevant trigger you created to it, as shown in the following screenshot:

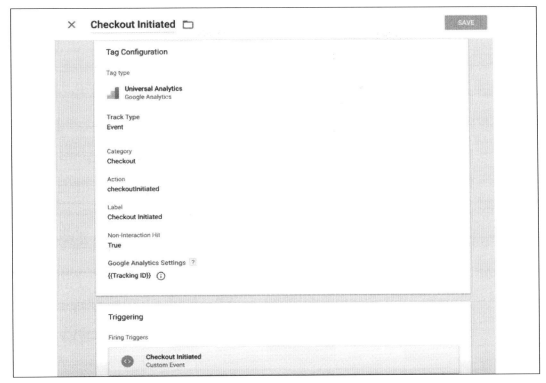

Figure 14.21: Trigger setup

11. Submit and publish your workspace.

We are now ready to receive custom events in our analytics environment.

Adding custom events in Angular

Now, let's edit the Angular code to trigger the events:

1. Consider the POS template with a checkout button:

    src/app/pos/pos/pos.component.html
    ```
    <p>
      <img
        src="https://user-images.githubusercontent.
    com/822159/36186684-9f05fef8-110e-11e8-991f-fae6ca60fe5d.png" />
    </p>
    <p>
      <button mat-icon-button (click)="checkout(currentTransaction)">
        <mat-icon>shopping_cart</mat-icon> Checkout Customer
      </button>
    </p>
    ```

    The circular checkout button is indicated in the bottom-left corner of the following diagram:

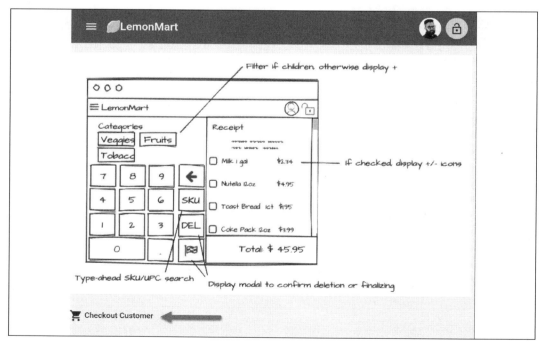

Figure 14.22: POS page with checkout button

Chapter 14

Optionally, you can add an `onclick` event handler directly in the template, such as `onclick="dataLayer.push({'event': 'checkoutInitiated'})"` on the checkout button. This pushes the `checkoutInitiated` event to the `dataLayer` object, made available by `gtm.js`.

2. Define an `ITransaction` interface:

   src/app/pos/transaction/transaction.ts
   ```
   ...
   export interface ITransaction {
     paymentType: TransactionType
     paymentAmount: number
     transactionId?: string
   }
   ...
   ```

3. Define a `TransactionType` enum:

   src/app/pos/transaction/transaction.enum.ts
   ```
   ...
   export enum TransactionType {
     Cash,
     Credit,
     LemonCoin,
   }
   ...
   ```

4. Implement a `TransactionService` that has a `processTransaction` function:

   src/app/pos/transaction/transaction.service.ts
   ```
   ...
   @Injectable({
     providedIn: 'root',
   })
   export class TransactionService {
     constructor() {}

     processTransaction(transaction: ITransaction)
         : Observable<string> {
       return new
         BehaviorSubject<string>('5a6352c6810c19729de860ea')
         .asObservable()
     }
   }
   ...
   ```

[735]

Google Analytics and Advanced Cloud Ops

> `'5a6352c6810c19729de860ea'` is a random string that represents a transaction ID.

5. In `PosComponent`, declare an interface for `dataLayer` events that you intend to push:

   src/app/pos/pos/pos.component.ts
   ```
   ...
   interface IEvent {
   event: 'checkoutCompleted' | 'checkoutInitiated'
   }
   declare let dataLayer: IEvent[]
   ...
   ```

6. Import dependencies and initialize `currentTransaction`:

   src/app/pos/pos/pos.component.ts
   ```
   ...
   export class PosComponent implements OnInit, OnDestroy {
     private subs = new SubSink()
     currentTransaction: ITransaction
     constructor(
       private transactionService: TransactionService,
       private uiService: UiService
     ) {}

     ngOnInit() {
       this.currentTransaction = {
         paymentAmount: 25.78,
         paymentType: TransactionType.Credit,
       } as ITransaction
     }

     ngOnDestroy() {
       this.subs.unsubscribe()
     }
   ...
   ```

7. Create the checkout function to call checkoutInitiated before a service call is made.
8. Simulate a fake transaction using setTimeout and call the checkoutCompleted event when the timeout ends:

   src/app/pos/pos/pos.component.ts
   ```
   export class PosComponent implements OnInit {
   ...
     checkout(transaction: ITransaction) {
       this.uiService.showToast('Checkout initiated')
       dataLayer.push({
         event: 'checkoutInitiated',
       })
       this.subs.sink = this.transactionService
         .processTransaction(transaction)
         .pipe(
           filter((tx) => tx != null || tx !== undefined),
           tap((transactionId) => {
             this.uiService.showToast('Checkout completed')
             dataLayer.push({
               event: 'checkoutCompleted',
             })
           })
         )
         .subscribe()
   }
   ```

> To prevent any data loss during your analytics collection, consider covering failure cases as well, such as adding multiple checkoutFailed events that cover various failure cases.

Now, we are ready to see the analytics in action:

1. Run your app.
2. On the POS page, click on the **Checkout** button.
3. In Google Analytics, observe the **REAL-TIME | Events** tab to see events as they occur.

4. After 5-10 minutes, the events will also show up under the **BEHAVIOR | Events** tab, as shown:

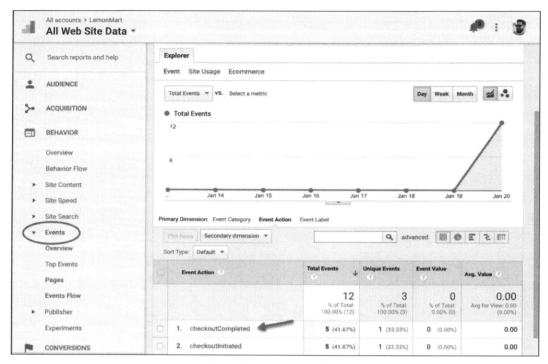

Figure 14.23: Google Analytics Top Events

Using custom events, you can keep track of various nuanced user behaviors happening on your site. By collecting `checkoutInitiated` and `checkoutCompleted` events, you can calculate a conversion rate of how many initiated checkouts are taken to completion. In the case of a point-of-sale system, that rate should be very high; otherwise, it means you may have systematic issues in place.

Advanced analytics events

It is possible to collect additional metadata along with each event, such as the payment amount or type, when checkout is initiated, or `transactionId` when checkout is completed.

To work with these more advanced features, I would recommend that you check out `angulartics2`, which can be found at `https://www.npmjs.com/package/angulartics2`. `angulartics2` is a vendor-agnostic analytics library for Angular that can enable unique and granular event tracking needs using popular vendors, such as Google Tag Manager, Google Analytics, Adobe, Facebook, Baidu and more, as highlighted on the tool's home page, shown here:

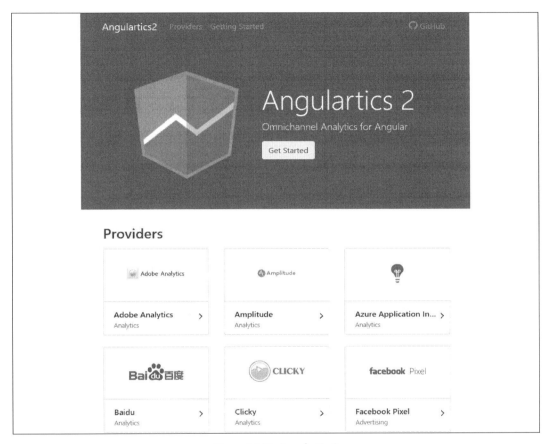

Figure 14.24: Angulartics2

`angulartics2` integrates with the Angular router and the UI router, with the ability to implement custom rules and exceptions on a route-per-route basis. The library makes it easy to implement custom events and enables metadata tracking with data binding.

Check out the following example:

```
<div angulartics2On="click" angularticsEvent="DownloadClick"
  angularticsCategory="{{ song.name }}"
  [angularticsProperties]="{label: 'Fall Campaign'}">
</div>
```

We can keep track of a `click` event named `DownloadClick`, which would have a `category` and a `label` attached to it for rich event tracking within Google Analytics.

With advanced analytics under your belt, you can use actual usage data to inform how you improve or host your app. This topic concludes a journey that started by creating pencil-drawn mockups at the beginning of this book, covering a wide variety of tools, techniques, and technologies that a full-stack web developer must be familiar with in today's web in order to succeed. We dove deep into Angular, Angular Material, Docker, and automation in general to make you the most productive developer you can be, delivering the highest quality web app, while juggling a lot of complexity along the way. Good luck out there!

Summary

In this chapter, you have rounded out your knowledge of developing web apps. You learned how to work with Google Tag Manager and Google Analytics to capture page views of your Angular application. Using high-level metrics, we went over how you can calculate the cost of your infrastructure per user. We then investigated the nuances of the effect that high availability and scaling can have on your budget. We covered the load testing of complex user workflows to estimate how many users any given server can host concurrently. Using this information, we calculated a target server utilization to fine-tune your scaling settings.

All of our pre-release calculations were mostly estimates and educated guesses. We went over the kinds of metrics and custom events you can use to measure the actual use of your application. When your application goes live and you start gathering these metrics, you can update your calculations to gain a better understanding of the viability and the affordability of your infrastructure.

Congratulations! You have completed your journey. I hope you enjoyed it! Feel free to use this book as a reference, including the appendices.

Follow me on Twitter @duluca and stay tuned to https://expertlysimple.io for updates.

Further reading

- Google Analytics and Google Tag Manager Blog, by Simo Ahava: https://www.simoahava.com.

Questions

Answer the following questions as best as you can to ensure that you've understood the key concepts from this chapter without Googling. Do you need help answering the questions? See *Appendix D, Self-Assessment Answers* online at https://static.packt-cdn.com/downloads/9781838648800_Appendix_D_Self-Assessment_Answers.pdf or visit https://expertlysimple.io/angular-self-assessment.

1. What are the benefits of load testing?
2. What are some of the considerations as regards reliable cloud scaling?
3. What is the value of measuring user behavior?

Appendix A

Debugging Angular

"A problem well-stated is half-solved." Charles Kettering, the head of research for GM in the early 20th century, said that to effectively find a solution to your problem, you must first be able to explain it well. In other terms, you must first invest the time to understand what the problem is and when you do you will be halfway to solving it.

Effective debugging is crucial in understanding why or how your software is failing. There are far better ways to debug you JavaScript code than using `console.log`. This appendix will cover various tools and techniques to introduce you to breakpoint debugging and browser extensions that can help you better understand the state of your application.

In this appendix, we cover:

- The most useful shortcut
- Troubleshooting errors in the browser
- Karma, Jasmine, and unit testing errors
- Debugging with dev tools
- Debugging with VS Code
- Debugging with Angular Augury
- Debugging with Redux DevTools
- Debugging RxJS

Let's start off by learning a keyboard shortcut that will make you way more productive.

The most useful shortcut

Finding your way around an unfamiliar or a large code base can be difficult, disorienting, and annoying. There is a keyboard shortcut that solves this problem, which is shared across multiple tools like VS Code and Chrome/Edge Developer Tools (dev tools).

To search for and open a file in VS Code or the **Sources** panel in dev tools, use the following shortcut:

On macOS: ⌘ + P

On Windows: *Ctrl* + *P*.

You'll quickly discover that this is the shortcut that you will be using the most.

Troubleshooting errors in the browser

In this section, you will intentionally introduce an easy-to-make mistake so that you can become familiar with real-life errors that can happen while developing your applications and gain a solid understanding of the tooling that makes you an effective developer.

Please refer to *Chapter 4, Automated Testing, CI, and Releasing to Production*, and the LocalCast Weather app to get a better context of the following code sample.

> The latest version of the LocalCast Weather app can be found on GitHub at `https://github.com/duluca/local-weather-app`.

Let's pretend that we made an innocent mistake when copying and pasting the URL from the API documentation page on `OpenWeatherMap.org` and forgot to add `http://` in front of it. This is an easy mistake to make:

src/app/weather/weather.service.ts
```
...
return this.httpClient
  .get<ICurrentWeatherData>(
`api.openweathermap.org/data/2.5/weather?q=${city},${country}&appid=${
environment.appId}`
  ).pipe(map(data => this.transformToICurrentWeather(data)))
...
```

Your app will compile successfully, but when you inspect the results in the browser, you won't see any weather data. In fact, it seems like the `CurrentWeather` component is not rendering at all, as you can see in the following image:

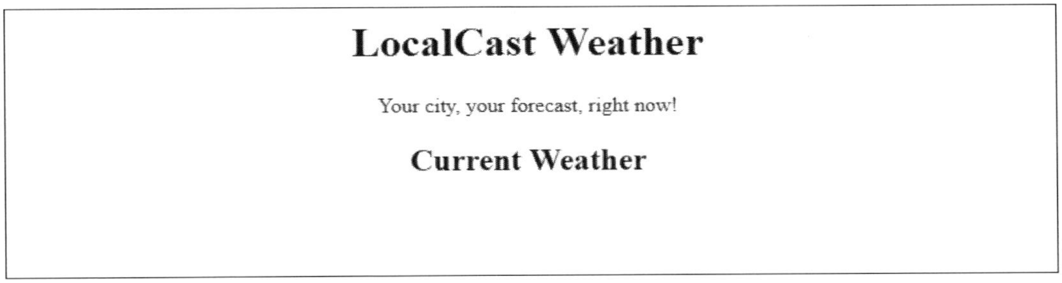

LocalCast Weather

Your city, your forecast, right now!

Current Weather

Figure 1: CurrentWeather does not render

To find out why, you will need to debug your Angular app.

Leveraging Browser DevTools

As a developer, I use the Edge or Google Chrome browsers because of their cross-platform and consistent developer tools with helpful extensions.

Open Edge/Chrome Developer Tools (dev tools) on macOS by pressing ⌥ + ⌘ + I, or on Windows by pressing *F12* or *Ctrl + Shift + I*.

As a best practice, I code with VS Code and the browser open side by side, while the dev tools are also open in the browser. There are several good reasons for practicing side-by-side development:

- **Fast feedback loops**: With live-reloading, you see the end result of your changes very quickly
- **Laptops**: A lot of developers now do most of their development on a laptop and a second monitor is a luxury
- **Attention to responsive design**: As I have limited space to work with, I constantly pay attention to mobile-first development, fixing desktop layout issues after the fact

Debugging Angular

- **Awareness of network activity**: To enable me to quickly see any API call errors and ensure that the amount of data that is being requested remains in line within my expectations
- **Awareness of console errors**: To enable me to quickly react and troubleshoot when new errors are introduced
- **Disabled cache**: So you know you are always getting all of your changes and not fighting with the browser's cache

Observe what side-by-side development looks like:

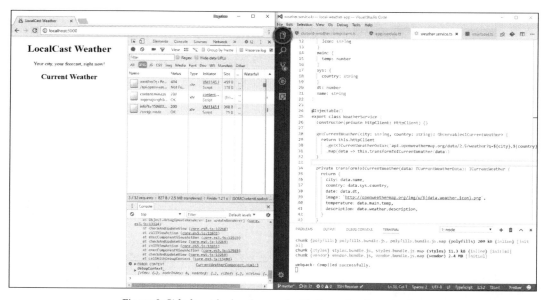

Figure 2: Side-by-side development with live-reloading running

Ultimately, you should do what works best for you. With the side-by-side setup, I frequently find myself toggling VS Code's Explorer on and off and resizing the dev tools pane to a larger or smaller size depending on the specific task at hand. To toggle VS Code's Explorer, click on the Explorer icon circled in the preceding screenshot.

Just as you can do side-by-side development with live-reloading using `npm start`, you can get the same kind of fast feedback loops for unit testing using `npm test`:

Appendix A

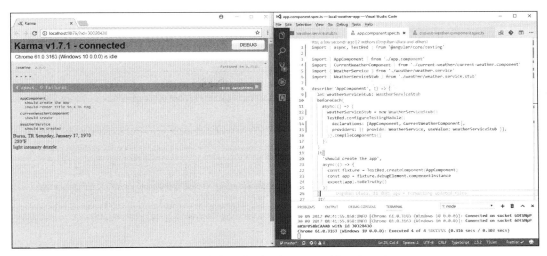

Figure 3: Side-by-side development with unit testing

With the side-by-side unit testing setup, you can become highly effective in developing unit tests.

Optimizing dev tools

For side-by-side development with live-reloading to work well, you need to optimize the default dev tools experience:

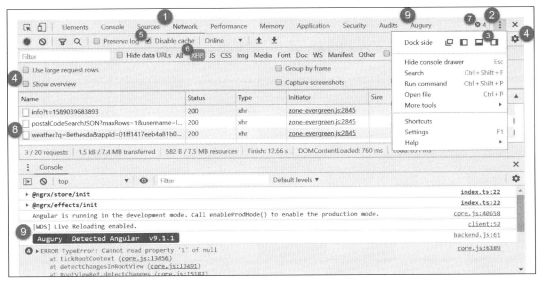

Figure 4: Optimized Chrome Developer Tools

Looking at the preceding screenshot, you will note that numerous settings and information radiators are highlighted:

1. Have the **Network** tab open by default so that you can see network traffic flowing.
2. Open the dev tools settings by clicking on the ⋮ button.
3. Click on the **right-hand side** icon so that dev tools dock on the right-hand side of Chrome. This layout gives more vertical space, so you can see more network traffic and console events at once. As a side benefit, the left-hand side takes the rough size and shape of a mobile device.
4. **Toggle on** large request rows and **toggle off** overview to see more of the URL and parameters for each request and gain more vertical space.
5. Check the option to **Disable cache**, which will force reload every resource when you refresh a page while the dev tools are open. This prevents bizarre caching errors from ruining your day.
6. You will mostly be interested in seeing XHR calls to various APIs, so click on **XHR** to filter results.
7. Note that you can glance the number of console errors in the upper-right corner as **12**. The ideal number of console errors should be 0 at all times.
8. Note that the top item in the request row is indicating that there's an error with status code **404 Not Found**.
9. Since we are debugging an Angular application, the **Augury** extension has been loaded. This tool is covered in more detail later in this chapter, using the more complicated LemonMart app.

With your optimized dev tools environment, you can now effectively troubleshoot and resolve the application error from earlier.

Troubleshooting network issues

There are three visible issues with the app at this stage:

- The component details aren't displaying
- There are numerous console errors
- The API call is returning a **404 Not Found** error

Appendix A

Begin by inspecting any network errors, since network errors usually cause knock-on effects:

1. Click on the failing URL in the **Network** tab
2. In the **Details** pane that opens to the right of the URL, click on the **Preview** tab
3. You should see this:

   `Cannot GET /api.openweathermap.org/data/2.5/weather`

   By just observing this error message, you will likely miss the fact that you forgot to add the `http://` prefix to the URL. The bug is subtle and certainly not glaringly obvious.

4. Hover over the URL and observe the full URL, as shown:

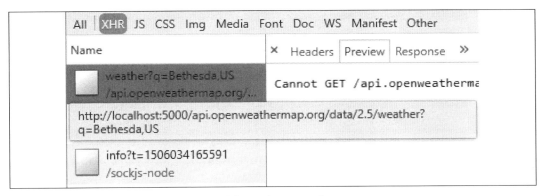

Figure 5: Inspecting network errors

As you can see, now the bug is glaringly obvious. In this view, we get to see the full URL, and it becomes clear that the URL defined in `weather.service.ts` is not fully qualified, so Angular is attempting to load the resource from its parent server, hosted on `localhost:5000`, instead of going over the web to the right server.

Investigating console errors

Before you fix this issue, it is worthwhile understanding the knock-on effects of the failing API call:

1. Observe the console errors:

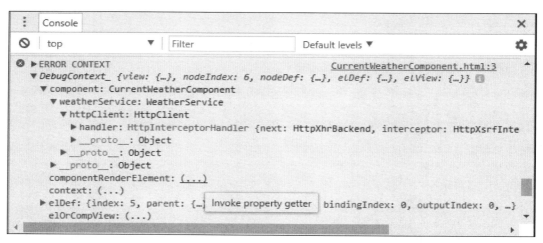

Figure 6: Dev tools Console Error Context

The first element of note here is the `ERROR CONTEXT` object, which has a property named `DebugContext_`. `DebugContext_` contains a detailed snapshot of the current state of your Angular application when the error happened. The information contained within `DebugContext_` is light years ahead of the amount of mostly unhelpful error messages AngularJS generates.

> Properties that have the value (...) are property getters, and you must click on them to load their details. For example, if you click on the ellipsis for `componentRenderElement`, it will be populated with the `app-current-weather` element. You can expand the element to inspect the runtime condition of the component.

2. Now scroll to the top of the console
3. Observe the first error:

   `ERROR TypeError: Cannot read property 'city' of undefined`

You have probably encountered the `TypeError` before. This error is caused by trying to access the property of an object that is not defined. In this case, `CurrentWeatherComponent.current` is not assigned to an object because the HTTP call is failing. Since `current` is not initialized and the template blindly tries to bind to its properties like `{{current.city}}`, we get a message saying **property 'city' of undefined** cannot be read. This is the kind of knock-on effect that can create many unpredictable side-effects in your application. You must proactively code to prevent this condition.

Karma, Jasmine, and unit testing errors

When running tests with the `ng test` command, you will encounter some high-level errors that can mask the root cause of the actual underlying errors.

The general approach to resolving errors should be inside out, resolving child component issues first and leaving parent and root components for last.

NetworkError

Network errors can be caused by a multitude of underlying issues:

`NetworkError: Failed to execute 'send' on 'XMLHttpRequest': Failed to load 'ng:///DynamicTestModule/AppComponent.ngfactory.js'.`

Working inside out, you should implement test doubles of services and provide the fakes to the appropriate components, as covered in the previous section. However, in parent components, you may still encounter errors even if you correctly provided fakes. Refer to the section on dealing with generic error events to uncover the underlying issues.

Generic ErrorEvents

Error events are generic errors that hide the underlying cause:

`[object ErrorEvent] thrown`

To expose the root cause of a generic error, implement a new `test:debug` script:

1. Implement `test:debug`, as shown, in `package.json`:

    package.json
    ```
    ...
      "scripts": {
        ...
        "test:debug": "ng test --source-map",
    ```

        . . .
    }

2. Execute `npm run test:debug`
3. Now the Karma runner will likely reveal the underlying issue
4. If necessary, follow the stack trace to find the child component that may be causing the issue

 If this strategy is not helpful, you may be able to glean more information on what's going wrong by breakpoint debugging your unit tests.

Debugging with Dev Tools

To `console.log` or not to `console.log`; that is the question. For the record, let me state that `console.log` statements will never be checked in to your repository. In general, they are a waste of your time, because it requires editing, building, and running code to bring value, not to mention the cost of cleaning up your code later.

The preferred method of debugging is breakpoint debugging, which is a way to pause the execution of your code, and inspect and manipulate the state of it while your code is running. You can conditionally set breakpoints, walk through your code line by line, and even execute statements in the console to try out new ideas.

Angular 9 and Ivy bring in many debugging improvements that makes it possible to debug asynchronous code and templates. In addition, the stack trace generated by Angular 9 is far more useful in pinpointing the root cause of an error.

There are some niche use cases where `console.log` statements can be useful. These are mostly asynchronous workflows that operate in parallel and are dependent on timely user interaction. In these cases, console logs can help you better understand the flow of events and interaction between various components. You can see this in action in the *Debugging RxJS* section later in this chapter.

For common cases, we should stick with breakpoint debugging. Using dev tools, we can observe the state of properties as they are being set, and be able to change their values on the fly to force the code to execute branching logic in `if-else` or `switch` statements.

Let's presume that some basic logic exists on `HomeComponent`, which sets a `displayLogin` boolean, based on an `isAuthenticated` value retrieved from an `AuthService`, as demonstrated:

Appendix A

```
src/app/home/home.component.ts
...
import { AuthService } from '../auth.service'
...
export class HomeComponent implements OnInit {
  displayLogin = true
  constructor(private authService: AuthService) {}

  ngOnInit() {
    this.displayLogin = !this.authService.isAuthenticated()
  }
}
```

Now observe the state of the value of `displayLogin` and the `isAuthenticated` function as they are being set, and then observe the change in the value of `displayLogin`:

1. Switch to the **Sources** tab in dev tools
2. Using the most useful shortcut, *Ctrl* + *P* or ⌘ + *P*, search for `HomeComponent`
3. Drop a breakpoint on the first line inside the `ngOnInit` function
4. Refresh the page
5. You'll see your breakpoint hit, as highlighted in blue here:

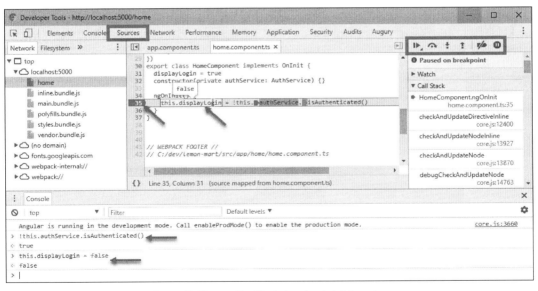

Figure 7: Chrome DevTools breakpoint debugging

6. Hover over `this.displayLogin` and observe that its value is set to `true`

7. If hovering over `this.authService.isAuthenticated()`, you will not be able to observe its value

   While your breakpoint is hit, you can access the current scope of the state in the console, which means you can execute the function and observe its value.

8. Execute `isAuthenticated()` in the console:

   ```
   > this.authService.isAuthenticated() true
   ```

   You'll observe that it returns `true`, which is what `this.displayLogin` is set to. You can still coerce the value of `displayLogin` in the console.

9. Set `displayLogin` to `false`:

   ```
   > this.displayLogin = false false
   ```

If you observe the value of `displayLogin`, either by hovering over it or retrieving it from the control, you'll see that the value is set to `false`.

Leveraging breakpoint debugging basics, you can debug complicated scenarios without changing your source code at all. You can debug templates as well as complicated callbacks with RxJS statements.

Debugging with Visual Studio Code

You can also debug your Angular application, Karma, and Protractor tests from directly within Visual Studio Code. First, you need to configure the debugger to work with a Chrome debugging environment, as illustrated:

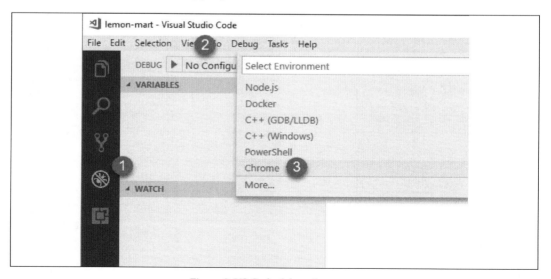

Figure 8: VS Code debugging setup

Appendix A

1. Click on the **Debug** pane
2. Expand the **No Configurations** dropdown and click on **Add Configuration...**
3. In the **Select Environment** checkbox, select **Chrome**

    This will create a default configuration in the .vscode/launch.json file. We will modify this file to add three separate configurations.

4. Replace the contents of launch.json with the following configuration:

    .vscode/launch.json

```
{
  "version": "0.2.0",
  "configurations": [
    {
      "name": "Debug npm start with Chrome",
      "type": "chrome",
      "request": "launch",
      "url": "http://localhost:5000/#",
      "webRoot": "${workspaceRoot}",
      "runtimeArgs": [
        "--remote-debugging-port=9222"
      ],
      "sourceMaps": true,
      "preLaunchTask": "npm: start"
    },
    {
      "name": "Debug npm start with Edge",
      "type": "edge",
      "request": "launch",
      "version": "dev",
      "url": "http://localhost:5000/#",
      "webRoot": "${workspaceRoot}",
      "sourceMaps": true,
      "preLaunchTask": "npm: start"
    },
    {
      "name": "Debug npm test with Chrome",
      "type": "chrome",
      "request": "launch",
      "url": "http://localhost:9876/debug.html",
      "webRoot": "${workspaceRoot}",
      "runtimeArgs": [
        "--remote-debugging-port=9222"
      ],
      "sourceMaps": true,
```

```json
      "preLaunchTask": "npm: test"
    },
    {
      "name": "Debug npm test with Edge",
      "type": "edge",
      "request": "launch",
      "version": "dev",
      "url": "http://localhost:9876/debug.html",
      "webRoot": "${workspaceRoot}",
      "sourceMaps": true,
      "preLaunchTask": "npm: test"
    },
    {
      "name": "npm run e2e",
      "type": "node",
      "request": "launch",
      "program": "${workspaceRoot}/node_modules/protractor/bin/protractor",
      "protocol": "inspector",
      "args": [
        "${workspaceRoot}/protractor.conf.js"
      ]
    }
  ]
}
```

Note that we also added debuggers for Microsoft's new Chromium-based Edge browser.

5. Execute the relevant CLI command, like `npm start`, `npm test`, or `npm run e2e`, before you start the debugger
6. On the **Debug** page, in the **Debug** dropdown, select `npm start` and click on the green play icon
7. Observe that a Chrome instance has launched
8. Set a breakpoint on a `.ts` file
9. Perform the action in the app to trigger the breakpoint
10. If all goes well, Chrome will report that the code has been **Paused in Visual Studio Code**

Appendix A

 For more information, refer to the Angular CLI section on VS Code Recipes on GitHub at https://github.com/Microsoft/vscode-recipes.

Debugging with Angular Augury

Augury is a Chrome DevTools extension for debugging and profiling Angular applications. It is a purpose-built tool designed to help developers visually navigate the component tree, inspect the state of the router, and enable breakpoint debugging by source mapping between the generated JavaScript code and the TypeScript code that the developer coded in.

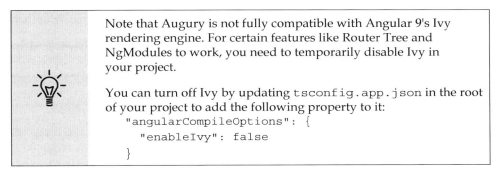 Note that Augury is not fully compatible with Angular 9's Ivy rendering engine. For certain features like Router Tree and NgModules to work, you need to temporarily disable Ivy in your project.

You can turn off Ivy by updating tsconfig.app.json in the root of your project to add the following property to it:
```
"angularCompileOptions": {
  "enableIvy": false
}
```

You can download Augury from https://augury.angular.io. Once installed, when you open Chrome DevTools for your Angular app, you'll note a new tab for Augury, as illustrated:

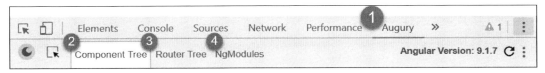

Figure 9: Chrome DevTools Augury

[757]

Debugging Angular

Augury provides useful and critical information in understanding how your Angular app is behaving at runtime:

1. The current Angular version is listed, in this case, as version **9.1.7**
2. **Component Tree** show all Angular components that rendered in the app
3. **Router Tree** shows all the routes that have been configured in the app
4. `NgModules` shows the `AppModule` and feature modules of the app

Component Tree

The **Component Tree** tab shows how all app components are related and how they interact with each other:

1. Select a particular component, such as `HomeComponent`, as follows:

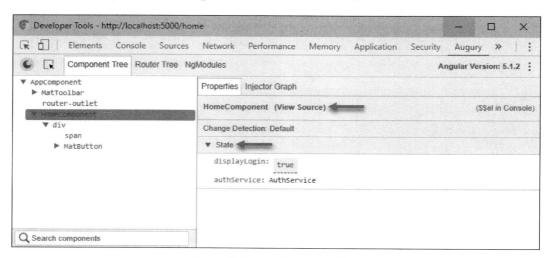

Figure 10: Augury Component Tree

The **Properties** tab on the right-hand side will display a link called **View Source**, which you can use to debug your component. Further below, you will be able to observe the state of properties of the component, such as the `displayLogin boolean`, including services that you have injected into the component and their state.

Appendix A

 You can change the value of any property by double-clicking on the value.

For example, if you would like to change the value of `displayLogin` to `false`, simply double-click on the blue box that contains the `true` value and type in `false`. You will be able to observe the effects of your changes in your Angular app.

In order to observe the runtime component hierarchy of `HomeComponent`, you can observe the **Injector Graph**.

2. Click on the **Injector Graph** tab, as shown:

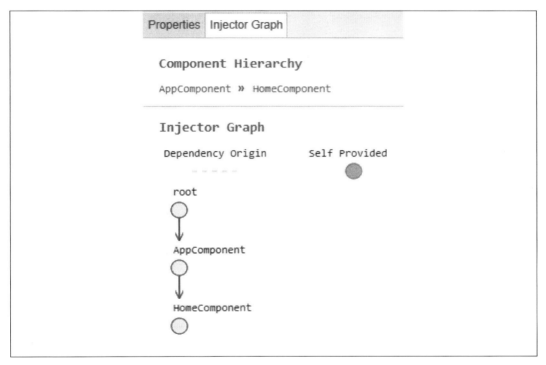

Figure 11: Augury Injector Graph

This view shows how your selected component came to be rendered. In this case, we can observe that `HomeComponent` was rendered within `AppComponent`. This visualization can be very helpful in tracking down the implementation of a particular component in an unfamiliar code base or where a deep component tree exists.

[759]

Router Tree

The **Router Tree** tab will display the current state of the router. This can be a very helpful tool in visualizing the relationship between routes and components, as shown:

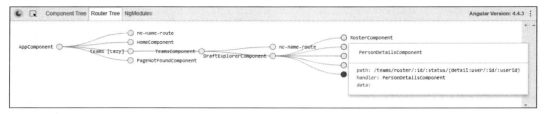

Figure 12: Augury Router Tree

The preceding router tree demonstrates a deeply nested routing structure with master-detail views. You can see the absolute path and parameters required to render a given component by clicking on the circular node.

As you can see, for `PersonDetailsComponent`, it can get complicated to determine, exactly, the set of parameters needed to render this detail portion of a master-detail view.

NgModules

The **NgModules** tab displays the `AppModule` and any other feature module that is currently loaded into memory:

1. Launch the `/home` route of the app and hit enter on the address bar, so Augury registers the navigation event
2. Observe the **NgModules** tab, as follows:

Appendix A

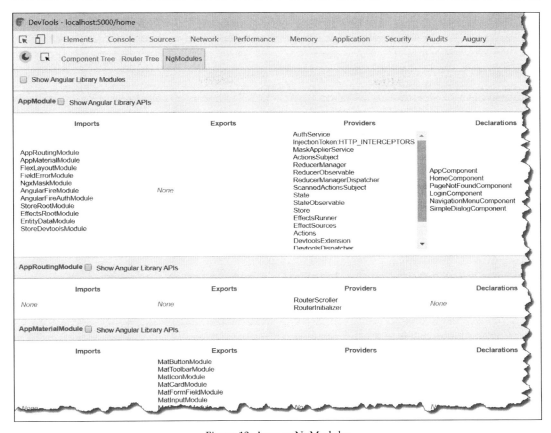

Figure 13: Augury NgModules

You'll note that all root-level modules, including the AppModule, are loaded. However, since our application has a lazy-loaded architecture, none of our feature modules are loaded yet.

3. Navigate to a page in `ManagerModule` and hit enter on the address bar
4. Then, navigate to a page in `UserModule` and hit enter on the address bar
5. Finally, navigate back to the `/home` route and hit enter on the address bar
6. Observe the **NgModules** tab, as shown:

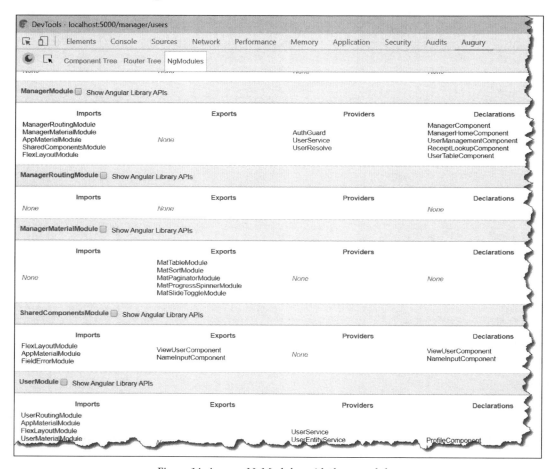

Figure 14: Augury NgModules with three modules

7. Now, you'll observe that `ManagerModule` and `UserModule`, along with all of their related modules, have been loaded into memory.

NgModules is an important tool to visualize the impact of your design and architecture.

Debugging with Redux DevTools

There are two major strategies to debug and get instrumentation from NgRx.

1. Implement a console logger for debugging
2. Configure Store DevTools for rich instrumentation

Let's start with the simple debugging solution.

Implement NgRx Console Logger

In `app.module`, `StoreModule` is configured to inject a `MetaReducer` into your configuration. Meta-reducers are able to listen to all events happening in the action-reducer pipeline, thereby giving you the ability to preprocess actions. We can use this hook to implement a simple logger.

1. Implement a function called `logger` in `reducers/index.ts`:

    src/app/reducers/index.ts

    ```
    export function logger(reducer: ActionReducer<AppState>):
    ActionReducer<AppState> {
      return (state, action) => {
        const result = reducer(state, action)
        console.groupCollapsed(action.type)
        console.log('prev state', state)
        console.log('action', action)
        console.log('next state', result)
        console.groupEnd()

        return result
      }
    }
    ```

2. Configure the `logger` with `metaReducers` and only in non-production mode:

    src/app/reducers/index.ts

    ```
    export const metaReducers: MetaReducer<AppState>[] =
    !environment.production
      ? [logger]
      : []
    ```

Now give it a whirl and you should be able to observe NgRx right in your console, shown as follows:

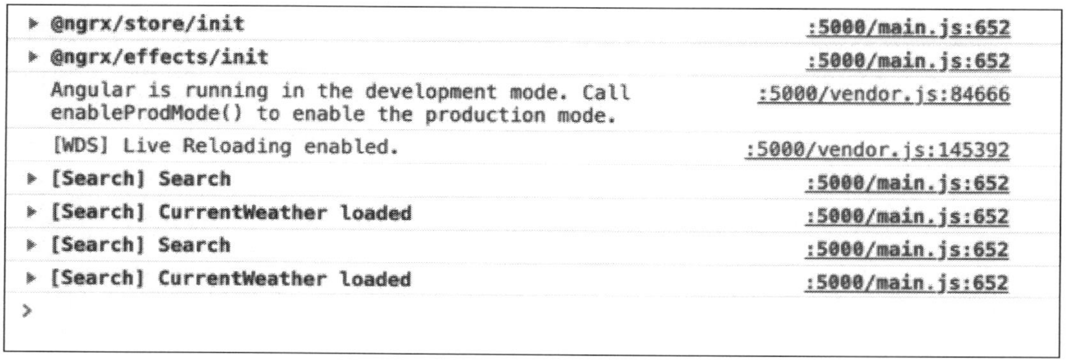

```
▶ @ngrx/store/init                                          :5000/main.js:652
▶ @ngrx/effects/init                                        :5000/main.js:652
  Angular is running in the development mode. Call          :5000/vendor.js:84666
  enableProdMode() to enable the production mode.
  [WDS] Live Reloading enabled.                             :5000/vendor.js:145392
▶ [Search] Search                                           :5000/main.js:652
▶ [Search] CurrentWeather loaded                            :5000/main.js:652
▶ [Search] Search                                           :5000/main.js:652
▶ [Search] CurrentWeather loaded                            :5000/main.js:652
>
```

Figure 15: Console view with NgRx logs

Configuring NgRx Store DevTools

The NgRx Store Devtools package can also assist with our debugging efforts during development or provide instrumentation of our production builds. Add the package by running the following command:

```
$ npx ng add @ngrx/store-devtools
```

You will notice that the package will automatically add production instrumentation rules in `app.module`, so that only the last 25 events are captured. This is necessary to avoid performance issues.

Once installed, in order to leverage the instrumentation generated and to be able to debug NgRx, you will want to install the Redux DevTools extension for Chrome or Firefox, found at https://github.com/zalmoxisus/redux-devtools-extension or http://extension.remotedev.io.

Once you launch your application, activate the extension and observe that detailed instrumentation over time is being captured by Redux DevTools, shown as follows:

Appendix A

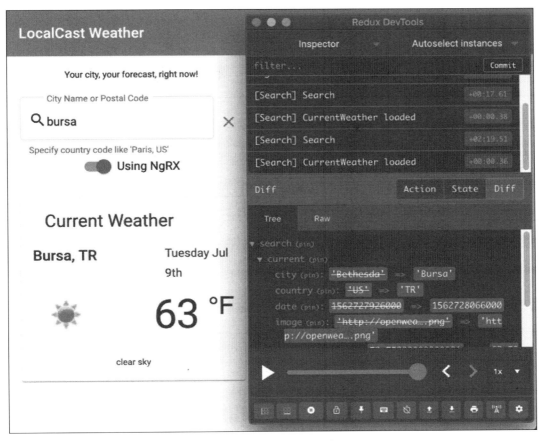

Figure 16: Redux DevTools

Redux DevTools gives you the capability to play back events and view state changes. This is demonstrated in the bottom-right quadrant of the preceding screenshot. You can observe the current city as **Bursa** and its previous value, **Bethesda**.

Debugging RxJS

There are two major strategies to debug and get information about what's happening inside an RxJS pipe:

1. Tap into the event stream and console log the event data at a particular point in the stream
2. Execute breakpoint debugging in dev tools

Let's start with using the `tap` operator.

Tapping an RxJS Event Stream

In *Chapter 6, Forms, Observables, and Subjects*, we introduced the RxJS `tap` operator as a way to direct the flow of user input from our search input's stream of change events, and eventually call our `doSearch` function. When an RxJS stream doesn't seem to be behaving as you'd expect, you can combine the `tap` operator and `console.log` to log each event's data, so you can see it over time. Since `tap` captures the data in the stream based on where it falls in the order of operations, once added to the stream, you can simply use VS Code's line movement keyboard shortcuts to move it around and test the flow.

 To move a line of code up or down, use *Alt* + ↑ and *Alt* + ↓ on Windows or ⌥ + ↑ and ⌥ + ↓ on macOS.

The following `tap` in `CitySearchComponent` will log to the console every change event coming from the input:

```
this.search.valueChanges
  .pipe(
tap(console.log),
    debounceTime(1000),
    filter(() => !this.search.invalid),
    tap((searchValue: string) => this.doSearch(searchValue))
  ).subscribe()
```

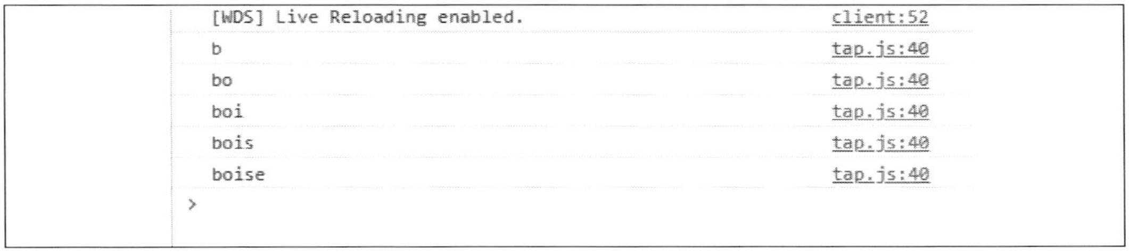

```
[WDS] Live Reloading enabled.                client:52
b                                            tap.js:40
bo                                           tap.js:40
boi                                          tap.js:40
bois                                         tap.js:40
boise                                        tap.js:40
>
```

Figure 17: RxJS logging every event

If we move the `tap` down one line, instead of getting every user input, we will get only the debounced events:

```
this.search.valueChanges
  .pipe(
    debounceTime(1000),
    tap(console.log),
    filter(() => !this.search.invalid),
    tap((searchValue: string) => this.doSearch(searchValue))
  ).subscribe()
```

```
enableProdMode() to enable the production mode.
[WDS] Live Reloading enabled.                client:52
bo                                           tap.js:40
boise                                        tap.js:40
>
```

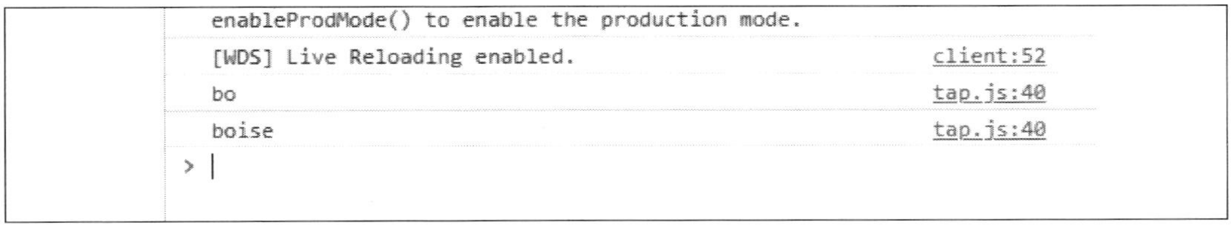

Figure 18: RxJS logging only debounced events

One more line down, and we see the events after being debounced and filtered:

```
this.search.valueChanges
  .pipe(
    debounceTime(1000),
    filter(() => !this.search.invalid),
    tap(console.log),
    tap((searchValue: string) => this.doSearch(searchValue))
  ).subscribe()
```

Debugging Angular

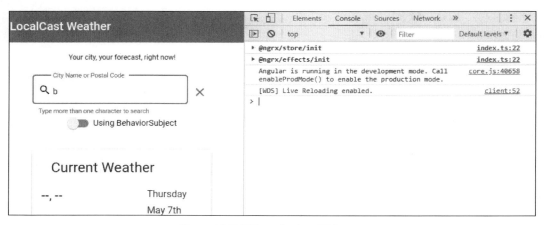

Figure 19: RxJS ignoring invalid inputs

Note that since one character is invalid, the filter has caught this event and not allowed it through, thus we see no data in the console.

While it can be very confusing in the console, you can also log many things at once, utilizing a callback instead of just passing the `console.log` callable:

```
this.search.valueChanges
  .pipe(
    debounceTime(1000),
    tap(debouncedData =>
      console.log('debounced: ', debouncedData)
    ),
    filter(() => !this.search.invalid),
    tap(debouncedAndFilteredData =>
      console.log(
        'debounced + filtered: ',
        debouncedAndFilteredData
      )
    ),
    tap((searchValue: string) => this.doSearch(searchValue))
  ).subscribe()
```

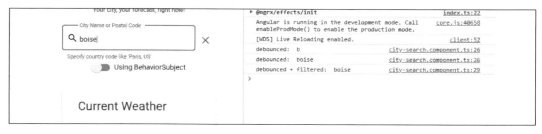

Figure 20: RxJS logging multiple events

Next, let's see how we can leverage breaking debugging.

Breakpoint debugging an RxJS Event Stream

Refer to the *Debugging with DevTools* section earlier in the chapter to learn more about breakpoint debugging. The important bit in debugging RxJS is to understand what the blue carets are for in the debugger.

When a line of code has multiple points that can be used to pause execution, these are indicated with the square-sided carets. These can be toggled on (dark, solid) or off (light, transparent) to indicate where in the line of code you want the browser to stop, as shown in the following screenshot:

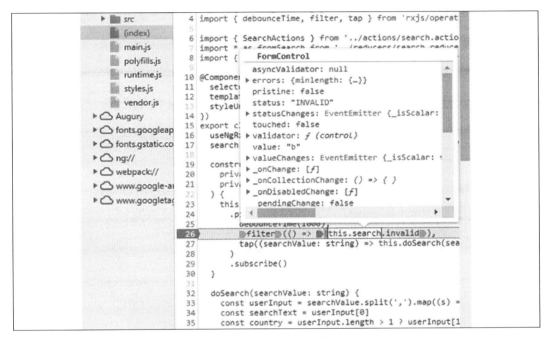

Figure 21: RxJS breakpoint debugging

The carets can be used to stop the browser mid-stream, inside a callback where work is done, to examine the data or even manipulate it. In the preceding example, I've set the breakpoint debugger to break inside the filter function, so I can examine the state of the search input field.

Experiment with debugging to learn more about it.

Further advice

If you're still stuck, don't get frustrated. Even the best of us spend countless hours on minor issues at times. However, if you need it, you can ask for help. Angular has a rich and supportive community online.

It does matter a lot how you go about asking for help. First replicate your issue using `https://stackblitz.com/`. Half the time, you will figure out your issue in the process of replicating it. Next, ask a question on `https://stackoverflow.com`. If you can provide the StackBlitz link to your issue, your problem will likely get answered quickly. If it turns out there might be an issue with the framework itself, then create a GitHub issue on the correct repository (in other words, Angular, CLI, Material, NgRx, RxJS, and so on) detailing your problem. If you found a bug in the framework, then you've officially contributed to the development of the open source project:

Otherwise, you can also use Twitter and search for help on the `@angular` or `#angular` handles. Personally, I'm a big fan of Googling. My philosophy is that someone else probably ran into the same issue as I did, and believe me when I say this -- a well-formed Google query is a problem half-solved.

Appendix B

Angular Cheat Sheet

Here is a quick reference cheat sheet for you to familiarize yourself with common Angular syntax and CLI commands. Take some time to review and orient yourself with new Angular syntax, major components, CLI scaffolds, and common pipes.

You may find the list especially useful if your background is with AngularJS, since you will need to unlearn some old syntax.

If you are new to Angular or simply not a fan of CLI commands, check out Nx Console at https://nx.dev/angular/cli/console, an awesome desktop app, and a Visual Studio Code extension, that can write your CLI arguments for you. That said, I do recommend that you first gain familiarity with the CLI commands and force yourself to use them for a bit, so you have a better understanding of how Nx Console works.

Binding, or data binding, refers to an automatic one or two-way connection between a variable in code and a value displayed or inputted in an HTML template or another component:

Type	Syntax	Data direction

Interpolation Property Attribute Class Style	`{{expression}}`
	`[target]="expression"`
	`bind-target="expression"`
		One-way,
		from data source to view target

Event	`(target)="statement"` `on-target="statement"`	One-way, from view target to data source
Two-way	`[(target)]="expression"` `bindon-target="expression"`	Two-way

Built-in directives

Directives encapsulate coded behaviors that can be applied as attributes to HTML elements or other components:

Name	Syntax	Purpose
Structural Directives	`*ngIf` `*ngFor` `*ngSwitch`	Controls the structural layout of the HTML and if elements get added or removed from the DOM
Attribute Directives	`[class]` `[style]` `[(model)]`	Listens to and modifies the behavior of other HTML elements, attributes, properties, and components, such as CSS classes, HTML styles, and HTML form elements

Common pipes

Pipes (known as filters in AngularJS) modify how a data-bound value is displayed in an HTML template:

Name	Purpose	Usage
Async	Manages subscriptions to observables, and provides synchronous access to the variable in the template	`someVariable$	async as someVariable`
Date	Formats a date according to locale rules	`{{date_value	date[:format]}}`
Text Transformation	Transforms text to uppercase, lowercase, or title case	`{{value	uppercase}}` `{{value	lowercase}}` `{{value	titlecase }}`
Decimal	Formats a number according to locale rules	`{{number	number[:digitInfo]}}`
Percent	Formats a number as a percentage according to locale rules	`{{number	percent[:digitInfo]}}`
Currency	Formats a number as currency with a currency code and symbol according to locale rules	`{{number	currency [:currencyCode [:symbolDisplay [:digitInfo]]]}}`

Starter commands, major components, and CLI scaffolds

Starter commands help generate new projects or add dependencies. Angular CLI commands help create major components by automatically generating boilerplate scaffolding code with ease. For the list of the full set of commands, visit https://github.com/angular/angular-cli/wiki.

Starter commands

Here are the most basic commands, which you will probably memorize over time and use the most often. Remember never to install `@angular/cli` globally as covered in *Chapter 3, Creating a Basic Angular App*:

Name	Purpose	CLI command
New	Creates a new Angular application with an initialized Git repository, `package.json`, with routing already configured and Ivy enabled. Run from the parent folder.	`npx @angular/cli new project-name --routing`
Update	Updates Angular, RxJS, and Angular Material dependencies. Rewrites code, if necessary, to maintain compatibility.	`npx ng update`
Add Material	Installs and configures Angular Material dependencies.	`npx ng add @angular/material`

Major component scaffolds

Use the following commands during your daily workflow to add new components, services, and other major components to your Angular application. These commands will save you serious time and help you avoid simple configuration mistakes:

Name	Purpose	CLI command
Module	Creates a new `@NgModule` class. Uses `--routing` to add routing for submodules. Optionally, import the new module into a parent module using `--module`.	`ng g module my-module` `ng g m my-module`

Angular Cheat Sheet

Component	Creates a new `@Component` class. Uses `--module` to specify the parent module. Optionally, use `--flat` to skip directory creation, `-t` for an inline template, and `-s` for an inline style.	`ng g component my-component` `ng g c my-component`
Directive	Creates a new `@Directive` class. Optionally, uses `--module` to scope directives for a given submodule.	`ng g directive my-directive` `ng g d my-directive`
Pipe	Creates a new `@Pipe` class. Optionally, use `--module` to scope pipes for a given submodule.	`ng g pipe my-pipe` `ng g p my-pipe`
Service	Creates a new `@Injectable` class. Uses `--module` to provide a service for a given submodule. Services are not automatically imported to a module. Optionally use `--flat false` to create a service under a directory.	`ng g service my-service` `ng g s my-service`
Guard	Creates a new `@Injectable` class, which implements the Route lifecycle hook `CanActivate`. Uses `--module` to provide a guard for a given submodule. Guards are not automatically imported to a module.	`ng g guard my-guard` `ng g g my-guard`

In order to properly scaffold some of the components listed earlier under a custom module, such as `my-module`, you can prepend the module name before the name of what you intend to generate, for example, `ng g c my-module/my-new-component`. The Angular CLI will properly wire up and place the new component under the `my-module` folder.

TypeScript scaffolds

If you are not familiar with the TypeScript syntax, these TypeScript-specific scaffolds will help you create classes, interfaces, and enums, so you can leverage object-oriented programming principles to reduce the duplication of code and implement code behavior like calculated properties in classes rather than components:

Name	Purpose	CLI command
Class	Creates a barebones class	`ng g class my-class`
Interface	Creates a barebones interface	`ng g interface my-interface`
Enum	Creates a barebones enum	`ng g enum my-enum`

Common RxJS functions/operators

In order to become an effective Angular developer, you need to become an RxJS master. Here are some of the most common and useful RxJS operators for quick reference:

Functions

Name	Purpose
`pipe`	Takes one or more observables as input and generates an observable as output, allowing you to build custom data streams.
`subscribe`	Required to activate an observable. It is an anti-pattern to extract the value of an observable data stream from a `subscribe` operation. An Async pipe or the `tap` function can be used to inspect or use the current value.
`unsubscribe`	Releases resources and cancels observable executions. Not unsubscribing can lead to performance problems and memory leaks. Use the Async pipe or the `SubSink` library to manage subscriptions.

Operators

Name	Purpose
`of`	Converts the provided value to an observable sequence. Useful for integrating synchronous code into an observable data stream.
`from`	Creates an observable from an array, an iterable object, or a promise.
`map`	Allows you to iterate through every value that is emitted by the observable.
`merge`	Creates an output observable that concurrently emits all values from every given input observable. Useful for triggering an action based on multiple observables.
`combineLatest`	Combines values from multiple observables with the latest value from each observable. Useful when used in tandem with the `merge` operator.
`filter`	Filters values in the data stream. Useful to ignore null values or only execute the rest of the pipeline when some condition is met.
`concat`	Sequentially emits values from multiple observables. Useful for synchronizing multiple operations. Variants like `concatMap` can also flatten the observable, which is useful for iterating over values of collections.
`take`	Given a count, automatically completes the observable after consuming the prescribed number of times.
`catchError`	Catches errors on the observable to be handled by returning a new observable or throwing an error.
`scan`	Using an accumulator function, it can process data incrementally. That is, getting a running subtotal as numbers are added. Useful for long-running operations where you need an update.

Thanks to Jan-Niklas Wortmann for reviewing this section. Keep up with him on Twitter: `@niklas_wortmann`.

Further Reading

- *Bindings*, https://angular.io/guide/template-syntax#binding-syntax-an-overview
- *Structural Directives*, https://angular.io/guide/structural-directives
- *Attribute Directives*, https://angular.io/guide/template-syntax#built-in-attribute-directives
- *Pipes*, https://angular.io/guide/pipes
- *CLI Commands*, https://angular.io/cli
- *Learn RxJS switchMap, mergeMap, concatMap, and exhaustMap, FOREVER!*, https://medium.com/@shairez/a-super-ninja-trick-to-learn-rxjss-switchmap-mergemap-conc atmap-and-exhaustmap-forever-88e178a75f1b
- *Reactive Extensions Library for JavaScript*, https://rxjs.dev
- *This is where we write about RxJS. It's meant to be a place for everyone who is interested in RxJS*, https://dev.to/rxjs

Another Book You May Enjoy

If you enjoyed this book, you may be interested in these other books by Packt:

Django 3 By Example - Third Edition

Antonio Melé

ISBN: 978-1-83898-195-2

- Build real-world web applications
- Learn Django essentials, including models, views, ORM, templates, URLs, forms, and authentication
- Implement advanced features such as custom model fields, custom template tags, cache, middleware, localization, and more
- Create complex functionalities, such as AJAX interactions, social authentication, a full-text search engine, a payment system, a CMS, a RESTful API, and more
- Integrate other technologies, including Redis, Celery, RabbitMQ, PostgreSQL, and Channels, into your projects
- Deploy Django projects in production using NGINX, uWSGI, and Daphne

Leave a review - let other readers know what you think

Please share your thoughts on this book with others by leaving a review on the site that you bought it from. If you purchased the book from Amazon, please leave us an honest review on this book's Amazon page. This is vital so that other potential readers can see and use your unbiased opinion to make purchasing decisions, we can understand what our customers think about our products, and our authors can see your feedback on the title that they have worked with Packt to create. It will only take a few minutes of your time, but is valuable to other potential customers, our authors, and Packt. Thank you!

Index

Symbols

80-20 solution 274
401 Unauthorized response 372
403 Forbidden response 372

A

A11Y project
  reference link 219
abstract auth service
  implementing 361-364
abstract caching service
  localStorage, using 368-371
abstract functions
  defining 364-368
abstraction 358, 360
accessibility (A11y)
  about 219, 220
  automated accessibility tool,
    configuring 220-222
advanced analytics events 739, 740
Advanced Angular architecture 23, 24
advanced continuous integration
  about 465
  build environment, containerizing 466
  multi-stage Dockerfiles 466, 467
advanced load testing
  about 719
  OctoPerf, using 719-723
Ahava, Simo 729
Ahead-of-Time (AOT) 444
Amazon Web Services (AWS)
  about 51, 52, 667
  AWS account 670-672
  AWS billing 702
  AWS Lambda 667

analytics
  collecting 707-710
Angular
  about 10-12, 489
  configuring 290, 291
  custom events, adding 734-738
  headless browser, configuring 469-471
  null guarding 121
  null guarding, with *ngIf 124
  property initialization 122
  safe navigation operator 123
  used, for optimizing VS Code 70
Angular 6 30, 31
Angular 8 32
Angular 9 32, 33
Angular application
  Angular CLI, installing 58
  Angular reactive forms, adding 237, 238
  code, committing with VS Code 67, 68
  component interaction, with
    BehaviorSubject 249
  components, adding 238-241
  components, verifying 238-241
  error messages 246, 247
  executing 68, 69
  generating 58
  input validation 246, 247
  package.json, inspecting 62-66
  package.json, updating 62-66
  search, implementing 243, 244
  search option, adding to weather
    service 241-243
  user inputs, limiting with
    throttle/debounce 245, 246
**Angular application, component
  interaction techniques**

child-parent relationships, with
    event emitters 250, 252
  global events 249
  parent-child relationships with
    input binding 252, 253
  sibling interactions, with subjects 253-257
Angular application, multiple API calls
  about 264
  chaining 267-269
  postal code service, implementing 265, 267
**Angular application, reactive style
    implementation**
  about 261
  observable, binding with async pipe 261, 262
  observable stream, tapping 263, 264
Angular application, subscriptions
  about 258
  managing 258
  memory leak, exposing 258
  unsubscribing from 259
  unsubscribing, with SubSink 260, 261
Angular architecture 17-19
Angular Augury
  Component Tree 758, 759
  debugging 757
  NgModules 760, 762
  Router Tree 760
Angular CLI
  about 57-61
  development directory, setting up 57
  installing 58
  proxy, configuring 660, 661
Angular CLI autocomplete
  configuring 80
Angular CLI, on VS Code
  reference link 757
Angular documentation
  reference link 12
Angular e2e tests
  about 152, 153
  executing 154
  page object 154, 156
  spec 154, 155
Angular Evergreen
  about 14, 15
  URL 15
Angular Flex Layout
  about 185-187
  alignment 201
  APIs, for DOM containers 190
  APIs, for DOM elements 191
  APIs, for element 191, 192
  basics 189
  installing 189
  reference link 187
  responsive layouts 187-189
  rough scaffolding, implementing 203-205
  working 202
Angular Material
  about 173-176
  automatically, adding 178-180
  components 181
  configuring 182, 291, 292
  icon font, adding 185
  installing 178
  manually, adding 181
  modules, importing 182, 183
  performance 176-178
  setting up 176-178
  theme, importing 184
  unit testing 217-219
Angular Material cards
  about 195-197
  header and content 198, 199
  reference link 197
Angular Material components
  using 192
Angular Material Design Color Tool
  reference link 215
Angular Material, icons
  reference link 185
Angular Material schematics 192, 193
Angular Material theme
  about 212-217
  reference link 214
Angular Material Toolbar
  used, for modifying landing page 193-195
Angular Material typography
  about 199
  applying 200
  reference link 200
Angular Material updates
  reference link 30
Angular reactive forms, types

reactive forms 237
template-driven forms 237
Angular releases
  reference link 13
Angular Router 24, 25
Angular Services
  creating 106, 107
  dependencies, injecting 107, 108
  using 105
Angular Styles 291, 292
Angular's philosophy 13, 14
angular-unit-test-helper 147, 151
Angular unit tests
  about 132, 133
  Jasmine 133
  TestBed, configuring 139
  test doubles 143
  unit test execution 136
API layer 519
architectural nuance, with illustrations
  reference link 95
Artifacts tabs 476
Artifacts Wiki
  creating 335-337
assertion
  expect() 134
  fail(message) 134
Asynchronous JavaScript and XML (AJAX) 4
attribute directives 576
Augury
  download link 757
auth guards 409-413
auth provider service
  selecting, with factory 424, 425
auth service
  creating 360, 361
auth service fake 413, 414
auth workflow
  designing 343, 344
auto-generated unit tests
  anatomy 135, 136
Automated Acceptance Tests (AAT) 152
automated installation scripts
  reference link 38
automation
  setting up, for macOS 52
  setting up, for Windows 52

auxiliary routes
  used, for implementing master/detail view 629, 630, 631, 632
availability zones (AZs) 724
AWS Elastic Container
  Registry (AWS ECR) 449
AWS Elastic Container
  Service (AWS ECS) 440, 459
Azure Container Registry (ACR) 459

B

backlog
  creating, for Local Weather app 89, 90
Balsamiq
  URL 223
Base form component
  building, as abstract class 597-599
Bash Script 54, 56
BehaviorSubject
  versus NgRx 646, 647
bigtestjs.io
  reference link 155
BModule 310
branding 302
browser DevTools
  leveraging 745-747
browser manifest and icons
  implementing 303, 305
build environment
  containerizing 466
  debugging 469
builder 467, 468
built-in directives
  about 772
  attribute directives 772
  structural directives 772

C

cached data
  restoring 615-618
CanActivateChild guards 408
CanActivate guards 408
CanDeactivate guards 408
CanLoad guards 408
Chocolatey for Windows
  installing 39

reference link 40
CircleCI
  about 158, 160, 161, 699
  reference link 456
  used, for deploying CD to
      Vercel Now 456-459
CircleCI config 498, 500
CircleCI container-in-container 473- 476
Clarity
  reference link 176
Class Under Test (CUT) 129
CLI package managers
  about 38
  Chocolatey for Windows, installing 39
  Homebrew for macOS, installing 40
CLI scaffolds 773
cloud
  deploying 166
  Dockerfile, deploying to 449
cloud environment
  scaling 717
cloud Run
  used, for configuring Docker 453
cloud Services
  about 50
  Amazon Web Services (AWS) 51, 52
  Google Cloud 51
  Google Firebase 50
  Vercel Now 50
code coverage reports
  about 476-478
  in CI 478-480
code linting
  scripting 75, 76
code styling
  scripting 75, 76
Color Blender
  reference link 306
color palette 302
command-line interface (CLI) 38, 172
common testing providers function 413, 414
Component Development Kit (CDK) 31
components (Cmp) 281
Component Tree 758, 759
conditional navigation 391, 393

conditional or ternary operator 349, 350
console errors
  investigating 750, 751
container, build and deploy
  reference link 452
Content Delivery Network (CDN) 673
continuous deployment (CD)
  about 429, 455, 456
  deploying, to GCloud with orbs 459-463
  deploying, to Vercel Now with
      CircleCI 456, 458
  Gated CI workflows, defining 464, 465
Continuous Integration (CI)
  about 50, 157, 429
  CircleCI 158-161
  code coverage reports 478-480
  GitHub flow 161-165
Cookies 368
cost per user calculation, scalable
      environment
  about 724
  estimates, revising with metrics 728
  target server utilization, calculating 725-727
Coveralls
  URL 479
CRUD (Create, Retrieve, Update,
      and Delete) 658
CSS
  elements, aligning 205, 206
CurrentWeatherComponent
  registering, with appStore using
      selector 653, 654
current working directory (CWD) 468
custom events
  adding, in Angular 734-738
  creating 729-733
custom icons 306, 307
custom rating control
  implementing 606-611
custom themes 305
custom user controls
  creating, with ControlValueAccessor 606
  using, in forms 611, 612
Cypress
  URL 481

D

data
  loading, with resolve guard 624-626
  transforming, with RxJS 117
data handling
  TypeScript operators, using 347, 348
data table
  implementing, with pagination 632-640
declarations 139, 140
DeepScan
  URL 166
dependency injection (DI) 18
development tools
  Git 41
  GitHub Desktop 41
  installing 41
DevOps 432, 433, 434
dev tools
  debugging 752, 753
  optimizing 747, 748
disciplined and balanced approach 277-279
Distributed Denial-of-Service (DDoS) 667, 724
Docker
  about 49
  configuring, with Cloud Run 453
  installing 49, 439
  URL 434
  used, for containerizing web apps 434
Docker Compose
  about 500
  environment variables, configuring with DotEnv 503-505
  executing, on CircleCI 508, 509
  launch, orchestrating 507, 508
  Nginx, using as web server 501
  reference link 501
  server, containerizing 502, 503
docker-compose.yml file
  defining 505, 506, 507
Docker extensions
  implementing, in VS Code 448, 449
Dockerfile
  deploying, to cloud 449
  reference link 436
Dockerfile, anatomy
  about 434-439

CMD 434
COPY 434
FROM 434
SETUP 434
Docker Hub
  image, building 440-446
  image, publishing 440-446
  reference link 439
Document Object Model (DOM) 5
DocumentTS library
  about 528, 529
  features 528
  filtering 556-558
  IDocument, defining 531, 534, 535
  pagination 556-558
  reference link 490
  used, for implementing MongoDB ODM 527
duluca/minimal-node-build-env
  about 467
  reference link 467
dumb-init process 450
Dynamic UI components 385
Dynamic UI navigation 385

E

Eager loading 314-317
ECS Fargate 676, 691
Elastic Container Service (ECS) 166
Elastic File System (EFS) 506
elements
  aligning, with CSS 205, 206
  design, matching 209-212
  styles, fine-tuning 207, 208
  styling 206, 207
entities
  defining 334, 335
entity relationship diagram (ERD) 334
Entity Service
  customizing 663-665
  using 661-663
enums
  defining 353
environment variables
  storing 111, 112
errors
  troubleshooting, in browser 744, 745
events

configuring 728, 729
expansion panels
    reference link 615
Express 489
Express.js
    routes and versioning 521-523
    server, bootstrapping 520, 521
    services 523, 524
    URL 490
    used, for implementing RESTful APIs 517-520

F

feature modules
    configuring, with components and routes 312, 313
    lazy loading, using 309, 311
field error attribute directive 576-583
filters 772
Firebase
    URL 414
Firebase authentication recipe
    about 414, 416
    application, adding 416, 417
    configuring 418, 419
    implementing 419-423
Firebase console
    reference link 415
fixtures
    about 133
    afterAll() 134
    afterEach() 134
    beforeAll() 134
    beforeEach() 134
Flexbox
    reference link 188
Flux pattern 27
forms
    validations 394
full-stack architecture
    about 487
    Docker Compose 500, 501
    minimal MEAN 488, 489
    monorepo, configuring 491
functional prototype
    exporting 228-230
Function Under Test (FUT) 129

G

Gated CI workflows
    defining 464, 465
gcloud run deploy
    reference link 454
generator schematics
    reference link 192
Generic ErrorEvents 751, 752
GET
    used, for implementing user service 563, 565
Git
    installing 43, 44
Git Bash
    reference link 43
GitHub
    need for 42
GitHub Credentials
    using, in Git 44, 45
GitHub Desktop
    installing 43, 44
    need for 42, 43
GitHub flow 161-165
GitHub projects
    setting up 86, 87
    used, for planning 85
Git repository
    publishing, with GitHub Desktop 61
Git submodules 492-494
Glacier service 724
Global npm packages 47, 48
Google Analytics
    facets 707
    reference link 713
    setting up 713, 714
Google Analytics Tag
    configuring, in Tag Manager 714, 716
Google Cloud 51
Google Cloud Platform Console
    reference link 454
Google Cloud Run
    about 449-452
    troubleshooting 454, 455
Google Container Registry (GCR) 459
Google Firebase 50
Google Search Console dashboard

reference link 716
Google Tag Manager
  adding, to Angular app 710
  Google Analytics Tag, configuring 714, 716
  reference link 729
  setting up 710-713
Graphical User Interface (GUI) 38
grid list
  reference link 615
  using, for layouts 612-615
guards
  role-based routing, using 407, 408

H

headless browser
  configuring, for Angular 469-471
high-level UX design
  defining 335
Homebrew for macOS
  installing 40
home route
  default routes, setting up 300
  designing 298, 299
  RouterLink 301
  Router outlet 301
HttpClient
  OpenWeatherMap APIs, discovering 111
  using, to retrieve data 105
HTTP GET operation
  implementing 112-114
HTTP interceptor 383-385

I

IDocument
  defining, in DocumentTS library 531-535
image
  building, to Docker Hub 440-446
  publishing, to Docker Hub 440-442
images, push and pull
  reference link 453
images, stages
  builder 466
  tester 466
  web server 466
imports 142
infrastructure
  per-user cost, calculating 717, 718
Infrastructure-as-Code (IaC) 429
inheritance 358, 360
in-memory auth service
  implementing 373-376
  login 376-379
  logout 379, 380
input masking 604-606
**Integrated Development
    Environment (IDE) 41**
interactive prototype
  adding 227
  building 223
interfaces
  defining 353
intermediary language (IL) 16
Internet Engineering Task Force (IETF)
  about 343
  reference link 344
Internet Explorer (IE) 4
inventory module 326-329

J

Jasmine
  about 133
  fixtures 133
  matchers 134
  reference link 133
Jasmine, behavior-driven development
  reference link 151
Jasmine, matchers
  reference link 134
Jasmine test framework 751
JavaScript classes 353-358
JSON Web Token (JWT) 343
JWT auth
  custom server auth provider 543-546
  GET User by ID, implementing 546, 547
  implementing 536, 537
  login API 537, 538, 539
  middleware, authenticating 539-543
JWT auth, packages
  bcryptjs 536
  jsonwebtoken 536
  uuid 536
JWT caching 371, 372

JWT life cycle 344-347
JWT session
   resuming 380-383

K

Kanban board
   configuring 87, 88
   used, for planning 85
Karma test framework 751
keyboard shortcut 744

L

landing page
   modifying, with Angular Material Toolbar 193-195
lazy loading
   about 25, 26, 317-319
   feature modules 309-311
lazy loading components, creating
   reference link 312
LemonMart
   creating 287
   designing 292
   high-level modules, identifying with site map 293-295
   NgRx/Data library, implementing 658-660
   reference link 303
   URL 417
   user roles, identifying 293
LemonMart project
   reference link 155, 481
lemon-mart-server 574
lightweight testing environment
   configuring 471
Line-of-Business (LOB) applications 275, 277, 429
lint checker
   implementing 79, 80
lint fixer
   implementing 79, 80
LocalCast Weather 90
localStorage
   about 368
   using, with abstract caching service 368-371
Local Weather app
   backlog, creating 88, 90
   features 89
   high-level architecture 91, 92
   planning, with GitHub projects 85
   planning, with Kanban board 85
   reference link 90
   Wireframe design 90
login component
   implementing 386-391
Long-Term Support (LTS) 2

M

macOS
   automation, setting up 52
major component scaffolds 773, 774
major data entities
   designing 334
manager module 320-323
master/detail view
   implementing, with auxiliary routes 629-632
matchers 134
MatDialog documentation
   reference link 396
Material Design Theme Palette Generator
   reference link 305
material icons
   about 302, 307-309
   reference link 307
Material Theme Builder
   reference link 305
mat-error, properties
   appFieldError binds 577
   group binds 577
   input binds 577
MatSnackBar documentation
   reference link 396
Message Authentication Code (MAC) 343
metrics 707
minimal MEAN
   about 488, 489
   Angular 489
   Continuous Integration (CI) 491
   Docker 491
   Express 489
   GitHub 491

Jasmine 491
Mongo 490
Node 490
npm 491
reference link 489
tooling 490
TypeScript 491
VS Code 491
minimal MEAN, packages
  cors 489
  morgan 489
minimal-node-web-server
  reference link 438, 503
mixed content
  reference link 157
mock components 147
MockFlow WireframePro
  about 223
  URL 223
mock services 148-151
MockStore
  used, for updating unit
      testing components 656, 657
mock-up
  building 223, 225
  home screen 225
  leveraging, in app 338
  search results 225
  settings pane 226
Models layer 519
Model-View-Controller (MVC) 7, 94
Model-View-ViewModel (MVVM) 8, 94
Mongo 490
MongoDB
  URL 490
MongoDB aggregation
  reference link 535
MongoDB ODM
  connecting, to database 529-531
  implementing, with DocumentTS library 527
MongoDB's Node.js driver
  reference link 527
Mongoose
  URL 529
monorepo
  CircleCI config 498, 500
  configuring 491

Git submodules 492-494
Node project, configuring
    with TypeScript 494-498
structure 492
multi-root workspaces
  reference link 491
multi-stage builds
  reference link 467
multi-stage Dockerfiles 466, 467
multi-step responsive forms
  about 566-569
  calculated properties 584-586
  data, reviewing 592-594
  data, saving 592-594
  DatePicker 584-586
  dynamic form arrays 587-590
  form controls 569, 570
  form groups 569, 570
  repeating template behavior, reusing with
      directives 576
  responsive layout 571-575
  shared components, creating 590, 592
  stepper 571-575
  typeahead support 586, 587

N

Nest.js
  URL 517
NetworkError 751
network issues
  troubleshooting 748, 749
ngModel
  reference link 248
NgModules 760, 762
NgRx
  implementing, for LocalCast
      Weather 644, 646
  setting up 648
  versus BehaviorSubject 646, 648
NgRx actions
  defining 648, 649
ngRxBasedSearch function 654
NgRx code samples
  reference link 139
NgRx Console Logger
  implementing 763

NgRx Data
  about 658
NgRx/Data library
  implementing, in LemonMart 658, 659, 660
NgRx Effects
  about 643
  implementing 650, 651
NgRx, elements
  action 644
  dispatcher 644
  effect 644
  store 643
NgRx library
  about 27, 28
  reference link 29
NgRx Store 643
NgRx Store DevTools
  configuring 764, 765
ng-tester library
  about 151
  reference link 151
ngx-mask library 604
Node 490
Node.js
  about 45
  installing 46, 47
Node Package Manager (npm) 41, 691
Node project
  configuring, with TypeScript 494-498
non-blocking I/O
  reference link 490
notable Angular features
  about 30
  Angular 6 30, 31
  Angular 8 32
  Angular 9 32, 33
npm packages, used for scripting cross-conf-env
  reference link 496
npm scripts
  implementing, in VS Code 447
npm scripts, for Docker
  about 439, 449
  setting up 439
npxs readme
  reference link 61
null and undefined checking 348, 349

null coalescing operator 350
nullish coalescing operator 350, 351

O

Object-Oriented Programming (OOP) 18
Object Relational Mapper (ORM) 527
OctoPerf
  reference link 719
OOP concepts
  leveraging, reusable services 352, 353
OpenAPI specification
  reference link 516
OpenWeather API 645
OpenWeatherMap 92
OpenWeatherMap APIs
  discovering 108-110
operating system (OS) 434
optional chaining operator 351, 352
Orb registry
  reference link 459
orbs
  circleci/aws-cli 459
  circleci/aws-ecr 459
  circleci/aws-ecs 459
  circleci/azure-acr 459
  circleci/azure-cli 459
  circleci/gcp-cli 459
  circleci/gcp-cloud-run 459
  circleci/gcp-gcr 459
  used, for deploying CD to GCloud 459-463

P

Pa11y
  URL 220
page views
  tracking 728
pagination
  used, for implementing data table 632-640
personally identifiable information (PII) 345, 423
Pilot Light service 724
pipes 772
POS module 295, 326, 327
postman
  Put User 556
Postman

configuring, for authenticated calls 548-550
Put User 555, 556
reference link 547
requests, automating 550-555
used, for generating users 547
PowerShell Gallery
reference link 54
Powershell Script 52, 54
Prebuilt Sample Container, deploying
reference link 452
pre-request scripts
reference link 551
pricing, for Cloud Run
reference link 449
PrimeNG
reference link 176
production readiness
about 156
building 156
environment variables, setting up 157
Progressive Web Apps (PWAs) 28
project's billing settings
reference link 451
providers 141, 142
provisioning time 718
proxy
configuring, in Angular CLI 660, 661
prune command
reference link 446
Pull Requests (PR) 86
PUT
implementation, with caching 565
Put User 555, 556

R

React
reference link 29
Reactive data streams 21-23
reactive development paradigm 19, 20
Reactive Extensions (RxJS) 21
reactive forms
about 237
reference link 237
versus template-driven forms 236, 237
Reactive transformations
implementing 117-121

React.js architecture 29
Receipt Look-up 321
recovery point objective (RPO) 723
recovery time objective (RTO) 723
reducers
implementing 652, 653
Redux DevTools
debugging 763
Redux DevTools extension
installation link 764
reliable cloud scaling 723, 724
Representational State Transfer (REST) 8
resolve guard
used, for loading data 624-626
Resolve guards 408
Responsive APIs
reference link 192
RESTful APIs
about 510, 511
implementing, with
  Express.js 517-520
Swagger, configuring with Express 524-526
web API, designing with Swagger 511, 512
reusable form part
implementing 599-604
role-based routing
with guards 407, 408
router-enabled modules
generating 295, 297
home route, designing 298
Router-first app
creating 288, 289
Router-first architecture
about 279, 280
code reuse, maximizing with ES 285, 286
code reuse, maximizing with
  TypeScript 285, 287
data-driven design, achieving 283
decoupled component architecture,
  enforcing 284
feature modules 280-282
lazy loading, designing 282, 283
roadmap, developing 282
scope, establishing 282
user controls and components,
  differentiating 285
walking-skeleton, implementing 283

router guards 408
router tree
  about 314, 760
  inspecting 329, 330
RxJS
  debugging 766
RxJS Event Stream
  breakpoint, debugging 769
  tapping 766-768
RxJS functions 775
RxJS operators 775, 776

S

salted password hashing
  reference link 345
scalable environment
  cost per user, calculating 724
scaling architecture
  with reusable form parts 595, 596
Scoop
  installation link 40
search engine optimization (SEO) 716
secure sockets layer (SSL) 345
Self Hosting section
  reference link 307
semver
  reference link 10
Separation of Concerns (SoC) 118
service data
  retrieving, from component 114-116
Services layer 519
services (Svc) 281
sessionStorage 368
side-by-side development
  practicing 745, 746
side navigation 400-406
Single File Component (SFC) 299
single-page applications (SPAs) 24
SiteMap tool
  reference link 294
Stack Overflow
  reference link 42
StandardJS
  reference link 75
starter commands 773
state management
  about 26
  Flux pattern 27
  NgRx library 27, 28
Static APIs
  reference link 192
static files
  deploying 166-169
store actions
  dispatching 654, 655
Studio 3T
  URL 555
style checker
  implementing 78, 79
style fixer
  implementing 78, 79
Swagger
  configuring, with Express 524-526
  used, for designing web API 511, 512
Swagger YAML file
  defining 512-515
  preview 516
  reference link 512, 516

T

target server utilization calculation
  about 725, 727
  blue/green deployments 728
  prescheduled provisioning 727
template-driven forms
  about 237
  using, with two-way binding syntax 247, 249
  versus reactive forms 236, 237
template literals
  reference link 97
TestBed
  configuring 139
TestBed, features
  declarations 139, 140
  imports 139, 142
  providers 139-142
test doubles 143
test doubles, types
  about 143
  fakes 144, 146
  mocks 146
  spies 146

stubs 146
test-driven development (TDD) 478
tester 469
testing module 331-334
time to interactive (TTI) 33
**token-based authentication
   scheme, components**
  auth service 344
  client-side 344
  server-side 344
tooling
  about 490
  configuring 76, 78
transport layer security (TLS) 345
Trilon
  URL 517
troubleshooting, Google Cloud Run
  reference link 455
TypeScript 16, 17
TypeScript operators
  conditional or ternary operator 349, 350
  null and undefined checking 348, 349
  null coalescing operator 350
  nullish coalescing operator 350, 351
  optional chaining operator 351, 352
  used, for data handling 347, 348
TypeScript scaffolds 775

U

UI elements
  Angular component, adding 94-98
  Angular component, demystifying 99
  crafting, with components and interfaces 93
  model, defining with interfaces 100-105
UI service 395-399
unit test execution
  about 136, 137
  compilation error 137, 138
  test results 138, 139
unit testing
  about 129-131
  components, updating with
     MockStore 656, 657
  implementing, for reducers
     and selectors 655, 656
unit testing errors 751

unit tests
  updating 641-643
unit tests, in Angular
  reference link 139
update from master feature 165
User Account Control (UAC) 39
User entity 347, 351
user experience (UX) 7, 26
user interface (UI) 6
User Management 321
user module 324, 326
users
  editing 624
  generating, with Postman 547
user service
  implementing, with GET 563, 565

V

validations
  for forms 394
Vercel Now
  about 50, 166
  URL 166
Vercel Now, documentation
  reference link 168
viewUser component
  reusing, with binding data 627-629
  reusing, with route data 627-629
Virtual Machines (VMs) 434
Visual Studio Code (VS Code)
  about 48
  auto save, enabling 72
  code linting, scripting 75, 76
  code styling, scripting 75, 76
  configuring 71, 290, 291
  debugging 754, 756
  Docker extensions, implementing 448, 449
  IDE extensions 74
  IDE settings 72, 74
  installing 48, 49
  npm scripts, implementing 447
  optimizing, for Angular 70
  URL 49
VS Code Auto Fixer 81
VS Code's Source Control 494

W

walking skeleton 320
web API
  designing, with Swagger 511, 512
web apps
  containerizing, with Docker 434
Web Content Accessibility Guidelines (WCAG) 219
WebDriver
  reference link 152
web frameworks
  history 4-9
web server 472, 473
web server budget
  calculating 717
Windows
  automation, setting up 52
Windows Subsystem for Linux (WSL) 42
Wireframe design 90
World Wide Web Consortium (W3C) 4

Y

yet another tool (YAT) 90